# THE ROMANTIC PERIOD

EDITED BY

## DAVID B. PIRIE

VOLUME 5 OF THE
*Penguin History of Literature*

PENGUIN BOOKS

PENGUIN BOOKS

Published by the Penguin Group
Penguin Books Ltd, 27 Wrights Lane, London W8 5TZ, England
Penguin Books USA Inc., 375 Hudson Street, New York, New York 10014, USA
Penguin Books Australia Ltd, Ringwood, Victoria, Australia
Penguin Books Canada Ltd, 10 Alcorn Avenue, Toronto, Ontario, Canada M4V 3B2
Penguin Books (NZ) Ltd, 182–190 Wairau Road, Auckland 10, New Zealand

Penguin Books Ltd, Registered Offices: Harmondsworth, Middlesex, England

First published 1994

3 5 7 9 10 8 6 4 2

Copyright © David Pirie, 1994
All rights reserved

Filmset in 10/11 pt Monophoto Ehrhardt by
Datix International Limited, Bungay, Suffolk
Printed in England by Clays Ltd, St Ives plc

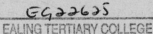

# CONTENTS

# INTRODUCTION

None of the writers now classified as 'Romantic' ever used that word to describe either their own work, or each other's, or the age (roughly 1780–1840) in which they lived. As a term of cultural history, 'Romantic' did not emerge until much later in the nineteenth century, and only gained full currency in the early years of the twentieth. Since then the word has probably contributed to the widespread delusion that writers of the Romantic period spent much of their lives day-dreaming. What does the Romantic Poet, of popular myth, look like? He is a surreal hybrid, ardently clutching an old Greek pot in one hand whilst dangling a daffodil from the other. He chatters a lot; but – since his favourite topics include the ugliness of the modern world, the beauty of solitude and, above all, the majesty of his own soul – he is often talking to himself. Being a naïve optimist, he grins; but hypersensitivity makes him volatile, and he may suddenly burst into tears, or even faint. Yet, should a thunderstorm seem imminent, he will instantly put to sea in a frail boat, or go prancing up the nearest mountain. Whichever of these routes to intensity he takes, he will still be distracted by dreams of lovelier places and better times. So he may well stumble, while touchingly young, into an early grave.

This, of course, is not exactly how the so-called Romantics saw themselves. William Wordsworth (who, incidentally, dodged the grave until he was eighty) claimed in one poem to be 'Dismissing . . . all Arcadian dreams,/All golden fancies of the golden age' ('Home at Grasmere', MS B, 829–30). Elsewhere he pointed out that he and his contemporaries had been able to live 'upon dreams' only in 'their childhood'. As young adults they were confronted by the fact of a political cataclysm: revolution erupted just across the Channel and left England itself quaking for many years. Wordsworth's generation had to survive in a society that was undeniably seismic – rumbling with what was for some the threat, but for many others the promise, of massive, irreversible change. Faced by such challenge in the real world, they

> Were called upon to exercise their skill
> Not in Utopia . . .

But in the very world which is the world
Of all of us, the place in which, in the end,
We find our happiness, or not at all.

(*The Prelude*, 1805, 709–27)

Twenty years later another young poet was arguing that, for his generation too, 'The poet and the dreamer' were not just 'distinct' but 'sheer opposite'. According to John Keats, who had trained as a doctor, 'a poet' should, by definition, work as 'physician to all men'. The best writers are 'those to whom the miseries of the world/Are misery and will not let them rest'; they 'Labour for mortal good', as if they were virtual 'slaves to poor humanity'; they 'are no vision'ries . . . no dreamers weak' (*The Fall of Hyperion*, i. 148–200).

Both poets might dismiss the label 'Romantic' as puzzling or even perverse. Both would, however, accept – along with the vast majority of their contemporaries – that theirs was a 'revolutionary' age. In science and technology, in agriculture and industry, in transport and commerce, revolutions transformed the map of Britain and ensured that much of the world would soon be mapped as belonging to the British Empire. The war against France was, in a bloodily real sense, a 'world war' (for instance, at least 50,000 British lives were lost in the struggle for control of the West Indies), partly because two imperialist nations were battling for the right to exploit the non-European globe. Yet at the outset Britain's conservative government had set out to defeat an egalitarian France that represented the most dangerous revolution of all: a revolution of ideas, an explosion of hope that ordinary men and women, empowered by democracy, could build a just society – that, as one of the period's seminal texts had phrased it back in 1776, 'all men are created equal'. And so it is 'the right of the people to alter or abolish' any regime whose actions do not have 'the consent of the people', and 'to institute new government . . . on such principles . . . as to them shall seem most likely to effect their safety and happiness' (Thomas Jefferson and others, 'Declaration of Independence'). The exhilaration or panic with which the English heard, in the late 1780s and early 1790s, that such ideas had exploded again (and this time so much closer to home, in France) reverberated for decades. In 1816, for instance, one English poet, in a letter to another, could still refer to 'the master theme of the epoch in which we live – the French Revolution'.[1]

1 *The Letters of Percy Bysshe Shelley*, ed. Frederick L. Jones, Oxford, 1964, i. 504 (to Byron).

A quarter of a century earlier, in 1791, when the English had first been required to make war against French democracy, their enthusiasm for the project was, to say the least, variable. The navy, for instance, could recruit in sufficient numbers only by the kidnapping and enslavement which was institutionalized in the press-gang. Mass mutiny immobilized both major fleets in home waters for some months in 1797, until the hanging of thirty-six sailors encouraged the others to remember their royalist duty. In the very next year, 1798, a poem appearing in the first edition of *Lyrical Ballads* focused on just one of the young sailors who had stayed in the Royal Navy, continuing to risk life and limb in battle against the French. As to his motivation for doing so, readers were left to supply their own – cynical or patriotic – theories. The poem's closing lines insist only on the fact that the lad is now about to die of his wounds, and that the 'Old Man Travelling', of the poem's title, is hoping to reach the Falmouth hospital in time to take a last farewell of his only son.

That grieving father is making the journey of 'many miles' on foot; and he respectfully addresses the genteel poet as 'Sir'. It was often the ordinary people of Britain rather than the relatively privileged, poetry-buying élite who had to pay the human price of war. As the conflict dragged on for over twenty years, from 1793 to 1815, its funding deformed the economy. The war's annual cost, as a proportion of the gross national product, was as great in 1811 as it would prove to be, over a century later, at the height of the 1914–18 war. In the worst years of 1794–6 and 1799–1801 recession and rocketing food prices crushed not only labouring families but many highly skilled workers and even small tradesmen. Money to purchase absolutely essential food could often only be raised through clothes and blankets being sold or pawned by those who had to weigh the relative risks of malnutrition and hypothermia. In writings of the time, references to hunger or to nakedness that the modern reader may mistake for mere metaphor can have bitterly literal resonances. There is no romance in the contemporary reports of emaciated children, clothed only in rags, picking over kitchen scraps that had been discarded on dunghills, or fighting dogs for bones that had been thrown into the street.[1]

Samuel Coleridge, in the title of a dissident poem of the 1790s, yoked such 'Famine' to 'Fire' and to 'Slaughter'. The fire is partly explained by the scorched earth policy of the English authorities in

1 See Roger Wells, *Wretched Faces: Famine in Wartime England 1793–1801*, Gloucester, 1988.

Ireland. There, the poem protests, the crops and cottages of 'many a naked rebel' are being burnt. The 'Slaughter' is that of the war against revolutionary France, which, according to the poem, had already cost almost a million lives. For all three nightmares the people of England should supposedly blame the Prime Minister, William Pitt, and the English ruling class that he embodies. Since 'Wisdom comes with lack of food' the exploited 'multitude' must soon recognize their true enemy and act. Once their 'cup of rage' has overflowed, 'They shall seize him and his brood – They shall tear him limb from limb'. The final lines suggest that even this brutal death-penalty is insufficient punishment. For such a mass murderer as Pitt, nothing less than an afterlife in which he burns 'everlastingly' will do.

The bitterness of Coleridge's 'Fire, Famine and Slaughter' may shock some modern readers, but it is not likely to have shocked Pitt himself. Such ferocious invective was common enough in literature at that time. A flood of anti-Government posters and pamphlets supplied an increasingly literate population with protest poems. Many of these anonymous ballads adopted a tone that was just as homicidal as Coleridge's. One, addressed to the Somerset textile workers in 1800, offered this rallying-cry:

> Then Rouse your drooping Spirits up
> Nor Starve by Pitt's Decree,
> Fix up the Sacred Guillotine
> Proclaim French Liberty.[1]

This poet and Coleridge and Pitt – and all their potential first readers – were having to face a wholly new possibility: that Britain's future might soon be determined not by the preferences of a tiny minority but by the opinions of ordinary people. The only mass medium then available was the printing-press, and, in this novel war for hearts and minds, literature was the arsenal of all combatants – whether they wrote with delight or in panic about the prospect that, any day now, 'the starving multitude would rush in and confound all orders and distinctions'.[2]

Pitt himself was an author, and published energetically, if anonymously, his own diatribes. Aided by his Under Secretary of State for Foreign Affairs, George Canning (who would later himself become Prime Minister), Pitt composed much of the polemic printed in the

1 Quoted in Wells, *Wretched Faces*, pp 154–5.
2 P. B. Shelley, 'An Address to the People on the Death of the Princess Charlotte' (1817; published 1843), ix.

pages of the conservative weekly the *Anti-Jacobin*. Here, published in the same year as 'Fire, Famine and Slaughter', was an equivalently specific denunciation of Coleridge himself, detailed enough to jeer at his Devonshire birthplace, Ottery St Mary.[1]

Twenty years later, in 1819, the greatest of the poems provoked by Peterloo (the army's massacre of political demonstrators at Manchester) would also name names. Percy Shelley's *Mask of Anarchy* accuses each government minister of personal responsibility for the barbarisms that are wrecking the country. It explicitly and specifically identifies 'Fraud' with the name of the Lord Chancellor, Eldon; it defines 'Murder' as the Foreign Secretary, Castlereagh; it makes 'Hypocrisy' synonymous with Sidmouth, the Home Secretary who, through an elaborate system of spies and *agents provocateurs*, waged a terrorist campaign against English democrats while publicly spending a million pounds building churches for the spiritual welfare of the masses.[2] However, the poem attacks all three politicians not as individual personalities but for the positions of privilege and the policies of repression that they represent.

On the other side the *Anti-Jacobin* attacked each of its opponents for articulating the supposedly dotty ideas of that all-purpose '*Jacobin* poet' whose egalitarian positions (or posturings) it so amusingly (if unfairly) anatomized in the Introduction to its very first issue. So too, a couple of decades later, the magazine article that is often misleadingly described as 'Lockhart's attack on Keats' was in fact published anonymously, under the pen-name 'Z', and its target was explicitly an entire 'cockney school'. This school supposedly taught a new and dangerous style not only 'of poetry' but also 'of Politics', and it mattered because Keats was not the only pupil there who had 'learned to lisp sedition'. Similarly, Lord Byron, to the ageing and reactionary Robert Southey, seemed a threat worth denouncing not because his flamboyant eroticism defined him as uniquely diabolical but because it typified an entire coven of sexual subversives, 'a satanic school'. Byron, travelling around Europe in 1816 with Mary Godwin and her stepsister and her future husband, Percy Shelley, represented a veritable 'League of incest'. Conversely, Byron himself tended to deride not just Southey or Wordsworth or Coleridge but what he saw as the clique of 'Lakers' to which these poets in

1 See Jonathan Wordsworth's introduction to the Woodstock Books 1991 reprint of George Canning's and John Hookham Frere's *Poetry of the Anti-Jacobin* (1799).
2 See Alasdair D. F. Macrae (ed.), *Percy Bysshe Shelley: Selected Poetry and Prose*, London and New York, 1991, p 273.

northern England belonged;[1] and, to the extent that Southey, like the others, had betrayed his youthful radicalism and matured into a Tory, he belonged, in the disgusted eyes of Byron, with a whole pack of 'renegado rascals'.[2]

What twentieth-century criticism, with its emphasis on the individual sensibility, has often underestimated is how communal and even impersonal the production of literature could still seem to those who were generating and consuming it in the late eighteenth and early nineteenth centuries. Consider, for instance, the extraordinary number of works that matter for us now because of their authors but which were then published anonymously. Wordsworth, when publishing the first edition of *Lyrical Ballads*, chose with his co-author to remain anonymous. Twenty-two years later Keats chose not to include his name when 'La Belle Dame sans Merci' was first published, amongst so many other journalistic and literary pieces, in an issue of a magazine called the *Indicator*. Readers of Jane Austen's first published novel, *Sense and Sensibility*, could discover from the title-page only that it was written 'by a lady' and readers of *Pride and Prejudice* only that it was 'By the Author of *Sense and Sensibility*'. Shelley, a few years later in 1821, chose to remain anonymous when *Epipsychidion* was first published in Pisa. The frequency with which writers at that time worked together on collaborative projects suggests that they were often more interested in what they had in common than in any supposedly unique sensibility that set each of them apart. Coleridge, for instance, before collaborating with Wordsworth on *Lyrical Ballads*, had already worked with Southey to produce *The Fall of Robespierre*, a verse play, in 1794. Keats's major attempt at poetic drama was a joint venture with Charles Brown – *Otho the Great: A Tragedy in Five Acts*, which they had hoped Edmund Kean would perform in 1819. Shelley was expelled from Oxford with his fellow student T. J. Hogg after they had together produced *The Necessity of Atheism*; and Shelley died travelling back from a business meeting to finalize arrangements for a collaborative journal, the *Liberal*, in which he, Leigh Hunt and Lord Byron would henceforward publish all their new poems.

1 The *Edinburgh Review* as early as 1802 had christened them 'Lake poets' and defined them as 'a literary faction'; see James K. Chandler, '"Wordsworth" after Waterloo', in *The Age of William Wordsworth: Critical Essays on the Romantic Tradition*, ed. Kenneth R. Johnston and Gene W. Ruoff, New Brunswick, N J, 1987, p 93.

2 Byron, *Letters and Journals*, ed. Leslie A. Marchand, London, 1973–82, vii. 253; *Don Juan*, Dedication, i. The Lakers are also 'Renegadoes' in *Don Juan*, IV. cxvi and X. xiii.

Byron, in this as in so much else, typifies the age's capacity to foster both co-operativeness and individualism. His agreeing to participate in the joint venture of the *Liberal* is wholly typical not only of his energies in personal friendship, but also of his concern for the larger community whose interests might be promoted by the new magazine's liberal politics. With most of his contemporaries he assumed that the health of literature, like that of society itself, was a shared responsibility – that culture survived and developed, to a large extent, through ventures that were essentially co-operative. On the other hand, Byron's participation in the team producing the *Liberal* was sought so eagerly because his name had a unique power. He had, whether intentionally or not, invented a new kind of personality cult, one where the infamy of the author's sex life ensures massive sales of his fictional narratives. The more that potential readers heard about the scandals which ended his marriage in 1816 and the more they were warned that the man was 'mad, bad and dangerous to know', the more they rushed to familiarize themselves with his works. Byron's canny manipulation of his own image did, at best, become so inventive that it can seem another aspect of his creative art.

However, no poet dependent solely on his own efforts could ever have concocted a myth like Byronism. Its growth and manipulation depended on numerous social, commercial and cultural changes. These shifts were so vast and complex that any one individual could not hope even to recognize, let alone manipulate, all their pervasively creative effects. For instance the very word 'genius', which in the middle of the eighteenth century had meant no more than 'talent', had by the 1820s acquired much of the more exalted role it occupies for us today. It was already helping to dematerialize literary artefacts, and to mystify not only their consumers but sometimes their producers too into believing new superstitions about the creative process.

'Poets', as Shelley remarked, 'are, in one sense, the creators and, in another, the creations of their age.' This last quotation comes from the Preface to *Prometheus Unbound*, written, like most of Shelley's works (and indeed most of Byron's) not in London, the hub of the society that both poets addressed, but in Italy. Such exile was in both cases, to some extent, a self-inflicted wound (or even, in some respects, a self-indulgent retreat). Nevertheless it too was partly the creation of the age. So was the oddly comparable remoteness of Wordsworth and Coleridge and Southey, living so far north that they could only be reached from the capital by a journey that was then far, far more difficult and time-consuming than it is today.

The vision of a scarcely populated wilderness of mountains and lakes as a good base for a writer has since become familiar. But the idea that one could produce literature relevant to one's fellow-citizens by living near as few of them as possible might have seemed odd, perhaps even downright crazy, to Shakespeare, or to Pope at the beginning of the eighteenth century – even, in Wordsworth's own day, to Blake or to Keats (who both spent most of their working lives in London).

Modern habits of reading – the conventions through which we decide what a work means and whether it is any good – often involve unconscious, unquestioning acceptance of premises about the nature of literature (and of course about life; and indeed – at least since the Romantic age – about 'Nature' itself). These almost intuitive methods of interpretation and evaluation can feel so natural that we regard them as the products of mere common sense; yet many of these premises were invented only around two centuries ago, in the decades that are explored by this volume. One idea that was largely concocted then is the notion that poetry is particularly suitable for solitary introspection. Consider too the related beliefs that such introspection is healthy, and that human consciousness, at its most vividly and intensely alive, is not a communal response to a shared experience but is instead the isolated insight of an essentially individualized self. Such ideas are still, in many markets, best sellers, and may now seem to evoke a wholly positive pursuit of peace. But at the time when such ideas were new (a time of violent revolution and bloody war), they were developed, at least partly, as negative reactions to apparent disaster. They were sometimes almost desperate manœuvres by which to manage and survive crisis: strategies for self-preservation in emergencies that were at once political and moral and psychological. Writers who in their youth had focused on the prospects for their community, their nation, even their entire species – when it had seemed possible that humanity itself would at last become wholly humane – found within a relatively few years that their dreams had become nightmares. Eventually some of them chose to look elsewhere.

In fact the numbers choosing to look elsewhere, in that age of paradoxes, made solitude itself an overpopulated zone, and many rival voices contended for control of its meaning. The vigour and complexity with which numerous works debate the implications of solitude is such that relationship, far from being some excluded opposite, is nearly always foregrounded as a key component of the emergent definition. It is not surprising: the starting-point for nearly all the important writers of the time had not been solitude but society; and the questions that continue to echo through much of their work are how society should develop under the inspiration of the French experiment, or how it might protect itself from the threat posed by that corrupting example – in other words, how communities, friendships and even loves of the most intimately personal kind could support, and be supported by, one's larger commitments to class, nation, humanity.

Of course there were retreats into egotism, as individuals aged and as causes that had seemed to promise so much developed in directions so unpredictable that their values seemed to have been redefined, even reversed. There were retreats too into the fanciful, the sentimental. There were withdrawals to contemplate ideals, not as targets to be attained but as fantasies to distract. At worst, perhaps, there was despair. 'Gloom and misanthropy', complained Shelley, 'have become the characteristics of the age in which we live' and 'tainted the literature of the age with . . . hopelessness . . . Our works of fiction and poetry have been overshadowed by the same infectious gloom.'[1] Shelley, the most radical of the age's better-known authors, was an extremist, and he may well be meaning to exaggerate here, acting the alarmist because a proportionate warning might go unnoticed. In fact the age was at least as strikingly prolific in the range and quality of works whose vision is inspiringly optimistic. Indeed the unprecedented diversity that marks the writings of the time is such that it was also an age of comedy, not only in the wit of its more humorous novels but also in verse. Shelley himself, Blake, Wordsworth, Coleridge, Keats – and supremely, of course, Byron – all wrote comic poems that succeed in being funny. What amounts to a second renaissance in English writing, an eruption of bewilderingly varied skills and energies over an extraordinary range of forms, ensures that any one-volume account can only suggest a tiny fraction of what the period's literature has to offer.

Writings reach their readership – or are prevented from doing so – by a complex range of forces. Inventors of improved printing-presses, reformers of old laws governing copyright, police officers enforcing new laws of censorship, publishers, distributors, booksellers and many others helped to mould the age's literature (as the opening essay here, on 'Reader Relations', shows). To write is to hypothesize potential readers, and the work shapes itself in anticipation of their real or imagined demands, interests, knowledge, prejudices, tastes.

1 Preface to *The Revolt of Islam* (1818).

So literature is partly produced by its consumers. Literary history can legitimately focus on examples that typify the facts – and indeed the fashions – that made the Romantic age's definition of literature so different from our own. The Table of Dates included in this volume aims to reflect some of that period's broad-mindedness about the parameters of the literary. There was intense awareness then of how historical events and verbal artefacts intimately shape each other. There was also a far more inclusive view of just how varied and numerous were the texts that deserved to be read attentively and treated as literature.

The Table of Dates specifies a number of scientific discoveries, technological advances and political events, as well as the more predictable dates of birth and death for writers. Moreover, it includes far more writers than the more traditionalist literary historian's league table would deign to mention. It also gives forenames, as well as surnames, to all these authors. It thus gives the forename, not just of Mary Shelley, the novelist, but also of her husband, P. B. Shelley. The practice aims to do more than just gesture towards equity between the genders; it also suggests a proper tentativeness about whose writings matter most. Which author deserves to be a household name, that should roll easily off even the least expert tongue, is often debatable. Here this volume deviates from convention, aiming to be a little humbler in its implied judgements and a little more egalitarian in the etiquette with which it introduces each author to the new reader. So too the Table of Dates lists the titles and publication dates for far more books than the few that are now most celebrated as great works of art. To these it adds not only many novels, plays and volumes of verse that have fared less well in recent fashion, but also other kinds of text that by some modern definitions are not 'literary' works at all – works that might now be allocated to philosophy or economics or politics or history or popular culture. Many titles included in the Table would be regarded by some modern scholars as too factual or polemical or popular to be included in 'English Literature', however influential they may have been in altering the lives of English people.

The rapid spread of literacy during the period covered by this volume produced an explosion, not just in the amount but also in the variety, of writings being produced; and in that less specialized age writings of any kind – however prosaically factual or passionately partisan – seemed as potentially valuable as those that the modern academy would privilege as 'literary'. Byron published his own learned notes with his verse. He supported his hugely popular poem

*Childe Harold's Pilgrimage*, in its first published form, with so many original notes that they print out in one modern edition to no less than seventy-eight pages. In them Byron ranges over geography, history and anthropology, and he even includes a thirty-three-page essay on Romaic linguistics. Similarly, anyone in 1810 wondering whether to buy a copy of Walter Scott's newly published poem, *The Lady of the Lake*, was offered by the author not only 290 pages of verse, spreading itself in generously large type, but also prose footnotes so voluminous that, though close-printed, they run to an extra 140 pages.

The juxtaposition of examples from different *œuvres* can save us from becoming obsessive about what is peculiar to a single writer. It may lead us to discover also a little of what typifies the age, or at least characterizes the work produced by a particular kind of writer in the period. Authors can, for instance, be grouped according to their social class (as in this volume the essay on working-class authors demonstrates) or gender (as the essay on Jane Austen shows by relating her work to that of some other women writers). Alternatively, what typifies work in a particular genre can be as interesting and matter as much, as exemplified by the essay that surveys the novel from 1780 to 1830. More specifically, that essay is about how prose fiction treated a particular topic; though, since that topic is as large as politics, and the period was one in which nearly all literature was arguably reacting to political crisis, the essay explores, for all its particularity, what is tellingly pervasive. Grouping literary works according to their subject-matter allows illuminating examples to be chosen from different genres and by diverse authors. One essay here, 'Representing the People', investigates the ways in which the working class were represented or misrepresented, in verse and prose, by writers as distinct as Crabbe, Southey and Hazlitt. Another essay, on 'Orientalism', explores the variety, complexity and recurrent intensity with which English writing of the period confronted the larger, enticingly and yet alarmingly alien, world that lay beyond Europe, to the East.

Some works, far from typifying the thoughts and language of whole generations, matter because they are so idiosyncratic. They represent deviant intellectual voyages, undertaken in defiance of currently recommended maps and resulting in wholly new ways of charting the world. But discovery, to be useful, must become disclosure. Valuably original minds are not just explorative; they are also expressive. Some authors have an unparalleled ability to choose and use words for particular effects. They create works whose beauty and power are not just extraordinary but, in a precise sense, unique. So in seven of the essays here the focus is upon work by just one author. The choice of the seven writers is wholly conventional: Blake, Wordsworth, Coleridge, Byron, Shelley, Keats and Austen – the 'six great poets and one woman' formula that traditional criticism, at risk of undervaluing so much else, has made famous (and that more progressive criticism is beginning to make infamous). However, the treatment accorded to this predictable group may surprise. There is much in all seven essays about how these famous authors relate to the society in which they lived and worked – and to which they addressed their writings; but there is relatively little about the intimate details of their personal lives. The notion that a mere massing of biographies could constitute the history of literature would have struck many in the Romantic age as distinctly odd. Wordsworth may have written an autobiography in verse, but he did not want it published in his lifetime; and some of its most famous passages explicitly foreground feelings that, far from being peculiarly his own, were shared with his contemporaries. To him, the light of liberty bursting forth to end France's long night of ignorance and injustice had not been some private revelation. Wordsworth described that glimmer of a real, earthly paradise as an excitement shared with an entire generation: 'Bliss was it in that dawn to be alive/But to be young was very heaven' (*The Prelude*, 1805, x. 692–3).

Over twenty years later Wordsworth had become the wealthy friend of aristocracy and was accepting pay from the Tory Government as one of their tax collectors. When a liberal who favoured moderate reform of Parliament dared to challenge the local land-owner's right to represent the area, Wordsworth became the Tory candidate's election agent and speech-writer. At much the same time Keats, who like the vast majority of his fellow-citizens still had no vote, was also contemplating the proposed reforms that would extend the franchise. An irresistible tendency towards a more egalitarian and inclusive society struck Keats as a 'grand' vision. It seemed to him a necessary progress, one for which more remote and élitist figures – even those whose talents towered as high as Wordsworth's – must give way; then 'every human might become great, and Humanity, instead of being a wide heath . . . with here and there a remote Oak or Pine, would become a grand democracy of Forest Trees'.[1]

1 Letter to J. H. Reynolds (19 February 1818), in *Letters of John Keats*, ed. H. E. Rollins, Cambridge, Mass., 1958, p 232.

This volume offers a few, unavoidably modern maps to just some of the ways in which writing at the time sought to describe and influence such volatile and hotly contested terrain. Maps, by definition of course, are confessedly selective. They are designed to report and recommend particular ways of seeing. Certainly any attempt to introduce a literary period of such massive fertility and diversity within the limits of a single volume can only aim to hint at how much it must omit. However, the essay-writers here have been free to decide what, in the areas that they introduce, matters most; and the sheer variety of cartographical method should prove suggestive. The literary landscape, like any other, does not change only as time passes. It also changes whenever we choose a different chart with which to select and arrange its supposedly significant features. Such landmarks can, of course, be shown here only in outline and only from a relatively few – and arguably partisan – points of view. Nevertheless the volume's dual aim is to help modern readers appreciate a little of the sheer scale and range of writing produced throughout that extraordinary period, as well as the individual contributions made by its most renowned authors. In the terms quoted above, from Keats's vision of future growth, we can try to see the wood as well as the trees.

DBP

# 1

## 'EVENTS... HAVE MADE US A WORLD OF READERS':[1] READER RELATIONS 1780–1830

### Kathryn Sutherland

The impulse to explain later events in terms of a clear beginning, a momentous date, and a significant actor is strong. Poised between the eighteenth and the nineteenth centuries, between a decaying traditional world of ranks and orders and its recategorization in terms of the concepts and language of class, the year 1800 carries a special commission: to appear to originate the new social formations and to bring to birth the world of nineteenth-century mass relations from the ruins of eighteenth-century privilege. One of the favourite 'facts' of literary history records that the democratization of literature is signalled in the year 1800 with the publication of the revolutionary 'Preface' to *Lyrical Ballads*. But the popular imagination of the age, as recorded in its radical journalism, tells a different story, that the year 1800 signals the democratization of literature because it saw the building of the first hand-operated iron-frame printing-press. Often metamorphosed in contemporary prints into a mechanical man, the iron hand-press became the commanding symbol of its own graphic and typographic omnipresence. In the search for heroes, it may be that Charles Earl Stanhope, the press's inventor, inaugurates the modern age of literature, and not William Wordsworth, though it is Wordsworth's rather than Stanhope's name which endures.

### THE IMPACT OF TECHNOLOGICAL CHANGE

As material objects as well as ideological constructs, books reflect events and changes in historical reality. Promising good literature in attractive form at the price of a packet of cigarettes, the Allen Lane/

---

1 From *Lectures on Shakespeare and Milton* (1811–12), in *Collected Works of Samuel Taylor Coleridge*, V, ed. R. A. Foakes, Princeton and London, 1987, i. 186.

Penguin paperback revolution of the mid-1930s cannot be divorced from the interwar expansion of an intellectually active, socially mixed readership, concerned to make sense of the large political movements in which it felt entangled. Part of the evidence which we need to train ourselves to see in interpreting literary works is the evidence of literature's material relations to society; more specifically, how the details of history inform not only the subject-matter of books (which in some part we recognize) but also dictate the conditions under which books are produced and read, then forgotten, or institutionalized and handed on to later generations. What we are not accustomed to considering, in general terms, is what publishing history and the physical constituents of books can tell the *critical* reader: what evidence lies in the history of printing technology, in paper, type design, illustration, binding, format, methods of issue (as volumes, magazine contribution, serial instalment, etc.) and cost. In spite of, or perhaps because of, the existence of a scholarly discipline – bibliography – whose end it is to anatomize works in terms of their materiality, such investigations have tended to be seen almost exclusively as a matter of internal rather than external relations: a science of book *making*, all too often geared to the editorial entombment of 'great' works, rather than a social history of book *reading*, intimately and necessarily occupied with questions of how and why as well as what people read. To learn to see and interpret such evidence is to begin to gain access to literature's living relation to the societies which produce and reproduce it, and its relation to those forces which we are ready to admit shape all aspects of reality except literature. Literature, we have been taught for much of the twentieth century, transcends reality. But depending on its status within a material structure, literature will be read either as an index of private sensibility or as a social or political statement. In looking beyond literature's traditional oppositional relation to reality, we can see that, like everything else, literature is shaped by fashions and market forces and, if usually more obliquely, by larger social, cultural and political realities.

While it is true that if such general statements are valid, then they will always be so, it is nevertheless possible to isolate certain periods as providing proof in especially vigorous form. The fifty years from 1780 to 1830 are just such a period, with technological changes promoting a rapidly expanding publishing industry and a consequent questioning and attempted reordering of the relations between kinds of reading-matter and classes of readers, changes which in their turn fuel further manufacturing advances and an increasing commitment to a written culture. It is interesting, therefore, to note that it is precisely the literature of this period which has assumed under the traditional critical gaze the appearance of essential purity, sealed off from the destabilizing crises of the world of its production. 'Romantic' literature, we are now beginning to realize, is a relatively limited and defensively self-regarding phenomenon within the diverse kinds of literary activity of the period 1780 to 1830.

Although books had been among the first commodities to benefit from mass production, for a number of reasons the trade lagged behind other industries in Britain at the close of the eighteenth century, and prices remained high until well into the new century. In part this can be explained by economics – by Britain's financial instability during the Napoleonic wars and postwar era – and by the traditional conservatism of a book trade characteristically slow to speculate on the changing requirements of the reading public. That insatiable appetite for newness, which was a feature of the commercialization of leisure among the affluent in eighteenth-century England, continued to thrive and to ensure a steady market for the tokens of conspicuous wealth, among them the purchase of exclusive editions of expensively produced books, while an avid, expanding readership turned to the growing number of borrowing outlets to satisfy its literary needs. This purchaser/reader distinction looked set to remain, with the publisher-bookseller (the two functions were joined at this time) reluctant to exchange assured high profit margins on small runs for the more precarious returns of a cheaper, larger issue. According to the poet Robert Southey, writing in the war year of 1805, 'books are now so dear that they are becoming rather articles of fashionable furniture more than anything else; they who buy them do not read them, and they who read them do not buy them.'[1] Further, Britain's virtual dependence for paper on imported rags from France led to an acute paper shortage throughout the war, at the very time when demand was rising. Paper contributed the highest proportion (one-half to two-thirds) of the cost of printing a book, even higher than labour, and that was also high, printing-house compositors being the best-paid skilled workmen in early nineteenth-century London. But the same years saw, too, a series of innovations which would eventually turn the tide and lead, by the 1830s, to a revolution in printing, changing it from a craft into a technology.

1 *The Life and Correspondence of the Late Robert Southey*, ed. Charles Cuthbert Southey, London, 1849–50, ii. 329–30.

In 1800 Earl Stanhope built a hand-operated printing-press with a full-sized platen in a cast-iron frame. Extremely durable and precise in the impressions it could produce (though it did not substantially increase the *rate* of production), the Stanhope replaced, by the mid-1820s and in the larger centres of printing, the wooden (or common) press, which had changed little since Caxton's time. In 1801 an English patent was taken out on a French invention, a paper-making machine, and within two years the Fourdrinier stationers had mechanized the manufacture of paper in England. Soon their machine was capable of producing six continuous miles of paper a day, and by 1825 over half the paper in England was machine made. A third development, though not invention, of the early 1800s, the plaster-mould stereotype, was perfected in 1802, enabling the printer to produce new impressions of a work after the type had been redistributed. 1780 to 1830 also saw great experimentation and improvement in graphic processes: aquatint, a tonal extension of etching, facilitating the production of luxury volumes with hand-coloured plates; lithography, a versatile and simple process by which a printed impression is taken from an ink drawing made upon stone; and developments in wood engraving, largely pioneered by the Newcastle artist Thomas Bewick. Bewick's subtly toned small-scale wood blocks paved the way for a refined but cheap conjunction of image and type which revolutionized communication in the new popular market, wood engravings playing a significant part in newspapers, religious tracts, political cartoons and theatrical cuts from the early nineteenth century.

Such developments spawned an information explosion in the period 1780 to 1830, with a steady rise in provincial printing and a considerable rise in London-based printers – from 124 letterpress printers in London in 1785, to 316 in 1824. Pamphlets and reprints apart, the yearly average for new titles quadrupled between 1792 and 1802, from under a hundred to 372, and by 1827 the figure stood at around 580. While the stereotype, the paper-making machine and the subsequent development of the steam-powered press promised a more flexible response to the demand for books and made a truly mass supply feasible by the mid-nineteenth century, it was Stanhope's iron hand-press which came to symbolize mass demand most potently.

The problems of determining the extent and directions of growth in the reading public in the period 1780 to 1830 are compounded, in particular, by the difficulty of gauging competing interpretations of literacy below the middle social strata in England and Wales. (The same arguments do not apply for the Scottish Lowlands, where, thanks to the strict Calvinist emphasis on Bible-reading, a flexible education had been long available to all social levels, as well as a compulsory elementary school system, so that profound illiteracy was virtually unknown there in the second half of the eighteenth century, and social mobility through education was a real possibility.) Literacy is itself a precarious term, conveying with certainty throughout the period no more than the capacity to sign one's name, and thereafter implying only an imprecise relation to what might be called 'active' literacy, the ability to use the written word for communication. Further, the church schools, whether Anglican or Dissent, established throughout England at the beginning of the nineteenth century to provide elementary education for the labouring poor, commonly distinguished between the skills of reading and writing; and while reading of suitable works was generally encouraged, writing was judged unnecessary for most to learn, and even dangerous to social stability, except as it was allied to certain trades. The Anglican National Society for the Education of the Poor in the Principles of the Established Church (1809) was careful to point out that in its schools the children of the poor would not be taught 'to write and cipher', and the Wesleyan Methodists placed a total ban on writing in their schools. Consequently, a rise or fall in the numbers of those able to sign their names can at best indicate only a rough proportionate change in (but no total identity with) the numbers able to read after a fashion; such evidence is no reliable indication of, for example, the ability to understand or formulate consecutive written argument.

However they distil the evidence, what most historians agree is that after a long period of educational stagnancy, from about 1675 to 1775, literacy among the rural and urban middle classes (yeomen and shopkeepers, and probably falling as low as the more highly skilled artisans) rose from 75 to 95 per cent during the next sixty years. In the case of the lowest social groups, no real rise can be registered until about 1800, when literacy reached a level of 35 to 40 per cent, with a significant and substantial improvement to as much as 60 per cent in the early decades of the nineteenth century. Alongside this percentage rise in basic literacy, however, needs to be set an increase in the actual number of illiterates, the result of an enormous growth in population, especially concentrated in the big new urban centres, like Leeds, Manchester and Preston, where facilities of all kinds, from housing and sanitation to religious institutions and schools, were woefully inadequate. Between 1780 and 1830 the population of Great Britain had doubled, from approximately 7 to 14 millions, with the greatest national rate of increase between 1811 and 1821. Between 1801 and 1821 the population of Greater London expanded by over 40 per cent, while Liverpool and Manchester each grew by over 40 per cent in the one decade 1821 to 1831. The reading public, it is estimated, quintupled in the whole period 1780 to 1830, from 1½ to 7 millions.

On the strength of these various calculations, certain broad statements can be made. Firstly, it was the achievement of the late eighteenth century to consolidate and extend the literacy of the middle classes, so that by 1800 most would have been able to read and write with a relative degree of accomplishment. Secondly, in spite of the temporary setback to mass literacy caused by social strains on the expanding cities of the period, the written word was firmly established at this time as the basic unit of communication and exchange, with by 1830 a significant proportion of the working classes having the rudiments of literacy and forming what might best be described as a potential and sporadically active reading public. Though literacy was by no means universal, the social composition of the national readership was comprehensive, members of every class now having the ability to identify themselves as readers. Indeed, the eventual supremacy in these years of the language and categories of class to describe the social structure, imprecise and unstable though the usage was throughout the period, is itself traceable to the new literacy. Emerging tentatively in the late eighteenth century alongside traditional terminology of ranks and orders, the shift, linguistic and socio-conceptual, was not properly accomplished until after 1830. Nevertheless, the compounds 'working classes' and 'middle classes' (usually plural) can be discovered carrying modern connotations by the 1820s, and perhaps even earlier (*OED* cites 'working classes' in 1813). Thirdly, and consequently, it came to be recognized in these years that it would be in terms of reading and mass education that social and political battles at home would now be lost or won. The benefits of promoting reading as a form of social control, and the need to censor reading because of its dangerous tendency to encourage a critical inquiry into the basis of that control, are argued and counter-argued throughout these fifty years, with debate focusing closely on the latest, largest, and potentially most threatening readerships to emerge, the urban middling and working classes (petit bourgeois, artisans, factory workers).

Social commentators were swift to grasp the connection between political revolution and the revolution in print during the turbulent 1790s. Drawing his conclusions from the recent upheavals in France, the bibliophile Isaac D'Israeli observed that 'within the present century a great *Revolution* was effected in the human mind. Philosophers ceased to be isolated. It is but of late that the people have been taught to *read*, and still later, that they have learned to think.'[1] James Currie of Liverpool, in a letter of 1792, outlines the close connection between reading and political radicalism, citing as proof the topical example of Thomas Paine, the pro-French champion of the people and author of the best-selling *Rights of Man* (1791–2): 'The cause why Paine takes so much in Scotland is simply because the *bodies* can all read. Among the manufacturers [workers] of Manchester and Birmingham, not one in a hundred of whom know their alphabet, Paine has hitherto done little harm, though I am told he now begins to operate.'[2] As the Society for Promoting Christian Knowledge records in its minutes for 21 May 1832, 'the population of this country is for the first time becoming a *reading* population, actuated by tastes and habits unknown to preceding generations, and particularly susceptible to such an influence as that of the press.'

At all levels of society a link was newly forged between reading and commercial and industrial expansion. Behind the monitorial schooling systems of Andrew Bell and Joseph Lancaster, the two leading promoters of mass education in the early nineteenth century (Bell with Church of England support and Lancaster with that of the Nonconformists), was the idealized mechanical model of an emergent industrial nation. Like the efficient factory, the monitorial schoolroom combined high production with small outlay, using a hastily trained group of pupil-monitors to teach the children under them, and employing only one teacher, as foreman, to oversee as many as several hundred learners. '[T]his incomparable machine, this vast moral steam-engine' was Coleridge's unironic comment on Bell's literacy factory.[3] Further, thanks to a comparable technology, a public which is itself, through industrial pressure and urbanization, increasingly stratified and defined in terms of its images as readers has its analogue in the diversified formatting and kinds of printed material available. Writing in 1781, the poet George Crabbe might seem to anticipate the later connection between membership of a social group, reading and the physical appearance of books:

> Lo! all in silence, all in order stand
> And mighty folios first, a lordly band;

1 Isaac D'Israeli, *Domestic Anecdotes of the French Nation . . . Indicative of the French Revolution*, London, 1794, sig. A5.
2 Cited in Lawrence Stone, 'Literacy and Education in England, 1640–1900', *Past and Present*, xlii (1969), 85–6.
3 *The Statesman's Manual* (1816), in *Collected Works*, VI, ed. R. J. White, 1972, p 41.

> Then quartos their well-order'd ranks maintain,
> And light octavos fill a spacious plain;
> See yonder, ranged in more frequented rows,
> A humbler band of duodecimos;
> While undistinguish'd trifles swell the scene,
> The last new play and fritter'd magazine.
> Thus 'tis in life, where first the proud, the great,
> In leagued assembly keep their cumbrous state;
> Heavy and huge, they fill the world with dread,
> Are much admired, and are but little read:
> The commons next, a middle rank, are found;
> Professions fruitful pour their offspring round:
> Reasoners and wits are next their place allow'd,
> And last, of vulgar tribes a countless crowd.
>
> (*The Library*, 127–42)

But by 1810, when he published *The Borough*, the link between literacy and social divisions is less speculative, more proliferative, and politically more vital:

> To every class we have a school assign'd,
> Rules for all ranks and food for every mind . . .
>
> (*The Borough*, xxiv. 'Schools', 1–2)

It seems that as the reading public expanded to include the lowest levels of society, the size and appearance of books too tended to descend, a link being forged at this time between a book's format, its targeted readership, and even its political impact: the smaller, the more dangerous. Those connected evidences of an aggressive commercialism – restricted output and mass output, the exclusive item and the everyday product – played their part in the reassessment and wide exploitation of the markets for print, regulating relations within an expanding cultural economy in terms not only of kinds of reading-matter but also of its physical constituents and of access.

At the higher end of the market, the profitable early nineteenth-century fashion for rare and antiquarian books and for book auctions among the wealthy created a demand for new books in the same 'antique' style. Walter Scott, himself an antiquary and the best-selling poet of the early years of the nineteenth century, issued his first long poem, a modern medieval romance, *The Lay of the Last Minstrel* (1805), as a luxury quarto volume. A tale focusing on the retrieval of a long-buried magic book, the *Lay* plays self-consciously with its internalized medieval model in its address to an aristocratic patron and in its simulation of the sumptuous appearance and format of an early printed book. Priced at a guinea (£1.05) a copy, when London skilled artisans, the highest-paid workmen in the country, were earning between twenty and (very exceptionally) forty shillings (£1.00 and £2.00) for an average seventy-two-hour week, and agricultural workers nine shillings (£0.45) or less a week (wage rates which remained applicable into the 1830s), Scott's *Lay* fell into that category of books celebrated by the collector Thomas Frognall Dibdin in his *Bibliomania; or Book Madness; A Bibliographical Romance* (1809). Cataloguing the symptoms of bibliomania, or 'the BOOK disease', Dibdin explains:

. . . it has almost uniformly confined its attacks to the *male* sex, and, among these, to people in the higher and middling classes of society, while the artificer, labourer, and peasant have escaped wholly uninjured. It has raged chiefly in palaces, castles, halls, and gay mansions; and those things which in general are supposed not to be inimical to health, such as cleanliness, spaciousness, and splendour, are only so many inducements towards the introduction and propagation of the BIBLIOMANIA!

(1876 edition, p 11)

Not only were new books expensive, but during the war years (1793 to 1815) and up to about 1820 the standard of living for the vast majority of the population was probably lower than at any time since the war years of the early eighteenth century, with real wages of London artisans falling by as much as a quarter and non-food purchases remaining at a minimum. At the opposite end of the market from rare books, experimentation with new typefaces and graphic processes led to a huge expansion of wall posters, cheap pictorial prints, and political cartoons. Even the illiterate, particularly in London, were increasingly addressed as 'readers', of pictures if not of words; while the proliferation of poster literature, 'the language of the walls' as it was called, seemed set to turn the urban landscape into a textual field, a book for all to read. Playbills, civic notices and trade advertisements established written communication at this time at the heart of cultural practices whose traditional meanings were not primarily textual. Wordsworth is not the only commentator to observe how every available space on London street walls was now plastered with this visually aggressive reading material, 'telegraphing' in dense black titles its essential message to a new semi-literate public:

> Here files of ballads dangle from dead walls;
> Advertisements of giant size, from high
> Press forward in all colours on the sight –
> These, bold in conscious merit – lower down,

That, fronted with a most imposing word,
Is peradventure one in masquerade.
(*The Prelude*, 1805, vii. 209–14)

## ANTICIPATING A MASS MARKET (I): MIDDLE- AND MIDDLING-CLASS READERS

While the greatest reading explosion took place among the newly affluent commercial and industrial middle sector, this still did not extend the potential purchasers of books beyond the upper 10 per cent of the population. Booksellers, at this time the moguls of the trade, kept tight control on prices, preferring to sell little and high until well into the 1820s. The rise over this period in book prices was larger than that in the price of other commodities, with the average octavo volume costing ten to fourteen shillings in 1780, twice what it had in 1700. Keats's *Endymion* sold for nine shillings in 1818, the two volumes of the agricultural worker John Clare's *Village Minstrel* cost twelve shillings in 1821 (far beyond the reach of any labourer's purse), and, most expensive of all, in the same year Walter Scott's new three-volume novel *Kenilworth* cost a guinea and a half (31s 6d). Not only was this equivalent to a top London workman's weekly wage, but even in the 1830s a family was considered 'respectable' with a weekly income of forty-eight shillings. Faced with such stiff prices for the latest publications, those who had acquired the reading habit sought alternative means than purchase of feeding it.

There were throughout the period various and proliferating methods of borrowing new works of fiction and non-fiction, usually by subscription membership of a non-profit proprietary library, like those attached to the 'literary and philosophical societies' established in the larger towns in the second half of the eighteenth century, or through the profit-making commercial outlets. The printed catalogue (1819) of the library of the Literary and Philosophical Society of Newcastle Upon Tyne (the Society had been founded in 1793) lists no novels among its eighteen classes of books and sets an annual contribution of one guinea and a half for all members except a few (no more than four at any one time) impoverished 'deserving persons who discover a taste for literature'. Some 'ladies' were to be admitted as 'reading members', but without voting rights or the right to attend meetings of the Society; and of its 524 members in 1819, only seven are listed as 'lady reading members'. At these meetings, 'on the first Tuesday in every month', a paper would be read, the subjects for discussion comprehending most branches of knowledge; 'but Religion, the practical branches of Law and Physic, *British Politics*, and indeed *all Politics of the day*, shall be deemed prohibited subjects of discussion.'[1] No one was to borrow more than one book at a time, unless the second book was a bound review volume or from the less entertaining categories of mathematics, chemistry, mineralogy, medicine and so on (this was a lending convention still in operation in public libraries in the 1950s). Such proprietary libraries were socially exclusive, charging a high initial admission fee as well as an annual subscription, and their governing committees saw it as a necessary part of their duties to the serious reader to vet new publications. James Losh, who had long abandoned his early French Revolutionary sympathies, noted in his diary for 8 January 1820 the Newcastle Literary and Philosophical Society's decision not to stock Byron's *Don Juan*, the first two cantos of which had appeared in 1819. Losh himself chaired the 'stormy debate' during which it was agreed 'by a majority of 20 to 1 that Lord Byron's *Don Juan* was an unfit book for our Library in which opinion I entirely concur'.[2]

In contrast to the Literary and Philosophical Society's grave cultivation of learning, the Newcastle 'General Circulating Library' lists over 4,500 entries under 'Novels, Romances, Adventures, Tales, Poetry, Plays, Miscellanies, etc.' in its printed catalogue of 1824, and among them is *Don Juan* in six volumes. Shelley and several of the radical writers of 1816 to 1820 (William Cobbett, T. J. Wooler and William Hone), none of whom appear in the catalogue of the Literary and Philosophical Society, also have entries. The remainder of the Newcastle Circulating Library's nearly 8,000 titles comes within the equally popular categories of biographies and travels, with a good selection of the latest magazines and reviews. The annual subscription in 1824 was fourteen shillings, which entitled each member to borrow two volumes at a time. For an extra six shillings, however, the subscriber was allowed to carry away all the volumes of any one book, particularly desirable when selecting from the library's shelves an intriguing title like *Amonaida, or the Dreadful Consequences of Parental Predilection*, a romance in four volumes.

One of the most successful purveyors of reading at commercial rates was William Lane, whose Minerva Press and Library specialized in the most sensational Gothic romances and sentimental novels, and

1 'Rules of the Society', *Catalogue of the Library of the Literary and Philosophical Society of Newcastle Upon Tyne*, Newcastle, 1819, pp v–vii.
2 *The Diaries and Correspondence of James Losh*, ed. Edward Hughes, Durham and London, 1962, i. 107.

offered from the 1790s to the 1820s complete circulating libraries, ranging from a hundred to ten thousand volumes, for sale to grocers, tobacconists and haberdashers eager to extend their trade into the profitable area of book-lending. Lane was an acute businessman, switching early in life from poultry to books. Controlling both publication and distribution from his base in London's Leadenhall Street, he made a huge fortune. He had grasped that in an under-capitalized industry fiction was a lucrative and marketable product, another consumer good, for which the fashion-conscious and the pleasure-seeking would pay highly; but that being an essentially ephemeral and lightweight commodity, profit and the healthy growth of the product lay in circulation figures and not in actual sales. Lane's annual subscription fee was high, between one and three guineas in 1798, depending on the type of subscription, and in 1814 two to five guineas. Obviously, such charges placed the circulating libraries beyond the reach of those below the middle classes, but it was through Lane's entrepreneurial drive that such libraries, in existence in certain urban centres since early in the eighteenth century, penetrated to the provinces.

Significantly, Lane's 'fiction manufactory' infiltrated too the sensitive network of the novel's inner organization: Jane Austen, in *Northanger Abbey* (1818) and the unfinished *Sanditon*, is only the most famous author to find in the circulating library, its categories of titles, its opportunities for chance meetings, and the distinctions it both makes and denies between classes of subscribers, a model of the larger social and moral economy as a complex circulatory system of readings and communications. The library offers a sentimental exchange of more than books, where books and their interpretation can be literally the *pre*texts for subsequent happenings, the paper currency which substitutes for and promises (to characters and readers) a profitable emotional expenditure.

Elsewhere Lane's successful marketing of lurid Minerva titles like Regina Maria Roche's *Children of the Abbey* (1796), Mary Charlton's *The Philosophic Kidnapper, a Novel, altered from the French* (1803), and Agnes Maria Bennett's *Vicissitudes Abroad, or the Ghost of my Father* (1806) raised fears for the welfare of his large, semi-literate reading audience and saw the beginnings of that moral and literary dismissal of the popular novel by the established guardians of taste which has dogged much fiction, and certainly best-selling fiction, ever since. The Revd Edward Mangin provided a representative diagnosis when he located that section of society most at risk from the disease of novel-reading, a disease which, significantly, attacks the circulatory system. 'The sons and daughters of the gentleman and the tradesman, who are, as it were, the very life-blood of the realm, become,' Mangin warned, 'the principal victims of this idle literature; which is so universally diffused, so easy of access, and of so insidious a nature, as nearly to preclude the possibility of safety.'[1] But here, as in many other instances, Coleridge is the fiercest cultural watchdog and commentator on the problems of social reading, fulminating in *Biographia Literaria* (1817) against the 'devotees of the circulating libraries':

. . . I dare not compliment their *pass-time*, or rather *kill-time*, with the name of *reading*. Call it rather a sort of beggarly daydreaming, during which the mind of the dreamer furnishes for itself nothing but laziness and a little mawkish sensibility; while the whole *materiel* and imagery of the doze is supplied *ab extra* by a sort of mental *camera obscura* manufactured at the printing office, which *pro tempore* fixes, reflects and transmits the moving phantasms of one man's delirium, so as to people the barrenness of an hundred other brains . . .[2]

In his town guide *A Picture of Manchester*, Joseph Aston leads the admiring stranger around those literary institutions and libraries which witness to the city's burgeoning importance in England in 1816. Among them are the seventeenth-century 'public' (in fact, exclusive) library at Chetham's Hospital (with at this time about 18,000 volumes), the Literary and Philosophical Society (established 1781, admission fee two guineas, annual subscription one), the Circulating Library (established 1757, with, in 1816, about 370 subscribers and nearly 10,000 volumes, admission fee five guineas, annual subscription one pound), the New Circulating Library (established 1792, with nearly 4,000 volumes, admission fee four guineas, annual subscription twelve shillings), and the Portico Library (established 1803, now with 400 subscribers, admission fee twenty guineas, annual subscription two guineas). Aston also draws the visitor's attention to 'several other libraries in the town, attached to the societies of different religious persuasions; and . . . several extensive circulating libraries . . . which hire out the various literary novelties of the day'.[3] With an admission fee equivalent to half the yearly income of many skilled workmen, the Portico Library was clearly far beyond the means of the lower reading audience; and, indeed, so

1 Edward Mangin, *An Essay on Light Reading, as it may be supposed to influence Moral Conduct and Literary Taste*, London, 1808, p 12.
2 *Collected Works*, VII, ed. James Engell and W. Jackson Bate, 1983, p 48n.
3 Joseph Aston, *A Picture of Manchester*, ed. C. E. Makepeace, Manchester, 1969, pp 179–80.

were all but the most modest subscriptions of the city's other libraries. Fixing prices upon the complex social divisions of class and sex, these early libraries memorialize the prosperity of the developing city. Significant clues to the right reading of the civic guidebook, they map cultural growth in terms of social exclusiveness.

The last decades of the eighteenth century saw the proprietary-library principle adapted on a modest scale to the needs of a so-called middling-class and serious-minded artisan readership. In the early decades of the nineteenth century, fashionable circulating libraries had their humbler counterparts attached to tobacconists' and barbers' shops in London and provincial towns. To cater for the urban dweller of limited means they offered novels, travel memoirs and biographies at a rental of as little as a penny a volume. However, throughout the period the vast majority of working-class readers were at the mercy of voluntary philanthropic schemes and religious organizations, whose concern it was to regulate the reading of the poor. The small factory libraries and Mechanics' Institutes beginning to appear in the 1820s (like the London Mechanics' Institution, 1823, forerunner of Birkbeck College) often excluded works of 'controversy' (politics and theology) and fiction. The 1820s saw, too, the establishment of alternatives from within the working class itself: cheap newsrooms where working men, upon the payment of a small fee, might have access to several papers; and in the same years 'Mutual Improvement Societies', like that described by Thomas Cooper, an apprentice shoemaker in Gainsborough and later a Chartist poet. Among the Gainsborough members in 1822 were a draper's assistant and a grocer's apprentice. The group made a joint subscription to the dissenting *Eclectic Review*, held weekly meetings for debate and formed 'an Adult School, on Sundays, for teaching the poor and utterly uneducated to read'.[1] Cooper also describes the 'Book Society' begun by the local 'gentry' at Mrs Trevor's stationer's shop. At two guineas a year the subscription was far beyond his means, but for the reduced rate of ten shillings he was allowed to exchange books in the evenings as the shop closed and when 'none of the genteel subscribers would be in the way' (p 52). Public libraries serving the poorer reader's needs did not develop until well after the Public Libraries Bill of 1850.

Apart from the borrowing outlets, there were several other means of cheapening literature in the period. A key date in the history of mass reading is 1774, when the concept of perpetual copyright

1 *The Life of Thomas Cooper, Written by Himself*, London, 1872, pp 46–7.

(already denied by an act of 1709) was finally overturned. Thereby the monopoly of a few powerful booksellers who kept prices high by claiming copyright in perpetuity was loosened, and the way was opened for the reprinting of any book whose copyright (a maximum of twenty-eight years from first publication) had expired. The result was a flood of cheap reprint series in the last decades of the eighteenth century. With the exception of new works, still protected by copyright, there inevitably followed an erosion in terms of available literature of the previous distinction between refined and vulgar readers. Leading the way were the major series from John Bell, among them *Poets of Great Britain Complete from Chaucer to Churchill* (1777–83), in 109 volumes, at 1s 6d a volume, and later reissued on coarse paper at 6d a volume. In the 1780s, John Harrison had enormous success with his *Novelists' Magazine*, issued in octavo with double columns, in 6d weekly numbers, and in the 1790s John Cooke's editions of British poets, prose writers and dramatists appeared, also in 6d weekly numbers. Books on the instalment plan, paperbound abridgements, and publications like Harrison's *British Classics*, which reprinted extracts from the *Spectator, Tatler, Guardian, Connoisseur* and other quality eighteenth-century periodicals, brought 'standard' literature within the purchasing power of the many. As William Hazlitt recalled of the reading revolution such publications caused in his childhood, 'the world I had found out in Cooke's edition of the British Novelists was to me a dance through life, a perpetual gala-day.'[1]

A comparable service was performed by James Lackington from 1780 to 1798 at his splendid 'Temple of the Muses' in Finsbury Square, London. A cut-price remainder and cash-and-carry emporium, Lackington's warehouse claimed to be, as the motto over the entrance blazoned, 'cheapest booksellers in the world'. Like many current marketers of books in the United States or the recent infringers of the Net Book Agreement in Britain, Lackington inverted the normal booksellers' practice, retailing new books at well below the advertised price and relying on the size of his turnover to make his huge profits. His was a lucrative if technically illegal venture. A Methodist shoemaker turned bookseller, Lackington combined a crusading zeal on behalf of the popular reader with a keen business sense. His frankly self-aggrandizing *Memoirs of the forty-five first years of the life of J. Lackington, bookseller, Finsbury Square, London;*

1 'On Reading Old Books' (1821), in *The Complete Works of William Hazlitt*, ed. P. P. Howe, London, 1931, xii. 223.

*written by himself* (1791) describes in some detail the 'reformed' state of the public as a result of the boost his trade in books gave to reading:

. . . it affords me the most pleasing satisfaction, independent of the emoluments which have accrued to me from this plan, when I reflect what prodigious numbers in inferior or *reduced* situations of life, have been essentially benefited, in consequence of being thus enabled to indulge their natural propensity for the acquisition of knowledge, on easy terms: nay, I could almost be vain enough to assert, that I have thereby been highly instrumental in diffusing that general desire for READING now so prevalent among the inferior orders of society: which must certainly, though it may not prove equally instructive to all, keeps [*sic*] them from employing their time and money, if not to *bad*, at least to *less rational* purposes.

(1803 edition, p 224)

In discovering and exploiting the large market for such previously exclusive material, Bell, Cooke, Harrison, Lackington and others helped forge a link between literary production and other forms of mass production in an emergently industrial society. It was a link which would be fully extended in the 1820s – in the career of Britain's first best-selling novelist, Walter Scott, in the grand publishing empire of Archibald Constable, in the fiction reprint libraries, like Charles Whittingham's Pocket Novelists, which began to appear as the price of new novels reached a peak, and in the grubbily mercantile dealings of that Dickensian figure Thomas Tegg, reprint merchant and absorber of bankrupt stock.

## ANTICIPATING A MASS MARKET (II): MIDDLING- AND LOWER-CLASS READERS

While the family bible remained the chief work of serious literature in the homes of the poor in the eighteenth century, reserving to itself the full authority and presiding power of print, it could be supplemented from the chap-books, broadsheet ballads and almanacs which featured among the wares of itinerant hawkers, and from the 1790s by various other kinds of material aimed at a low popular readership. Richard D. Altick notes the temporary 'surge of popular interest in reading during the 1790s',[1] linked to the accelerated political activity of the period. To the British government, at war from 1793 against revolutionary France, an emergent mass press, already characterized

---

1 Richard D. Altick, *The English Common Reader: A Social History of the Mass Reading Public 1800–1900*, Chicago, 1957, p 72.

by seditious and atheistical activities, was cause for extreme disquiet. Behind what developed in the 1790s into the first socially comprehensive war of printed propaganda in Britain was the popular chapbook. Traditionally the 'little books' of the poor, though enjoyed too by a multilayered audience, as the childhood reading of many of the major writers of the period attests,[1] chap-books became at this time the site of a fierce textual confrontation between diverse groups anxious to shape an emergent working-class reading public and competing, through radical and conservative discourses, to adapt its popular heroes to new ends.

Chap-books are modestly sized pamphlets, of anything between four and twenty-four pages, paper-covered and usually illustrated with crude woodcuts. Folk heroes like Jack the Giant Killer, Saint George, Robin Hood, and the pugnacious Long Meg of Westminster figure in chap-book adventures, but so too do unauthorized abridgements of works by Bunyan and Defoe. Many Bible narratives, Bunyan's allegorical romances, and early novels like *Robinson Crusoe* share a common concern with life as an embattled journey and with fiction as merely a cloak for truth. 'The Story, although allegorical, is also historical . . . one whole scheme of a real life of eight and twenty years, spent in the most wandering, desolate and afflicting circumstances that ever man went through', writes Defoe in the Preface to *Serious Reflections during the Life and Surprising Adventures of Robinson Crusoe* (1720). Such imaginative transformations of hardship and endurance stand as ur-texts or palimpsests behind the autobiographies of working men who grew up into literacy in the early years of the nineteenth century – behind *The Life of Thomas Cooper, Written by Himself* (1872) and behind *The Life and Struggles of William Lovett in His Pursuit of Bread, Knowledge, and Freedom* (1876). Archetypal fictions, they confer literary authority on the worker's heroic realities, since to record a life in print is to validate and preserve it. Thomas Cooper called *Pilgrim's Progress* 'my book of books', and E. P. Thompson writes that 'it is above all in Bunyan that we find the slumbering Radicalism which was preserved through the eighteenth century and which breaks out again and again in the

1 Walter Scott began collecting chap-books in childhood, buying them from the baskets of travelling pedlars. Bound in six volumes in 1810, his collection was influential in the development of his adult imagination. Both Wordsworth and Coleridge recommend the traditional tales found in chap-books as the best early reading for children: see *The Prelude* (1805), v. 364–9, part of a critique of modern education; and Coleridge's 1808 lecture on the education of children, in *Collected Works*, V, i. 108. There is also the description of Wordsworth's own early reading in Mary Moorman, *William Wordsworth: A Biography*, Oxford, 1957, i. 9–10.

nineteenth. *Pilgrim's Progress* is, with *Rights of Man*, one of the two foundation texts of the English working-class movement.'[1] First published in 1678–84, *Pilgrim's Progress* had gone through 160 editions by 1792. Echoes in such narratives of social oppression as Charlotte Brontë's *Jane Eyre* (1847) and Thomas Hardy's later, but obviously backward-looking, *Jude the Obscure* (1895) provide fictional confirmation of its politicized rereading throughout the nineteenth century.

The first part of Thomas Paine's *Rights of Man* appeared in 1791, asserting the relevance of the American and French revolutions to British political life, and directly opposing Edmund Burke's evolutionary conservative vision of *Reflections on the Revolution in France* (1790). Against Burke's primitive and emotional invocation of hereditary principle, native country, family and property, Paine sets, here and in Part Two issued the following year, an appeal couched in the direct language of the practical man of superior skills. Impatiently brushing aside the irrational obfuscations of argument from tradition (hereditary monarchy is declared to be no more than 'a system of *mental levelling* . . . Kings succeed each other, not as rationals, but as animals'),[2] Paine replaces them with plain analysis and tables of figures. Nevertheless he counters rhetoric with a heightened utterance of his own, drawn from the shared imaginative topography and popular biblical and chap-book heroes of the working man: the fall of the Bastille signified the downfall of despotism, he explains, for the two are 'as figuratively united as Bunyan's Doubting Castle and Giant Despair' (p 74); in imitation of a multitude of sub-Bunyan moral fables, he argues '[t]he duty of man is not a wilderness of turnpike gates, through which he is to pass by tickets from one to the other' (p 89); and he inserts a portrait of his own early seafaring and subsequent trials which reads remarkably like the unpromising start of Robinson Crusoe's career (p 240–41). Realizing new correspondences between the language of popular fiction and material reality, Paine inevitably destabilizes the sense of order and meaning in the social structure and threatens a more pervasive dissolution of relations. Specifically, his condemnation of the primitive conservatism of argument from hereditary principle finds a topical illustration in the remark that '[a]n hereditary governor is as inconsistent as an hereditary author' (p 198). For one far-reaching consequence of

1 E. P. Thompson, *The Making of the English Working Class*, rev. edn, Harmondsworth, 1968, p 34.
2 Thomas Paine, *Rights of Man*, ed. Henry Collins, Harmondsworth, 1969, p 194.

*Rights of Man* was to expose and so open up the closed world of political debate to a broader cross-section of writers and readers. In so doing, Paine presented the possibility of authorial identity to many working people.

With assisted free distribution to the workers through the republican London Constitutional Society, 50,000 copies of the original three-shilling edition of Part One of the *Rights* were sold in a few weeks (dwarfing the huge sales figure of 30,000 copies over two years of Burke's *Reflections*, also priced at three shillings). Part One was reprinted when Part Two was published in 1792, both selling in cheap format at six pence; over 32,000 copies of this cheap edition went in a month. The contemporary report that by 1793 there were 200,000 copies of *Rights of Man* in circulation, and by 1809 as many as 1,500,000 (Paine's own estimate, suggesting an improbable one copy for every ten people in the United Kingdom), including foreign translations, is treated sceptically by modern historians; but, however circulation figures are moderated, the joint sale of the two parts was formidable. More than any other single work in the period, it activated lower-class literacy as a political weapon. Part Two – with its crucial fifth chapter proposing a programme of social reforms such as a graduated income tax (rising to twenty shillings in the pound at £23,000 per annum), the revenue to finance the alleviation of the poor, family allowances for the encouragement of a minimal education for all children, and old-age pensions – sold higher than Part One and led to Paine's trial and sentence in his absence for seditious libel in December 1792. Paine found safety in flight; but some of his publishers and distributors fared worse: like H. D. Symonds, a publisher in London's Paternoster Row, sentenced to four years in prison and given a fine of £200 for printing the cheap edition of *Rights of Man*.

Paine's trial precipitated a series of repressive steps by the Pitt administration to curb the spread of radical writing and, more particularly, the self-identification of a radical reading audience at this sensitive time. It is crucial in the context of his contemporary political climate to weigh not merely the intellectual significance of Paine's ideas, but also the impact of *Rights of Man*, as book, on a wider system of material relations and social alignments. At the time, the cheap price of the sixpenny issue was possibly considered more dangerous than its content; so too was its instrumentality in bonding together a vulgar, thinking reading public. In an emergently literate society like working-class England, reading is primarily an associative activity, and therein lay its danger. Paine found his audience in the alehouses where artisans and labourers met to read and discuss *Rights of Man* or have it read to them for a few pennies, illiteracy being no bar to written communication in a society which at this stage defined reading as a socializing attribute.

The London Corresponding Society was established in January 1792, and, unlike earlier radical groups, it was not drawn from the relatively compromised and assimilated middle-class liberal circles but from a workforce which threatened, with all the zeal of the fundamental convert, to find its image within a specific written discourse, a new 'book of books'. With a subscription of a penny a week and unlimited membership, the London Corresponding Society held discussions and mass meetings, and formed links with radical movements elsewhere in Britain and in France. It was the single most important radical society of the period. According to one member, the tailor Francis Place, writing in his *Autobiography*, the London Corresponding Society 'induced men to read books, instead of wasting their time in public houses, it taught them to respect themselves, and to desire to educate their children. It elevated them in their own opinions.'[1] Reading conferred human dignity on the lowest section of society. They took to themselves, virtually as an incitement to effective group consciousness and as a spur to political definitiveness, Burke's inflammatory label 'a swinish multitude'. (Burke's famous reference is to a time when, civilization tossed aside, 'learning will be cast into the mire, and trodden down under the hoofs of a swinish multitude.'[2]) Radical journals like Thomas Spence's weekly *Pig's Meat; or, Lessons for the Swinish Multitude* (1793), Daniel Eaton's *Politics for the People: or, a Salmagundy for Swine* (1793), and provincial publications like the *Patriot* (1792) from Joseph Gales, the Sheffield master-printer, attempted to address and inform this post-Paine reading audience and to consolidate the radical network.

But 1792 saw the beginning of a full-scale pamphlet war with the formation in November of the Association for Preserving Liberty and Property against Republicans and Levellers. Their loyalist campaign of censorship and cheap distribution of anti-radical tracts was conducted after the style of the London Corresponding Society. But oiled by government assistance and grounded in those old-established values still largely regarded as 'natural', its propaganda machine had

1 *Autobiography of Francis Place*, ed. Mary Thale, Cambridge, 1972, p 198.
2 Edmund Burke, *Reflections on the Revolution in France*, ed. Conor Cruise O'Brien, Harmondsworth, 1969, p 173.

the advantage over its radical counterpart. The frequent arrests of radical booksellers (Eaton was arrested six times and Spence four between 1792 and 1795) and the state trials in 1794 of Thomas Hardy, John Horne Tooke and John Thelwall were aimed less against individuals than at defining the acceptable operation and sphere of mass reading and its agency in forming the social character. Repressive government measures of the late 1790s point to the directness of the link between reading and social action, and the consequent need to reaffirm readerly identifications along exclusive lines, in terms of boundaried (and so controlled) audiences.

The fear that an emergent multilayered readership would promote a dangerous proliferation of oppositional discourses, an explosive rivalry of 'truths', was matched by an equal concern that a radical literature would act as cement to otherwise scattered grievances. In particular, the concept of class below the middle is itself to a large extent the consequence of literacy, the act of reading serving to bind men and women across traditional skill and trade divisions. The last year of the eighteenth century saw the passing of the Corresponding Societies Act, suppressing political organizations with branches, forbidding public lectures on history and imposing a strict control by local magistrates on the whole printing trade. It also saw the foundation of the Religious Tract Society, an interdenominational organization whose redirection of an expanding readership had been anticipated by Hannah More's Cheap Repository Tracts (1795–8).

There are two compatible ways of interpreting Hannah More's counter-revolutionary zeal: as out-and-out conservatism in the face of those anarchic, pro-French sympathies which threatened to destroy Britain's social stability from below; or as the traditionally confined woman's domestic alternative to political questioning, a literary counterpart to her own extensive charity work among the rural labourers of Somerset. Just as it would be a mistake to assume that the radical movements of the period promoted as a matter of course the rights of women, so it would be historically short-sighted to lose More's practical feminism in her political conservatism. For three and a half years More waged war in the Cheap Repository Tracts against those radical pamphleteers who, in her words, had brought 'speculative infidelity . . . down to the pockets and capacities of the poor'.[1] According to one 'Advertisement' in the 1818 collected edition of More's writings, the Cheap Repository project 'was

1 *Memoirs of the Life and Correspondence of Mrs Hannah More*, ed. William Roberts, 2nd edn, London, 1834, ii. 458.

undertaken with an humble wish to counteract, not only vice and profligacy on the one hand, but error, discontent and false religion on the other'.[1] A long series of tales and ballads with a simple moral appeal, the tracts were formatted and styled, down to eye-catching title and crude woodcut, in close imitation of the pamphlets and coarse chap-books they meant to oust. Under the brief but authoritative persona of 'Z', More herself wrote forty-nine of the first one hundred and fourteen, with self-explanatory titles like these three for March 1795: *The Carpenter; or, the Danger of evil company*; *The Gin-shop; or, a Peep into a prison*; and *The Market Woman, a true tale; or, Honesty is the best policy*. Her best-known tract, *The Riot; or, Half a loaf is better than no bread* (August 1795), is reported to have stopped a riot among colliers near Bath. Retailing at the initially subsidized prices of a halfpenny or a penny, a staggering 2 million tracts had been distributed after only one year. But this high figure needs to be seen in the context of circulation methods: the tracts were given away through large institutions, the army and navy, prisons, factories, workhouses and charity schools. In addition, More's fictionalized and tamed lower-class communities had greater appeal for their upper- and middle-class distributors than for the poor themselves, and as early as January 1796 More was worried that titles were not reaching her targeted readership.

Characteristically, and to the confusion of many of our own cruder assessments of the sexual politics of the past, More turns the language of political agitation into a feminized discourse of caring, enduring and making the best of things. In place of the public reorganization demanded by the radical pamphleteers, she sets a plea for private regeneration. Earlier, in *Village Politics. Addressed to All the Mechanics, Journeymen, and Day Labourers, in Great Britain* by 'Will Chip, a Country Carpenter' (1793), the most famous of the Association for Preserving Liberty tracts, More presented a dialogue between a Paineite mason, Tom Hod, and Jack Anvil, a blacksmith, whose commonsensical political uninvolvement and cheerful confidence that those set above him know best are signs of his true patriotism:

> TOM  I'm a friend to the people. I want a reform.
> JACK  Then the shortest way is to mend thy self.
> TOM  But I want a *general reform*.
> JACK  Then let every one mend one.

> (*Works*, i. 346–7)

---

1 *The Works of Hannah More*, London, 1818, iv. iii.

From the historic and the public, More turns to the family and the unhistoric, the exchange often mediated through the author's representative in the text, the middle-class female philanthropist, the private, moral revolutionary whose mission is reading itself. Such a heroine is Mrs Jones the merchant's widow, who features in *The Cottage Cook; or Mrs Jones's Cheap Dishes; shewing the way to do much good with little money* (January 1797). It is Mrs Jones's practice 'never to walk out without a few little good books in her pocket to give away' (*Works*, iv. 337). She is an ardent believer in the saving power of controlled reading, arguing in *The Sunday School* (May 1797), against one contemporary conservative faction, represented by Farmer Hoskins, that 'to teach good principles to the lower classes, is the most likely way to save the country. Now, in order to do this, we must teach them to read' (*Works*, iv. 376). Mrs Jones champions the 'rights of man' too, in her own modest way, bringing to justice a dishonest baker who has cheated the local poor. More particularly, she advocates the 'rights of woman', to useful, practical education and to a sober, home-centred husband. If Paine took men to the alehouses, as one contemporary argument went, then More campaigns on behalf of women and children against the divisiveness and misery of drink. In her battles with tradesmen, farmers and small businessmen, Mrs Jones is clearly a forerunner of the middle-class female agents of the mid-nineteenth-century novel of social concern, possessing with the heroines of Elizabeth Gaskell, for example, an apolitical affinity with children, semi-literate labourers and the insecure middling class – all those who share their own absence from history. It was More's task, as she saw it, to feminize the political and in so doing to promote the family as a model of non-violent reorganization, an alternative to revolution.

Bringing to a close a turbulent decade in print, More's tracts were enormously comforting to the middle ranks, for whom the socially cohesive ideology of the family and family reading were to take on ever greater power in the early decades of the nineteenth century. In working to sever the rhetoric of popular democracy from its revolutionary roots and to appropriate it to the family unit, it could be argued that More was paving the way for the language of middle-class liberal reform of the new century. But we must be careful not to overestimate the extent to which the labouring poor identified with their literary inscription either as Paineite worker-scholars or as members of a growing family of the morally regenerated. In their campaign to colonize the emergent readership, political pamphleteers and disseminators of improving tracts engaged in intertextual warfare, mapping new ideological positions on to an older framework of popular social reading. But there is much evidence to suggest that this so-called 'sub-literary' prototype lost none of its appeal. Broadsheet ballads, lurid accounts of 'true' crimes and cheap reprint libraries competed on easy terms throughout the period with works of a political and moral revolutionary nature, revealing that reading was as much an escape from social tension as a route to confrontation or reconciliation.

## CRITICAL REVIEWS, LITERARY MAGAZINES AND CHEAP JOURNALS

Partly owing to the slowness of the book trade to exploit the combined expansions in technology and literacy, the early nineteenth century witnessed an unprecedented explosion in all kinds of periodical publication. Magazines, reviews and journals came to dominate the market. With large print runs, lower prices, and high standards for manufacture and contributions, these periodicals achieved wide circulation and influence (readerships of five to fifteen thousand and more each) and in many cases became the mainstay of publishing firms. In particular, periodicals locate one of the most complex issues of a mass reading age: the problem of whether a readership is discovered or made. Behind the variety of the early nineteenth-century periodicals lies a common task to mould a receptive readership by means of a unification of writer, format and reader. This is usually not so straightforward a matter as isolating and addressing a single social interest. The most powerful journals targeted the gentry, rich manufacturers and top professionals as their prime purchasers. Francis Jeffrey, the first editor of the hugely influential Whiggish *Edinburgh Review* (1802–1929), saw as his particular cultural charge the untutored resources of the 'middling classes'. Lesser clergy, teachers and shopkeepers, reading 'for amusement or instruction', they formed a potential readership of 200,000, ten times the number of the higher audience, according to Jeffrey's 1812 estimate. It was here in the middle, which he further defined as 'almost all those who are below the sphere of what is called fashionable or public life, and who do not aim at distinction or notoriety beyond the circle of their equals in fortune and situation', that Jeffrey considered lay the nation's best hope. These were the protectors of social stability and civilized decency, awaiting their full initiation via reading. For, as Jeffrey argued, 'though their taste may not be so correct and fastidious, we are persuaded that their sensibility is greater . . . [their emotions] the more powerful' (*ER*, xx, 1812: 279–81). His own task was to render culturally and politically potent the concomitant social virtues – industriousness and high moral purpose – of this responsive and responsible middle ground, and to do so by means of a careful diet of approved literature, current affairs and economic analysis. In reality, of course, the *Edinburgh*'s readership comprised the high and ambitious as well as the undistinguished and content, but Jeffrey's 'middling class' readers and their characteristic values were a political resort, a notional grouping, in part at least the creations of the periodical itself as well as the recipients of its middle-of-the-road ideology.

Characteristically, the early nineteenth-century periodicals are multi-voiced *and* univoiced. A comprehensive or miscellaneous coverage by several anonymous, and therefore representatively diverse, contributors is in its turn authorized by the centralizing editorial personality. Further, in the typographic presentation of contributions, knowledge is seen as a matter of contexts, of graphic alignments and juxta-positions, which foster connective links between the act of reading within the periodical and the interpretation of society's juxtaposed 'texts' beyond it. Towards this end the periodical is itself the instructor. In the early eighteenth century the *Spectator* had initiated a specific readership of 'well regulated Families', 'contemplative Tradesmen' and the 'Blanks of Society' into a community of 'sound and wholesom Sentiments' and habitual daily reading (*Spectator*, x). A century later such precise targeting is no longer possible. In an age of political turmoil and social insecurity, and later of bewildering urban and technological expansion, the periodicals re-quired a more flexible discourse. According to Jon P. Klancher in his recent inquiry into the making of reading audiences in the period, 'after 1790 [the 'reading habit'] became the scene of a cultural struggle demanding a new mental map of the complex public and its textual desires, a new way to organize audiences according to their ideological dispositions, their social distances, and the paradoxically intense pressure of their proximity as audiences.'[1]

One challenge posed to the modern reader by the early nineteenth-century periodicals is to distinguish the limits of an addressed audience, the manner of its invocation and representation in print in an age of shifting and competing literacies. Another is the challenge to rethink the reading process itself, in particular to assess

1 Jon P. Klancher, *The Making of English Reading Audiences: 1790–1832*, Madison, Wis., 1987, p 20.

the significance of what Jerome McGann has called 'spatial' or 'radial' reading,[1] a procedure which involves recovering for interpretation the printed relation of texts one to another across the regulated columns of the periodicals. As one site of radial reading, the periodical makes available to the student of literature unexpected textual alliances, rendering richly unfamiliar those works which are better known in the self-regarding format of single-author volumes and scholarly editions. The *Examiner* (1808–81), for example, was founded as a London weekly dedicated, in the words of its co-editor Leigh Hunt, primarily to 'Reform in Parliament, liberality of opinion in general (especially freedom from superstition), and a fusion of literary taste into all subjects whatsoever'.[2] While Hunt's political journalism resulted in imprisonment in 1812, it was in the pages of the *Examiner* from 1816 that an audience for the poetry of Shelley and Keats was created. The issue of 1 December 1816 printed Hunt's essay 'Young Poets', on Shelley, Keats and John Hamilton Reynolds. Keats's first published poem, 'O Solitude', appeared in the *Examiner*, on 5 May 1816; so too did Shelley's 'Hymn to Intellectual Beauty', on 19 January 1817, and 'Ozymandias', on 11 January 1818. To read Shelley's lyrics in the *Examiner*'s radical context is to recover different, political meanings. 'Ozymandias', for example, makes its first appearance in print in the top left-hand corner of a two-column page of the *Examiner* and fills, under the general heading of 'Original Poetry', little more than a quarter of the column. The rest of the page is taken up with an article entitled 'The Poor Laws', on the overburdened and inadequate provision for the poor in the Plymouth dockland, an area of radical unrest for much of the period. The lyric's comment on the nature (and transitoriness) of human power gains particular resonances in the light of the following article. This exercise in recovery is a useful reminder that works of literature share a synchronic existence with other, non-literary texts and events as well as a constituent place in the development of an author or a literary canon.

'On the Reciprocal Influence of the Periodical Publications and the Intellectual Progress of This Country', an article in *Blackwood's Edinburgh Magazine* for November 1824, argues in Humean fashion that the market forces of supply and demand are equally prescriptive of society's material *and* intellectual progress. Here the specialist

---

1 Jerome McGann, 'Theory of Texts', *London Review of Books* (18 February 1988), 21.
2 *The Autobiography of Leigh Hunt*, London, 1860, p 172.

reader and the specialist periodical are seen to be twin consequences of that division of labour and universal advancement which necessarily attends society's investment in literacy:

Hence the contents of the Magazines became divided; and instead of a Magazine being the repository of papers on a great variety of topics, literary, technical, domestic, &c., it was found that almost every one department was sufficient to support and fill its own peculiar Magazine. Thus, we now see such a variety of these periodical publications . . . [which] by the extent of their sale, sufficiently prove the extent of dominion which intellect of some kind and degree at present possesses in this country. It has insinuated itself into every nook and corner; and as, like caloric, it expands whatever it enters into, it must enlarge the capacity of the human mind, create new intellectual desires and wants, and the means of satisfying them.

(*Blackwood's*, xvi, 1824: 524)

*Blackwood's'* contributor traces to the periodical form pre-eminently that interactive relationship between information, economic expedience and public taste in terms of which a culture prospers. He locates the trigger for this mutually refining process in the crisis of the French Revolution, but for which intellectual life in England 'would have still lain dormant' (p 522) and the periodical press remained unregenerated.

The variety of the early nineteenth-century periodicals and their imaged readers is to be understood through ideas of directed discourses, of audience classification, and of the economic laws and market forces which forge the links between the anonymous magazine contributors and their unknown readers. The magazine is the quintessential commodified text. Namelessly multivoiced, it addresses sectors of an emergent reading public in their own style and language. And the writer–reader boundaries can be further dissolved by the common editorial practice of communicating with contributors too through the magazine's columns. As early as 1790–94 Edinburgh had been home to a weekly venture, the *Bee*, in some ways a consciously eighteenth-century venture but in others the forerunner of many Victorian miscellanies. It was, unusually for the time, copiously illustrated, wide-ranging in its scope and targeted readership, and it offered, through prizes and other enticements, the opportunity for its readers to exchange roles and become writers. London-based, from the house of John Bell, *La Belle Assemblée* (1806–32) was a monthly magazine for ladies, with a stimulating coverage of material, from articles on science, mathematics and politics, to serious reviews and anonymous serialized novels, and to fashion features, lavish engraved plates and illustrated needlework patterns. Priced at an expensive three shillings, *La Belle Assemblée* also included two separate supplements, one literary and the second an advertisement section, designed to build up into a permanent directory. With its seemingly comprehensive coverage, the magazine offered throughout the period 'an amusing and instructive emporium of elegant erudition', representing, by its totalizing power, its female reader to herself as an 'elegant, polite, and economical' shop-window of attractive and marketable talents.[1] Later, magazines like John Limbird's *Mirror of Literature, Amusement, and Instruction* (1822– 47), for most of its life issued weekly, and later still *Chambers's Edinburgh Journal* (1832–1956, weekly until 1854) brought cheap periodical literature and sanitized entertainment to a lower-class mass audience bent on dutiful self-improvement. Priced at two pence for sixteen pages of reprinted miscellaneous contents (along the lines of the modern *Reader's Digest*), the *Mirror*'s weekly circulation – 150,000 copies of the first issue and settling around 80,000 per issue in 1825 – easily dwarfed the sales of the middle-class journals.

But it was in the proliferous middle-class journals that intellectual battles raged and the acceptable perimeter of early nineteenth-century culture was drawn and debated, often along strictly party-political lines. 'But now the sun of criticism is ever shining upon us' comments one sardonic reviewer in the *Guardian* for 6 August 1820. Some literary and critical journals, like the *Edinburgh Review*, its Tory rival the *Quarterly Review* (1809–1962) and *Blackwood's Edinburgh Magazine* (1817–1980), were founded in the early nineteenth century but can lay equal claim to being classified as Victorian and twentieth-century journals. Others, like the short-lived *Honeycomb* (1820), the *Indicator* (1819–21) and the *Literary Speculum* (1821–3), attest to the impermanence and insecurity behind the apparently adapted language and format of such ventures: as many as thirty-eight which began publication after 1798 had disappeared by 1825.

As a centre of intellectual activity and publishing innovation, Edinburgh led in the field of periodical literature in the early nineteenth century. Issued quarterly, expensive (six shillings in 1809) and widely circulated (print runs of 13,000 in 1814, and an estimated three or four readers to each copy), the *Edinburgh Review* departed radically from eighteenth-century reviewing formulas, setting new standards in the critical rigour of its judgements on

---

1 Quoted phrases are from the magazine's editorials, as included in Alison Adburgham, *Women in Print: Writing Women and Women's Magazines from the Restoration to the Accession of Victoria*, London, 1972, pp 220–22.

contemporary literature and in the financial remuneration of its contributors. Where the Whig *Edinburgh* issued from the powerful publishing house of Archibald Constable, *Blackwood's*, a monthly magazine offering a variety of creative pieces rather than a critical review, was the organ of the rival Edinburgh house of the Tory William Blackwood. Assiduous, if often hostile, in its coverage of the work of Wordsworth, Coleridge, Shelley and Keats, *Blackwood's* was an important disseminator of Romantic poetry, in the form of lengthy quotations, to the reading public. De Quincey published in its pages, and, more particularly, *Blackwood's* provided a forum for original fiction, often serialized – John Galt's Scottish novels in the 1820s, and George Eliot's *Scenes of Clerical Life* in 1857.

The monthly *London Magazine* (1820–29) requires consideration alongside *Blackwood's* because of the literally deadly feud which the two periodicals waged over the value of contemporary poetry: John Scott, the *London*'s first editor, was fatally wounded in a duel with J. H. Christie of *Blackwood's*. It was in the *London* that Hazlitt's *Table-Talk* (1821–2), Lamb's Elia essays (1820–22) and De Quincey's *Confessions of an English Opium-Eater* (1821) appeared. In its pages the *London* sought to establish fair critical principles for the assessment of current literature (in its 'Living Author Series') and, famously, for the poetry of Keats.

Both John Gibson Lockhart in *Blackwood's* (iii, 1818: 519–24) and John Wilson Croker in the *Quarterly* (xix, 1818: 204–8) base their dismissal of Keats's newly published *Endymion* on his poetic association (and presumed political sympathies) with the reformist Leigh Hunt, leader of the scornfully named 'Cockney School of Poetry'. In fact it is Hunt and his politics rather than Keats and his poetry which are the real target of the Tory reviewers, unless we include the reiterated gibe that neither Hunt nor Keats was a 'gentleman', tantamount by itself to proof of radical collusion. In Lockhart's vituperative personal attack, 'the calm, settled, imperturbable drivelling idiocy of "Endymion"' is symptomatic of the late stages of that severe illness of '*Metromanie*' (poetical mania). 'Whether Mr John had been sent home with a diuretic or composing draught to some patient far gone in the poetical mania, we have not heard. This much is certain, that he has caught the infection, and that thoroughly' (p 519). Indulging the analogy between illness and 'bad' poetry, grounded in Keats's known apprenticeship as an apothecary, Lockhart invites Shelley's subsequent romantic diagnosis of death by review in the preface to *Adonais* (1821), his elegiac tribute to Keats, as well as Byron's more flippant verdict in *Don Juan* (1823) ('''Tis strange the mind, that very fiery particle,/Should let itself be snuff'd out by an article', XI. lx).

A vigorous promoter of critical integrity divorced from political allegiance and personal attack, John Scott champions Keats against the 'cold-blooded conscious dishonesty' of the *Quarterly* and the 'merry ruffianism' of *Blackwood's* (*London*, ii, 1820: 315–21). He attacks *Blackwood's* as 'a publication, in which . . . the violation of decency was to render it *piquant*, and the affectation of piety render it persuasive, and servility to power, render it profitable'. Scott's own death by reviewer witnesses to the zeal with which the major periodicals pursued their mission of cultural control, and the protective vigilance (wittily or ponderously articulated) with which the partisan politics of reading was decreed and enforced. Looking back from the middle of the century at these early reviewing feuds, Leigh Hunt summarized what seemed to him, as one sufficiently persecuted, the mood of the times:

> Readers in these kindlier days of criticism have no conception of the extent to which personal hostility allowed itself to be transported, in the periodicals of those times. Personal habits, appearances, connections, domesticities, nothing was safe from misrepresentations, begun, perhaps, in the gaiety of a saturnalian licence, but gradually carried to an excess which would have been ludicrous, had it not sometimes produced tragical consequences.
>
> (*Autobiography of Leigh Hunt*, p 218)

As editor and chief literary reviewer for the *Edinburgh Review* from 1802 to 1829, Francis Jeffrey was among the most powerful arbiters of national taste. His authoritarian posturing proved an irresistible satiric target to the young Byron ('O'er politics and poesy preside,/Boast of thy country, and Britannia's guide!' *English Bards and Scotch Reviewers*, 1809, 500–501). Jeffrey's sense of the critic's public responsibilities as cultural leader and literary censor in a country at war explains his privileging of literature's social relevance over narrower aesthetic criteria. It also exposes the political expedience of his campaign against much contemporary poetry and his ridicule of Wordsworth's experimental verse in particular. What he calls Wordsworth's 'childish and absurd affectations' and his 'poor ambition of originality' offend Jeffrey's belief in the necessary subordination of individual talent to the common sympathies of 'ordinary minds' (*ER*, xii, 1808: 137; and xx, 1812: 374). Where the prevailing fashion among twentieth-century critics and readers, schooled in the interiorized idealisms of the Romantic imagination, has been to find in the sympathetically isolated poet one who transcends history, politics and social circumstance, Jeffrey judges the poet as he addresses and accommodates his vision to his times, and his poetry not as an insight into the workings of the poet's mind but as a socially accountable artefact.

Despite many reservations, Jeffrey could therefore declare of Walter Scott, the best-selling poet of the war years, that '[a] popularity so universal is a pretty sure proof of extraordinary merit' (*ER*, xvi, 1810: 263). What amounted in the early years of the nineteenth century to a reviewing crusade against Wordsworth and an overestimation of Scott as poet was not free from political presuppositions. But in this Jeffrey valuably reminds us that the questions asked by any and every critic are never exclusively aesthetic but have to do with audience and reception – who will read the work, and how. The fluctuating success of British efforts to control French imperialism in Europe and the need to maintain a united war-spirit at home provided a fostering environment for the strong alliance of a national taste and a national voice in a national poet. Scott, an openly political poet allied to Scotland's dominant Tory interest by family connections and for professional preferment as a lawyer, combined unprecedented popularity with strong patriotic fervour. The Whig Charles James Fox and the Tory William Pitt, arch-opponents in the Commons, were united in admiration of Scott's *Lay of the Last Minstrel* (1805). *Marmion*, his second long poem, was the best-seller of 1808 – 2,000 copies in the first month, and 11,000 in the first year, despite the exorbitant price of 31s 6d.

Though separated by political differences (in 1808 there was still serious opposition among the Whigs to the continuation of the economically crippling war with Napoleon, and from 1807 the *Edinburgh* began carrying articles in favour of peace), the liberal Jeffrey saw in the Tory Scott the poet who appealed pre-eminently to the vast middlebrow public, readers of the *Edinburgh Review*, on whom Britain's future seemed to depend. In pressing in its pages, after 1808, for a judicious parliamentary reform, Jeffrey bowed to historical inevitability and to the justice of political change as the only means to preserve Britain from the internal turmoils of France. Far from being a headlong democrat, he saw in the swelling ranks of the middle classes (many of them as yet disenfranchised)[1] the

1 The eventual Reform Act of 1832 enlarged the borough franchise to include £10 a year male householders (men who occupied as owners or tenants of one landlord buildings with an annual value of £10), thus attaching the interest and loyalty of a broad-based, property-centred, 'respectable' middle, much as Jeffrey had argued was necessary. The qualification still effectively excluded the working classes and, of course, all women.

guardians of the arts, of industry and morality against the encroach-
ments of despotism from the Crown or insurrection from below.
Like the Victorians, whose cultural values he so often anticipates,
Jeffrey saw refinement in the arts as bound up with a society's
progress towards commercial civilization and its production of other
commodities. Scott's poetic voice, like his personal ambitions, chimed
with the aspirations of the rising middle classes, as Scott the man,
his politics aside, was a model of professional industry, a perfect
example of the artist as representative in the great age of commercial
civilization. His did not seem a divisive poetry. An uncomplicated
backcloth of bold deeds and unreflecting action, its effect was
salutary, temporarily neutralizing the partisan climate and policy
indecision of the war years.

In contrast, Wordsworth's democratic claim to have found true
poetry in his oppositional scrutiny of the language and situations of
'common life' appeared to threaten social disunity and subversion of
all decent order. So Jeffrey seems to understand it when he attacks
the Lake School (so-called) in a review of Southey's *Thalaba* (1801)
in the very first issue of the *Edinburgh*. Wordsworth and his Lake
School adherents 'constitute, at present, the most formidable conspiracy that has lately been formed against sound judgment in
matters poetical'. Wordsworth dangerously suggests a universally
applicable poetry in the passions of 'a clown, a tradesman or a
market-wench', and he and his followers display

[a] splenetic and idle discontent with the existing institutions of society . . .
at the bottom of all their serious and peculiar sentiments. Instead of
contemplating the wonders and the pleasures which civilization has created
for mankind, they are perpetually brooding over the disorders by which its
progress has been attended.

(*ER*, i, 1802: 64–71)

To Jeffrey, Wordsworth's poetic experiments have a political immediacy dangerously akin to the radical mouthing of Paineite French
Revolutionary precepts in Britain. Believing, as he did, in the
significance of literature as a record of a given time and in the
primacy of its social usefulness in its own time, it was crucial to
Jeffrey that the spirit of the war years be strengthened and reflected
in a particular kind of public statement. It is a measure of the
seriousness with which he assumed his guardianship of contemporary
culture that his private opinions (among which was an admitted
enjoyment of some of Wordsworth's poetry) did not override what
he believed was his public duty. Amply endowed with that robust

sanity which Jeffrey considered the very antithesis of true genius (with all its, for him, disquieting connotations of social disease and political instability), Scott was a man for the time, a representative voice. It was inevitable that such an ambiguously founded reputation would not survive its enabling context.

Alongside the periodical expansion of the early nineteenth century there was too a commensurately rapid growth in newspapers. The last decades of the eighteenth century saw the introduction of Sunday and evening daily papers to supplement the existing London morning dailies, the less frequent evening papers and the provincial weeklies, which had been up to this time little more than rehashes of metropolitan features, their local flavour gathered from advertisements. Between 1801 and 1831, when heavy taxation held production back, officially stamped copies alone more than trebled. An average of forty newspapers and periodicals were started each year during the first decade of the nineteenth century; in 1832 the average was 250. However, the frequent increase in stamp taxes meant that newspapers were prohibitive as purchases to any below the reasonably well off. Even then it was common to share the expense of a paper, and hiring, illegal since 1789, continued. By 1815 stamp tax on newspapers was four pence per sheet – that is, for every four pages of advertisements and compressed news items – a sum which inevitably denied the working classes lawful access to up-to-date information. In pubs and workshops, clubs were formed to read or hear news read on a regular basis, each copy of a paper having, it has been suggested, a reading or 'hearing' public of as many as thirty.

In a society in which the printed word possessed a (to us) scarcely comprehensible power to soothe or incite and an alarmingly mercurial identity, it is difficult to overestimate the influence of the news-sheet in the hands of an emergent lower-class readership. Twin growths of the new technology of steam press and cylindrical platen, the newspaper and the mass reading public threatened in concert an explosive information alliance. A repository of current events and organ of opinions, the newspaper's regular punctuation of the working week and its centralizing overview formatted the new readership as an informed collective consciousness, and hence a potentially dangerous dissonant voice. With press production on *The Times* accelerated in 1816 to 900 perfected sheets an hour, the State viewed censorship and audience restriction as the corollary of the print expansion, part of the necessary redefinition of the exclusivity of public affairs in a depressed postwar economy. One consequence was that the years

1816 to 1820 saw an intense outburst of radical journalism, a reawakening of the spirit of Paine and the 1790s in a generation now more confident in its literacy and in the amalgamating agency of a demotic press in the struggle for constitutional reform.

In the war of the 'unstamped' press, William Cobbett's weekly *Political Register* (1802–35) led the way, issued from 1816 not only in its expensive form of a shilling halfpenny, but as a twopenny pamphlet. Originally a Tory news-sheet, the *Register* had long exposed to reformist rhetoric the corruption of the Establishment (which Cobbett dubbed the 'System' or the 'Thing'). Avoiding stamp duty by omitting the direct reporting of news, the entire issue of 2 November 1816 was an open-sheet address 'To the Journeymen and Labourers of England, Scotland and Ireland', dedicated to awakening them to their right to full social participation. Cobbett claimed that 200,000 copies were sold in two months (a figure which invokes the contemporary estimate of sales of Paine's *Rights of Man* after, in the case of Part One, not two months but two *years*). Subsequent circulation of the twopenny *Register* stood at 40,000 or 50,000, and perhaps as high as 70,000, representing sales beyond every other journal of the day.

Resetting the price of the paper, Cobbett, himself the son of a small farmer and innkeeper, attempted to redefine not only the reading of politics but the politics of reading. An ambiguous Tory-Radical (Hazlitt called him 'a kind of *fourth estate* in the politics of the country'),[1] he united in himself the purposes of Paine and Hannah More, bringing the worker-politician out of the pub and into the home. Where the home becomes the site of radical reading – represented in the *Register*'s first cheap issue (2 November 1816) as a place affording 'the time for reflection, and opportunity of reading over again' – it can seem that the quiet power of grammatical association is to replace the potentially violent conjunction of man with man in clubs and other public meeting-places. Now the ability to wield language becomes the worker's best means of political assertion. In his *Grammar of the English Language in a Series of Letters* (1817), Cobbett identifies access to the skill of writing as well as that of reading as socially empowering, a political rite of passage.

After 1816 social tensions and political agitation gathered momentum. The suspension of the Habeas Corpus Act in 1817 gave the Government the opportunity to threaten Cobbett, who had so far offered no specific grounds for prosecution, with arrest. He fled to

1  *Table Talk* (1821), in *Complete Works*, viii. 50.

America. The next two years witnessed a bolder metropolitan and provincial radical journalism with papers like T. J. Wooler's *Black Dwarf* (1817), John Wade's *Gorgon* (1818), William Hone's *Reformist's Register* (1817), James Wroe's *Manchester Observer* (1819) and, latterly under the editorship of Richard Carlile, *Sherwin's Political Register* (1817), renamed from 1819 the *Republican*. Some of these publications, like the *Black Dwarf*, gained a weekly circulation of around 12,000. By following Cobbett's lead, they evaded the effects of stamp duty and appeared as political pamphlets rather than as what might legally be defined as newspapers. Among government attempts to suppress lower-class political reading at this time and the spread of radical literature ('Twopenny Trash' as it was familiarly called, after Cobbett's price-setting *Register*) were the unsuccessful 1817 prosecutions of Hone, on three counts of blasphemous libel, for printing parodies based on the Book of Common Prayer. Hone's tracts are unsubtle in their satire and direct in their exposure of injustice, as befits political journalism aimed at a mass and insecurely literate readership – as, for example, this passage from the *Political Litany*, addressed to the Prince Regent:

> From all the deadly sins attendant on a corrupt method of election;
> from all the deceits of the pensioned hirelings of the press,
> *Good Prince, deliver us!*
> . . .
> From a Parliament chosen only by one tenth of the tax-payers;
> from taxes raised to pay wholesale human butchers their subsidies . . .
> *Good Prince, deliver us!*
> *(The Political Litany, diligently revised; to be said or sung,*
> *until the appointed change come*, 1817, p 4)

The cheap price of twopence a copy only aggravated the offence of such topical invective. After the infamous attack by government troops in August 1819 on an outdoor mass meeting for reform in Manchester's St Peter's Fields (the Peterloo massacre), further legislation was introduced and passed in only one month in an attempt to curb unrest. Two of the 'Six Acts' were aimed specifically at the radical press. By the Seditious Publications Act, the 'newspaper' was freshly defined to include those cheap journals which had proliferated by circumventing the stamp. Now a fourpenny tax was imposed on any periodical containing news or comment, published more frequently than every twenty-six days, printed on two sheets or less, and costing sixpence or under, exclusive of the tax. Effectively this reinforced the illegal status of political journals within the working-class price range and maintained tax as a convenient weapon of censorship. No longer a tax on news, as the earlier stamp duty had been, this was a tax on anti-Government views.

Richard Carlile, who had been on the platform at Peterloo, was indicted and imprisoned in October 1819 for publishing and selling seditious material, including his 1818 reprint of Paine's forbidden classic *The Age of Reason* (1794–5). For a period after 1820, the literature of radical protest, raised to a minimum price of sixpence, was reduced to a trickle. Throughout his imprisonment, Carlile's Fleet Street shop continued to defy further prosecutions by issuing seditious and blasphemous reprints. Carlile had shot to prominence in 1817 as one of the piratical publishers of Robert Southey's *Wat Tyler*, about the popular leader of the late fourteenth-century Peasants' Revolt. Written and left unpublished in the 1790s, it was a youthful and recanted piece. As Poet Laureate, Southey was, in 1817, comfortably ensconced on the other side and had tried unsuccessfully to block its publication. Now it was followed by pirated editions of Shelley's *Queen Mab* and *The Necessity of Atheism*, and Byron's *Cain*. If the perseverance of Carlile and others like him ultimately made a nonsense of government censorship, the libel trials of 1817 and 1819 and the events of St Peter's Fields nevertheless brought home the emptiness of the vaunted freedoms of the British people. Freedom of the press, freedom of speech and the right of assembly: all had been decisively undermined in the very years which saw the proliferation of middle-class journals.

## THE ECONOMICS OF LITERATURE AND THE GLAMOUR OF THE PRESS

As the economics of censorship suggest, the models of commerce and industry, closely identified from the start with projects for mass education, became impressed upon all aspects of the trade in reading. These are the 'machines' which, in Thomas Carlyle's gloomy interpretation, make of instruction 'a secure, universal, straightforward business, to be conducted in the gross, by proper mechanism' ('Signs of the Times', *ER*, xlix, 1829: 443). By the same forces the publisher was transformed during the early nineteenth century from relative insignificance in the process of turning manuscript into printed book into a powerful entrepreneur, capable of 'making' authors and creating markets for their wares. Constable and Blackwood in Edinburgh, and a fellow Scot, Murray, in London established their formidable publishing networks around the critical periodicals they each launched (the *Edinburgh Review, Blackwood's Edinburgh Magazine* and the *Quarterly Review* respectively). The big periodicals attached to themselves schools of reviewers, selectively accommodated new authors, and attempted to set the cultural and political horizons of their readers. According to Thomas Cadell, writing to Blackwood in 1821, 'Murray's procuring the publication of almost all the new Works of consequence . . . is occasioned by the extensive literary connexion attached to the publication of the "Quarterly Review", the character of which for sterling merit is now firmly established, and the sale of it known to be preeminently successful.'[1] A closed-circuit model of literary relations in an industrial age (from generation, through production, marketing and consumption), the periodical was confirmed as the shop-window of its publishing-house, advertising ('puffing') its goods, fashioning the taste for their reception, and decrying those of its competitors.

Summing up the success of Constable, the so-called 'Napoleon of print', Henry Cockburn had this to say:

Abandoning the old timid and grudging system, he stood out as the general patron and payer of all promising publications, and confounded not merely his rivals in trade, but his very authors, by his unheard-of prices. Ten, even twenty, guineas a sheet for a review, £2000 or £3000 for a single poem, and £1000 each for two philosophical dissertations, drew authors from dens where they would otherwise have starved, and made Edinburgh a literary mart, famous with strangers, and the pride of its own citizens.

*(Memorials of His Time*, 1856, pp 168–9)

Some would-be authors were not so fortunate. Jane Austen wrote in April 1809, in a letter which she signed M. A. D., reminding the publisher Richard Crosby of his purchase for only ten pounds, six years previously, of the manuscript of a novel 'Susan' (*Northanger Abbey*), still unpublished. Crosby replied, 'there was not any time stipulated for its publication, neither are we bound to publish it, Should you or anyone else (*sic*) we shall take proceedings to stop the sale. The MS. shall be yours for the same as we paid for it.'[2] He continued to refuse to publish, and the copyright was not recovered until 1816. The novel finally appeared in 1818 from the house of Murray, a year after Austen's death. The £400 which Austen left in her will represents, it has been suggested, a considerable part of her earnings as a novelist. But in many cases vast sums of money were now paid to authors for copyright, and the

---

1 *The Publishing Firm of Cadell and Davies, Select Correspondence and Accounts, 1793–1836*, ed. Theodore Besterman, London, 1938, p 65.
2 *Jane Austen's Letters*, ed. R. W. Chapman, 2nd edn, London, 1952, pp 263–4.

publisher's place of business became a literary *salon* where authors and critics met.

If Scott was the star of Constable's stable, Byron held the same high place in Murray's, until they fell out over the publication of *Don Juan*. Scott's and Byron's careers coincided with and helped to fuel the unprecedented popularity and sales of volumes of verse in the first twenty years of the nineteenth century. A poetry boom, it can be linked to the continuance of manufacturing constraints on the production of more diffuse literary forms as well as to the high fashionable status enjoyed by poetry and poets, a genteel respect which was not accorded to the novel, with its origins in trade and its acknowledged democracy of readers. Between them, Scott and Byron forced up the market value of new poetry. Scott received an unprecedented £4,000 for *The Lady of the Lake* (1810), which sold over 20,000 copies in the first year. In 1812 Murray sold 4,500 copies of the first two cantos of *Childe Harold* in less than six months, and on the day of publication alone 10,000 copies of *The Corsair* (1814). Subsequently he felt able to offer Byron 1,000 guineas for *The Siege of Corinth* and £2,000 for Canto III of *Childe Harold*, both published in 1816. It is no coincidence that Byron, the born aristocrat, and Scott, the aspirant aristocrat, established the contemporary definition of poetry as a judicious blend of (financially) expensive and (socially) exclusive adventure. Only a few years previously urban nostalgia for an agrarian world had brought a transient fame and fortune to the labourer-poet Robert Bloomfield, paid £4,000 as a sign of his temporary stature. His *Farmer's Boy* appeared in 1800, originally in sumptuous quarto, and broke all records, selling 26,000 copies in under three years. But such success belies any concept of a free market in literature: Bloomfield's was an uprooted and kidnapped discourse, his orthography and grammar 'corrected' for publication. A sentimentalized commodity for a middle-class audience, his poetry prompted no mobility of consciousness across the social divide of rich and poor, appearing though it did at a time of agricultural crisis.

'Gentlemen, persons of fortune, professional men, ladies, persons who can afford to buy, or can easily procure, books of half-a-guinea price, hot-pressed, and printed on superfine paper. These persons are, it is true, a part of human nature, but we err lamentably if we suppose them to be fair representatives of the vast mass of human existence.'[1] So wrote Wordsworth in June 1802 to John Wilson,

1 *The Letters of William and Dorothy Wordsworth, 1787–1805*, ed. Ernest de Selincourt, rev. Chester L. Shaver, 2nd edn, Oxford, 1967, p 355.

later the influential journalist and editor for *Blackwood's*, expressing at once his unhappiness with the reading taste of the so-called 'Public' and his dissatisfaction with the narrow bounds within which that public is defined. 'People in our rank in life are perpetually falling into one sad mistake,' he continued, 'namely, that of supposing that human nature and the persons they associate with are one and the same thing.' Those readerly responses which we would wish to gloss as humanly representative and socially unconstrained serve, in fact, Wordsworth suggests, a particular class interest. While Scott and Byron set a higher and higher value on poetry, so too did Wordsworth. Until well into the nineteenth century, London and Edinburgh dominated the book trade, and non-metropolitan publication was commercial suicide. In arranging publication of *Lyrical Ballads* in 1798 through the radical Bristol bookseller Joseph Cottle, with London distribution by Longman, Wordsworth and Coleridge may have been making a political point: the connection between a provincial imprint, radical literature, and books for children and the poor was well established. In a later letter of June 1808, on reading and the poor, addressed to the Revd Francis Wrangham, Wordsworth confesses to a long-standing desire that some of his own poetry might 'supplant', in the peasant culture it seeks to record, the traditional reading of 'half-penny Ballads, and penny and twopenny histories'.[1] Wordsworth's two statements, admittedly separated by six years, shift uneasily between a call to a broader democracy in publishing and a self-confessed plan for colonizing a lower-class culture.

However interpreted, the Bristol publication of *Lyrical Ballads* (advertised at five shillings in small octavo, and so in this form well beyond a labourer's pocket) was instrumental in Cottle's financial downfall, and almost the whole edition of 500 copies had to be sold to the London bookseller Arch only five days after publication. *Lyrical Ballads* subsequently achieved a modest success, though one remarkable in Wordsworth's publishing career, going through four editions by 1805. But even when public demand for poetry was at its height (between Scott's *Marmion*, 1808, and Byron's *Don Juan*, 1819–23), Wordsworth's sales generally were low, only in part the result of the hostile reviewing campaign which Jeffrey led against him; for at least the *Edinburgh*'s attacks kept Wordsworth's name before the public. In 1814 Longman still had 230 copies of the *Poems* of 1807 to shift. The 500 copies of *The Excursion* (1814) lasted

---

1 *The Letters of William and Dorothy Wordsworth, 1806–1811*, ed. Ernest de Selin-court, rev. Mary Moorman, 2nd edn, Oxford, 1969, p 248.

for six years, and the second edition of 500 in 1820 lasted another seven. Nor did Keats and Shelley, entering the market in the second decade of the new century, find fortune in poetry. Taylor and Hessey paid Keats £100 for the copyright of *Endymion* in 1818 and the same amount for *Lamia, Isabella, and Other Poems* (1819) together with *Poems* (1817), taken over from C. and J. Ollier. None of these volumes went into a second edition; the story is similar for Shelley, all of whose poems published with C. and J. Ollier lost money.

If Scott, Byron, Tom Moore and others gave to exotic and alien subjects a common poetic currency, a robust and easy idiom, and a wide public appeal, Wordsworth is responsible for a counter-development which is now the poetic norm: the simultaneous idealization of shared communal models and the intellectual isolation of the actual reader of poetry. In addressing, in 1815, his democracy of readers as 'the People, philosophically characterized . . . the embodied spirit of their knowledge',[1] Wordsworth practises a universalizing and dehistoricizing exercise sufficiently familiar to us from traditional literary criticism and explainable in terms of the rise of a common reader. Partly economically, partly politically and philosophically, and partly class ordered, a mass reading population challenges the author to identify and constitute his/her own readerly reception in the face of its unknowable heterogeneity. Faced with Coleridge's 'multitudinous PUBLIC',[2] the author (Wordsworth, Coleridge, Keats and Shelley) withdraws from the threatened instability of his discourse to the security of the ideal, the text-created reader. Re-imagining the poet's relation to his audience, Wordsworth retreats from what he interprets as insensitivity and lack of taste in 'that small though loud portion of the community, ever governed by factitious influence, which, under the name of the PUBLIC, passes itself, upon the unthinking, for the PEOPLE'. He attempts, instead, to shift the economics of literary relations from the fluctuating fortunes of the populous market-place to the nobler, family labour of the agrarian community. What the bankrupt economy of poems like 'Michael' reveals to be historically obsolescent in an age of industrial progress – the self-sufficient pastoral unit – is, interestingly, the model which the modern reader has most profitably internalized, making of the poem a private plot, defended by familial contract, on which author and reader successively labour for reward. Paradoxically, and after Wordsworth,

1 'Essay, Supplementary to the Preface' (1815), in *The Prose Works of William Wordsworth*, ed. W. J. B. Owen and Jane Worthington Smyser, Oxford, 1974, iii. 84.
2 *Biographia Literaria*, in *Collected Works*, VII, p 59.

poetry's potential for private investment has for us become the exclusively representative dictum of an age which ostentatiously celebrated (and carefully censored) its public value.

Poetry's pre-eminence did not outlast the 1820s. In 1818 Byron could write 'I've half a mind to tumble down to prose/But verse is more in fashion – so here goes!' (*Beppo*, lii); but his death in 1824 marks a reordering of relations among literary forms. According to Ian Jack, 'Within a few weeks of Byron's death we find a writer in *Blackwood's* remarking that nowadays "few write poetry . . . and nobody at all reads it. Our poets . . . have over-dosed us."'[1] Longman, Murray and John Taylor, the friend and publisher of Keats and Clare, all withdrew over the next few years from financial investment in poetry. Although the slow spread of technological innovation into the book trade meant that verse was still cheaper to turn out in the early years of the century, at the same time the proliferation of magazines which had initially given a boost to new poetry soon began to run short stories and serialized fictions as a serious challenge. It is possible to link poetry's dwindling status to advancements in technology, the consequent diversification and cheapening of print for a growing reading public, and the lifting of restrictions on a purchasing public. If between them Constable and Scott made of poetry a best-selling business pre-1820, together they capitalized on and helped to shape the technological revolution whereby the novel became the dominant literary form post-1820.

'They talk of a farmer making two blades of grass grow where one grew before but you my good friend have made a dozen of volumes where probably not one would have existed', wrote Scott to Constable in March 1822.[2] The first true best seller (as early as 1818 his annual novel profits were estimated at £10,000), Scott comes to locate the work of fiction within the world of production and exchange, and to incorporate metaphorically the pressures of literature's industrialization in an age of mass reading. As the preface to his novel *The Betrothed* (1825) suggests, in its proposal for the formation of a joint-stock company to turn out future fiction by machinery, the modern author is now just one on the production line. In the same important year of 1825 Scott was negotiating with Constable a revolutionary venture to flood the market with cheap reprints of his best-selling Waverley Novels. Scott and his publisher

1 Ian Jack, *English Literature 1815–1832*, Oxford, 1963, p 421.
2 *The Letters of Sir Walter Scott*, ed. H. J. C. Grierson, Edinburgh and London, 1932–7, vii. 104.

had forced up the standard price set for new fiction with *Kenilworth* in 1821 (sold at 31s 6d, 10s 6d per volume); but now their ambitious plan was to combine narrow profit margins with huge sales and so to bring recent fiction within the price range of the lowest classes. Forestalled by the great financial crash of 1825–6, the project only came to birth much modified as the 48-volume collected edition of the Waverley Novels, advertised in the *Literary Gazette* for 18 April 1829 as designed to enlarge Scott's reading public, previously confined to 'the wealthier ranks of society', to include 'readers of all classes'. Issued by Robert Cadell from 1829–33 at monthly intervals, sales were estimated at 35,000 copies a month as early as the end of 1829; but at a cost of five shillings a volume, it still would not have percolated much below the middle. Extensively annotated, handsomely produced in a uniform format and ensured of limited mass circulation, the collected edition of the Waverley Novels for the first time raised a living author to institutional status and, also for the first time, canonized the work of a novelist. The success of the *Magnum Opus* edition, as Scott liked to call it, paved the way for the high Victorian assessment of the contemporary novelist and helped to turn the novel into a new paper currency, whose identified literary and monetary value Dickens, Thackeray and Trollope were to exploit later in the century.

At the same time Constable's original plan for the cheapening of print to the common reader spawned a whole flood of 'Family Libraries', 'Miscellanies', 'Cabinet Libraries' and 'Libraries for the People' from the major publishing houses, offering new works as well as fiction reprints at low prices (from sixpence to five shillings). Such series were not simply money-spinners for their publishers, but national encyclopaedias collectivizing the new mass audience between their covers and proffering 'cheap knowledge' (the slogan of the late 1820s) as the social panacea. Chief among them was the Library of Useful Knowledge, an austere diet of science and technology (topics included differential and integral calculus, and 'animal mechanics') issued from early 1827 in fortnightly instalments of densely printed text, priced sixpence, by the newly formed Society for the Diffusion of Useful Knowledge. Two years later it was supplemented by the hardly more digestible Library of Entertaining Knowledge (subjects like 'insect architecture', 'vegetable substances' and the Elgin Marbles[1]).

---

1 These were the much-discussed sculptures removed by Lord Elgin from the Parthenon in Athens. They were offered for sale to the British Government in 1811

Under the weight of such systematically 'diffused' instruction the popular radical press, which had itself campaigned for a wider access to knowledge, was, ironically, neutralized. Henry Brougham, founder of the SDUK, was also, with Francis Jeffrey and others, one of the leading intelligences of the *Edinburgh Review*, whose liberal support for a system of universal education was underpinned by a developed interest in political economy and a belief in the socially unifying role of the middle classes. The contemporary debate over the potential for social subversion within an educated lower class should be set against that appeal to determined economic laws which drives Brougham's scheme: by means of education, the rightness and necessity of society's division of labour and opportunity is liberally diffused from the middle through the whole system. The SDUK is only one consequence of a general promulgation post-1820 of the new economic order (see, for example, the founding in 1820 of the Political Economy Club, and the rash of economics textbooks in these years). Education of the poor in all branches of knowledge, including party politics, argued Brougham in 1824, is the best security for 'the peace of the country, and the stability of the government' (*ER*, xli: 101). It seems agreed by 1830 that ignorance and illiteracy are at the root of crime and social dissidence. Brougham's 'Steam Intellect Society', as Peacock satirized the SDUK in *Crotchet Castle* (1831, Chapter 2), seemed set to turn print into the profitable producer of social good and of advancing economic prosperity. Stemming social decline, literacy offers integral calculus and the Elgin Marbles as the routes to social cohesion in a world of mechanical relations.

There was throughout the period 1780 to 1830 an urgent awareness that society, its ranks and relations, its modes of communication, and even its fantasies were being reordered by the printing-press, and that something amounting to a revolution in consciousness was taking place. Some things, like the potent rallying power of the symbolized press itself, are difficult for us as we enter a post-literate age to understand. The dazzling rays of light emitted in popular

---

and were eventually purchased for the nation in 1816 and housed in the British Museum. Byron attacked Elgin's acquisition of the Marbles in *Childe Harold's Pilgrimage* (1812), II. xi–xv. George Cruikshank's satiric print of 10 June 1816 is glossed 'The Elgin Marbles! or John Bull buying Stones at the time his numerous Family want Bread!!' The intensity of Keats's imaginative response is recorded in several poems (for example, his 1817 sonnet 'On Seeing the Elgin Marbles'). In view of the early canonization of the Marbles in poetry and painting on the one hand, and their history as a focus for contemporary political unrest on the other, it is interesting to note their prominence in programmes for mass education.

iconography by the simple iron-frame hand-press, most notably in the prints executed by the caricaturist George Cruikshank for William Hone's polemical satires of 1819–21, witness to the settled conviction that, in Richard Carlile's words written from Dorchester Gaol, 'the right application of the Printing Press was the remedy' (*Republican*, vii, 30 May 1823: 683). A people's press partakes of that same glamour (a word introduced at this time by Walter Scott, deriving from 'gramarye' and ultimately from 'grammar') that the penknife possessed in the pre-literate tradition of folk ballad. In ballads, murders are committed with penknives (originally knives for making or mending quill pens); for, belonging to the book learned, penknives have special potency. Cruikshank's all-seeing press is one element in a radical romance which articulates, in word and picture, the campaign for access to the near-magical salvatory power of print.

Another element is the unlikely creation of the conservative Burke, whose fear of the revolutionary zeal of a people transformed into 'a swinish multitude' had unleashed a whole farmyard of pig allegories from the radical press of the 1790s: in journals like *Politics for the People: or, a Salmagundy for Swine* and *Pig's Meat; or Lessons for the Swinish Multitude*; in pseudonyms like 'Gregory Grunter' and 'Gruntum Snorum'; and in songs like that of 1795, satirically entitled 'Wholesome Advice to the Swinish Multitude', which identifies its readers as 'You lower class of human race, you working part I mean'. How pigs turn human – how the working class is graphically embodied in these its formative years by means of a visual syntax of group identity and social differentiation – is a narrative of political struggle which can be followed through the prints of the age. Nor is the pig analogy party allied, all political hues being content to employ its persuasive imagery. Consequently, it is traceable from the frontispiece to the first issue and collected edition of Thomas Spence's radical *Pig's Meat* (1793–6), through the anti-radical propaganda of *The Loyal Man in the Moon* (February 1820) (a riposte to Hone's *The Man in the Moon*, January 1820), with its aggressive pig-faced mob, and on to the sentimentalized though impoverished confusion of the piggy-featured working-class Nubbles family in H. K. Browne's woodcut illustrations to Dickens's *Old Curiosity Shop* (1840–41). The reformist and democratic journals of the second decade of the nineteenth century, Wooler's *Black Dwarf* (1817) and Hunt's *Yellow Dwarf* (1818), and in reply Gibbons Merle's Tory *White Dwarf* (1817), add another thread to the intertextual allusions of radical romance, dwarfs having a long traditional association with underground and subversive night-time activities. All-seeing presses, humanized pigs and anarchic dwarfs weave a fairy-tale weft into the fabric of early radical literature, a further reminder of the potency of its chap-book origins.

Working-class autobiographies of the period attest to the near-religious illumination which print brought. Thomas Cooper made himself a daunting educational programme to learn Latin, Greek, Hebrew, French, Italian and German; and he set about the systematic acquisition of English Literature, soon having *Hamlet* and four books of *Paradise Lost* 'entirely and perfectly by heart' (*Life of Thomas Cooper*, p 68). To the question where did poetry fall to when it fell out of fashion in the 1820s, one answer might be to Thomas Cooper. The Chartist Cooper was one of that group of politicized working-class poets for whom Byron's technically imitable verses became a model. According to Engels, it was among the urban poor that both Shelley and Byron found their most appreciative mid-century audience, the middle classes owning at this time only expurgated, 'family' editions.[1] If Shelley's *Queen Mab* (1813) became the 'Chartist Bible', then Byron's poetry 'seemed to create almost a new sense' in the young Cooper (p 35). Radical enthusiasm for Byron and Shelley amply justified the many attempts to censor their works for a mass audience. When in 1819–20 Shelley planned a volume of political poems for popular publication (including *The Mask of Anarchy* and 'Song to the Men of England'), his publisher refused to accept it. In the same year Murray's approved and anonymous quarto (large and expensive) edition of Cantos I and II of Byron's *Don Juan* met with little critical disfavour, but the flood of duodecimo (small and cheap) piracies, the inevitable consequences of Murray's attempt to limit publication, were greeted with moral outrage by the reviewers. Behind the marginalization of poetry and the promotion of 'useful knowledge' at the close of the period there may even lie a suspicion of poetry's dangerous portability. The justified blocks of prose represent an ordered and contained communication, firmly embedded in its context, whereas poetry, and certainly Byron's idiomatic stanzas, is an easily liberated and relocated discourse.

Surveying the literary scene in 1832, Thomas Frognall Dibdin could find no trace of that 'bibliomania', the craze for expensive books, which had governed publishing trends twenty years earlier. Now the illustrious house of Murray appeals to the family market,

1 Frederick Engels, *Condition of the Working Class in England* (1845), ed. Eric Hobsbawm, London, 1969, p 265.

and Murray himself is 'the greatest "FAMILY" man in Europe . . . surrounded by an extensive circle of *little ones*'. Now, as Murray regretfully observes, 'the love of quartos [is] well nigh extinct . . . the dwarf [has] vanquished the giant . . . Laputa [is] lording it over Brobdingnag.'[1] But what might seem like a victory, in terms of the age's active bibliopolitics, for the radical over the reactionary format – a battle of the books in which Cobbett's 'TWOPENNY TRASH, dear little twopenny trash' (*Political Register*, 6 January 1820) vanquishes the 'proud quarto, with a rivulet of text meandering through a wide plain of margin'[2] – is in fact its opposite. An assimilation of the cheap radical model to conservative ends, the 'Family Library' and its imitators aim to reunite a society dangerously divided over issues of political reform and to do so, rather as Hannah More had successfully proposed in the 1790s, through an equation of reading and the family unit. This rather than Victorian Britain, we should remember, is the age of Dr Thomas Bowdler and the expurgated classics. It is both ironic and totally symptomatic that Byron's publisher should be in the forefront when it comes to adapting texts 'for Family Reading'.

What we see happening in Britain between the dates 1780 and 1830 is the emergence of (working-) class consciousness as a potentially revolutionary force, and its gradual absorption into a transformed model, one which resubmits to the designatory and assimilative powers of the middle, newly confirmed as *the* class in its prescriptive rights over society.[3] The twin agents of this process are literacy and the press: identifying the nature and outer limits of a popular press is crucial to the establishment of class identity in the period. For most of the age the words 'Reading Public' (to Coleridge 'as strange a phrase . . . as ever forced a splenetic smile on the staid countenance of Meditation')[4] tend to signal their curiosity value by capitalization, italics or other typographic fireworks. One reviewer in the Tory *Quarterly* registers his attempt to win order from the potential confusion of a mass literacy when he writes of 'those publishers whose market lies among that portion of the people who are

---

1 Thomas Frognall Dibdin, *Bibliophobia, Remarks on the Present Languid and De-pressed State of Literature and the Book Trade*, London, 1832, p 31.
2 Charles Knight, *Passages of a Working Life*, London, 1864–5, i. 276.
3 This removal of reforming initiative from the working to the middle class has been variously considered by historians and literary critics. See Thompson, *The Making of the English Working Class*, pp 887–915; and David E. Musselwhite, *Partings Welded Together: Politics and Desire in the Nineteenth-Century English Novel*, London, 1987, pp 31–6.
4 *The Statesman's Manual*, in *Collected Works*, VI, pp 36–7.

below what is called the public, but form a far more numerous class' (xi, 1814: 78). Posed in 1817 at the height of reformist unrest, Hazlitt's question 'What is the people?' (in an essay of that title) reveals that dangerous fluidity and competitiveness of definition, one result of a widespread popular press which government would soon attempt to contain. Under the proliferated weight of print, meanings have become notoriously unstable. In Hazlitt's essay, *'vox populi vox Dei'*, the 'lower classes' and 'a *Reading Public*' threaten the 'mob of Lords and Gentlemen' '"stying us" in the den of legitimacy'.[1] An unshackled press, a free language, a contained culture and a universally sanctioned social model are revealed in these years as explosively incompatible with a mass reading public.

The various attempts throughout the period in the field of cheap publishing – from radical pamphlets through evangelical tracts and sensation fiction and on to 'useful knowledge' – witness to the competing interests of those who saw in print a remedy for social and political evils, those who saw an extension and consolidation of the guardianship of the middle, and those who viewed print for the people with élitist horror or regret as a mass anodyne. A psychological gulf separates a reading and a non-reading public, together with new systems of communication and new social structures and cultural institutions. Significantly, reading shifts the impulse to social assembly from the actual world to the printed text. In a literate society, reading – 'information' – can come to predict all possible experience, to intercept and inflame or dissolve material grievances. As Britain moved towards the limited concessions of the 1832 Reform Bill, the need to take account of 'the principle of numbers'[2] was never more urgently felt. A mass purchasing and reading public required to be decisively shaped.

Brougham, addressing Parliament during the reading of the Reform Bill in 1831 with the declaration that 'by the people . . . I mean the middle classes, the wealth and intelligence of the country, the glory of the British name',[3] makes no secret of the shape he has in mind. Two major tasks emerged from the period 1780 to 1830: one was to image a middle-class readership to itself as the custodians of society; the other was to contain a working-class readership, to censor its associative identity and to establish its social frame of reference. As the early competition to appropriate the mass readership

1 'What is the People?' (1817), in *Complete Works*, vii. 259–81.
2 Charles Knight's phrase in the lead article of the first issue of *The Printing Machine: A Review for the Many* (15 February 1834), 5.
3 Brougham is quoted under *OED*, 'Middle class'.

reminds us, establishing a frame of reference is as much a matter of disassociations as associations. After 1830 the address to the *problem* (as it so clearly remained) of reading came to be sited in the private rather than the public space: reading as an act of individuation rather than of group identification. To the extent that reading was defined as the route to quiet self-possession, its revolutionary force was internalized and the problem successfully negotiated. Buying identity through reading becomes an act of self-purchase in a world of mass production and anonymous relations. But the private reader is a disempowered reader, whose characteristic sense of apartness and redemption from the many is both a tacit act of compensation for and of conformity to a class-structured reality: buying out is in fact oddly close to buying in. Signalling anarchy and collapse in the 1790s, universal literacy seemed, by the mid-nineteenth century, the precondition for stability, the surest social cement and the most effective political solvent.

# POLITICS AND THE NOVEL 1780–1830

## Peter Garside

'So far from reading political pamphlets, I hunt for any books, except modern novels, that will not bring France to my mind, or that at least will put it out for a time.'[1] So Horace Walpole, well into his seventies, wrote at the beginning of 1794, having heard rumours of a defeat suffered by allied troops at the hands of the republican French army. For the past four years the British public had been overwhelmed by news of the revolution in France. At an early stage, enthusiasm for French constitutionalism encompassed a broad span of 'middle' opinion. Events such as the election of the National Legislative Assembly in October 1791 encouraged liberal thinkers to hope for reform at home, and Burke's anti-revolutionary *Reflections on the Revolution in France* (1790) was effectively countered by Mary Wollstonecraft's *Vindication of the Rights of Men* (1790), Mackintosh's *Vindiciæ Gallicæ* (1791) and Paine's wide-selling *Rights of Man* (1791). In 1792, with the 'September Massacres' in Paris and the declaration of France as a republic, positions became more entrenched. As reforming Whigs and radicals actively embodied themselves in the Constitutional and Corresponding societies, an increasingly nervous Government initiated the prosecution of booksellers for selling Paine's works. The execution of Louis XVI in January 1793 further alienated middle-of-the-road sympathizers (the poet Cowper declared himself 'sick of the very name of liberty'),[2] and more common readers responded loyally to the latest sensation. In addition to manufacturing novels, William Lane at the Minerva Press was busily hawking broadsheets such as 'The trial of Thomas Paine for certain false, wicked, scandalous and seditious libels ...' and 'Glorious victory over the French, or the British tars triumphant'.

1 *Correspondence of Horace Walpole*, ed. W. S. Lewis et al., xxxix, New Haven, 1974, p 509.
2 *Correspondence of William Cowper*, ed. Thomas Wright, 4 vols, London, 1904, iv. 364.

Thomas Hookham, who specialized in elegant sentimental fiction, co-published numerous pamphlets for the 'Association for Preserving Liberty and Property against Republicans and Levellers'. By February 1793 Britain had declared war on France. March that year marked the establishment of Robespierre's Committee of Public Safety: reports of the Terror gave vivid pointers to what might happen if sansculottism broke loose at home.

Walpole's resolve to exclude novels from his reading was not based on any apprehension of political content, but reflected a more general weariness with the form. Writing to Hannah More in 1788, he declared himself 'nauseated by . . . the host of novel-writers in petticoats'.[1] In the early 1780s fiction was generally abused as the lowest of literary genres, only a handful of titles trickling from the presses, to receive condescending abuse or faint praise in the reviews. Nevertheless a distinct upsurge in production is discernible in the second half of the decade. According to a notice in the *Monthly Review* for January 1788: 'The Reviewer of the modern novel is in the situation of Hercules encountering the Hydra. – One head lopped off, two or three immediately spring up in its place' (p 82). Impression numbers remained small, only exceeding 1,000 in the case of a known author or assured sale. The price too was relatively high, and rose in the 1790s from 2s 6d to 4s per volume, before spiralling in the new century. Purchasing works whose interest was normally considered to be ephemeral, but which easily could extend to four or more volumes, was well out of most people's reach. But access to fiction became easier, mainly through a proliferation of circulating libraries. Large London libraries, such as Lane's and Hookham's, appear from their catalogues to have carried approximately 25 per cent fiction, though the stocking of multiples probably made this larger in practice. William Rusher's library, at the Market Place in Banbury, *circa* 1798 held 450 novels out of a total of 670 items. Rusher's subscription rate was five shillings a quarter, though he is also likely to have lent many of his books singly for a few pence.

Unfortunately no record of borrowing at commercial circulating libraries has survived. Contemporary satire is filled with stories of farmers' daughters and apprentices corrupted by novels so obtained. Circumstantial evidence, however, points to a more 'respectable' audience, with a preponderance of female readers. Jane Austen was not alone amongst the daughters of the gentry when, in 1798, candidly proclaiming her family 'great Novel-readers & not ashamed

1 *Correspondence of Walpole*, xxxi, 1961, p 271.

of being so'.[1] Catalogues from the proprietary subscription libraries, where members were shareholders, indicate the growing acceptability of more 'serious' kinds of fiction to the professional classes. While still frequently reviled, the novel clearly enjoyed a wider distribution from the 1790s. Accepting as a rough marker Burke's estimate of 80,000 readers in Britain, Richard Lovell Edgeworth's Preface to his daughter's *Popular Tales* (1804) targeted a large underbelly especially susceptible to works of fiction: '. . . we may calculate that ten thousand are nobility, clergy, or gentlemen of the learned professions. Of seventy thousand readers which remain, there are many who might be amused and instructed by books which were not professedly adapted to the classes that have been enumerated. With this view the following volumes have been composed.' A novel 'by an author of reputation', Zachary Macaulay observed in 1809, was 'likely to pass through the hands of nine-tenths of the reading part of the community'.[2]

Underlying Edgeworth's and Macaulay's comments – and evidently absent in Walpole – is a new awareness of the novel's capacity for influencing public opinion. Relatively free of classical rules, it offered a malleable medium. It also provided access to the 'middle' rank, whose opinion was increasingly canvassed from the 1790s. Unsuspected by officialdom, for a time it remained virtually free of censorship. Indeed, if Walpole had looked at novels in 1794, he might have found them already deeply involved in the contemporary 'paper war'.

1

## JACOBIN FICTION

The first shots were fired by the group now commonly described as the 'Jacobin' novelists. At the immediate centre stood three philosophical reformers: Thomas Holcroft (1745–1809), William Godwin (1756–1836) and Mary Wollstonecraft (1759–97). Associated with them, but working more within the literary mainstream, were Robert Bage (1728–1801), Charlotte Smith (1749–1806) and Elizabeth Inchbald (1753–1821). All were conscious, in varying degrees, of exploiting the novel to promulgate 'revolutionary' ideas. Modern interpreters have pointed to a dynamic fusion between ideas and fiction, leading to a renovation of the English popular novel. Such an

1 *Jane Austen's Letters*, ed. R. W. Chapman, 2 vols, Oxford, 1932, i. 38.
2 *Christian Observer*, viii (December 1809), 781.

approach, however, underestimates the extent to which Jacobin fiction inherited tendencies already established in the form.

This is best illustrated in the case of Bage and Smith, both of whom had acquired a popular reputation before the Revolution. Bage wrote four novels in the 1780s: *Mount Henneth* (1782), *Barham Downs* (1784), *The Fair Syrian* (1787) and *James Wallace* (1788). All were handled by publishers specializing in fiction, Bage with the fourth moving over to William Lane, then busily cornering the novel market. The proprietor of a small paper-mill in Staffordshire, Bage had close ties with the Dissenting tradition through membership of the Derby Philosophical Society. From the start, his novels projected a variety of liberal attitudes (against duelling, gaming, mercenary marriage, etc.) in multivocal epistolary narratives, linking them with a tradition of discursive fiction which from Smollett's day had characteristically taken an independent stance against governmental corruption. Even so, on some fronts Bage can seem unusually daring and waspish. More than any other male novelist, he spoke frankly about women's rights. His novels also offered trenchant observations on recent public events, notably the American war, and gave withering pictures of ministerial bungling. Such criticisms, however, usually came as it were obliquely through views expressed by a variety of characters, and any malice was apparently offset by the good humour of the authorial persona.

Though in many ways the four-volumed *Man as He Is* (1792) follows the same pattern, its Paine-like title and prefatory humouring of 'twenty thousand fair readers' immediately set a new tone, providing an appropriate point of entry for a narrative which becomes increasingly controversial. Sir George Paradyne, having recently inherited the family estate, resists patronage from his ministerialist uncle, Lord Auschamp. Instead, he selects his own tutor in Mr Lindsay, an impoverished scholar, who propounds liberal Whig views with a distinctly republican flavour. On a 'tour' of Britain, Paradyne meets Miss Colerain in Hampshire (a locale which provides a relatively stable country base in an otherwise ambulatory novel). Impoverished by her father's failure as a merchant, Miss Colerain still asserts her independence by refusing financial help from an amorous Sir George. Paradyne in turn is pressurized to marry Lady Ann Brixworth, an heiress, his sister having previously formed an alliance with Mr Birimport, another ministerialist. Whilst Sir George mostly shuns London, enough scenes take place there to give a sense of the prevailing political atmosphere. Against Paradyne's 'humane sentiment', a Count Colliano argues the ideology of the *ancien régime* in terms which echo Burke: 'The common herd want nothing more than mere animal gratification' (ii. 129).[1] Shades, too, of Burke's alleged apostasy are traceable in Birimport's wildly fluctuating pronouncements on Warren Hastings. Before the end of the second volume Sir George has visited Birmingham. Here he finds Miss Colerain not only earning her own living as a painter of toys, but – more daring yet – enjoying the company of unconventional intellectuals: the poet Erasmus Darwin and scientist Joseph Priestley (whose house, in actuality, had been attacked by a 'loyalist' mob in July 1791).

With the third volume Sir George's tour extends to Europe. In pre-revolutionary Paris, he expounds English 'liberty' to enlightened members of the French nobility, albeit not without some difficulty in finding recent exemplification: 'At present, the art seems to be declining amongst us. Indeed our practice is now principally confined to the game laws and laws of excise' (iii. 116). At this point Bage's (direct) narrative shifts perceptibly to a present which appears to be 1791: 'The Count had a select party to sup with him that night. He cordially invited Sir George. It consisted of patriots whose names have been since famous. Never before had Sir Geo. heard the science of government so freely canvassed; the rights of men so deeply appreciated' (iii. 118). Baillé, Lafayette, Mirabeau are subsequently named – unlike Burke. However, there can be no doubt of his presence in an interlude where a Miss Zaporo speaks against rebellion in Transylvania (the bizarre names form part of a strategy to associate his *Reflections* with the Gothic and outlandish): 'These enlarged and liberal sentiments . . . have always struck me as being the true foundation of most of the existing governments of this our globe. A book which has lately enchanted all kings, all queens, all bishops – save one – all good old women, and half an university, has been wrote to amplify, and to sublime them' (iv. 71–2). Ironically, the authorial persona accedes to the rhetoric, which is reinforced by direct quotation from Burke's celebrated homage to Marie Antoinette ('I thought ten thousand swords must have leaped from their scabbards, to avenge even a look that threatened her with insult', iv. 72); but he is answered by a Bageian 'friend', who, in opposition to Burke's lament for 'chivalry', applauds instead the commencement of an 'age of truth and reason'. Having announced the return of the married Sir George and Miss Colerain and friends to a France now

1 Page references in parentheses refer to editions asterisked in the Bibliography, pp 455–9.

distinctly post-revolutionary, Bage's peroration closes with a paean to liberty reminiscent in its intensity of Blake's contemporary 'Song of Liberty' in *The Marriage of Heaven and Hell*:

... when an English senator had said in a book, supposed to contain the collected wisdom of the nation – 'That man has no rights,' – the whole French people fell into a violent fit of laughter, which continues to this day ... But if, said they, men have no rights, they have wills at least, and Kings, Lords, and Priests, shall know it.

(iv. 272)

Charlotte Smith wrote three popular sentimental novels – *Emmeline* (1788), *Ethelinde* (1789) and *Celestina* (1791) – before politics entered directly into her writing. True to the mode, each had shown 'orphan' outsiders clinging to the shreds of their gentility in a hostile materialistic world, hopelessly in love with their male counterpart – that is, until fame and fortune are fortuitously found. While recommending quiescence, and ultimately applauding rank, the form also offered a vent for the expression of a more profound malaise. For nine-tenths of their stories Smith's heroines are suffocated by a hostile world, prey to unwanted male suitors, fated to play humble cousin to moral inferiors. In celebrating intuitive feeling, as opposed to social convention, sentimentalism was also a potentially 'revolutionary' mode. Bernardin de St Pierre's *Paul et Virginie*, which contrasted love on an island with the false social standards of pre-revolutionary France, went through at least three English translations between 1789 and 1795 – the last by the then notorious Francophile, Helen Maria Williams. Williams's *Julia: A Novel* (1790) had earlier shown its heroine painfully suppressing a love made impossible by prior engagement, in a world where nature is opposed by art and sensibility by selfishness.

From the beginning Smith wrote under her own name, as a separated woman raising her numerous children independently. Though probably already known to her readers, her plight was first publicly announced with *Desmond* (1792) ('... I am become an *Author by Profession*'). In the same Preface, dated June 20, 1792, she asserted her right as a woman to comment on public events: 'As to the political passages dispersed through the work, they are for the most part, drawn from conversations to which I have been a witness in England, and France, during the last twelve months ... But women it is said have no business with politics – Why not?' The 'political passages' mostly concern events in France, as described in a series of letters dated from mid-1790 to early 1792, spanning roughly the period from the abolition of hereditary titles to the Legislative Assembly. Desmond, the main correspondent, is platonically in love with Geraldine Verney (née Waverly), the victim of a tyrannical and profligate husband. In strict Jamesian terms *Desmond* is dismissible as an unsatisfactory hybrid, awkwardly grafting partisan politics on to a sentimental story of frustrated love. Viewed more flexibly, however, Smith can be seen to have tapped the hidden revolutionary element in sentimentalism by associating a domestic story with a nation's struggle for freedom. Public and private events are both parallel and contiguous, since the common factor is an unfeeling patriarchal power. Geraldine's eventual freeing by her husband's death, allowing the fulfilment of Desmond's love, matches France's liberation from tyranny. Having earlier contradicted prejudiced reports of 'anarchy and confusion' in France, Desmond's voice at one point merges with Smith's in parodying Burke: 'I foresee *that a thousand pens will leap from their standishes* to answer such a book . . . and therefore I rejoice that it has been written, since, far from finally injuring the cause of truth and reason against which Mr Burke is so inveterate, it will awaken every advocate in their defence' (ii. 63).

Though Holcroft and Godwin had both written novels in the 1780s, it was as mainly jobbing authors, and each turned to the form more deliberately after the Revolution as a vehicle for the expression of philosophical ideas. Holcroft's *Anna St Ives* (1792), which has been described as the 'first full-blown revolutionary novel',[1] was written with Godwin's active encouragement. Adopting a Richardsonian epistolary apparatus, it focused attention almost exclusively on the interaction of three characters: Anna, Frank Henley and the aristocratic Coke Clifton. Like his creator (the son of a shoemaker), Frank is a hero from the people; there are no 'mysterious' origins, his father being palpably Abimelech Henley, the embezzling steward of Anna's father. Frank's rationality, nevertheless, allows him to share the moral high ground with Anna. His active courage too compares favourably with the frenetic and self-centred 'chivalry' which characterizes Clifton. Anna tries to reconcile the difficulties of her situation by reforming Clifton into marriageability, so as to please her father, while remaining friendly with Frank. Yet Clifton seems to be irredeemably conditioned by his upbringing, while Frank asserts a more legitimate love based on truth and reason.

1 J. M. S. Tompkins, *The Popular Novel in England: 1770–1800*, London, 1932, repr. Lincoln, Nebr. 1961, p 300.

Frank's claim tolls like a bell throughout: 'I claim relationship to your mind; and again declare I think my claims have a right, which none of the false distinctions of men can supersede'; '*To the end of time I shall persist in thinking you mine by right . . .*' (pp 133, 136). Unable to control his passions, Clifton resorts to abducting Anna, who fends off her would-be rapist by coolly talking him out of it. Anna and Frank are then free to enter into a union untrammelled by traditional ties ('how poor how insignificant are they, when compared to the claims of eternal justice', p 382). Holcroft's rationalism flies in face of the sentimental tradition, but not without causing some technical difficulties. Emotionally, the nature of Frank and Anna's relationship remains problematical, the lovers more than once employing the language of sensibility in self-expression. Moreover, in a curiously abstract setting, much of the plot's energy and psychological interest would seem to stem from Clifton. *Anna*'s singularity made it more obtrusive, and so arguably less effective, than other Jacobin novels. The *Critical Review* (April 1792) confidently surmised that 'the period of philosophical lovers will probably begin and end with Frank Henley' (p 461).

In the Preface to *Caleb Williams* (1794), omitted by the nervous publisher of its first edition, Godwin presented his work as a fictional embodiment of 'the modes of domestic and unrecorded despotism by which man becomes the destroyer of man'. Faced with its complex narrative and psychological intensities, modern critics have tended to dismiss this as an over-deliberate statement of authorial purpose. Yet the very strengths of the work – its coherence, commitment and unity – derive to a significant degree from its faithfulness to ideas Godwin had strenuously excogitated in his *Enquiry Concerning Political Justice* (1793). The novel's full title, *Things as They Are; or, the Adventures of Caleb Williams*, sets out the dual forces which will govern its action. Caleb Williams (the names are elemental, yet allusively potent) suggests unaccommodated man, his energy and potential; 'things as they are', chosen possibly after Godwin's reading of *Man as He Is*, adumbrates an existing state of affairs in which the human spirit is found to lie crushed and perverted. Mr Collins's retrospective narrative, describing events up to Caleb's engagement as Mr Falkland's secretary, assails the reader with two cases of social injustice committed by Barnabas Tyrrel, Falkland's neighbouring landowner. Tyrrel first offers refuge to his tenant Hawkins, then wilfully condemns him to ruin, by due process of law. He similarly drives to death Miss Melville, an orphan dependant, having attempted to force her into a degrading match.

Both fall helplessly as victims of 'order and subordination' (p 71), though Tyrrel's own passions – his inability to brook opposition and self-destructive jealousy – are ultimately traceable to the same pernicious source. The ramifications are apparently endless. If Tyrrel's egregious behaviour ultimately alienates the neighbourhood, the atmosphere conveyed by Godwin is one of misdirected rage rather than cohesive opposition: 'It seemed as if the sense of public resentment had long been gathering strength unperceived, and now burst forth into insuppressible violence' (p 96).

While Tyrrel makes an obvious villain, Ferdinando Falkland at first sight could be the hero: an enlightened version of Fielding's Allworthy set against a peculiarly debased Squire Western. His chivalry is stressed from the start, and upheld by him as a social code capable of mitigating the injustices attendant on a 'necessary' 'distinction of ranks' (p 80). Yet it is the chivalric code, in the shape of an inflated sense of 'reputation', that leads Falkland to triple murder: the assassination of Tyrrel, who has insulted him in public, and his passive collusion in the execution of Hawkins and his son for the offence. The suppression of truth furthers Falkland's moral corruption; just as Caleb's curiosity, triggering an involuntary confession, locks the two characters into a seemingly endless chain of accusation and recrimination, oppression and exasperated self-defence. The ease with which Falkland can imprison Caleb is symptomatic of an English legal system whose root purpose is to serve as an agency of property, and which, in operation, proves as inhumane as anything in despotic France: 'Is that a country of liberty, where thousands languish in dungeons and fetters? . . . show me the man shameless enough to triumph, and say, England has no Bastille!' (p 188). In addition to providing an emblem for 'the whole machine of society' (p 190), Caleb and Falkland's relationship enacts a more insidious poisoning of the mind by the forces of repression. As Falkland's degeneration turns him into an object of pity, Williams is drawn himself into a kind of vindictive counter-tyranny. In the original manuscript end of the novel, closure came with Caleb's failure to incriminate Falkland at the court of justice, his own imprisonment and descent into madness. The final printed 'Postscript' describes Falkland's confession before the magistrates and reconciliation with Caleb on a humanitarian plane, shortly before Falkland's death. The published ending is perhaps more optimistic in celebrating the potential which underlay Falkland's character, and might well have embodied Godwin's hopes for a last-minute reconciliation in the public sphere. In so far as it ties in with a pervading sense of endless human waste, however, it remains enduringly pessimistic.

Notwithstanding its reputation as the one Jacobin novel to have successfully transcended its immediate background, *Caleb Williams* vibrantly reflects the traumatic events which overtook Britain in 1793–4. Far from nailing the novel down, resurrecting its topicalities can make it crackle and sparkle as an imaginative and courageous text written in the face of mounting danger. Its Preface was dated on the exact day (12 May 1794) of the arrest of Thomas Hardy, as a member of the Corresponding Society, which led to the Treason Trials of 1794, at which Holcroft stood indicted. As well as offering the most trenchant Jacobin exposé of 'things as they are', Godwin's story was first to identify the bitter reaction which would soon negate English Jacobinism itself.

The period 1796–8, while still perilous for writers with liberal sympathies, saw a brief resurgence of the Jacobin novel. In her one explicit Jacobin fiction, *Nature and Art* (1796), Elizabeth Inchbald delivered a withering parable of social injustice, the climax of which sees a bishop's son made good (as a judge) condemning the mother of his illegitimate child. Holcroft, in the final volumes of *Adventures of Hugh Trevor* (1794–7), turned a heavy if predictable fire on the forces of counter-revolution: 'Innovation struck the ball at first too impetuously; but Establishment took it at the rebound, and returned it with triple violence' (p 339). More elusively Bage used humour to maximum effect in *Hermsprong; or, Man as He is Not* (1796), a last novel featuring a delightful triad of young women in varying states of emancipation and some of his funniest anti-Establishment satire.

Charlotte Smith strove likewise to keep her principles intact through waves of reaction which must have seriously disturbed the readers on whom she depended. *Marchmont* (1796), via its eponymous hero, supplied views of France in devastation, while insisting that as bad (if not worse) was to be found in England: 'whether I am to pass my life in the Fleet, or the Abbaye – whether I am to exist under the tyranny of Robespierre, or a victim to the chicanery of Vampyre [a lawyer], seems to me a matter so immaterial, that it ought not to induce me to cross the water to embrace the one, or escape the other' (ii. 162). *The Young Philosopher* (1798), her last complete novel, returned to the fray with renewed vigour. Lampooning reactionary types *passim*, it finally directs its hero, heroine and family to America: the last hope now, for many English liberals, of an ethically grounded society. As with *Desmond*, the coexistence of liberal argumentation – a Mr Armitage sets out at length why he is a reformist, not a Jacobin – with a full-blown sentimental plot is likely to confuse modern readers. Sympathetic contemporaries no doubt knew how to decode it. In this novel, too, one senses a dovetailing of sentimentalism with a more conscious feminism. At a time when genteel ladies took delight in Mary Wollstonecraft's misfortunes, Smith's Preface bravely acknowledged 'a writer whose talents I greatly honoured, and whose untimely death I deeply regret'.

An account of Jacobin fiction would be incomplete without discussion of Wollstonecraft, whose two novels were more pointedly committed to portraying the condition of women. In *Mary: A Fiction* (1788), the heroine finds herself contracted into a loveless marriage of convenience. Travelling to Lisbon, prior to its consummation, she forms a sentimental friendship with the consumptive Henry. 'Sensibility' proves at once Mary's leading strength – aiding self-definition and inspiring benevolent action – and a vulnerability or weakness, undermining fortitude and provoking suicidal feelings. Unlike Smith, Wollstonecraft invents no *deus ex machina* such as inheritance. Henry dies, and the marriage must be faced. The female predicament is pictured in even more oppressive terms in the unfinished *Wrongs of Woman*, whose fractured narratives involve a succession of used and abused women, from the maritally mistreated Maria to her brutalized wardress Jemima, an ex-prostitute. Wollstonecraft makes more tangible than any other contemporary novelist the physical irksomeness of male harassment. At the same time, almost paradoxically, the heroine's sensibility is more closely associated than ever with feelings of a distinctly *sexual* nature. According to its plan, Henry Darnford (a fellow-prisoner and escapee) was to prove unfaithful, leaving Maria derelict: 'Her lover unfaithful – Pregnancy – Miscarriage – Suicide' (p 147).

As a *novelist* Wollstonecraft failed to enter the mainstream like other Jacobins: *Mary*, technically ingenuous, was not reprinted; and *The Wrongs of Woman* first appeared in Godwin's edition of her *Posthumous Works* (1798). The more indirect influence of her life and works on contemporary women novelists, on the other hand, was extensive. In particular, work remains to be done in charting a school of advanced female fiction which burned brightly but briefly near the end of the century. Mary Hays's *Memoirs of Emma Courtney* (1796), a surviving example, bravely centres on a woman's struggle for moral independence – including sexual self-expression – in an atmosphere of stifling social convention, whose pressures make her actions seem increasingly frantic. The work had a mixed reception, inevitably running the gauntlet of the male reviewers. Like most fiction, however, it passed into the circulating libraries, to be read both by those aware of the author's notoriety and others simply in search of a fresh title. Hays's next novel, *The Victim of Prejudice* (1799), appears from surviving catalogues to have fallen like a stone – almost as if there were something self-prophetic in the title. By 1800 the Jacobin novel in its pure form was extinct.

2

## *ANTI-JACOBINISM*

On 9 July 1798 the *Anti-Jacobin, or Weekly Examiner* published a long fold-out cartoon by Gillray entitled 'The New Morality'. Its caption indiscriminately blurred English reformers with French Jacobins. A highly motivated organ of political propaganda, with Young Turks such as George Canning amongst its contributors, the *Anti-Jacobin* was coming to the end of a short but effective eight-month run. The cartoon, a kind of pictorial politicization of the fourth book of Pope's *Dunciad*, displays a swirling mass of insubordination presided over by three muses in Gallic caps. Philanthropy, in the centre, hugs a globe to her chest like a greedy child. To her right, with *Égalité* emblazoned on her belt, the scrawny figure of Justice holds a dagger aloft. On her left, Sensibility nurses a dead pigeon and clutches a copy of Rousseau – her right foot pressing on a decapitated head. Before them lies an assorted pile of publications, amidst which can be discerned Charlotte Smith's *Young Philosopher* and Wollstonecraft's *Wrongs of Woman*.

In effect, the novel's capacity for influencing opinion had been found out. Gillray's cartoon also featured in the first number of the monthly *Anti-Jacobin Review*, which in its second issue (August 1798) included an attack on *The Young Philosopher*. Advising its author to 'abstain from politics', it proposed Fanny Burney as an exemplary model: 'The best of our female novelists interferes not with Church nor State. There are no politics in Evelina or Cecilia' (p 189). The *Anti-Jacobin Review* also took upon itself the task of policing the reviews, accusing them of bestowing bland praise so that the political content of novels could circulate freely. The campaign was clearly designed to match the administration's actions on the ground. Subscription libraries (with their strong professional membership and liberal Dissenting roots) were placed under immense pressure from within and without. In 1798 the annual general meeting of the Greenock Library recommended against the purchase of 'political party books', and in the following year the committee withdrew *Caleb Williams* from stock.[1] An act passed in 1799 'for the more effectual Suppression of Societies established for Seditious and Treasonable Practices' made it illegal to run a circulating library or a reading-room unless a licence was granted by two magistrates.[2] The period saw a new wave of arrests amongst the London trade, where nearly all novels were published. Joseph Johnson, the publisher of Godwin, Wollstonecraft and Hays, spent ten months in prison in 1798–9 for publishing a 'seditious' pamphlet against the Bishop of Llandaff, a noted Tory polemicist. Having identified its leading enemies, the *Anti-Jacobin Review* turned to reviewing favourably novels of a manifestly 'anti-Jacobin' nature, at least one of which was written under its own aegis.

The *Anti-Jacobin* campaign of 1797–9 would not have worked without a widespread slippage of 'middling' opinion towards the Establishment position. The arrival of large numbers of émigrés brought the 'Terror' into respectable living-rooms, and must have inspired a good deal of tremulous self-identification. Stories of outrage suffered at the hands of revolutionaries soon found their way into fiction. An interesting overlap with the Gothic is found in Harriet Lee's 'Frenchman Tale' (one of her eminently respectable *Canterbury Tales for the year 1797*, 1797), which perilously places its dispossessed heroine between a usurping tyrant and vengeful peasantry 'dyed with blood'. By 1797 England had come under direct threat of invasion; 1798 saw rebellion in Ireland, and an incursion by French troops into Wales. In *Mordaunt* (1800), Dr John Moore retracted his earlier Whig enthusiasm for the Revolution, castigating Robespierre as 'an obscure, canting, capricious madman' (p 23).

Meanwhile, the aristocracy and gentry closed ranks. A desire to sponsor fiction of an 'exemplary' nature is evident in the relatively large number of subscription novels published in the last years of the century. The 1,058 subscribers to Fanny Burney's *Camilla* (1796), including Burke (five sets) and Canning, would have been aware of the authoress's recent marriage to the eminent but impecunious General D'Arblay. An even more celebrated exile, the Comte D'Artois (Charles X to be), co-headed 1,217 Whig and Tory subscribers to Sir Samuel Egerton Leigh's *Munster Abbey* (1797). Subscription fiction usually featured settled country neighbourhoods, governed by

1 An account of the incident, slightly misdated, appears in John Galt's *Autobiography*, 2 vols, London, 1833, i. 38–42.
2 See Donald Thomas, *A Long Time Burning: The History of Literary Censorship in England*, London, 1969, p 142.

benign patriarchs. In Egerton Leigh's novel, the proprietor of Munster Abbey marries an impoverished but morally fine Miss Melville, whose name might have brought back to some readers the saddest victim in *Caleb Williams*.

More effective in the market place was a school of anti-sentimental 'domestic' fiction, whose main exponent was Jane West (1758–1852). Self-educated, loyally married to a yeoman farmer, adopting the persona of 'Prudentia Homespun', Mrs West was the antithesis of Mrs Smith: plain Jane to fancy Charlotte. In *The Advantages of Education* (1793) the heroine resists the blandishments of an unreformed rake, who keeps a mistress, and marries plain Edmund Herbert instead. Such tales were popular with anxious mammas, and the novel did well enough in the commercial libraries. *A Gossip's Story* (1796) in its Dedication broadcast an intention 'to illustrate the Advantages of CONSISTENCY, FORTITUDE, and the DOMESTIC VIRTUES' while exposing 'AFFECTED SENSIBILITY' – terms which by now were politically loaded. In concentrating on the careers of two sisters, its plot effectively turned the 'sentimental' novel inside out. Marianne resists her father's advocacy of the sensible Mr Pelham ('an indulgent landlord, an obliging neighbour, and a steady active friend' (i. 93)) on the grounds that their 'sentiments' make them unsuited: '". . . there was no similitude of soul, nothing to form that strong tie of sympathy which you know," said she, "must exist, or else there can be no certain expectation of felicity"' (i. 92–3). Instead she marries the aristocratic Clermont, who declares his love on a 'picturesque' tour. West carefully avoids making Clermont a villain, but his inability to exert himself helps doom the marriage to failure. Louisa actively cares for their father in reduced circumstances, tends the local poor, before literally espousing Pelham's virtues: 'As he led her the tour of his pleasure grounds, she was particularly pleased with a long avenue, sloping down the declivity of a hill, on the summit of which a fine Dorick temple was dedicated to Integrity and Fortitude' (ii. 212).

In some respects the strategies used by the two camps were not dissimilar. Both through their titles (cf. Alethea Lewis's *Plain Sense*, 1795) attempted to project an aura of uncomplicated veracity. Each, too, tended to fix their heroes and heroines firmly in the 'middle' rank, reserving the bulk of their satire for mendacious aristocrats and showy *arrivistes*. One positive advance achieved by Mrs West was her creation of Danbury ('a small market town . . . in the north of England') as a permanent setting for her 'homely' narrator. However lightly sketched, the voices of its gossips give the sense of a *de facto* community, in which the actions of the main characters must take place and where they will necessarily be judged.

Mrs West's next two novels, *A Tale of the Times* (1799) and *The Infidel Father* (1802), openly signalled her commitment to Morality and Religion in the struggle against 'New Philosophy'. Both included a new kind of Gallicized infidel villain. In the first, the unstable but tenable marriage between Geraldine and the Earl of Monteith is wrecked by a freethinking libertine, Lord Fitzosborne. While highly implausible, Fitzosborne's compound of revolutionary ideology, irreligion and sexual abandon was well formulated to stick in plain English gullets. Geraldine dies the victim of unjust scandal, reconciled at the last hour with her husband. Her destroyer lives to swallow his own medicine, imprisoned in Robespierre's France: 'In the gloom of the Abbaye prison . . . surrounded by the instruments of despotism, Fitzosborne might have seen the refutation of that false philosophy which, founded upon the visionary perfectibility of the human species, rejects the wise restrictions which Infinite Wisdom has contrived as a barrier against the extreme atrocity of a fallible creature' (iii. 373). Death is by now the inevitable consequence of ideological/sexual aberration. In *The Infidel Father* Lord Glanville expires as an unrepentant atheist, having earlier witnessed his daughter's suicide. As before the survivors stick religiously to their determined social niche, unless properly elevated by marriage or inheritance. West's satire in this later novel is mainly aimed at the *nouveau riche* Sir Peter and Lady FitzJohn, in origin a farmer's daughter and an ironmonger. Lady FitzJohn's ambition for her daughter, Melisandriania (a '*bourgeois fillette*'), leads to the appointment of a tutor who improbably spouts a bizarre mixture of Godwinian and Rousseauist ideas. Melisandriania rewards her parents, not unexpectedly, by eloping to Scotland with 'the most *charmingest* man in all the world'. Lady FitzJohn receives the news on her sofa, where she has been reading 'The Victim of Generosity'.

Mrs West's darker fiction shows an affinity with a more acerbic kind of anti-Jacobin satirical novel which came to the fore in the last few years of the century. A typical example is *The Vagabond* (1799) by George Walker, in which Godwin appears as false tutor (Stupeo) to the anti-hero, Frederick Fenton. Intent on spreading the truth, Fenton sparks off an uprising in London by a mob misled into believing the cause is 'No Popery'. The later stages are set in America, where 'primitivist' Indians burn Stupeo at the stake. Returning home to 'the land of genuine liberty', Fenton accepts his own human frailty: '*All that I know, is that I know nothing.*' As an aspiring young bookseller in London, Walker knew the market well, and the novel went through four editions in less than three years. Robert Bisset's *Douglas; or, the Highlander* (1800), printed at the Anti-Jacobin Press, was actively promoted by the *Anti-Jacobin Review*. Set in 1792, to accentuate the threat of revolution, it excoriated in pseudo-Fieldingesque caricature Holcroft (Tom Croft), Godwin (William Subtlewould) and Smith (Charlotte Self-Praise). Mary Hays, in turn, became the butt of Elizabeth Hamilton's more accomplished *Memoirs of Modern Philosophers* (1800), in the person of Bridgetina (née Bridget) Botherim. Bridgetina's inability to embarrass herself gives her a durability which to some extent overrides the satirical function. Otherwise Hamilton's plot goes according to form. Godwin (as Myope) is taken as a mentor, while sensible advice is spurned; a low-born swindler (Vallaton), posing as an aristocrat, applies 'revolutionary' ideology to the purposes of seduction; a sentimental heroine (Julia), weaned on Rousseauism, dies in circumstances which strongly echo Mary Wollstonecraft's death in childbirth.

3

## REGIONALISM AND EVANGELICALISM

The novel's return to public respectability, and the development of fresh channels of expression, can be traced in the careers of two novelists whose reputation stood at its height in 1812: Maria Edgeworth (1767–1849) and Amelia Opie (1769–1853). Edgeworth is now best known as the innovator of a new kind of 'regional' fiction. Opie's later domestic novels share a number of characteristics with a wave of moral evangelicalism which swept Britain in the second decade of the century. Though developing separately, the modes in which they worked both provided outlets for impulses which had been severely impeded by the anti-Jacobin reaction of the 1790s. In each case sentiment might be said to have found a place.

Both writers, through their upbringing, could claim links with the liberal tradition of the 1780s. Maria's father, Richard Lovell Edgeworth, enjoyed the friendship of the Rousseauist educationalist Thomas Day, had campaigned for reform in Ireland in 1782–3, shortly after having moved to his family estates there, and was undoubtedly instrumental in choosing Joseph Johnson as his daughter's publisher. On the other hand, Maria Edgeworth's earliest fiction is strongly anti-sentimental in character and follows the pattern set by the conservative novelists of the late 1790s. In 'Angelina; or, l'Amie Inconnue', one of her *Moral Tales* (1801), an *ingénue* quixotically pursues the authoress of 'The Woman of Genius', which she has found in the circulating library. After 'inglorious' adventures in Wales, where Angelina's 'romantic' expectations are constantly denied, 'amiable Araminta' is finally discovered in the person of the brandy-swilling, slatternly and masculine Miss Hodges – currently soliciting subscriptions for 'The Sorrows of Araminta, a novel in nine volumes'.

*Belinda* (1801), in describing its heroine's début in 'fashionable' London, gave fuller vent to Edgeworth's vitality and quasi-anarchic sense of comedy. Nevertheless, a more programmatic design is never far from the surface, not least in the author's projection of alternative models for female behaviour. Clarence Hervey raises an 'ideal' Rousseauist protégée in the person of Virginia (named after *Paul et Virginie*), in a way which threatens to produce a hapless automaton. Another radical prototype is travestied in the shape of Harriet Freke, who wears men's clothes, advocates female duelling and somewhat erratically expounds the 'Rights of Woman'. In the middle, Edgeworth firmly places her Belinda: naïve and gullible, vulnerable to misinterpretation, yet basically rational in decision-making. Withstanding a society suitor and the allurement of first impressions, she eventually discovers Hervey's true disposition and a relationship founded on 'esteem and love' (p 220). Against the false glitter of London, personified by the conventional marriage of Lord and Lady Delacour, the author sets the rational-domestic society of the Percival family at Oakly-Park, where Lady Ann Percival's role is that of a 'partner' (p 197) to her husband.

If Maria Edgeworth had confined herself to English 'domestic' fiction, she would certainly figure less prominently in literary history. *Leonora* (1806), her next full novel, in several ways represents a regression. Bowed down with moral purpose, it shows its heroine stoically enduring her husband's seduction by a novel-reading, Francophile 'friend', eventually to be rewarded by the return of the same errant spouse (himself chastened by the experience of living with a *femme fatale* more conscious of 'the rights of woman than of her duties'). Even before *Belinda*, however, Edgeworth had stumbled on a more innovatory mode. *Castle Rackrent: An Hibernian Tale* (1800) broke with protocol by employing as its narrator an idiosyncratic 'vernacular' Irish character – Thady Quirk, long-standing steward to the Rackrent family. Thady relates an unswerving loyalty to a succession of Rackrents, each singularly undeserving of his attention.

To some extent the creation overtook the author's intention, which was to expose the social irresponsibility of landlords in Ireland's bad old days. In such a frame of reference, blind fealty merely upholds the Rackrents' selfishness and dereliction of duty. On the other hand, the rapport existing between Thady and his superiors gives a sense of communal relations stronger than those imposed by legal and monetary considerations. His willingness to stick with Sir Condy, the most human and vulnerable of the Rackrents, contrasts with the grasping, mercenary behaviour of Jason (Thady's lawyer son). Above all Thady extended the *range* of the novel, introducing a voice and mentality (albeit ideologically mediated) hitherto excluded from fiction.

Edgeworth gave a fuller airing to her Irish materials in *Ennui* (1809) and *The Absentee* (1812), two of the most popular stories in *Tales of Fashionable Life* (1809–12), a collection which marked the high point of her reputation as a novelist.[1] In *Ennui* the enervated Earl of Glenthorn runs up debts, weds and loses a fashionable wife, before returning to his native Ireland, his curiosity whetted by a mysterious Irishwoman (Ellinor) who has nursed him in illness. His journey into the hinterland uncovers an alien and unknown culture, the progress involving a comic chaise-ride, at the hands of Paddy, a postilion, which delighted contemporaries and made jokes about Irish subordinates all the rage in polite company. Condescension apart, Paddy remains illogically true to himself and speaks richly in a dialect which reinforces a sense of difference. At Glenthorn Castle, the culture gap leads Glenthorn into making a number of mistakes. An English-style cottage for Ellinor predictably degenerates into a 'comfortable' Irish pickle. Correct procedure is exemplified by the Scottish agent, Mr M'Leod, who cites Adam Smith in arguing for gradualism and non-denominational education. Once again, however, one senses a pull towards the more emotional responses of tenants. In a threatened uprising (based on the 1798 rebellion) Ellinor and her 'son' Christy remain loyal. Even when it is revealed that Glenthorn is not the Earl (Ellinor, his real mother, having switched him for Christy at birth), the tenants remain grateful for past

---

1 For the second series of *Tales* (3 vols, 1812) Maria Edgeworth received £1,050, and for *Patronage* (1814), a less popular work, £2,100. This compares with the £700 reputedly offered by Constable for the copyright of *Waverley* (1814), and the paltry £110 Jane Austen received for *Pride and Prejudice* (1813). The figures for Edgeworth are taken from Appendix B of Marilyn Butler's *Maria Edgeworth: A Literary Biography*, Oxford, 1972.

kindnesses, and so emotionally primed for Glenthorn's eventual restoration through marriage.

The sense of a reservoir of loyal feelings capable of being tapped in favour of enlightened landlordism finds more overt expression in *The Absentee*. As its title indicates, the story exemplifies the advantages to be gained by a return of the Anglo-Irish aristocracy to their native estates. Lord and Lady Clonbrony live a wasteful existence amongst the London beau monde, where they are privately ridiculed. In an effort at retrenchment and impelled by 'patriotic' feelings, Lord Colambre (their son) pays an extensive visit to Ireland, taking in a developing Dublin, good and bad country houses, and even a member of the Catholic gentry (Count O'Halloran). On home ground, the rationally administered Colambre estate compares favourably with the corruption rife on the larger Clonbrony estate, which has been milked dry by the grasping Nicholas Garraghty ('Old Nick'). The scope of *The Absentee*, embracing a variety of manifestations of Irish life, makes it a fuller if more deliberate 'regional' (or 'national') novel than either of its predecessors. Its concluding scenes also conveyed an idea of social solidarity, the implications of which stretched beyond the ostensible 'Irish' purpose. After an emotional appeal from Colambre, Lady Clonbrony finally forsakes the false world of fashion. To describe the family's return Edgeworth used the vernacular voice of Terry Brady, another postilion, in the form of a letter to his brother in London:

Ogh, it's I driv 'em well … and the birds were singing, and I stopped whistling, that they might hear them; but sorrow bit could they hear when they got to the park gate, for there was such a crowd, and such a shout, as you never see – and they had the horses off every carriage entirely, and drew 'em home, with blessings, through the park. And, God bless 'em! when they got out, they didn't go shut themselves up in the great drawing-room, but went straight out to the *tir*rass, to satisfy the eyes and hearts that followed them … O, there was great gladness and tears in the midst …

(p 343)

The use of the rustic narrator allows the tenantry a resonant voice, rhetorically validating their superiors' paternalism, at the same time offering an appealing microcosm for a fuller 'union' of British ranks.

A different line of development can be traced in the career of Amelia Opie, daughter of a Norwich doctor, though the starting-point was not dissimilar. As a young woman she mixed freely in Dissenting society and married the painter John Opie in 1798. Through her father and husband she was acquainted with the Godwin circle in London, enjoying the friendship of Elizabeth

Inchbald and Mary Wollstonecraft. Her public appearance as a novelist, however, coincided with the anti-Jacobin reaction; and such 'liberalism' as can be found in her earliest works exists in the harshest of worlds, where death is the usual penalty for social deviancy. In *The Father and Daughter* (1801) Agnes Fitzhenry is inveigled away from her tradesman father by an irresponsible young aristocrat, Clifford, who tricks her into an alliance without marriage, from which she eventually flees in desperation with her illegitimate child. Struggling homeward, she finds her father, an escaped lunatic. The magnitude of Agnes's offence prohibits any immediate reintegration into the community. On the contrary, she must bear the brunt of indignant disapproval and malicious slander while supporting (through needlework) her father and child in an isolated cottage. Even then Agnes's fate is to die in painful rapture shortly after having been recognized again by her dying father. Contemporary readers would almost certainly have seen a parallel between Agnes's fate and Mary Wollstonecraft's recent history, and a stony moral law behind the pathos. Only after a 'long and painful probation', the constant practice of 'self-denial, patience, fortitude and industry' (3rd edn, 1802, p 191), will society receive its prodigals back into the fold. In other respects *The Father and Daughter* fails to match the strict anti-Jacobin rule. If Agnes's death prevents rehabilitation, at least that prospect is held out in principle: the sharpest barbs are reserved for her detractors. In bereavement, too, one senses a reassembling of communal values based on *feeling* ('Even those who had distinguished themselves by their violence against Agnes at her return, dropped a tear as they saw her borne to her long home', p 221). The longevity of the story's success (a seventh edition by 1813) indicates that it was well pitched to meet new moral intensities.

In *Adeline Mowbray* (1804), a full-scale novel, Opie returned more overtly to the Wollstonecraft story. Pursued by a libidinous step-father, her heroine seeks the protection of Frederic Glenmurray, living with but refusing to marry him, having previously imbibed his anti-marriage philosophy. As a result both suffer the slings and arrows of outraged society, Adeline on Glenmurray's death finding herself with the status of a discarded mistress. In applauding Adeline's refusal to bow to stultifying convention, some recent inter-preters[1] have discounted too lightly a doctrinal element capable of satisfying Mrs West's most draconian readers. Adeline's vulnerability is laid squarely at the door of an indulgent mother, raised on

1   See e.g. Dale Spender, *Mothers of the Novel*, London, 1986, p 322.

'theoretical' politics, who has shunned the 'good sense and sober experience' (p 14) of a Dr Norberry in favour of Glenmurray's abstruse metaphysics. Adeline herself finally recants, tracing the source of her tribulations to false philosophy: '. . . I bitterly regret the hour when, with the hasty and immature judgement of eighteen . . . I dared to think and act contrary to the opinion and the reverend experience of ages . . .' (p 244). Nevertheless, *Adeline* still reads as more than just a 'thesis' novel. Humanized to an extent quite uncharacteristic of anti-Jacobin satire, Glenmurray wishes to marry Adeline for her sake, and generally gives an impression of being prepared to modify his earlier idealism to fit the way of the world. Adeline's suffering at the hands of outraged convention goes far beyond desert, and her detractors/betrayers are infinitely more noxious than Mrs West's gossips. It is Adeline, not the guardians of morality, who champions human rights by rescuing a mulatto (Savanna, later a loyal servant) from distress.

Despite returning once more to the plight of the single woman of conscience in an alien-seeming society, Opie managed only to give tenuous expression to feelings so recently suppressed by rigid anti-Jacobinism. Neither *The Father and Daughter* nor *Adeline* offers its protagonists any tangible alternative in the form of a suitable lover (a Colonel Mordaunt is excruciatingly unattainable *because* of Adeline's lapse). In this sense the death suffered by both heroines represents a sort of impasse, symptomatic of the author's inability to find a moral centre in which they can engage.

In *Temper, or Domestic Scenes* (1812), Opie's next full novel, one notes a new tone as well as a significant shift in the relation between generations. Agatha Torrington elopes with a Mr Danvers, suffers his attempt to wipe their marriage from the record, and dies of a fever. Emma, her daughter, is brought up under the preceptorship of Mr Egerton (a clergyman) in Cumberland, learning through him to overcome her petulance. Her reward is to marry a fellow-pupil, Henry St Aubyn, whose rumoured 'engagement' she had previously patiently endured. Compared with the nominal presence of Norberry in *Adeline*, Egerton is a dominant figure for the bulk of the book, offering advice that is always taken. This includes steering Emma away from Richardson's *Clarissa* until later in life, and advocating an active career in Parliament for St Aubyn. The more obtrusive religious tone to be found in Opie's later fiction has been associated with the death of John Opie in 1807 and her conversion to Quakerism in 1825. *Temper*, if far from her best novel, helps place the shift more precisely.

In particular it follows the pattern set by Hannah More's *Coelebs in Search of a Wife* (1808), which was entering its fourteenth edition in 1813. In keeping with the evangelical aim of reforming the 'respectable' classes, *Coelebs* contrasts the lifestyle of 'nominal' Christians in London, vitiated in varying degrees by an adherence to fashion, with the moral probity of its 'real' Christians, the Stanleys. Having journeyed from his northern estates, Charles (More's young hero) survives the temptations of Cavendish Square prior to securing the hand of Lucilla Stanley, whose suitability is vouchsafed by the cheerful but pious ethos of Stanley Grove. Much of the later narrative is filled with religious discourses, invariably involving the correctly 'serious' Mr Stanley. The broad appeal of the evangelical movement in the Regency is easily underestimated. Promising to re-sanction Establishment's authority, it advocated moral standards more immediately associable with the middle 'ranks', combining conservatism (Wilberforce, its leading parliamentary spokesman, was a Tory) with the espousal of long-standing 'liberal' causes such as the abolition of slavery. While temperamentally and culturally distant from the 'hard-core' evangelicalism of the Clapham Sect, Opie in 1816 felt no need to resist the idea of her having become 'enlist[ed] under the banner of Mr Wilberforce & Hannah More'.[1]

*Temper* is only one of a number of novels in the early nineteenth century which can be broadly designated 'moral-evangelical'. Some are little more than novel-tracts: Henry Kett's *Emily: A Moral Tale* (1809), for example, incorporates letters from a father to his daughter, guiding her survival in London. In other hands the mode provided a fresh outlet for psychological analysis and moral discrimination. Mary Brunton's *Self-Control* (1811) follows with great sensitivity its heroine's resistance of a match, backed by her father and able to offer protection on his death, with an attractive suitor whom she nevertheless feels to be 'unprincipled'. So frustrated is Colonel Hargrave that he resorts to kidnapping Laura and imprisoning her in the wilds of Canada, a predicament from which she escapes by shooting the rapids.

This lapse into melodrama was jokingly recorded by Jane Austen,[2] whose *Mansfield Park* (1814) nevertheless suggests an indebtedness to Brunton's technical originality in describing subjective thought. The issue of whether the first of Austen's novels

1  Letter to William Hayley, 28 February 1816, quoted by Margaret Eliot MacGregor, *Amelia Opie: Worldling and Friend*, Smith College Studies in Modern Languages, XIV (October 1932–July 1933), i. 64.
2  *Jane Austen's Letters*, ii. 344; cf. ii. 278.

apparently not to originate in the 1790s was influenced by evangelicalism is too complex to be dealt with here in detail. Certainly Mansfield itself resembles an evangelical battleground. Fanny Price, from a less privileged background and motivated by 'principle', vies with the sophisticated but immoral Crawfords for possession of the socially respectable, but only nominally Christian, Bertrams. The novel also focuses on a number of issues which would have been recognized as typically evangelical by contemporary readers, though Austen refrains from directly advocating them: 'ordination', in the form of Edmund's ambition to take his profession as a clergyman seriously; the dangers of 'acting', both in the sense of amateur theatricals and role-playing; and the slave-trade, which Sir Thomas wishes to discuss on his return from Antigua. Fanny also resists an 'advantageous' match on the grounds of autonomous moral scruple. Like other inheriting young couples in 'evangelical' fiction, both she and Edmund move outward from private discrimination to constructive social action.

The 'regional' and 'moral-evangelical' schools developed not only separately but with an element of mutual hostility. Edgeworth's rationalism made her a continuing object of suspicion amongst more austere evangelicals. And it would be difficult to think of a novelist less sympathetic to evangelicalism than Lady Morgan (née Sydney Owenson), whose *Wild Irish Girl* (1806) deserves consideration as one of the first 'national' novels. A 'radical slut, and a great Bonapartist',[1] according to her facetious sister, Morgan in her fiction lambasted placemen, absentee landlords, lady evangelists and other abusers of Ireland's past, often in the form of outrightly polemical footnotes. Her Whig 'radicalism', however, was of a different order to that which had fired Godwin and Holcroft in the 1790s. The Catholic hero of *O'Donnel: A National Tale* (1814) wears, on his neck, a ring presented him during service in the Irish Guard by Marie Antoinette ('the loveliest sovereign that ever received the affections of a devoted and loyal people', ii. 103). He also earnestly seeks *rapprochement* with London, looking to 'a spirit of *accommodation* and *conciliation in all parties*' (iii. 275).

Such a message was well geared to suit a society which, after twenty years of almost continuous war, was beginning to sense national solidarity in victory. It also points to a more profound similarity between the two traditions. Just as the regional novel held out appealing images of social cohesion and far-flung loyalty, so

1 Quoted by Lionel Stevenson, *The Wild Irish Girl: The Life of Sydney Owenson, Lady Morgan 1776–1859*, London, 1936, p 250.

moral-evangelical fiction allowed access to a moral field of activity where energy was potentially directed into social channels. With similar roots, some cross-fertilization was inevitable. Elizabeth Hamilton's *Cottagers of Glenburnie* (1808) leavened its strong moral-religious purpose with a pioneering description of Scottish 'manners'. The evangelicals' distaste for the London *haut ton* often led them northwards in pursuit of suitably pure environments. In *Self-Control* Laura returns to her native glen with full patriotic vigour: '. . . the tears of rapture dimmed her eyes, when every voice at once shouted, "Scotland!" . . . Land of my affections! . . . Blessed be thou among nations!' (p 428). The heroine's mentor and eventual husband, in the same author's *Discipline* (1814), is transfigured by its finale into a Highland clan leader: 'Many a smoke, curling in the morning sun, guides my eye to the abode of true, though humble friends; for every one of his romantic race is united to me by the ties of relationship' (p 375). The ingredients, needless to say, mixed awkwardly.

4

## SCOTT AND THE HISTORICAL NOVEL

Shortly before the publication of *Waverley* on 7 July 1814, James Ballantyne (its printer) wondered whether he should order paper for an impression of 750 or 1,000. The incident serves as a useful reminder of the hesitancy with which Sir Walter Scott (1771–1832) and his coadjutors approached the novel market. According to the 'General Preface' (1829) to the first collected Waverley Novels (*Magnum Opus*) its earliest 'English' chapters had been written in 'about the year 1805'. There is evidence, too, of another phase of activity in 1810, with Scott possibly taking the narrative on as far as its early Highland scenes. Even when returning to the project in 1813–14, Scott's primary consideration seems to have been his waning star as a poet. Public approval was more immediate: within a month Constable had ordered a second edition of 2,000, to be followed by five more within three years. In the case of *Rob Roy* (1818), the publishers ventured on an unprecedented first edition of 10,000, having agreed to advance Scott £4,000. The Hollywood-type sums involved become clearer if allowance is made for more than a twenty-fold inflation since.

In such a short space Scott had established himself as the first regular best-selling novelist. While sustaining and developing the novel's new-found reputation for seriousness, he added a dash and vigour which attracted readers from a wide spectrum, many of whom had previously held themselves distant from fiction. The extent of the sale of first editions indicates a large proportion of privileged individual purchasers, willing and able to pay the increasingly large sums demanded (reaching a ceiling with 31s 6d for the three-volumed *Kenilworth* in 1821). In effect, Scott attracted and expanded the 'soft' readership targeted by R. L. Edgeworth in 1804, while drawing back to the novel large elements of the 'polite' literary audience. At the end of Scott's career the monthly publication of the *Magnum Opus* (1829–33) brought yet another wave of readers to the Waverley Novels, with sales soon settling down in the region of 30,000.

In the early twentieth century Scott's reputation suffered a decline, with the souring of a generation weaned on 'chivalric' novels. Even now it takes a degree of historical imagination to appreciate how the early Waverley novels enraptured their first Regency readers. The way back will be made easier when we are supplied with modern texts liberated from the textual accretions of later editions and set apart from the sometimes cumbersome historical frames added by the *Magnum Opus*. On the other hand, it was undoubtedly the fusion of history and fiction which most interested Scott's earliest reviewers. By 1830 it had become a critical *donnée* that Scott was the founder of a new historical novel, surpassing much formal historiography in its ability to revitalize the past.

Scott's centrality has since been reaffirmed by Georg Lukács's *Historical Novel* (1937), the English translation of which, early in the sixties, helped generate a revival of scholarly interest in the Waverley Novels. For Lukács, Scott was the first novelist to depict history as a complex, impersonal process, dwarfing individual protagonists: a viewpoint traceable, in his opinion, to the French Revolution and a new sense of history as 'mass experience'. While assimilating much of Lukács's historicism, recent Anglo-American commentators have looked closer to home in explanation. A firm intellectual influence can be found in a school of Scottish 'philosophical' history, developed by leading figures of the Enlightenment such as Adam Smith, David Hume and Adam Ferguson, which was still taught at Edinburgh University when Scott was a student. Unlike other contemporary ideas of progress, it claimed an economic motivation for social transition, leading to a development through distinct 'stages' of society, from the patriarchal or feudal to modern commercial 'refinement'. More immediately, Scotland in living memory had undergone a series of sweeping changes: from the loss of independence with the

Union of 1707, at first widely resented; through two Jacobite risings in 1715 and 1745; to a period of 'improvement' in the later eighteenth century, marked by Edinburgh's emergence as an 'Athens of the North'. Scott's own life expressed a dualism deep in Scottish culture. The son of a Writer to the Signet (Scottish solicitor), trained to the law himself, as a Clerk to the Court of Session he spent the Edinburgh legal terms resident in a neoclassical New Town residence at 39 Castle Street, supporting unfailingly the dominance of the Pittite (Tory) Dundas family in Scottish affairs. On the other side, there is the Scott who assumed an almost clan-like allegiance to the Dukes of Buccleuch: the ballad collector, laird of Abbotsford, lifelong antiquarian, and passionate opponent of any attempted Anglicization of Scottish institutions. To a degree, these oppositions found a direct *literary* expression in the Scottish Waverley Novels, where the 'correct' English speech of the narrator and hero can sound hollow compared with the vernacular Scots usually found in the mouths of Scott's 'lower' characters.

It is also essential to bear in mind the immediate 'British' context in which the Waverley Novels first appeared. The last two volumes of *Waverley* were written in a burst of a few weeks in the early summer of 1814, shortly after Napoleon's first abdication and the triumphal entry of the allies into Paris. A final 'Postscript, which should have been a Preface' buoyantly pulls the narrative up from 1745 in terms well calculated to match the mood of national euphoria: 'The gradual influx of wealth, and extension of commerce, have since united to render the present people of Scotland a class of beings as different from their grandfathers, as the existing English are from those of Queen Elizabeth's time.' The completed novel also inherited from its opening an 'anti-romantic' attitude reminiscent of the 'moral education' tale in the first decade of the century. Left to his own devices in the quasi-Jacobite ambience of Waverley-Honour, his uncle's estate, Edward Waverley acquires a potentially dangerous view of the past from family legend and an untutored reading. Waverley takes this with him to Scotland, where on military leave he visits the North Lowland estate of Baron Bradwardine, a family ally since the abortive '15, before crossing the Highland Line to confront the clan presided over by Fergus Mac-Ivor and his sister Flora. The more open narrative style at this point partly follows the pattern of the gentlemanly 'tour', a form which had flourished in blockaded Britain, though Waverley's journey is more *historical* than geographical in nature. Scott's narrator, here at his most 'philosophical', observes the economic stagnation which underlies the squalor seemingly endemic in the village of Tully-Veolan. Topography too plays an important part in 'sociological' analysis: the 'formal gardens' surrounding Bradwardine Hall provide a correlative for the stratified feudal observances so cherished by the baron; the 'solitary tower' constructed by Fergus's forefather symbolizes an essentially different 'patriarchal' system, centred exclusively on the clan leader.

Waverley's confrontation with operative instances of 'past' societies is frequently expressed in terms of sudden collision with what had been held picturesquely 'at a distance' (p 76). The 'blue hills' scanned from Bradwardine Hall prove, close up, to be a 'black bog . . . full of large pit-holes' (p 77); on arrival, his feet are washed not by a Homeric 'damsel' but 'a smoke-dried skinny old Highland woman' (p 95). Mixing Fieldingesque irony with Smithian analysis, Scott demystifies the 'romance of the Highlands' by exposing more elemental features of 'patriarchal' society. Fergus – a cultural hybrid, spurred by a more 'modern' type of ambition – artificially fosters his overpopulated clan as a war machine. Flora cultivates a Highland 'garden' redolent of eighteenth-century sentimentalism, where she attempts to entice Waverley into joining the Jacobite cause. Bustled along by events out of his control, Waverley finally finds himself inside Holyrood Palace:

A long gallery, hung with pictures, pretended to be the portraits of kings, who, if they ever flourished at all, lived several hundred years before the invention of painting in oil colours, served as a sort of guard-chamber, or vestibule, to the apartments which the adventurous Charles Edward now occupied in the palace of his ancestors.

(p 191)

The 'biscuit tin' image of Charles Edward casts yet another alluring and deceptive picture, belying the raw mechanism of rebellion. Motivation sways between vaulting ambition (Fergus's earldom) and human pique, from feudal prejudice (the baron's boot-fetishism) to economic deprivation and sheer coercion. On the march into England, the internecine squabbling of clans (less effective as they move further from home) anticipates only too clearly the inevitability of failure. Fergus is one of Scott's *fated* characters, haunted by the ghost of his ancestor and doomed by irresistible social forces. Detached from the army at Penrith, Waverley acknowledges the end of 'the romance of his life' and the beginning of its 'real history'.

History, however, demands one last exorcism. After his own rehabilitation, Waverley witnesses the trial (but not execution) of

Fergus at Carlisle. It is here that one senses an undertow from Scott's deeper feelings about the clan. Evan Dhu's offer to fetch six clansmen to suffer in Fergus's place is misunderstood by a court whose first inclination is to laugh, until awakened to a loyalty outside its normal experience:

'. . . if they laugh because they think I would not keep my word, and come back to redeem him, I can tell them they ken neither the heart of a Hielandman, nor the honour of a gentleman.'

There was no farther inclination to laugh among the audience, and a dead silence ensued.

(p 320)

Waverley's promise to guard over the surviving clan smacks of disingenuity on Scott's part in the light of the subsequent clearances, and is anyway effectively squashed by Fergus's pessimism ('You cannot be to them Vich Ian Vohr; and these three magic words . . . are the only *Open Sesame* to their feelings and sympathies . . .' p 325). Otherwise, Scott's narrative works hard to communicate the assimilation of older virtues into a 'new' Anglo-Scottish society. Bradwardine's tenants remain true to their laird, and Bradwardine Hall is renovated with the help of English money. The baron's response to Waverley's request for his daughter's hand signals a release of feelings, previously held in narrow channels, into a broader range of social activity: 'the pride of birth and rank were swept away; – in the joyful surprise, a slight convulsion passed rapidly over his features as he gave way to the feelings of nature . . . Edward returned the embrace with great sympathy of feeling . . .' (p 316).

The pursuit of 'union' could be seen as the guiding impulse in Scott's life and work. The discovery of the Scottish Regalia early in 1818, orchestrated by Scott on behalf of the British authorities, recalled his pleasure at hearing of Napoleon's defeat at Waterloo. Yet Britain's more tangible post-Waterloo experience was one of increasing disunion. Returning soldiers failed to find employment in an industrially depressed economy; an unpopular Tory administration held up land prices by restricting the import of grain; bad harvests in 1816 and 1819 were followed by rumours of imminent insurrection. Convinced that stability was only attainable by co-operation between 'moderate' Whigs and Tories, Scott complained bitterly of a new breed of 'reforming' Whigs and their readiness to deal with the 'demagogic' leaders of a resurgent radicalism.

Signs of a disruption are already manifest in *Old Mortality* (1816), where Scott turned back in Scottish history to the religious wars of the later seventeenth century. More palpably *historical* in subject-matter than its predecessors, this could also claim to be his most deliberately *political* novel. A sense of parallelism between the seventeenth and nineteenth centuries was not confined to Scott and his peers: in June 1815 a group of working people had assembled at Drumclog, the site of a famous Covenanting victory over the royalist forces, to celebrate Napoleon's escape from Elba. It is in the direct wake of Drumclog that Henry Morton, Scott's hero, reluctantly decides to join the Covenanters' council of war. Once we are alive to this level of possibility, all kinds of lost topicalities are retrievable. Morton and his royalist (Tory) counterpart, Evandale, can be seen as surrogate 'moderates', unwillingly implicated in an atmosphere of mounting party enthusiasm. Similarly, the more extreme Covenanters could be Scott's radicals: embroiling, then overwhelming more ortho-dox Whigs while inciting 'the mob of the insurgents, always loudest in applause of those who push political or religious opinions to extremity' (pp 310–11). At intense moments the narrative appears to lose the confidence of an allegorical relation, as the world of acceler-ating fanaticism is telescoped into a nightmarish version of Scott's present. Increasingly internalized, Morton's moderacy proves not only non-communicable, but itself seems to lose inner coherency. Only in dialogic exchanges with social subordinates, notably Cuddie (his rustic 'wally-de-shamble'), does he achieve anything like a meaningful reciprocity. Even in the post-1688 sequence, a politically vindicated Morton remains painfully alienated – his long-awaited 'union' with Edith Bellenden strangely private and disconnected from the social realm.

In *The Bride of Lammermoor* (1819) a different tone is immediately felt with the elegiac-cum-heroic burial of the last of the barons of Ravenswood, one of Scotland's most martially celebrated families. The surviving representative of the line, Edgar, is called Master of Ravenswood only out of courtesy. Of all his hereditary possessions Wolf's Crag alone remains. Small, dilapidated, perched as if it were falling into the North Sea, it represents a moribund 'old' Scotland. The land has been lost to Sir William Ashton, the Lord Keeper, whose star has risen from low Presbyterian origins through a self-aggrandizing career in law and politics (in its pre-*Magnum* form, the plot is consistently set immediately *before* the Union of 1707). Ashton is despised by his huntsman, who receives gratuities like a waiter in a fashionable hotel. Old Alice resists Ashton's explanation of the changes:

'Yet you knew that they must needs arrive in the course of years?' said the statesman.

'Ay; as I know that the stump, on or beside which you sit, once a tall and lofty tree, must needs one day fall by decay, or by the axe; yet I hoped my eyes might not witness the downfall of the tree which overshadowed my dwelling.'

(p 50)

In a letter on 1 January 1819 Scott used the same metaphor to describe Buccleuch's *protectiveness* in the late economic distresses: 'The Duke is one of those retired and high-spirited men who will never be known untill the world asks what became of the huge oak that grew on the brow of the hill and shelterd such an extent of ground.'[1] Scott's private concern for the ailing Buccleuch combined with broader anxieties about a crisis in paternalist landlordism, the linchpin of his conservatism. Most painful of all Ravenswood's deprivations is the loss of the social function which went with his lands.

A particularly strong sense of disparity is evident in scenes at Ravenswood Castle – the ancestral home of the Ravenswoods, refurbished to match the social pretensions of the new possessors – during a temporary alliance between the Master and Keeper. In contrast with the penury of Wolf's Crag, the visitor is regaled with a feast of showy profusion. In *The Antiquary* (1816) the Earl of Glenallan, having vegetated in the past, is integrated into a busy if less grandiose 'new' society. Here the possibility of *rapprochement* is dashed by the intervention of Lady Ashton – an inveterate Whig. Whereas in earlier novels the Alice-figure usually hands on a talisman to the emergent generation, in this case there is no transference; instead Alice laments the subversion of 'ancient houses' and vehemently warns Ravenswood against treating with the Ashtons. 'Romance' elements remain distinct from a series of 'realistic' cameos depicting the corruption of 'patronage' politics. The only diachrony in an otherwise 'static' scenario charts the rise of Wolf's Hope, emancipated from feudal control, in terms which suggest a profound distaste on Scott's part for naked bourgeois acquisitiveness. The tragic denouement of *The Bride* brutally shatters the 'ideal' union proposed between Ravenswood and Lucy Ashton.

At the beginning of the 1820s, a classic in his own time, Scott stood at the height of his literary success. New ground was found

1 *The Letters of Sir Walter Scott, 1787–1832*, ed. H. J. C. Grierson, 12 vols, London, 1932–7, v. 286.

with *Ivanhoe* (1820), and for a while an extended popularity with English readers. Though Scott returned occasionally to Scottish subjects (notably with *Redgauntlet*, 1824), for the most part the later novels satisfied a taste for historical exoticism, with 'chivalry' and historical personages prominent. First editions rose to 12,500, but began to drop with *Peveril of the Peak* (1822). In Scott's later career it is possible to trace a widening rift between political and literary priorities. Concerned for the sales of the *Magnum*, Robert Cadell (his publisher after the bankruptcy of 1826) sought to prevent any public intervention in the Reform controversy. Perhaps needlessly: the gallery at Jedburgh which hooted down Scott's anti-Reform speech in 1831 were kith and kin with the Waverley Novels' earnest new subscribers, by and large oblivious to their original political import.

5

## PEACOCK'S SATIRICAL FICTION

A different outlook on Britain between Waterloo and the Reform Bill of 1831 is found in the satirical novels of Thomas Love Peacock (1785–1866). While eventually finding a stable social role through an appointment at India House in 1819, Peacock spent his early manhood in insecurity and financial hardship. Sporadically educated – his father, a glass-merchant, apparently left the family when he was three – he was relatively unconnected and had little hope from the 'interest' system in finding a fulfilling career. A naval post, secured presumably through his mother's relatives, was relinquished in favour of literary pursuits, which brought scant recognition. Two narrative poems, *The Genius of the Thames* (1810) and *The Philosophy of Melancholy* (1812) failed to make money, notwithstanding the spectacular contemporary successes of Scott and Byron; Drury Lane turned down at least two of the farces Peacock was working on in 1812–13. Several appeals were made on his behalf to the Literary Society; the third, by his friend Thomas Hookham, reported that he was 'reduced to a state of utter distress'.[1]

A gifted autodidact, Peacock taught himself classical literature, developing a special fondness for 'peripheral' authors (the idea of a

1 See Nicholas Joukovsky, 'Peacock before *Headlong Hall*: A New Look at His Early Years', in 'Thomas Love Peacock: Special Number', *Keats–Shelley Memorial Bulletin*, xxxvi (1985), 1–40, esp. p 30.

more harmonious, humanly vigorous Greek culture is tacitly present throughout his work, finding its most complete expression in *Gryll Grange*, 1861). In 1809–10 Peacock was reading his way through philosophy, old and new, good and indifferent – Locke, Berkeley, Hume, Horne Tooke, Payne Knight, Sir William Drummond – much of it while footloose in 'picturesque' Wales. Contact with real-life intellectuals came through his introduction in 1813 to the Shelleyan circle at Bracknell, an experience later recalled in his *Memoirs of Shelley*:

At Bracknell, Shelley was surrounded by a numerous society, all in a great measure of his own opinions in relation to religion and politics, and the larger portion of them in relation to vegetable diet. But they wore their rue with a difference. Every one of them adopting some of the articles of the faith of their general church, had each nevertheless some predominant crotchet of his or her own, which left a number of open questions for earnest and not always temperate discussion. I was sometimes irreverent enough to laugh at the fervour with which opinions utterly unconducive to any practical result were battled for as matters of the highest importance to the well-being of mankind . . .

*(Works*, viii. 70–71)

If in the monomania of the crotcheteers it is possible to trace a 'source' for the later satires, due allowance needs to be made for the retrospective 'practical' air cast by the *Memoirs*, both here and in its larger account of Peacock's emerging friendship with Shelley. Certainly it is necessary to resist a common image of Peacock as the cold scholar, dispensing Greek, mutton chops and an easily circumvented wisdom to poetical genius. One meeting-point was a mutual interest in sceptical philosophy, perceived by both as an invaluable weapon in the fight against the tyranny of opinion. Even forty years on, in defending Voltaire and Lucian, Peacock can sound surprisingly close to radical Shelley: 'To clear the ground of falsehood is to leave room for the introduction of truth . . . The main object of both was, by sweeping away false dogmas, to teach toleration' (*Works*, x. 225).

*Headlong Hall* (1816) established the familiar Peacockian pattern whereby a group of intellectuals congregate in a remote country house. Little attempt is made at character analysis or environmental explanation; instead Peacock uses the disembodied voices of his speakers to parody modish theories of the day. Psychologically, the formula allowed a release from a potentially incapacitating awareness of the *artificiality* of writing which continued to subvert Peacock's efforts at formal exposition, as in his theoretical *Four Ages of Poetry* (1820). Now the word-directed, all-explaining philosophy could range freely, with the 'real' Peacock silently and sceptically in control. One might legitimately talk of two categories of meaning: the verbally explicit/typographically evident, and the unspoken implication which exists literally between the lines. In attempting a cross-section of ideas, *Headlong Hall* splits its debaters into two broad groups, main theoreticians and minor specialists. The first grouping contains three figures: Foster (a 'perfectibilian'), Escot ('deteriorationist') and Jenkison ('status-quo-ite'). Escot and Foster (anagramatically almost interchangeable) counter each other using similar logical methods, in rhetoric which is diametrically opposite yet employs equivalent linguistic devices. Jenkison's metronomically balanced statements, claiming to reconcile difference, smack both of intellectual and political complacency. Through the trio's predictable patterns Peacock not only questions the deadlocked stereotypes of philosophy in the eighteenth-century manner, but also implicitly points to the dangers of a newer radical 'thought' becoming rhetorical habit.

A different sound originates from the novel's 'specialists'. In shorter interchanges, an assortment of landscape gardeners, *littérateurs*, reviewers and a phrenologist (Mr Cranium) obsessively stake out claims while undercutting their fellows, occasionally falling foul of less interested bystanders. The Reverend Doctor Gaster lapses into a doze on hearing Miss Philomela Poppyseed detail the plan of her latest novel:

'Will you have the goodness to inform me where I left off?'

The Doctor hummed a while, and at length answered: 'I think you had just laid it down as a position, that a thousand a-year is an indispensable ingredient in the passion of love, and that no man, who is not so far gifted by *nature*, can reasonably presume to feel that passion himself, or be correctly the object of it with a well-educated female.'

'That, sir,' said Miss Philomela, highly incensed, 'is the fundamental principle which I lay down in the first chapter, and which the whole four volumes, of which I detailed to you the outline, are intended to set in a strong practical light.'

'Bless me!' said the Doctor, 'what a nap I must have had!'

(p 34)

The exchange gives a good example of the diversity of a work which has been too easily dismissed as a rickety prototype. Miss Poppyseed is at once Amelia Opie (etymologically) and the 'moral' female novelist (generically). Her duplicitous moral standards are undercut by an Anglican divine, himself the butt of Peacock's satire as a complacent sinecurist. Gaster's response none the less contains the seeds of a fiercer castigation of the age's mercenary priorities, from which Peacock had personally suffered.

Since James Spedding noted in 1839 a preference for 'the pulling down of other men's systems instead of building up a better of his own',[1] an influential body of opinion has declared Peacock's a 'negative voice' and so inherently conservative. This, however, overlooks the radical impulse behind the scepticism. With *Melincourt* (1817), his only three-decker novel, Peacock directed attention more squarely at current social issues. In Mr Fax and Mr Forester he brought together representatives of the two main 'progressive' strands of political thought in the Regency: the utilitarian–Malthusian school, with its faith in scientific analysis, and the more literary philanthropic humanism of Shelley. Each character frequently undercuts the other to the point of negation; and both run the gauntlet of a world equally oblivious to reason and idealism – sometimes joyously so – or where more cynical voices identify interest and custom as the main behavioural determinants. According to Sir Telegraph Paxarett, '*l'homme moyen sensuel*', 'most of us go on with the tide'. But later Paxarett accepts (in principle) ecological arguments about the wastefulness of his barouche, and joins the emancipatory 'Anti-saccharine Society' apparently inspired by a 'BELIEF IN HUMAN VIRTUE' (*Works*, ii. 43, 298). Unlike Escot and Foster, Peacock's twin spokesmen are also prepared to concede ground to each other, their developing argument at least holding out the *possibility* of a productive cross-fertilization of ideas.

*Melincourt*'s completion ran parallel with a succession of repressive measures early in 1817, thwarting the reformist optimism of the preceding year, and culminating in the Habeas Corpus Suspension Act and William Cobbett's flight to America. In scenes at Mainchance Villa, Peacock turned his most corrosive satire on the orchestrators and apologists of Tory reaction: Mr Vamp (Gifford, editor of the *Quarterly Review*), Mr Feathernest (Southey), Mr Paperstamp (Wordsworth), Mr Anyside Antijack (Canning) – fingers all unashamedly in the civil 'CHRISTMAS PIE' (*Works*, ii. 416–17). Antijack's display of his old political repertoire includes an acknowledgement that war had been fomented in the 1790s as a means of avoiding domestic reform. This engages Peacock on a level of anti anti-Jacobin satire which would have been unthinkable ten years earlier. But the sting was attached to the tail of a novel which had already passed its topical hour. Peacock's views, moreover, were largely anathema to the 'polite' audience whose sponsorship was increasingly necessary for profitable sales in fiction.

1 *Edinburgh Review*, lxviii (January 1839), 447.

That 'fashionable' literary scene subsequently became the focus of attention in *Nightmare Abbey* (1818). Its year of publication coincided with Austen's *Northanger Abbey*, and both works have enjoyed a continuing reputation as spoofs of Gothic extravagance, each depicting a character (Catherine Morland/Scythrop) detrimentally affected by a literary fashion inappropriate to their true circumstances. Here, however, the resemblance largely ends. Originating in the late 1790s, the posthumously published *Northanger Abbey* had set its sights on the relatively decorous 'horrid' fiction of Mrs Radcliffe and her imitators; *Nightmare Abbey* took as its target an essentially different Gothicism, in the process locating a new species of 'Byronic' hero. Mr Flosky – by far Peacock's fullest and most complex portrait of Coleridge – observes the change:

The ghosts . . . have been laid . . . and now the delight of our spirits is to dwell on all the vices and blackest passions of our nature, tricked out in a masquerade dress of heroism and disappointed benevolence; the whole secret of which lies in forming combinations that contradict all our experience, and affixing the purple shred of some particular virtue to that precise character, in which we should be most certain not to find it in the living world . . .

(p 68)

This is not Coleridge of the 1790s and Pantisocracy, but the 'intellectual' figurehead of *Lay Sermons* (1816, 1817) and *Biographia Literaria* (1817) – a transcendental philosopher, neo-feudalist and (such is Peacock's imputation) the self-appointed guru of counter-revolutionism.

Amongst his multifarious roles Flosky claims the right of divining the taste of the 'reading public'. Surveying a parcel of books just received by the Honourable Mr Listless – Peacock's enervated 'aristocratical' reader – he skims '"Devilman, a novel." Hm. Hatred – revenge – misanthropy – and quotations from the Bible. Hm. This is the morbid anatomy of black bile' (p 60). In one sense Flosky's politics and relish for *sauce piquante* are not at odds. The work alluded to is Godwin's *Mandeville: A Tale of the Seventeenth Century in England* (1817), a psychological study of hatred set amidst bigotry and civil antagonism during the Civil War. Tricked out as a 'fashionable' novelist, with a Scottian subtitle, Godwin represented little threat to the status quo; and, indeed, through his determinism might have been seen as condoning passive obedience. Listless's lassitude in the first half is matched by the dramatic appearance of Mr Cypress (Byron) in the second, a *tour de force* in which Peacock ingeniously mixes parody and direct quotation from the fourth canto of *Childe Harold*. On the point of departing the country (Byron had already left, forsaking a Whig seat in the House of Lords), Cypress veers drastically between misanthropic generalization and portentous self-observation: 'Sir, I have quarrelled with my wife; and a man who has quarrelled with his wife is absolved from all duty to his country' (p 99).

The extent to which the more brooding presence of Scythrop, self-destructively caught between two women (Marionetta and Stella/Celinda), is based on Shelley and his elopement with Mary Godwin has puzzled Peacock's critics. In more generic terms, the portrait meshes with Peacock's analysis in two important ways. Scythrop's esotericism (seven copies of *Philosophical Gas* sold) throws a satirical light on the widening rift between literary exponents of 'liberty' and the reading audience at large; while his self-immersion in a private dilemma, likely to be judged merely as scandalous by the public, adds range and depth to the critique of solipsism which underlies nearly all the literary parody. In fine comedy Peacock sounded the death-knell of the second phase of Romanticism as an active libertarian force.

Published in 1831, *Crotchet Castle* followed *Headlong Hall* in attempting to encompass an entire milieu, though the world it addressed had substantially changed. In immediate political terms, during the course of its writing the Wellington government had collapsed, to be replaced by Grey's reform-bent administration. Whigs 'born to opposition' were now in positions of influence, and liberalism (if of a changed tenor) had become orthodoxy. An imminent new world is evident in the Reverend Doctor Folliott's opening tirade against his 'learned friend' (Henry Brougham) and the 'Steam Intellect Society' – the Society for the Diffusion of Useful Knowledge, whose aim was the 'practical' education of the non-voting artisan class. Again the satire is double-edged: the heavy ironies ('equally well qualified ... every branch of human knowledge') partly convey Peacock's own scepticism about mass educationism; but Folliott's overall dismissiveness, mirroring High Anglican opposition, is patently self-interested. Peacock's unerring eye for the topical picks out new intellectual configurations as well as a redisposition of old battle-lines. Foster–Fax has hardened into Mr Mac Quedy, a fully-fledged 'utilitarian' political economist. Mr Chainmail opposes with a new kind of medievalism, founded on an idea of the twelfth century as a communally unified and more spiritual society. In the polarization, Scott has become an irrelevance. For Chainmail, his pictures of the Middle Ages are too harsh: 'No one would infer from his pictures that theirs was a much better state of society than this which we live in' (p 202). With eyes only for the present, Mac Quedy inevitably claims the obverse, albeit in terms which might have been culled entirely from a prejudiced reading of *Ivanhoe*!

The second half of *Crotchet Castle* incorporates a long Welsh idyll, in which Peacock temporarily retreats into pastoralism for stability. Elsewhere the utilitarian ethic goes hand in glove with an enacted middle-class practice, leading to a smudging of 'ideas' and 'reality' unusual in Peacock's satire. Lady Clarinda is both a latter-day Mary Crawford, viewing marriage as a manoeuvring business, and an incipient Louisa Gradgrind, a sacrificial offering to Mammonism: 'I dare say, love in a cottage is very pleasant; but then it positively must be a cottage ornée: but would not the same love be a great deal safer in a castle, even if Mammon furnished the fortification?' (p 149). The last chapters describe an assault by insurrectionaries on Chainmail Hall, with Peacock's own position at its most tantalizingly elusive. Hints are thrown out of a possible collaboration between Chainmail and Mr Toogood (the paternalist factory-owner Robert Owen); but then Chainmail's guests are all property-owners, holding out a mob bent presumably on their own, more extensive implementation of the utilitarian pleasure principle.

The early 1830s also threw up prophets of a kind unanticipated by Peacock. Thomas Carlyle in 1833 was calling for writers of fiction to 'sweep their Novel-fabric into the dust-cart, and betake them with such faculty as they have, to understand and record what is *true*'.[1] With *Pickwick Papers* (1837) Dickens found the pulse of an expanded readership, shifting from parody of fads in some ways reminiscent of Peacock to the vibrant presentation of a 'bourgeois' society – one to be characterized by doubts and by dogmas that were quite different from those of the Regency. In *Crotchet Castle*, Peacock had again placed his finger on an important turning-point in the British intellectual scene, but one which was to isolate even further his own outlook and medium. The circumstances of the age demanded different forms and an essentially new kind of novel.

---

1 *Foreign Quarterly Review*, xi (April 1833), 262.

# 3

# JANE AUSTEN: QUESTIONS OF CONTEXT

## Margaret Kirkham

'Yes, I am fond of history.'

'I wish I were too. I read it a little as a duty, but it tells me nothing that does not either vex or weary me. The quarrels of popes and kings, with war or pestilences, in every page; the men all so good for nothing, and hardly any women at all – it is very tiresome: and yet I often think it odd that it should be so dull, for a great deal of it must be invention.'

*Northanger Abbey*, p 108[1]

## INTRODUCTION

In 1975, two hundred years after her birth, George Steiner voiced what had long been a common view: 'At the height of political and industrial revolution, in a decade of formidable philosophic activity, Miss Austen composes novels almost extra-territorial to history.'[2] In the same year Marilyn Butler, in *Jane Austen and the War of Ideas*, re-examined the novels in the light of contemporary ideological conflict and found in them a clear, partisan commitment to reactionary social and moral values. Few would now be likely to endorse the older view of Austen, as outside the historical conflicts and pressures of her time, yet it is not altogether easy to place her in relation to them. Austen's silence on major public events cannot be ignored, especially now that it has been made clear, through such studies as Warren Roberts's *Jane Austen and the French Revolution* (1979) as well as by recent biographers,[3] that it was not the result of ignorance, but of deliberate choice. Some naïve remarks of Catherine Morland,

---

1 Page references to Jane Austen's novels refer to R. W. Chapman's Oxford edition. Page references to her letters refer to *Jane Austen's Letters*, ed. R. W. Chapman, Oxford, 1948.

2 *After Babel: Aspects of Language and Tradition*, Oxford, 1975, p 9.

3 For example, John Halperin, *The Life of Jane Austen*, Brighton, 1984; Park Honan, *Jane Austen: Her Life*, London, 1987.

the heroine of *Northanger Abbey*, are quoted at the start of this chapter, since they draw attention to difficulties about women and history, relevant to discussion of the Austen novels in their historical context.

Catherine is bored by history and alienated from it, because it excludes women. She thinks it odd that she should find it so dull since, like the novels she can't put down, it must include a great deal of invention. Catherine is the least sophisticated of Austen's heroines, and the feminist scepticism shown here has often been seen simply as a mark of her childishness; but, as Tony Tanner (1986) says, it 'anticipates a complaint which has become much more articulate in our own times, namely that "history" has been traditionally written from an almost exclusively male point of view'.[1] Nor was the complaint a new one. Right at the start of the eighteenth century, Mary Astell, in *The Christian Religion as Profess'd by a Daughter of the Church of England* (1705) spoke of women's inability to profit from study of a branch of writing which excluded them:

History can only serve us for Amusement and a Subject of Discourse. It cannot help our Conduct or excite in us a generous Emulation . . . the Men being the Historians, they seldom condescend to record the great and the good Actions of Women; and when they take notice of them, 'tis with this wise Remark, that such Women *acted above their Sex*. By which one must suppose they would have their Readers understand that they were not Women who did those Great Actions, but they were Men in Petticoats.

(pp 292–3)

Since 1975 critical interest in the ideological placement of the Austen novels has continued, but it is only quite recently that the history of early modern feminism has begun to re-enter the history of politics and ideology.[2] Strange though it now seems, Raymond Williams did not include an entry under 'feminism' in his *Keywords* (1976), nor was the anti-Romanticism of some early feminist writing mentioned under 'Romantic'. There is little disagreement about the importance of Austen's anti-Romanticism, but a good deal about what it signifies. Differences depend to a large extent on the way in which we construct the ideological context. If emphasis is placed on similarities between Mary Wollstonecraft and Jane Austen, as rational, feminist moralists, and upon Harriet Martineau's admiration

1 *Jane Austen*, London, 1986.
2 See Gerda Lerner, *The Majority Finds Its Past: Placing Women in History*, Oxford, 1979; and Jane Rendall, *The Origins of Modern Feminism: Women in Three Western Societies, Britain, France and the United States 1780–1860*, Cambridge, 1984.

of the Austen novels, we are more likely to discover a 'liberal' rather than a 'conservative' novelist, perhaps even, at times, a 'radical' one. To say this, however, is not to suggest that Austen was either a covert sympathizer with Godwin or Paine, or a 'Benthamite'; it is merely to cast doubt on how far the simple opposition of revolutionary versus reactionary is useful, and on whether, as a social novelist, Jane Austen's point of view should be assimilated to the line of conservative romantic thought associated with the later Burke and Carlyle.[1]

Jane Austen's a-centricity, as an anti-Romantic, in an age we habitually define as Romantic, must be a major concern of contextual criticism and was closely examined by Marilyn Butler in what proved to be the most stimulating and thought-provoking of the many studies marking the bicentenary of the novelist's birth. Bringing formidable erudition to bear on her subject, Butler traced the growth of Sentimentalism, the precursor of full-blown Romanticism, in the England of Jane Austen's youth, arguing that, from the time of the French Revolution, the novel was polarized between the forces of revolution and reaction. Sentimentalism amounted to more than a literary fashion. It was, and was understood to be, a means of questioning and reinterpreting traditional ideas about human nature. It was associated with fundamental changes of thought and feeling about society and the individual, and about morals. It was for this reason that the Jacobin novelists, including William Godwin, Robert Bage and Thomas Holcroft, wrote within the sentimentalist tradition of the novel, and that opponents of revolution attacked it. After 1797, with the intensification of hostility between France and England, a reaction against revolutionary impulses of any kind set in, and remained strong until after Austen's death. Her works may be seen as 'belonging generically . . . to a movement that defines itself by opposition to revolution'.[2]

Coming four years after Alistair Duckworth's *Jane Austen and the Improvement of the Estate*, the *War of Ideas* consolidated a critical view of Austen as a conservative novelist, strongly influenced by the political views of Edmund Burke. Her command of narrative authority could now be seen as united with a political partisanship. The irony which had earlier led D. W. Harding and Marvin Mudrick to discern a subversive novelist hiding behind a conformist mask had, if Butler's view were accepted, to be dismissed as little

---

1 Outlined in Raymond Williams, *Culture and Society 1780–1950*, London, 1958.
2 *Jane Austen and the War of Ideas*, Oxford, 1975, p 123.

more than surface decoration.[1] The formal structure of the novels, which was indubitably anti-sentimental, must be held as decisive evidence of conscious political commitment of a strongly reactionary kind.

Both Duckworth and Butler discuss Austen's handling of the individual in relation to society, but without special consideration of her emphasis on women as having the rights and responsibilities of discrete individuals. Discussing *Mansfield Park*, Duckworth says:

> From *the individual himself* must come the affirmative response, and the courage to maintain faith in 'principles' and 'rules of right' even when these are everywhere ignored and debased. Such qualities, represented quietly but firmly in Fanny's nature . . . suggest an author whose deepest impulse was not to subvert but maintain and properly improve a social heritage.
>
> (p 80, my emphasis)

Here it is recognized that Fanny Price's moral nature is such that she incurs the rights and responsibilities appropriate to 'the individual', but not that this carries feminist implications about the right ordering of domestic government and, indirectly, about the 'improvement of the estate', in both its literal and figurative meanings.

It is an essential argument of *A Vindication of the Rights of Woman* (1792) that women share the same moral nature as men, and have the same kind of individual rights and obligations. As Wollstonecraft, who refers to herself as 'a moralist', puts it: 'Surely there can be but one rule of right, if morality has an eternal foundation, and whoever sacrifices virtue, strictly so called, to present convenience, or whose *duty* is to act in such a manner, lives only for the passing day, and cannot be an accountable creature' (p 120). Whatever their other differences, Wollstonecraft and Austen are alike in their treatment of women as 'accountable creatures', and in drawing on eighteenth-century moralists in framing their ethical viewpoint. Austen's indebtedness to Bishop Butler, discussed by Philip Drew, is particularly interesting, since it suggests a parallel with Wollstonecraft's reliance on Richard Price, a moralist of the same school. Janet Todd points out that 'Part of her tribute to Price is found in her use of his philosophy, especially in her dependence of morality on reason.'[2] As early as 1973 Lloyd W. Brown had demonstrated

---

1 D. W. Harding, 'Regulated Hatred: An Aspect of the Work of Jane Austen', *Scrutiny*, viii (1940), 346–62; Marvin Mudrick, *Jane Austen: Irony as Defense and Discovery*, Princeton, 1952.
2 Janet Todd, *A Wollstonecraft Anthology*, Indiana, 1977, p 4; Philip Drew, 'Jane Austen and Bishop Butler', *Nineteenth-Century Fiction*, xxxv (1980–81), 127–49.

similarities of thought between Wollstonecraft and Austen, some of them striking enough to suggest direct indebtedness, and they are further discussed in a number of later studies, including Leroy W. Smith's *Jane Austen and the Drama of Woman* (1983) and my *Jane Austen, Feminism and Fiction* (1983).[1]

David Spring, writing as a social historian, has suggested that literary critics have not paid enough attention to Jane Austen's precise social placement in what he calls 'the clerical pseudo-gentry'. Discussion of how far her novels affirm the traditional values of the landed gentry or give preference to those of the rising bourgeoisie are, in his view, based on false assumptions about conflict between the two. There was, he maintains, no landed crisis in the England of her time, since landowners were becoming successful agricultural businessmen. The professional class held much the same view of society and, since both groups were doing well, there was no conflict of interest. Dismissing class conflict as the subject of the Austen novels, he speaks of 'the fate of women' in the social group to which she belonged as her major preoccupation.[2]

In this essay the controversy about the nature of woman and her role as an individual in society is treated as central to the historical context of the Austen novels. This is not to deny that class attitudes, interests and assumptions come into the picture, for it is clear that they do. Austen's viewpoint is that of a daughter of the pseudo-gentry, the group Virginia Woolf was later to call 'the daughters of educated men',[3] but because she writes as a self-conscious daughter, not a son, her perspective does not quite fit that of her class in general. Although, as Gilbert Ryle said, she takes an interest in some quite general philosophical problems about sense and sensibility, or reason and feeling,[4] there is a specific, feminist edge to her interest. Feminist concern takes Austen into the sexual/textual politics of her time, and consideration of the ideological meaning of her novels should begin here. Richardson's *Sir Charles Grandison* (1754), Rousseau's *Émile* (1762), Wollstonecraft's *Vindication* (1792) and Germaine de Staël's *Corinne* (1807) are especially important.

Jane Austen was closely acquainted with *Sir Charles Grandison*,

---

1 See also Julia Prewett Brown, *Jane Austen's Novels: Social Change and Literary Form*, Cambridge, Mass., 1979.
2 'Interpreters of Jane Austen's Novels', in *Jane Austen: New Perspectives*, ed. Janet Todd, Women and Literature, NS, iii, New York, 1983, p 68.
3 *Three Guineas*, London, 1938, p 10.
4 'Jane Austen and the Moralists', in *Critical Essays on Jane Austen*, ed. B. C. Southam, London, 1968.

but her admiration was far from uncritical. Richardson wrote this novel largely in response to female criticism of his two earlier works, *Pamela* and *Clarissa*, where he had seemed tacitly to accept the double standard of sexual morality. Because *Sir Charles Grandison* attempted to meet such objections, it had a place of special importance to women, for several generations. Nevertheless, Austen, like other women of her generation, did not find its idealized vision of patriarchal authority convincing. Its hero, Richardson's 'Good Man', was intended to be a credibly drawn, 'unmixed' character, whose sexual conduct came up to the standards required of a 'virtuous' heroine, but a good many readers found him absurd.[1]

Neither *Émile* nor the *Vindication* is mentioned by Austen in her novels or letters, but there is indirect evidence that she had read Wollstonecraft and shared, to a large extent, her objection to Rousseau's treatment of Sophie, the ideal wife for his ideal man. In *Émile*, Rousseau takes the view that men and women have fundamentally different mental qualities and therefore fundamentally different moral natures. It was widely believed to have influenced those who drew up the Revolutionary Constitution in France against granting rights of citizenship to women, as well as providing quite unrevolutionary writers of conduct-books and sermons for the fair sex with the underlying view of female nature that informed their recommendations. For both reasons it is the main target of Wollstonecraft's attack in the *Vindication*. In Chapter 5, which is in effect a piece of feminist literary criticism, Wollstonecraft directs her 'animadversions' against sentimental literature, on the grounds that it degrades women by denying them the rational powers of mind which she, like Rousseau, accepts as the proper qualification for those who claim the rights of the individual moral agent. Rousseau, by denying that such powers are natural to women, became for Wollstonecraft the foremost writer to have 'rendered women objects of pity bordering on contempt'. A number of English 'conduct-book' authors, including James Fordyce, of whom Mr Collins in *Pride and Prejudice* shows approval (I. xiv), are also censured as disciples of Rousseau. Without supposing that Austen had the least sympathy for Wollstonecraft's revolutionary politics, it is clear that, as a feminist moralist, she shared her objection to Rousseau's view of female nature. There is also common ground in attitudes to female education

1 See Edward Copeland, 'The Burden of Grandison: Jane Austen and Her Contemporaries', in *Jane Austen: New Perspectives*; and Margaret Kirkham, *Jane Austen, Feminism and Fiction*, Brighton, 1983, and New York, 1986, pp 27–32.

and in the belief that 'affection and esteem', rather than passionate love, should form the essential basis of 'respectable' marriage.

Among the women authors censured in the *Vindication* is the 'rhapsodist' Germaine de Staël, whose novel *Corinne* (1807) was of some importance to Austen, though there is no reason to think she admired it. Since anti-*Corinne* elements are of some importance in the construction of the later Austen novels, de Staël's ambiguous position in relation to the sexual/textual politics of her time needs clarification. Wollstonecraft's condemnation of de Staël was based on a perception of her as an enthusiastic admirer of Rousseau – one whose admiration led to an acceptance of the exclusion of women from the political rights of citizenship. Her special bitterness, in the fifth chapter of the *Vindication*, resulted from the pain of seeing a woman who, like herself, supported the French Revolution standing against the enfranchisement of women. Olympe de Gouges, whose *Déclaration des droits de la femme et de la citoyenne* (1792) placed her with Wollstonecraft and other rational feminists, went to the guillotine in 1793 for 'having forgotten the virtues which belong to her sex'. Wollstonecraft, at the time she wrote *Vindication*, saw that revolutionary France had already betrayed the hopes of women demanding the rights inherent in an acceptance of their discrete status as 'individuals'. De Staël was felt to have associated herself with that betrayal. Some women in England, by no means revolutionaries in the accepted sense, though they might be thought of as daughters of the Enlightenment, continued, after Wollstonecraft's death and despite the scandal about her life, to sympathize with her view of women's nature, and to see de Staël with hostile eyes. Opposing attitudes to Wollstonecraft and de Staël also took on nationalistic overtones in the long period of war with France and its aftermath. Wollstonecraft, whatever her faults, could be seen as representing English honesty, against the Gallic acceptance of duplicity in sexual attitudes. Mary Russell Mitford, for instance, contrasted Wollstonecraft's 'pure and perfect style' in English with de Staël's 'miserable bombast' in French, claiming that, 'married or not married', Wollstonecraft 'wrote like a modest woman – was a modest woman'.[1]

As Marilyn Butler says, the English Jacobins were not in sympathy with Rousseau, Goethe, or Kotzebue, and 'refused to exploit sexual passion as a powerful natural ally against a moribund society and its

---

1 *Life and Letters of Mary Russell Mitford*, ed. A. G. L'Estrange, London, 1870, i. 305–6.

repressive conventions. At a conscious level, they could not use the libido because they believed in reason.'[1] This may be seen simply as the effect of English middle-class prudery, associated with the puritanism of eighteenth-century Dissenters and early nineteenth-century Evangelicalism, but it must be remembered that the women's rights movement owed a great deal to such a tradition and that, as some saw it, women in France owed their inferior status to a Rousseauist view of female nature. The divisions which opened between literary women at this time arose from opposed responses to two of Rousseau's works. Whereas *Émile* provoked feminist antagonism, *Julie, ou la Nouvelle Héloïse* (1762) established the type of the *femme de génie*, whose largeness of soul, sensibility and suffering, displayed through her letters, gave her an equivalence to the Romantic artist.[2]

This figure, developed by de Staël in *Delphine* (1802) and more powerfully in *Corinne*, was inspirational to women writers of the Romantic movement and may be seen as 'feminist', in that it was used to reveal the intolerable restrictions placed on outstanding women and to associate their need to express themselves through art with the need for sexual liberation. Romantic concentration on women of genius could, however, lead to social élitism, to a snobbish scorn of 'ordinary' women in the middle class and adulation of aristocracy allied with talent. It is against such a background that Austen's refusal to meet de Staël (Mitford did the same) and her one known, mocking reference to *Corinne* must be seen, together with de Staël's dismissal of *Pride and Prejudice* as '*vulgaire*'.[3]

Jane Austen and Germaine de Staël, who was some eleven years her senior, died within a week in July 1817, de Staël, as it happened, on the fourteenth, the twenty-third anniversary of the storming of the Bastille. De Staël was then clearly established as the foremost 'literary woman' of the Romantic movement, having written a major critical work, *De L'Allemagne*, as well as one novel of great importance to later women novelists and poets, in England and America, as well as in France. *De L'Allemagne* was first published in England in 1813, the 1810 edition having been suppressed in Napoleonic France. It was while de Staël was being lionized in London in 1813 by, among others, Scott and Coleridge that Austen declined to meet her. Henry Austen, in the 1833 revision of the 'Biographical Notice',

---

1 *Jane Austen and the War of Ideas*, pp 44–5.
2 See Ellen Moers, *Literary Women*, New York, 1977, pp 151–8.
3 See *Memoirs of Sir John Mackintosh* (1805), quoted in B. C. Southam, *Jane Austen: The Critical Heritage*, London, 1968, p 110. For Austen's reference to *Corinne*, see *Letters*, p 242.

used his sister's deliberate avoidance of de Staël to illustrate her dislike of the public world of literary fame. However, given the marked differences between the two authors, it may well indicate a more specific antipathy.

## JANE AUSTEN'S NOVELS

Jane Austen wrote the original versions of her first three novels between 1795 and 1799, though none of them was published until 1811. It may be useful to give the earlier titles and the publication dates of all six novels here: 'Elinor and Marianne', retitled *Sense and Sensibility*, 1811; 'First Impressions', retitled *Pride and Prejudice*, 1813; 'Susan', retitled *Northanger Abbey*, accepted for publication and advertised in 1803, but withdrawn and published posthumously in 1818; *Mansfield Park*, 1814; *Emma*, 1816; *Persuasion*, 1818. The gap between the inception of the early novels and their final revision and publication created some anomalies in the way they were received by contemporary reviewers and readers, discussed in the Conclusion. They are here considered in the order in which they were published, except that *Northanger Abbey* is treated as though it had actually appeared in 1803, when it was accepted and advertised, but unaccountably withdrawn from publication.

### Northanger Abbey

*Northanger Abbey* is comparatively unguarded in exposing the author's feminist viewpoint: not only are there outspoken authorial comments on male vanity as requiring female ignorance, if not outright imbecility, to minister to it (p 111), but in Chapter 5 there occurs the 'Northanger Defence of the Novel', the only statement about fiction Austen ever intended for publication. Markedly different from the low-keyed remarks scattered in her family letters, it is less a general defence of the novel than of the novel as written by women. Fanny Burney's *Cecilia* and *Camilla*, and Maria Edgeworth's *Belinda* are picked out for praise, no male novelist being mentioned. It is by implication women novelists who are called on to stand by their own and other people's heroines, in a sisterly solidarity: 'Let us not desert one another; we are an injured body.' The merits of a good novel as a 'work in which the greatest powers of the mind are displayed, in which the most thorough knowledge of human nature, the happiest delineation of its varieties, the liveliest effusions of wit and humour are conveyed to the world in the best-chosen language' are contrasted with 'a volume of the Spectator', and an assortment of characteristically male literary hack work, generally praised at the expense of 'performances which have only genius, wit and taste to recommend them' (pp 37–8). *Sir Charles Grandison* is not defended and later it is carefully placed as a novel denigrated by the anti-heroine, Isabella Thorpe, much admired by Mrs Morland, whose literary taste is suspect, and merely found 'entertaining' by the heroine, even though it isn't like *Udolpho* (pp 41–2).

Tension between the formal *part* of the heroine and the character who does not quite fit it is frequently found in the Austen comedy. Exploited to the full in *Mansfield Park*, it is found more light-heartedly in *Northanger Abbey*, where it is used to change the meaning of the type of burlesque it superficially resembles, and to develop heroineship as a metaphor for the acquisition of female false consciousness. Charlotte Lennox's *The Female Quixote* (1752), Colman's *Polly Honeycombe* (1760), Sheridan's *The Rivals* (1775), Beckford's *The Elegant Enthusiast* (1796) and Maria Edgeworth's *Angelina* (1801) are all examples of burlesque in which a naïve heroine is misled by romantic reading into delusions about the real world and, as a rule, misconduct towards those to whom she owes obedience. Eaton Stannard Barrett's *The Heroine* (1813) is a late example, in which Cherubina has her kind old father shut up in a lunatic asylum. Such burlesques deny value to the novel, especially the novel of female authorship; the heroine's delusions are unambiguously corrected by the superior wisdom of the hero and she herself is simply a figure to be mocked. *Northanger Abbey* differs in important ways: the value of the novel, especially as written by women, is pointedly affirmed – even Mrs Radcliffe is given her due, the hero being made to assert that only a stupid reader could fail to find pleasure in her works (p 106); the deluded Catherine is never so far deluded as to abuse or disobey her genuinely affectionate (if rather dim) parents; and a balance, characteristic of Austen, is set up between hero and heroine, so that his superiority of age, education and sex does not get unqualified validation.

Catherine's language is sometimes ludicrously naïve, but also disconcertingly direct; as she says, 'I cannot speak well enough to be unintelligible' (p 133). She speaks, even at her most absurd, the language of 'truth and nature', whereas the hero's language is frequently too clever and confident, 'more nice than wise', as his sister tells him (p 108). Henry Tilney has the easy command of a clever young man over the generalized language of public moral and political discourse, but his author adopts a position of ambiguous critical distance towards it. This is particularly apparent in the passage at the end of Chapter 9, Volume II which has become something of a crux of critical discussion. Having disposed of Catherine's horrid suspicion that General Tilney had murdered his wife, Henry poses a series of rhetorical questions:

Does our education prepare us for such atrocities? Do our laws connive at them? Could they be perpetrated without being known, in a country like this, where social and literary intercourse is on such a footing; where every man is surrounded by a neighbourhood of voluntary spies, and where roads and newspapers lay everything open?

Catherine is obliged to see that the answer is 'no', the murder of unloved wives is not tolerated in 'the midland counties of England'. Yet Henry's questions do raise doubts about how far all is well in 'the country and the age in which we live', at least for readers sensitive to linguistic difficulties inherent in generalized language, which obliterates differences between men and women. What does 'our' education prepare us for? What do 'our' laws connive at? Is social and literary intercourse on a sound footing? Is every woman 'protected' by a neighbourhood of voluntary spies and by what is 'laid open' in the gossip columns of newspapers? Austen's novels show a clear awareness of ways in which education, the law, and the manners and customs of the age differentiate between the two sexes, and wholly soothing answers to Henry's rhetorical questions are undermined in *Northanger Abbey*. In so far as it validates part of Catherine's suspicion of the General, it keeps them reverberating. After all, her view of him as an irascible domestic tyrant was partly based on clear-sighted observation of his treatment of his children, especially his daughter. When General Tilney turns Catherine out of his house because she is not an heiress, the element of good sense in her perception of him is confirmed.

Besides being a naïve reader of Gothic romance, Catherine is a heroine not quite grown out of honest childhood. 'Becoming a heroine' is used in this novel as a metaphor for acquiring the artificial characteristics of an objectionable stereotyped femininity, for 'growing down' rather than growing up.[1] Though 'in training' from fifteen to seventeen, Catherine's progress is limited. She secures the love of the hero by breaking one of the cardinal rules of heroineship, enshrined in *Sir Charles Grandison* and endless conduct-books: she falls in love first and fails to disguise her

---

1 Annis Pratt and Barbara White, 'The Novel of Development', in *Archetypal Patterns in Women's Fiction*, ed. Annis Pratt, Brighton, 1981, p 14.

feelings. She is unlike the Arabellas and Cherubinas of the classic anti-sentimental burlesque, in that the soundness of her heart is never in doubt, nor is her honesty.

In *Vindication* Wollstonecraft takes particular exception to Rousseau's belief that duplicity, together with a love of dolls, dress and needlework, are natural attributes of the female character in childhood. She says:

a girl, whose spirits have not been damped by insensitivity, or innocence tainted by false shame, will always be a romp, and the doll will never excite attention unless confinement allows her no alternative.

(p 129)

*Northanger Abbey* opens with an account of Catherine's childhood in which we learn:

She was fond of all boys' plays, and greatly preferred cricket, not merely to dolls, but to the more heroic enjoyments of infancy, nursing a dormouse, feeding a canary bird, or watering a rose-bush . . . she was moreover, noisy and wild, hated confinement and cleanliness, and loved nothing so well as rolling down the green slope at the back of the house.

(pp 13–14)

Catherine's nature and her advantage, in having been allowed the rough-and-tumble of an unrestricted childhood, make it difficult for her to 'grow down' into womanhood, though, as she becomes a young lady and heroine, she does her best to acquire the trimmings of a 'femininity' clearly seen as artificial by her author. Irony is directed against the part, not against the 'natural girl' who can't act it properly. This is particularly apparent in the handling of Catherine's response to her brother's letter, informing her that he has been jilted by the hypocritical Isabella Thorpe (pp 202–7). Here Catherine's concern for her brother, despite her naïve display of it, is shown as giving pause to the hero. For once he does not express himself with the eloquence of a clever young man, who knows more than the heroine does. He says: 'You feel, as you always do, what is most to the credit of human nature. – Such feelings ought to be investigated, that they may know themselves' (p 207). It is, of course, impersonal enough, but the slightly unclear syntax registers a point at which the balance between hero and heroine is changed. What Catherine knows and feels has become worth Henry's respect and 'investigation', his self-knowledge has been advanced by her simplicity, but it is the simplicity of a 'natural' version of the female character in youth that produces this effect.

Catherine is, to be sure, a bit of a clown, simple in ways which make us smile at such innocence in one who aspires to heroineship; but then, in the hands of this author, her failure, even so late as seventeen, to become a mysterious exemplar of the female character is made to evoke deeper levels of intelligence in the hero. *Northanger Abbey*, for all its youthful high spirits, goes quite deep into what Catherine knew, and what Henry comes to know after he falls in love with her.

## Sense and Sensibility

In *Sense and Sensibility*, which makes use of schematized heroines drawn from the didactic tradition of women's writing, it proved difficult to bring the necessary irony to bear upon their contrasted roles without 'deserting' the characters who play them. Published in 1811, its origins go back to as early as 1795, and its similarities to Maria Edgeworth's *Letters of Julia and Caroline* (1795) and Jane West's *A Gossip's Story* (1796) are plain. That its title and its treatment of reason and feeling are directly relevant to contemporary feminist debate is, perhaps, now generally accepted.

*Sense and Sensibility* opens with the ejection from the family estate of the widowed Mrs Dashwood and her daughters, and it includes some brilliantly satirical passages in which the meanness of their half-brother, who has inherited virtually everything, is displayed. Urged on by his totally unscrupulous wife, he reinterprets the promise given to his dying father to make proper provision for them, whittling down his original notion of giving them three thousand pounds to 'some little present of furniture' when they find, as best they may, somewhere else to live. Here Austen's scenario implies a criticism of that adopted by Richardson in *Sir Charles Grandison*. The Dashwood sisters *cannot* depend upon their brother to secure their rightful place in the world, and it is in a society where sensitive, intelligent and non-exploitive women are shown as peculiarly vulnerable that Austen sets her story of devoted, and schematically contrasted, sisters.

Elinor Dashwood, at nineteen, is the representative of female rationality and prudence. Marianne, at seventeen, carries, in her response to life and her way of seeing the world, an essentially poetic sensibility. Elinor's attitudes and conduct are shown to be more worthy of respect than Marianne's, and in this the novel conforms to the conservative, didactic models on which it is based – but there are important modifications. Both Austen heroines are allowed enough complexity to prevent them from becoming simple *types* of either Sense or Sensibility. In the first chapter we are told of Elinor's 'excellent heart' and 'affectionate disposition', while it is Marianne who is said to be 'sensible and clever'. Besides being contrasted with one another, Elinor and Marianne are contrasted with the common run of less intelligent, less sensitive and less morally scrupulous characters who make up the society in which they live; the half-brother who inherits the Dashwood estate, Sir John Middleton the benevolent but brainless baronet, and their defective wives – the mean and narrow-minded Mrs John Dashwood, the silly Lady Middleton. Beside them the superior qualities of both the Miss Dashwoods stand out, and are further accentuated by the lack of heroes quite equal to them. Elinor's Man of Sense, Edward Ferrars, cuts rather a foolish figure for the greater part of the novel, and Colonel Brandon, the respectable Man of Feeling whom Marianne eventually accepts, remains a slightly comic figure, his flannel waistcoat being quite as memorable as his delicate feelings.

The schematic design of *Sense and Sensibility* requires the exposure of Willoughby, the anti-hero, as corrupt, but it is between Elinor, Marianne and Willoughby that deeper levels of feeling and more complex moral responses are suggested. This is well illustrated in Chapter 7 of the third volume, where the repentant Willoughby explains himself to Elinor. The novel closes in a curiously cool way, with as much emphasis on the continuance of the relationship between the two sisters as on their marriages. Austen has let us hear silences that speak beyond the 'argument', and beyond the formal comic conclusion of this novel.[1]

## Pride and Prejudice

Elizabeth Bennet, the heroine of *Pride and Prejudice*, is intelligent; of that there can be no doubt. She sparkles with confidence in her own intellectual ability and the knowledge of the world she has acquired through it. However, she was originally conceived as the heroine of 'First Impressions', and her role in the early part of the novel owes something to that of the deluded sentimental heroine of burlesque literature. She betrays a romantic prejudice in favour of first impressions, and this, together with pride in her own cleverness, leads her to misjudge Mr Darcy, whom she eventually marries, and to be taken in, at first, by the charming but disreputable Mr Wickham. Able not only to think, but to formulate an argument with the fluency of a clever undergraduate, Elizabeth is inclined to trust her

---

1 Angela Leighton, 'Sense and Silences: Reading Jane Austen Again', in *Jane Austen: New Perspectives*, p 140.

own judgements without enough self-criticism, or awareness of her personal advantages. Angry when her friend, Charlotte Lucas, becomes engaged to the ridiculous clergyman, who had a few days earlier proposed to herself, she says to her sister:

'My dear Jane, Mr Collins is a conceited, pompous, narrow-minded, silly man; you know he is, as well as I do; and you must feel, as well as I do, that the woman who marries him, cannot have a proper way of thinking. You shall not defend her, though it is Charlotte Lucas. You shall not, for the sake of one individual, change the meaning of principle and integrity, nor endeavour to persuade yourself or me, that selfishness is prudence, and insensibility of danger, security for happiness.'

(pp 135–6)

Later she modifies this condemnation – 'My friend has an excellent understanding' – but, at the time, Elizabeth, not yet twenty-one, with her fine eyes and conversational brilliance, does not know the danger she herself is in from a lack of 'understanding', both of herself and other people. A mixed character, not a picture of perfection, Elizabeth Bennet demonstrates those powers of mind that feminist moralists claimed for women. She undergoes the education of experience with credit to her head as well as her heart, weighing up evidence and submitting her first impressions to rational examination.[1]

To have created such a heroine was a major achievement, and Austen's letters show she knew it. Yet the work was 'too light and bright and sparkling'.[2] *Pride and Prejudice* originated in 'First Impressions', begun in 1796, and it may be that in its earlier form the schema, still recognizable in the novel as it was published in 1813, entailed a more ironic and mocking control. Darcy, perhaps, stayed nearer to the rather wooden figure of the early chapters. However, as the novel stands, the heroine's second attachment provides no mocking correction of her earlier and more romantic one. Darcy has no flannel waistcoat. Morally superior to Wickham, and less flashy, he is young, quite as attractive and with a great landed estate to boot. The happy marriage lacks ironic distancing, and, as Rachel Browenstein puts it, the reader is invited to escape from reality through identification with Elizabeth, who turns out to be 'a novel heroine after all'.[3]

1 Martha Satz, 'An Epistemological Understanding of *Pride and Prejudice*', in *Jane Austen: New Perspectives*, pp 171–83.
2 *Letters*, p 299.
3 Rachel Browenstein, *Becoming a Heroine: Reading about Women in Novels*, Harmondsworth, 1984, p 134.

Marilyn Butler finds the form taken by intelligence in the novel seductive, though in her view it is treated negatively. One might say that the author is seduced by the intelligence of her heroine, and ends up rewarding it as extravagantly as Richardson rewards the restricted 'virtue' of his Pamela. There are fairly clear indications that a correction of *Sir Charles Grandison* is intended. The hero of *Pride and Prejudice* has faults matching those of the heroine, and she is allowed the liveliness and wit censured in Grandison's sister Charlotte. Yet this adds to a sense that there is something excessive and over-indulgent in Elizabeth's staggeringly 'great' marriage. Her husband is rich and influential, without being perfect, and has fallen in love with her 'lively mind' as well as her fine eyes. No wonder, then, that *Pride and Prejudice* has always been the most popular of the novels, or that Austen in her next two novels found ways of keeping her heroines at a distance, and managing their happy marriages in such a way as to retain an element of mocking alienation. The long gap between inception and final revision detach *Pride and Prejudice* from the literary context of 1813. The mature Austen is evident in the command with which it is executed, but its allusive focus is early, Fanny Burney's *Cecilia* (1782) being the most important novel, apart from *Sir Charles Grandison*, in relation to which its meanings are formed.[1]

## Mansfield Park

*Mansfield Park*, begun in 1811, was published soon after completion in 1814, the same year as Edgeworth's *Patronage*, Burney's disturbed late novel *The Wanderer* and Scott's *Waverley*, and a more ambitious engagement with the contemporary world is apparent. Yet this has led to difficulty in twentieth-century interpretation of its heroine. Austen thought no one but herself would like Emma Woodhouse, but it is Fanny Price who has proved unlikeable.[2] Trilling, however, was wrong in supposing no one had ever liked her. A critic of 1852 called her 'a bewitching "little body"', and Richard Whately, the first reviewer to notice *Mansfield Park*, in 1821, found her sympathetic.[3] Even more surprising in view of the modern critical literature, he picked out Miss Price to illustrate her author's departure

---

1 See Jan Fergus, *Jane Austen and the Didactic Novel*, London, 1983, pp 61–86.
2 J. E. Austen-Leigh, *A Memoir of Jane Austen*, London, 1870, repr. 1906, p 148.
3 Richard Whately's review of *Northanger Abbey* and *Persuasion*, originally published in the *Quarterly Review*, January 1821, is included in Southam, *Critical Heritage*, Item 16; see also Item 31, 'The mid-century view', p 138.

from the usual practice of women novelists, in showing her heroines as 'mixed characters'.

Fanny is not a 'picture of perfection',[1] but she is something of a paradox. One of the earliest readers of *Mansfield Park*, Henry Austen, was puzzled by her,[2] and she is presented from the start as posing problems for other characters. Sir Thomas Bertram is worried initially about preserving a distinction of social status between his daughters and the niece without fortune who is to grow up with them. Mary Crawford cannot decide whether Fanny has 'come out' (p 48), that is, whether she has a recognizable adult place in Mansfield society. There are also problems about Fanny's abilities and character. Set down as ignorant and stupid by her girl cousins and Aunt Norris (pp 18–19), she is discovered by her cousin Edmund, who effectively takes on the task of educating her, 'to be clever, to have a quick apprehension as well as good sense, and a fondness for reading' (p 22).[3] Yet, as the novel develops, even Edmund fails to understand her fully. The reader alone is given access to her inner mental life and enabled to recognize a strength of mind at odds with her physical appearance and demeanour, and unsuspected by either her uncle or the anti-hero, Henry Crawford. Through the indirect free style of narration and the use of interior monologue, we are shown Fanny's jealousy and the pain she suffers under humiliating treatment, especially at the hands of Mrs Norris, but we also see her attempts to cope with difficult and painful emotions, and the 'powers of mind' which make it proper for her to insist on the exercise of her own judgement where her own interest is so much at stake as in the acceptance of a husband. Fanny observes, weighs up evidence, remembers and subjects her experience to rational reflection, and this necessitates eventually that she becomes a 'moral agent'.

Further paradoxes are developed through allusion to the theatre and acting, especially through the amateur theatricals got up by the young people during Sir Thomas Bertram's absence. Opposed to the whole enterprise and unwilling to take part, Fanny nevertheless finds an appreciative interest in the art of acting, and takes pleasure in

1 In a letter to her niece Fanny Knight, written in March 1817, Austen wrote 'pictures of perfection as you know make me sick and wicked' (*Letters*, pp 486–7).
2 See *Letters*, pp 376, 378 and 381.
3 Fanny's reading evidently included Cowper (p 56) and Dr Johnson (p 156), but she is also in possession of more recent works, like Crabbe's *Tales*, published in 1812, and her interest in travel literature is shown in a reference to Lord Macartney's *Embassy to China*, 1807 (p 156 and note).

attending rehearsals. She believes herself to 'derive as much innocent pleasure from the play as any of them' (p 165). In the highly dramatic scene at the start of Volume III, where she offends her uncle by refusing to marry Henry Crawford, there is something theatrical about the roles played by both uncle and niece. Sir Thomas finds himself, most unexpectedly, playing something like the stock part of the angry father or guardian, to an apparently irrational and 'headstrong' niece.[1] The girl who earlier 'cannot act' now confronts and disobeys her awesome benefactor. Immediately afterwards she is shown dramatizing herself in a way worthy of many a heroine of the contemporary stage: ' "I must be a brute indeed if I can really be ungrateful!" said she *in soliloquy*: "Heaven defend me from being ungrateful!" ' (p 323, my italics).

The choice of *Lovers' Vows*, Elizabeth Inchbald's translation of Kotzebue's *Das Kind der Liebe*, for performance at Mansfield also has a strong bearing on the way in which Fanny is portrayed. Despite his revolutionary sympathies, made much of in the twentieth-century critical literature on *Mansfield Park*, Kotzebue enjoyed a popular success in England which rested mainly on his sentimental treatment of women and sexual relationships.[2] *Lovers' Vows* was put on six or seven times while Austen lived in Bath, no more then than now a hotbed of revolution. No doubt she disapproved of his politics, but her objection to him as a Rousseauist in his sexual attitudes is more directly relevant to Fanny Price, and to the way in which she is perceived by Henry Crawford. Not knowing what she thinks or feels, he mistakes her for a perfect, early nineteenth-century English version of the ideal woman of the sentimental male imagination. Young, childish in appearance, physically frail, pretty, timid, with a strong wish to be approved of, and often in tears of acute sensibility, Fanny scarcely ever strings two sentences together in his presence. He is, understandably, quite unaware of the strong feelings, or the critical, rational mind, lurking behind her innocent appearance.

It is because he does not know what to make of 'Miss Fanny' that Henry begins to take an interest in her, planning in a light-hearted, irresponsible way to make her fall in love with him: 'I do not quite know what to make of Miss Fanny. I do not understand her. I could

---

1 Cf. Sheridan's *The Rivals* (1775), Prince Hoare's *Lock and Key* (1796), Garrick's *The Guardian* (1759). Eaton Stannard Barrett's prose burlesque *The Heroine* (1813) mocks these same *types*.

2 L. F. Thompson, *Kotzebue: A Survey of His Progress in England and France*, Paris, 1928.

not tell what she would be at yesterday. What is her character? – Is she solemn? – Is she queer? – Is she prudish?' (p 230). Henry does not solve the conundrum of Miss Price, for his preconceptions make it impossible for him to recognize or respect her true nature. In Chapter 12 of the second volume his passion for Fanny is at its height, and he declares his intention of marrying her to his sister. Attractive though his warmth of feeling is, he betrays throughout this chapter attitudes which condemn him. He sees himself as 'fairly caught', and dwells on Fanny's 'charms'. In the long paragraph on p 294 he paints a portrait of her as a Rousseauist hero sees her, ending by placing a high value on her being 'well principled and religious'. Rousseau had also insisted that the wife of Émile should be 'religious', but with this proviso: 'As a woman's religion is controlled by authority it is more important to show her plainly what to believe than to explain the reasons for belief . . .'[1] Henry glories in his power to protect Fanny and improve her status in the world, and sees her as likely to improve him through his love for her, but it does not occur to him to ask if she likes or respects him. He takes her acceptance of him entirely for granted. What he does not know is that Fanny's nature is not that of a Sophie, and that her principles are not merely learned in obedience to authority, but tested and applied in the light of her own rational judgement.

*Mansfield Park* opens with an ironic reference to the success of Miss Maria Ward of Huntingdon in the marriage stakes. Some thirty years ago she 'had the good luck to *captivate* Sir Thomas Bertram' (my emphasis). The language of capture and captivation, of enslavement and conquest, is used unselfconsciously by both Henry and Mary Crawford, but it is not countenanced by Fanny or the author. Maria Bertram has pulled off a great 'catch' in getting engaged to the stupid Mr Rushworth, the owner of Sotherton Court, but at Sotherton she sees herself as caged in. Rushworth himself has already spoken of the house as looking like a prison, 'quite a dismal old prison' (p 53); and Maria, passionately in love with Henry Crawford, compares herself to the starling shut up in the Bastille and endlessly repeating 'I can't get out. I can't get out' (p 99). Here the more serious dangers of a love-game played for catches and conquests is allowed to make itself felt.

Fanny's inability to play such a game is connected with her moral

1 J. J. Rousseau, *Émile*, ch 5; in the English translation by Barbara Foxley, London, 1974, p 340.

status, which, for all his kindness, her uncle misunderstands. Having married a wife who takes no decisions for herself, and having overlooked the need to educate his daughters as accountable beings, Sir Thomas is unprepared for Fanny's insistence that, in accepting a husband, she must be allowed to make her own decision, in the light of her own conscience. Dependent on Sir Thomas as she is, she nevertheless supposes that she has some of the rights appropriate to an individual. The good baronet, whose plantations in Antigua are worked by slaves, is far from thinking of the women in his family in the same way; but still, the domestic government at Mansfield Park is not founded on recognition of women as moral equals or as potential partners in life. Among the women who welcome Sir Thomas back from the West Indies, Fanny alone shows any interest in his experiences there, and goes so far as to ask him a question about the slave trade (p 198). Although we are not told what he said in reply, the question itself is significant. In a low key it suggests an analogy, made by feminists from Mary Wollstonecraft to the early advocates of women's rights in America, between the moral status of women and slaves. A similar comparison is made in *Emma* (see below, p 110). Austen was an admirer of Thomas Clarkson, who wrote in 1808, of the Act of Abolition, that it had recorded 'as a principle of our legislation that commerce itself shall have its moral boundaries' and had 'restored the rational creature to his moral rights'.[1] *Mansfield Park* asks, 'And hers?'

It was around the same time that Austen read *Corinne*, a novel in which de Staël takes over contrasted heroines, one dark-eyed and Italian, the other light-eyed and English, from *Sir Charles Grandison*, giving them new meanings. Corinne, the *femme de génie*, is both a projection of her author and an embodiment of woman as Romantic artist. She is betrayed by her English lover, Lord Nelvil, who marries her insipid half-sister Lucille, a spiritless, conforming nonentity, and the novel includes a wholesale attack on English society as mercenary and hypocritical. De Staël was painted as Corinne, holding a lyre, in which pose the beauty of her white arms showed to advantage, as do Mary Crawford's as she plays her harp.

In *Mansfield Park* Austen cuts the 'woman of genius' down to size and valorizes the ordinary (English) 'woman of sense', but not without some playful mockery of the trope of the paired heroines itself. She gives her anti-heroine dark eyes and flashes of genius, but

---

1 Thomas Clarkson, *The Abolition of the African Slave-Trade by the British Parliament*, 2 vols, London, 1808, ii. 583.

makes her self-regarding, slightly devious and, in the end, a victim of a calculating prudence which prevents her from marrying the man with whom she is half in love. Fanny's 'soft light eyes' are treated mockingly when, in the final chapter, the hero at last notices them. Sitting in the shrubbery at Mansfield Parsonage, Mary compares herself with the 'famous Doge at the court of Lewis XIV', declaring she sees no wonder in the shrubbery equal to seeing herself in it. By contrast, Fanny's genuine, if slightly absurd, sensibility is shown in her musings on memory and plants, and in her eulogy on the name Edmund, as breathing 'the spirit of chivalry and warm affections'. Mary says cynically that while *Lord* Edmund or *Sir* Edmund would sound delightful, *Mr* Edmund, the name of a younger son, is pitiful (pp 209–10). Although both girls are English, Mary is tainted by the cosmopolitan world of smart London, while Fanny belongs to the 'true' England and, as Henry Crawford is ironically made to say, 'ought never to be long banished from the free air and liberty of the country' (p 411).

## Emma

In *Emma*, begun in 1814 and published early in 1816, there is comparatively little direct allusion, but, as in *Mansfield Park*, true English values and attitudes are established partly through a critical reshaping of figures and situations from sentimental and romantic literature. When we first see George and John Knightley together, the brothers greet one another undemonstratively in 'the true English style' and settle down to a discussion of drainage, fencing and turnip-growing on the 'Donwell' land. There is no doubt they are held up for approval, but there is a humorous placing of their low-keyed merit against something false and foreign. Sentimental comedy of the time had many examples of family estrangements over apparently trifling quarrels, followed by excessively tearful reconciliations. The manly reticence of the two Knightleys disguises genuine brotherly affection, the more admirable since one is now the owner of the family estate, the other a younger son, still sharing an interest in its improvement. Their behaviour is in marked contrast to that of the two brothers in Kotzebue's *Die Versohnung*, translated into English by Thomas Dibdin as *The Birthday*. Jane Austen saw an early performance of this play, which was even more popular than *Lovers' Vows*, in Bath in 1799, and seems to have drawn on it in constructing *Emma* many years later.[1] The heroine of *The Birthday* is called

1 Kirkham, *Jane Austen, Feminism and Fiction*, pp 121–4.

Emma Bertram and, like Emma Woodhouse, supposes herself unable to marry on account of her devotion to her invalid father. Austen corrects the sentimentality of Kotzebue's father and daughter by making Mr Woodhouse a hypochondriac and by showing Emma's faults as partly derived from her early aggrandizement as mistress of his house. Miss Bates provides a more realistic example of the devoted daughter. Plain, middle-aged and impecunious, she cares for her aged mother without any such rewards as Emma enjoys.

As Trilling rightly saw, 'Emma has a moral life . . . as a man has a moral life . . . as a given quality of her nature.'[1] And this is an aspect of her 'true English style' of heroineship. 'Handsome, clever and rich', as she is described in the opening sentence of the novel, she is placed in a situation where she has uncharacteristic social influence, especially over other women. Her moral education consists largely in learning to use it responsibly. We are assured from the start that she will do so, since she is loved and admired by the former governess who is her closest friend. Mrs Weston knows 'she has qualities that may be trusted' (p 40), but they are severely tested in her dealings with the two most vulnerable young women in her circle, Harriet Smith and Jane Fairfax.

Harriet is the 'natural daughter of somebody' and, at seventeen, is still a parlour boarder at Mrs Goddard's school. Pretty and silly, she is easily manipulated by Emma, who concocts grandiose fantasies about her parentage and attempts to cast her in the role of romantic heroine. Abusing her power by making a plaything of Harriet, Emma is blind to the claims that Jane Fairfax, her equal in talents and education, but not in fortune, ought to have upon her sympathy and friendship. While Emma is an exemplary daughter, sister and aunt, she is shown as having social responsibilities beyond her family and, at first, failing to fulfil them. The emphasis placed on extrafamilial relationships enlarges the moral dimension in which Emma is seen, and Austen also develops a new configuration of heroines through these three.

It is Mrs Weston who dwells on Emma's appearance, in terms which connect with, and distinguish her from, Corinne. Her eyes are 'brilliant'; neither the dark eyes of genius and sensibility nor the blue eyes of insipidity, they are 'the true hazle' and go with an 'open countenance', 'a firm and upright figure' and 'the idea of being the

1 Lionel Trilling, '*Emma* and the Legend of Jane Austen', originally published as an introduction to the Riverside edition of *Emma*, New York, 1957; reprinted in *Jane Austen: Emma*, ed. David Lodge, Macmillan Casebook Series, London, 1968, p 154.

complete picture of grown-up health' (p 39). The baby-blue eyes of mindless conformity go to Harriet Smith; to Jane Fairfax, the dark eyes, superior musicianship and strong feeling of a potentially tragic heroine of sensibility. Although Jane is presented with some sympathy, she is nevertheless censured for a lack of openness and for her marriage to a man she loves but cannot respect, which leaves her future happiness in doubt. We last see Frank Churchill gloating over her angelic beauty and resolving to have his aunt's jewels set in an 'ornament for the head' (p 479). By contrast, Emma is rewarded, once she has learned from her mistakes, with a marriage of mutual affection and esteem. She, with some justification, thinks of herself as, like Churchill, marrying a superior, but Mr Knightley, effectively anticipating the ideal of marriage to be put forward by J. S. Mill fifty years later, speaks of 'our having every right that equal worth can give, to be happy together' (p 463). Mill thought that the 'moral regeneration of mankind will only really commence, when the most fundamental of the social relations is placed under the rule of equal justice, and when human beings learn to cultivate their strongest sympathy with an equal in rights and cultivation'.[1]

In both *Mansfield Park* and *Emma* allusion is made to the role of the hero as guardian to the heroine-pupil, but in such a way as to criticize the many sentimental treatments of this figure. A particular target is the Rousseauist fantasy of the innocent girl to be turned into the ideal wife. Frank Churchill teasingly suggests to Emma that she should find a wife for him to come back to after two years abroad. 'Adopt her, educate her', he says (p 373). It is no more than a rather devious joke, since he is already secretly engaged to Jane, but in a light way it hints at what is wrong in his attitude to women. Austen's true heroes have too little vanity to think of women as 'relative creatures', existing only for the good of man. Edmund Bertram's part in Fanny's education comes about as a result of his affectionate response to her as an adopted sister, and is without design on her. As she grows up, he implicitly accords her the status of an equal, seeking her 'advice and opinion' (*Mansfield Park*, p 153) and defending her right to refuse to take part in the theatricals. Reproving Mrs Norris, he says, 'It is not fair to urge her in this manner. – You see she does not like to act. Let her choose for herself as well as the rest of us. – Her judgement may be quite as safely trusted' (pp 146–7). Mr Knightley eventually acknowledges that he

1 J. S. Mill, *The Subjection of Women* (1869), repr. in John Stuart Mill, *Three Essays*, ed. Richard Wollheim, Oxford, 1975.

has been in love with Emma since she was thirteen. Earlier he recollects a book-list she compiled at fourteen, 'which did her judgement so much credit' he preserved it (p 37). This is amusing in showing how little he has known his real feelings, and also in reversing the stereotype in which the guardian-hero prescribes the heroine's reading.

*Emma* is sometimes read as a novel in which the heroine alone undergoes the education of experience through which she arrives at self-knowledge, but Mr Knightley, despite his superiority of age and experience, is also lacking in self-knowledge. Early in the novel he says, 'I should like to see Emma in love, and in some doubt of a return; it would do her good' (p 41). He is quite right, but the irony is that it is only when he becomes jealous of Frank Churchill that he begins to understand his own feelings. Emma is rude to Miss Bates, while flushed with the pleasure of showing off with Churchill, and gets properly corrected for it by Mr Knightley, but he, under the pressure of jealousy, is quite rude to her himself. Angry at seeing 'that fellow Churchill showing off his own voice', he says, 'Miss Bates, are you mad, to let your niece sing herself hoarse in this manner? Go and interfere' (p 229). At the end of the novel he claims no serious part in Emma's education: 'Nature gave you understanding; – Miss Taylor [Mrs Weston] gave you principles' (p 462). We may think he underestimates the influence he himself has had, but his implicit acceptance of the equal moral status of men and women is affirmed here, not only through his recognition of Emma's 'understanding', but also in his respect for her governess as a moral guide.

Mrs Weston's part in *Emma* is important. She is not, any more than Mr Knightley, a wholly reliable character, since her view of Emma is biased by strong affection. Yet that, in itself, speaks volumes about the good qualities of the imperfect heroine. This is made all the more apparent since, through Jane Fairfax, the humiliations to which governesses were commonly subjected are allowed to bring to the surface a comparison between the 'governess-trade' and the 'slave-trade'. It is Jane Fairfax who distinguishes and connects the two: '"I did not mean, I was not thinking of the slave-trade," replied Jane; "governess-trade, I assure you, was all that I had in view; widely different certainly as to the guilt of those who carry it on; but as to the greater misery of the victims, I do not know where it lies"' (pp 300–301).

## *Persuasion*

Begun in 1815 and never finally revised, *Persuasion* is generally seen as taking a new direction, and some critics have spoken of it as Jane Austen's one Romantic novel. This view gains support from the character of the heroine and the way in which she is presented, but, if sensibility is given an enhanced value in *Persuasion*, it is not at the expense of sense. Anne Elliot, the heroine, is comparable with Jane Fairfax in her superior cultivation and sensibility, but, unlike Jane, whose secret engagement implies an error of judgement, Anne makes no serious mistakes. As the first reviewer of *Persuasion* put it, she 'is the only one in the family possessed of good sense (a quality which Miss Austen is as sparing of in her novels, as we fear her great mistress Nature has been in real life)'.[1]

Austen spoke of Anne Elliot as a heroine 'almost too good for me',[2] and she is carefully presented as combining sensitivity with thoughtful intelligence. At twenty-seven she is a little too old for the part of heroine in 'true laughing comedy' and her father sees her as 'faded and thin . . . haggard' (p 6). We are given a brief account of how, seven years ago, she had broken off her engagement to the young Captain Wentworth and of the pain this brought her: 'Her attachment and regrets had, for a long time, clouded every enjoyment of youth; and an early loss of bloom and spirits had been their lasting effect' (p 28). But Anne is not shown as at fault in having acted as she did. At the end of the novel she says that, although the advice she had received had been wrong, she was, while under age, right to accept it. The hero, not the heroine, is called on to re-examine past conduct and acknowledge mistakes. Captain Wentworth is forced to contrast his success as a naval officer with his failure to judge Anne's conduct aright. He says, with a nice touch of self-mockery: '"I have valued myself on honourable toils and just rewards. Like other great men under reverses," he added with a smile, "I must learn to brook being happier than I deserve"' (p 274).

The Grandisonian figure of the Good Baronet, undermined in *Mansfield Park*, is annihilated in *Persuasion*. Anne's father, Sir Walter Elliot, is given the character of one of the most despised female stereotypes, the ageing woman of fashion. Obsessed by his appearance and incapable of managing his estate properly, he is

1 Richard Whately, in Southam, *Critical Heritage*, p 102.
2 *Letters*, p 487.

shown as unfit for authority of any kind. His heir, the cousin to whom Anne is briefly attracted, is also revealed as not merely incapable of protecting the interests of women, but of cynically disregarding them.

Austen's feminism is also shown in a remarkable remoulding of the figure of the 'mannish' woman, whose affectation of male dress and manners made her an object of ridicule and discredited her feminist opinions. Elinor Harleigh in Burney's *The Wanderer* is such a character, but probably more important to Austen was Mrs Freke in Edgeworth's *Belinda*. Mrs Croft, Captain Wentworth's sister, is not a freak, but she is clearly designed to contravene sentimental notions of femininity, and has been described as 'a tactful and subtle portrait of the "new woman"'.[1] With nice irony Austen gives Mrs Croft the Christian name Sophy and portrays her as the perfect wife for the endearing but erratic Admiral, to whom she has been happily married for fifteen years. Mocking the assumptions made by Rousseau in *Émile*, Mrs Croft is shown as still retaining her husband's affection though, at thirty-eight, her face is merely 'agreeable' and her complexion as 'reddened and weather-beaten' as his. Nor is this surprising, for she says the happiest part of her life has been spent at sea, and she has 'crossed the Atlantic four times . . . been once to the East Indies . . . besides being in different places about home – Cork and Lisbon and Gibraltar' (p 70). She rebukes her brother for misplaced gallantry: 'But I hate to hear you talking so, like a fine gentleman, as if women were all fine ladies, instead of rational creatures. We none of us expect to be in smooth water all our days' (p 70).

Early in the novel Anne is amused by the Crofts' style of driving a gig, Mrs Croft 'coolly giving the reins a better direction herself' when 'my dear Admiral' is 'in danger of hitting a post or running foul of a dung-cart'. She sees it as 'no bad representation of the general guidance of their affairs' (p 92). Later, in Bath, she finds pleasure in observing them:

She always watched them as long as she could; delighted to fancy she understood what they might be talking of, as they walked along in happy independence, or equally delighted to see the Admiral's hearty shake of the hand when he encountered an old friend, and observe their eagerness of conversation when occasionally forming into a little knot of the navy, Mrs Croft looking as intelligent and keen as any of the officers around her.

(p 168)

---

1 Nina Auerbach, 'O Brave New World: Evolution and Revolution in *Persuasion*', *ELH*, xxxix (1972), 123.

In Mrs Croft Austen creates the most clearly feminist portrait of any in her novels, but it is Anne who voices a feminist perception of male bias in literature. Speaking with gentle authority, she says: 'Yes, yes, if you please, no references to examples in books. Men have had every advantage of us in telling their own story. Education has been theirs in so much higher a degree; the pen has been in their hands. I will not allow books to prove anything' (p 234). It is, perhaps, only because she is 'almost too good' for Austen that she can be allowed to make so clear a point, which the reader is not permitted to dismiss as easily as Catherine Morland's comments on history.

Naval officers and life at sea play an important part in *Persuasion*, but the role of the navy in the war with France is almost entirely excluded. The merits of sailors as husbands, brothers and friends is what matters. The possibility of female participation in a freer, more open life, through a naval marriage, is what is foregrounded. The novel opens with a depressed heroine, undervalued in the country house where Sir Walter Elliot sits reading Debrett's Baronetage of England; it closes with her marriage to Mrs Croft's brother and the happy prospect of being 'a sailor's wife'. Curiously, in the last sentence, she is spoken of as though she herself had entered the navy: she 'must pay the tax of quick alarm for belonging to that profession which is, if possible, more distinguished in its domestic virtues than in its national importance'.

## CONCLUSION

Jane Austen's earliest attempt at publication was made in 1797, a few months after the death of Mary Wollstonecraft. Had 'First Impressions' been accepted, it would have come out at about the same time as Godwin's *Memoirs of the Author of a Vindication of the Rights of Woman*, in which, as one of her defenders said, he exposed 'the very circumstances, which he must have known would injure her credit with the respectable part of the community, and thus undermine the influence she had been labouring to acquire'.[1] The outrage provoked ensured that Wollstonecraft's name could be mentioned only to be abused and that her writings could no longer be openly discussed on their merits. Female biography, already sensitive, became even more delicate, respectable women being shown as

1 *A Defence of the Character and Conduct of the Late Mary Wollstonecraft Godwin*, Anon., London, 1803, pp 52–3.

either having disapproved of Wollstonecraft or as never likely to have heard of her.[1] By the time *Northanger Abbey* was eventually published with *Persuasion* in 1818, after Austen's death, it was prefaced by her brother's 'Biographical Notice', in which she was portrayed as pious, self-effacing and as having led an exemplary life of contented domestic usefulness, remote from any controversial aspect of literature in her time. The 'Biographical Notice' was reprinted in the Bentley edition of Austen's novels in 1833 and remains to the present time a part of the standard Oxford edition.

Q. D. Leavis questioned the reliability of Austen's 'life', and later biographers have shown that much was left out of the family biography as it was created in the nineteenth century. Deborah Kaplan relates the problems of the Austen biography to more general questions about her location in history. Terry Eagleton, writing in 1975 on the Brontës, sought to reclaim authorial biography, as a link between 'the unique artistic product' and 'historical structures' determining the individual life,[2] but female 'lives', as they were written in the early nineteenth century, call for careful scrutiny. The 'Biographical Notice' conceals Austen's awareness of the public world of literature and inhibits interest in how her novels engage with it.

Scott's review of *Emma* is the only important piece of criticism written before 1818, and before the influence of the 'Biographical Notice' began to make itself felt. It gives generous and perceptive praise to the three works considered – *Sense and Sensibility*, *Pride and Prejudice* and *Emma* – but there is, at the end, a note of unease. Placing emphasis on these novels as belonging to a new kind of fiction, Scott says that it is 'in these times of revolution' that 'moral authors' (implicitly female) have brought a disquieting realism into their treatment of sexual relationships, assailing 'Cupid, king of gods and men' even in 'his own kingdom of romance'. Such authors are liable to encourage 'selfishness' and 'calculating prudence' in the young.[3] What is interesting about this is that Scott raises doubts

1  See Claire Tomalin, *The Life and Death of Mary Wollstonecraft*, London, 1974, ch 19, 'Aftermath and Debate'.
2  Q. D. Leavis, 'A Critical Theory of Jane Austen's Writings, III: The Letters', first published in *Scrutiny*, xii (1944), reprinted in *A Selection from Scrutiny*, ed. F. R. Leavis, Cambridge, 1968, ii. 66–7. Deborah Kaplan, 'The Disappearance of the Woman Writer: Jane Austen and Her Biographers', *Prose Studies*, vii (1984), 129–47. Terry Eagleton, *Myths of Power*, London, 1975, p 7.
3  Review of *Emma*, first published in the *Quarterly Review*, March 1816; Item 8 in Southam, *Critical Heritage*, p 68.

about the moral tendency of the Austen novels, not because they embody traditional, perhaps rather narrow attitudes, but because there is something radical about them. His remarks suggest he had experienced a little of the shock later felt by W. H. Auden, who was made uncomfortable to see:

> An English spinster of the middle class
> Describe the amorous effects of 'brass',
> Reveal so frankly and with such sobriety
> The economic basis of society.
>
> ('Letter to Lord Byron', 1937)

In 1816, when she was again hoping to see *Northanger Abbey* in print, Jane Austen wrote an 'Advertisement' giving its curious history and pointing out how it had become separated from the context in which it was written and should have been published. It was another two years before it at last appeared, and the author's fear that it had missed its moment was partly justified. However, interest in the Gothic tale had by no means ended. In 1818 Peacock's *Nightmare Abbey*, in which Coleridge is satirized as Mr Flosky, a reactionary Germanist, was published, and so was the most disturbing of all the English tales of terror, Mary Shelley's *Frankenstein*. Both authors were on the left in politics, but in these works rationalist criticism of some aspects of Romanticism is apparent.

*Frankenstein* embodies in a new and powerful way tensions apparent in women's writing over the previous thirty years. As the child of William Godwin and Mary Wollstonecraft, as well as Shelley's second wife, its author was placed in a position to feel acutely the contrary influences of Reason and Romanticism, especially as they affected women. In *Frankenstein* the idealistic man of genius pursues his scientific interests without regard for the effect upon his family or society in general. He produces a monster through whom a series of innocent victims, including his bride, are destroyed. Subtitled 'The Modern Prometheus', *Frankenstein* develops one of the central myths of the Romantic movement, but here Promethean vision brings disaster rather than benefit to humankind. Repulsive as the monster is – and at one level it is its creator's *alter ego* – it is not treated without sympathy, especially during the brief period when it experiences the pleasures of human relationship with a blind man, not terrified by its appearance.

As myth, *Frankenstein* cannot be pinned down to any one interpretation, and feminist critics are no more in agreement about it than anyone else. The view of Gilbert and Gubar, that the monster is a projection of female isolation, rejection and rage is, despite its attractions, beset with difficulties.[1] What is clear, however, is that *Frankenstein* combines a Gothic nightmare with strong elements of the moral tale, and in this it reveals feminist ambivalence about how far the liberating forces of Romanticism, unrestrained by Reason, could be trusted to bring women greater freedom.

Although it is no more than a freak of publishing history that *Northanger Abbey*, *Persuasion* and *Frankenstein* came out in the same year, the coincidence points to the need to construct a context in which women's writing can be considered in relation to the troubled history of feminist ideas at the end of the 'Age of Reason' and the beginning of 'The Romantic Period'.

1 Sandra Gilbert and Susan Gubar, *The Madwoman in the Attic*, New Haven and London, 1979, ch 7, 'Horror's Twin: Mary Shelley's Monstrous Eve'.

# 4

## WILLIAM BLAKE

### Stewart Crehan

I

Relatively unknown as a poet during his lifetime, Blake is now canonized as a major figure in Western literature. The past thirty years have, however, produced considerably divergent accounts of Blake, from the political allegorist to the master of an occult tradition, from the radical social critic to the orthodox Christian. Canonization has not only restored Blake to complete mental health; much of the mystical obscurity has been dispelled, his strangeness and eccentricity have given way to an extraordinary contemporaneity, and the apparent chaos of the longer works has been revealed as a new kind of order, though requiring a way of reading for which few, if any, of Blake's contemporaries could have been prepared.

The son of a hosier, Blake was born in Broad Street, Soho, London in 1757. He received no formal education except as an apprentice to the engraver James Basire, whose somewhat unfashionable linear style was to form that of London's most neglected genius. Apart from three years in Felpham, Sussex, where he was a protégé of the minor poet William Hayley from 1800 to 1803, Blake's entire working life was spent either in, around or a few minutes' walk from the house in Soho where he was born. In this artisan, shopkeeping environment, always on the fringe of cosmopolitan gentility and elegance, Dissent and plebeian radicalism thrived, and Blake's radical sympathies went deep, especially in the revolutionary years 1789–93.

Artists also frequented this part of London: the painter Henry Fuseli, who once said that Blake was 'damned good to steal from', lived in nearby Poland Street between 1771 and 1781. Blake wrote that

> The only Man that eer I knew
> Who did not make me almost spew
> Was Fuseli . . .

(MS Notebook, 1808–11)[1]

1 *The Complete Poetry and Prose of William Blake*, ed. David V. Erdman, New York, 1982, p 507. Hereinafter referred to as 'Erdman, 1982'.

Yet Fuseli's later world of bankers, businessmen, scholars and art collectors; of heated drawing-room discussions, dinner parties and visits to the theatre, was rather different from the alehouses, meeting-rooms, workshops and streets one associates with Blake. Blake's remarks on London's social and artistic life are frequently bitter. In 1803 he asked Hayley how it was possible that a man of his age and experience could

be inferior to a boy of twenty who scarcely has taken or deigns to take a pencil in hand but who rides about the Parks or Saunters about the Playhouses who Eats & drinks for business not for need how is it possible that such a fop can be superior to the studious lover of Art can scarcely be imagind Yet such is somewhat like my fate & such it is likely to remain.[1]

He reached the private conclusion that

The Enquiry in England is not whether a Man has Talents. & Genius? But whether he is Passive & Polite & a Virtuous Ass: & obedient to Noblemens Opinions in Art & Science. If he is; he is a Good Man: If Not he must be Starved

(Annotations to *The Works of Sir Joshua Reynolds*)[2]

The first genteel circle that patronized him was that of the Reverend and Mrs A. S. Mathew, whose salon for bluestockings and literati had Mrs Barbauld and Hannah More among its members. Mathew and Flaxman helped to finance the printing of Blake's *Poetical Sketches* in 1783, but the collection was not published. Something must have happened, because Blake was given copies to distribute himself. J. T. Smith wrote that 'in consequence of his unbending deportment, or what his adherents are pleased to call his manly firmness of opinion', his visits 'ceased'.[3] Blake's support for the American War of Independence might have been a point of contention, but Blake is also known to have accompanied a crowd of Gordon rioters in 1780 from Broad Street to Newgate, where he witnessed the burning of the prison and the release of three hundred prisoners. Topics such as these may have disturbed the atmosphere of pious philanthropy, moral earnestness and polite wit that reigned at Rathbone Place.

1 Erdman, 1982, p 736.
2 Erdman, 1982, p 642.
3 G. E. Bentley, *Blake Records*, Oxford, 1969, p 457.

The second coterie to which Blake became attached was that of the radical bookseller and publisher Joseph Johnson. Its members included Thomas Paine, Mary Wollstonecraft, William Godwin, Joseph Priestley, Dr Price and Thomas Holcroft. As before, Blake never became an integral part of this radical, highly educated and highly political circle. Although he did some engravings for Mary Wollstonecraft's *Original Stories from Real Life* (1791), and clearly had a great admiration for Paine, he is not mentioned in Godwin's diary. The first book of his *French Revolution*, printed by Johnson in 1791, was not published, possibly because Blake feared the consequences.

From 1790 to 1793 Blake and his wife were almost prosperous, occupying a Georgian terraced house with a garden in Lambeth until 1800. The years 1793–5 were perhaps the most creative in his whole career, for they saw the appearance of the revolutionary satire *The Marriage of Heaven and Hell* (1793), the prophecies *Visions of the Daughters of Albion* (1793) and *America* (1793), the well-known *Songs of Innocence and of Experience* (1794) and a parody of the Book of Genesis called *The Book of Urizen* (1794), as well as the 1795 colour prints, which include two of his most famous designs, 'The Ancient of Days' and 'Newton'. The war, anti-Jacobin repression and the financial crisis took their toll, however, and by the late 1790s Blake began to experience hardship. Between 1797 and 1800, marginalized by events and yet determined to set these events as well as his own sufferings in a cosmic perspective, he wrote a huge mythological epic, *Vala, or The Four Zoas*, which he continued to revise (the poem remained in manuscript at Blake's death). Thomas Butts and George Cumberland, two old friends who were now at the War Office, became his patrons, and in 1800 he told Cumberland that he was emerging from 'a Deep pit of Melancholy'. An incident with a soldier in his garden at Felpham in 1803 led to his trial for treason at Chichester in 1804. Blake was acquitted, but the experience, compounded by artistic disappointments, wounded him. As his notebooks show, no matter what *Jerusalem* (1808–20) might have to say about forgiveness of sins and the brotherhood of man, 'when it is a matter of his own wrongs, or what he conceives to be his wrongs, Blake forgives nobody'.[1] His last years nevertheless give an impression of spiritual serenity and dignified poverty. In the 1820s he acquired his own circle of admirers: the 'Shoreham Ancients', a group of young painters whose leading figure was Samuel Palmer. Blake died in his

1  Jack Lindsay, *William Blake: His Life and Work*, London, 1978, p 196.

two-room apartment at Fountain Court, the Strand, in 1827 and was buried at Bunhill Fields, alongside Bunyan, Defoe, Isaac Watts and Thomas Hardy, the radical shoemaker and founder of the London Corresponding Society.

The revolution in taste towards the end of the eighteenth century, which owed much to Macpherson's Ossian poems and Percy's *Reliques*, and which associated simple language with purer feelings and purer forms of society, was partly initiated by Blake's lyrics. Yet from *Songs of Innocence* (1789) to *Songs of Experience* (1794) and the later lyrics, we find a naked directness and honesty, a forceful and at times almost cryptic brevity and compression that is qualitatively different from anything in Gray, Smart or Cowper – the last two, like Blake, greatly affected by the new mood of religious enthusiasm. Cowper's 'On a Goldfinch Starved to Death in His Cage', which is 'spoken' by the departed soul of the bird, reconciles us to familiar responses (such as 'better to be put out of one's misery'):

> More cruelty could none express,
> And I, if you had shewn me less
> Had been your pris'ner still.

Blake's 'Auguries of Innocence' does not compromise, but responds to cruelty with an intransigent empathy:

> A Horse misusd upon the Road
> Calls to Heaven for Human blood
> Each outcry of the hunted Hare
> A fibre from the Brain does tear
> A Skylark wounded in the wing
> A Cherubim does cease to sing

$$(11–16)[1]$$

In a unified creation the smallest event sends ripples throughout the cosmos. This is the unanswerable, almost unbearable logic of a poet who sought 'to open the immortal Eyes/Of Man inwards into the Worlds of Thought: into Eternity/Ever expanding in the Bosom of God' (*Jerusalem*, v. 18–20); for once we have glimpsed the Eternal Idea, in which nothing is ever forgotten, a tear becomes 'an Intellectual Thing' ('The Grey Monk', 29).

Blake has often been called a 'mystic'. Historically he belonged to a Dissenting fringe of antinomians, millenarians and mystics who

1 Erdman, 1982, p 490.

became active during the period 1788–95. An unbroken tradition connected these sects and individuals of the 1790s with the libertarians who had flourished during the Leveller-republican upsurge of the late 1640s and early 1650s. Antinomianism in particular rejected notions of original sin, moral law and eternal damnation, regarding hell as a mental state, or as a purely figurative entity. Antinomian groups such as the Muggletonians (who nourished 'a highly intellectual anti-intellectualism'[1], continued to meet in public houses in London during Blake's time, asserting that 'morality is an unnecessary thing', and that holiness 'can be no evidence of faith'.[2] In 1788 Blake writes: 'Active Evil is better than Passive Good', and 'all Act is Virtue' (annotations to Lavater's *Aphorisms on Man*). By 1790 he is enunciating a dialectical philosophy: 'Without Contraries is no progression. Attraction and Repulsion, Reason and Energy, Love and Hate, are necessary to Human existence' (*The Marriage of Heaven and Hell*, iii).

Blake's perception of 'contraries' is often conveyed with such intensity, and involves such a strong reaction against mimetic theories of art, that one suspects he sometimes found it hard to distinguish Wordsworthian sensitivity from Lockian sensation, which he linked with Baconian reasoning and the 'single vision' of Newtonian mechanics. The intensity lies not just in some posited intensity of feeling, but operates figurally. Paradox and antithesis combine with the aphoristic statement and the universalizing proposition. The oxymoron in 'Excess of joy weeps' ('Proverbs of Hell', *The Marriage of Heaven and Hell*, viii); the moral contradiction in 'Pity would be no more,/ If we did not make somebody Poor' ('The Human Abstract', *Songs of Experience*, 1–2); and the astounding collocation 'Marriage hearse' in the last line of 'London' (*Songs of Experience*) defamiliarize our perception of the world. Likewise this, from Blake's last epic poem *Jerusalem*:

> Embraces are Cominglings: from the Head even to the Feet;
> And not a pompous High Priest entering by a Secret Place.
>
> (lxix. 43–4)

Here the wit lies not merely in a clever juxtaposition, revealing in the manner of John Donne the unexpected appropriateness of yoking two apparently remote ideas, but functions more radically to assert

---

1 E. P. Thompson, letter in *The Times Literary Supplement*, 7 March 1975.
2 W. Hurd, *A New Universal History of the Religions, Rites, Ceremonies, and Customs of the Whole World* (1811), quoted in Lindsay, *William Blake*, p 49.

the real yet hidden unity between the private and the public spheres, where secrecy in the latter is mirrored as a repressed sexuality and vice versa.

Blake's poetry resembles Donne's more closely, perhaps, in the way it compels the reader to enact its own operations. One of the ways it 'rouzes the faculties to act' (letter to Dr Trusler, 23 August 1799) is by deliberately frustrating our urge to close off meanings, to fix what cannot be fixed. Framing, for example, is what we try to do as readers of 'The Tyger' (*Songs of Experience*) once we start asking the questions that the poem's speaker asks. In 'The Smile' (Pickering Manuscript) the first two stanzas lead us to expect symmetrical closure. But the second stanza runs into the third, breaking the symmetry:

> There is a Smile of Love
> And there is a Smile of Deceit
> And there is a Smile of Smiles
> In which these two Smiles meet
>
> And there is a Frown of Hate
> And there is a Frown of disdain
> And there is a Frown of Frowns
> Which you strive to forget in vain
>
> For it sticks in the Hearts deep Core
> And it sticks in the deep Back bone
> And no Smile that ever was smild
> But only one Smile alone
>
> That betwixt the Cradle & Grave
> It only once Smild can be
> But when it once is Smild
> Theres an end to all Misery

Since this last smile is not named, one is tempted to speculate. Could it be the Smile of Jesus? The Smile of Innocence? But the 'Smile of Love', had we but noticed, has already been incorporated into life's treacherous masquerade. By inviting us to attach another label the poem exposes our own complicity in the game of reification through naming, at the same time as the uniqueness of the unnamed smile is preserved. Moreover the move towards symmetry was, we realize, deceptive: 'Hate' and 'disdain' are not contrasted like 'Love' and 'Deceit', while 'a Smile of Smiles' cannot be quintessential here, even if 'a Frown of Frowns' can.

An important aspect of Blake's poetry is its interrelated symbolism, the rich patterns of meaning that grow from certain words such as *veil, chain, net, fibre, circle, plague, tree, river* and *grave*.[1] The experienced reader learns to appreciate these patterns in all their subtlety – though there are some scholars for whom the temptation to classify the fluid interrelations into a synchronic 'system', complete with charts and tables, has proved too strong. 'The suggestion', as D. G. Gillham has said, 'is that Blake discovered how to interpret symbols in terms of a traditional body of knowledge, but the best poets do not work in this way; their images are flexible, change significance in various contexts and discover new directions on different occasions.'[2] Blake's symbolism is 'visionary' in that it implies an autonomous world of the imagination, something that can neither be paraphrased, systematized nor reduced to a set of mundane references. One could add that reading Blake's symbolic narratives also involves us in strange mental journeys, as in 'The Mental Traveller', a poem which has so far defied systematic interpretation. In 'A Poison Tree' (*Songs of Experience*) the speaker's repressed wrath turns into a poison tree. The poem cannot be read merely as the account of a metamorphosis happening to someone else, for the reader is also involved in the process. At the line, 'And I waterd it in fears', we must renegotiate the meaning of 'it', reinterpreting 'wrath' (the co-referent of 'it') as something that can be watered; in this way we perform the very act of metaphorization that the poem's self-alienated speaker is narrating.

Whereas the lyrics can condense a symbolic process into a few words (thirty-four in 'The Sick Rose'), the prophecies expand into 'sublime allegories'. Greater metrical freedom was offered by Blake's adoption of the septenary line, treated 'as if it were already traditional', so that 'he virtually invents his own'.[3] An Ossianic, bardic style fuses with the style of biblical prophecy, which Lowth's *Lectures on the Sacred Poetry of the Hebrews* (1787) had shown to be the Hebraic form of sacred poetry, working, as Oliver Elton puts it, 'through figures, apostrophes, and passionate separate affirmatives, and not by the chainwork of reasoned Western oratory'.[4] This in turn combines with a somewhat overblown Miltonic style, where we find adverbialized adjectives ('swagging heavy'), nominalized

1 See Nelson Hilton, *Literal Imagination: Blake's Vision of Words*, Berkeley, Calif., 1983.
2 D. G. Gillham, *Blake's Contrary States: The 'Songs of Innocence and of Experience' as Dramatic Poems*, Cambridge, 1966, pp 174–5.
3 Alicia Ostriker, *Vision and Verse in William Blake*, Madison, Wis., 1965, p 132.
4 Oliver Elton, *A Survey of English Literature 1780–1830*, i, London, 1912, p. 156.

adjectives ('thro the immense') and adjective-noun-adjective con-
structions ('dismal torment sick'). Grand, dangerously toppling
Gothic edifices that house a protean and unruly mythology, the epics
work on a different scale from the shorter prophecies. They make
more use of the long verse-paragraph, whose length is extended by
anaphora, parallel clauses, and a succession of noun phrases and
non-finite clauses, two of Blake's favourites being participle and
infinitive clauses. It is in the epics that Blake's mythopoeic, philosophic and cosmological concerns are most prominent. They also
present most problems for the general reader, who may find them
boringly opaque at first. Later acquaintance reveals a fertile matrix
of ideas for which allegory proves to be the only mode possible.

After *Poetical Sketches* Blake's career as a poet was conditioned –
in some ways positively, in others negatively – by an important
technical invention. First mentioned in the incomplete fictional
satire *An Island in the Moon* (1784–5), it is announced in the 1793
Prospectus as 'a method of Printing which combines the Painter and
the Poet'. Jean H. Hagstrum describes it as follows:

The text was thickly lettered in a varnish impervious to acid on a paper
coated with gum arabic. That paper was then soaked, laid face down on a
heated copperplate, and rolled under pressure . . . The paper being removed,
the letters were transferred in reverse to the copper, where they were given
such retouching as necessary . . . The surface of the metal was then treated
in a solution that ate away the unvarnished portions, leaving design and
letter in low relief. Ink and colour were delicately transferred to the etched
block from the smooth metal surface of another block against which it was
pressed. Proof on 'beautiful wove paper' was then taken, and additional
colour and highlights added. No two copies being alike, colour was changed
with each issue.[1]

Blake's decision to print, publish and sell his works in this form was
a declaration of artistic independence from the publishers and booksellers. This 'craftist' resistance to the spectre of commerce pushed
the Romantic principle of freedom further than anyone else, and
ensured complete control over the work's material production.

The text was not merely decorated or illustrated but 'illuminated',
as in 'The Blossom' (*Songs of Innocence*), where meanings that are
only latent in the poem are made visually explicit in the design. The
illuminated plates also foreground the materiality and the fluidity of
the Blakian text. Lettering, such as the sombre roman capitals used
for the titles of poems in *Songs of Experience*, contribute to the

1 Jean H. Hagstrum, *William Blake: Poet and Painter*, Chicago, 1964, p 4.

meaning, while variations in graphic detail and in the colouring are not only significant in themselves, but, like Blake's idiosyncracies of orthography and punctuation, seem almost calculated to perplex and annoy modern editors, scholars and critics. As in the oral tradition, where each live performance has its unique and transient significance, so in Blake there is no 'authentic original' or 'standard text'. When we consider that some of the poems in *Songs of Innocence and of Experience* were transferred from the earlier to the later series, and that the arrangement of the plates varies in every copy of the book until about 1815, the Blakian text becomes even harder to pin down. 'The essence of Romanticism', says Mario Praz, '. . . comes to consist in that which cannot be described. The word and the form are only accessories.'[1] For Blake, the printed word and the form of the book contaminate essence by seeking to bind it, thereby destroying 'the winged life'. But they live 'in eternity's sun rise' when they kiss 'the joy as it flies'.[2]

The most obvious disadvantage of Blake's method of printing was that it drastically curtailed his readership at a time when the popular reading public was rapidly expanding. In 1793, a year after its publication, the second part of Paine's *Rights of Man* had sold 200,000 copies. The number of surviving copies of Blake's entire poetic works as they appeared during his lifetime comes to less than two hundred. *Vala, or The Four Zoas* exists only in manuscript, and would no doubt have perished had Tatham, and not Linnell, acquired it; *The French Revolution* exists in one printed copy, *Jerusalem* in six illuminated copies, only one of which is coloured, and *The Marriage of Heaven and Hell* in nine illuminated copies. Blake's marginalization as a poet during his lifetime is sometimes blamed on a reading public that misunderstood him. Yet in many ways Blake was so dissentient that he became a one-man sect. His determination to create a system rather than 'be enslav'd by another Mans' (*Jerusalem*, x. 20) applies to every aspect of his art, from metrics to mythology, from punctuation to printing technique. Yet having created a system, he does not allow it to ossify.

Blake's divorce from the popular reading public also went with an inability, or more likely a refusal, to develop the public voice of an individualized self, to cultivate a subjectivity that was both public and personal – in other words, a Romantic persona. There are hints of one in *The Marriage* ('I have also: The Bible of Hell: which the

1 Mario Praz, *The Romantic Agony*, New York, 1950, p 14.
2 'Eternity', in Erdman, 1982, p 470.

world shall have whether they will or no'), and there are strong autobiographical elements in the epics; but the *Songs of Innocence and of Experience* are dialogic and dramatic, not expressions of a Romantic ego. To read Blake as a self-expressive Romantic poet is to forget how closely, in this period, expressive individuality was tied to the values and assumptions of the middle class, a class in relation to which Blake never occupied much more than a marginal or dependent position. The growing middle-class reading public was helping to create its own national 'I' elsewhere. Through Wordsworth, for instance, this 'I' would say to them in 1798: 'Once again/Do I behold these steep and lofty cliffs';[1] and in 1807: 'Inland, within a hollow vale, I stood',[2] and: 'I'll think of the Leech-gatherer on the lonely moor!'[3] The solitary Wordsworth's precise landscaping of England would in any case have been easier to grasp for an empirical-minded readership than Blake's involved and suspect mythology of Urizen, Orc, Los and Albion.

An enigma except perhaps to a few close friends and admirers, Blake either had his image created for him or was judged according to the 'spectrous' masks he wore. Loyal patriot, astonishingly, was one of them. It is a macabre joke of literary history that Robert Hunt's famous *Examiner* attack on Blake in 1809 as 'an unfortunate lunatic' (which Blake neither forgave nor forgot) was due, not simply to prejudice (Leigh and Robert Hunt were principled radicals), but also to Blake's ill-advised gambit of presenting to the public – with an irony too subtle for most observers – pictures of Nelson and Pitt as national heroes, and even quoting Nelson's famous signal as if supporting the war: 'England expects that every man should do his duty, in Arts, as well as in Arms, or in the Senate.'[4] It betrayed whatever radical following he might have had, as well as his own beliefs. Hiding opinions that might otherwise alienate his patrons, who thus had little idea what their apparently zealous but harmless engraver was thinking, seems to have become a habit. One could of course attribute to the later, 'mystical' Blake a steadfast refusal to become a fashionable 'Selfhood', a recognizably bourgeois-Romantic ego; but only fear, and confusion in the limelight, can explain some of the false selves he presented to the world and to others.

1 'Lines Composed . . . above Tintern Abbey', 11 4–5.
2 'September, 1802. Near Dover', 1 1.
3 'Resolution and Independence', 1 140.
4 *A Descriptive Catalogue*, in Erdman, 1982, p 549.

II

*Poetical Sketches*, which marks Blake's emergence as a poet, reflects the wide reading of its 'Untutored' author: Shakespeare, Spenser, Gray, Collins, Macpherson and Chatterton. In the four poems to the seasons there is something more mythopoeic than the usual obligatory personification. 'Summer' and 'Winter' are, in fact, 'contrary' poems, in which the oppositions of the later poetry – fire and stone, water and ice, Energy and Reason – are already present in embryonic form. The two ballads, 'Fair Elenor' and 'Gwin, King of Norway', combine the current interest in the ballad as a serious poetic form with familiar 'northern' effects and themes: blood-curdling Gothicism, and the overthrow of a cruel tyrant by a giant who is just as bloodthirsty. It is in the songs, however, that Blake's lyric powers begin to manifest themselves, especially in 'How sweet I roam'd', with its simple diction, end-stopped lines and subtle rhythmic effects, and in 'Mad Song', with its striking last stanza. The decline of the lyric in neoclassical verse is summed up in 'To the Muses':

> How have you left the antient love
>   That bards of old enjoy'd in you!
> The languid strings do scarcely move!
>   The sound is forc'd, the notes are few!

In 1789, at the beginning of his most prolific and creative period, Blake issued *Songs of Innocence*, a masterpiece of his illuminated art. Its pastoral idiom is not that of neoclassicism, but derives from biblical sources and the native English tradition of nursery rhymes, songs and moral hymns for children. The children's hymn-books of Isaac Watts, Charles Wesley and Laetitia Barbauld are transcended, however, not only artistically (some of Watts's stanzas in *Divine Hymns for Children*, 1715, are little more than versified prose) but ideologically, since their heavily didactic and condescending tone is implicitly rejected. Watts's doctrine of inherited guilt, his all-seeing, somewhat terrifying God the Father who punishes the disobedient, and his insistence on dutiful, virtuous industry, are entirely absent from the spirit, if not from the world, of Blake's songs. (The line 'So if all do their duty, they need not fear harm' in 'The Chimney Sweeper', *Songs of Innocence*, has a potentially sinister implication.) The traditional insect emblem is thus transformed. The ant or 'Emmet' is no longer an emblem of middle-class thrift in 'A Dream', but a lost, travel-worn mother who activates the practical compassion of the 'Angel-guarded' dreamer. (Blake later undercut the 'business' morality of the busy bee who 'improves each shining hour' when, in *The Marriage*, he wrote: 'The busy bee has no time for sorrow'.)

It would not be quite true to say that *Songs of Innocence* merely celebrate 'instinctive behaviour' and 'reject the very act of teaching'.[1] The religious teaching in 'The Divine Image', 'A Cradle Song' and 'The Little Black Boy' verges on the sentimental, though there is a sense in which songs such as 'The Blossom', 'Infant Joy', 'Spring' and 'Laughing Song' simply delight in their form rather than advocating anything. Blake's songs subvert the sugared-pill approach to education by removing the pill altogether, and by offering the pleasure of the composite, illuminated text to adults as well as to children. Innocence is not just a childhood state through which we all pass, but a set of relationships, implying something more social and organized, like the 'echoing' identifications in 'The Echoing Green'. It is not the child who must be socialized into the world of the educator, but the educator who needs to be led into the world of the child. This sounds like Wordsworth, but, in Blake, Rousseauism's encounter with Watts and Wesley has nourished, not an innocence perceived through, and hence positioning the reader inside, a 'fallen' adult consciousness (as in Wordsworth's 'We are Seven'), but songs whose simple diction, musical rhythms, self-contained lines, repetitions and even narrative structure cunningly mimic or suggest songs *of* children (rather than songs written *for* children – children too can be independently creative); songs whose 'Introduction' reverses 'normal' adult–child relations by having the piper obey the child's commands.

Although the speaker of the 'Introduction' is an adult, his viewpoint is informed by visionary energy instead of a fallen empiricism. This is felt in the trochaic repetition of 'Piping', and in the bouncy, skipping rhythm – an energy that breaks the first stanza's syntactic frame. From piping the speaker is told to sing, then to write:

> Piper sit thee down and write
> In a book that all may read –
> So he vanish'd from my sight.
> And I pluck'd a hollow reed.
>
> And I made a rural pen,
> And I stain'd the water clear,

1 Nick Shrimpton, 'Hell's Hymnbook: Blake's *Songs of Innocence and of Experience* and their models', in R. T. Davies and B. G. Beatty, eds, *Literature of the Romantic Period*, Liverpool, 1976, pp 25–6.

And I wrote my happy songs,
Every child may joy to hear

The poem narrates its own creation. But why does the child vanish? The obvious answer is that the song moves from the immediacy of the oral situation to the solitary, unreciprocating, sedentary act of writing, which is no longer spontaneously playful, but a deliberate and serious labour: 'And I pluck'd . . . And I made . . . And I stain'd . . . And I wrote . . .' Another implication could be that the initial inspiration has been replaced by the 'I'. (An ambiguity has even been noted in 'stain'd the water clear'.)[1] The last line raises hopes of the book's potential audience ('Every child'), but 'may' could also imply that a book guarantees neither listeners nor joy.

The only example in *Songs of Innocence* of an empirical adult viewpoint is in 'Holy Thursday', whose speaker sees 'innocent' charity-school children, not a stage-managed show on Ascension Day:

Twas on a Holy Thursday their innocent faces clean
The children walking two & two in red & blue & green
Grey headed beadles walkd before with wands as white as snow
Till into the high dome of Pauls they like Thames waters flow

His attitude is subtly revealed in his admiration for public demonstrations of visible purity ('innocent faces clean', 'wands as white as snow'). The simile 'like Thames waters' is more ambiguous. For Erdman, the lines of verse in the design are 'kept as open as "Thames waters"',[2] but the vines and leaves flowing across the page between the iambic septenaries that rhyme 'two & two' are also being channelled. In 'London' the free-flowing, purifying stream of Innocence turns into 'the *charter'd* Thames', a river whose embankments, lined with the quays and wharves of chartered companies, provided little opportunity for the kind of spontaneous baptismal immersion enacted in the run-on lines of 'Summer'.

In fact, the speaker in 'Holy Thursday' sees, or rather hears, more than the heart knows. Language unfiltered by a repressive urge seems to make him the unconscious transmitter of imaginative truth, betraying his receptivity into an apocalyptic vision:

1 See Heather Glen, *Vision and Disenchantment: Blake's 'Songs' and Wordsworth's 'Lyrical Ballads'*, Cambridge, 1983, p 66.
2 David Erdman, ed., *The Illuminated Blake*, London, 1975, p 61.

> Now like a mighty wind they raise to heaven the voice of song
> Or like harmonious thunderings the seats of heaven among
> Beneath them sit the aged men wise guardians of the poor
> Then cherish pity, lest you drive an angel from your door

The lines are prophetic of another kind of 'Ascension': a vast human force that is no longer docile, but elemental. In this context, the moral tag in the last line is curiously dislocated and comes as an anticlimax. Conventionally sincere, the artless speaker muffs the effect of the preceding lines, as if trying to muffle the truth he has let through. Just as 'the high dome of Pauls' is there to hold in thunderous voices ascending up to heaven's dome from the 'seats of heaven' (the children sat in high wooden galleries), so the last line, in seeking to contain heavenly thunder, reveals the limits of homiletic wisdom. A 'mighty wind' and 'harmonious thunderings' do not really call for 'pity'.

The last line of 'The Chimney Sweeper' performs a similar function. The new sweep, 'little Tom Dacre', cries when his head is shaved, but is consoled by his friend (the speaker of the poem). Tom dreams of 'thousands of sweepers' locked up 'in coffins of black' who are set free by an Angel. The sweeps 'wash in a river and shine in the Sun'.

> Then naked & white, all their bags left behind,
> They rise upon clouds, and sport in the wind.
> And the Angel told Tom if he'd be a good boy,
> He'd have God for his father & never want joy.
>
> And so Tom awoke and we rose in the dark
> And got with our bags & our brushes to work.
> Tho' the morning was cold, Tom was happy & warm,
> So if all do their duty, they need not fear harm.

Instead of inspiring revolt, Tom's dream of freedom serves as a comforting illusion that enables him to carry on working without complaint. The Angel who frees the sweepers is Tom's own imprisoning trust, restoring his faith in a surrogate loving father. (The speaker's father 'sold me while yet my tongue/could scarcely cry weep weep weep weep'.) But the 'coffins of black' are also the chimneys of eighteenth-century London houses. How, from these coffins, can the moralizing Angel free Tom and his fellow sweepers? The framing narrative gives the answer: its grim reality ('in soot I sleep . . . we rose in the dark') remains unaltered.

If we ask how such a poem can be a song of Innocence, we should remember that Innocence is a state of the human soul. The speaker and Tom are not simply victims of an illusion. Tom's inner warmth has a real cause: the speaker's solicitude ('There little Tom Dacre . . . Hush Tom never mind it . . .'). Though inured to his lot ('So *your* chimneys I sweep' – note how this implicates the reader), the speaker has not become hardened like the cynical sweeper in *Experience*, who has been reduced to 'A little black thing' in the eyes of the adult speaker. Tom's dream, which the speaker relates to us, already evinces a personal solidarity with 'thousands of sweepers Dick, Joe, Ned & Jack' (the speaker's enthusiasm breaks the metre). The last line can be read as a parroted maxim, as a bounded (and spiritually binding) piece of morality stuck on like a dead appendage, satirically exposed, or as a mark of psychological realism (harm may come, but with a fate collectively shared and a toddy of illusions inside them, obedient victims 'need not *fear* harm'). However we read it, the speaker retains his positive innocence. Yet the text is there to be read as the speaker cannot know it: as a poignant and sharply ironic comment on the way ideology works.

Blake's poetry characteristically concerns itself with 'spiritual' states and dramatic situations. Contrary viewpoints are opposed in paired poems such as 'The Lamb' and 'The Tyger', or within a single poem. Since this practice involves the use of personae, of 'voices' and dialogues, it often becomes facile or perverse to read a particular poem as an expression of the author's own views and feelings. Blake's poetry is *dialogic*, unlike descriptive and reflective poetry, which invites the reader to identify the viewpoint enounced in the poem as that of the poet. Readers of Blake should thus be on guard against a lingering Romantic ideology[1] that finds the genesis or meaning of a work in the poet's mind or soul, as in: 'In the *Songs* Blake pursued a more traditional and more lyrical art, *because some deep need in him* called for this kind of expression'; 'in ["London"] *he gives his own view* of that "chartered liberty" on which his countrymen prided themselves'; or, '[*Songs of Experience*] were born of a deep anguish, *from a storm in the poet's soul*'.[2] Blake's poetry is multivocal, allusive and intertextual rather than directly expressive; philosophic rather than experiential; variously mediated rather than immediately intelligible. Since it confronts a whole range of contemporary ideological discourses, it operates on different referential levels

---

1 See Jerome J. McGann, *The Romantic Ideology: A Critical Investigation*, Chicago, 1983.

2 C. M. Bowra, *The Romantic Imagination*, Oxford, 1961, pp 27, 42, 45–6. (My emphasis.)

simultaneously, seeking to transcend these discourses through a series of relativizing literary strategies.

*The Book of Thel* (1789) has been read as a debate between Neoplatonism (which views the transient world of matter as 'mere mire') and alchemy (which perceives the divine as working within matter). On this reading, Thel is the female soul unwilling to join the cycle of life.[1] She hears the Lilly claim to be 'visited from heaven' (i. 19); the Cloud, that he passes away 'to tenfold life' by marrying 'the fair eyed dew' (iii. 11–13); the Clod of Clay, full of maternal love for the infant worm, that he who 'loves the lowly' kisses her. Yet how, says the Clod, 'I know not, and I cannot know' (v. 1–5). Thel, however, laments: 'And all shall say, without a use this shining woman liv'd,/Or did she only live. to be at death the food of worms' (iii. 22–3). Imagining what 'all shall say', she is unable to forget her special status as the only daughter of 'Mne Seraphim'[2] who does not tend sheep. The Cloud replies: 'Then if thou art the food of worms. O virgin of the skies,/How great thy use. how great thy blessing' (iii. 25–6). The wit of turning Elizabethan melancholy's favourite image of death into a cause for celebration, and the humour of summoning a worm as the next witness to refute an 'astonish'd' Thel, belong to gentle satire rather than philosophical debate, while Thel's over-refined attitude of self-conscious melancholy is hardly innocent. Set against her sentimental responses, which are as easily spilled out as they are liberally misplaced (pitying others out of self-pity), the Lilly's modest deference, the Cloud's light mockery, and the homely realism and respectful hospitality of 'matron Clay' are amusingly appropriate. But a jarring note intrudes when, coming to 'her own grave plot', Thel hears a 'voice of sorrow' ask: 'Why a tender curb upon the youthful burning boy!/Why a little curtain of flesh on the bed of our desire?' (vi. 19–20) – whereupon Thel flees 'with a shriek' back into 'the vales of Har'. These two lines, erased in two copies,[3] make Thel's shriek doubly discordant. Her blinkered sense of futility is caused by a lack of experience in loving and protecting others (as opposed to pitying them from afar). Performing acts of self-sacrifice brings to the giver a corresponding

1  See Kathleen Raine, *Blake and Tradition*, London, 1969, i. 99–100.
2  'Mne' suggests 'Mnemosyne'. Blake later wrote that 'the Greek Muses are daughters of Mnemosyne ... or Memory'; Thel would thus seem to be associated with classical culture and its limitations.
3  Erdman, in *The Illuminated Blake* (p 40), suggests there were 'persons who asked Blake to erase references to the boy's "tender curb" and the girl's "curtain of flesh"'

feeling of being loved and protected, which is what, essentially, the state of Innocence is all about. Yet Thel's moral lack is somewhat reductively exposed as a virgin's hysterical fear of sex – of sex viewed as perverted desire, a destroyer of life (like the worm in 'The Sick Rose') rather than its creator.

Intertextually, the poem is linked to Erasmus Darwin's *The Loves of the Plants* (1789). Thel wipes 'her pitying tears with her white veil' (v. 7); Darwin's Anemome (a Nymph who 'shines . . . in beauty's blushing pride') prays for Zephyr to tear 'with rude kiss her bosom's gauzy veil'.[1] But she still lives in a 'fair mansion', unlike the 'Retiring Lichen', whose 'flinty bed' is gilded by 'the cold moon-beam'. A note on lichen reads: 'after it perishes, earth enough is left for other mosses to root themselves; and after some ages a soil is produced sufficient for the growth of more succulent and large vegetables.'[2] Living and dying for others becomes a blessing in *The Book of Thel*, a poem that raises Christian humility above classical beauty, the loving interdependence of the 'meanest things' above a lonely, artificially genteel existence. Thel cannot enter the world of the humble, but behind the comic pathos of her plight there may be a real pathos. For what, after all, did the 'shining lot' of the average 'lady of quality' in Blake's England really amount to?

According to Mary Wollstonecraft, very little except comfortable slavery. In *A Vindication of the Rights of Woman*, published in 1792, women are called slaves 'in a political and civil sense'; they are 'slaves of casual lust', slaves to their own feelings, and 'in the same proportion the slaves of pleasure as they are the slaves of men'.[3] Blake's *Visions of the Daughters of Albion* (1793), whose closest intertext is Wollstonecraft's feminist treatise, begins: 'ENSLAV'D, the Daughters of Albion weep'. The feminist theme is linked to the campaign against slavery: women are also treated as property by Albion's slave-trading, slave-owning Englishmen. (In 1791 Blake did engravings for Stedman's *Narrative of a five years' expedition, against the Revolted Negroes of Surinam, in Guiana*.) Unlike Thel, Oothoon, 'the soft soul of America', plucks the flower of experience. She wings over 'the waves' of Theotormon in 'exulting swift delight', only to be rent by the thunders of Bromion, who boasts: 'Stampt with my signet are the swarthy children of the sun' (i. 21). A ravished prisoner in his caves, Oothoon is bound back to back with Bromion

---

1 Erasmus Darwin, *The Botanic Garden*, ii (1794), l 341.
2 Ibid., p 36.
3 *A Vindication of the Rights of Woman*, London, 1792, pp 386, 345, 402.

while the jealous Theotormon, tormented by a hypocritical religion, sits wearing 'the threshold hard/With secret tears' (ii. 6–7), unable to free Oothoon or to accept her avowals of purity now that she has been raped. The story also has a Neoplatonic reference. In Thomas Taylor's *Dissertation on the Eleusinian and Bacchic Mysteries* (1791) the Persephone myth is interpreted as the descent of the soul into a sorrowful corporeal existence: 'Proserpine . . . as she was gathering tender flowers, in the new spring, was ravished from her delightful abodes by Pluto; and being carried from thence through thick woods, and over a length of sea, was brought by Pluto into a cavern.'[1] The other intertext is Macpherson's 'Oithona: A Poem' in *Poems of Ossian* (1762). While her lover is away, Oithona is carried off by a rejected suitor and concealed in a cave. ('Oithona', we are told, means 'the virgin of the wave'.) The scenery of *Visions* is Ossianic: mountains, valleys, flowers, clouds, sea, waves, thunder and a Hebridean cave. Oothoon's 'lamentations' – continuing those of Thel at a higher emotional level – also derive, ultimately, from the elegiac laments in Macpherson's Ossian.

Various strands have been interwoven: feminism, anti-slavery, the Persephone myth and the wild (albeit spurious) primitivism of an ancient northern bard. If Oothoon is less sharply characterized than Thel, it is because her main function is to serve as the mouthpiece for a passionate polemic that addresses the sexual crisis as a whole: women's degraded status, false notions of purity, 'the burning fires/ Of lust', the enslavement of the marriage bed, the hypocritical cult of modesty, and the cry for a love 'free as the mountain wind' (vii. 16) – a love never called for on Ossian's mountains. Above all, it is the assertion of a 'pure' female sexuality that strikes twentieth-century readers as so modern. That, and the extraordinary connection drawn between what are now called masturbation fantasies, and religious ideology:

> the youth shut up from
> The lustful joy. shall forget to generate. & create an amorous image
> In the shadows of his curtains and in the folds of his silent pillow.
> Are not these the places of religion? the rewards of continence?
> The self enjoyings of self denial? Why dost thou seek religion?
> Is it because acts are not lovely, that thou seekest solitude,
> Where the horrible darkness is impressed with reflections of desire.
>
> (vii. 5–11)

---

1 *Thomas Taylor the Platonist: Selected Writings*, ed. Kathleen Raine and George Mills Harper, London, 1969, p. 385.

*Visions* can be read, then, as a propagandist work memorable for its sustained passages of impassioned rhetoric; as an argument in favour of free love and women's liberation (though bringing the two together could be seen as confusing the feminist issue). But it can be read in other ways. For all its persuasiveness, Oothoon's rhetoric of innocence and purity falls on deaf ears. This indicts the stubbornness of male reaction – Theotormon is unable to cross 'the threshold hard' into a new relationship with Oothoon – but there may be flaws in Oothoon's rhetoric. She asks: 'How can I be defild when I reflect thy image pure?' (iii. 16). This martyr-like faith in Theotormon's purity (his 'black jealous waters' are not pure; moreover, he and Bromion could be aspects of the same person) prostrates Oothoon before an image *she herself* has created, perhaps seeing her own 'image pure' reflected in Theotormon while offering herself as the reflection of *his* 'image pure'. Either way, the rhetoric evokes those very 'places of religion' Oothoon later condemns. The youth's 'amorous image' has a narcissistic aura. Echo pined for Narcissus; Oothoon pines for Theotormon, and her laments are echoed back by the Daughters of Albion.

The climax of Oothoon's long speech is an imagined scene offered to Theotormon as proof of a selfless love free of jealousy:

> But silken nets and traps of adamant will Oothoon spread,
> And catch for thee girls of mild silver, or of furious gold;
> I'll lie beside thee on a bank & view their wanton play
> In lovely copulation bliss on bliss with Theotormon:
> Red as the rosy morning, lustful as the first born beam,
> Oothoon shall view his dear delight, nor e'er with jealous cloud
> Come in the heaven of generous love; nor selfish blightings bring.
>
> (vii. 23–9)

The 'purity' of this vision of 'lovely copulation' is arguably vitiated by its voyeuristic and, from a male point of view (given Theotormon's privileged place in it), its narcissistic overtones: copulation is 'lovely' to the viewer, and hence to the viewed. Theotormon's paralysis when sitting near Oothoon (who cannot weep, but 'can howl incessant writhing her soft snowy limbs') is dispelled in this vision, which provides, however, no compensating freed activity for Oothoon, whose 'lustful' desire is confined to the 'self enjoyings of self denial' as she vicariously views Theotormon's 'dear delight'. Perhaps the road to a higher innocence is not as straightforward as Oothoon's impassioned vision might have led us to believe.

In Blake, the desire for sexual and psychological liberation is inseparable from the desire for political freedom. By 1793 the combined cause of political and sexual repression has become mythologized as a reactionary, frozen patriarch called Urizen (from 'horizon' and Greek *horizein*, 'to limit', also from 'Your reason – Your reason?' said by Inflammable Gass – Joseph Priestley? – in *An Island in the Moon*). A combination of Jehovah, priest, scribe, king and lawgiver, Urizen is the archetypal jealous father, the sensitive rebel's universal authority figure. In *Visions* he is addressed by Oothoon as 'Creator of men! mistaken Demon of heaven' (v. 3). In *America* (1793) his arch-antagonist is another 'Demon', the roaring, raging, fiery Orc. At the end of the prophecy Orc is still raging, but Urizen's 'leprous head' has emerged from 'his holy shrine', his tears 'in deluge piteous/Falling into the deep sublime' (xvi. 3–5) and his brows covered with snow. Orc is hidden in 'clouds & cold mists' until France receives 'the Demons light' (xvi. 13–15). Urizen's pity only serves, in Nietzschian fashion, to freeze up energy.[1]

As a fusion of prophecy and historical narrative, *America* is both more successful and more mythopoeic than Blake's previous 'political' prophecy, *The French Revolution* (1791), whose imagery, although conveying the feeling of enormous energies being unleashed, at times becomes strident and inflated. The spirit of revolution found more appropriate expression in a work whose aphoristic concentration, irreverence and daring make it unique even in the Blakian *œuvre*: The Marriage of Heaven and Hell (1790–93), which T. S. Eliot called 'naked philosophy',[2] though it is much more than that.

The immediate conjuncture of *The Marriage* was twofold: the events in France, and Blake's disaffection with the Swedenborgian New Jerusalem Church. Blake and his wife were, it seems, members of the New Church in April 1789, but by 1790 his reservations about the principles of its founder had hardened into strong disagreement with Swedenborg's predestinarian notions. Swedenborg's claims to have conversed with angels, set forth in his 'Memorable Relations', are parodied in *The Marriage*'s 'Memorable Fancies'. His dry, unemotional and pedantic style is also parodied. More important, Swedenborg's faith in gradual enlightenment and constant improvement towards spiritual perfection, stemming from his doctrine of degrees, is rejected in favour of sudden illumination and apocalyptic change. Finally, his depiction of Hell is satirically revealed as the

1 'Christianity', says Nietzsche, 'is called the religion of *pity*. – Pity stands in antithesis to the tonic emotions which enhance the energy of the feeling of life: it has a depressive effect.' *The Anti-Christ*, in *Twilight of the Idols and the Anti-Christ*, tr. R. J. Hollingdale, Harmondsworth, 1968, p 118.
2 In *The Sacred Wood*, London, 1920, p 142.

'spiritual' precipitate of class prejudice.[1] There were others who became disillusioned with the New Jerusalem Church in 1788–9. One was John Wright, a carpenter; another was William Bryan, a copperplate printer. Wright visited the Great Eastcheap chapel in 1788 and 'saw nothing but old *forms* of worship established'.[2] Blake, however, attacks the source: Swedenborg's writings and their enervating metaphysics. 'Swedenborg is the Angel sitting at the tomb; his writings are the linen clothes folded up.'

*The Marriage* moves towards the monism of Joseph Priestley (who published his *Letters to Members of the New Jerusalem Church* in 1791, the year in which a Church and King mob destroyed his library and laboratory in Birmingham) without adopting Priestley's materialism. For Priestley, it is matter that thinks; for Blake, 'Man has no Body distinct from his Soul'. Philosophically, however, *The Marriage*'s most original contribution is its elaboration of the dialectic:

But the Prolific would cease to be Prolific unless the Devourer as a sea recieved the excess of his delights.

Some will say, Is not God alone Prolific? I answer, God only Acts & Is, in existing beings or Men.

These two classes of men are always upon earth, & they should be enemies; whoever tries to reconcile them seeks to destroy existence.

Religion is an endeavour to reconcile the two.

(16–17)

In applying the dialectic to the social domain, Blake anticipates Marx.

In the seventeenth century Jakob Boehme had viewed everything in the universe as a dynamic interplay of opposing forces or principles. In *Aurora* (1612), however, Boehme had bracketed good and evil with love and wrath, sympathy and antipathy. For Blake, good and evil are not true 'contraries'. Their opposition is a rationalized abstraction, a mere 'negation'. In *The Marriage* they are displaced by Reason and Energy: 'Good is the passive that obeys Reason. Evil is the active springing from Energy' (v). Blake's redefining of terms is a satiric exposure of ruling-class moral hypocrisy. Later he writes

1 G. R. Sabri-Tabrizi, in *The 'Heaven' and 'Hell' of William Blake*, New York, 1973, observes that Swedenborg's Hell bears an uncanny resemblance to the coalmines he owned, whereas his Heaven is remarkably like the spacious world of the leisured upper classes.
2 John Wright, *A Revealed Knowledge*, London, 1794, p 4.

that 'Goodness is the cloke of knavery', the 'Moral Virtues ...
continual Accusers of Sin', promoting 'Eternal Wars & Domineering
over others'.[1] Like Nietzsche, he deconstructs the whole moral
system of good and evil as – to quote Fredric Jameson – 'the
sedimented or fossilized trace of the concrete praxis of situations of
domination', where the 'Good' is simply 'my own position as an
unassailable power centre' in terms of which the Other (as 'Evil') is
repudiated.[2]

When Blake writes that 'Energy is the only life and is from the
Body and Reason is the bound or outward circumference of Energy'
(*The Marriage*, iv) he reminds us of Energy's subversive connotations. An 'energumen' or 'energumenist' in the seventeenth century
meant 'one actively possessed by the devil'.[3] Salmasius saw Milton as
belonging to the Diabolical Party, and the connection made between
active devils and political radicals continued into the later eighteenth
century with 'that Devil Wilkes', together with the English Jacobins'
ironic boast that the Devil was the first Jacobin. It is in this
historical context that Blake's assumption of the satiric 'Devil'
persona in *The Marriage* can be understood as a tactic in a long-
standing ideological war.

Apart from being a treasury of quotations, a source of revolutionary ideas (it even enunciates a psychological theory of repression)
and a stupendous lava flow of sententious prose, *The Marriage* is a
unique literary intervention in terms of genre. It has no discernible
progression or narrative structure; it mixes modes and genres
('bardic' verse, aphorism, tractate, essay, mock-anecdote, travelogue,
prosaic report, allegory); and it moves from one topic to another
without any bridging transition. It thus seems to elude any formal or
generic classification. In fact *The Marriage* belongs to an ancient
classical genre: that of the old Roman *satura*, or satiric medley, in
which intellectual errors are ridiculed – a kind known as Menippean
satire. According to Bakhtin, Menippean satire's main aim is to
subvert the monologism of official discourse. Hence its radical shifts
and metamorphoses; its cynical exposés and debunking of official
dogma; its deliberate rejection of stylistic unity through the mixing

1 Erdman, 1982, pp 269, 664.
2 *The Political Unconscious: Narrative as a Socially Symbolic Act*, London, 1983, p
117.
3 'The active Witch I conceive to Act together with the Divell; but the Passive Witch
to be Acted rather by him ... The mearly Passive be simply daemoniacks, but not
Energumenists.' John Gaule, *Select Cases of Conscience Touching Witches and
Witchcraft*, London, 1646, p 37.

of genres; its parodic debasing of 'high' genres, and its 'carnivalistic logic of "a world upside down"' . . . The carnivalistic nether world of the menippea determined the medieval tradition of representations of *joyful hell*, a tradition which found its culmination in Rabelais.'[1] The satiric element is to the fore in *The Marriage*'s use of the Devil as a satiric persona and two Swedenborgian Angels as satiric *adversarii*, whose self-righteous dogmatism is twice refuted in a comic reversal. Thus the conservative Angel's lurid vision of the French Revolution as a 'nether deep . . . black as a sea' from which 'a monstrous serpent' emerges (xviii) turns out to be a projection of the Angel's own diseased psyche, for the vision disappears when the narrator, left alone and no longer 'imposed' upon by the Angel, finds himself 'on a bank by moonlight hearing a harper' (xix).

Formally, *The Marriage* consists of two parts, each containing seven sections, not including 'A Song of Liberty', which was added later. The sections in the second half correspond thematically to those in the first half but in reverse order. The text thus forms a chiasmus or mirror-correspondence — 'what amounts to a formal parody of Swedenborgian "correspondence"', as Graham Pechey, who discovered this structure, puts it.[2] In the fifth section of the first half the Swedenborgian narrator, a mock-genteel persona, tells us how he has collected some 'sayings' of Hell. Coming home, he saw 'a mighty Devil' who, 'with corroding fires' (Blake's acid, used for relief etching), wrote a sentence 'now percieved by the minds of men' (vi–vii). The corresponding section in the second half is another 'Memorable Fancy' in which the narrator relates: 'I was in a Printing house in Hell & saw the method in which knowledge is transmitted from generation to generation' (xv). A brief, complex allegory follows, ending in bathetic clarity: the molten 'metals', cast 'into the expanse' by 'Unnam'd forms', 'were reciev'd by Men . . . and took the forms of books & were arranged in libraries' (xv). Each of the two sections is an aetiology of written forms, but whereas in the first 'Infernal wisdom' is preserved by 'the mighty Devil' at his engraver's table, in the second imaginative labour is reified as 'books', institutionally classified.

*The Marriage* argues that a historic usurpation has led to the present upside-down state of affairs, a topsy-turvydom that is also

1 Mikhail Bakhtin, *Problems of Dostoevsky's Poetics*, Manchester, 1984, p 133.
2 Graham Pechey, '*The Marriage of Heaven and Hell*: A Text and Its Conjuncture', *Oxford Literary Review* (Spring 1979), 60.

ideological. In this it resembles other 'liberation' texts such as Winstanley's *The True Levellers' Standard Advanced* (1649), in which the non-producing 'teacher and ruler' have expropriated the productive tillers of the land, and Rousseau's *Dissertation on the Origin and Foundation of the Inequality of Mankind* (1754), in which the artificial rationalized hegemony of the propertied classes has restrained the instinctual freedom of the natural man. The free-verse 'Argument' of *The Marriage* tells how the 'just man' has been driven into 'barren climes' by 'the villain'. Having usurped the place of desire, Reason falsifies its legitimacy; the abstract 'system' of a usurping Priesthood has taken the place of the animist imagination of the 'ancient Poets'; Mosaic law has subjected 'the deities of surrounding nations', 'weak and tame minds' have chained prolific Giants, and Angels have supplanted Devils. The text ends with the carnivalistic de-conversion of the Tory Angel, who becomes the plebeian Devil's 'particular friend'. Blake may not have been entirely satisfied with *The Marriage*'s impact as a liberation text, however, for between 1792 and 1793 he appended a series of declamatory verses entitled 'A Song of Liberty'. Politically more explicit and stylistically simpler than the rest of *The Marriage*, the Song's imperatives, apostrophes, exclamations and affirmations are in the high bardic style similar to that of Orc's long speech in *America*, which even makes the same splendidly antinomian assertion that 'every thing that lives is holy'.

By 1793–4 Blake had written *Songs of Experience*, and, although he continued to issue *Songs of Innocence* as a separate collection, the two were bound together in 1794 under the title *Songs of Innocence and of Experience, Shewing the Two Contrary States of the Human Soul*. The nature symbolism of *Songs of Experience* is postlapsarian: the 'dismal shade' of the tree of mystery, the 'dread' tiger, the 'sick' rose, the caterpillar and the raven have replaced the shade of 'leaves so green', the 'woolly' lamb, the 'happy' blossom, the maternal 'Emmet' and the 'Merry' sparrow. Oppressive patriarchy and an interfering, mystifying priesthood have replaced caring parents and 'the human form divine' of a loving Jesus. In the world of Experience there is neither an inner warmth nor any outer defence against harsh social realities. The communal concern and mutual obligation of the democratic community have gone. In 'Holy Thursday' it is not just poverty that appals, but the lack of any love or concern. This becomes clear in the designs, whose borders lack the interweaving trunks, entwining branches and coiling tendrils that grace the humanized world of Innocence, where the weak are protected and natural instincts are given free play. As in *Visions*, the sexual crisis – male possession ('Earth's Answer'), pining, unfulfilled desire ('Ah! Sun Flower'), fearful chastity ('The Angel'), 'unacted' desire ('My Pretty Rose Tree'), the suppression or outlawing of desire ('A Little Girl Lost', 'The Garden of Love') and a destructive, guilty lust ('The Sick Rose') – is enmeshed with social and political oppression, dealt with in 'Holy Thursday', 'The Chimney Sweeper', 'The Little Vagabond', 'London', 'The Human Abstract' and 'A Little Boy Lost'.

As in *Songs of Innocence*, the speaker's viewpoint is crucial, though a single speaker does not necessarily mean a univocal or monologic viewpoint. 'The Tyger', for example, seems to speak with two voices.[1] The first is the voice of a deeply anxious observer whose belief in a God of love and pity is being seriously challenged; the second is the voice of a doer, whether an artisan (who seizes, twists and grasps), or a demonstrator shouting the apostrophic slogan 'Tyger Tyger, burning bright'. The first tries to contain or 'frame' the Tyger's energy by asking questions, viewing the beast with a fearful incomprehension bordering on hysteria, like those anti-Jacobins who tried to explain the republican wrath of the 'tygerish multitude' in 1792–3;[2] the second simply celebrates the Tyger's energy, subverting the voice of the questioner by beating out the relentless trochaic rhythms, resonating with a force whose energy, however violent, outweighs all other considerations. Seen this way the poem becomes an equivocation on the destructive energy of power. We need not accept either viewpoint as valid or true, for in dialectical terms both are true; what we as readers of the poem cannot avoid is our own response, either as potential makers (of 'The Tyger' as well as of the Tyger) or as potential restrainers.

'London' begins with weary reiterations symptomatic of the speaker's tired and blunted humanity. He inscribes with careless absolutism 'Marks of weakness, marks of woe' (his own?) into 'every' face he meets. The workings of society revealed in the poem have an apocalyptic logic. After marking faces, the speaker chains each heard cry to the next by repeating 'every'; in every cry he hears

1 See Stewart Crehan, 'Blake's *Tyger* and the "Tygerish Multitude"', *Literature and History*, VI. ii (Autumn 1980), 151–60.

2 'Exception has been taken at Mr Burke's opprobrious term Swinish multitude. I am ready for one . . . to change the epithet to tygerish multitude . . . The fact is, the Monkey-compound has disappeared with the Aristocratical part of the Community, and left the wanton cruelty of the Tyger to be claimed exclusively by the Democracy.' *The Anti-Gallican*, London, 1793, pp 22–3.

'mind-forg'd manacles'.[1] More specified (yet still representative rather than individual) voices next modify his powers of perception in such a way that the heard is metamorphosed into the seen: the sweeper's cry into a pall, the soldier's sigh into blood, the harlot's curse into plagues that turn the monogamous marriage bed into a hearse. The perception is both prophetic and visionary. The lines

> And the hapless Soldiers sigh
> Runs in blood down Palace walls

can be read primarily as a rhetorical figure intended to produce guilt (and fear – whose blood?) in the promoters of the war with France, but they also trigger a startlingly surrealistic image of red blood suddenly materializing out a 'sigh' and then running down high stone walls. By the end of the poem other voices merging with that of the speaker have drastically altered his tone of voice: from the tired monologism of the aimless wanderer to the hyperbolic fury associated with a cursing harlot. Urban alienation so 'becomes' the speaker that his voice builds up to a climax of murderously expletive rage, not so much through a deliberate protest but rather in response to an inescapably oppressive environment of sights and sounds. Taking this poem with 'The Tyger', which arguably takes us through a complementary process of apocalyptic changes, we can perhaps begin to see why revolutionary 'tygers of wrath' (*The Marriage*, ix) burn so bright in the oppressive forests of 'midnight streets'.

T. S. Eliot spoke of Blake's 'peculiar honesty', saying that *Songs of Innocence and of Experience* 'are the poems of a man with a profound interest in human emotions, and a profound knowledge of them. The emotions are presented in an extremely simplified, abstract form.'[2] In 'A Poison Tree', simplicity of language and form give the emotional process described (a suppressed, hidden anger that grows into a murderous hate) a paradigmatic intensity, raising it to the level of a universal truth. Herein lies Blake's 'prophetic' strength. 'Every honest man is a Prophet he utters his opinion both of private & public matters/ Thus/If you go on So/the result is So/He never says such a thing shall happen let you do what you will'.[3] The poem begins:

1 In 1767 the French jurist O. M. Servan wrote: 'a stupid despot may constrain his slaves with iron chains; but a true politician binds them even more strongly by the chain of their own ideas . . . on the fibres of the brain is founded the unshakeable base of the soundest Empires.' Quoted in Michel Foucault, *Discipline and Punish: The Birth of the Prison*, Harmondsworth, 1979, pp 102–3.
2 *The Sacred Wood*, p 139.
3 MS annotation to *An Apology for the Bible* by R. Watson, Bishop of Llandaff (1797); in Erdman, 1982, p 617.

> I was angry with my friend;
> I told my wrath, my wrath did end.
> I was angry with my foe:
> I told it not, my wrath did grow.

The parallel syntax of the antithetic couplets is broken in the fourth line, whose own antithesis contains pressing narrative implications. It is the speaker's failure to speak, his 'omission of act in self'[1] that makes the wrath grow. Keeping it to himself, he nurtures it like a loved possession:

> And I waterd it in fears,
> Night & morning with my tears:
> And I sunned it with smiles,
> And with soft deceitful wiles.

This peculiarly 'honest', yet peculiarly unrepentant confessant relives the pleasure of nurturing his repressed anger without realizing what has happened to him, for the abstracted 'it' has acquired a mysterious independence from his will: 'And it grew both day and night./Till it bore an apple bright.' Not until the last word of the poem is the metamorphosed 'it' actually named: 'In the morning glad I see;/My foe outstretchd beneath the tree.' The sense of release in the final iambic line is counteracted by the stress on 'tree', while the change from the simple past ('stole') to the timeless present ('I see') betrays an obsessive fantasy which the deluded speaker merely projects as an accomplished fact. Still unconsummated, such a desire for revenge will only grow more pestilential through the 'omission of act'.

The notebook title of the poem is 'Christian Forebearance'. The poem alludes not just to the duplicity of 'Christian manners' but to the forbidden fruit placed in the Garden of Eden by, presumably, a vindictive God of Genesis. Blake had also read of the poisonous upas tree of Java, which gained a legendary reputation for killing all those who fell asleep beneath it (hence the last line of the poem). Mahomet, so the story ran, had applied to God to punish certain sinners, 'upon which God caused this tree to grow out of the earth, which destroyed them all, and rendered the country for ever uninhabitable'.[2] It may be objected that Blake's poem deals with human actions and human psychology, not divine matters. On the other hand, 'God only Acts & Is, in existing beings or Men' (*The Marriage*, xvi).

---

1  Erdman, 1982, p 601.
2  Darwin, *The Botanic Garden*, p 188.

III

Five related prophecies are the product of the years 1794–5. These are: *Europe* (1794), *The Book of Urizen* (1794), *The Song of Los* (1795), *The Book of Ahania* (1795) and *The Book of Los* (1795). The Urizenic creation of the material world, really a dividing off from Eternity, is the subject of *The Book of Urizen*, itself a Urizenic 'book' whose plates are divided into two columns of numbered, pseudo-biblical verses. A fiercely ironic, parodic rewriting and revision of the Book of Genesis, yet in some ways a tragic reproduction of its limiting monotheism, *The Book of Urizen* may have been intended as the first book of Blake's projected 'Bible of Hell', announced at the end of *The Marriage*.

Urizen, as Gnostic demiurge, begins his career somewhat inauspiciously as 'a shadow of horror', a solitary, secretive power whose 'silent activity' reminds us of those 'places of religion' pinpointed by Oothoon:

> 4. Dark revolving in silent activity:
> Unseen in tormenting passions;
> An activity unknown and horrible;
> A self-contemplating shadow,
> In enormous labours occupied

(i. 4)

Clusters of participles and abstract nouns devoid of any concrete reference suggest a purely mental consciousness, a superego detaching itself from the rest of the psyche into 'I alone, even I!' (ii. 5), repressing hostile energies and passions. Dividing and limiting, Urizen establishes a world whose legitimating authority, inevitably, is a book, or rather *The* Book of Urizen, which proclaims the monologic dogma of 'One King, one God, one Law' (ii. 8).

A catastrophic yet dynamic separation has now occurred. The poem proceeds through vertiginous downfall and enormous cosmic wrenchings to a countermovement of laboured reparation which, ironically, results only in further division. The 'Eternals' mistakenly try to contain the horror by spurning it; Urizen is rent from the side of Los, whose loss of Eternity can never be redeemed through his energetic labours, creating, as they do, the mind-forged links of time and causality, whose terrible logic suggests a continuous movement away from Eternity. A human body emerges, complete with skull, writhing spine, ribs that shoot like 'a bending cavern', a heart, eyes, ears, nostrils and tongue – the caverned senses of fallen man, no

sooner created than already fallen, since it is Urizenic creation that
Los is compelled to undertake. Shrinking from his task, Los begins
to feel pity, which materializes as the female Enitharmon. We now
have sexual division. In a defensive reflex, the Eternals weave a
puritanical curtain round the pair, calling it Science. Los, echoing
Urizen's self-contemplating activity, begets 'his likeness,/On his own
divided image' (vi. 2). Eternity shudders. Enitharmon brings forth
Orc, and a new cycle, that of familial conflict, begins.

The poem's outcome is the Net of Religion; more specifically, the
Judaeo-Christian religion:

> A cold shadow follow'd behind him
> Like a spiders web, moist, cold, & dim
> Drawing out from his sorrowing soul
> The dungeon-like heaven dividing.
> Where ever the footsteps of Urizen
> Walk'd over the cities in sorrow.
>
> 7. Till a Web dark & cold, throughout all
> The tormented element stretch'd
> From the sorrows of Urizens soul
> And the Web is a Female in embrio
> None could break the Web, no wings of fire.
>
> 8. So twisted the cords, & so knotted
> The meshes: twisted like to the human brain
>
> 9. And all calld it, The Net of Religion

(viii. 6–9)

With dialectical irony, moist sorrow has metamorphosed into the
twisted cords and knotted meshes (reminding us of fishing-nets,
even fishers of men) of cruelty. Since Urizenic pity induces a
shrunken perception by freezing up energy, its grotesque combination of cruelty and pity is not perceived:

> 2. Till the shrunken eyes clouded over
> Discernd not the woven hipocrisy
> But the streaky slime in their heavens
> Brought together by narrowing perceptions
> Appeard transparent air . . .

(ix. 2)

The stated theme of Blake's mythological narrative is 'the primeval
Priests assum'd power', but in *Vala, or The Four Zoas*, begun
around 1797, the theme is no less than 'a cosmic history of Mankind
and his universe, from initial collapse and division among his primal

energies, to final regeneration'.[1] Whether or not *The Four Zoas* (one of whose early titles was *Vala or The Death and Judgement of the Ancient Man a DREAM of Nine Nights*) was also part of Blake's 'Bible of Hell' (a title found on the back of one of his drawings reads: 'The Bible of Hell, in Nocturnal Visions collected'), it belongs essentially to the Christian tradition of the 'divine epic', whose narrative scope was that of the Bible itself, stretching from the Creation to the Day of Judgement. The scheme of *The Four Zoas* is also a refinement of Hippocratic, medieval and Elizabethan psychology, which explained mental illness as an imbalance of the body's four humours. The humours correspond to the 'Zoas' as follows: melancholy, which is cold and wet (Tharmas: water); blood, which is hot, the seat of passion (Luvah/Orc: fire); phlegm, the cold humour of rational self-possession (Urizen: air); and choler, which is dry, the seat of wrath (Urthona/Los: earth). Attempts by each of the four Zoas to usurp power results in war, division and sickness in the Eternal Man. This parallels in some ways a schizophrenic psychosis, where the 'system of functions . . . is shattered into a multiplicity of warring functions . . . the various parts of the system function in relative independence, and are apt to come perpetually in conflict with one another.'[2] Only in Night IX is unity restored following the Man's command:

> In Enmity & war first weakend then in stern repentance
> They must renew their brightness & their disorganizd functions
> Again reorganize till they resume the image of the human . . .
>
> (ix. 370–72)

The opening dialogue between Tharmas and Enion, his emanation (each 'Zoa' has his female emanation), is filled with gloomy terror. Tharmas complains to Enion:

> Why wilt thou Examine every little fibre of my soul
> Spreading them out before the Sun like Stalks of flax to dry
> The infant joy is beautiful but its anatomy
> Horrible Ghast & Deadly nought shalt thou find in it
> But Death Despair & Everlasting brooding Melancholy
> Thou wilt go mad with horror if thou dost Examine thus
> Every moment of my secret hours . . .
>
> (i. 48–54)

1 Alicia Ostriker, ed., *William Blake: The Complete Poems*, Harmondsworth, 1977, p 921.
2 William McDougall, *An Outline of Abnormal Psychology*, 2nd edn, London, 1933, pp 395–6.

How does Tharmas know that Enion is doing this? To ask such a question presupposes that Tharmas is an ego-bounded psyche, and that he and Enion are two separate people. The dialogue throws doubt on this. Tharmas's identity has become vulnerable, it seems, because his ego boundaries have collapsed, leaving his inner self unprotected; he imagines that Enion has total access to his innermost thoughts and that she is thus able to lay them bare before the world. Later, Enion confesses that, having murdered the 'Emanations' of Tharmas, she now finds 'that all those Emanations were my Childrens Souls' (i. 165). Tharmas and Enion begin to appear like divided parts of one self speaking as separate selves; in which case the dialogue looks more and more like a schizophrenic persecution anxiety. One defence against such an anxiety is to create a false self. Enion draws out Tharmas's Spectre, which assumes the form of a stern superego detached from what have come to be regarded as sinful libidinous drives:

> If thou hast sinnd & art polluted know that I am pure
> And unpolluted & will bring to rigid strict account
> All thy past deeds . . .

> (i. 130–32)

Paraphrasing the narrative of *The Four Zoas* (much of it expands the Urizen myth, told in *The Book of Urizen*) serves little purpose; not only was it continually revised, to be abandoned in its incomplete manuscript state, but – as some commentators have noticed – it resists interpretation by traditional critical methods, for the poem is not the work of an authoritative, stable ego, but of a fluid and divided one. The act of reading the poem, according to one critic, 'desubstantializes the independently existing Newtonian reader'.[1] Nevertheless, even the un-deconstructed reader can appreciate the imaginative power and critical force of certain episodes and passages, such as the building of the Mundane Shell in Night II, lines 135–286, or Urizen's exploration of the Abyss in Night VI, lines 72–228, where, unable to find a fixed vantage point for Lockian observation and objectivity, he desperately 'regulates' his books, hoping to fix 'many a Science in the deep' (vi. 187), like a one-man army of moral philosophers and historians. The metaphorical landscape is Miltonic and eludes any topographical identification or spatial orientation. In the 'Abyss' which Urizen has unknowingly created, he beholds 'ruind spirits once his children & the children of Luvah':

---

1 Donald Ault, 'Re-Visioning *The Four Zoas*', in Nelson Hilton and Thomas A. Vogler, eds, *Unnam'd Forms: Blake and Textuality*, Berkeley, Calif., 1986, p 130.

> Beyond the bounds of their own self their senses cannot penetrate
> As the tree knows not what is outside of its leaves & bark
> And yet it drinks the summer joy & fears the winter sorrow
> So in the regions of the grave none knows his dark compeer
> Tho he partakes of his dire woes & mutual returns the pang
> The throb the dolor the convulsion in soul sickening woes
>
> (vi. 94–9)

A temptation here might be to read off meanings like answers to clues – to provide empirical references. Thus, if the 'Abyss' equals the lower-class environment, and 'ruind spirits' refer to all the burnt-out revolutionaries and radicals, then the passage could be describing their demoralized, schizoid withdrawal under Pitt's repression in the late 1790s. However plausible, this interpretation cannot explain the poetic effect of the passage, and many others like it, where comparison and metaphor continually suggest and yet continually defer the possibility of their being tied down to such empirical points of reference. Both the somewhat anthropomorphized tree and the metaphorical 'regions of the grave' are brought in as comparisons, the latter returning us to an 'Abyss' that is itself a metaphor. In other words, we keep moving from one metaphor to another. Nothing is ever 'merely' metaphorical either: the tree's bounded sensitivity acquires its own strangely vivid suggestiveness.

The meeting of Urizen and Orc in Night VII jolts the poem into dramatic life. Orc, a Christlike and Prometheus-like figure, is all passion, wholly incapable of *not* being sensitive to the suffering around him. 'What dost thou in this deep', he asks Urizen. 'I rage in the deep for Lo my feet & hands are naild to the burning rock' (vii. 69–70). He continues:

> . . . yet thou dost fixd obdurate brooding sit
> Writing thy books. Anon a cloud filld with a waste of snows
> Covers thee still obdurate still resolvd & writing still
> Tho rocks roll oer thee tho floods pour tho winds black as the Sea
> Cut thee in gashes tho the blood pours down around thy ankles
> Freezing thy feet to the hard rock still thy pen obdurate
> Traces the wonders of Futurity in horrible fear of the future
>
> (vii. 80–86)

Urizen's devotion to writing might begin to seem almost heroic were it not for his reply, breathtaking in its unyielding, unhearing obtuseness, and one of the best moments in the poem: 'Urizen answerd Read my books explore my Constellations' (vii. 89). Posing as science, Urizen's writing is merely a shield against reality.

Blake wrote two more epics: *Milton*, completed in 1804, and

*Jerusalem*, completed in 1820. Whereas *The Four Zoas* has a strong narrative interest, in *Jerusalem* narrative progression gives way to a somewhat cyclic schematism. Jerusalem's lament, 'Then was a time of love: O why is it passed away!' (xx. 41), recurs in one form or another throughout the poem. Admission of guilt, an avowed sense of shame, despair of redemption and the impulse to confess afflict Albion right from Chapter 1, so that his repentance and conversion in Chapter 4 come as no surprise. The theme of Jerusalem and Albion derives to some extent from the current mythology of 'British Israelism', yet unlike Richard Brothers, who believed that the ten lost tribes had settled in ancient Britain, Blake sees Britain itself as 'the Primitive Seat of the Patriarchal Religion'; Jerusalem is thus 'the Emanation of the Giant Albion'. The poem articulates a profound faith in the change from a society of cruel exploiters, 'natural' enemies and competing monads to a society of loving brothers and sisters. It is a fitting conclusion to the work of an artist whose ideological and artistic struggles were waged under conditions of insecurity, fear of persecution and frequent poverty. Like the blossom-seeking 'Merry Sparrow' we return, at last, to a world of Organized Innocence.

# 5

## WORDSWORTH

### J. H. Alexander

I

The most celebrated poem of the British Romantic period is certainly the untitled piece popularly known as 'Wordsworth's "Daffodils"'. It is one of the handful of poems that almost everybody who reads poetry at all thinks they know. The picture of Wordsworth most readers will take away from 'I wandered lonely as a Cloud' is that of a solitary man at home with the pleasures afforded by the contemplation of nature. This is not essentially a false impression, though it is a simplified and partial one. We know that when Wordsworth actually saw the daffodils, his sister Dorothy was with him: her journal includes an account of the occasion,[1] which contributed so much to her brother's poem that the lyric probably ought to be accounted a joint production. But Keats was to call the older poet an egotist,[2] and this poem is a small-scale example of Wordsworth's absorbing interest in the way that his own past experiences interacted with his present mood.

His long autobiographical poem *The Prelude* is an infinitely more complex investigation of the same area, exploring ways in which 'spots of time', moments enshrining ordinary but strangely impressive events,

> with distinct pre-eminence retain
> A renovating Virtue, whence, depressed
> By false opinion and contentious thought,
> Or aught of heavier and more deadly weight
> In trival occupations, and the round

---

1 *Journals of Dorothy Wordsworth*, ed. Mary Moorman, Oxford, 1971, p 109 (Thursday 15 April 1802).
2 *The Letters of John Keats 1814–21*, ed. Hyder E. Rollins, 2 vols, Cambridge, 1958, i. 223 (3 February 1818, to J. H. Reynolds).

> Of ordinary intercourse, our minds
> Are nourished and invisibly repaired . . .
>
> (xi. 258–65: 1805 version)[1]

The particular 'spot of time' that Wordsworth chooses to introduce immediately after these remarks involves a boyhood encounter, during a horseback outing near Penrith, with the name of a murderer carved in the turf where he had been hanged. The narrative continues:

> forthwith I left the spot
> And, reascending the bare Common, saw
> A naked Pool that lay beneath the hills,
> The Beacon on the summit, and more near,
> A Girl who bore a Pitcher on her head
> And seemed with difficult steps to force her way
> Against the blowing wind. It was, in truth,
> An ordinary sight; but I should need
> Colours and words that are unknown to man
> To paint the visionary dreariness
> Which, while I looked all round for my lost guide,
> Did at that time invest the naked Pool,
> The Beacon on the lonely Eminence,
> The Woman, and her garments vexed and tossed
> By the strong wind.

Wordsworth goes on to recall revisiting the common repeatedly in young manhood with his sister and his wife-to-be:

> When, in a blessed season
> With those two dear Ones, to my heart so dear,
> When in the blessed time of early love,
> Long afterwards, I roamed about
> In daily presence of this very scene,
> Upon the naked pool and dreary crags,
> And on the melancholy Beacon, fell
> The spirit of pleasure and youth's golden gleam;
> And think ye not with radiance more divine
> From these remembrances, and from the power
> They left behind? So feeling comes in aid
> Of feeling, and diversity of strength
> Attends us, if but once we have been strong.
>
> (xi. 302–28)

Thus the strange, dreary, naked power sensed in the original experi-

---

1 Wordsworth's poems are quoted from the Oxford Authors *William Wordsworth*, ed. Stephen Gill, Oxford and New York, 1984.

ence of what to any other observer would have been unremarkable, 'An ordinary sight', lends spiritual depth to a later and very different experience. By exploring such incidents from the past, and their interaction with each other and with the present, the poet seeks to investigate 'the hiding-places of [his] power' (336), the foundations on which his life is built.

Those experiences near Penrith are of a different order from the linking of past and present in 'I wandered lonely as a Cloud', but in both works the imagination penetrates to the essence of a windswept scene: in the one, the daffodils and the waves danced, and the poet's heart dances with them in recollection; in the other, a bleak landscape is the background for the exercise of youthful vigours. The passage from *The Prelude* may suggest a poet capable of more visionary grandeur (and of more sociability) than 'Wordsworth's "Daffodils"' reveals.

Several critics have emphasized this visionary or 'apocalyptic' side of Wordsworth, his increasing tendency to exalt the self-sustaining imaginative mind as 'lord and master' at the expense of 'outward sense', which is 'but the obedient servant of her will' (*Prelude*, xi. 271–3). Apart from the later books of *The Prelude*, the *locus classicus* for the visionary Wordsworth is the poem generally known as the Immortality Ode. In this, the most Blakian of his poems, Wordsworth unusually adopts a myth to express his conviction that the child has more immediate access to spiritual reality than the adult. In mythical terms, the child comes into the world of time 'trailing clouds of glory' from a previous eternal existence. Gradually the world makes the child forget its spiritual origins, and the adult has to be content with glimpses:

> Hence, in a season of calm weather,
>     Though inland far we be,
> Our Souls have sight of that immortal sea
>     Which brought us hither,
>     Can in a moment travel thither,
> And see the Children sport upon the shore,
> And hear the mighty waters rolling evermore.

                                                    (164–70)

Other critics have distrusted this visionary Wordsworth and have tended to emphasize the poet of 'The Ruined Cottage' and some of the *Lyrical Ballads* and the other shorter poems, with their intense interest in ordinary humanity. For them Wordsworth is at his greatest when he observes faithfully and respectfully men and women hitherto generally deemed unworthy of serious treatment in English poetry.[1] Perhaps the most striking of all such observations is to be found in 'The Matron of Jedborough and Her Husband', where the paralysed husband follows his wife's dancing with his uncertain eyes:

> Ah! see her helpless Charge! enclosed
> Within himself, as seems; composed;
> To fear of loss, and hope of gain,
> The strife of happiness and pain,
> Utterly dead! yet, in the guise
> Of little Infants, when their eyes
> Begin to follow to and fro
> The persons that before them go,
> He tracks her motions, quick or slow.
> Her buoyant Spirit can prevail
> Where common cheerfulness would fail:
> She strikes upon him with the heat
> Of July Suns; he feels it sweet;
> An animal delight though dim!
> 'Tis all that now remains for him!
>
> (48–62)

So honest is Wordsworth in this poem that he goes on to note the matron's history of mental disturbance.

The delighted observer of the natural world; the solitary investigator of his own mind past and present; the brother and husband; the visionary apocalyptic; the poet of humanity: all these are vital components of Wordsworth the major poet. But one crucial element remains to be added, and that is to be the main subject of this essay.

## II

It will come as a surprise to many readers, even those familiar with Wordsworth's major poetry, to learn that in 1833 he told an American visitor, Orville Dewey, that 'although he was known to the world only as a poet, he had given twelve hours thought to the conditions and prospects of society, for one to poetry.'[2] The assertion can hardly have been literally true; but it suggests vividly the extent to which a profound concern with social and political theory underlines many of his poems. It is significant that at the beginning of *The Prelude*, of the topics considered as possible subjects Wordsworth

1 This had not been the case in the Scottish tradition: witness most notably Robert Burns, to whom Wordsworth acknowledged he owed a massive debt.
2 Quoted in F. M. Todd, *Politics and the Poet: A Study of Wordsworth*, London, 1957, p [11].

gives most attention to the progress of 'the Soul/Of Liberty' in political history (i. 185–219). The poetry of Wordsworth's 'great decade' (1797–1807) is flanked by two major political prose pamphlets: *A Letter to the Bishop of Llandaff*, written in 1793 (but not published until 1876, a quarter of a century after the author's death); and *The Convention of Cintra*, begun in 1808 and completed in 1809 (the year in which it was published). The main part of this essay will characterize the two pamphlets briefly, setting them in the context of Wordsworth's career, and will go on to approach some of the major poems by tracing in them the leading socio-political ideas discussed in the pamphlets.

When he wrote *Llandaff*, probably in the spring of 1793, Wordsworth was almost twenty-three. He had grown up in the Lake District and attended the ancient grammar school at Hawkshead; he had spent three years at Cambridge, and in 1790 he had travelled through France in the first enthusiastic celebration of the Revolution; and he had returned to France for a year (1791–2), in the course of which he had associated with revolutionary activists. In 1793 he was back in England, which soon found itself at war with France and bitterly divided internally between those who supported the Revolution, as Wordsworth passionately did, and those who endorsed the Pitt government's equally passionate counter-revolutionary ideologies. *Llandaff* was an outspoken, somewhat Rousseauistic, and probably potentially treasonable, contribution to 'the science of government . . . the most fruitful field of human knowledge' (640–42), an anti-monarchical response to the erstwhile liberal Bishop of Llandaff, Richard Watson, who, 'thoroughly shocked at the course of events in France . . . hurriedly composed an indignant protest, larded with fervent praise of the British Constitution' in an appendix to a published sermon on *The Wisdom and Goodness of God in having made both Rich and Poor*.[1] The complacency of the bishop's argument may be gathered from the following sentence from the appendix:[2]

Other nations may deluge their land with blood in struggling for liberty and equality; but let it never be forgotten by ourselves, and let us impress the observation upon the hearts of our children, that we are in possession of both; of as much of both, as can be consistent with the end for which civil society was introduced amongst mankind.

1 *The Prose Works of William Wordsworth*, ed. W. J. B. Owen and Jane Worthington Smyser, 3 vols, Oxford, 1974, i. 19. References to *Llandaff*, *Cintra* and the other prose works are to the line numbers in this edition.
2 Quoted in *ibid.*, i. 63.

In the mid-1790s Wordsworth suffered what we would nowadays call a mental breakdown, caused in part by the development of the French Revolution from an initial popular emancipatory movement which British liberals could wholeheartedly endorse, to the 'Terror' – when the guillotine was thirsty for any blood suspected of being tainted with counter-revolutionary tendencies. His sister Dorothy was instrumental in helping him in Dorset to re-establish links with the natural and human world of his childhood in a valuable personal therapy; and after a period of close association with Coleridge in 1797–8, at Nether Stowey in Somerset, that resulted in the *Lyrical Ballads*, and a winter spent in Germany, he retired with Dorothy to the Lake District at Christmas 1799 to pursue his poetic career and comment on political developments from a distance. The 'great decade' saw the composition of Wordsworth's major poems: the *Lyrical Ballads*, published as a single volume in 1798 and in an extended two-volume form in 1800, with which are to be associated in particular 'The Ruined Cottage', written in 1797,[1] and 'Peter Bell', written in 1798; *The Prelude*, begun in 1798 and completed in 1805, but published in an extensively revised and generally less vital form only after the poet's death in 1850; and the *Poems, in Two Volumes*, published in 1807.

The *Cintra* pamphlet (which Coleridge asserted had been maturing as something of a joint conception for twelve years before its 1808–9 composition)[2] is a very different affair from *Llandaff*. For one thing, whereas *Llandaff* is an attractive, brisk and eminently readable (though incompletely preserved) document, adopting a plain style influenced by that of the leading radical Thomas Paine, *Cintra* is long, somewhat repetitive and couched in a portentous neo-Miltonic prose style. Although Wordsworth did worry about the possible legal repercussions of one passage, *Cintra* is emphatically not in the least treasonable. Wordsworth is now an ardent Tory patriot, stirred to assert the basic principles that make for national identity by what he saw as the slighting of Britain's Portuguese allies in the terms of the agreement concluded by the British generals with the Napoleonic invaders of the Peninsula. The title-page asserts that the publication

1 'The Ruined Cottage' was not published as a separate entity during Wordsworth's lifetime; consequently, it does not appear in many editions of Wordsworth, but it can be found in the Oxford Authors *William Wordsworth*, in Jonathan Wordsworth's *The Music of Humanity*, in his advance text of the poem for the Cambridge *Wordsworth* and in the Penguin Poetry Library *William Wordsworth*: see Bibliography, p 466–9.
2 *Collected Letters of Samuel Taylor Coleridge*, ed. Earl Leslie Griggs, 6 vols, Oxford, 1956–71, iii. 216.

brings the Convention of Cintra 'to the test of those Principles, by which alone the Independence and Freedom of Nations can be Preserved or Recovered'. These basic principles, Wordsworth asserts at the beginning of the work, have been adhered to since the Revolution by 'the body of the people' (80), among whom he himself is evidently proud to be numbered. Originally they had opposed the war with France because that country seemed to be liberating itself from ancient tyranny, and the early years of the Revolution remain in some ways an attractive model for nations seeking liberation (4502–6). It was in 1797, when the French invaded Switzerland, that their allegiance necessarily shifted:[1]

Their conduct was herein consistent: they proved that they kept their eyes steadily fixed upon principles; for, though there was a shifting or transfer of hostility in their minds as far as regarded persons, they only combated the same enemy opposed to them under a different shape; and that enemy was the spirit of selfish tyranny and lawless ambition.

(83–9)

Wordsworth's position has undoubtedly altered in the years since *Llandaff*: he has abandoned his early rationalism, his readiness to accept a temporary moral coarsening as the price of political innovation, and his rejection of central elements in the British constitution. But there is much truth in his assertion that the essential change has been in external circumstances rather than in his own fundamental beliefs, and several of the most profound emphases of *Llandaff* recur in *Cintra*, modified in tone and application by the political and poetic developments of the fifteen intervening years.

The full title of *Llandaff* announces the pamphlet to be 'by a Republican'. Wordsworth's republicanism was influenced *inter alia* by the English seventeenth-century political writers whom he had probably read in France, by his own experience of the Revolution, and by the classical authors of the Roman republic;[2] but it had its origin in the comparatively egalitarian Lake District where he grew up. It was this upbringing, as he explains in *The Prelude*, reinforced

---

1 Coleridge's 'France: An Ode', of 1798, offers in its fourth stanza a parallel recantation to Wordsworth's:

> Forgive me, Freedom! O forgive those dreams!
> I hear thy voice, I hear thy loud lament,
> From bleak Helvetia's icy caverns sent –
> . . . forgive me, that I cherished
> One thought that ever blessed your cruel foes!

2 *Prose*, i. 23; *Llandaff*, 524–5.

by the academic egalitarianism of Cambridge, where he soon dismissed the 'glitter' and 'dazzle' of fashionable undergraduate circles (iii. 94–5), that prepared him to sympathize with the French Revolution:

> For, born in a poor District, and which yet
> Retaineth more of ancient homeliness,
> Manners erect, and frank simplicity,
> Than any other nook of English Land,
> It was my fortune scarcely to have seen
> Through the whole tenor of my School-day time
> The face of one, who, whether Boy or Man,
> Was vested with attention or respect
> Through claims of wealth or blood. Nor was it least
> Of many debts which afterwards I owed
> To Cambridge and an academic life,
> That something there was holden up to view
> Of a Republic, where all stood thus far
> Upon equal ground, that they were brothers all
> In honour, as in one community
>             . . .
>
> It could not be
> But that one tutored thus, who had been formed
> To thought and moral feelings in the way
> This story hath described, should look with awe
> Upon the faculties of Man, receive
> Gladly the highest promises, and hail
> As best the government of equal rights
> And individual worth.

(ix. 218–49)

The first book of *The Prelude* contains a good-natured parody of the card-game in Pope's aristocratic mock-heroic poem *The Rape of the Lock*: the cards undergo confusion of rank, and both royalty and upstart plebeians suffer grave indignities, all in one of those 'lowly Cottages' of 'plain and seemly countenance' that punningly 'dealt out . . . plain comforts' (i. 525–62). The remarkable subsequent lines place the whole matter in an awesomely deflating natural perspective:

> Meanwhile, abroad
> The heavy rain was falling, or the frost
> Raged bitterly, with keen and silent tooth,
> And, interrupting oft the impassioned game,
> From Esthwaite's neighbouring Lake the splitting ice,
> While it sank down towards the water, sent,
> Among the meadows and the hills, its long

> And dismal yellings, like the noise of wolves
> When they are howling round the Bothnic Main.

(i. 562–70)

In the following book Wordsworth goes on to explain how

>                the pride of strength,
> And the vain-glory of superior skill
> Were interfused with objects which subdued
> And tempered them, and gradually produced
> A quiet independence of the heart . . .

(ii. 69–73)

Brought up thus, Wordsworth, while reverencing the great heroes of the past, found nothing to dazzle him 'in the regal Sceptre, and the pomp/Of Orders and Degrees' (ix. 201–217).

Although Wordsworth's anti-monarchical and anti-aristocratic convictions faded with the years, he remained a republican in the wider sense that he trusted the instincts of the common person (while deeply distrusting and fearing the mass instincts of the radical 'mob'). At no time had he any time for the views of a fashionable metropolitan élite. When *Lyrical Ballads* appeared, several reviewers were uneasy at what they (with some justice) took to be the subversive political overtones in the new serious sympathy with which figures hitherto deemed marginal in society were presented, and a decade later Wordsworth believed that *Cintra* would 'create me a world of enemies, and call forth the old yell of Jacobinism'.[1] The two political pamphlets allow us to explore different facets of this fundamental egalitarianism, which lies close to the heart of many of Wordsworth's finest poems.

III

Among the criticisms that Wordsworth levels at the Bishop of Llandaff is one prompted by the cleric's sympathy for the fate of Louis XVI:

At a period big with the fate of the human race, I am sorry that you attach so much importance to the personal sufferings of the late royal martyr and that an anxiety for the issue of the present convulsions should not have

---

1 *The Letters of William and Dorothy Wordsworth*, ed. Ernest de Selincourt, 2nd edn, ii (*The Middle Years, Part I: 1806–1811*), rev. Mary Moorman, Oxford, 1969, p 312.

prevented you from joining in the idle cry of modish lamentation which has resounded from the court to the cottage.

(52–6)

Wordsworth always opposed the 'modish', the fashionable, in form and concept (and here he seems to acknowledge that at any rate some cottages will be tainted by courtly falseness). In *Cintra* he recognizes that the most difficult readers to convince will be those 'who are mere slaves of curiosity, calling perpetually for something new' (250–51), and he reverts again and again in that work to fundamental, enduring human feelings: 'the common feelings of [a man's] social nature' (1754–5) and 'the supremacy of [men's] common nature' (2686).

The word 'common' is among Wordsworth's most significant. On occasion it is used in a pejorative sense,[1] but it is usually a resonant, positive, campaigning word, reminding the reader of the daring of this poet's belief in the ordinary as opposed to the modish. In his 1819 revision of 'Peter Bell' he proclaims:

> The common growth of mother-earth
> Suffices me – her tears, her mirth,
> Her humblest mirth and tears.

(133–5)

He wishes to believe and demonstrate (though he may not always succeed in doing both of these) that the ordinary can satisfy the demands of the most ardent imaginative energies, that the paradise which he seeks in setting up house in Grasmere, in the Lake District, will be 'the growth of common day' ('Home at Grasmere', MS B, 1001), for it was in this same region that as a child he had experienced

> The admiration and the love, the life
> In common things; the endless store of things
> Rare, or at least so seeming, every day
> Found all about me in one neighbourhood . . .

(*Prelude*, i. 117–20)

In formal and stylistic matters Wordsworth even teases his fashion-

---

1 The most notable use of 'common' in a derogatory sense occurs in 'Hart-Leap Well', 170. In the 1850 version of *The Prelude* Wordsworth twice substitutes another word for 1805's derogatory 'common' (1805: ii. 319, 405), suggesting that at one stage in his career he may have wished to develop his characteristic use more exclusively.

able readers: the Advertisement to the 1798 *Lyrical Ballads* imagines readers 'accustomed to the gaudiness and inane phraseology of many modern writers' (fashionable writers of the time involved in the dying throes of post-Augustan poetic diction) frequently having 'to struggle with feelings of strangeness and aukwardness: they will look round [in *Lyrical Ballads*] for poetry, and will be induced to enquire by what species of courtesy these attempts can be permitted to assume that title' (11–14). Wordsworth and Coleridge reclaim in this volume the right of great poetry to use the simplest language, as the 'elder writers' (such as the authors of the classic ballads) had done, with precise, pathetic or haunting effect. Such poetry, the Preface to the 1800 *Lyrical Ballads* argues, will be 'in its nature well adapted to interest mankind permanently' (553–4), being immune from passing fashions in sentiment and expression.

The challenge to polite readers to examine their prejudices is evident in several of the *Lyrical Ballads*. It is there very explicitly in 'Simon Lee, the Old Huntsman' and implicitly in 'Michael': in both poems Wordsworth makes a point of not gratifying his readers' lust for sensational stories. It can be seen too in 'A Poet's Epitaph', with its satirical characterization of fashionable professions, and in 'The Brothers', with its anti-tourist sentiments. But probably the most sustained assault on the reader's expectations comes in 'The Idiot Boy'. Not only is the language of the simplest, descending even to Johnny's sub-linguistic burring, but the central figure is a child (children had been confined strictly to the nursery by Augustan literary convention); and not only a child, but a mentally handicapped child; and not only a mentally handicapped child, but one living in the country far from the metropolitan centre of fashionable taste, and of much humbler stock than most of Wordsworth's anticipated readership. To assert that a subject marginalized in so many ways is actually of central importance is a deliberately shocking act, though one undertaken with great good-humour and glee. The final stanza sums up the humour, the mock-heroic narrative element, the sympathetic, fussy narrator, the unflinching understanding of the actualities of mental handicap, and the conceptual freshness and splendour that Wordsworth discerns in one whose essential imaginative life is, as he put it, '*hidden with God*':

> And thus to Betty's question, he
> Made answer, like a traveller bold,
> (His very words I give to you,)
> 'The cocks did crow to-whoo, to-whoo,

> And the sun did shine so cold.'
> – Thus answered Johnny in his glory,
> And that was all his travel's story.

Johnny as perpetual child shows that spontaneous 'mystical' response to the natural world which the adult can glimpse only in a more distant, meditative, 'sacramental' manner.[1]

Wordsworth's retirement to the Lake District involved the toleration (by middle-class standards) of financially straitened circumstances by himself and his family until his acceptance of the office of Distributor of Stamps for Westmorland in 1813.[2] In the opening exordium of *The Prelude* he refers to Grasmere as his 'hermitage' (i. 115), with connotations of dedicated austere seclusion, and in his discussion of Cambridge two books later he recalls with a good deal of admiration the venerable scholars of former times,

> When all who dwelt within these famous Walls
> Led in abstemiousness a studious life,
> . . .
> Trained up, through piety and zeal, to prize
> Spare diet, patient labour, and plain weeds

(iii. 461–70)

– the contrast being with fashionable undergraduate life described in terms of alluring surface attraction and serpentine temptation (the reader is referred by implication to the fall of Eve in *Paradise Lost*):

> The surfaces of artificial life
> And manners finely spun, the delicate race
> Of colours, lurking, gleaming up and down
> Through that state arras woven with silk and gold;
> This wily interchange of snaky hues,
> Willingly and unwillingly revealed . . .

(iii. 590–95)

To praise virtuous and dedicated abstinence is quite different from glorifying the grinding poverty which enslaved so many in his time, a far cry from his own genteel straitened circumstances. In *Llandaff* Wordsworth recognizes that 'the extremes of poverty and riches have

1 For these terms see David Ferry, *The Limits of Mortality: An Essay on Wordsworth's Major Poems*, Middletown, Conn., 1959, *passim*.
2 This post was by no means a sinecure, but it was the basis of one of the main charges levelled against Wordsworth, as presumed turncoat, by the poets of the younger generation.

a necessary tendency to corrupt the human heart' (436–8), and towards the end of *The Prelude* he sees that

> labour in excess and poverty
> From day to day pre-occupy the ground
> Of the affections, and to Nature's self
> Oppose a deeper nature . . .

(xii. 197–200)

making love impossible. But this is not to agree with those polite theorists who argue that the growth of love

>                                        requires
> Retirement, leisure, language purified
> By manners thoughtful and elaborate,
> That whoso feels such passion in excess
> Must live within the very light and air
> Of elegances that are made by man.

(xii. 188–93)

Although Wordsworth is in general far from being an Augustan, there is often a good deal of the Augustan avoiding of extremes and a cultivation of Horatian detachment in his political and social thinking. Extreme poverty and luxury are always to be attacked, whereas a healthy but not extreme abstinence will favour both virtuous living and an art immune from the passing concerns of metropolitan fashion.

IV

An argument central to both *Llandaff* and *Cintra* is that rulers should take care to maintain contact with the experience of ordinary people. This conviction underlies the earlier pamphlet's attack on the institution of the monarchy. According to *Llandaff*, it is not modish, but legitimate, to feel 'sorry that the prejudice and weakness of mankind have made it necessary to force an individual into an unnatural situation, which requires more than human talents and human virtues, and at the same time precludes him from attaining even a moderate knowledge of common life and from feeling a particular share in the interests of mankind' (80–85). *Cintra* develops the theme already touched on in *Llandaff* that the general on the field of battle acts, just as much as the private citizen does, 'under the obligation of his human and social nature' (46–7).

In an eloquent passage Wordsworth attacks the blindness to basic moral obligations of 'the majority of men, who are usually found in high stations under old governments' (3466–7). He goes on:

The progress of their own country, and of the other nations of the world, in civilization, in true refinement, in science, in religion, in morals, and in all the real wealth of humanity, might indeed be quicker, and might correspond more happily with the wishes of the benevolent, – if Governors better understood the rudiments of nature as studied in the walks of common life; if they were men who had themselves felt every strong emotion 'inspired by nature and by fortune taught;' and could calculate upon the force of the grander passions.

(3488–96)

One of the aims of several of Wordsworth's finest poems is to educate those in authority in just this way. 'The Old Cumberland Beggar', written in 1797 and included in the 1800 *Lyrical Ballads*, is unusually open in its didacticism. After tellingly describing the old beggar's laborious progress on his rural circuit, the narrator is made to exclaim:

> But deem not this man useless. – Statesmen! ye
> Who are so restless in your wisdom, ye
> Who have a broom still ready in your hands
> To rid the world of nuisances; ye proud,
> Heart-swoln, while in your pride ye contemplate
> Your talents, power, and wisdom, deem him not
> A burthen of the earth. 'Tis Nature's law
> That none, the meanest of created things,
> Of forms created the most vile and brute,
> The dullest or most noxious, should exist
> Divorced from good, a spirit and pulse of good,
> A life and soul to every mode of being
> Inseparably linked. While thus he creeps
> From door to door, the Villagers in him
> Behold a record which together binds
> Past deeds and offices of charity
> Else unremembered, and so keeps alive
> The kindly mood in hearts which lapse of years,
> And that half-wisdom half-experience gives
> Make slow to feel, and by sure steps resign
> To selfishness and cold oblivious cares.

(67–87)

Some readers have felt that this passage, which continues for almost a hundred lines, is crudely expressed; but it is full of words that are to recur frequently, with subtle variation of context and emphasis, in Wordsworth's best poetry: 'meanest', 'forms', 'spirit', 'life', 'soul', 'being', 'mood', 'hearts' and 'feel'. Against the restless, interfering, self-admiring tidiness of government officials with their schemes for workhouses, and against cold selfishness, are set the inner spirit and pulse of this decrepit man and his vital usefulness in preserving social relationships. In *Llandaff*, four years earlier, Wordsworth had envisaged the abolition of mendicancy (460–63). Now in 1797 his humane egalitarianism may be seen as moving in a more conservationist and ultimately conservative direction; the conservatism being founded on a catholic understanding of usefulness which is essential if a society is to be truly civilized.

In the majestic blank-verse narrative 'Michael', written three years later, another superficially unattractive countryman, the shepherd of the title, is implicitly recommended to the reader as worthy of the most sympathetic and intelligent attention; but in this case the explicit exhortation to politicians, or a politician, is to be found not in the poem itself but in a letter from Wordsworth to the Whig leader Charles James Fox. The whole document will repay careful reading, but for present purposes it is enough to note that Fox is being educated in the importance for 'small independent *proprietors*' of a modest holding of land, under threat from apparently progressive rural policies: 'Their little tract of land serves as a kind of permanent rallying point for their domestic feelings, as a tablet upon which they are written which makes them objects of memory in a thousand instances when they would otherwise be forgotten', and consequently it preserves 'the bonds of domestic feeling' which are at the heart of a nation's life.[1] This is how Michael experiences these feelings:

> Fields, where with chearful spirits he had breathed
> The common air; the hills, which he so oft
> Had climbed with vigorous steps; which had impressed
> So many incidents upon his mind
> Of hardship, skill or courage, joy or fear;
> Which like a book preserved the memory
> Of the dumb animals, whom he had saved,
> Had fed or sheltered, linking to such acts,
> So grateful in themselves, the certainty
> Of honorable gain; these fields, these hills
> Which were his living Being, even more
> Than his own Blood – what could they less? had laid
> Strong hold on his affections, were to him

---

1 *The Letters of William and Dorothy Wordsworth*, ed. Ernest de Selincourt, 2nd edn, i (*The Early Years: 1787–1805*), rev. Chester L. Shaver, Oxford, 1967, pp 312–15.

> A pleasurable feeling of blind love,
> The pleasure which there is in life itself.
>
> (65–79)

In *The Prelude* Wordsworth recalls how during his time at Cambridge

> those spiritual Men,
> Even the great Newton's own etherial Self,
> Seemed humbled in these precincts, thence to be
> The more beloved, invested here with tasks
> Of life's plain business, as a daily garb;
> Dictators at the plough, a change that left
> All genuine admiration unimpaired.
>
> (iii. 269–75)

Those closing lines refer to Cincinnatus, who, it is said, was at the plough when summoned to assume the dictatorship of Rome. The importance of political activists and leaders keeping in touch with humble life is a central theme of Wordsworth's characterization later in the poem of the French revolutionary soldier Beaupuy:

> By birth he ranked
> With the most noble, but unto the poor
> Among mankind he was in service bound
> As by some tie invisible, oaths professed
> To a religious Order. Man he loved
> As Man, and to the mean and the obscure,
> And all the homely in their homely works,
> Transferred a courtesy which had no air
> Of condescension, but did rather seem
> A passion and a gallantry, like that
> Which he, a Soldier, in his idler day
> Had payed to Woman.
>
> (ix. 309–20)

It was because Napoleon lacked this ability to relate to common life, this understanding that 'Wisdom doth live with children round her knees', that Wordsworth grieved for him ('I grieved for Buonaparte', 9). His own ideal 'Happy Warrior' (thought to be based partly on Beaupuy, as well as on Nelson and on Wordsworth's sailor brother John) stands in significant contrast: though formed to cope with 'storm and turbulence', he

> Is yet a Soul whose master bias leans
> To home-felt pleasures and to gentle scenes . . .
>
> ('Character of the Happy Warrior', 57–60)

The degree of explicitness varies; but, in nearly all of Wordsworth's major poems, genteel readers are being educated, at least by implication: and what they most need to learn is the virtuous dignity evident in many of society's humblest members.

V

Wordsworth's high estimation of the domestic and local affections, and his concern for their preservation at a time when their traditional embodiments were under threat, helps to explain the emphasis in the political pamphlets and in the poetry on the 'moral'. In *Llandaff* he sees that the violent events inevitable during a time of revolutionary struggle 'must of necessity confuse the ideas of morality and contract the benign exertion of the best affections of the human heart'. 'Political virtues are developed at the expence of moral ones', but in course of time the 'mild and social virtues' will return (110–18). While rejecting such concessions to revolutionary processes, *Cintra* has at its centre a celebration of this morality of social relationship, adding to it the relationship between present and past and future. The peasant is intimately linked with 'the soil of which he is the growth'. Hence:

These sensations are a social inheritance to him; more important, as he is precluded from luxurious – and those which are usually called refined – enjoyments.
  Love and admiration must push themselves out towards some quarter: otherwise the moral man is killed. Collaterally they advance with great vigour to a certain extent – and they are checked: in that direction, limits hard to pass are perpetually encountered: but upwards and downwards, to ancestry and to posterity, they meet with gladsome help and no obstacles; the tract is interminable. – Perdition to the Tyrant who would wantonly cut off an independent Nation from its inheritance in past ages . . .
                                                              (4324, 4330–40)

At the end of the 1800 Preface to *Lyrical Ballads* Wordsworth hopes that he may have produced genuine poetry 'important in the multiplicity and quality of its moral relations' (554–5), and earlier in the document he proclaims (in a long passage inserted in 1802 into the 1800 piece) that the poet 'is the rock of defence for human nature; an upholder and preserver, carrying everywhere with him relationship and love' (1850 text: 444–6). For Wordsworth, vital, loving relationships among humankind (living and dead) and between humanity and the natural world are at the heart of the moral.

Nowhere is Wordsworth's understanding of the moral more eloquently expressed than in 'The Brothers', the companion pastoral narrative to 'Michael'. The title already suggests that this is to be a poem about relationship, centring most obviously in the returned sailor Leonard's inquiries of the parish priest about his brother James, who turns out (at the end of a characteristically indirect narration) to have perished, probably while sleepwalking on the mountains, and probably seeking Leonard. The literal family relationships, the intricacies of 'the family heart' (208), are traced with great delicacy, and the terms of relationship are allowed to spread to embrace the priest's years which 'make up one peaceful family' (119) and the two symbolic 'brother fountains' (141). James's story, the priest says, is 'but/A fellow tale of sorrow' to that of Leonard (325–6). As an orphan, Leonard had been, like Johnny the idiot boy, 'the child of all the dale' (338); and he found 'that time/Is a true friend to sorrow' (384–5). The relationship unites not only the brothers and the living inhabitants of the vale, but also the living and the departed: rural folk have no need of churchyard memorials because they 'in each other's thoughts/Possess a kind of second life', in the communal memory (181–2).

Both the French revolutionaries and then Napoleon had aimed to divorce, not only their own nation, but also those societies that they conquered, away from their past – to tear apart the tightly woven world of 'The Brothers', so as to reorder matters on rational principles. In the early days of the Revolution that had seemed to Wordsworth an attractive prospect:

> Bliss was it in that dawn to be alive,
> But to be young was very heaven! O times,
> In which the meagre, stale, forbidding ways
> Of custom, law, and statute took at once
> The attraction of a Country in Romance;
> When Reason seemed the most to assert her rights
> When most intent on making of herself
> A prime Enchanter to assist the work
> Which then was going forwards in her name.
> Not favored spots alone, but the whole earth
> The beauty wore of promise . . .

> (*Prelude*, x. 692–702)

The millenarian enthusiasm recalled in that passage clearly informs *Llandaff*, written at 'a period big with the fate of the human race' (52). But with hindsight the previous book of *The Prelude* has already hinted at the damage such an over-rational disjunction from the past did to Wordsworth himself. When he arrived in France in 1792, his own sense of links with earlier times had still been powerful enough to insulate him from the excesses of those who were obsessed with the present:

> I, who at that time was scarcely dipped
> Into the turmoil, had a sounder judgment
> Than afterwards, carried about me yet
> With less alloy to its integrity
> The experience of past ages, as through help
> Of Books and common life it finds its way
> To youthful minds, by objects over near
> Not pressed upon, nor dazzled or misled
> By struggling with the crowd for present ends.
>
> (ix. 339–47)

When, with Dorothy's help, Wordsworth worked his way back to such a sense of continuity with the past, the revolutionary millenarianism transformed itself into something subtler and more gradual.

Grasmere was one of those new 'favored spots' in which Wordsworth hoped that a model for human life might be found. We have seen that both *Llandaff* and *Cintra* set much store by the mild domestic virtues, which had indeed motivated some of the original revolutionaries, 'of gentle mood . . . schemers more mild' (*Prelude*, x. 716, 718). 'Home at Grasmere' recalls an important incident during William and Dorothy's journey to the vale in December 1799:

> when the trance
> Came to us, as we stood by Hart-leap Well,
> The intimation of the milder day
> Which is to come, the fairer world than this,
> And raised us up, dejected as we were
> Among the records of that doleful place
> By sorrow for the hunted beast who there
> Had yielded up his breath, the awful trance –
> The vision of humanity, and of God
> The Mourner, God the Sufferer when the heart
> Of his poor Creatures suffers wrongfully –
> Both in the sadness and the joy we found
> A promise and an earnest that we twain,
> A pair seceding from the common world,
> Might in that hallowed spot to which our steps
> Were tending, in that individual nook,
> Might even thus early for ourselves secure,
> And in the midst of these unhappy times,

A portion of the blessedness which love
And knowledge will, we trust, hereafter give
To all the Vales of earth and all mankind.

(MS B, 236–56)

This incident, with its anticipation of the spread of virtuous, sympathetic mildness from favoured spots such as Grasmere 'To all the Vales of earth', is the subject of one of Wordsworth's finest poems, 'Hart-Leap Well'. In the first part, the arrogant and immoral Earl Walter (ancestor of Shelley's Ozymandias) anticipates that the pleasure-house which he builds to commemorate the mighty leap of the hart he has hunted to its death will endure 'Till the foundations of the mountains fail' (73). In the second part, the poet-narrator proclaims (echoing *Othello*, I, iii, 135) that 'The moving accident is not my trade' (97), and takes delight in a shepherd's understanding of the significance of the ruined pleasure-house, expressed partly in the form of a superstition. He foresees 'the coming of the milder day' (175) – a time when domestic humbleness will have replaced aristocratic arrogance and aggression as the norm for human conduct, 'a temperate shew/Of objects that endure' (*Prelude*, xii. 35–6). Wordsworth has rejected the 'effective' for the 'affective', in the hope that the affective will, in the fullness of time, be more effective than schemes for sudden revolution.[1]

VI

For Earl Walter, killing harts was a way of killing time. The same function, for himself and his paramour, is served by telling the story of the hart's leap 'in the summer-time when days are long' ('Hart-Leap Well', 69). One of the reasons Wordsworth gives in *Llandaff* for attacking the nobility is particularly significant in the light of this and other poems:

I have another strong objection to nobility which is that it has a necessary tendency to dishonour labour, a prejudice which extends far beyond its own circle; that it binds down whole ranks of men to idleness while it gives the enjoyment of a reward which exceeds the hopes of the most active exertions of human industry. The languid tedium of this noble repose must be dissipated . . .

(532–9)

Boredom is a major cause of evil in life and letters. The attempt to

1 Michael H. Friedman, *The Making of a Tory Humanist: William Wordsworth and the Idea of Community*, New York, 1979, *passim*.

relieve ennui leads to that frivolity which Wordsworth had experienced as tedium on his arrival in France (*Prelude*, ix. 114–26). To describe it he uses images of rankness and stagnation (ix. 357; x. 21, 436–9); and he amusingly introduces the poetic diction of 'silent zephyrs' sporting with the dust of the Bastille to suggest both the leisured privilege that has been swept away and also his own self-conscious 'enthusiasm' (ix. 63–71). Ennui in polite rural England is memorably conjured up in a stanza eventually deleted from 'Peter Bell':

> Is it some party in a parlour
> Crammed, just as they on earth were crammed,
> Some sipping punch, some sipping tea,
> But, as you by their faces see,
> All silent and all damned?

> (MS, 531–5)

One of the main thrusts of Wordsworth's poetry is towards the cultivation of

> a mind whose rest
> Was where it ought to be, in self-restraint,
> In circumspection and simplicity . . .

> (*Prelude*, x. 152–4)

When he heard of the death of Robespierre he was moved to say of him and the violent men associated with him:

> 'Their madness is declared and visible,
> Elsewhere will safety now be sought, and Earth
> March firmly towards righteousness and peace.'
> Then schemes I framed more calmly, when and how
> The madding Factions might be tranquillised,
> And, though through hardships manifold and long,
> The mighty renovation would proceed . . .

> (*Prelude*, x. 550–56)

The safety foreseen will not be the parody afforded by the French Revolutionary 'Committees of Safety' but true security, beyond the temporary madness of revolutionary excess; and it will be worked out, as the echo of Gray's *Elegy in a Country Churchyard* makes clear, 'Far from the madding crowd's ignoble strife'.[1]

---

1 Wordsworth attacked Gray for his use of poetic diction, but he admired him when he wrote in what the later poet took to be a natural fashion. Wordsworth's uses of 'mean' and 'common' in a positive sense, as in 'Hart-Leap Well' and the Immortality Ode, probably derive from Gray's 'Ode on the Pleasure arising from Vicissitude': see Mary Moorman, *William Wordsworth: A Biography*, 2 vols, Oxford, 1965, ii. 24n.

*Cintra*, an unashamedly 'consolatory' document by this pre-eminent poet of healing (259–60), is concerned to define a blend of secure repose and virtuous activity that may be considered the opposite of fashionable ennui. Wordsworth has 'been carried forward by a strong wish to be of use in raising and steadying the minds of my countrymen' ('steady' being one of the massive stable words that support the fabric of his verse), for 'all knowledge of human nature leads ultimately to repose' (538–41). This repose, and the eager and hopeful activity for which it forms a basis, are described in a memorable passage:

The great end and difficulty of life for men of all classes, and especially difficult for those who live by manual labour, is a union of peace with innocent and laudable animation. Not by bread alone is the life of Man sustained; not by raiment alone is he warmed; – but by the genial and vernal inmate of the breast, which at once pushes forth and cherishes; by self-support and self-sufficing endeavours; by anticipations, apprehensions, and active remembrances; by elasticity under insult, and firm resistance to injury; by joy, and by love; by pride which his imagination gathers in from afar; by patience, because life wants not promises; by admiration; by gratitude which – debasing him not when his fellow-being is its object – habitually expands itself, for his elevation, in complacency towards his Creator.
                                                                    (4267–78)

The word 'complacency' there means 'tranquil satisfaction', not 'self-satisfaction', but its occurrence in connection with the biblical allusions may lead some readers to recall the Bishop of Llandaff. Wordsworth's analysis, though, is much subtler than the bishop's had been, and his commendation of 'firm resistance to injury' is far from a complacent acceptance of the rightness of things as they are.

It is clear from the opening of the twelfth book of *The Prelude* that Wordsworth has looked into his own mind, discovered the importance for himself of such a blend or 'interchange' of calm and movement (there is no Augustan middle way *here*), and interpreted the lives of humble folk in the light of his personal discoveries. This passage is one of the most central in Wordsworth's thinking, demonstrating the extent to which his social thought grows from his own experience:

> From Nature doth emotion come, and moods
> Of calmness equally are Nature's gift,
> This is her glory; these two attributes
> Are sister horns that constitute her strength;
> This twofold influence is the sun and shower

Of all her bounties, both in origin
And end alike benignant. Hence it is,
That Genius, which exists by interchange
Of peace and excitation, finds in her
His best and purest Friend, from her receives
That energy by which he seeks the truth,
Is rouzed, aspires, grasps, struggles, wishes, craves,
From her that happy stillness of the mind
Which fits him to receive it, when unsought.

Such benefit may souls of humblest frame
Partake of, each in their degree; 'tis mine
To speak of what myself have known and felt . . .

(xii. 1–17)

During the period of Wordsworth's principal creative achievement the 'interchange/Of peace and excitation' referred to was fully operative. One of the central questions raised by his work is the extent to which the virtuous hopes and joys celebrated in his poetry can indeed suffice to banish ennui and to occupy the energies of the human soul. Wordsworth is here reworking Milton's rejection, as a subject for his epic poem, of 'Wars, hitherto the only argument/ Heroic deemed' (*Paradise Lost*, ix. 28–9). His friend Walter Scott chose to write about conflicts from the past, but raised the same question as to the adequacy of mild domestic occupations for an age that was in the process of substituting bourgeois values for aristocratic ones. The problem remains central for the happiness, and indeed the survival, of our race.

## VII

Wordsworth is even more conspicuously at one with Scott in an area where *Cintra* markedly departs from *Llandaff*, though he would certainly wish to argue for an underlying continuity. *Cintra* is an early document in the developing theory of nationalism which, for better or worse, became one of the dominant political developments of the nineteenth century. The main subject of *Cintra* is the right of a nation to self-determination. Wordsworth's understanding of Portugal's and Spain's cause is based on the development of his own British patriotism in the years after 1797, when the French invaded Switzerland (whose idyllic pastoral independence he had celebrated in the *Descriptive Sketches*, written in 1792, and in *Llandaff*, 301–6). Many of the shorter poems written after the publication of the 1800 *Lyrical Ballads* are overtly patriotic. Although it is not by any means his best sonnet, 'England! the time is come', written in 1802, introduces with unusual clarity the two strands, critical and celebratory, of the patriotic argument. The octave laments in general terms Britain's domestic and imperial 'trespasses' in preparation for a shift of tone in the course of the sestet:

> England! all nations in this charge agree:
> But worse, more ignorant in love and hate,
> Far, far more abject is thine Enemy:
> Therefore the wise pray for thee, though the freight
> Of thy offences be a heavy weight:
> Oh grief! that Earth's best hopes rest all with Thee!

The positive aspect of Wordsworth's new view of his country is unambiguous: she acts, however imperfectly, as the bastion of national freedom against Napoleon's imperialist subjugations in the name of enlightenment. *Cintra*'s emphasizing of the domestic virtues as the backbone of the nation's liberty is anticipated by the elegiac lyric 'I travelled among unknown Men', in which the speaker discovers on his return from abroad a hitherto unknown depth of love for England, because his love had 'turned her wheel/Beside an English fire' and because, in the poignant ending, 'thine is, too, the last green field/Which Lucy's eyes surveyed!'

Wordsworth's chief criticism of contemporary Britain centres on a peculiarly virulent form of greediness prevalent in the opening years of the new century, when war had brought prosperity for many. The last eight lines of the sonnet 'Written in London: September, 1802' are at once a blazing denunciation of current materialism and an elegy for the old virtues:

> The wealthiest man among us is the best:
> No grandeur now in nature or in book
> Delights us. Rapine, avarice, expence,
> This is idolatry; and these we adore:
> Plain living and high thinking are no more:
> The homely beauty of the good old cause
> Is gone; our peace, our fearful innocence,
> And pure religion breathing household laws.

Underlying all of these complaints against his beloved and invaluable homeland is *Cintra*'s diagnosis of radical selfishness. Spain had responded to the Napoleonic menace with a unanimous feeling uniting all ranks: 'If there have been since individual fallings-off; those have been caused by that kind of after-thoughts which are the bastard offspring of selfishness.' In the sonnet 'October, 1803', Wordsworth had alluded to the threatened Napoleonic invasion of Britain and commented in its opening line that 'These times touch moneyed Worldlings with dismay'. Now, in *Cintra*, he addresses himself directly to 'the worldlings of our own country', advising them that 'there is no true wisdom without imagination' and that 'the man, who in this age feels no regret for the ruined honour of other Nations, must be poor in sympathy for the honour of his own Country' (4370–79). He is here joining forces with Scott, whose poems *The Lay of the Last Minstrel* (1805) and *Marmion* (1808) were in part designed to unite the country in unselfish patriotic feeling.[1] One of the most impressive elements in the early days of Wordsworth's residence in France had been the display of 'patriot love/ And self-devotion' in the service of

> a cause
> Good, and which no one could stand up against
> Who was not lost, abandoned, selfish, proud,
> Mean, miserable, wilfully depraved,
> Hater perverse of equity and truth.
>
> (*Prelude*, ix. 278–93)

At one stage in his thinking, stimulated in 1799 by a letter from Coleridge and adopting its terms, it had seemed to Wordsworth that the failure of the French Revolution to live up to people's expectations had resulted in a particularly subtle form of selfishness disguising itself 'in gentle names/Of peace, and quiet, and domestic love', using these vital elements as an excuse for political apathy (*Prelude*, ii. 448–56).[2]

It was clear to Wordsworth that the attack on selfishness should begin with education: in the fifth book of *The Prelude*, entitled 'Books', he advocates the generous provision of romances on the grounds that

> The child, whose love is here, at least, doth reap
> One precious gain, that he forgets himself.
>
> (v. 368–9)

It is to the exposure of selfishness, whether open or covert, and the

---

1 See especially the celebrated Introduction to the sixth canto of *The Lay of the Last Minstrel*.
2 The surviving extract from Coleridge's letter of *c*. 10 September 1799 is to be found in *Collected Letters of Coleridge*, i. 527.

recovery of patriot love and self-devotion in Britain that many of Wordsworth's shorter poems contemporary with the composition of the 1805 *Prelude* are directed.

### VIII

Three objections may be raised to the foregoing argument. Some will complain that Wordsworth has been taken too much on his own terms. For them the crucial political issues in an author are those of which the writer is unaware. That there is a degree of truth in such an assertion is undeniable. Michael Friedman claims convincingly that Wordsworth, in common with all of his contemporaries to a greater or lesser extent, was very imperfectly aware of the complexity of class interests and interrelationships in France and Britain, and of the subtle pervasiveness of bourgeois capitalism.[1] But it may be doubted if the most profitable reading of (say) 'Lines Written a Few Miles above Tintern Abbey' is one that focuses on what is *not* included in the poem, for example the signs of rural poverty that Wordsworth must have encountered in the course of his walk in the Wye valley.[2] One may suspect that such a reading – charging Wordsworth with mystification, displacement and miscellaneous swervings – is itself a materialist avoiding of another sort of reality, with its own challenging and disturbing validity:

> And I have felt
> A presence that disturbs me with the joy
> Of elevated thoughts; a sense sublime
> Of something far more deeply interfused,
> Whose dwelling is the light of setting suns,
> And the round ocean, and the living air,
> And the blue sky, and in the mind of man,
> A motion and a spirit, that impels
> All thinking things, all objects of all thought,
> And rolls through all things.

('Tintern Abbey', 94–103)

Some readers may feel that to present Wordsworth as a lifelong republican and egalitarian is to ignore disconcerting evidence of his later high Toryism (not least the dismay of Keats and Shelley)[3] and

---

1 Friedman, *The Making of a Tory Humanist*, pp 101–2.
2 See for an uncompromising example of the 'new historicism' Marjorie Levinson, *Wordsworth's Great Period Poems*, Cambridge, 1986.
3 *Letters of Keats*, i. 298 (25–27 June 1818, to Tom Keats), i. 335 (17 July 1818, to Tom Keats); Shelley's 'Peter Bell the Third' (1819), 634–92.

even suggestions of a strong disposition in that direction earlier, during his great decade. Although *Llandaff* openly attacks Edmund Burke, Friedman has plausibly seen a Burkian fear of the mob in the image of a revolutionary people as an 'animal just released from its stall', exhausting 'the overflow of its spirits in a round of wanton vagaries' (278–9); and James Chandler has suggested that Wordsworth was essentially a Burkian conservative from the time of 'The Old Cumberland Beggar' in 1797, concerned to advocate a moral rather than a political egalitarianism.[1]

There is truth in these contentions also. Wordsworth's own mental collapse and the course of the Revolution made him wary, before the turn of the century, of rapid and radical political change. The weariness of prolonged war reinforced this fear. Advancing age, persistent illness, bereavement and declining energy brought a degree of timidity. For instance, at election time in 1818, he supported the Tory Lonsdales in their campaign to retain control of the Westmorland parliamentary seats; and he wrote articles in a local newspaper attacking the Whig Henry Brougham's attempt to diminish that family's influence. In these articles Wordsworth argued for an aristocratic hegemony which would defend the way of life that he most valued against deracinated city radicalism. The concrete realities of local continuity could thus be protected from 'the vanities of a system founded upon abstract rights'. That last phrase indicates what Whig doctrine had become in his eyes, in some measure as a result of the party's failure to support the struggle against Napoleon.[2]

Wordsworth's opposition to reform may be considered unfortunate with hindsight, but it was not unthinking (any more than Scott's was). And in 1835 he appended to *Yarrow Revisited and Other Poems* a lengthy postscript arguing against the workhouse inhumanities of the new (Whig) Poor Law, significantly quoting a couplet from the most unquestionably radical of all his poems, 'Salisbury Plain' of 1793, with its attacks upon 'engrossing, enclosing landlords; the horrors of war; kidnapping by press gang; a society so callous that it leaves a homeless woman to starve; and capital punishment':[3]

---

1 Friedman, *The Making of a Tory Humanist*, p 99; James K. Chandler, *Wordsworth's Second Nature: A Study of the Poetry and Politics*, Chicago and London, 1984, pp 84–92, and, for the attack on Burke in *Llandaff*, pp 15–25.
2 *Two Addresses to the Freeholders of Westmorland* (in *Prose*, iii), 196–7.
3 Friedman, *The Making of a Tory Humanist*, p 110.

> Homeless, near a thousand homes they stood,
> And near a thousand tables pined, and wanted food.[1]

To argue, as Heather Glen has done, that Wordsworth's cast of mind tends inevitably to promote conformism while Blake's is always open to the possibility of radicalism is to oversimplify Wordsworth's position in the great debate to which his work contributes. That debate, according to Coleridge in a discussion of Scott's novels, is no less than 'the contest between the two great moving Principles of social Humanity – religious adherence to the Past and the Ancient, the Desire & the admiration of Permanence, on the one hand; and the Passion for increase of Knowledge, for Truth, as the offspring of Reason – in short, the mighty Instincts of *Progression* and *Free-agency*, on the other ... two polar Forces, both of which are alike necessary to our human Well-being, & necessary each to the continued existence of the other'.[2] Like every serious contender in that infinitely complex contest Wordsworth had to weigh gains and losses. While recognizing that he was both limited by and partly unaware of the class structures of his time, one should not underestimate his daring and his achievement in according ordinary people a fitting place at the very centre of some of the finest poetry in an age of fine poetry. His attention to those apparently marginal figures that people his poems – beggars, discharged soldiers, gypsies, leech-gatherers and the like – can be as instructive to the late twentieth-century urban socialist as to the genteel *rentier* at the beginning of the last century.

Some readers, finally, may wish to argue that to take Wordsworth at his word by regarding him as a political poet is a fundamentally mistaken project. One freely grants that neither 'Salisbury Plain' nor most of the political sonnets written a decade later are among his greatest poems. Some will insist that he is essentially a nature poet, an expressionist, a man obsessed by words (and by a limited number of words in infinitely variable combinations), a sentimental tragedian, a religious-moral rather than a political-moral or social-moral writer, or an apocalyptic visionary. What political content, the new historicism apart, is there (it will be asked) in 'The Ruined Cottage', 'The Thorn', 'Tintern Abbey', 'Peter Bell', the Lucy poems, 'Resolution

---

1 *Postscript, 1835* (in *Prose*, iii), 152–3. Cf. 'Salisbury Plain', 386–7. For the later textual history of the poem see *The Salisbury Plain Poems of William Wordsworth*, ed. Stephen Gill, The Cornell Wordsworth, Ithaca, NY, and Hassocks, 1975.
2 *Collected Letters of Coleridge*, v. 35 (8 April 1820, to Thomas Allsop). For the contrast between Wordsworth and Blake see Heather Glen, *Vision and Disenchantment: Blake's 'Songs' and Wordsworth's 'Lyrical Ballads'*, Cambridge, 1983, *passim*.

and Independence', 'Peele Castle', the Immortality Ode, three-quarters of *The Prelude*, or, for that matter, 'I wandered lonely as a Cloud'? This final objection could be partly answered by tracing some of the terms and fundamental concepts explored in this essay through most of these poems, and the exercise would be valuable in confirming the interconnectedness of Wordsworth's moral, social and political vision. One could point in the Immortality Ode to the significance of an increasingly conservative poet first attacking the growing domination of the child's imagination by the weight of 'custom' (130) and then deriving adult comfort from living beneath the 'more habitual sway' of the natural world; or in 'I wandered lonely as a Cloud' to the hint of social criticism offered by that natural world in the description of the 'host of dancing daffodils' and their 'show' in terms of a fashionable ball. But in the last analysis it is freely admitted that the approach adopted here is partial and inadequate, as is inevitable with a writer of this stature and variety. Perhaps a quarter of the major poems emphasize the political dimension; in maybe another quarter a political subtext is discernible; the remaining half have their being in worlds from which political considerations are excluded, or in which they are effectively suppressed. Others have written penetratingly and eloquently on the crucial non-political aspects listed above. As a hint of what may be held to lie largely and essentially beyond the political dimension in Wordsworth the essay concludes with a brief analysis of 'The Ruined Cottage'.

IX

'The Ruined Cottage' was written in 1797, but published only in 1814 as part of the first book of *The Excursion*, and then in a greatly altered version.[1] Many of the concerns explored above can be easily traced in the original pathetic narrative. Margaret had functioned, like the Old Cumberland Beggar, as an important part of the web of rural social relationships, regularly offering travellers cups of water from the cool spring beside her cottage, and in such a manner that

> no one came
> But he was welcome, no one went away
> But that it seemed she loved him . . .
>
> (101-3)

1  Line numbers cited in this essay refer to MS D of 'The Ruined Cottage'.

Her husband led a 'steady' and industrious life (120–30) of the sort praised in *Cintra*. That pamphlet is anticipated further when the pedlar Armytage notes that, when war brought poverty, Margaret was 'gladly reconciled/To numerous self-denials' (145–6), and when he chronicles the gradual loss of that vital social ingredient of hope by means of the eloquent recurrence of the word 'hope' itself (132, 148, 246, 277, 359, 390–91, 428). The calamitous social effects of 'the plague of war' are vividly described at several points in the narrative, and John Turner has noted the remarkably penetrating analysis of the effects of long-term unemployment.[1] Taken as a whole the poem could be seen as implicitly a socially educative document, a 'simple', 'common', 'homely' tale, anticipating 'Hart-Leap Well' in being 'By moving accidents uncharactered' (203, 209, 231–2).

Few readers will feel, though, that an analysis in these terms, however true and illuminating, really penetrates to the heart of this poem. Four factors may be identified as leading beyond the political and social dimension, however widely conceived.

As so often in Wordsworth, the natural world plays a crucial role. The poem opens oddly, with an apparently irrelevant description of a pleasant, stable natural scene as seen by a putative figure taking his ease in 'dewy shade' (13). The narrator himself, in striking contrast, turns out to be making his way with some difficulty across a bare, slippery common, annoyed both by insects and by 'the tedious noise/ Of seeds of bursting gorse that crackled round' (25–6). This latter landscape is linked, as the venerable Armytage's narrative gets under way, with superficial and unfeeling people 'whose hearts are dry as summer dust' (97).

The cool, steady aspect of nature introduced in the opening lines quickly becomes dominant, firstly in the 'shadows of the breezy elms' that dapple Armytage's face (47–8), and then in the focusing on the cool spring: when Margaret dies 'a bond/Of brotherhood is broken' between herself as representative of the human world and this spring as representative of the natural world (84–5). By the end of the first part of the narrative the natural world (not excluding the flies) has become a source of calm wisdom and consolation to be set against 'the weakness of humanity' (187–98). This theme is continued at the end of the poem: at line 104 the worm was on Margaret's cheek, but now 'She sleeps in the calm earth' (512), the weeds are 'silvered o'er' (515) and the air, as the narrator and his companion

---

1 John Turner, *Wordsworth: Play and Politics – A Study of Wordsworth's Poetry, 1787–1800*, London, 1986, p 96.

leave, is 'milder' (533). The sense of consoling fittingness here anticipates the celebrated lines at the end of 'Home at Grasmere' which appeared, somewhat altered, as the 'Prospectus' to the unfinished philosophical poem *The Recluse*:[1]

> . . . my voice proclaims
> How exquisitely the individual Mind
> (And the progressive powers perhaps no less
> Of the whole species) to the external World
> Is fitted: — and how exquisitely, too —
> Theme this but little heard of among men —
> The external World is fitted to the Mind . . .

Blake scribbled on reading these lines: 'You shall not bring me down to believe such fitting & fitted I know better & Please your Lordship'.[2]

One may conjecture that Blake would certainly have extended his censure to the conclusion of Margaret's story, but that he would have responded more positively to at least two passages in the narration which have decidedly apocalyptic overtones, as he did to the Immortality Ode. Armytage says that the story of Margaret is

> A tale of silent suffering, hardly clothed
> In bodily form, and to the grosser sense
> But ill adapted . . .
>
> (233–5)

and at the end he asserts that

> all the grief
> The passing shews of being leave behind,
> Appeared an idle dream that could not live
> Where meditation was . . .
>
> (521–4)

Much of Wordsworth's poetry is permeated by a sense that consciousness has only a tenuous connection with the natural world in which it is for a time embodied. There is often at the heart of his work a tension between the apocalyptic and the natural, which is connected

1 The 'Prospectus' was published with *The Excursion*, the only part of *The Recluse* to be satisfactorily completed, in 1814. The lines quoted are 62–8 of the 'Prospectus', corresponding to 'Home at Grasmere', MS B, 1006–11.
2 *The Poetry and Prose of William Blake*, ed. David V. Erdman, New York, 1965, rev. 1970, p 656.

with the parallel tension between social radicalism and religious quietism.

That in this poem natural piety and quietism come to dominate is due more than anything else to the *sound* of the verse, to its music. As later in 'Resolution and Independence', so here the speaker hears a tale not so much as separate words as undifferentiated sound: 'that simple tale/Passed from my mind like a forgotten sound' (203–4). And Armytage feels 'The story linger in my heart', as his 'spirit clings/To that poor woman' (362–5): the verbal echoing of 'linger' by 'clings' (cf. 256) reinforces the point, and the poem is full of human and natural clingings. The haunting presence of this story is due above all to Wordsworth's masterful handling of the blank verse:

> Meanwhile her poor hut
> Sunk to decay, for he was gone whose hand
> At the first nippings of October frost
> Closed up each chink and with fresh bands of straw
> Chequered the green-grown thatch. And so she lived
> Through the long winter, reckless and alone,
> Till this reft house by frost, and thaw, and rain
> Was sapped; and when she slept the nightly damps
> Did chill her breast, and in the stormy day
> Her tattered clothes were ruffled by the wind
> Even at the side of her own fire.
>
> (476–86)

These lines are linked by three sets of unobtrusive alliterations and assonances: 'nippings', 'chink', 'Chequered', 'chill'; 'Sunk', 'sapped', 'slept'; and 'fresh', 'reckless', 'reft', 'frost', 'ruffled', 'fire'. Behind the last of these sequences there may be glimpsed the ghostly presence of 'suffer', confirmed by the echo in lines 477–8 of lines 374–5: 'when he shall come again/For whom she suffered'. The recurrence of the personal pronoun, without the need for any specified 'husband', takes the reader to the heart of this personal tragedy. The same quiet intensity pervades all of this verse with its subdued but constantly varied movement, its eloquent handling of line-endings (for example, 350/1, 354/5), and its echoing repetitions of 'human', 'hope', 'heart', 'waste', 'calm', 'mild', 'nook', 'spot', and 'power'.

The last word in that list, 'power', is specially significant. For though the narrator's grief at Armytage's story is impotent (500), this is in truth a powerful tale. The speaker asks the pedlar to continue the story 'for my sake' (219), and the element of personal consolation is important. But Armytage warns him against indulgent sentimentalism (anticipating the parallel rejection in 'Hart-Leap Well'). He maintains that the story of Margaret possesses 'A power to virtue friendly', and adds:

> were't not so,
> I am a dreamer among men, indeed
> An idle dreamer . . .

(229–31)

When Keats read these lines in the first book of *The Excursion*, which he called (in spite of the egotism and the Tory ideology) one of 'three things to rejoice at in this Age',[1] they must have touched on his own surgeon-poet's developing sense of the possible conflict between tragic feeling and social usefulness, which was to play a major part in his brief creative life and find tentative expression in *The Fall of Hyperion*.[2] That was an early stage in a continuous process whereby Wordsworth has been educating his readers both as he intended to do and in ways beyond the grasp of his conscious understanding.

The year after Wordsworth's death a memorial tablet was erected in Grasmere church. Its tribute does not by any means tell the whole story, but it tells a good deal of it, in terms that he would have approved at any period in his life, and which modern readers may find unexpectedly challenging to a number of their prejudices:

To the memory of
WILLIAM WORDSWORTH

a true philosopher and poet,
who, by the special gift and calling of
almighty God,
whether he discoursed on man or nature,
failed not to lift up the heart
to holy things,
tired not of maintaining the cause
of the poor and simple;
and so, in perilous times was raised up
to be a chief minister,
not only of noblest poesy,
but of high and sacred truth.

---

1 The other two were Haydon's pictures and 'Hazlitt's depth of Taste': *Letters of Keats*, i. 203 (10 January 1818, to B. R. Haydon).
2 See especially lines 147–202.

# 6

## COLERIDGE

### Paul Hamilton

The most difficult and important aspect of Coleridge's writings to capture in any summary is their range: poems of all sorts, plays, lectures on politics, religion, literature, criticism and philosophy, the two periodicals *The Watchman* and *The Friend*, a *Theory of Life* in the esoteric idiom of contemporary German *Naturphilosophie*, lay sermons, homiletic theological reflections and meditations on the English Church and Constitution. These combine to express a range of interest only partly resumed in Coleridge's portmanteau intellectual autobiography, *Biographia Literaria*. His published opinions are supported and contradicted by numerous unpublished researches, not just in letters, notebooks and literary remains, but in a manuscript treatise on logic and in writings towards an encyclopaedic *'opus maximum'*.

At different times Coleridge was as avant-garde as any post-modernist hopes to be now, and as staunchly conservative as any pre-Thatcherite high Tory. He was strikingly original and provocatively eclectic, a dazzling expositor of ideas and also an élitist insistent on the need for intellectual speculation. Above all he was an 'intellectual', a description which only became current at the end of the nineteenth century, but which already denoted a nostalgia for the unity of a Latin culture in which men of ideas were thought to possess an easy and disinterested expertise in all kinds of mental discipline. That ideal was, in the parlance of Romantic philosophy, 'transcendental': it aspired to knowledge of a universal human character lying behind all particular sciences and discourses. It provided the germ by which Coleridge's poet activated 'the whole soul of man', his philosopher deduced reality, and his intellectual caste, the 'Clerisy', were to educate us in the cultivation of our humanity.

Characteristic of the 'intellectual' interest which Coleridge first represented in its modern form in English is the belief in a kind of investigation which is, in the philosopher Richard Rorty's phrase, 'foundational in respect to the rest of culture'.[1] This explains Coleridge's confident and extravagant vision of the philosophical poem he encouraged William Wordsworth to write, in preparation for which Wordsworth produced *The Prelude* and offered *The Excursion* as the first part of such a project, to be called *The Recluse*. Coleridge explained to Wordsworth why *The Excursion* fell short of the vast collaborative enterprise he had envisaged. Had *The Excursion* measured up to Coleridge's expectations, Wordsworth, according to a letter of May 1815, would have confidently ranged through 'every thing that is most worthy of the human intellect' in a manner corrective of an inherited 'philosophy of mechanism'. Coleridge's target is British empiricism and French Enlightenment thought, whose radical moral and political implications he presents as reductive and overcomes rhetorically by a breadth of interest 'adequate to the majesty of the Truth'.[2]

However, he had given equally strong expression to a sense of the incompatibility of poetic and philosophical interests, and the demoralizing effect of their conflict upon sensibility, in 'Dejection: An Ode' in 1802. In *Biographia Literaria* (1817), arguments are left incomplete, deductions fluffed, plagiarisms veiled; and gestures towards a saving irony, or sketches of untold expertise, suggest that the intellectual project is in some difficulties. Autobiography is an incorrigible mode of writing, expressive of its author's character in his failures as much as in his successes. *Biographia*'s revelations, however digressive, forestall categorical objections and secure for the work its lasting fascination. But the reader is torn between accepting either that Coleridge is defining the self as incoherent, or that he is giving reasons for abandoning *Biographia*'s intellectual pluralism for an increasingly abstract and religious foundationalism.

The first option is the most popular among our contemporary critics, some of whom have argued with great ingenuity for Coleridge as a precursor of modern theorists of the self as processual and decentred rather than a stable, achieved identity, and for the need, as a result, to ironize traditional forms of self-definition, literary and philosophical. The second option appears to resolve the discursive conflict only by abandoning its rich variety. In order to preserve consistency between his different disciplines, Coleridge increasingly abstracts and refines. His transcendentalism, his philosophical interest in the conditions logically necessary for experience to be possible, becomes more and more formal as he moves behind conflictual uses of language to consider their ultimate theological rationale in pure Reason.

Unitarianism provided Coleridge's earliest ideology or historically working definition of the unity he continuously sought as the foundation of all theory and practice. Unitarianism was the religious, political and philosophical movement which governed Coleridge's first departure from his cultural background. He was born in 1772 into an Anglican family in Devon. On the death of his father, the local vicar at Ottery St Mary's, Coleridge was boarded at Christ's Hospital school in London. He remembered his childhood as mainly unhappy. The youngest member, teased and bullied, of a large family, he grew progressively more bookish and introverted, and accounts of his reading habits at Christ's Hospital, both by himself and his fellow pupil Charles Lamb, even if exaggerated, suggest extraordinary erudition. His breadth of acquaintance with the history of literature and philosophy from Plato and his followers through to the latest twists of the British empiricist tradition enhanced his traditional classical education with a speculative cosmopolitanism. In the 1790s Coleridge's freethinking, encyclopaedic habit found an echo in Unitarianism as much as it was later to do in the plan for an *Encyclopaedia Metropolitana* to which he contributed a 'Treatise on Method' in 1817. Debating whether or not to accept a likely invitation to a Unitarian charge at Shrewsbury, Coleridge wrote to a potential benefactor, Josiah Wedgwood, early in 1798, that 'the *necessary* creed in our sect is but short – it will be necessary for me, in order to my continuance as a Unitarian Minister, to believe that Jesus Christ was the Messiah – in all other points I may play off my intellect *ad libitum*.'[1] Eventually he turned down the Unitarians, accepted Wedgwood's patronage and gradually moved towards a 'higher' version of the Anglicanism of his upbringing. But the attractions of Unitarianism at this stage did not seem to differ substantially from Coleridge's later ambitions, through for example *The Friend*, to find an audience to whom, as he told his brother George in 1808, he could 'play off my whole mind'.[2]

Originally Unitarianism was a specifically anti-Trinitarian religious movement, but it dissented from doctrinal exclusiveness of any kind and encouraged a religious community founded on belief in an underlying consensus of theological opinion. This credo had both moral and metaphysical implications. It argued a spirit of toleration

1 Ibid., i. 366.
2 Ibid., iii. 133.

and love in which theological difference could be acknowledged without reviving the violent oppositions which bloodied the history of Christianity. It also implied a trust in the ultimate convergence of apparently different knowledges: competing views reveal only different aspects of a universe activated by a single mind in whose larger, comprehensive principle their differences would be reconciled. As Coleridge put it in 'Religious Musings', the climactic poem at the end of his first published poetic collection:

> 'Tis the sublime of man,
> Our noontide Majesty, to know ourselves
> Parts and proportions of one wond'rous whole:
> This fraternises man, this constitutes
> Our charities and bearings.
>
> (135–9)[1]

Unitarians varied in their views on the liberality of opinion thus licensed. Coleridge was happy to enliven his poetry, as in the poem expanded into 'The Destiny of Nations' from lines first included in Southey's *Joan of Arc* in 1796, with what 'Others boldlier think' – metaphysical theories verging on pantheism. A Unitarian leader like Joseph Priestley was admired by Coleridge in letters and a sonnet for his expertise both in theological dispute and scientific experiment. But Priestley, like Newton and David Hartley before him, sought scriptural corroboration for all his discoveries. He could have inspired the apocalyptic tone of 'Reflections on Having Left a Place of Retirement' or 'Ode to the Departing Year' as much as Coleridge's rationalist championing of freedom of debate in 'The Fall of Robespierre' of 1794, in his 1795 lectures on politics and religion, and, a year later, in *The Watchman*.

Dissent, in other words, was a relative business, and favoured forms of writing as eager to create their own partisan audience as to be dissociated from an exclusive orthodoxy. At Jesus College, Cambridge, Coleridge quickly found his place within such an audience, that commanded by one of its fellows, William Frend, who had already written in favour of Unitarianism and moved in radical circles which supported the principles of the French Revolution despite the Terror of 1792–3. Frend was tried and expelled by the university court for the allegedly seditious content of his pamphlet of 1793, *Peace and Union*, advocating political reform and attacking the war with France. Two years later, addressing the same subject, 'On

1 Coleridge's poems are quoted from *Poems*, ed. John Beer, London, 1974.

the Present War', in his *Conciones ad Populum*, Coleridge emphasized that the friends of liberty 'should be bold in the avowal of *political* Truth only among those whose minds are susceptible of reasoning . . . the Conduct of the speaker is determined largely by the nature of his Audience.'[1]

However, in the same lecture Coleridge concedes that even 'the *attempt* to promote Discussion will be regarded as dangerous'.[2] In his poetry of 1793–8 he therefore frequently writes in apostrophic vein – in a manner, that is, conspicuously concerned with foregrounding its mode of address. Generally, his poems meditate on the political as well as the philosophical significance of writing poetry which solicits a sympathetic audience by reflecting on its own imaginary status. Coleridge's poetry has always been regarded as having as one of its main concerns the imagination which produced it. Recent, more sociologically minded studies of his work have laid heavier stress on the way such reflexivity draws its implied audience into its own ideal realm. To read a reflexive poem with understanding, you must retrospectively collaborate in its vision. But this fantastic solution is very much expressive of a historical dilemma. Its tactics are finely poised between political transformation and idealist escape, between a positive belief in the practical power of poetry to change the hearts and minds of those who strive to become its sympathetic readers, and a negative belief in the need to preserve an ideal form of dissent in a society which does not allow it any more realistic breathing-space.

Pitt's administration unscrupulously manipulated English fears of imported revolutionary violence in order to discredit discussion of any reform whatsoever. In the early 1790s, across a wide intellectual and class spectrum, Pitt's tactics were seen for what they were. To maintain free speech with which to attack his government's censorship became the common, liberal concern of working-class activists in the Corresponding Societies, religious Dissenters of all complexions, radical intellectuals like the brilliant etymologist Horne Tooke and the novelist Thomas Holcroft, respectable philosophers like Sir James Mackintosh and less respectable ones like the anarchistic William Godwin, Foxite Whigs, feminists like Mary Wollstonecraft, and, of course, poets such as Wordsworth and Coleridge. The collective consciousness of so disparate an opposition might seem to

---

1 *Lectures 1795 on Politics and Religion*, in *The Collected Works of Samuel Taylor Coleridge*, Bollingen Series lxxv, 14 vols, London and Princeton, 1969–, I. 51.
2 Ibid., I. 52.

have to be ideal or imagined. Only by the late 1790s, when Pitt's own 'Terror' had won the battle against the liberals, would this imaginariness appear a consequence of their recent defeat rather than the sign of the alternative consensus which had preceded it.

The reason for taking Coleridge's envisioned and envisioning audiences seriously is the extent to which the Revolution controversy was explicitly ideological – one waged at the level of discourse. The book and pamphlet wars between Richard Price, Edmund Burke, Thomas Paine, Godwin, John Thelwall and a host of others achieved enormous publicity. Paine's radical reply in *Rights of Man* to Burke's *Reflections on the Revolution in France* was even ritually burned by the mob. Mostly, though, the battle was about preserving the meanings each side claimed the other ignored. Burke's richly metaphorical conservative rhetoric was set against Paine's common sense. Coleridge, though always appreciative of Burke, as late as 1800 took a Paineite line against the systematically misleading language of Tory ministers like Pitt, Greville and Wyndham. In his political essays and lectures he had persistently discussed those topics obscured by or irrationally associated with the Revolution: the slave-trade, Greville's and Pitt's 'Two Bills', public expenditure, the political theories of Paine and Godwin, opposition to the war with France, and the whole quality of contemporary civic and religious life. Yet this very practical agenda is at least initially complemented by his poetic invitations to participate in envisioning a community generous enough to contemplate the reform and betterment which, according to Government propaganda, would lead to social dissolution.

Coleridge the poet leapt into print in 1796 with *Poems on Various Subjects*. His prose reputation went before him, established, as the *Analytical Review* noted, by the eloquence of the lectures he had given in Bristol the previous year. Coleridge had left Cambridge in academic disarray, without a degree but with considerable debts, which at one stage drove him to enlist pseudonymously in the 15th Light Dragoons. Under the influence of Robert Southey, he progressed from playing the failed hero of a picaresque novel to become a radical orator. One of his addresses, in a year of spectacular public utterances by other radicals, was described in a newspaper report as 'most sublime'.[1] Also with Southey he planned, or rather, as his

1 *The Romantics Reviewed: Contemporary Reviews of British Romantic Writers*, ed. Donald H. Reiman, New York and London, 1972, Part A, i. 6; N. Roe, *Wordsworth and Coleridge: The Radical Years*, Oxford, 1988, pp 149–59.

sonnet on 'Pantisocracy' has it, indulged his 'Visionary Soul' in the direction of a small community on the banks of the American river Susquehanna. On the strength of breakfast with an acquaintance of Priestley, Coleridge was persuaded that 'the Doctor will join us'. He later quarrelled with Southey, as both pioneers got cold feet. Defined by Coleridge to the reneging Southey in November 1795, Pantisocracy was a kind of domestic communism based on the elimination of 'the *selfish* Principle'. This fundamental tenet required both the abolition of property and an equality overriding ties of kinship and marriage among the participating families.[1]

Coleridge's enthusiasm is amusing now, but his visionary impracticality translated into progressively more accomplished poetry, raising the question we have been considering about the relation between poetry and politics. Coleridge unites metaphysical speculation and domestic sympathies to authenticate his visions. When unsure of his commitment to his future wife, Sarah Fricker, also a sometime candidate for Pantisocracy by the Susquehanna, Coleridge had written to an unsympathetic Southey of 'having mistaken the ebullience of *schematism* for affection'.[2] However, the fulsome love for 'Sara', to which so many of the 1796 poems testify, is frequently the test of Coleridge's schemes. Thus he writes without any sense of incongruity lines 'To a Young Lady with a Poem on the French Revolution'. The dislocated and unargued appeal to Sara at its end, 'Nor, SARA! thou these early flowers refuse –/Ne'er lurk'd the snake beneath their simple hues', is a frequent gambit. Other poems, like the sonnet 'Pity', where the homely couple are to restore public virtue, develop the domestic transition until, in 'The Eolian Harp', it can become the model for Coleridge's serious and continual pondering on the social value of poetic speculation.

That speculation is seen in its least diluted form in 'Religious Musings'. Its predominantly religious idiom may stem from Coleridge's response to having met the radical philosopher and lapsed Dissenting Christian, William Godwin, a few days before composing it. The poem assertively retains the theological context which Godwin's comparable progressivism had abandoned. In 'Religious Musings' the 'elect . . . Treading beneath their feet all visible things/ As steps, that upward to their Father's Throne/Lead gradual' (52–9), follow a sublime life of 'subliming import' (116). Sublime self-knowledge comes from a conscious participation in nature which

1 *Letters*, i. 98, 163–4.
2 Ibid., i. 132.

dissolves nature's otherness in order to reconstitute it on a higher level instantiating 'one Mind'. In a footnote to the poem, Coleridge attributes this idea of loss of self-consciousness in a sublime awareness of God to the philosophy of David Hartley, main precursor in the Dissenting tradition of philosophers of human perfectibility like Priestley and Godwin. Distinctive in Coleridge's version was the extraordinary elevation of language which accompanied accession to the elect. The *Critical Review*'s notice complained that Coleridge 'too frequently mistakes bombast and obscurity for sublimity'; but Coleridge's old school-friend, Charles Lamb, read 'Religious Musings' as 'a Gigantic hyperbole by which you describe the Evils of existing Society'.[1] Coleridge is very much aware of the rhetorical risks in writing a poem which maps the book of Revelation on to the present state of society by way of Unitarian metaphysics. His epigraph from Akenside agrees with Lamb that historical circumstance justifies the poem's elevated diction; and throughout, Coleridge inserts caveats about his 'young anticipating heart' (369), resolving to discipline his 'young noviciate thought/In ministeries of heart-stirring song' (429–30).

'Religious Musings' could hardly be more ambitious in scope, so it is its occasionally chastening idiom, rather than its afflatus, which can be developed in the subsequent, better-known conversation poems. This chastening is an especial feature of both the production and the theme of 'The Eolian Harp', allegedly written at Clevedon, Somerset, in August 1795, although it reads as though composed after Coleridge's marriage to Sarah in October. In 'The Eolian Harp' the Miltonic blank verse is more relaxed, if never quite colloquial, and the central visionary speculation, while comparable in ambition to that of 'Religious Musings', is presented as the more accessible progression of an individual fantasy which may or may not coincide with the 'thought' of 'one intellectual Breeze,/At once the Soul of each, and God of all' (47–8). The poem's conversation is with 'Sara', who clearly thinks this coincidence unlikely, and whose reproachful verdict on the narrator's theological adventure at the end is supported by his imagery of illicit departure from the initial paradigm of the 'Family of Christ' represented by herself, the narrating Coleridge and their cottage at Clevedon. The conspicuous predating of the poem to the marriage may also stress the Christian precedent of a virginal rapport between husband and wife. Coleridge

1 Reiman, *Romantics Reviewed*, i. 304; *The Letters of Charles and Mary Lamb*, ed. E. W. Marrs, Jr., Ithaca, NY, and London, 1975, i. 10.

added a short passage on 'the one Life within us and abroad' (26) for the version included in *Sibylline Leaves* in 1817, further defusing that erotic approach to the Unitarian plateau during which the wind apparently makes love to the harp, whose 'long sequacious notes/ Over delicious surges sink and rise' (18–19). The later addition refines this intercourse into a theology which still, however, is allowed to retain that exciting impulse:

> And what if all of animated nature
> Be but organic Harps diversely fram'd,
> That tremble into thought, as o'er them sweeps
> Plastic and vast, one intellectual Breeze,
> At once the Soul of each, and God of all?
>
> (44–8)

The tensions in 'The Eolian Harp' reveal Sara ostensibly objecting to Coleridge's attempt to gain public credence for a too private, too heterodox speculation. The force of the imagery deconstructs this stated verdict, and suggests instead that the failure to gain an assenting *public* masks the poem's greater disturbance: the discovery of an indeterminacy or failure of *private* allegiance as soon as it touches on the erotic. In other words, if Sara's doctrinal disapproval at the end is the poem's only goal, then there seems little justification for having entertained at such length 'These shapings of the unregenerate mind' (55). This disparity remains a problem unless we take it to parallel structurally the gap between conscious and unconscious motive in the narrator's theological desire.

The reader's sensation of being conducted into a public sphere of debate incapable of resolving the previous private one is a feature of the conversation poems, poems which G. M. Harper, generalizing from Coleridge's description of 'The Nightingale', first grouped as a genre of occasional, locodescriptive poems of friendship. Harper thought that Coleridge 'could not even think without supposing a listener', but did not speculate about the nature of the society postulated by Coleridge's sociability. Subsequent commentators have noted the poems' typical pattern of expansion and contraction; sometimes seeing in this attempt to carry his audience with him on his mental voyages that reconciliation of opposites which Coleridge later argued was the natural movement of imagination; at other times suspecting that the imaginative idiom perhaps covers a political impasse or private incoherence. For example, readers from the poem's first publisher, Joseph Cottle, to Albert Gérard have been undisturbed by the untruth of the climactic assertion of 'Reflections on Having Left a Place of Retirement': 'I therefore go, and join head, heart, and hand,/Active and firm, to fight the bloodless fight/ Of Science, Freedom, and the Truth in Christ' (60–62).[1] The impecunious Coleridge left Clevedon for the libraries of Bristol, lectures and journalistic employment.

Aside from its biographical reductiveness, this objection misses the poem's equation of imagination and reality, seeming and being. When the narrator ascends from his dell, he so enjoys the view that 'No *wish* profan'd my overwhelmèd heart./Blest hour! It was a luxury, – to be!' (41–2). But the landscape *is* wishful thinking: 'It seem'd like Omnipresence! God, methought,/Had built him there a Temple: the whole World/Seem'd *imag'd* in its vast circumference' (38–40). Conversely, the wish which should have 'profan'd' the poem's conclusion ('Let thy Kingdom come') cannot be disentangled from the experience of the place of retirement. The dell and its cottage, the sublime moment and its view, turn out to *be* the end-points of millenarian desire.

> And I shall sigh fond wishes – sweet Abode!
> Ah! – had none greater! And that all had such!
> It might be so – but the time is not yet.
> Speed it, O Father! Let thy Kingdom come!
>
> (68–71)

The indirections needed to find this out suggest that the narrator is not distressed by the possible unreality of his hopes, the untruth which did trouble subsequent readers. The poem's rhetorical equivalences imply rather that it is the sufficiency of the experience described, collapsing imagination into luxuriant being, which might be unsettling. The narrator may avowedly suspect, in the penultimate verse-paragraph, the escapism of his pastoral; but the only idea of political transformation he possesses is just this domestic retreat: the creation of a universal place of retirement from whatever stands in need of reform.

When Coleridge first published it in the *Monthly Magazine* in October 1796, anxiety about the poem's exclusive self-sufficiency was expressed in the subtitle: 'A Poem which affects not to be

---

1 Contrast the approaches of Kelvin Everest in *Coleridge's Secret Ministry*, Brighton, 1979, and Kathleen Wheeler in *The Creative Mind in Coleridge's Poetry*, London, 1981. The example from 'Reflections' is discussed in Albert Gérard, 'The Systolic Rhythm: The Structure of Coleridge's Conversation Poems', in *Coleridge: A Collection of Critical Essays*, ed. K. Coburn, Englewood Cliffs, NJ, 1967, pp 78–88.

Poetry'. The plenitude of the conversation poems, their circular return upon their own private discourse to guarantee the reality of their vision, is both their intriguing problem and their means of generating allegorical content: this is what the paradoxes of parental love ('The Nightingale', 'Frost at Midnight'), religious and erotic love ('The Eolian Harp', 'Dejection: An Ode') feel like. We wish the fulfilment of others in our own image, just as a conversation poem authenticates its dialogue with another in its own terms. The problem here is clearly stated by the *Critical Review*'s difficulties with 'France: An Ode', whose last stanza recants Coleridge's political radicalism by keeping the final apostrophe to freedom lodged within a nature purified of allegorical content or political application. Nature remains symbolic in the Coleridgian sense of being consubstantial with this 'Liberty', their features blended in poetic ejaculation:

> Yes, while I stood and gazed, my temples bare,
> And shot my being through earth, sea and air,
> Possessing all things with intensest love,
> O Liberty! my spirit felt thee there.

> (102–5)

'The conclusion', wrote the reviewer, 'is very ridiculous . . . what does Mr Coleridge mean by liberty in this passage? Or what connexion has it with the subject of civil freedom?'[1] In symbolic response, the private and imaginary remain firmly in their place: their appeal to nature does not activate a recognizably public audience whose civil sense is transformed by participating in the freedom of poetic apprehension.

Here, Coleridge's new symbolic accent announces a *poetic* emancipation from his former support for anti-British, Francophile radicalism, now characterized as the poetic imprisonment of when 'I sang, amid a slavish band' (27). The ode's imagined sympathy with English landscape releases Coleridge's ideal of liberty from disreputable association with the terroristic aftermath of the French Revolution. However, this unabashedly aesthetic escape from a compromised historical example appears to leave Coleridge's 'Liberty' without any political application at all, a natural rather than a social franchise, hence the reviewer's perplexity. Participation in the poetic vision no longer assures a readerly solidarity with the potential to become a politically significant grouping. The ode's lyrical apostrophe is not keyed into other radically programmatic discourses in

1 Reiman, *Romantics Reviewed*, i. 302.

the way that the Unitarian poems were. As we shall see, though, Coleridge, throughout his writings, precisely challenges readers to revise existing political economies in order to imagine new ones in which the audience his writing attempts to create would have a part to play.

The confident but less discursive appeal to nature in 'France: An Ode' can be usefully contrasted with the beginning of the earlier 'Ode to the Departing Year', published two years before, in 1796. The latter's inspired opening apostrophe to the 'Spirit who sweepest the wild Harp of Time' powerfully anticipates Shelley's 'Ode to the West Wind'. Coleridge's poem similarly identifies an elevated, private poetic self with the trumpet of public prophecy:

> When lo! its folds far waving on the wind,
> I saw the train of the Departing Year!
>   Starting from my silent sadness
>   Then with no unholy madness,
> Ere yet the enter'd cloud foreclos'd my sight,
> I rais'd the impetuous song, and solemniz'd his flight.
>
> (7–12)

The later 'France: An Ode' naturalizes rather than solemnizes the narrator's apotheosis; its quieter confidence shows the influence of Wordsworth and has its advantages.

Wordsworth's influence on Coleridge could be simplistic, as in 'The Three Graves' and 'The Old Man of the Alps', or part of a complex personal and poetic dialogue between the two poets which Coleridge found alternately enabling and damaging. He tried to address it conclusively in various poems to his friend, especially the verse 'Letter to Sara Hutchinson' which was the ur-text of 'Dejection: An Ode', and, after hearing *The Prelude* in January 1807, 'To William Wordsworth: Composed on the Night after His Recitation of a Poem on the Growth of an Individual Mind'. Coleridge had met Wordsworth briefly in Bristol in September 1795, but, as far as we know, they did not meet again until Coleridge took the Wordsworths from Racedown, in Dorset, to visit his new home at Nether Stowey in March 1797. 'Ode to the Departing Year' was written in the interim. The renewed acquaintance was celebrated in 'This Lime-tree Bower My Prison', written in July 1797, just after William and Dorothy had begun living at nearby Alfoxden, and sent in a conciliatory letter to Coleridge's former mentor, Southey. 'Henceforth I shall know/That Nature ne'er deserts the wise and pure' (59–60) anticipates the conviction of 'Tintern Abbey' a year later 'that Nature

never did betray/The heart that  loved her' (123–4). No need now
for proto-Shelleyan strenuosities if nature can appear in Coleridge's
poetry as the self-evident tutelary spirit of 'The Dungeon'. But of
course Coleridge retained the theoretical and political ambitions
which his pre-Wordsworthian rhetoric had telegraphed through Unitarian, apocalyptic and Miltonic idiom.

'Fears in Solitude' is Coleridge's last conspicuous attempt to
combine the older metaphysics with the new domestic idiom. The
poem explains his less radical stance and encourages opponents of
the French Revolution to join in 'Repenting of the wrongs with
which we stung/So fierce a foe to frenzy!' (152–3). He was to satirize
those who called this complex admission mere recantation or apostasy
in a slightly later poem called 'Recantation: Illustrated in the Story
of the Mad Ox'. In 'Fears in Solitude', though, the refusal simply to
disown earlier positions is shown by the persistence of the visionary
licence which supported them – 'Religious meanings in the forms of
Nature!' (24). The poem insists on tracing abstractions back to their
origins in sensation, and abandons a language which floats above
recent political events 'As if the soldier died without a wound' (117).
Yet this new realism sits uneasily beside the poem's attempts to
grasp in vision a universal purpose behind historical change. Once
more, the locodescriptive 'burst of prospect' only 'seems like society'
(215–18), and this imagined reality or political future is finally
locked up in Stowey's domestic, Wordsworthian seclusion where the
narrator is 'made worthy to indulge/Love, and the thoughts that
yearn for human kind' (231–2).

Conversation poems like 'This Lime-tree Bower My Prison', 'The
Nightingale' and 'Frost at Midnight' narrow the former range and
openly specify a coterie audience. They are influenced by Wordsworth, and to some extent they are about the initial artistic stability
and contentment Coleridge found in his company. He is happy to
write about the new centre 'In the deep Sabbath of meek self-
content' desired at the end of the 'Ode to the Departing Year' and
now confirmed by the contrast of Wordsworth's companionship to
all the radical projects and sociability of Bristol. 'Frost at Midnight'
appears the most successful because it is most at ease with its genre's
characteristic savouring of its own ways of seeing a nature which it
'By its own moods interprets, every where/Echo or mirror seeking of
itself,/And makes a toy of Thought' (21–3). Like 'The Nightingale',
it is 'a father's tale' of desire to evoke a completely natural franchise different from the oppressive city childhood of the narrator,
one surpassing even the rural infancy described in the second

verse-paragraph. Yet that freedom leads into a recognizably Coleridgian preoccupation with nature as the language of God: in willing betterment for the baby the poem tells us more of the origins of the father's solicitude and the imaginative resources for his vision. By the end of the poem the deceptively simple opening image of the 'silent ministry of frost' encapsulates the poem's discovery. The frost makes a tangible object, icicles, out of a medium of transparency. To call the crystallization of its own element a 'ministry' connects it with the way in which the narrator's ministrations on behalf of his child become the imaginative substance of the poem rather than, as he desires, a transparent window looking on to an order of freedom different from his own experience. This unstated theme, and so 'secret' and 'silent', forms the poem into an expressive object: its reflection upon its own vision also gains allegorical reference to the common dilemma of a parenthood bound to constrict even in its attempts transparently to transform and ameliorate. This was sadly true in the case of Coleridge's son Hartley, to whom the poem, biographically read, refers, and whose muddled life certainly bore his father's imprint. But the poem does not need special corroboration, and applies generally to the way in which the human subject locates itself in specific symbolic orders – patriarchal, philosophical, religious, political – even as it imagines a natural freedom from their constraint.

In this kind of conversation poem, an implausible public is replaced by a like-minded coterie ('This Lime-tree Bower'), a child's future self ('Frost at Midnight') or both ('The Nightingale'). The genre assures a sympathetic audience in advance, rather than making it subject to the poem's rhetorical success in transforming its listeners. This more relaxed framework makes for poems of less spectacular reach, but with more subtle powers to evoke in self-sufficient domesticity symbols for the circularity of understanding and an imaginative source for all reality. 'Frost at Midnight', for example, domesticates the harsher paradoxes of the changeling in 'The Foster-mother's Tale', extracted for *Lyrical Ballads* from the drama *Osorio* which Coleridge had written in the summer of 1797. The changeling is a comparably contradictory free spirit, 'unteachable', whistling 'as if he were a bird himself', yet soon becoming 'a very learned youth', full of 'heretical and lawless talk'. He escapes civilization, but only for its reactionary mirror-image 'among the savage men'. The confidence of 'Frost at Midnight', boosted by neighbourhood with the poet Coleridge was coming to regard as the greatest since Milton, compensates for such retreats from the task of envisaging radical political transformation.

'The Nightingale' progresses from Milton's description of the bird in 'Il Penseroso' as 'most musical, most melancholy' to natural relish for the bird's song, artfully artless, mediated by the company of the Wordsworths. In 'This Lime-tree Bower' the narrator is doubly sequestered: firstly in his coterie, secondly in the bower while his friends make the familiar journey out of a dell to higher ground and a climactic view of the surroundings. Under the pressure of his doubled confinement, his vision universalizes its enforced vicariousness, making the friends' immediate experience of the view as symbolic as the narrator's projected substitute has to be:

> So my friend
> Struck with deep joy may stand, as I have stood,
> Silent with swimming sense; yea, gazing round
> On the wide landscape, gaze till all doth seem
> Less gross than bodily; and of such hues
> As veil the Almighty Spirit, when yet he makes
> Spirits perceive his presence.

(37–43)

In the earlier version of these lines in the letter to Southey, Coleridge called their sentiment Berkeleyan. If nature is, as the philosopher George Berkeley supposed, always sustained by God's perception of it, then we do always see it at second hand, the perception of a perception. The private imagination, referring openly to the canon of Coleridge's conversation poems ('as I have stood'), is now the confident agent of Coleridge's desire to know 'something *great* – something *one & indivisible*', as he told the radical activist John Thelwall in a letter quoting these lines.[1] Thelwall might have been forgiven for thinking that the balance between retreat from and criticism of society had shifted considerably in favour of the former. The double retreat in 'This Lime-tree Bower' is, however, into what Coleridge, describing 'The Rime of the Ancient Mariner' to Mrs Barbauld, called 'pure imagination':[2] a faculty which he increasingly saw as the matrix of all the public concerns he might otherwise have been thought to have left behind. After all, his contributions to political journalism were renewed in the long service he gave from 1799 onwards to the *Morning Post* and afterwards to the *Courier*, reprinted by his daughter Sara as *Essays on His Own Times*. Nevertheless, the kind of archetypal poetic writing one encounters in the mystery poems of 1797–8 does appear to avoid the politics, as well as

1 *Letters*, i. 349.
2 *Table Talk*, 31 May 1830.

the infelicities, resulting from the strenuous interaction of public and private in the poems we have looked at so far.

It is undeniable that the mystery poems – 'The Rime of the Ancient Mariner', 'Kubla Khan' and 'Christabel' – are usually thought to be the poems on which Coleridge's reputation ought to rest. If this view is justified, it is because they have internalized the breadth of historical concern in the rest of Coleridge's poetry in order to reproduce it as though stemming from archetypal sources. Two of the poems, 'Kubla Khan' and 'Christabel', are fragments and were not published until 1816. Then the Whiggish *Edinburgh Review* found their mystery full of 'bathos' and their publication an 'impertinence',[1] showing how quickly they had lost the historical relevance inscribed in other Coleridgian poems of the period, a loss which most subsequent commentary has been slow to redeem. In the earlier poem 'The Destiny of Nations: A Vision', Coleridge first cites the fanciful power which 'Emancipates [the dark mind] from the grosser thrall/Of the present impulse' (85–6). The power becomes an excuse to present his own reading, here learned tracts on Lapland and 'the Greenland Wizard', as relevant for understanding the original motives to social government:

> If there be Beings of higher class than Man,
> I deem no nobler province they possess,
> Than by disposal of apt circumstance
> To rear up kingdoms . . .

> (127–30)

In the bookish search for the apparently unlimited sources of the mystery poems, such a feature of Coleridge criticism, this continuing political orientation of their heightened imagination and literariness tends to get overlooked. Yet the mystery of these poems makes authority their theme. The 'Rime' is framed by images of community, wedding and worship, a subtle adjustment which initiates the reader's revaluation of the Mariner's tale. 'Kubla Khan' forces us to compare the deployment of the same energies towards cultivation, government and fantasy. 'Christabel' examines how absolute values of purity and innocence can mask the inability to act because of an unwillingness to confront and think through a previous history which, as a result, can only break through this repression in inarticulate shapes of Gothic horror.

When 'Kubla Khan' and 'Christabel' were published in 1816, the

1 Reiman, *Romantics Reviewed*, ii. 469, 473.

'Rime' being first acknowledged by Coleridge a year later in *Sibylline Leaves*, they slipped easily into the context of Coleridge's writings of this later period. In 1816 he had published the first of his lay sermons, *The Statesman's Manual*, and the second, *Blessed are ye that sow* . . ., which was 'On the Existing Distresses and Discontents', followed in 1817. In the lay sermons Coleridge tried to work out in detail a kind of transcendental politics based on an a priori understanding of the proper disposition of the mental faculties. He argued that philosophically to deduce this universal grid through which we are obliged to apprehend the world was not to retreat into a detached realm of pure logic or metaphysics, but to make possible a specific historical intervention within the troubled political world of Britain after the Napoleonic wars. In *The Statesman's Manual* he wrote that 'all the *epoch-forming* Revolutions of the Christian world, the revolutions of religion and with them the civil, social, and domestic habits of the nations concerned, have coincided with the rise and fall of metaphysical systems.' Again, he insisted that this perception was not peculiar to philosophers but was the experience of political activists: 'in periods of popular tumult and innovation the more abstract a notion is, the more readily has it been found to combine, the closer has appeared its affinity, with the feelings of a people and with all their immediate impulses to action.'[1] Later views like these suggest that the mystery poems do not eschew politics, but that they prefigure the change to come in Coleridge's political views. He frequently attacks the Unitarians in the lay sermons, at one point condemning their 'antipathy to *mysteries*', which he glosses as 'all these doctrines of the pure and intuitive *reason*, which transcend the understanding'.[2] The Unitarian who, in the *Monthly Repository*, replied with dignity to Coleridge's attacks urges him to remember that he 'thought and felt with us in the vernal freshness of [his] genius', and claims, perhaps disingenuously, that 'it is not to us, but to poetry that I should most cordially hail your return.'[3] However, the 'mysteries' of the 'Rime', 'Kubla Khan' and 'Christabel' had already shown how poetry can engage with those 'pure and intuitive' elements which in 1816–17 power Coleridge's conservatism.

In Appendix C to *The Statesman's Manual*, Coleridge describes conscience as 'the coincidence of the human will with reason and religion'. He is tempted to call this 'a *spiritual sensation*', but

1 *Lay Sermons*, in *Collected Works*, VI. 14–15.
2 Ibid., VI. 56.
3 Ibid., VI. 259–60.

hesitates over defining 'that, which being unique, can have no fair analogy'.[1] In the 'Rime', the Mariner recovers a comparable harmony in his life, yet remains unique rather than straightforwardly exemplary. Coleridge published a marginal gloss accompanying the 1817 version which emphasized the moral interpretation of the tale: 'He prayeth best, who loveth best/All things both great and small.' The obvious failure of this homily to cover the significance of the Mariner's story is shown by the way in which the Mariner repeatedly loses his repose and is compelled to tell his tale to yet another audience. His conscience cannot be shrived once and for all by the hermit at the end of his voyage, but must be restored again and again through penitential repetition of the 'Rime'. This circular solution stresses the uniqueness of the poem, the impossibility of unpacking its meaning in other terms, and its anticipation of the proverbial status awaiting its protagonist in future English usage. Although the Mariner's understanding of what he has experienced belongs to the Christian community he describes at the end, his impulse to redemption was aesthetic, a feeling for the beauty of the water-snakes generating love, then benediction and the intercession of 'Mary Queen', the gloss's 'holy Mother'. The search for his saving motive, therefore, returns us to the poem's specifics: the language and imagery in which the creatures appear to the Mariner as aesthetically persuasive. Mystery supervenes, as we are told 'no tongue/Their beauty might declare' (282–3), and the reader, like the Mariner, is led rhetorically into repeating the words whose lack of explanatory conclusion send one back to look for clues to their sequence. The most prominent patterns in the poem are strikingly elemental – heat and cold, light and dark, sun and moon – so that one is again deprived of plot and invited to ascribe to the poem an absolute appositeness of language. The 1798 version accentuates this from the start in a buttonholing shorthand:

> Listen, Stranger! Storm and Wind,
>   A Wind and Tempest strong!
> For days and weeks it play'd us freaks –
>   Like Chaff we drove along.
>
> Listen, Stranger! Mist and Snow,
>   And it grew wond'rous cauld:
> And Ice mast-high came floating by
>   As green as Emerauld.

(45–52)

1  Ibid., VI. 66–7.

Presence is all in this kind of writing. Its artful simplicity conjures the illusion of immediacy: its apparent poverty of description, or nominalism, is compensated for by its gestural authority. The less the Mariner elaborates, the more his rhetoric suggests he is making the stranger 'hear' the elements at work rather than merely his names for them. Again, though, it is worth stressing that the ballad's transparency is paradoxically what forces the reader to ponder its poetry. There isn't really anything visible behind words, and since this poetry is especially closed to other explanatory discourses and poses, as we saw happen in 'France: An Ode', as symbolically replete, it focuses *itself* with unignorable sharpness. Like the Wedding Guest, readers are wilfully cut off from other forms of communication, temporarily suspended from all social obligation or determination. The 'Rime''s presentation of poetic autonomy or 'pure imagination' has therefore been used by critics over the years either to exemplify their own aesthetic priorities, or to attack the idea of a poetic isolated from other orders of significance. For some the poem becomes a self-sufficient symbolic system; its albatross, guilt, purgatorial voyage, demonology and cosmic play are parts of a self-regulating ecology. For others this self-sufficiency is just the problem, as the poem confusedly appropriates as its own a significance which lies outside poetic jurisdiction and under that of religious, moral or political discourses. Historically to recreate Coleridge's poetic ideology, however, is to bring these opposed readers closer together. We begin to see how Coleridge could have thought that poetic internalization did not withdraw from wider concerns. Instead, poetry exposed their archetypal, mental sources, and, most importantly, helped define an audience interested in this kind of higher, transcendental knowledge.

What is the audience implied by a poem like this? The ambience of coterie is revived by Coleridge in *Sibylline Leaves* with a footnote to the lines 'And thou art long, and lank, and brown,/As is the ribbed sea-sand' (226–7) which acknowledges them as Wordsworth's and dates the plan and partial composition of the poem from 'a delightful walk' in his company in November 1797. The reader aspires to belong to the company of poets and poetic spirits who can recognize what Coleridge calls in *Biographia Literaria* the 'logic' of poetry, readers who are willing to submit to the jurisdiction of poetic imagination.[1] When Southey called the poem 'a Dutch attempt at German sublimity' in the *Critical Review* of October 1798, he

1 *Biographia Literaria*, in *Collected Works*, XI. i. 9.

shrewdly linked the poem's balladic populism to its pretensions to transcendental authority.[1] The reader, that is, who is silenced by the poem's simplicity of description is invited to attribute this to the poem's rhetorical feat in having its imaginary logic accepted as natural. Awareness and resentment of this artful imposition of authority are evident in the *British Review*'s comment in August 1816 on 'Christabel':

A witch is no heroine, nor can we read a tale of magic for its own sake. Poetry itself must show some modesty, nor be quite unforbearing in its exactions. What we allow it the use of as an accessory it must not convert into a principal, and what is granted to it as part of its proper machinery it must not impose upon us as the main or only subject of interest. But Mr Coleridge is one of those poets who if we give him an inch will be sure to take an ell . . .[2]

The audience variously implied or 'exacted' by poems like these is one flattered to be thought able to recognize an image of poetry written for its own sake. Similarly, in the elaborately presented fragmentariness of 'Kubla Khan', they would be pleased to be thought capable of appreciating the constitutional incompleteness of an 'Idea' containing, as *The Statesman's Manual* has it, 'endless power of semination'.[3] The ability to recognize an Idea, though, is just what the lay sermons set out to revive through their address to the higher and middle classes of society rather than a 'promiscuous audience' or 'Reading Public'. Poetry written to foreground its own archetypal imaginative power turns out to be a genre, not an absolute. The audience it specifies as competent to recognize its authority turns out to be the social classes with which it enjoys a cultural solidarity.

The late publication of the mystery poems in the context of Coleridge's lay sermons lays bare a political tendency dormant in 1798. The detection of the partisanship of 'pure imagination' is like *The Statesman's Manual*'s discovery that the Bible (Old Testament) provides lessons in political economy and the 'Elements of Political Science'. Coleridge argues on the first page against an unhistorical transcendentalism, which leaves the Bible in 'a dead language', and for an appreciation of the need to historicize and relativize scriptural interpretation: 'the very excellence of the Giver has been made a

1 Reiman, *Romantics Reviewed*, i. 309.
2 Ibid., i. 239.
3 *Lay Sermons*, in *Collected Works*, VI. 24, 36.

reason for withholding the gift.'[1] Equally, the stylistically anachronistic Elizabethan gloss to the medieval 'Rime' may be ironically incomplete, demonstrating the irreducible authority of the verse;[2] but it points readers in the right direction, which is to ask what historical audience or culture *is* defined by the ability properly to recognize the 'Rime''s poetic authority. Coleridge still maintains that the original words of the Bible are literally and philosophically true. Their benefits for his contemporaries come from inspiring a learned class, who can distinguish biblical symbols from the normally exhaustive alternatives of literal and metaphorical usage, a self-fashioning activity indirectly applying the Bible to contemporary events without threat to its authenticity. Coleridge frequently asserts that 'Reason and Religion are their own evidence' and employ symbols consubstantial with their truths. What this means within the overall strategy of *The Statesman's Manual* is that the clerkly reflective and philosophical habits such studies encourage within the professional classes will counter their current subjection to a predominantly 'commercial spirit', which is the immediate occasion of existing social distresses. To become a clerk or member of the learned class has an inherently beneficial social effect, is its own reward or 'evidence', irrespective of the doctrinal details which the new skills in symbolic interpretation might elicit. It alters the social mix on analogy with a revivified aristocracy or supra-mercantile class. When Coleridge begins to deploy some of the 'mysteries' to which his Clerisy might be privy, the result is faintly ridiculous, as when he claims that 'the Prophet Isaiah revealed the true philosophy of the French revolution more than two thousand years before it became a sad irrevocable truth of history', or when he ponders with some irony the practicability of elevating 'even our daily newspapers and political journals into COMMENTS ON THE BIBLE'.[3]

Direct applications like these appear as fallible as Charles Lamb thought mere publication would render the mystery of 'Kubla Khan'. In a letter he told Wordsworth that 'there is an observation Never tell thy dreams, and I am almost afraid that Kubla Khan is an owl that wont bear day light, I fear lest it should be discovered by the lantern of typography & clear reducting to letters, no better than nonsense or no sense.'[4] Of course the poem itself already expresses this fear, and 'in holy dread' proposes the devout but cautionary

1 Ibid., VI. 5.
2 Wheeler, *The Creative Mind*, pp 51–64.
3 *Lay Sermons*, in *Collected Works*, VI. 34, 35.
4 Lamb, *Letters*, iii. 215.

sequestration of the charismatic poet transported by its vision. However, this ambiguous respect would only be merited 'if' the poet could reconstitute Kubla's civilizing 'decree', a materialist aesthetic, in his own imaginary terms. It would be anachronistic to try to reconstruct Kubla's achievement in a more literal way, although its misprision may be the conflict prophesied by the 'ancestral voices'. Researches such as Elinor Shaffer's, which see 'Kubla Khan' as modelling Coleridge's plans for an ultimate epic on 'the Fall of Jerusalem', explicitly link mystery poem and German 'higher' Biblical criticism within a single ideal of clerical learning.[1] The poet in 'Kubla Khan' gains respect for his modern envisioning of Xanadu, his own recreation of the Khan's culturally formative ideals rather than a pale imitation of their historical particulars. The preface of 1816 tells denigratory stories which privilege the 'psychological curiosity' of the piece over 'any supposed *poetic* merits'. It throws an emphasis, as ironically misguided as the 'Rime''s gloss, on the process rather than the content of the poem. Readers, by contrast, can ponder the ideal nature of the magnetic poet's socially encompassing vision, and make themselves the higher critics or contemporary translators of that.

On the other hand, this interpretation copes with the complexity of image and structure in 'Kubla Khan' by disappointing the traditional critical expectations justifiably raised by the poem's richly allusive style: expectations of a definite meaning achieved through symbolic decoding, allegorical unravelling or the unmasking of explanatory sources. Yet the alternative is more responsive to the way the poem expresses the loss incurred by being true to any past meaning in terms significant for the present. To this extent Coleridge's prefatory remarks about losing inspiration in its composition are doubly ironic. The framing tale of the poet's failure is ironically belied by the poetic product. The Crewe manuscript of the poem in the British Library suggests that, far from being a spontaneous effusion, an attenuated but effortless recall, the 1816 poem we read was carefully edited, polished and shaped out of several versions. However, the higher-critical reading which exonerates the poem's fragmentariness as a finished modernism also ironically implies an inherently inconclusive dialectic of truth – how truth is gained through loss, is recreated through translation into other terms, and is made significant through infidelity to an original.

The poem exhibits this primarily by making its structure, in the

1 E. Shaffer, '*Kubla Khan' and the Fall of Jerusalem*, Cambridge, 1975.

form of a progressively diminishing echo, dependent on its faithfulness to an original, confused resonance. For behind the figure of the Khan lies the source of the river which enables his plan of cultivation. And that 'deep romantic chasm' of the second stanza releases an image of creativity which is a violent, obscure, sexually inchoate, and inexpressive harvest, until its principal emission, the river Alph, subsides into productive irrigation.

> And from this chasm, with ceaseless turmoil seething,
> As if this earth in fast thick pants were breathing,
> A mighty fountain momently was forced:
> Amid whose swift half-intermitted burst
> Huge fragments vaulted like rebounding hail,
> Or chaffy grain beneath the thresher's flail:
> And 'mid these dancing rocks at once and ever
> It flung up momently the sacred river.
>
> (17–24)

Subsequently the poem lists successive mediations of this creation: the Khan's pleasure-dome, his 'miracle of rare device', and its more and more distant afterlives in the imagined subject of the song of the Abyssinian maid, seen in the poet's vision, which he would like to 'revive within', internally. But his picture of what that would entail summons an image of poetic possession far in excess of the Abyssinian muse-figure's conventional female ministrations, one recalling instead the original, sexually undifferentiated forces of the 'romantic chasm'.

Those whom the poet can make see *his* pleasure-dome are immediately compelled to contemplate the energies which created it, 'momently' reversing the journey of the entire poem away from the originary.

> I would build that dome in air,
> That sunny dome! those caves of ice!
> And all who heard should see them there,
> And all should cry, Beware! Beware!
> His flashing eyes, his floating hair!
>
> (46–50)

At the poem's furthest distance from the contingent natural powers which the Khan's culture materially deploys, the modern poet's internalized, idealist echo nevertheless recalls their bewildering effect. The critic has to remain flexible: between readings which emphasize the poet's authority, and those which stress the confusing indeterminacy of his supposedly timely grasp of transcendental ideals prior to their historical and cultural determination.

'Christabel' dramatizes, among other things, the lack of just that critical flexibility. Its characters are monstered by their fixations. In *The Statesman's Manual*, Coleridge described life without access to a transcendental idea, when 'Experience itself is but a cyclops walking backwards, under the fascination of the Past'.[1] William Hazlitt, reviewing 'Christabel' in the *Examiner*, predictably had no truck with the politics of Coleridge's imagination – 'this pretended contempt for the opinion of the public' – but caught at its method in his perception that 'Mr Coleridge's style is essentially superficial, pretty, ornamental, and he has forced it into the service of a story which is petrific.'[2]

A story which turns its characters to stone is bound to reduce everything to attractive surface irony and arabesque. Christabel is eventually characterized by her potential to match or fit Geraldine. Her innocence is the transparency and superficiality, the childlike octosyllabic lines, the eerie Gothic nothingness through which we see and recognize the realistic adult motivations of Geraldine and Sir Leoline. Christabel finds Geraldine petrifying:

> So deeply had she drunken in
> That look, those shrunken serpent eyes,
> That all her features were resigned
> To this sole image in her mind . . .
>
> (601–4)

Geraldine may have the power to fixate Christabel, but only as a consequence of Christabel's unchanging, childlike perspective on her adulthood. Geraldine's spell, sealed in a masterful erotic encounter –

> Then suddenly as one defied
> Collects herself in scorn and pride,
> And lay down by the Maiden's side! –
> And in her arms the maid she took
>
> (260–63)

– has the effect of rendering Christabel inarticulate, Geraldine now becoming the 'lord of thy utterance' (268) as well. Christabel is made *infans*, a babe in (Geraldine's) arms, incapable of dissociating herself from the words and images Geraldine gives her. Her passive imitation and 'unconscious sympathy' with Geraldine make it increasingly difficult to separate them, as Sir Leoline's reading of Bracy the bard's dream of snake and dove intertwined testifies. They also

1 *Lay Sermons*, in *Collected Works*, VI. 43.
2 Reiman, *Romantics Reviewed*, ii. 530–31.

remind us of the nugatoriness of Christabel's character before Geraldine substituted for her absent lover, supplanted the memory of her dead mother and became her father's favourite.

Readers look for what Hazlitt called 'something disgusting at the bottom of his subject', but to be horrific the poem does not need the description of Geraldine's naked deformity which Hazlitt complained was cut from the 1816 version. Geraldine is a future self presented as utterly determined rather than chosen, commandeering all the sexual and parental influences to which the self should respond with its own defining choices. The past she offers to Sir Leoline, for whom since his wife's death 'Each matin bell . . ./Knells us back to a world of death' (332–3), is one apparently open to reinterpretation, and so rejuvenation, through the recovery of his youthful friendship with her father, Lord Roland de Vaux. He can only enjoy this benefit, though, by repudiating Christabel. Presumably still the victim of Geraldine's ventriloquizing ('lord of thy utterance'), Christabel asks him to banish Geraldine, a request which he takes as a slight on his hospitable nature. He loses his wife over again by leaving 'the babe for whom she died,/[and prayed] Might prove her dear lord's joy and pride!' (630–31) in disgrace.

Geraldine thus draws another circle tight, having Sir Leoline reincur the cause of his misery and substitute her for Christabel as its palliative. The second 'Conclusion' suggests ironic reconciliation in the picture of the father who 'Must needs express his love's excess/With words of unmeant bitterness' (664–5), but it is precisely the way in which Geraldine *is* an ironic figure, reconciling or immobilizing opposite characters in herself, that has been the problem. The only way out is, as Marjorie Levinson suggests, to read 'Christabel' as a genuine fragment of something larger. In this case we are really *not* given the full story: we cannot adopt 'contradiction as the work's organizing principle . . . naturalizing the poem (and one's response to it) through some notion of irony or dialectic'.[1]

Denied this context, the work retains its status as 'mystery'; and denied the irony of the 'Conclusion', we readers are also denied the richer, many-sided content which irony's expressive tolerance of contradiction produces. We become the readership of a mode of writing which keeps its own counsel. We can see its slipping of all explanations as the wilful egotism or even 'nonsense' deplored by many of the reviews of 1816. Or else the story of 'Christabel', in

1 M. Levinson, *The Romantic Fragment Poem*, Chapel Hill, NC, and London, 1986, p 85.

which all interpretations are trapped by the petrifying Geraldine, can be understood as lending an historical point to what would otherwise be an empty transcendental freedom. This point is in keeping with the one being developed in Coleridge's other writings of this time for those learned in a kind of higher criticism above interpretation and direct application; one whose consequently disinterested discipline ought to be its own political reward.

Definitive interpretation is in this way undercut by the method the mystery poems employ to solicit an audience capable of accepting them on 'their own evidence', and capable of recognizing the social role specified for themselves as a result – membership of a learned class whose reflective habits and cultural priorities differentiate them from the predominantly commercial interests of the rest of contemporary society. The same logic fuels Coleridge's praise in *Biographia Literaria* of Wordsworth's *'untranslatableness'* and of his characterization of the Immortality Ode's 'intended' readership as one whose symbolic expertise was above 'ordinary interpretation'.[1] He elaborated further on the nature of this learned class or Clerisy in *Biographia* and placed it within his full-blown political theory in *On the Constitution of the Church and State According to the Idea of Each* in 1830. By then the cat was out of the bag: transcendental politics described the placé of those who studied the 'Ideas' from which derived the form of political organization of which Coleridge approved. Those learned in 'Ideas' cultivated that knowledge of humanity which made citizens aware of the point of the institutions to which they were subject, and thus grounded their social obligations to Church and State in a higher freedom. Radicals like Hazlitt understood this to be no more than an elaborate apology for Coleridge's conservatism, and tried to discredit his political theory by discovering the idiom of the mystery poems at the heart of its philosophical prose: 'for greater nonsense the author could not write, even though he were inspired expressly for the purpose'.[2] In retrospect we can have more admiration for Coleridge's breadth of rhetorical resources and regret the progressive neglect of that professionally cultivated range in subsequent conservative thinking.

Another critical vocabulary used against the lay sermons and *Biographia* deplores his use of German philosophy and terminology. In 1825 Coleridge wrote that, as well as personal attacks, 'the mistaken notion of my German Metaphysics . . . rendered my au-

1 *Collected Works*, XI. ii. 142, 147.
2 Reiman, *Romantics Reviewed*, ii. 537.

thority with the TRADE worse than nothing.'[1] Authority of a
peculiar kind was clearly the thing at stake here, an authority whose
Coleridgian idiom did not fit or was even thematically opposed to
commercial considerations of what would sell. 'Mr Coleridge', wrote
Hazlitt, supposes his audience 'intuitively to perceive the cabbalistic
visions of German metaphysics.'[2] Coleridge had travelled to Germany with the Wordsworths in September 1798, and leaving them at
Goslar moved on to the more philosophically active environment of
the university town of Göttingen. He began reading voluminously in
German philosophy and literature, translating and imitating poems
by Goethe, Gessner, Stolberg and Schiller, translating Schiller's
plays *The Death of Wallenstein* and *The Piccolomini* in 1800. In
February 1801 he wrote to his friend Poole that 'Change of Ministry
interests *me* not – I turn at times half reluctantly from Leibniz or
Kant even to read a smoking new newspaper/such a purus putus
Metaphysicus am I become.' A few days later he sent the first of a
series of philosophical letters to Josiah Wedgwood, arguing that
'Locke's *System* existed in the writings of Descartes.'[3] Coleridge's
eagerness to detect plagiarism in others has often been linked to his
anxieties about acknowledging his own eclecticism, especially debts
to A. W. Schlegel in his literary lectures, and to Schelling and the
German historian of philosophy Tennemann in *Biographia* and his
philosophical lectures of 1818–19. Equally, the 'pure' transcendental
ground sought by German idealism would both render agreement
between Coleridge and other thinkers unsurprising, like the 'genial
coincidence' between himself and Schelling coolly conceded in *Biographia*.[4] It would also vindicate that typically retreating movement
in his thought and poetry towards a coincidence with its imaginative
sources. Reality was not necessarily abandoned as a consequence, but
its logically necessary congruence with our powers of comprehending
it was poetically symbolized. Schelling's post-Kantianism explained
this congruence as the result of an underlying Absolute activity
which expressed itself through both mind and nature, the active and
the passive, the conscious and the unconscious, seeking their eventual
reconciliation within a universal poetic pattern. Our intermediate
grasp of this final harmony in art makes imagination the arbiter of
ultimate reality, spectacularly exonerating it from escapism. Coleridge
later fears that pantheism will result from extending imaginative

1 *Letters*, v. 421.
2 Reiman, Romantics Reviewed, ii. 480.
3 *Letters*, ii. 676, 686.
4 *Collected Works*, XI. i. 160–64.

authority so far: there is no logical room left for God or anything else. On the other hand he increasingly wished to retain that authority for the Clerisy, the transcendental linchpin of his social theory. Opposition to his attempts to expound the German sources of his idealism exhibited a mixture of cultural xenophobia and genuine insight into the political designs which his German obscurity appeared to disguise or discredit.

The continuity between imagination, German idealism and constitutionalism in Coleridge's thought was temporarily but memorably interrupted by the verse letter he wrote to Sara Hutchinson on 4 April 1802. He had met Sara in October 1799 and fallen in love with her at the same rate that he had become estranged from Sarah Fricker. His relationship with Sara remained unconsummated, partly, as far as one can tell, from Coleridge's religious and social inhibitions, and partly from Sara's less than totally committed response. It produced, as well as happier 'Asra' poems, his furthest-reaching investigation in verse of his imagination's power to compensate or undercut public disappointment. The poem is about Coleridge's ill health, loss of inspiration, marital misery and, above all, the intolerableness of the vicariously imaginative existence which he defends with such poetic conviction on other occasions. In contrast to that redemption, the 'Letter to Sara Hutchinson' shows, in David Pirie's words, that 'in facing the full extent of his misfortunes, Coleridge regains the capacity to feel, which had seemed the central loss.'[1] Like *The Prelude* (and the poem was at one stage addressed to Wordsworth) the 'Letter' can be placed within the Romantic convention of poems lamenting the loss of the powers which have produced them. But this redeeming irony is not adequate to the miseries this poem describes. It is not the case that the narrator can imaginatively conjure the absent Sara's reality in a more permanent form than he can experience in transient social encounters with her. He certainly tries to argue this, but success turns out to depend on whether or not she is well or ill. Her illness provokes his irrepressible need for intimacy, not to be satisfied in imagination, but at one with his desire for physical union expressed vividly in his notebook jottings and acrostics.

> But (let me say it! for I vainly strive
> To beat away the Thought) but if thou pin'd,
> Whate'er the Cause, in body or in mind,

1 See D. Pirie, 'A Verse Letter to [Asra]', in *Bicentenary Wordsworth Studies*, ed. J. Wordsworth, Ithaca, NY, and London, 1970.

I were the miserablest Man alive
To know it & be absent! Thy Delights
Far off, or near, alike I may partake –
But O! to mourn for thee, & to forsake
All power, all hope of giving comfort to thee –
To know that thou art weak & worn with pain,
And not to hear thee, Sara! not to view thee –
    Not to sit beside thy Bed,
    Not press thy aching Head,
    Not bring thee Health again –
    At least to hope, to try –

(169–82)

The fact that Sara's indisposition was caused by receiving an earlier importunate letter from Coleridge adds further poignancy to the self-laceration of his writing.

The value of this kind of verse is not in its own metaphysical certainty, its imagination's reassuring coincidence with itself even *in extremis*. Passages like this one evoke the hermeneutical circle of Romantic poetry and philosophy as a genuine prison, imposed by circumstance and personal difference, not the springboard to the universal communion celebrated in 'This Lime-tree Bower'. However, the version of the 'Letter' edited, cut and published in the *Morning Post* six months later restores the Romantic orthodoxy. The publicly acceptable version gains formality from the exclusion of potentially embarrassing personal details: it becomes an 'ode' rather than a 'verse letter', and the new genre implies that a disciplined processing of personal content for public consumption has taken place. 'The dark distressful Dream' of Coleridge's dilemma is therefore expanded to 'Reality's dark dream' and a theory of Romantic irony. Ironically, that is, the dramatis personae which art and imagination create for nature – her wedding garment, her shroud, her voices – startle the narrator into a more attentive, feeling observation which an unsung literal reality could not attract, appearing dreamlike by comparison. This pivotal irony of the 'Ode' then redeems the relationship with the 'Lady'. The histrionics of the ode's description of the wind – 'Lutanist', 'Actor', 'Poet' – is the sign of the poet's revived sensibility, just as the final benediction on the 'Lady' envelops her in joyful, satisfied well-wishing as if in fact 'we receive but what we give/And in our life alone does Nature live'. It is eerie to contrast this confidence with the conclusion of 'The Pains of Sleep', written within the year, which protests *against* natural subjection to an absolute imagination. Its power indifferently to create both object and subject is measured this time by its alternation between the roles of victim and torturer: '. . . all confused I could not know,/Whether I suffered, or I did' (28–9). This sado-masochistic characterization of Schelling's active, passive, inescapable Absolute is countered feebly but unignorably at the end with the unassimilable pain of the 'Letter': 'To be beloved is all I need,/And whom I love, I love indeed.'

Later poems like 'Limbo' and 'Constancy to an Ideal Object' similarly reflect adversely upon central positions in Coleridge's public thought. In 'Limbo', the ultimate, awful fear is of '*positive negation*'. This notion is the parodic inverse of Coleridge's attempt to give substance to 'Ideas' which explain experience but can themselves only be experienced as contradictory and negative. In 'Constancy to an Ideal Object' the 'enamoured rustic', deceived by the broken spectre, represents the transcendental project as requiring an escape from self-consciousness in order to be able to work its sublimations. The mystifying rustic can figure either Coleridgian humility before ultimately religious authority or expose as an illusion the ideological machinery of Coleridgian transcendental superiority.

Nevertheless, despite 'The Pains of Sleep', it is the friendship in which the 'Ode' concludes that shades into the aims of Coleridge's next journalistic attempt to create the public audience by which his work might be enjoyed. *The Friend* was first published in June 1809 and abandoned in March 1810. It was reissued in 1812 and reworked into a three-volume edition of 1818. Coleridge's final choice of title for his 'Weekly Essays' conciliates timid readers in advance. Barbara Rooke pointed out in her edition a relevant remark of Coleridge's in a letter to Southey of 1794: 'I love my *Friend* – such as *he* is, all mankind are or *might* be.'[1] But this lasting ambition of moulding an ideal audience now goes with Coleridge's growing awareness of what might be called the pathology of his transcendental detachment from the constraints of any single discipline. In the 'prospectus' he conjures up a public which understands his problem of finding definitive expression for his thought: 'tempted onward by an increasing Sense of the imperfection of my Knowledge, and of the Conviction that, in Order fully to comprehend and develope any one Subject, it was necessary that I should make myself Master of some other, which again as regularly involved a third, and so on, with an ever-widening Horizon'.[2]

1 *Letters*, i. 86.
2 *The Friend*, in *Collected Works*, IV. ii. 16.

Excuses for the vacillations of the philosophical mind now accompany its logical justifications. When Coleridge writes in the issue of 11 January 1810 that 'There is nothing, the absolute ground of which is not a Mystery', he is conscious of the discouragement which might be experienced by the reader of the transcendental philosopher of the 'absolute ground' or the untranslatable poet of its 'Mystery'. He reprinted the claim, its context slightly revised, in *Aids to Reflection*, a book whose primarily aphoristic discourse is etymologically glossed by Coleridge as 'circumscribing and detaching' from that 'ever-widening Horizon' of meaning.[1] *Aids* tries to furnish his formal philosophical analyses with a more readable, memorable idiom. Nevertheless, *The Friend* did prove obscure to many of Coleridge's correspondents and perhaps forced him to consider more popular ways of communicating his transcendental project. The 1809 *Friend* had discussed Coleridge's difficulties of communication, casting them as a critique of 'the epigrammatic unconnected periods of the fashionable *Anglo-gallican* Taste'.[2] The 1818 *Friend* added 'Essays on the Principles of Method' – to be, as a letter of 1819 asserts, 'the first elements, or alphabet, of my whole system',[3] the difficulty still remaining for his readers that the first elements of his system claimed acquaintance with the Ideas motivating the 'method' of any system.

In striking contrast to his earlier journalism, *The Friend* scarcely dealt with contemporary events at all. Yet Coleridge originally planned to call it 'The Advocate' or 'The Upholder',[4] and just the lack of political criticism in an author by now so famous for it must have instantly communicated a positive attitude towards Government. The 'Prospectus' announced forthcoming essays primarily on moral philosophy. Yet a political aim is again kept paramount when these turn out to concern the proper sphere of moral ideals and critiques of those who, like Rousseau or the *philosophes* of the French Revolution and unlike Kant, are argued to have deduced forms of government from pure reason. The ideal political models grasped in transcendental philosophy need rather to be reinterpreted from age to age in accordance with historical needs and circumstances. In fact this turns out to be *The Friend*'s argument against universal suffrage, a liberty banished to the ideal realm for being, in keeping with the

1  *Aids to Reflection* (1825): see the footnote to Introductory Aphorism xxv, 15n.
2  *Collected Works*, IV. ii. 150.
3  Ibid., IV. ii. 504.
4  *The Notebooks of Samuel Taylor Coleridge*, ed. K. Coburn, 6 vols, London, 1957–, iii. 3366, 3390.

argument of 'Kubla Khan', too pure or untranslated to be currently significant.[1] To those who found this conclusion not timely but straightforwardly reactionary, Coleridge's transcendentalism could only appear authoritarian. In effect, it undercut radical reform by legitimating the conservative interest as the authentic modern embodiment of a universal political model.

In a notebook entry of November 1803, presumably still in the mood of the 'Letter' and 'The Pains of Sleep', and before his recuperative travels to Malta and Italy from 1804 to 1806, Coleridge had given a pathological account of the difficulties we have just seen him try to rationalize as philosophical method:

with a deep groan from the Innermost of my Heart, in the feeling of self-humiliation, & a lively sense of my own weakness, & the distraction of my mind, which is indeed 'always doing something else', I yet write down the names of the Works that I have planned, in the order in which I wish to execute them, with a fervent prayer that I may build up in my Being enough of manly Strength & Perseverance to do one thing at a time.[2]

As expected, though, the catalogue which follows is so comprehensive that we can only make sense of the ambition by again postulating some transcendental approach in possession of the principles fundamental to each subject. Coleridge's method, in other words, would not reform but exonerate his neuroses, turning his apparently shiftless transitions between different subjects into a logical map of their common ground. At one point, though, the entry refers to the 'work which I should wish to leave behind me, or to publish late in Life, that On Man, and the probable Destiny of the Human Race, followed & illustrated by the Organum vere Organum, & philosophical Romance to explain the whole growth of Language, and for these to be always collecting materials'.[3] Now, if the 'Letter' established anything, it was that Coleridge's poetic involvement in language was in excess of any formal purpose he might propose for it, such as the revised 'Ode'. The linguistic project described in the notebook entry similarly threatens to outdistance any transcendental scheme it might be thought to illustrate. But it is in *Biographia Literaria* and his *Logic* that Coleridge concedes most to language. In this he implicitly follows an already existing pattern of linguistic critique of the transcendental tradition: the 'meta-critiques' of less well-known

1 *Collected Works*, IV. ii. 135.
2 *Notebooks*, i. 1646.
3 Ibid.

German thinkers like Hamann and Herder, which argued that human language carried its thought-forms in itself, and that any philosophical scheme that (like Kant's) ignored the formative language in which it was expressed contradicted itself.

In his 'Elements of Discourse' or *Logic*, Coleridge conceded that 'what is a fact of all human language is of course a fact of all human consciousness.' His decision, dating from 1803, 'to write my metaphysical works, as *my Life*, & *in* my Life' suggests some level of awareness at which philosophy can no longer distance itself from all the neurotic untidiness of self-expression, or from the hope that language itself will show some philosophical initiative when conscious philosophical purpose fails.[1] Hence we find Coleridge conceding in *Biographia* that 'in all societies there exists an instinct of growth, a certain collective, unconscious good sense working progressively to desynonymize those words originally of the same meaning.'[2] This in fact describes the critical effort of *Biographia* as accurately as any of its unrealized transcendental plans for a grand deduction of rules of criticism from philosophical principles. Desynonymy – the detection of a difference of meaning between words originally thought synonymous – allows Coleridge to distinguish imagination from fancy early in the first volume. It is a further refinement of this desynonymy into two imaginations, one perceptual and the other poetic or idealizing, which constitutes 'the main result' of the missing deduction excused by a fictitious letter to the author.

*Biographia* was written when Coleridge was under considerable pressure, personal, psychological, medical and financial. These were somewhat relieved when, in 1816, he was accepted as house guest and patient at the home of Dr James Gillman in Highgate. Begun as a preface to *Sibylline Leaves*, the work bears the marks of procrastination, lack of confidence and repeated rejigging to compensate for the printer's miscalculations of length. Every infelicity, though, has the disconcerting power to make the reader wonder if it can be assimilated to an overarching methodology. Once it was realized that the transcendental build-up, Chapters 5–13, contained significant plagiarisms, most notoriously from Schelling, the work's reputation gradually sank throughout the nineteenth century, as did that of idealist philosophy in an increasingly scientific and positivist age. Those who, like Mill, tried to revive the humanist bias of the Romantics

1 *Logic*, in *Collected Works*, XIII. 82; *Notebooks*, i. 1515.
2 *Collected Works*, XI. i. 82–3.

found more help in Coleridge's explicitly cultural theory than in his great critical work. Fundamentally, *Biographia* justifies and elucidates the aesthetic status of poetry which, Coleridge argues, was threatened by Wordsworth's attack on poetic diction in the Preface to *Lyrical Ballads*. Responding further to Wordsworth's more recent Preface and Supplementary Essay to his *Poems* of 1815, Coleridge departs from Wordsworth's more traditional description of poetry in terms of genres or kinds, and emphasizes conventional expectations raised in readers of poems. Poems should be complete, whole and resistant to paraphrase – as if the real were being experienced entire, under ideal conditions, rather than being reproduced in the partial copies resulting from mere observation or 'the despotism of the eye'. This recalls the elemental achievement of the 'Rime', but also connects up with *Biographia*'s claim that 'the poet, described in *ideal* perfection, brings the whole soul of man into activity.'[1] Coleridge's poet becomes acquainted with the 'Ideas' which give, as he puts it in *On the Constitution of the Church and State*, the '*ultimate aim*' of human activities only through becoming proficient in 'PHILOSOPHY, or the doctrine and discipline of *ideas*'; for 'no man', writes Coleridge in *Biographia*, 'was ever yet a great poet, without being at the same time a profound philosopher.'[2] To avoid collapsing into philosophy, poetry must be able to foreground the aesthetic status of its archetypal understanding. Coleridge must keep separate the ideal vision of the poet and the philosophical intuition of ideas. The difficulty in sustaining this act of desynonymy beyond the close readings of Shakespeare, Milton and Wordsworth in *Biographia* helps explain his subsequent turning to theology and political theory for the main focus of his thought.

None the less, Coleridge's attitude towards language still remains central to his writings. His *Logic* is definitively split by the fact that there is no guarantee that the power it concedes to language will back up its authoritarian design to teach 'that sort of *Knowledge* which is best calculated to re-appear as Power – all that a Gentleman ought to possess'.[3] Again one feels that significance here lies not in what is said but in the gentlemanly readership implied by what is said; but this dissociation allows what is said to interfere with Coleridge's symbolic purposes for it. His plagiarisms, in the *Logic* as

1  Ibid., XI. ii. 15–16.
2  Ibid., XI. ii. 25–6.
3  *Letters*, v. 220.

much as elsewhere, tend to remain just that, and cannot be transformed by Coleridge's symbolic use of them to identify a particular audience.

In *Aids to Reflection*, Coleridge appears to abandon an overarching system for a more informal kind of philosophizing, truer to the creative indirections of language and the self. He argues for a religion answering a need or want, the acknowledgement of which produces its own evidence – participation in a satisfying way of life. 'Christianity is not a Theory or a Speculation; but a *Life*; – not a *Philosophy* of Life, but a Life and a living Process ... TRY IT.'[1] In the same section he rather cramps this openness with more scholastic distinctions describing the logic of religious language, this time distracting less successfully from its exclusive Christian basis. In 'Reason', a poem published as the conclusion to *On the Constitution of the Church and State*, Coleridge writes:

> Whene'er the mist, that stands 'twixt God and thee,
> Defecates to a pure transparency,
> That intercepts no light and adds no stain –
> There Reason is, and then begins her reign!

Or as he puts it succinctly in *Aids*, 'there is ... no *Human* reason.'[2] Reason is now a faculty whose self-validation lies in its purification of the typically human rather than its incorporation of it in a uniquely satisfying way of life.

Coleridge began his career as a democrat and a Unitarian. He finished a Tory and a Trinitarian. This progress can be presented as a narrowing betrayal of earlier radical and more generous ambitions. Yet its development widened the horizons of English (and American) thought, introducing German philosophy, theology and criticism to contemporary debate, and in its attention to the language of religion setting precedents for Victorians like John Keble, F. D. Maurice, John Sterling and John Henry Newman. The influence of Coleridge's theoretical constitutionalism extends from John Stuart Mill to Michael Oakeshott, and its insistence on a Clerisy, or criticism institutionalized in a learned class, is reflected in cultural theory from Arnold to Leavis. At its best, the more his writing claimed to supply its own evidence, the more it symbolized an ideal range of thought and concern, persuading that it could resume all the sources of its historical moment. When Coleridge's

1 *Aids*, p 134.
2 Ibid., p 144.

ambition fails, the consolation for his readers is that his transcendental ambition is outmanoeuvred by his expressiveness in a language we all share.

# REPRESENTING THE PEOPLE:
## CRABBE, SOUTHEY AND HAZLITT

### Jon Cook

I

What is meant by 'the people' can be notoriously vague, or obscure to us because of historical distance from a particular use, and critical analysis, my own included, will soon be embarrassed by this. 'The people' is one of those terms which can be used with assurance and vigour, implying a consensus of understanding; but there is a suspicion about the word because of the frequency of its use by professional politicians, eager to lay claim to their 'representativeness'. We suspect a deceptive use of language, a pretence of democracy which masks the exercise of domination. Some of this complexity is illustrated in a parliamentary speech of 1776 by John Wilkes. Wilkes assumes the role of 'man of the people', occupying an ambiguous position which implies that the speaker is at once one of the people, and therefore intimate with their interests and needs, and set apart from them by virtue of being their representative:

I will at this time, sir, only throw out general ideas, that every free agent in this kingdom should in my wish, be represented in parliament . . . I wish, sir, an English parliament to speak the free, unbiased sense of the body of the English people, and of every man among us . . . The meanest mechanic, the poorest peasant and day labourer, has important rights respecting his personal liberty, that of his wife and children, his property however inconsiderable, his wages, his earnings . . . Some share therefore in the power of making those laws which deeply interest them, and to which they are expected to pay obedience should be reserved to this inferior, but most useful set of men in the community. We ought always to remember this important truth, acknowledged by every free state, that all government is instituted for the good of the mass of the people to be governed; that they are the original fountain of power, and even of revenue and in all events the last resource . . .[1]

Wilkes's speech is worth quoting at length for a number of reasons. It is an important historical marker: the first time a speech calling for an extension of the franchise had been made to Parliament in the eighteenth century. It reminds us that, in the period under consideration, there were various campaigns for parliamentary reform which had at their base the claim that parliament should more adequately represent 'the people'. More radical demands included a call for all adult males to be entitled to vote regardless of property qualification. There were even intermittent and half-apologetic arguments that the franchise should be extended to women. And by the early 1790s a few radicals, such as the young Coleridge, and Thomas Spence, extended the argument about an equality of political rights to an argument about equality of condition. Spence's proposals for the redistribution of land were based upon the conviction that there could be no equality of political rights without an equitable distribution of wealth and property.

These campaigns required a terminology which would legitimate claims to popular representation. Wilkes's speech is rich in examples of this terminology. When he hopes that 'every free agent . . . should . . . be represented in parliament', he is referring to a central concept in eighteenth-century debates about political representation: only 'free agents' were entitled to take part in the political process, and, in a dominant version of the argument, 'free agents' were necessarily male and property-owning. Property ownership was held to be a precondition of freedom because without it a man would be dependent for his livelihood on others. His capacity to make the kinds of independent judgement appropriate to a politically responsible citizen would be jeopardized by his dependence upon his employer. Clearly, what is meant by property in this argument is something extensive enough and productive enough to give a significant measure of economic independence. In another influential version of the argument, the ownership of an extensive property was necessary to free an individual from the need to make a living. Without this freedom he would not have the leisure to take part in politics, nor the capacity to develop a comprehensive view of the public good unconstrained by the partial perspectives and narrow interests that followed

---

1 John Wilkes, *Speeches in Parliament* (1777), i. 85 *et seq.*; this passage is reprinted from a text of the speech in *The English Radical Tradition*, ed. S. Maccoby, London, 1966, pp 31–2.

inevitably from participation in a particular trade. These arguments were at one with the necessity of being male. By legal definition only men could own property and therefore only men could be free to take part in public, political life. To give oppression its proper fullness, women were also thought, because of their sexual identity, to be incapable of achieving the comprehensive views of the public good appropriate to the good citizen.

This reminds us that being one of the people could be hedged round with qualifications. The idea that a person had to own property to be one of the people was not just a conservative view. A number of radicals in this period distinguished the 'People' from the 'illiterate rabble'. One of them, Christopher Wyvill, feared that the ideas of Thomas Paine might 'rouse up the lower classes' and threaten private property and liberty.[1] Property gave a person a stake in the political game, a durable interest in the conduct of the nation. Contemptuous references to the 'illiterate rabble' reminds us of another qualification: political capacity was based upon education. In this view the people are those who can read and write, those whose property affords them the leisure for education.

Wilkes's claim that 'every free agent' should be represented in Parliament is followed by his wish that 'an English parliament' should speak 'the free, unbiased sense of the body of the English people'. He seems to be repeating the view which identifies the people as those with the legal, and propertied, identity of free agents, as well as assuming what was often assumed: that what makes *a* people *the* people was its participation in a national identity. But Wilkes goes on to include the 'meanest mechanic, the poorest peasant and day labourer' in the constituency deserving representation. These were far from being traditionally identified as free agents. Wilkes invokes a range of arguments in defence of their claim: that anybody whose activities are affected by the decisions of Parliament should have some say in its composition; that the rationale of government is in promoting the well-being of the majority of the governed; that the people are the sovereign power in any political state and that any government has to proceed with their tacit or active consent; that, as a source of revenue, the people should be represented in the Parliament, which decides on the kind and level of taxation – 'no taxation without representation' being an important radical slogan of the period, and a central argument put forward

---

1 Christopher Wyvill, *Political Papers* (1794–1804), v. 23; quoted in H. T. Dickinson, *Liberty and Property*, London, 1977, p 240.

by the American colonists in their struggle with the Government of George III.

However, though Wilkes addresses Parliament on behalf of the people, the structure of his speech makes clear that he distinguishes both Parliament and himself from them. Parliament is addressed in the terms of gentlemanly courtesy: Wilkes's interlocutor is 'sir'; Parliament is 'every man among us' distinct from 'the body of the English people'. The 'people' is a device for equivocation: a sovereign power, the locus of denied rights, and yet waiting for someone to speak on their behalf to audiences who are not exactly the people themselves. They are the prototype of the silent majority, waiting for professional politicians, or professional literary men for that matter, to both give them voice and claim their authority for doing so. Sentences about the 'people' arise in a complex negotiation of the rival demands of equality and hierarchy: sometimes they are 'us'; but, in the background, 'we' always have the security of knowing they can become 'them'.

The 'people' have many attributes, but no certain definition. The strategic potential of the term, whether for implying alliances or asserting discriminations, depends upon its vagueness. But, however vaguely defined, the people are not indistinct. As we have seen, the 'people' can be distinguished from the 'illiterate rabble', although it is exactly a part of the term's strategic vagueness that Wilkes's different use can include the labouring poor, that 'inferior, but most useful set of men', in the popular constituency claiming the franchise. At the other end of the social scale, the 'people' can be distinguished from the aristocracy, as in this example from the Report of the Sub-Committee of Westminster, written in 1780, and also demanding electoral reform: '. . . the alarm of the nobility for the very existence of their present splendid distinctions will co-operate with the poignant feelings of the people; and every rank and description of men will feel the propriety, the necessity of establishing that plan of parliamentary reform . . .'[1]

The aristocracy can be mocked, but, in the perspective of reform in 1780, their distinction is not threatened as long as they co-operate with the people. This idea of reforming co-operation became much harder to entertain after the French Revolution. What Wilkes and the Westminster Sub-Committee included amongst the people became Edmund Burke's 'swinish multitude', threatening to level aristocratic distinction and destroy the culture maintained by gentle-

1 Maccoby, *The English Radical Tradition*, pp 35–7.

men and priests. The people did not disappear from Burke's political writings, but they had to be represented in a way which separated them from revolutionary or even reforming ambitions. Prior to 1789 the 'people' demand reform; after the French Revolution they are increasingly ready to be recruited to the causes of conservatism and patriotic war, fearful that their own cultural and political advance will be threatened by revolution from 'below'.

Burke's example may seem to give the game away. The 'people' are the middle class writ large, bounded by the aristocracy above them in the social scale and a rural or urban proletariat below. But the problem with an analysis which explains the 'people' as an item in the lexicon of bourgeois ideology is that it can overlook the politically contested history of the term, the ways in which conservative and radical writers vie for the claim to be the representatives of the people. The term may be used to give a capacious feeling to what turn out to be the particular interests of a specific class or group, but it works this way because it carries a mythical charge. This can be identified, for example, in radical myths about the historical past: the 'people' carry with them the traces of society in its natural state, prior to corruption by the evils of government and artificial social distinctions. In this natural state the people were benevolent and reasonable. They represent what society once was and what it should become again. The people are invested with the pathos of origins, always in need of recovery, representation or redress. They are at work in that part of imaginative discourse called lost and found, where losing and finding are compulsively repeated actions.

Whether in radical or conservative forms, the representation of the people in political discourse was intimately connected with the literary genre of pastoral. Wilkes's speech has affinities with Empson's analysis, in *Some Versions of Pastoral*, of the typical structure of the pastoral work: about the people but not 'by' or 'for' them. Both his speech and the report of the Westminster Sub-Committee propose a pastoral ideal of political relations: balanced between the interests of rich and poor, establishing co-operation rather than conflict between different social groups. As in pastoral, the people are often invoked as bearers of some fundamental truth about what society should be like. They witness what we all have in common and may be in danger of forgetting amidst the distinctions of a corrupt and artificial society.

As Empson argues, pastoral was a literary genre always likely to carry powerful political messages, especially as the form suggests an ideal of social life: 'The essential trick of the old pastoral, which was felt to imply a beautiful relation between rich and poor, was to make simple people express strong feelings (felt as the most universal subject, something fundamentally true about everybody) in learned and fashionable language (so that you wrote about the best subject in the best way).[1] In the eighteenth century this kind of pastoral ideal entered into a complicated negotiation with a demand for greater realism. What this meant was that pastoral should be nationalized: it should be about the people in recognizably English rural settings. What it also meant was that pastoral should concern itself with the representation of labour as well as leisure, especially as that could be made, as it is in James Thomson's *The Seasons*, the basis of a celebration of England's growing economic power, a power which the different social classes combined to produce.

But, as John Barrell and Roger Sales have argued in their studies of pastoral, this realism was prescriptive: what should be masquerading as what is.[2] The people in their identity as the rural poor were acceptably represented as industrious because to show them otherwise provoked anxieties not only about their moral degeneration but also about their possible involvement in political conspiracy. Their industry also made them worthy objects of charity when times were hard. Similarly, to show the poor as domestically settled, confined to home or village, assuaged anxieties about the possibility that they were developing a consciousness of their own interests as a class opposed to other classes. Representation, here, was not so much about what was real as what was acceptable in a cultural atmosphere increasingly charged with political and social tensions. If the trick of the old pastoral was to combine simplicity and sophistication, strength of feeling with articulate language, the trick of the new pastoral was to mediate between realism and acceptability, making the people fit to be seen, interpreted, and – sometimes – heard. The politics of pastoral can be discerned in this interplay between representation and exclusion. Another way of stating the problem is to ask how pastoral responds once the people become, as they did in eighteenth-century radical thought, the subjects not just of natural feelings but also of natural and inalienable rights to life, liberty and happiness. In what follows I want to analyse how three writers – Crabbe, Southey and Hazlitt – respond to the emergence of the people as politically sovereign subjects.

1  William Empson, *Some Versions of Pastoral* (1935), Harmondsworth, 1966, p 17.
2  John Barrell, *The Dark Side of the Landscape*, Cambridge, 1980; see, for example, pp 6–16. Roger Sales, *English Literature in History, 1780–1830: Pastoral and Politics*, London, 1983; see, for example, pp 15–51.

II

Political radicalism haunts the margins of Crabbe's poetry. There is the unnamed father at the end of Part I of *The Parish Register* (1807). He is represented as a social outcast, refusing the Anglican Communion, living, literally, on the margins of society: 'His, a lone house, by Deadman's Dyke-way stood' (791).[1] Crabbe surrounds the figure with an aura of wildness. He is beyond the pale, without a Christian name, a rabble-rouser who calls 'the wants of rogues the rights of man'. The neat, satirical renaming of the 'rights of man' would have been a sufficient reminder to Crabbe's original audience of the version of the people he opposes with his own. The unnamed father represents Paineite radicalism, the people as the subjects of unalienable natural rights. He is a freethinker who 'deem'd the marriage-bond the bane of love' (815–17). And he comes to a bad end, of course: drowned in a ditch one night, out poaching.

The vicar poet of *The Parish Register* has to tidy up after him. He gives his five sons the Christian names their father denied them, and they become one of the round of baptisms recorded in Part I of the poem:

> These have we named; on life's rough sea they sail,
> With many a prosperous, many an adverse gale!
>
> (824–5)

The authority of the good poet, like the authority of the good vicar, is to give things their Christian names, and doing this depends, as the couplet implies, on taking what is claimed as a balanced view: there are 'prosperous' as well as 'adverse' gales, although it is important to remember that the sea is basically rough.

The same point is made, with less emphasis, in Crabbe's depiction of Hammond, the radical orator, in a later work than *The Parish Register*, the *Tales* of 1812. This particular tale, the first in the collection, is called 'The Dumb Orators'. Towards the end of it Hammond is shown by the poet as dispossessed of speech when confronted with a politically hostile audience:

> By desperation urged, he now began:
> 'I seek no favour – I – the Rights of Man!
> Claim; and – I – nay! – but give me leave – and I

---

1 Crabbe's poems are quoted from *Poems by George Crabbe*, ed A. W. Ward, 3 vols, Cambridge, 1905.

> Insist – a man – that is – and in reply
> I speak.' – Alas! each new attempt was vain:
> Confused he stood, he sate, he rose again;
> At length he growl'd defiance, sought the door,
> Cursed the whole synod, and was seen no more.
>
> (454–61)

The poem's level and dispassionate articulation contains Hammond's inarticulate attempts to voice the 'Rights of Man'. In one sense the poem is about Hammond's humiliation: its narrative shows that his command of a radical language cannot survive translation from a sympathetic to a hostile audience.

But Hammond's humiliation is also part of another story, of Justice Bolt, the Tory patriot. Like Hammond, but at an earlier stage of the tale, he finds himself unable to defend the Tory cause when he attends the meeting of a radical club in which Hammond is a leading figure. The balance, and by implication the authority, of the tale derives from the even-handed dealing with the Tory and the radical orator alike. Both exemplify the pride which Crabbe attributes to the political rhetorician; both are presented as small-town figures who cannot sustain their pretensions to influence a wider public sphere. In addition, Bolt is the focus of psychological interest. He begins to learn humility after his experience of being a lone Tory amongst the radicals, but this learning ends once his pride is restored by Hammond's humiliation. The story holds out the prospect of a change which doesn't, in the end, materialize. This indicates another aspect of Crabbe's realism: to know reality truly, according to Crabbe, is to be sceptical about the possibility of change at either an individual or social level.

The balancing of the Tory and the radical as both 'dumb orators' – dumb because foolish and because silenced – does not alter the underlying conservative force of the tale. Crabbe's narrative does not enter into any overt alliance with Bolt's King and Country Toryism, but there is no lack of secret sharing. Hammond's views are described quite unironically at line 270 of the poem as 'heresy and crime', and, if not delighting in his humiliation as much as Bolt does, the reader is invited to feel reassured. The radical Hammond is exorcized: he disappears at the end of the poem, 'seen no more'. What Crabbe keeps in view is Justice Bolt, with his failings, but felt to be more real, more representative of the English people than Hammond. In one respect the poem may be read as a cautionary mirror for Tory magistrates, a warning about the dangers of complacency in the political battle with radicalism. But this didacticism is absorbed in the measured calm of Crabbe's narrative, which dispels the fear of failure. Bolt's shortcomings do not seriously weaken the social fabric he claims to defend. As with the unnamed father in *The Parish Register*, the story wants to persuade the reader of the truth that political radicals bring about their own downfall. This is the pleasure of 'The Dumb Orators' for a conservative audience. It offers the reassurance that Crabbe's couplets can see off Hammond, even if Bolt lacks the resources to do it.

Crabbe's depiction of Paineite radicals is an example of his skill in passing off a pessimistic conservatism as a moderate and balanced realism. Those who seek change, desire a different world or simply refuse to accept the place assigned them are repeatedly punished by madness and death. The power of his conservatism derives from the thoroughness with which he imagines the insanity and suffering that follows from rebellion or deviance. There are plenty of broken or desperate minds on display in Crabbe's work, placed there for the reader's edification and pleasure. Some, like Peter Grimes, are presented as responsible for their downfall; others, like the unnamed vagrant woman in *The Hall of Justice*, are more obviously the victims of circumstance; a few are displayed to us because they are saved from their torment by Christianity. But, in every case, there is a quality of implacable demonstration: to ignore the reality of pain and 'care', one of Crabbe's favourite words, to act on desire or impulse, brings with it the inevitable consequence of intense mental or physical suffering. Crabbe's preferred form, the Augustan couplet, can be understood as contributing to this ideological work: it contains, and then subdues, aspiration.

This conservative vision was in place early in Crabbe's career. It informs the piece of finger-wagging which begins the second book of *The Village*, first published in 1783:

> No longer truth, though shown in verse, disdain
> But own the Village Life a life of pain . . .

As a number of critics have noted, Crabbe's target in *The Village* is an imagination of rural life shaped by pastoral expectations. It is these that separate 'truth' from 'verse', and Crabbe's intention in this poem, as elsewhere in his writing, is to purge poetry of what he takes to be false imaginings, and thereby bring it back into alliance with what Crabbe wants to believe is truth. Hence the first book of *The Village* is a point-by-point refutation of the conventions of the pastoral idyll. Belief in these conventions encourages an anachronistic or superficial and hedonistic attention to the lives of the rural poor.

Dedicated to truth, Crabbe's muse discerns the evidences of suffering which for him are intimately connected to seeing truly:

> I grant indeed that fields and flocks have charms
> For him that grazes or for him that farms;
> But, when amid such pleasing scenes I trace
> The poor laborious natives of the place
> And see the mid-day sun, with fervid ray
> On their bare heads and dewy temples play;
> While some with feebler heads and fainter hearts
> Deplore their fortune, yet sustain their parts:
> Then shall I dare those real ills to hide
> In tinsel trappings of poetic pride?

(39–48)

In these lines, finding pleasure in rural life is associated with the partial and interested perspectives of the shepherd or farmer. By contrast, the poet's disinterested gaze converts 'pleasing scenes' into sites of pain.

*The Village* inverts the priority of pleasure over pain which Crabbe associates with pastoral. It is this aspect of his work which has led a number of critics to describe him as a writer of 'counter' or 'anti' pastoral verse. Raymond Williams has argued that Crabbe's demolition of pastoral produced a poetry which can give the reader the 'real history' of rural labour in the late eighteenth century.[1] By providing 'real history' in verse, Crabbe invites his readers' compassionate attention for the plight of the rural poor. An alliance between reader and poet will create a fictional community to counter the negligence of the village doctor and the parish priest.

Crabbe may invite compassionate attention for the rural poor, but that compassion is selective and far from disinterested. The sufferings of the poor, in Crabbe's view, do not arise from a denial of their natural rights, and he does not want to argue like Wilkes that the peasantry are entitled to political representation or that, if they were represented, their condition would be improved. As we have seen, Crabbe associates that kind of thinking with a subversive radicalism which his poetry attempts to marginalize.

The significance of the poor in Crabbe's representation of the people can be discovered in the formal structure of poems such as *The Village*, *The Parish Register* and *The Borough*. All combine the forms of survey and of story in varying proportions, and in every

1 Raymond Williams, *The Country and the City*, London, 1973; see, for example, pp 87–95.

case the two forms are sustained by an Augustan poetic whose version of truth depends upon the discovery of unity in variety and the derivation of general truths from an accumulation of particular examples. The ambition of Crabbe's survey is to comprehend society in its diverse trades and professions, in the relation between work and leisure, and in the role of institutions such as the Church and the law. But survey has another purpose: to derive some general, unifying truth out of this diversity and so persuade readers of the poem that they are gaining a view of society as a whole. And, as John Barrell has argued, this means that the writer must command an observational vantage point, 'an Equal, Wide, Survey', which subsumes and, where necessary, corrects partial and potentially misleading points of view.

The knowledge afforded by the comprehensive view was linked in the eighteenth century with social advantage: it was the intellectual property of the gentleman or the aristocrat. This produces a tension in Crabbe's writing, which is especially marked in a relatively early poem like *The Village*. Crabbe, the poet of humble social origin, simulates the perspective of the aristocrat or gentleman at the same time as he begs their attention for his work. By the time of *The Parish Register* and *The Borough* the ground has shifted. The authority of the comprehensive view (although, as Crabbe's prefaces suggest, he was nervous about how comprehensive it was) is now claimed for people of lesser social standing: the conscientious parish priest of *The Parish Register*, or the 'residing burgess' whom Crabbe invents as a persona in *The Borough*.

Story offers an alternative but complementary resource to survey. Particular stories can stand as exemplifications of the general truths afforded by the comprehensive surveying view. This is the case with the story of the old labourer in *The Village*, and particular stories in *The Parish Register* help sustain the distinction made in the introductory section of the poem between the deserving and the undeserving poor. But stories are not just a subordinate resource in Crabbe's writing. They supply another kind of authority, one that places the poet not as the comprehensive observer of society but as the recorder of particular lives and places. What is mobilized in these stories is the authority of custom and tradition. Each one embeds the wisdom of an established narrative formula – 'pride before a fall', 'vice destroys itself', 'virtue is its own reward', 'the suffering innocent' – and they are narrated in such a way as to encourage the reader to feel that the particular story being told is a contemporary version of something that might be told in any generation.

The alliance of story and survey is by no means a static one in Crabbe's writing, nor is the combination of the two modes original with him: it is one aspect of the form of the eighteenth-century long poem which Crabbe engages with in the first half of his career as a writer. As an alliance it constitutes a form of pastoral, engaging the sophisticated resources of the comprehensive view with the more simple, heartfelt truths of the story. In *The Village* the two modes of story and survey combine to deliver a general truth which bears upon the poem's representation of the rural poor, and enables the poet to comprehensively address both 'the poor' and 'the great'.

Midway through the second book of *The Village* Crabbe turns on an imaginary reader to justify his descriptions of 'humble crimes':

> Yet, why, you ask, these humble crimes relate,
> Why make the poor as guilty as the great?
> To show the great, those mightier sons of pride,
> How near in vice the lowest are allied.
>
> (87–90)

The truth addressed to the great is that they share a common nature of vice with their social inferiors. The poet addresses a complementary and balancing truth to the poor about what they share with the great:

> And you, ye poor, who still lament your fate
> Forbear to envy those you call the great
> And know, amid these blessings they possess
> They are, like you, the victims of distress.
>
> (101–4)

This clinches the argument of the poem, although it may feel to a modern reader more like the slamming of a prison door. By refuting the delusions of what he identifies as pastoral, Crabbe has revealed to rich and poor what they share despite differences of wealth and power: an equality of vice and suffering. This is the unifying truth that underlies variety and difference. It is intended to have an immobilizing force. Once recognized there is no point in trying to change anything, and especially no point in challenging existing social and economic distinctions. After all, if the poor were to become rich, they would only find in the end a repetition of their suffering within their change of state. To which the poor might reply that they would still get a taste of the 'blessings' possessed by the rich. Crabbe ignores this possible response. The poor do not speak in his poem; the poet speaks on their behalf and, by doing this, forces out of them the general truth the poem recommends.

*The Village*, like many other poems by Crabbe, is an education in the necessity of diminished expectations. It is a necessity because only in a state of diminished expectation can we soberly recognize our common nature in vice and suffering. The truth is humbling, even humiliating. Its acceptance establishes a basis of equality, of the common identity which might constitute the people, but in a way that preserves social distinctions instead of threatening them. Crabbe did not tire of repeating it in poems and sermons alike, but its articulation is not always problem-free.

In *The Village* the problem has to do with the place of the aristocracy in Crabbe's scheme of society and of the poem. The poem ends with a eulogy on the death of Lord Robert Manners and some advice to his surviving brother, the Duke of Rutland, on the management of grief. Crabbe's précis of the second book of *The Village* suggests that the death of Manners exemplifies the sufferings of the great which the poor must recognize in order to be content with their lot. The eulogy fits naturally into the sequence of the poem and sustains the general truth it proposes. But Crabbe's précis ignores the shifting pattern of address at the end of the poem.

Manners is certainly offered to the poor as an example of suffering, and then of protective and self-sacrificing leadership. But he is offered to his fellow aristocrats, and to his brother in particular, as an example of heroic patriotism, which is associated with a future of progress and natural abundance. The Duke of Rutland is invited by the poet to 'expel' grief and contemplate the future glories of his family:

> And as thy thoughts through streaming ages glide
> See other heroes die as Manners died:
> And, from their fate, thy race shall nobler grow
> As trees shoot upward that are pruned below . . .

> (196–9)

The aristocracy bring strong magic into the poem. Their blood sacrifice, it is implied, will bring about a renewal of nature, which sweated labour never can. Their power carries the promise of an abundant world which contrasts with the representation of scarce resources at the beginning of the poem. What one aristocrat is invited to recognize in the death of another is very different to the general truth recommended earlier in the poem: not the monotonous repetition of vice and suffering, but the glamour of sacrificial death; not diminished expectations in an unyielding world, but a heroic aspiration which is felt to be intensely productive. The aristocracy, or at least that part of it represented by the dynasty of the Duke of Rutland, carry an exemption clause; they represent a truth and a relation to nature which much of Crabbe's poem seems devoted to denying.

The problem is that what is introduced into the poem as an example confirming a general truth turns into its opposite. Crabbe's original audience may have found nothing wrong with this. The poet recommends himself with a piece of responsible social analysis which shows the economic plight of the rural poor and the irresponsibility of the professions who should care for them. He derives from this an appropriate cautionary truth which may encourage greater responsibility amongst the guardians of the poor while showing the futility of radical change. But a poem is not only a representation of society: it is also an episode in a poet's career, and flattery directed at a prospective patron does not come amiss. If flattery disturbs the coherence of the poem's claim to represent a general truth, it also gives a new perspective: the aristocracy restore energy to a world otherwise in decline. If their attention is redemptive for the represented world of the poem, it works in a similar way for the poet's career. On the one hand Crabbe insists that poetry is an arduous, monotonous work of uncertain reward. In *The Village* he describes it as 'a poorer trade' than rural labour: the poet is down there, suffering and working with the people. But the humble circumstances of the poet are also a means of courting the attention of the aristocracy, or their equivalents in cultural power. They can elevate him to a fame which moves him, in fantasy, from being less than a peasant to being more than a professional, and thereby helps secure his authority as a critic of the professional classes.

Such, at least, is one image of the poet projected by Crabbe's early work, especially if his prefaces are taken into account, which were remarkably sycophantic, even by the standards of the day. Despite the way in which his poetry enforces social stasis, Crabbe saw his literary career as a means of escaping his own relatively humble social origins. This meant keeping his readership and their pleasures firmly in view. Flattery of an aristocratic patron or a powerful critic was one way of doing this, satisfying a relish for grim moral truths another. But it required the operation of a more or less discreet double standard: the representation of the people did not necessarily extend to identifying Crabbe's readership as the people, despite rhetorical flourishes which might suggest this. In order to take pleasure in Crabbe's joyless didacticism, the reader had to be allowed to feel that it really applied to others, that there was a society of poet and reader which worked to different rules and standards to the society represented in the poem. Crabbe's address to the Duke of Rutland at the end of *The Village* is a relatively crude example of this double standard. It is at work, too, later in his career, when he had abandoned the poetry of explicit survey – *The Village, The Parish Register, The Borough* – for the poetry of story: the *Tales* of 1812, and *Tales of the Hall*, published in 1819. Crabbe may well have been responding to a changing taste in his readership, an increasing demand for sentimental and didactic stories in verse. The precedents invoked for these collections are specifically English, and not neoclassical as with Crabbe's earlier work: the epigraphs come from Shakespeare rather than Ovid; Crabbe's couplets echo Chaucer as much as Pope or Johnson. But Crabbe's attention to the difference between the world represented in the *Tales* and the world of his readers remains constant, as is made clear in his Preface to the collection:

. . . I must allow that the effect of poetry should be to lift the mind from the painful realities of actual existence, from its everyday concerns and its perpetually occurring vexations, and to give it repose by substituting objects in their place, which it may contemplate with some degree of interest and satisfaction; but what is there in all this, which may not be effected by a fair representation of existing character? Nay, by a faithful delineation of those painful realities, those every-day concerns, and those perpetually-occurring vexations themselves, provided they be not (which is hardly to be supposed) the very concerns and distresses of the reader? for, when it is admitted that they have no particular relation to him, but are the troubles and anxieties of other men, they excite and interest his feelings as the imaginary exploits, adventures and perils of romance . . .[1]

The Preface to the *Tales* constitutes an extended justification of Crabbe's desire to tell the truth in verse. But the 'faithful delineation of those painful realities', which, according to Crabbe, follows from a commitment to realism, does not implicate the reader. Crabbe's poetic is not one of recognition or catharsis. He does not justify 'painful realities' by suggesting that readers might learn about their own suffering or face it with greater equanimity as a result of reading his work. His argument here seems absurdly literal. As long as a story is not precisely about a reader's experience, whatever painful material it contains will have 'no particular relation to him'. With this distance secured, 'the troubles and anxieties of other men', the one fate of suffering and vice, can become a kind of 'romance'.

1 Crabbe, 'Preface' to *Tales 1812*, in *Poems*, ii. 11.

Crabbe's version of readerly pleasure precludes the possibility of identification or empathy with the text. More pertinently, the reader is never directly implicated in the social world represented in his writing. His didacticism is a species of literary shadow-boxing: hard truths for other people who are thought to be at such a distance from his readers' own experience that they become equivalent to characters in a fairy tale. His poetic helps to explain the forensic detachment and eerie calm which informs his depiction of other people's suffering and failure. If anything unites the distinctions between Crabbe's reader and the world of his poems, it is the consistency of his conservatism. He no more wants to disturb or arouse his reader than he wants to disturb existing social arrangements. At the conclusion of the Preface to the *Tales* Crabbe insists that nothing in his work will militate 'against the rules of propriety and good manners', nothing will offend 'against the more important precepts of morality and religion'.[1]

The consistency of Crabbe's conservatism depended upon the successful demotion of certain cultural and political forces deemed to be extreme. These included, as we have seen, the radicalism of Paine's *Rights of Man*, and pastoral, especially as the latter encouraged desires of a life without hard labour. It also included identifying his own poetic as an alternative to the writing we have come to call Romantic. The Preface to the *Tales* is a not-so-veiled polemic against Wordsworth and Coleridge. Crabbe states that his work is addressed to 'the plain sense and sober judgement' of his readers. It is to be distinguished from the poetry of imagination, both in its attention to everyday reality and in its engagement with the reader. Although Wordsworth and Coleridge are not directly mentioned in the Preface, Crabbe was more explicit elsewhere. In a letter to Walter Scott, written in 1813, he criticized 'The Ancient Mariner' – which, incidentally, he thought written by Charles Lamb – as a description of madness not 'by its Effects but by imitation, as if a painter to give a picture of Lunacy should make his Canvas crazy, and fill it with wild unconnected Limbs and Distortions of features.'[2] 'The Ancient Mariner' was found guilty of disorderly behaviour. It disrupted the distance which Crabbe thought a poem should maintain between reader and subject. Unsurprisingly, he had more time for Wordsworth, seeing similarities between his own *Tales*

1 Ibid., ii. 12.
2 *Selected Letters and Journals of George Crabbe*, ed. T. C. Faulkner and R. L. Blair, Oxford, 1985, p 102.

and Wordsworth's contributions to the *Lyrical Ballads*, but he still found him obscure and described his example as a disease. Nor were influential judges slow to see the difference. Francis Jeffrey, founder of the *Edinburgh Review*, praised Crabbe for exhibiting 'the common people of England pretty much as they are, and as they must appear to everyone who will take the trouble of examining into their condition'.[1] Crabbe's poetry confirmed the classification of the people which accorded with the world-view of sane gentlemen like Jeffrey, and, as such, could be conveniently deployed in the latter's battle against the obduracy and eccentricity of Wordsworth's poetry. According to Jeffrey, Wordsworth makes the people opaque and enigmatic, falling outside what his review describes as 'the common sympathies of our nature, and our general knowledge of human character'. There is an air of confident possession in Jeffrey's statement, implying a consensus about what 'common sympathies' and 'general knowledge' are. Crabbe's strength is that he can be read in the terms of this consensus.

Jeffrey's review indicates something of Crabbe's authoritative status as a poet in the early nineteenth century. It also shows how this authority was connected to the reassurance provided by his representation of the people. Crabbe's career spanned different literary generations, which subsequent criticism has come to understand as a moment of cultural transformation, distinguishing Augustans from Romantics. What Crabbe's writing reminds us of is a consistency of taste which meant *The Village* could meet with the approval of Johnson in 1783 and Jeffrey in 1808. Crabbe recruited the powers of a conservative Augustan vision to the new demands of a counter-revolutionary epoch. He engaged an influential audience, who discovered in his work a bulwark against both literary and political innovation.

### III

Six years before his review of Crabbe, Jeffrey had used the publication of Southey's long poem *Thalaba* as an occasion to attack what he regarded as the pernicious tendency represented by Southey's poetry. Along with Wordsworth and Coleridge, Jeffrey labelled Southey as one of the 'followers of simplicity'. For Jeffrey, simplicity

1 Francis Jeffrey, *Edinburgh Review* (April 1808), in A. Pollard, ed., *Crabbe: The Critical Heritage*, London, 1972, p 56.

is motivated by a subversive view of the social order, and this in turn connects closely to arguments about the representation of the people:

A splenetic and ideal discontent with the existing institutions of society, seems to be at the bottom of all their serious and peculiar sentiments. Instead of contemplating the wonders and pleasures which civilization has created for mankind, they are perpetually brooding over the disorders by which its progress has been attended. They are filled with horror and compassion at the sight of poor men spending their blood in the quarrels of princes, and brutifying their sublime capabilities in the drudgery of unremitting labour . . .[1]

Jeffrey's is the classic authoritarian strategy of discovering the motive for criticism in the psychological malaise of the critic, not in social injustice. Writing in 1802, Jeffrey did not, as he would in 1808, have the example of Crabbe's work to hand. If it had been available to him, he would no doubt have favoured Crabbe's 'one-fate' version of suffering and vice, uniting rich and poor alike, to the idea he finds in the work of Southey and his allies, that the sufferings of the poor are distinctive, and distinctively the result of their exploitation by the rich and powerful.

The review of *Thalaba* gives an informative, if unsympathetic, picture of Southey's reputation at the beginning of the nineteenth century. Jeffrey links the socially critical content of the work he discusses with its threat to established literary standards. These connections are made without embarrassment: for Jeffrey, the quality of a literary language depends upon the language of the social class it takes as a model. Equally, the capacity of a literary work to deliver 'just taste and refined sentiment', and to excite 'admiration and delight', depends upon what social class it represents. Jeffrey is firmly of the view that the social classes are distinguished by idiom and by the quality of their passions:

Now, the different classes of society have each of them a distinct character, as well as a separate idiom . . . The love, or grief, or indignation of an enlightened and refined character is not only expressed in a different language, but is in itself a different emotion from the love, or grief, or anger of a clown, a tradesman or a market wench . . .[2]

In this view, love in a palace is definitely not the same thing as love in a hut, and any writer who persuades us that they might be

1 Jeffrey, *Edinburgh Review* (October 1802), in L. Madden, ed., *Southey: The Critical Heritage*, London, 1972, pp 76–7.
2 Ibid., pp 71–2.

misrepresents the world and confuses those distinctions of feeling which, in addition to distinctions of wealth, status and language, explain why the classes are separated one from another in the way they are. The connection between social and literary hierarchies is threatened by the literary experimentalism which Jeffrey associates with Southey.

The nature of the experiment had been announced by Wordsworth and Coleridge in their Advertisement to the first edition of *Lyrical Ballads*: '. . . to ascertain how far the language of conversation in the middle and lower classes of society is adapted to the purposes of poetic pleasure'. The statement may seem innocuous now, but, for Jeffrey, it was a cultural time bomb. It proposed a language which would represent the feelings of the poor or the ordinary as if they were exemplary of human feeling in general. Jeffrey concedes that the poor may be represented in literature through the transparent artifice of pastoral, when they are given the language and the character of the refined; he acknowledges that the poor may be interesting because of what he calls their 'situation'. But the idea that their feelings might be exemplary is simply absurd to him: 'poverty makes men ridiculous' – a fit subject for burlesque or parody perhaps – and, he adds, 'just taste and refined sentiment are rarely to be met with amongst the uncultivated part of mankind.'[1]

Representing the people in a literary version of their own language invites the reader to identify with them without that powerfully reserved distinction between reader and represented world which runs through Crabbe's pastoral of depression. What is at stake in the argument is the kind of cultural authority conferred upon a social group by the way in which it is represented. This may explain what seems an obvious contradiction in Jeffrey's position: he blames Southey, Wordsworth and Coleridge for failing to observe the distinctions of emotion and language which separate the social classes; but he also blames them for failing to observe what the different classes have in common: 'they are subject alike to the overruling influence of necessity, and equally affected by the miserable condition of society.'[2] On the face of it, this seems both startling and absurd. Jeffrey appears to sever any connection between material condition and the experience of constraint. He also denies any possibility that a common structure of feeling might follow from a common subjection to necessity; that, in this respect, the grief of the rich might be the

1  Ibid., p 72.
2  Ibid., p 77.

same as the grief of the poor. But these possibilities are necessarily excluded as Jeffrey seeks to further his argument about the obligations of the literary work to map social difference and identity in ways which will sustain the existing structure of society. The 'followers of simplicity' threaten an audience's sympathy with the powerful, and they do so in a language which refuses to model itself on what Jeffrey regards as the proper standard – the language of 'good society', free from those defects which characterize the language of the 'middling or lower order', 'the cant of particular professions, and of every impropriety that is ludicrous or disgusting.'[1] What Jeffrey cannot or will not allow is that the 'followers of simplicity' might be writing a form of pastoral which does not subvert social distinctions. The point can be followed through in more detail by an analysis of some of Southey's early work devoted to a representation of the people. Of these, the one that seems obviously subversive is *Wat Tyler*, a verse play set in the time of the Peasants' Revolt of 1381, and written by Southey over a few mornings late in 1794.

At the time of writing the play Southey was on the far left of English politics: a supporter of the French Revolution, a republican, and, with Coleridge, planning to found 'Pantisocracy', an experiment in living without private property. Given Southey's subsequent conversion to King and Country Toryism, these commitments can seem fragile and posturing, an example of late eighteenth-century radical chic. The few critics who have recently made a cautious reclamation of Southey's work either ignore the play or see it as a piece of immature if well-intentioned foolishness; it is excluded from the Oxford edition of his poems. In Southey's lifetime it was by far his most popular work, although not from any circumstances of the poet's choosing. Although written in 1794, the work was not published until 1817, in a move designed to embarrass the Poet Laureate with his radical past. Southey tried to withdraw the work from public circulation, but his legal case failed when Eldon, the Lord Chancellor, ruled that a work so seditious could not be protected by copyright law. The result was the production of numerous and increasingly cheap editions of the work. It sold in tens of thousands, reaching the same kind of audience that had made Paine's *Rights of Man* one of the most widely read books of the period.

The scandal provoked by the play's publication was no doubt one reason for its popularity. But another, at least for its radical artisan audience, would have been the play's sympathetic rendering of the

1   Ibid., p 72.

main arguments of Paine's *Rights of Man*. Southey uses the Peasants' Revolt in a similar way to Paine's use of the French Revolution: as a vivid historical case to develop arguments about political rights and justice. Like Paine, Southey is concerned with arguments about the necessity of revolutionary violence. In Act II, John Ball's speech to the insurrectionaries at Blackheath cautions them against a violent revenge on their oppressors. By Act III, with Wat Tyler murdered and the insurrection breaking up, he doubts the wisdom of his initial advice:

> I fear me I have been like the weak leech,
> Who, sparing to cut deep, with cruel mercy
> Mangles his patient without curing him.[1]

It does not seem surprising that Eldon found the play seditious. It is a piece of revolutionary literature, schematic in its presentation of action and motive, unambiguous in its sympathies. It seems designed to confirm an audience in its belief that unjust governments must be overthrown, by violent means if necessary. The play's schematic presentation appears to minimize the historical distance between 1381 and 1794. Southey represents the leaders of the Peasants' Revolt as examples of a Rousseauist republican virtue. Throughout the play the grievances common to 1381 and 1794 are stressed: an unnecessary war with France, excessive taxation and the threat of starvation. John Ball's last speech at the end of Act III establishes another kind of unstated connection between late medieval and late eighteenth-century England: he looks forward to a future when the unfinished work of the Peasants' Revolt will be completed and monarchy overthrown. Had the play been published in 1794, it is clear that Southey would have wanted his audience to finish reading it with a renewed sense of political obligation.

However, the play's subversive political advocacy is complicated by its reliance on pastoral convention and sentiment. It works upon two potentially incompatible representations of the people, each one assuming a different kind of cultural authority. On the one hand they are the bearers of reason, deducing the necessity of insurrection from principles of social justice, and possessing a comprehensive view of the social good unavailable to their rulers. But the people are also presented as the heroes of a Christian pastoral in which they

1 *The Poetical Works of Robert Southey*, collected by himself, 10 vols, London, 1837, ii. 49.

play the role of sacrificial victim, purging the socially powerful and privileged of the guilt induced by cruelty and exploitation.

The play's ending appears to guard against this understanding of the people's suffering in a way which only serves to confirm its power. Richard II's speech, which closes the play and follows immediately on John Ball's visionary anticipation of the just society, shows him completely unmoved by what has happened. He insists on the need to crush insurrection by violent means. But this serves to distance him from the audience's reaction to a central dynamic within the play. Wat Tyler and John Ball, the play's two main characters, are both Christian heroes; their poverty and suffering become emblematic of moral purity and elevation. Behind the play's overt political message – that poverty must be abolished in the just society – is the strong, covert feeling that this same condition is the occasion of Christian nobility and a source of heroic distinction. The problem here is not simply to do with a clash of ideas: Christian doctrine could be, and was, harnessed to revolutionary thought in the late eighteenth century, as it had been in other periods. The tension arises once these ideas become part of a symbolic action which establishes comparisons between the Peasants' Revolt and Calvary. The result is a play which oscillates between representing the people as the agents of political change and as the subjects of pious spectacle.

The presence of Christian pastoral in the play is sustained by other aspects of pastoral convention. The sense that the play is about a social class distinct from the author and audience is marked by Southey's treatment of the motives for insurrection. It is made plain that Wat Tyler and John Ball suffer hard and long before they are moved to political action. Neither of them is presented as out to make trouble. It seems that Southey needed to reassure himself, and whatever audience he might have intended for the play, that political insurrection was morally virtuous in a way they would readily recognize. Similarly there is a laborious didacticism in the characters' recounting of their social and economic oppression, implying an audience who needed convincing. This insistence on popular virtue is supported by a pastoral equation which identifies their goodness as an aspect of their closeness to nature. The play begins with a lyrical celebration of the coming of the spring, implying the people's traditional identity with the rhythms of nature. This pastiche of folk ceremony is then given a Rousseauist elaboration. The people are naturally benevolent, polite and sympathetic, exiled from happiness by an artificial, and therefore unnecessary, system of social privilege and economic exploitation. The idea sustained by the play is that they are naturally noble but socially humble, while the ruling élite is socially noble but naturally base. But these simple equivalences act like a strait-jacket on Southey's characterization. His people are debarred from anything like a desire for power, or a pleasure in subversion for its own sake.

The simplicity of the play's psychology and action is matched by the simplicity of its language. But this hardly corresponds to what Jeffrey disapproved of: a poetic style modelled on the language of 'the middle and lower classes'. The shift in the *social* affiliation of poetic style is made by way of invoking the authority of Shakespeare as a *literary* precedent. The characters speak in a pastiche of Shakespearian blank verse, and the play's structure is deliberately mixed, combining pastoral, lyric interludes with dramatic action in a way that is reminiscent of *The Winter's Tale*.

In the eighteenth century the invocation of Shakespeare carried various messages, but one recurs. Samuel Johnson was one of a number of critics who defined Shakespeare as 'the poet of nature', and, for Johnson, this meant that Shakespeare's characters and their language reminded us of what we all had in common.[1] This view is useful to a writer like Southey because it could be readily grafted on to a critique of aristocratic or monarchic government. Aristocrats preserved their distinction by denying their participation in a common human nature. Their distinction was based on artifice, a view sustained by a number of radical political and historical myths of the period, which claimed that aristocratic government was a corrupt addition to republican democracy, the natural form of the political state. Southey's imitation of Shakespeare was another means of identifying his characters as natural, and therefore giving a legitimacy to their social grievances by identifying them as natural feelings naturally expressed. In addition, Shakespeare's precedent combines nature with nation and, in doing that, anticipates any attempt to label radical critique as unpatriotic. Filtering the Peasants' Revolt through Shakespearian pastiche makes political subversion appear an honest English tradition.

Shakespeare enables Southey to counter what a critic like Jeffrey expects as an appropriate representation of the people and to create a space in which low-born characters like Wat Tyler can take on the dignity of representing common human nature. The problem is that

1 See, for example, *Preface to Shakespeare's Plays* (1765), in *Samuel Johnson on Shakespeare*, ed. H. R. Woudhuysen, Harmondsworth, 1989, p 122.

the space created is a frozen one. There are two main reasons for this, both of which have a general application beyond the particular example of the play. The first of these concerns the power of a convention which equates representing the people with exhibiting their condition. This does not matter to a conservative writer like Crabbe, because it fits readily with the project of his work: exhibiting the people is one way of inviting an audience to consider how they might be more effective if compassionately ruled, as well as making them a useful example in a sermon about suffering. But, for the radical Southey, exhibiting the people produces an insoluble dilemma. It puts a label on all the popular characters which reads 'please pity me'. The play thus constantly re-creates the social distance which its ostensible political commitments want to abolish. The audience is as likely to go away from it feeling a need to perform more good works as complete a piece of unfinished revolutionary history.

The second reason returns us to the cult of simplicity and Southey's imitation of Shakespeare. The change in eighteenth-century bourgeois taste which made simplicity a virtue by equating it with what was natural was accompanied by nostalgia, the sense that simplicity was an expression of former times, of archaic and backward cultures.[1] Johnson's recommendation of Shakespeare as the poet of nature has a melancholy grandeur about it. His example is unrepeatable in a complex, commercial society.

The fact that simplicity is accompanied by a sigh, however much it sustains a contrast between a bad, corrupt modernity and the virtues of the old days, fixes Southey's play in a paradox which threatens to short-circuit its radical pretensions. The simple language of nature is sustained in the medium of a complex, historically self-conscious culture which it purports to criticize. Nature is always in need of revival, a quality recovered against the grain of history, its very vulnerability to loss also acting as a source of its attraction. It was, perhaps, this hide-and-seek attitude towards nature which made it pleasurable to an audience who wanted both to enjoy the benefits of civilization and regret its costs. The effect on *Wat Tyler* is to make the play's appeal for revolutionary solidarity between the peasants of the late fourteenth century and the radicals of the late eighteenth appear to come from a world inevitably if regrettably lost, rather than from a historical situation which needs to be surpassed.

1 For a useful discussion of this aspect of eighteenth-century culture see Marilyn Butler, *Romantics, Rebels and Reactionaries*, Oxford, 1981, pp 11–39.

The sense of nature as simplicity at a distance was evident in another aspect of late eighteenth-century literary culture, reflected in Southey's *Poems*, a collection first published in 1799. Within the formal eclecticism which characterizes the collection there are a number of ballads, lyrics and metrical tales whose presence suggests that Southey is responding to a scholarly and imaginative fascination with the recovery or imitation of traditional popular forms. They are admired as the products of cultures geographically or historically removed from the artificial division and hierarchies of modern civilization. Whether they are directly about the lives of the people or not, they are felt to bring popular or collective attitudes to bear upon whatever subjects they treat. They also propose imaginative identities for the poet: as bard or minstrel, speaking to or on behalf of an individual culture, or, in some of Southey's poems, as the mediator of traditional and popular forms of expression and knowledge.

In his revivals of the ballad form Southey represents the people by implication: as subjects with a history of cultural invention, as a voice and a value worth the attention of civilized and sophisticated readers. So one of them, 'Lord William', is not a poem directly about the people at all, but it implies a popular judgement on an aristocrat who discovers that no amount of social privilege can exempt him from the moral law which, in the end, makes equals of us all. When the people are directly represented, as in Southey's lyric poem 'The Complaints of the Poor', the same ethos of simplicity is carried over from ballad to lyric. The poem is framed as a response to the question of the 'Rich Man' who doubts that the sufferings of the poor are genuine. The Poet, acting as guide, takes him on a tour of the 'frozen streets', where the condition of the poor is made visible through a series of cameo encounters with the 'old bare-headed man', the 'young bare-footed child', a vagrant woman and a prostitute. All become emblems of unjustifiable suffering and the moral corruption that poverty brings. The incremental effect on the 'Rich Man' is the equivalent of a refutation of his initial scepticism. At the end of the poem he is left in reflective silence.

The poem's basic idea is that the poor themselves constitute the best answer to the sceptical questions of the privileged. Their situation is best represented by the poetics of simplicity because the truth of their condition cannot be disclosed by what the poem implies as the idiom opposed to its own: the discursively elaborate and emotionally detached rhetoric of political and economic analysis. The last two lines of the poem's first stanza have the character of an unexpected response to the opening gambit in an argument which, if pursued in the usual way, would go on all night and get nowhere:

> And wherefore do the Poor complain?
> The Rich Man ask'd of me . . .
> Come walk abroad with me, I said
> And I will answer thee.[1]

The poem's form composes a little myth about its own status as a special discourse, outside the distorting trammels of other discourses. It becomes, by implication, the language of a truth that could only be destroyed by rhetorical adornment. The recognition of this truth depends upon the state of the perceiver: the poem's simplicity contributes to the Rich Man's feeling which acknowledges that what the poor say about themselves is true.

The three 'English Eclogues', also published in the 1799 edition of Southey's *Poems*, share a similar concern with attitudes that threaten or sustain the social bond. Like their classic Virgilian precedents, Southey's eclogues are concerned with rural dispossession, the loss of home and property. In two of the poems, 'Hannah' and 'The Ruined Cottage', the agent of loss is a heartless male sexuality which destroys a community of affection. Both are stories of seduction and betrayal, in which the eclogue drifts into elegy, commemorating the lives of the humble and virtuous poor. The poet looks compassionately on those who might otherwise be overlooked. He follows through the stories embedded in a particular occasion or scene – stories which, in their turn, lead to the pleasures of melancholy reflection on the transience of all things and the vulnerability of virtue.

In the first of the eclogues, 'The Old Mansion House', melancholy is invoked and then surpassed. Following the conventions of the classical eclogue, the poem takes the form of a dialogue between an old man, representative of the labouring poor, and a stranger, who responds to the old man's anxious story about the changed ownership of the local mansion. The old man interprets the improvement to the house and grounds made by the new owner as so many threats to a customary, traditional way of life, secured by paternalistic relations between rich and poor. The poem's narrative turns on a revelation which proves the old man's fears to be groundless. The stranger

---

1 Robert Southey, 'The Complaints of the Poor' (first published in the *Morning Post*, June 1798, and afterwards in *Poems*, 1799), in *Poems of Robert Southey*, ed. M. H. Fitzgerald, Oxford, 1909, p 387.

declares himself to be the new owner of the mansion and offers hospitality to the old man. The core of affectionate community survives what turns out to be only a superficial change of appearance. By withholding his true identity, the new owner of the mansion can at once observe and test the opinions of the old man. His loyalty to tradition is rewarded by benevolence.

What Southey's eclogues share with the lyrics and ballads is a piety towards an ideal of domestic affection, which is also proposed as the basis of social harmony. Only if rich and poor treat each other familiarly, with the rich playing the role of parents, the poor the role of children, can the social bond be maintained. The poems are pervaded by a sentiment, at first sight odd in an ostensibly radical poet, which is close to that of the counter-revolutionary ideologue Edmund Burke:

To be attached to the subdivision, to love the little platoon we belong to in society, is the first principle (the germ as it were) of public affections. It is the first link in the series by which we proceed towards a love to our country and to mankind.[1]

Burke's ideas about the development of attachment find a poetic equivalent in Southey's collection of 1799. The poems recommend the perspectives of 'the little platoon'; they invite us to admire what is humble, unassuming, attached to local memories rather than abstract principles, preferring elegiac softness to visionary fervour.

As in Burke's writings, so in Southey's, these recommendations are linked to a sense of what it means to be English. The resolution of change into continuity, of grief and abandonment into the delicacies of elegiac memory, contribute to the Englishness of Southey's eclogues as much as the language they are written in. Indeed, the compositional effect of the poems is to suggest that the values and feelings they recommend are incarnate in the language, the language incarnate in the values and feelings. In this sense Southey's eclogues are not classical imitations but English originals: the classical model is not so much imitated as transformed by what is proposed as a natural core of Englishness. At another level a myth of Englishness supplies a coherence to the stylistic eclecticism of Southey's style. Ballad, lyrics, sonnet and formal ode are not only the medium for displaying the skills of a professional poet: they become the literary equivalent of an ideal which can incorporate learned and popular

1 Edmund Burke, *Reflections on the Revolution in France* (1790), London, 1910, p 44.

cultures within a single national substance. The ornate and learned style of 'The Hymn to the Penates' coexists with lyric simplicity and the 'popular' directness of the ballad form, to sustain a piety towards the English virtues of domestic affection and a morality sanctioned by tradition. What threatens these English virtues is not political tyranny, but a generalized selfishness, whose particular incarnations are the heartless seducer or acquisitive businessman.

Southey's *Poems* of 1799 are then a staging-post in his passage from Jacobin radical to Tory. The poetry implies the paternalism and patriotism that was to become Southey's explicitly declared political stance by 1810. Jeffrey's unsigned 1802 review of Southey's *Thalaba* cannot or will not see that simplicity in poetry need not be socially subversive. But then Jeffrey was committed to stirring literary controversy as a means of promoting the *Edinburgh Review*, and, as he almost concedes in the review of *Thalaba*, his real target is not Southey's emollient poetry, but the more obdurate practice of Wordsworth.

IV

Hazlitt's writing is pertinent for the contrasting account it offers to both Crabbe and Southey of the relations between writing and the people. Although a contemporary of both men, Hazlitt's cultural formation was markedly different. He was born into the culture of religious dissent, the son of a Unitarian minister. In this milieu religious and political dissent were closely allied. Hazlitt's native culture educated him into an obligation to publicly criticize arbitrary power and to assert the twin freedoms of speech and conscience. The obligation stayed with him throughout his career and made him a more fiercely outspoken writer than many of his contemporaries. He remained an unswerving supporter of the libertarian goals of the French Revolution and shaped for himself an image of Napoleon as the hero of freedom. But his affiliation to religious dissent was complicated by his early attraction to the powers of art, whether this took the form of Renaissance painting, Shakespeare's drama, or the new poetry of Wordsworth and Coleridge. What Shakespeare represented pre-eminently to Hazlitt was a power and variety of communication which could not be found in the closed world of theological dispute and definition, which also characterized the culture of dissent. Hazlitt refused to follow his father's plan and become a Unitarian minister. After an unsuccessful attempt to earn a living as a portrait painter, he became a professional writer and lecturer. By 1820 his powers as a critic and essayist were recognized by the politically liberal side of English literary culture, but he had also attracted the intense hostility of counter-revolutionary conservatism.

Hazlitt often chose to define himself as an outsider. One of the things that he stayed outside was the conservative political and cultural consensus that emerged in the English gentry and aristocracy during the Napoleonic wars. He was certainly conscious of his difference to Crabbe and Southey, and polemicized against both of them. In both cases what is at issue for Hazlitt is the relation between the writer and the people. His account of Crabbe as a 'Malthus turned metrical romancer', a poet who 'describes the interior of a cottage like a person sent there to distrain for rent', gives in aphoristic form the substance of radical dissent from Crabbe's particular brand of literary and social conservatism. Southey's case was different. He was one of a generation of turncoat poets, ranked with Wordsworth and Coleridge. Hazlitt diagnosed Southey's move from Jacobin radical to Tory royalist as the product of self-interest, and not, as Southey claimed, of principle. The main principle at stake was the one that Southey had betrayed, and the one that Hazlitt defined as 'the cause of the people'.[1]

Hazlitt's version of what it could mean to write on behalf of the people is powerfully exemplified by his political essay 'What is the People?', first published in 1817. The essay begins dramatically, by turning on an imaginary interlocutor:

And who are you to ask the question? One of the people. And yet you would be something! Then you would not have the people nothing. For what is the People? Millions of men, like you, with hearts beating in their bosoms, with thoughts stirring in their minds, with blood circulating in their veins, with wants and appetites and passions and anxious cares, and busy purposes and affections for others and a respect for themselves, and a desire for happiness, and a right for freedom and a will to be free.[2]

The question which gives the essay its title unexpectedly becomes part of the essay itself. The conventions of printed writing are re-framed in a way that shifts them towards the situation of a dramatic dialogue. This opening gambit is characteristic of the rhetorical

---

1 For Hazlitt on Crabbe, see his *Lectures on the English Poets* (1818), in *The Complete Works of William Hazlitt*, ed. P. P. Howe, 21 vols, London, 1930, v. 97; and on Southey, see Hazlitt's review of *The Lay of the Laureate*, first published in the *Examiner*, 7 July 1816, and collected in *Complete Works of Hazlitt*, vii. 90.

2 First published in the *Champion* (October 1817), and collected in *Complete Works of Hazlitt*, vii. 259–81.

strategy of the essay as a whole, which works by reversals and redefinitions of what it takes to be established opinion. So, in this case, the tables are turned, the questioner is questioned, and this is part of a political intention which seeks to embarrass those uses of the term 'the people', which imply and legitimate social hierarchy and condescension. By contrast, the drive of Hazlitt's essay is towards an account of the people which stresses the primacy of social identity and equality. It restates the case for popular sovereignty in both culture and politics. But the context it evokes repeatedly implies an opposite and hostile understanding. Hence the ironies at work in Hazlitt's lengthy sentence defining the people. The definition, which is also an argument for the recognition of a basic human equality, is obliged to labour the obvious: the people are human beings like any others, and, under circumstances of political and social justice, common sense would carry that understanding. But the writer has to spell out what is obvious in a society whose political and cultural life are built around a denial of the recognitions of common sense.

A pattern of allusion and quotation in Hazlitt's essay gives a more specific reason why Hazlitt labours under this necessity; its name is Edmund Burke. 'What is the People?' is an attempt to exorcize the rhetorical and the intellectual power of Burke's conservatism. Hazlitt's method is homoeopathic. He acknowledges the power of Burke's language to be memorable and to shape imagination for political ends, while seeking to counter that power by witty inversion and parodic quotation. By appropriating Burke's language for the purpose of radical rather than conservative assertion, Hazlitt replaces Burke's pieties about history and society with others of his own.

Burke used the French Revolution as an occasion to define monarchy, aristocracy and established religion as the subjects of pathos, attracting the reader's compassion and horror at their treatment by the revolutionaries. His skill is to identify the individuals who represent these institutions not just as innocent victims but as the bearers of those values which are basic to the survival of society as such.[1] Hazlitt reverses these priorities. He defines the people as the subjects of pathos, and the 'great and the powerful' as the predatory and parasitic force. The threat they pose is threefold: politically, they deny the claims of popular sovereignty; economically,

---

1 For an example, see Burke, *Reflections*, pp 72–86, where Burke makes the removal of the King and Queen of France to Paris in October 1789 into a central image of the horrors of the new democracy.

they consume wealth they have not produced; culturally, they claim to be the sources of intellectual and artistic achievement. Hazlitt turns the suggestion that these arrangements might be divinely sanctioned into a comic absurdity: 'To be formally invested with the attributes of Gods upon earth they [the great and powerful] ought first to be raised above its petty wants and appetites; they ought to give proofs of the beneficence and wisdom of Gods, before they can be trusted with the power . . .'[1] Viewed comically, the social hierarchy that Burke argues is necessary to social order is disclosed by Hazlitt as a structure of exploitation which needs to be dismantled. The social classes which Burke would have us revere are made over into objects of comic mockery by Hazlitt, and so lose the distinction which Burke claims for them.

For Hazlitt, the necessary class is the people. Their labour guarantees social existence. The wealth they produce is both material and intellectual. Hazlitt is particularly insistent on this latter point:

Where are we to find the intellect of the people? Why all the intellect that ever was is theirs . . . All the greatest poets, sages, heroes are ours originally and by right. But surely Lord Bacon was a great man? Yes, but not because he was a lord . . . All discoveries and all improvements in arts, in science, in legislation, in civilization . . . have been made by this intellect . . .[2]

Hazlitt roots intellectual achievement and innovation in a collective human process. Once again he counters Burke's arguments – in this case the latter's view that the source of culture and learning is found in the gentleman and the priest. But Hazlitt's argument resonates beyond the specific contest with Burke. By implication, he opposes the intellectual and political stance which divides the people from 'the illiterate rabble'. He also opposes those systems of classification which would preclude any social group from political participation on the grounds of their lack of intellect, their inability to think rationally about what is good for society as a whole. The distinctions between political and non-political subjects, deeply embedded in the traditions of political thought derived from Aristotle and Plato, are precluded by Hazlitt's contention that intellect is a common human property.[3]

One other context is immediately relevant. 'What is the People?'

1 *Complete Works of Hazlitt*, vii. 262.
2 Ibid., vii. 269.
3 For a useful discussion of the political and intellectual context here, see John Barrell, *The Political Theory of Painting from Reynolds to Hazlitt*, New Haven and London, 1986, pp 7–8.

was written and first published in 1817, in the immediate aftermath of Napoleon's defeat, and in a political atmosphere defined by the restoration of the European monarchies and the attempt to suppress popular political initiatives in Britain. Hence the specifically political pathos of Hazlitt's representation of the people: the restoration of the European monarchies signified the exile of popular sovereignty. The people are a power banished from their proper inheritance of political liberty and cultural recognition. In Hazlitt's lexicon the 'people' wavers between a term of social description and a challenge to political and social identification. The answer to the question that gives his essay its title is, in the end, left to his readers and their decisions about affiliation and belief, about where they stand in what the writer presents as a momentous political and cultural struggle.

'What is the People?' is Hazlitt's most sustained and explicitly political defence of popular sovereignty. Its manner – dramatic, challenging, volatile – characterizes Hazlitt's other, less explicitly political, writings about what would now be called popular culture. One essay, 'The Fight', first published in 1822, can serve as an illustration.[1] The essay was occasioned by what was for Hazlitt at least a thoroughly absorbing performance: a prizefight that took place at Hungerford, in Berkshire, in December 1821. He presents the fight itself as an epic occasion, a powerful and at times horrifying demonstration of pride, courage and physical endurance. But the fight is not the only performance at work in the essay. Hazlitt is engaged by what precedes the fight and what follows it: a carnival-esque holiday when an urban culture moves out into the countryside and social existence takes on the character of theatre. This, in turn, is subject to the self-conscious performance of the writer himself, mediating a 'low-life' occasion to what he represents as a genteel and feminine audience. The interplay of these various performances illustrates how different Hazlitt is as a writer from Crabbe and Southey. He does not bring writing to popular life in order to propose moral and social norms, or to make reassuring noises about social stability. In 'The Fight' the writer is not projected as a wise observer: he is at once a witness to a carnivalesque occasion and a character within it.

The energies displayed by the people are displayed as something that the writer needs, exemplified in the encounter between Hazlitt and a 'tall English Yeoman' during a late-night drinking-session at

---

1 First published in the *New Monthly Magazine* (February 1822), and collected in *Complete Works of Hazlitt*, xvii. 72–86.

an inn in Newbury on the evening before the fight. The yeoman has been mocking a drunken farmer who falls 'quietly asleep with a glass of liquor in his hand':

His laughing persecutor made a speech over him, and turning to the opposite side of the room, where they were all sleeping in the midst of this 'loud and furious fun' said, 'There's a scene, by God, for Hogarth to paint. I think he and Shakespeare were our two best men at copying life.' This confirmed me in my good opinion of him. Hogarth, Shakespeare, and Nature, were just enough for him (indeed for any man) to know. I said 'You read Cobbett, don't you? At least', says I, 'you talk just as well as he writes.' He seemed to doubt this. But I said, 'We have an hour to spare: if you'll get pen, ink, and paper, and keep on talking, I'll write down what you say; and if it doesn't make a capital Political Register, I'll forfeit my head. You have kept me alive tonight, however. I don't know what I should have done without you.'[1]

Hazlitt presents himself as a kind of parasite, dependent for his life on the dramatic exuberance of his subject-matter. The writing intimates some psychological malaise in the writer, but it does not invade the text, because Hazlitt turns himself into a character in a comedy about representation. The comedy consists in Hazlitt's efforts to turn into writing a situation whose best representation (by Hogarth or Shakespeare, the 'two best men at copying life') has already been anticipated by a character within it. The writer's eager desire to prove a point about the coincidence between good prose style, exemplified by Cobbett, and conversational idioms, exemplified by the yeoman, introduces an uneasy constraint: the energies which he values, and which are captured by Shakespeare and Hogarth, are threatened once he proposes to write them down, in a literal-minded attempt to copy life. In what follows on from the passage quoted above, we discover that Hazlitt sets aside his proposed experiment in writing in favour of further conversation.

In 'The Fight', as in his other writings about popular culture, Hazlitt's representation of the people moves between his attraction to whatever energy or skill he can discover in a particular occasion on the one hand, and, on the other, his scepticism about the tendency of authors or intellectuals to confine particular experiences by finding precedents for them. In a letter of advice written to his son in 1822, Hazlitt gave a warning about the pathologies of the professional author:

1 *Complete Works of Hazlitt*, xvii. 78.

Authors feel nothing spontaneously ... Instead of yielding to the first natural and lively impulse of things, in which they would find sympathy, they screw themselves up to some far-fetched view of the subject in order to be unintelligible ... Their minds are a sort of Herculaneum, full of old petrified images; – are set in stereotype, and little fitted to the ordinary occasions of life . . .[1]

The passage provides a useful additional gloss to Hazlitt's encounter with the yeoman. The allusions to Hogarth and Shakespeare, which are part of the yeoman's pleasure in the situation he finds himself in, are converted by the writer into an obsession about 'copying life'. In finding an equivalence between the yeoman's speech and Cobbett's prose style, Hazlitt is caught in a paradox: in trying to prove a connection between vivid speech and the best prose style, he is in danger of fixing the 'natural and lively impulse of things' in 'stereotype'.[2]

Hazlitt's sceptical awareness of the dangers of professional authorship supplies a particular dynamic to his writing, swayed between the search for a style that will yield to 'the first natural and lively impulse of things' and the constant tendency of writing to regress to precedent and stereotype. This carries particular consequences for the representation of the people in Hazlitt's writing. The authority of the writer to represent his subject is put in question, sometimes directly, more frequently by implication. It is not assumed, as it is with Crabbe and Southey, that the writer is doing his subject a favour by bestowing literary attention upon it, even if that favour, as in the case of Crabbe, has to do with the teaching of what is claimed as a necessary discipline. Indeed, in Hazlitt's case, as we have seen, the favours can be altogether the other way round.

V

This necessarily summary account of Hazlitt's representation of the people has indicated some of the ways in which he differs from Crabbe and Southey. These differences open out into larger questions about the relations between politics and culture in the period, at the

1 The letter can be found in *The Letters of William Hazlitt*, ed. H. M. Sikes, W. H. Bonner and G. Lahey, New York, 1978; the excerpt quoted can be found on pp 233–4. Hazlitt published a revised form of the letter, excluding this passage, in *Table Talk* (first published 1825).

2 For a useful discussion of Hazlitt's attitudes to authorship, see Marilyn Butler, 'Satire and Images of the Self in the Romantic Period: The Long Tradition of Hazlitt's Liber Amoris', in *The Yearbook of English Studies*, iv (1984), 209–25.

same time as they return us to Hazlitt's status as an outsider. What he stood outside was a remarkable and durable cultural achievement, to which Crabbe and Southey in their different ways both contributed: the elaboration of a conservative ideology, which was closely tied to an understanding of literature and its responsibilities. The terms of this conservatism are indicated in both writers' work. For Crabbe, and increasingly for Southey, the main problem which writing encounters is presented as a threat to order. This threat can take on various forms and is variously named, but the underlying responsibility of the literary work is both to secure an image of social order against this threat, and to recommend the pleasure and the necessity of resignation and obedience. In a period when issues of popular sovereignty and representation recur, whether in the form of revolutionary action or pressures for reform, it is necessary to the success of this ideology that it should shape an image of the people as in need of government by others, if only, as always, for their own good. Crabbe and Southey are both engaged in a complex act of reassurance and admonition: reassuring their audiences that the social order can in the end be secured, admonishing them that there are people out there in need of government, whether this is done with a compassionate tear, an iron rod, or both.

Hazlitt's representation of the people is conditioned by a very different interpretation of the period. For him, what threatened social existence was not disorder but an excess of order, figured both in a conservative attack on popular political rights and in the erosion of communicative energy by a conformist culture. The main problem which his work confronts is figured as this excess of order and conformity; the main responsibility of the writer is to unsettle this order by creating pockets of turbulence and free speech, even when this seems a forlorn and hopeless task. In this perspective the people represent a liberty and an energy either threatened by the activities of government or happily persisting outside its scrutiny. Hazlitt sought to defend popular liberties and to give vivid witness to occasions of energetic communication, but always within the paradoxical knowledge that literary writing might threaten both.

# 8

## POOR RELATIONS: WRITING IN THE WORKING CLASS 1770–1835

### Roger Sales

1

### NOT UNWORTHY OF NOTICE

What happened in 1830? George IV died and was succeeded by his brother, William IV. Parliamentary reform became, once again, a burning political issue. William Cobbett's *Rural Rides*, originally published as articles in the *Political Register*, came out in book form. The Swing agricultural riots swept through many of the southern and eastern counties of England. The Government tried to convict Cobbett for seditious libel, claiming that his article on the 'Rural War' in the *Political Register* of 11 December was directly responsible for some of the rioting in Sussex. Chichester experienced the effects of the Swing riots before Cobbett's article appeared. A large group of agricultural labourers and others assembled on 16 November to try to persuade the local magistrates and farmers to redress their grievances.[1]

This group almost certainly did not include Charles Crocker, a shoemaker, whose first volume of poetry, *The Vale of Obscurity, The Lavant and Other Poems*, was published by subscription in Chichester in 1830. It was dedicated to the Bishop of Winchester, who purchased twelve copies. Crocker was born in Chichester in 1797 and spent the rest of his life in the locality. He was apprenticed at the age of eleven, after receiving a limited formal education. He nevertheless made amends by buying an English grammar book and learning, at first, how to discriminate between nouns and verbs. This enabled him to spend his brief leisure time 'reading some good poetry and a

---

1 For more details on the Swing Riots, see E. J. Hobsbawm and G. Rude, *Captain Swing*, London, 1969; and ch 4 of my *English Literature in History 1780–1830; Pastoral and Politics*, London, 1983.

few works of criticism' (page x). He began to acquire a 'relish for the productions of Genius and Taste' (page x). He committed long passages from such works to memory and then repeated them to himself while he was working. He graduated to writing imitations of his favourite authors, who included John Milton, Oliver Goldsmith and William Cowper. He was, nevertheless, quick to reassure the Bishop of Winchester and other readers that he regarded authorship as an 'innocent gratification' (p vii) rather than an attempt to improve his social status. He hoped that his readers would derive 'innocent amusement' (p xii) from the poems. He knew his place, and this is why a place was found for his poetry on the shelves of the local gentry. It was only after some of his poems had 'accidentally fallen into the hands of persons capable of judging such things, and been pronounced by them not unworthy of publication' (p viii) that he began to contemplate publication.

Crocker was patronized because his individualistic and domesticated leisure activities offered a comforting contrast to forms of communal agitation and protest. His cultivation of a polite, literary language separated him from the vernacular languages and politics of the streets. His particular version of pastoralism stressed links between poverty and virtue. He argued in 'To Poverty' that, though destined to be poor throughout his life, there were blessings in this situation. 'The Vale of Obscurity' involves a dialogue between the poet and Content about the nature of these blessings. Content assures the poet

> '. . . I will not forsake thee, but will cheer
> Thy hours, or dark, or cloudless, as they rise;
> Oft mid thy toil and care will I appear
> And bid my visions to thy view arise,
> Whose wondrous imag'ry, and rainbow dyes
> Shall charm thy inmost soul' . . .

(p 46)

Poetry itself allows the poet to remain contented with his station in life. This theme is developed in 'Kingly Vale', which was included in the third edition of *The Vale of Obscurity*, in 1841:

> For though nor fame nor lucre may attend
> My unobtrusive song, yet e'en on me
> In solitude and silence oft descend
> The exalting influences of Poesy:
> And these a sweeter recompense shall be
> Than aught that fame or fortune can bestow; –

And though the visions bright which oft I see,
In my unequal lay but faintly glow,
Yet on my path obscure a sunny light they throw.

(p 23)

Crocker's poetry continued to sell reasonably well, and in 1845 he became a sexton at Chichester Cathedral. He took great delight in showing visitors around it and published a number of tourist guidebooks.

The protesters who took to the streets of Chichester in 1830 to complain, in a vernacular language, about economic grievances, which included the oppression of the state church, were not granted a public voice. It was given instead to the isolated individual who learnt the literary language and then employed it to extol the blessings of poverty and obscurity.

2

## UPSTAIRS AND DOWNSTAIRS

Robert Southey, the Poet Laureate, was a great admirer of a patriotic poem by Crocker entitled 'To the British Oak'. Southey's earlier radicalism had been replaced by a reverence for traditional values. He devoted some of his time in 1830 to preparing for publication an edition of poems by John Jones, a domestic servant. It appeared in 1831 with the title *Attempts in Verse, by John Jones, an Old Servant; with Some Account of the Writer, Written by Himself: and an Introductory Essay on the Lives and Works of Our Uneducated Poets, by Robert Southey, Esq. Poet Laureate*. The subscribers included William IV's Librarian and William Wordsworth. Jones had approached Southey by letter in 1827, asking the Laureate to look at his verses. He described himself as a 'poor, humble, uneducated domestic' (p 1). Southey decided to help Jones to raise a little money through publication because the old servant raised hopes about the existence of a deferential working class. Such hopes appeared to be confirmed when Jones penned an autobiographical letter in which he referred to Southey as 'Sir' no less than thirty-three times (pp 171–80).

Jones was very modest about the merits of his work and refused to let it disrupt his domestic duties. This old retainer often had to retain a poem in his head for several days because he was unable to find the time to write it down. He did, however, find time to acquaint himself with Shakespeare's plays as he found an edition of them in the dining-room of one of his employers and set about reading them after he had set the table. He added that 'when I could not be in the dining-room I read in the Bible below stairs' (p 173).

Jones was published because he deferred to dominant cultural assumptions. Southey still feels it necessary to mediate his voice by placing it after the long introductory essay on the 'uneducated poets'. This essay claims that Jones is likely to be 'the last versifyer of his class' (p 12) as universal education threatened to destroy the social conditions that produced such poets. Southey's perspective is controlled by an antiquarian nostalgia. His essay is confined to the lives and works of six writers: John Taylor, Stephen Duck, James Woodhouse, John Bennet, Ann Yearsley and John Byrant. He devotes most space to Taylor, a seventeenth-century poet, and his accounts of some of the more contemporary writers are very sketchy by comparison.

Southey's perspective is also influenced by nationalism. He wants to establish a specifically English tradition of working-class writing in contrast with better-known Scottish traditions. This means that he is able to ignore Robert Burns and James Hogg and therefore to preserve his condescending, dilettante approach to the subject. He avoids having to deal with writers whose output and reputation threaten the security of his own position. Yet he also selects his English tradition to protect his power as a patron. He refers at the end of the essay to Robert Bloomfield, but is anxious to postpone a discussion of his life and works. John Clare is conspicuous by his absence.

A consideration of Bloomfield would have forced Southey to consider the working-class writer as a best seller. *The Farmer's Boy* (1800) sold twenty-six thousand copies and went through seven editions in three years. It became the talk of the literary reviews. Southey himself told the readers of the *Critical Review* that 'even trite circumstances appear original in the discriminating language of this poet' (xxix. 70). Bloomfield, an agricultural labourer who had migrated to London to work as a shoemaker, became a literary curiosity because of what were taken to be discrepancies between his life and work. He describes in the Preface how large parts of the poem were written in a 'Garret, amid six or seven other workmen' (page x), and yet, to everyone's astonishment, the poem employed a discriminating literary language. Bloomfield may have rejected some of the more heroic versions of pastoral to concentrate on what Southey refers to as 'trite circumstances'. Yet, as William Hazlitt pointed out in his *Lectures on the English Poets* (1818), Bloomfield became popular because he reproduced rather than challenged literary conventions. The content as well as the form of *The Farmer's Boy* was reassuring, because it endorsed social discriminations. The hero, Giles, leads a life of 'constant, cheerful, servitude' (p 5) on an estate characterized by benevolent paternalism:

> Where smiling EUSTON boasts her good FITZROY,
> Lord of pure alms, and gifts that wide extend;
> The farmer's patron, and the poor man's friend:
> Whose Mansion glitters with the eastern ray
> Whose elevated temple points the way,
> O'er slopes and lawns, the park's extensive pride, . . .
>
> (pp 67–8)

Bloomfield follows pastoral conventions by reserving his social critique for an alien commercial economy that threatens to destabilize the hierarchical harmony of the estate. Although he published four more volumes, he never repeated the success of *The Farmer's Boy*.

John Clare spoilt Southey's nostalgia by remaining alive. He was considering publishing a fourth volume of his poetry at the same time as John Jones was presented to the reading public as a curious survival from a bygone age. He nevertheless became disillusioned by the way in which his proposal for the new volume was wilfully misread: 'these reviewers who begin like bill stickers to vex me very much they would force it down the throat of the world that I am evoking charity when I am only seeking independance.'[1] He was also annoyed by the way in which some of the reviewers gave the false impression that he was well provided for by his patrons. Jones was prepared to accept charity and therefore allowed Southey, and his readers, to reinforce the security of their positions. Clare's struggle for literary and social 'independance', to 'stand on my own bottom as a poet without any apology as to want of education or anything else',[2] offered more of a challenge to a professional writer like Southey. It was therefore conveniently ignored. Clare responded by pointing out that Southey's essay held 'uneducated poets in very little estimation'. He also suggested that the question of possible increases in educational opportunities for the working class was dealt with in 'a sneering way'.[3] He was to argue later on in favour of the Government establishing schools in every village.

Clare came to the notice of the reading public at the beginning of

1  J. W. and Anne Tibble, eds, *The Letters of John Clare*, London, 1951, p 262.
2  *Letters of Clare*, p 275.
3  *Letters of Clare*, p 254. Clare was also angry because he felt that Jones had plagiarized one of his poems.

1820 with the publication of *Poems Descriptive of Rural Life and Scenery*. Although not as commercially successful as *The Farmer's Boy*, it nevertheless went through a number of editions and attracted a lot of publicity. Some reviewers and patrons attempted to recruit Clare to the ranks of the anti-radical crusade. This could only be achieved, however, through either editing or suppressing a number of poems which suggested that he was not a loyal, contented peasant. At one level, the cultural battle was fought over issues of content, such as explicit critiques of wealth and enclosure. One of his patrons was to demand the removal of all 'radical slang' from his second volume, *The Village Minstrel* (1821).[1] This phrase indicates that language and form were regarded as being just as important as content in the attempt to market Clare as a conspicuous example of the grateful poor. His patrons and publishers continually demanded the removal of either dialect words or what they regarded as 'slang' terms from his poetry, regardless of their explicitly political associations. His erratic spelling and punctuation also created problems. He was led on one occasion to equate the tyranny of grammar with governmental tyranny.

Clare's acceptance of many of the pastoral conventions, together with the way in which he became accustomed to acting as his own censor, nevertheless meant that this effort to make his poetry more literary was deemed to be worthwhile. There was, however, one important pastoral convention which he found difficult to accept. Pastoral was generally written from the point of view of the overseer, whose privileged position in, or often above, the landscape could produce hierarchies and other kinds of discriminations. Clare did not inhabit such a position socially and was often reluctant to adopt it in his poems. One of his correspondents remarked that 'Yours is not that Panoramic view of Nature, which (imposing while viewed at a distance) only gives an idea of the general effect of the landscape: but you have touched your miniature with the finest pencil . . . '[2] The poetry often contains a tension between panorama and 'miniature'.

1 'Letters Addressed to John Clare', British Museum Egerton Manuscripts 2245–50, 2245, fol. 272.
2 Egerton Manuscripts, 2245, fol. 192. Clare's complicated relationship to the panoramic perspective of the overseer is considered very skilfully by John Barrell, *The Idea of Landscape and the Sense of Place 1730–1840: An Approach to the Poetry of John Clare*, Cambridge, 1972. For more details on the editing of *The Shepherd's Calendar*, see Eric Robinson and Geoffrey Summerfield, 'John Taylor's Editing of Clare's *The Shepherd's Calendar*', in *Review of English Studies*, xiv (1963), 359–69. Ch 5 of my *Pastoral and Politics* considers Clare's politics and the political nature of his patronage.

Clare's failure to establish hierarchies and make discriminations led to the severe editing of his third volume, *The Shepherd's Calendar* (1827). Passages in which he offered what appeared to be indiscriminate catalogues of trifling events or trite items were suppressed on the grounds that they were merely descriptive rather than reflective. Yet these catalogues are linked to reflections about rural society. Clare represents, and therefore preserves, a rural society that is fading even from memory. The lists of wild flowers or the chronicles of old customs offer negative reflections upon the present:

> Old customs O I love the sound
> However simple they may be
> What ere wi time has sanction found
> Is welcome and is dear to me
> Pride grows above simplicity
> And spurns it from her haughty mind
> And soon the poets song will be
> The only refuge they can find . . .[1]

Clare's nostalgia is both conservative and radical. He may take personal refuge *in* the past, but he also provides a refuge *for* the past itself. The past, once it has been rescued and preserved in all its seemingly indiscriminate detail, can be employed as part of a critique of the present. By ignoring Clare, Southey was able to ignore questions not just about the politics of patronage but also ones concerned with the politics of literary language and literary form.

There are further problems about the way in which Southey organizes his essay. He ignores eighteenth-century women writers such as Mary Collier and Mary Leapor and, as will become more apparent later on, fails to acknowledge some early nineteenth-century examples of writing by working-class women.[2] Despite the emphasis

1 Eric Robinson and Geoffrey Summerfield, eds, *The Shepherd's Calendar*, London, 1973, p 126. The quotation is from December.
2 For a detailed account of Collier, see Donna Landry, 'The Resignation of Mary Collier: Some Problems in Feminist Literary History', in Felicity Nussbaum and Laura Brown, eds, *The New Eighteenth Century: Theory: Politics: English Literature*, London, 1987, pp. 99–120. Some working-class poetry is anthologized in Roger Lonsdale, ed., *The New Oxford Book of Eighteenth Century Verse*, Oxford, 1984. General accounts of eighteenth- and/or nineteenth-century working-class writings include: ch 4 of Nigel Cross's *The Common Writer: Life in the Nineteenth Century Grub Street*, Cambridge, 1985; H. Gustav Klaus, *The Literature of Labour: Two Hundred Years of Working-Class Writing*, Brighton, 1985; Martha Vicinus, *The Industrial Muse: A Study of Nineteenth Century British Working-Class Literature*, London, 1975. There is a good chapter on 'Peasant Poets' in Morag Shiach's *Discourse on Popular Culture: Class, Gender and History in Cultural Analysis, 1730 to the Present*, Cambridge, 1989. I am also using material from my 1976

on lack of education in the title o the essay, it only occasionally gestures towards forms of Romantic primitivism. The *Edinburgh Review* was right to notice that Southey was primarily concerned to show that most of the 'uneducated' writers whom he carefully selected possessed a 'reverence for antiquity, for social distinctions, and for the established order of things'.[1] The biographical sketches were primarily designed to show how such writers educated themselves, and were educated, into an acceptance of dominant cultural assumptions. Ironically, a volume which appeared at first sight to suggest that ignorance might be a virtue was in reality a plea for the necessity of forms of social education which endorsed 'the established order of things'. Southey believed that his own curiosity, and that of his readers, about working-class writers was the product of cultural benevolence. Clare suggests, by describing how he was expected to act out a 'strangers poppet show', what it was like to be the spectacle rather than the spectator.[2]

James Taylor was a Lancashire hand-loom weaver who only learnt to read and write at the age of twenty-four by attending a village school. His *Miscellaneous Poems* was published in Oldham in 1827. This event 'excited great attention, and many have condescended to visit him and his family in their mansion of poverty. In addition to this, several have had the noble resolution to invite the Poet, in his garb of labour, to their tables' (1830 edn, p vi). Those who did not retain a rhyming butler could still reassure themselves about the existence of a deferential working class by occasionally inviting a hungry poet for dinner. They could also, of course, read Southey's edition of John Jones's poetry. Working-class men who wrote poetry were a potential threat to a cultural Establishment which sought to privilege the voices of university men. They could, nevertheless, be tolerated by being represented as amusing curiosities. The university wits associated with *Blackwood's Magazine* enjoyed themselves by caricaturing James Hogg's table talk. The threat posed by working-class writers was also neatly contained by the way in which they were incorporated into arguments in favour of dominant cultural assumptions. Exceptions were used to prove rules.

---

unpublished Cambridge Ph.D. thesis 'The Literature of Labour and the Condition-of-England Question 1730–1860'.

1 *Edinburgh Review*, liv (1831), 76. The reviewer was T. H. Lister.

2 *Letters of Clare*, p 60.

## MODEST CONFIDENCE

Working-class women writers posed a threat to an Establishment which privileged male voices in general. Publication tended to happen only when the woman writer could also be placed within the category of the deserving poor. Her literary presumption was thus neatly contained. Charity was certainly an impetus behind the publication of writings by many working-class men, and yet it tended to be even more pronounced in the cases of women writers. More specifically, publication and the limited amount of money which could be made from it was often justified as the means towards the end of maintaining family values.

*Poetical Attempts, by Ann Candler, a Suffolk Cottager: with a Short Narrative of Her Life* was published by subscription in Ipswich in 1803. This was a method of publication which involved individuals undertaking to buy one or more copies of a book before it appeared. The subscribers' names were listed within the book itself, often at the beginning, and thus competed for attention with the author's own name and his or her work. Candler's narrative was clearly meant to establish her as a member of the deserving poor. She had spent over twenty years in the Tattingstone Workhouse, after she had been deserted by her drunken husband. The fact that, at one point in their stormy relationship, she had walked out on him was a potentially uncomfortable one for her gentry patrons. This is perhaps why she represents her time in the workhouse as her punishment. The editor of the volume stressed the way in which she had cultivated a 'steady unaffected Christian faith', as well as her poetic muse, during her years of confinement. It was argued that publication would provide her with 'a sum sufficient to furnish a room, and place herself, in a state of comparative happiness, near her married daughter, where she might spend the evening of her days in peace, supported by her own industry, and occasionally assisted by those friends who know, and respect, her unobtrusive good qualities' (p 17). As with Jones, it was her humility, or 'unobtrusive good qualities', rather than her literary merit which excited most interest. She was constructed as a conspicuous example of the cottager: 'she has never had a higher station, or, in this world, a higher aim' (p 1).

Some of Candler's poetry seems to have been written to order, or at least written with a knowledge of what would appeal to the gentry market. 'Reflections on My Own Situation' draws a sharp distinction between the sufferings of the isolated, poetic individual and those of the rude multitude with whom she was forced to live in the workhouse:

> Within these dreary walls confin'd
> A lone recluse, I live,
> And, with the dregs of human kind,
> A niggard alms receive.
>
> Uncultivated, void of sense,
> Unsocial, insincere,
> Their rude behaviour gives offence
> Their language wounds the ear.

(p 53)

This kind of writing, like the editor's introductory remarks, is meant to show why Candler, and Candler alone, deserves to be given 'a sum sufficient to furnish a room'. She differentiates herself from the other inmates in the same way that Crocker distances himself from the protesters in Chichester. Yet her poetry as a whole is not just a transparent and unproblematic endorsement of traditional values and categories. 'Serious Reflections on the Times Written during the Late War' rejects patriotic representations. Profiteering is attacked:

> May speculators, and oppressors, find
> The painful workings of a guilty mind,
> With same review their vile nefarious arts,
> Till conscience wound and humanize their hearts.

(p 33)

Both sides are criticized for 'their haughty pride' (p 33).

*Simple Poems on Simple Subjects, by Christian Milne, Wife of a Journeyman Ship-carpenter in Footdee* was published by subscription in Aberdeen in 1805. Before she married, Milne had been a domestic servant and had managed to acquire some knowledge of literature by dipping secretly into books owned by her employers. Secrecy, or inventing cover stories, characterized her whole educational history since her own family considered even basic reading and writing to be signs of idleness. Her early poetry found its way into the hands of members of the local Establishment, who encouraged her aspirations because she appeared to represent domestic virtues. She agreed to publication as she wanted to raise money so that her children could have a better education than her own. The volume made a hundred pounds, although Milne appears to have saved the money and invested it some years later in a share of a fishing port. She suffered a mild form of consumption before her poems were published, and illness continued to restrict her literary activities. She herself, rather than her writing, was the commodity in demand.

While some working-class writers like Crocker showed visitors around tourist attractions, others like Clare and Milne became the tourist attraction themselves. Elizabeth Isabella Spence was one of a number of travellers and social explorers who made a detour to discover Milne. She describes her visit in *Letters from the North Highlands during the Summer of 1816* (1817):

I found her seated in the midst of her children, clean, neat, and employed at her needle. Her homely apartment had none of the litter and disorder, seen in many of the dwellings of the poor in Scotland. Her countenance pale, melancholy, and sickly, is marked by intelligence. She rose, with timid surprise when I entered, accompanied by a friend, and addressed me, when drawn into conversation, with modest confidence.

(p 56)

Spence's pen portrait is contradictory. At one level it is almost as if Milne's sickly appearance complements her other virtues such as domesticity and deference. Her weaknesses become her strengths. Yet, at another level, it seems likely that Spence made the visit because of Milne's achievements as a woman writer. Spence was influenced by Mary Wollstonecraft and appears to be reproducing some of the contradictions to be found in *A Vindication of the Rights of Woman* (1792). She admires Milne's 'intelligence' and yet, like Wollstonecraft, does not challenge the socially perceived need for good domestic servants.

Elizabeth Bentley of Norwich published *Genuine Poetical Compositions on Various Subjects* in 1791. She used the proceeds to establish a school so that she could afford to look after her widowed mother. A second volume, *Poems, being the Genuine Compositions of Elizabeth Bentley of Norwich*, was published in 1821 with a view to raising money for her retirement. She was presented to the reading public as a deserving case because her writings showed an awareness of a great literary tradition: 'The minor poems of Milton, the graver compositions of Pope, the moral allegories and descriptive pieces of Thomson and Collins, of Gray and Goldsmith, had supplied her with those models which she felt most desirous to imitate' (pp xxi–xxii). Readers were reassured that her poetry contained none of the 'bolder style' (p xxi) associated with forms of Romanticism. At the same time as university men like Wordsworth were rejecting polite literary culture in favour of folk culture, working-class writers were being represented as rejecting either folk or popular culture in favour of polite literary culture. It is always useful to be reminded of the fact that much of the writing produced during what has become known as the Romantic period was untouched by Romanticism.

Working-class writers who were content to echo the literary assumptions of their patrons posed no threat, whereas those who sought to find their own voices were deemed to be anarchic. At first sight Ann Yearsley appeared to literary ladies like Hannah More and Elizabeth Montagu to offer a combination of exactly the right qualities. Her large family were desperately in need of financial assistance, and yet, despite work and worry, she still found time to write the kind of poetry which showed an awareness of literary traditions. She could therefore be represented as a conspicuous example of the deserving poor. *Poems on Several Occasions by Ann Yearsley, a Milkwoman of Clifton* was published by subscription in 1785 and quickly went through a number of editions. Hannah More gestured towards a form of primitivism in the Preface to Yearsley's second volume, *Poems on Various Subjects, by Ann Yearsley, a Milkwoman of Clifton . . .* (1787): 'You will find her, like all unlettered Poets, abounding in imagery, metaphor, and personification . . . I should be sorry to see the wild vigour of her rustic muse polished into eloquence, or laboured into correctness' (page x). Yearsley nevertheless found herself trapped within the same contradictions which Southey was to impose upon John Jones: the working-class poet was expected, at one and the same time, to be both culturally innocent and yet also aware of literary tradition. Simplicity was only acceptable in its more refined forms. More's affectations about 'wild vigour' were in fact coupled with strenuous attempts to instil both 'eloquence' and 'correctness'. She underlined the way in which Yearsley exhibited a 'justness' of literary taste as well as a familiarity with 'the opinions of the best critics' (p ix).

More and Yearsley disagreed about what was to happen to the money that had been raised through publication. More, like many philanthropists, believed that the working classes ought to be treated as children who might squander money in an improvident way unless they were restrained from doing so. She felt that Yearsley was too fond of expensive clothes. She therefore set up a trust fund, which was designed to benefit Yearsley's children at some unspecified date in the future. The publicity that surrounded this quarrel meant that Southey could not ignore Yearsley in *The Lives and Works of Our Uneducated Poets*. She became the token woman writer, whose career was dealt with very briefly. Southey often uses More's words to tell Yearsley's story and also takes More's point of view as far as the quarrel is concerned:

The whole transaction was vexatious to Miss More, whose benevolent intentions ought not to have been misunderstood; and it was unfortunate for Mrs Yearsley, who was now represented as a thankless and unworthy person, and who from that time considered as an enemy one who, but for this misunderstanding, would have continued to be her friend and faithful adviser.

(p 130)

This quarrel was not just about money, but also concerned Yearsley's desire to establish her own literary independence. Accordinging to Yearsley's own account in *Poems on Various Subjects*, More responded to her attempts to establish herself as a professional writer by calling her a 'savage' (p xx). More considered her ignorance of the cultural role which she was expected to perform to be neither noble nor virtuous. Primitive writers became savages if they vigorously pursued wild notions of cultural equality.

Ironically, Yearsley's struggle for independence only served to heighten her attraction as a tourist spectacle. As she noted in *Poems on Various Subjects*, 'My character, which in one moment appeared so bright, and in the next tinged with every vice that can disgrace the sex, excited many gentlemen and ladies to visit me' (p xxii). She nevertheless succeeded in emancipating herself from the confinements of the stereotype of the 'uneducated' or 'unlettered' writer. Her poetry, for instance *A Poem on the Inhumanity of the Slave-Trade* (1788), engaged in topical political debates. She established a circulating library and was therefore not totally dependent on the patronage system. She also experimented with new literary forms such as drama and prose fiction. *Earl Goodwin*, a historical play which was first performed in 1790, represented the tyranny of the 'Norman yoke'. This was a common theme in the radical writings of the 1790s. *The Royal Captives* (1795) is a melodramatic historical novel set in seventeenth-century France. It can be seen as both a release from the restrictions of the stereotype of the working-class writer and an exploration of them. It contains a number of variations on the themes of confinement and guardianship. The representation of the 'poetess of the mountain', who was mad enough to think for herself and who was thus torn apart 'by contending passions' (p 104), can be read as a self-portrait. There are also a number of occasions when the position of women in society is looked at in more general terms: 'oppression hangs on woman. Custom and law respecting her, are through the world unjust . . .' (p 198).[1]

Charlotte Richardson was another working-class writer whose work was modelled on the literary canon; it could therefore be used to suggest the universality of taste. Her first volume, *Poems Written on Different Occasions*, was published in York in 1806. It was edited by Catherine Cappe, the wife of a Unitarian minister, who provides a version of Richardson's own story. She was, according to Cappe, born in York in 1775 'under circumstances the most unfavourable' (p vii). She nevertheless managed to attend a Sunday school, at which she demonstrated 'uncommon quickness, docility, and a great desire for information' (p vii). Working-class writers were caught in a double bind: they were expected to be quick but docile, modest and yet also confident, attentive while remaining unobtrusive. These are all qualities which have traditionally been associated with the 'good servant'.

Richardson went into service, and then married a shoemaker in 1802. He died of consumption, and so she was left to support herself and her baby. It was at this point that Cappe decided that publication could be used to establish Richardson as a conspicuous member of the deserving poor. Richardson used the profits from *Poems Written on Different Occasions* to establish her own school. Her health deteriorated and so Cappe decided to make another appeal to the benevolence of the local reading public. According to Cappe, the message of *Poems Chiefly Composed during the Pressure of Severe Illness* (York, 1809) was that there was

no state of suffering . . . in which a heart sincerely devoted to its maker, may not seek for and obtain, support and consolation, for it cannot be without its use to see as in a mirror, that every thing, even in this world, does not depend upon riches, learning, rank, or station, but that energy of mind, supported and adorned by Christian piety and virtue, can raise its possessor to consideration and respect in circumstances the most indigent and depressing.

(pp iv–v)

Richardson's life was worthy of notice and this meant that her poetry was 'not wholly unworthy' (p vi) of consideration. She recovered from this severe illness, reopened her school and died in 1825. The patronage which she received was broadly similar to that which was given to Candler, Bentley and Milne. Her knowledge of Gray and Goldsmith exhibited what was deemed to be correct

1 For more details on Yearsley, see Moira Ferguson, 'Resistance and Power in the Life and Writings of Ann Yearsley', in *The Eighteenth Century: Theory and Interpretation*, xxvii (1986), 247–68.

literary taste. Her life was organized around religion, domesticity and service. Unlike Yearsley, she appeared to be quick but docile, confident and yet also modest.

4

## MARKETABLE ARTICLES

Southey, the professional man of letters, was sharply attuned to relationships between literary popularity and curiosity. He suggested that Henry Kirke White achieved a posthumous success because of the interest that was taken in his tragic life: 'For poetry is not a marketable article unless there be something strange or peculiar to give it a fashion; and in his case what money might possibly have been raised, would, in almost every instance, have been considered rather as given to the author than paid for his book.'[1]

Kirke White was the son of a small tradesman from Nottingham. He began work at fourteen on a stocking-loom and yet succeeded in gaining a place at Cambridge University through a combination of self-help and patronage. He died in his college rooms in 1806 at the age of twenty-one. Southey decided to raise money for the poet's family through the publication of *Poetical Works and Remains of Henry Kirke White, with a Life by Robert Southey* (1807). Southey usually managed to work his own name into a title. His commercial instincts proved to be correct: the first edition sold out relatively quickly and had to be reprinted several times. The story of Kirke White's literary aspirations appealed to middle-class and gentry readers. His remorseless pursuit of knowledge under difficulties also allowed him to become an important role model for working-class readers and writers. His premature death added poignancy and therefore marketability to his work.

Joseph Blacket was another working-class writer whose premature death made his writings more of a 'marketable article'. He was a London shoemaker whose wife died in 1807, leaving him to bring up his small daughter. The fact that he sought solace in writing poetry in the wake of this domestic tragedy meant that he could be presented as a deserving case for charity. His enthusiasm for Shakespeare, Milton and some of the leading eighteenth-century poets

---

1 C. C. Southey, ed., *The Life and Correspondence of Robert Southey*, 6 vols, London, 1849, iii. 212–13. This letter is addressed to Ebenezer Elliott and is an unsuccessful attempt to persuade him to abandon his dreams of becoming a writer. He went on to achieve success as the 'Corn-Law Rhymer'.

indicated traditional literary tastes. *Specimens of the Poetry of Joseph Blacket, with an Account of His Life and Some Introductory Observations, by Mr Pratt* was published in 1809. Blacket himself became consumptive while this volume was in preparation and, despite the attempts of his patrons to provide him with medical attention and a healthier environment, died in 1809. Samuel Pratt compiled *The Remains of Joseph Blacket* . . . (1811), which, because of high-society curiosity about the tragic story, raised five hundred pounds for Blacket's daughter.

Byron's response to *The Remains* was that 'Pratt has put Joe Blackett [*sic*] into two volumes as bad as Purgatory, Poor Joe, killed first & published afterwards, if the thing had been reversed the wonder had been less, but the cruelty equal . . .'[1] This represents a continuation of the argument of *English Bards and Scotch Reviewers* (1809), in which Byron satirizes the reading public for allowing wonder, curiosity and gossip to become substitutes for a concern with literary merit. His position is, as always, fraught with contradictions, since his own gossipy style and manner offers a celebration of what is also the object of his satire. He may have been the scourge of marketable articles, yet he fashioned his life and poetry into bestselling commodities. He took every opportunity to draw attention to the way in which Southey's radicalism had been replaced by an adoration for Church and State. The famous satires may foreground political disagreements, and yet it is also important to establish the similarities between Byron and Southey. They were both extremely skilled players of the literary market. Byron's obsessive crusade against Southey was motivated by a rivalry that recognized similarity as well as difference.

## 5

## TITLES AND ENTITLEMENT

The reading public was prepared to be charitable to literary curiosities provided that certain rules were observed. A claim for charitable status had to be clearly announced in the title of a volume. Christian Milne, it will be remembered, was introduced as the 'Wife of a Journeyman Ship-carpenter in Footdee'. The reader is made aware of her social background before he or she reads a single word of the

---

1 Leslie A. Marchand, ed., *Byron's Letters and Journals*, 12 vols, ii: *Famous in My Time*, London, 1973, p 132.

poetry. The fact that this poetry is advertised as *Simple Poems on Simple Subjects* also allows the reader to assume a position of cultural superiority.

Male writers were not required to parade their marital status, but they still had to agree to titles which clearly foregrounded their entitlement to be treated as curiosities. Another working-class poet from Aberdeen appealed to the generosity of the reading public by publishing under the title *Simple Strains; or, the Homespun Lays of an Untutored Muse by James Cock, Weaver* (Aberdeen, 1810). Such titles defined both the literary norm and its 'other'. Milne's place of residence is also highlighted in the title of her volume, but as this was published locally this was a way of making sure that local readers patronized a local writer. Similarly, the title of John Lucas's volume – *Miscellanies in Verse and Prose by John Lucas, Cobler [sic], a Pensioner in Trinity Hospital, Salisbury* (Salisbury, 1776) – invites local readers to be charitable towards a local writer. More specifically, Lucas's place of residence guarantees that he is a member of the deserving poor. The foregrounding of a writer's provincial origins in volumes that were published in London may, by contrast, be seen as an example of how a metropolitan-orientated literary Establishment defined its 'other'. The full title of Clare's first volume, published in London in 1820, was *Poems Descriptive of Rural Life and Scenery, by John Clare, a Northamptonshire Peasant*.

As indicated, working-class writers were expected to make a spectacle of what were taken to be their social handicaps and disadvantages. Physical handicaps were also used to make out a case for otherness and therefore for curiosity and charitable concern. *A Narrative of the Life of James Downing [a Blind Man], Late a Private in His Majesty's 20th Regiment of Foot. Written by Himself, in Easy Verse* (1815) was published with the intention of securing financial relief for the writer, and, as it went through three editions relatively quickly, probably achieved this objective. Downing was a shoemaker who ran away from home to join the army. He became blind while serving in Egypt and had to be invalided out of the army. His narrative is concerned with conversion: he only sees the religious light after he has been blinded. The title, with its condensed life history, serves the same function as the 'written paper' worn by the blind beggar in Book VII of Wordsworth's *The Prelude*: it explains 'The story of the Man, and who he was'. Wordsworth, cut adrift from his moorings and borne along by the tide of 'the overflowing Streets', manages to drop anchor by reflecting upon the emblematic significance of the immobile blind beggar and his story. The beggar's message is taken to be the only fixed, or stable, sign in an environment characterized by the fluid, mysterious and anarchic relationship between signs and meanings.[1] The full title of Downing's *Narrative* may not provoke this kind of philosophical speculation, but it too is making claims about the authenticity and therefore stability of a blind man's story.

Terms such as 'genuine' and 'authentic' were often used in titles to reassure the reading public that it was not being asked for charity under false pretences. *The Genuine Life of Robert Barker, Dictated by Himself while in a State of Total Darkness . . .* (1809) is another title which makes out a case for charitable entitlement.

Working–class writers like Yearsley were treated as if they were children, and so it is not surprising that the reading public also enjoyed discovering and patronizing child poets. Thomas Dermody, who was billed as the 'orphan poet' in much the same way as Candler was given the title of the 'workhouse poet', received a classical education from his father, who was a schoolmaster in Ireland. He was nevertheless reduced to poverty when his father died of drink. The Dublin literary establishment promoted his poetry on the well-founded assumption that the discrepancy between classical learning and poverty would make it a 'marketable article', which would raise money to rescue him from street life. The readers of his first volume were assured that he was still under fourteen, and his age was used more explicitly as a selling-point in his second volume, which was entitled *Poems, Consisting of Essays, Lyric, Elegiac &c by Thomas Dermody, Written Between the 13th and 16th Year of His Age* (1792). Just as Yearsley's patronage had little to do with primitivism, so Dermody was represented as a poet who imitated the best poetic models.

The sporting newspapers in the 1820s, for instance the *Weekly Dispatch* and *Bell's Life*, were filled with poems which claimed to be the genuine productions of Tom Cribb and other famous boxers. They were, in fact, produced by literary hacks. The joke depended on making the discrepancy between the pugilistic 'fancy' and the poetic fancy as great as possible; so ornate, well-wrought neoclassical poems were attributed to the bruisers.[2]

1 I am concerned here with the well-known passage towards the end of Book VII; in *The Oxford Authors: William Wordsworth*, ed. Stephen Gill, Oxford, 1984, ll 589–623.
2 Further details in John Ford, *Prizefighting: The Age of Regency Boxiana*, Newton Abbot, 1971, pp 56–7.

6

## COMPETING VOICES

Working-class writers were seldom allowed to address their readers directly. Their work was mediated and framed by introductions, prefaces and footnotes composed by their patrons. Perhaps the most extreme example of this kind of cultural mediation occurred in 1773 with the publication in London of *Poems on Various Subjects, Religious and Moral, by Phillis Wheatley, Negro Servant to Mr John Wheatley, of Boston, in New England*. Great care was taken to establish the authenticity of the poetry since it was believed that, in this particular case, the discrepancy between social position and cultural achievement was too great to be credible. The reader is presented with different types of documentary evidence before being allowed to read the poems. A drawing of Wheatley in the act of composition is followed by a statement from her master: 'PHILLIS was brought from *Africa* to *America*, in the year 1761, between Seven and Eight Years of Age. Without any Assistance from School Education, and by only what she was taught in the Family, she, in sixteen Months attained the English Language . . .' (p 6). Further proof is offered in the form of a guarantee signed by eighteen of 'the most respectable Characters in *Boston*' (p 7). They had examined Wheatley to make absolutely sure that both she and her poetry could be marketed as genuine articles.

The poetry itself, which included an imitation of Ovid, appeared to suggest the universality of neoclassical versions of literary taste. It also tended at times to reproduce a version of colonial discourse. Africa, because it is seen as unchristian, is represented as 'the land of errors, and Egyptian gloom' (p 15) and as '*Pagan*' (p 18). Some of Wheatley's more explicitly political poetry was not included in *Poems on Various Subjects*. When this is considered, together with some of her later poems and her letters, then it emerges that the reading public may have been offered a comforting, but not necessarily genuine, article.[1]

Conversion narratives offered working-class writers opportunities for publication, and yet their voices were subordinated to more authoritative ones. Mary Saxby's prose narrative *Memoirs of a Female Vagrant, Written by Herself* (Dunstable, 1806) was edited by Samuel

---

1 For more details about Wheatley's career, see *The Collected Works of Phillis Wheatley*, ed. John C. Shields, New York, 1988. I am grateful to Ros Ballaster for drawing my attention to this informative edition.

Greatheed. He chose to preface the *Memoirs* with a letter which he had written about his editorial policy to one of Saxby's patrons. He acknowledged that he had omitted material that he did not consider to be relevant to the main issue of religious conversion. His prejudices against vagrants are clearly visible throughout the letter. Saxby is therefore only allowed to speak within the narrow confines established for her by her editor. Her narrative is also frequently broken up with editorial footnotes, which are designed to make sure that not even the simplest soul misses the moral of the story. She is denied the last word as well as the first one: when the narrative breaks off, Greatheed closes the volume with his version of her story. She is allowed a voice only to be denied it.[1]

Wordsworth's representation of vagrants, solitaries and outcasts is, of course, more complex than this straightforward attempt to record how a sinner was saved. There are nevertheless some parallels that can be drawn between the *Memoirs* and, say, 'The Old Cumberland Beggar'. The poem appears to offer a critique of the workhouse system, whose monologic rules and regulations fail to recognize the importance of memory and custom. Yet there is also a sense in which Wordsworth's poem confines the beggar within what might be described as the workhouse of representation. Workhouses imposed rules of silence upon their inmates, but the interesting contradiction is that the poem also imposes a rule of silence on its inmate, the beggar. The poem can be read as a dialogue between Wordsworth and utilitarian statesmen, but not as a dialogue between Wordsworth and the beggar. Following on from this, the silent beggar can be seen as playing a carefully scripted part in Wordsworth's own version of a conversion narrative. The poem may not be designed to save sinners, but it is concerned to get statesmen to recognize the error of their ways.[2]

1 For a more detailed study of Saxby, see Regenia Gagnier, 'Social Atoms: Working Class Autobiography, Subjectivity, and Gender', in *Victorian Studies*, xxx (1987), 335–63. For more information on working-class autobiographies in general, see David Vincent, *Bread, Knowledge and Freedom: A Study of Nineteenth Century Working Class Autobiography*, London, 1982.
2 This is based on my reading of Wordsworth in Chapter 3 of *Pastoral and Politics*. I am, nevertheless, indebted to Nicola Trott, whose interesting paper at the 1989 'Reviewing Romanticism' conference at Winchester suggested this particular approach to 'The Old Cumberland Beggar' to me, even though it argued in favour of a quite different interpretation.

7

## KING AND COUNTRY

It is difficult even to estimate how many working-class writers there were in this period. The publicity that surrounded the discoveries of poets like Burns, Bloomfield and Clare encouraged a relatively large number of other working-class writers to declare their existence. Clare received letters from at least seven other working-class poets after the success of *Poems Descriptive*, and yet only two of them eventually had volumes published under their own names.[1] It is clear that the supply of such writers greatly exceeded the demand for them by the literary Establishment. It was essential that only a limited number of these poor literary relations were discovered in order to perpetuate mythologies which sought to contain and marginalize their writings. The reception of working-class writings was not just conditioned by negative versions of social control. As already suggested, appropriate writers were recruited through patronage and the promise of publication to show that literary tastes and judgements were universal rather than more narrowly class-based. These writers were also expected to come out positively in favour of the Church and State.

The Reverend Robert Storry reassured readers of *Poems, Chiefly on Religious Subjects, by John Forster, Shoemaker, of Winteringham in Lincolnshire, Late a Private in the N. Lincoln Militia* (1797) that the poems were 'the genuine production of the obscure person mentioned in the title-page' (p 7). Forster was represented as a deserving case because, like Crocker, he used acceptable versions of pastoral as the basis for poetic statements on the blessings of obscurity. His literary values were, as Storry was quick to point out, closely allied to his religious beliefs: 'The excellent matter contained in these little pieces seems well calculated to show the use and excellency of the gospel principles, and to promote the comfort and spiritual welfare of the serious reader' (p 8). Forster's religious beliefs were, in turn, related to his strong sense of patriotism. He had been invalided out of the local militia with 'a lingering and painful complaint which no medical advice can remove' (p 8). This mysterious illness, together with his 'declining age' (p 8) and the material needs of his large family, strengthened his claims to charity.

---

1 The letters of the working-class poets who wrote to Clare are in the Egerton Manuscripts 2245–50. For precise details, see my 'The Literature of Labour and the Condition-of-England Question 1730–1860', p 1.

Working-class writers were actively recruited into the literary campaign against forms of radicalism during the period of the Revolutionary and Napoleonic wars. Robert Buchanan's *Poems on Several Occasions* (Edinburgh, 1797) was dedicated to the 'officers and gentlemen who compose the honourable and patriotic band, the Wigtonshire Volunteers'. He declared his intention of doing all that he could in his 'humble station' to support 'that beautiful fabrick, the British Constitution, which disappointed and disaffected men would make totter and fall, that they amongst the ruins of the long and justly admired edifice, might bury all and everything that tended to thwart their ambitious designs' (page v). The poetry itself, in common with other forms of anti-Jacobin propaganda, clearly identified Tom Paine as being the destroyer of tradition.

Other writers reproduced the style and tone of some of Hannah More's counter-revolutionary tracts in their denunciations of Paine. William Edwards, in a volume entitled *A Collection of Poems on Various Subjects, In English and Scottish Dialects, by William Edwards, Gardener, Delgaty, Turreff* (Aberdeen, 1810), advised his readers to pay their taxes and 'From Paine and his plots to keep free' (p 66). Napoleon gradually replaced Paine in this demonology. Milne voiced her anger at Napoleon's coronation and Blacket, who was a member of his local volunteer corps, attacked France's imperial policies in a poem on 'The Fall of Zaragossa'. Jones was one of many working-class poets who delivered up thanks for the victory at Waterloo. Earlier on, several poets, including Bentley, Kirke White and Richardson, commented on the importance of Admiral Nelson's victories.

Patriotism continued to open the door to publication after the end of the Napoleonic wars. Old soldiers like Serjeant Butler and John Shipp, author of *Memoirs of the Extraordinary Military Career of John Shipp, Late a Lieutenant in His Majesty's 87th Regiment, Written by Himself* (1829), traded upon the generosity of the reading public. Poets were also anxious to parade their military service. Robert Millhouse was born in Nottingham and started work at the age of six. He was working on a stocking-loom by the time he was ten. He enlisted with the Nottinghamshire Militia in 1810 and spent the next two years serving in Ireland. Although he was not therefore called upon to act against the Luddites in Nottinghamshire, his duties in Ireland almost certainly involved surveillance of radical movements. He returned to his old job in Nottingham when the militia was disbanded, but then joined the Royal Sherwood Foresters. The colonel of the regiment took an interest in his poetry, which was influenced by Shakespeare, Milton and the leading eighteenth-century poets, and was instrumental in the publication of *Vicissitude ... by Robert Millhouse, Corporal of the Staff of the Royal Sherwood Foresters ...* (1821). A later volume, *The Song of the Patriot, Sonnets and Songs* (1826), offers an unproblematic version of 'plenty' by ignoring questions about ownership and agency. Social divisions are harmonized through an emphasis on national unity:

> Peasant and Peer are by one law control'd;
> And this it is, that keeps us great and grand:
> This is the impulse makes our warriors bold,
> And knits more close the bond of our father's seal'd of old.

(p 9)

The victories of the Napoleonic wars are related to a historical roll-call of honour, which includes the almost obligatory reference to Agincourt, in order to demonstrate the strength of this national unity.

A few working-class writers wrote explicitly party political poetry. John Nicholson, the Airedale Bard, came out strongly against Catholic emancipation. Robert Storey, who began his working life as an agricultural labourer in Northumberland, was proud of his title of 'the poet of conservatism', which he earned because of his writings against parliamentary reform. One of his songs, 'The Isles are Awake', was widely used by the Tories on the hustings during the 1835 general election.

The working-class poets who supported radical political movements inevitably stood less chance of getting published in book form; they therefore used the radical press as their platform. The volumes of radical poetry that were published were aimed, not at condescendingly curious gentry readers, but rather at the readers of the 'pauper press'. The *Poor Man's Guardian* carried an enthusiastic recommendation for George Petrie's *Equality: A Poem* (1832). Charles Cole's volume *Political and Other Poems, by Charles Cole, a London Mechanic* (1834) was aimed at the same audience. He was, like most radical working-class poets, strongly influenced by Shelley's political poetry, and tried to expose the masquerades of power. His critique of the monarchy contrasted with the songs of praise for King and country which attracted the attention of literary patrons.

8

## BEYOND THE PALE

The role of accident was frequently stressed in the narratives that were constructed around the discovery of working-class writers. The writers themselves were often represented as stumbling upon particular literary texts, which led to desires to acquire a more general knowledge of polite culture. Such accounts can be read as cultural, as opposed to more purely religious, conversion narratives. Patrons apparently stumbled upon these writers quite by chance. Manuscripts had a habit of falling miraculously into the right hands at precisely the right moment. This emphasis on accident, or the uniqueness and unpredictability of events, reinforced the attempts to promote ideas of individual authorship and special creation. A different interpretation of the process of discovery was suggested by Cobbett, who claimed that many working-class writers were 'taken in tow' by the Government to prevent them from participating in the radical movement.[1] He never knowingly understated his case. Direct governmental intervention was very rare, but Cobbett's remark might imply that individual patrons, publishers and reviewers ought to be seen in collective terms as cultural ambassadors for the Government. This in turn suggests that the individual discovery narratives were, in fact, institutionally authored.

Cobbett's remark, at a more general level, draws attention to the war of words between the Government and its enemies. Political polemic was not, of course, invented in this period, and yet the scale on which it was conducted began to change quite dramatically during the 1790s. The second part of Paine's *Rights of Man* (1792) probably sold upwards of two hundred thousand copies, and had a circulation which was far in excess of this figure. It can be argued that the size of Paine's audience, which he sustained through his aggressively populist rhetoric, was in the end more subversive than his political messages. Counter-revolutionary legislation in the 1790s and later was quite successful in policing audiences that were located beyond the pale of polite political and cultural discourses. Yet no amount of legislation and surveillance could render these large audiences knowable and therefore safe. The Government and its

---

1 Quoted in 'Robert Bloomfield, Correspondence with His Family and Others 1788–1823', British Museum Additional Manuscripts, 28, 268, fol. 423.

cultural ambassadors believed that readers, like authors, were isolated individuals. Paine's audience could not be thought about, or known, in these terms. This is not to deny Paine's readers their individuality, but rather to suggest that they also need to be seen as forming a community, held together by both gossip and conviction, around the text.

It was not just explicitly political texts like *Rights of Man* which found large audiences. The Catnach Press specialized in cheaply produced sensational and melodramatic publications. Catnach's version of the confession of William Corder, who was convicted for the murder of Maria Marten, sold over a million copies in 1828.[1] Criminal confessions, which often provided platforms for working-class voices, should not be seen as offering wholehearted support for the agencies of law and order. The criminal was often permitted a more direct form of address than was customary in religious conversion narratives. Although some confessions were obviously either ghosted or invented, this was not true of all of them. It is also dangerous to place too much emphasis on endings which appear to show the triumph of law and order. Criminal confessions dramatized a conflict between the criminal and society and were therefore open to conflicting readings.

Wordsworth and Coleridge reject the idea that popular literature could produce conflicting, or multiple, meanings in the 1800 Preface to *Lyrical Ballads*. They represent urban readers as being crazed addicts, who all respond in the same way to 'gross and violent stimulants'. Their construction emphasizes the ways in which readers are abused by popular literature rather than acknowledging the different ways in which it may be used: 'For a multitude of causes, unknown to former times, are now acting with a combined force to blunt the discriminating powers of the mind, and unfitting it for all voluntary exertion to reduce it to a state of almost savage torpor.' At one level, the expanding urban reading public is feared because it is seen as being indiscriminate. At a more complex level, it is feared because, if it does not discriminate, then it cannot be thought about or known, as knowledge depends upon, and is defined by, discrimination. The Preface itself discriminates between the work of named authors and what are represented as being anonymous categories of writing: 'The invaluable works of our elder writers, I had almost said the works of Shakespear and Milton, are driven into neglect by

---

1 Contemporary writings about the Corder case can be found in Louis James's useful collection *Print and the People 1819–1851*, London, 1976.

frantic novels, sickly and stupid German Tragedies, and deluges of idle and extravagant stories in verse.'[1] The patronage and promotion of working-class poets who were familiar with the works of Shakespeare and Milton was seen by many people as providing a way of stopping a flood of popular literature from reducing everyone, and everything, to the mainstream.

William Hone was a writer and publisher who inherited his readers from both Paine and the Catnach Press. His report on the trial and execution of Eliza Fenning belonged to the popular traditions of criminal confessions and gallows narratives. Fenning was a domestic servant who was publicly hanged in 1815 for allegedly trying to poison her master and his family. The case attracted wide publicity not just because of the incredibly flimsy and circumstantial nature of the evidence, but also because it dramatized tensions between 'upstairs' and 'downstairs'. The subscribers to volumes of working-class poetry were able to subscribe to the view that domestic servants spent their leisure time reading the works of Shakespeare and Milton. The Fenning case challenged such comforting images by suggesting the possibility that servants devoted their time and energy to plotting violent acts of revenge. Hone and other writers suggested that Fenning was the innocent victim of 'upstairs' anxieties about an unknowable 'downstairs' world. A number of the pamphlets on the case, for instance the anonymous *Affecting Case of Eliza Fenning Who Suffered the Sentence of the Law July 26, 1815* (1815), reprinted the letters that Fenning wrote both to newspapers and to her family protesting her innocence. She is therefore given some opportunity to tell her own story.

Hone's literary career provides a sharp contrast to the activities of many working-class writers. Although he was the son of a clerk and therefore probably not working-class by origin, he became a prominent figure in the political and literary underground culture of London. He was a member of the London Corresponding Society in the 1790s, and eventually established a precarious business as a bookseller and publisher. The ending of the Napoleonic wars in 1815 allowed radical writings, no longer so easily labelled as unpatriotic, to become more visible. Cobbett brought out a cheap version of the *Political Register*, known as 'twopenny trash', which achieved a weekly circulation of over forty thousand copies. Hone's *Reformists' Register* was one of a number of publications which articulated radical demands. Like some of Byron's satires, it took particular

1 All quotations from *The Oxford Authors: William Wordsworth*, p 599.

pleasure in baiting Southey by drawing attention to his changeable political allegiances. Hone was put on trial in 1817 by a Government which was determined to assert its authority over the political and literary activities that were taking place beyond the pale, and therefore beyond its knowledge.

9

## TRIAL AND ERROR

Hone was tried at the Guildhall on 18 December 1817 for publishing a version of John Wilkes's *Catechism*, which was held to be both blasphemous and libellous. Despite being acquitted, he found himself in court again the following day to defend the publication of *The Political Litany*. He was found innocent once more and yet was still forced to return to defend publication of *The Sinecurists' Creed*. He was acquitted again, so the Government's attempt to humiliate him and his readership resulted in its own humiliation.

The three consecutive trials followed a broadly similar pattern. Hone's younger brother staggered into the courtroom with a pile of books, prints and newspapers. Hone and his supporters succeeded in altering the appearance of the courtroom: '. . . the table within the bar has not the usual covering of crimson bags, but ever and anon a shabby boy arrives with an armful of books of all ages and sizes, and the whole table is strewed with dusty and tattered volumes that the ushers are quite sure have no law within their mouldy covers.'[1] The jury was sworn in, and then the Attorney-General proceeded to outline the case against Hone. This involved the Clerk of the Court in reading out the offending parodies, which caused laughter in the packed public galleries. Such carnivalesque reception was intensified by the fact that the Clerk probably delivered them in an official manner, despite having to do all the voices. These are performance details that need to be added to William Tegg's edition of *The Three Trials of William Hone . . .* (1876):

1 Charles Knight's comment, quoted in F. W. Hackwood, *William Hone: His Life and Times* (1912), New York, 1970, p 147. Chapter 5 of Olivia Smith, *The Politics of Language 1791–1819*, Oxford, 1984, offers a perceptive account of Hone's career as well as detailed commentary on the trials. E. P. Thompson, *The Making of the English Working Class*, Harmondsworth, 1968, provides some of the essential background on the postwar radical movement. Iain McCalman, *Radical Underworld: Prophets, Revolutionaries and Pornographers in London, 1795–1840*, Cambridge, 1988, gives an interesting account of the mentality of Hone's world. Part Two of *Pastoral and Politics* also deals with aspects of the radical underworld.

The alleged libel was then put in by the ATTORNEY-GENERAL, and read by the Clerk of the Court . . .

From an unnational debt; from unmerited pensions and sinecure places; from an extravagant civil list; and utter starvation,
   *Good Prince, deliver us.*

(p 78)

The stage was now set for Hone's defence. The length of his speeches ranged from six hours at the first trial to eight hours at the third one. He was primarily concerned to show that the parodies belonged to a tradition of writing which had previously not been prosecuted. He disregarded warnings about the inadmissibility of his evidence, and selected passages from the 'tattered volumes' in front of him to read out to the court. Sir Thomas Bertram in Chapter 20 of Jane Austen's *Mansfield Park* (1814) burns the unbound copies of *Lovers' Vows*: it can be assumed that the state of Hone's books gave similar offence to those who believed in the necessity of all forms of binding. Hone also displayed caricatures which had not been prosecuted. His examination of defence witnesses was brief and essentially tokenistic. The jurymen were then invited to bring in verdicts of guilty, but they, much to the jubilation of the crowds both inside and outside the courtroom, took a leaf from Hone's book and refused to take the legal advice that they were offered.

John Keats commented on the significance of Hone's victories in a letter to his brothers dated 22 December 1817: 'Hone the publisher's trial, you must find very amusing; and as Englishmen very encouraging – his *Not Guilty* is a thing, which not to have been, would have dulled still more Liberty's Emblazoning . . .'[1] The second trial in particular illustrates the connection that Keats suggests between laughter and liberty. Hone's prosecutors tried to prevent laughter in court from subverting the dignity of the proceedings. The Sheriff was forced, at one point, to warn that 'The first man I see laugh . . . shall be brought up' (p 90). The Attorney-General claimed at the start of the trial that the 'indecent conduct' of the spectators threatened to destroy 'the social bonds of society' (p 75).

Given the Establishment's fear of laughter, it is hardly surprising that working–class poets were seldom encouraged to experiment with comic idioms. One of the reasons for the popularity of Paine's *Rights of Man* was that it encouraged readers to laugh at the 'farce of

1 Maurice Buxton Fonman, ed., *The Letters of John Keats*, London, 1960, p 70. I am grateful to David Pirie for suggesting the importance of this letter.

monarchy and aristocracy' (ii. 161). Both Byron and Shelley used parody and mockery to deflate their enemies. Shelley's 'Peter Bell the Third' laughs at Wordsworth's solemnity:

> Peter was dull – he was at first
>   Dull – oh, so dull – so very dull!
> Whether he talked, wrote, or rehearsed –
> Still with this dulness was he cursed –
>   Dull – beyond all conception – dull.
>
> No one could read his books – no mortal,
>   But a few natural friends, would hear him;
> The parson came not near his portal;
> His state was like that of the immortal
>   Described by Swift – no man could bear him.[1]

Shelley mimics both the content and cadences of Wordsworth's poetry. Austen's critique of patriarchy is often set within a comic framework. She offers at least two accounts of Sir Thomas Bertram's return to Mansfield Park during the period of the rehearsals. The first, or official, script sympathizes with his bewilderment and his attempts to restore a sense of social binding. The second, or subversive, script casts him as a figure of fun in a brilliantly written and plotted domestic farce.

The second trial provides another example of anxieties about the reading habits of servants. The Attorney-General appealed directly to the paternal responsibilities of the members of the jury:

If there be any among you, which is doubtless the case, who is the father of children, and the master of a household, I will ask him, if he would suffer that publication to be perused by his servants, who are not so well educated as himself? Or if he would suffer his children for one moment to read it?

(p 75)

It was their duty to maintain surveillance over the servants' quarters and the nursery, both in their own houses and in their political house. Hone's later use of nursery rhymes to convey his political messages, for instance in the highly popular *The Political House that Jack Built* (1819), subverts this view.[2]

---

1 'Peter Bell the Third', in *Shelley: Poetical Works*, ed. Thomas Hutchinson, London, 1970, ll 703–12.
2 For modern reprints of some of Hone's political pamphlets, see Edgell Rickword, ed., *Radical Squibs and Loyal Ripostes: Satirical Pamphlets of the Regency Period*, Bath, 1971.

The Attorney-General went on to draw even sharper distinctions between educated and uneducated readers:

There may be many writings which sensible men may read in their closets; some of them may be highly improper for general circulation, although some may be properly open to a free discussion: but the subject of the present question is not to be looked at in this point of view, for the mode of publication plainly shows what the real object is, and fully proves that it was intended that it should find its way among the ignorant and uninformed, where it was calculated to have a gross effect.

(pp 75–6)

Hone's specific response to this charge was that the readership for the *Political Litany* was not confined to any one class. More generally, he responded to the charge by turning the Attorney-General's categories upside down. He proved that he had a better knowledge of polite culture than the closeted reader and yet established these credentials as part of his defence of the culture of the people.

Working-class writers were actively encouraged to produce reverential imitations of acceptable cultural models. Hone's imitations contained more parodic distance. His imitations of legal modes of address, for instance, always contained elements of irreverent mockery. He held up a newspaper during the second trial and claimed that, despite the verdict in his favour the day before, he was still being represented as a guilty man. The judge, Lord Ellenborough, who believed that newspapers were 'trash' (p 99), intervened to try to get Hone to stick to the legal point. Ellenborough's interventions may be compared to the ways in which the editors of working-class poetry and conversion narratives attempted to mediate and control voices:

*Lord Ellenborough*: Really, you are getting so far out of the case: what have I to do with the libels published against you? We are not trying that newspaper.
*Mr Hone*: I hope, and firmly believe, that I have an impartial jury, who will be unprejudiced by every thing they may have heard or seen in or out of court.
*Lord Ellenborough*: Why, nobody can have read that newspaper you speak of; what have I or the jury to do with –
*Mr Hone*: My lord! My Lord! it is I who am upon my trial, not your lordship. I have to defend myself, not your lordship.

Long-continued acclamations here interrupted the proceedings of the court.

(p 98)

Hone's imitation of quick-witted legal wordplay casts Ellenborough as a Dogberry-like figure who mistakenly believes that he is the person on trial. Such a carnivalesque reversal of roles creates laughter in the courtroom.

The second trial was carnivalesque in a general sense because it provided the audience with opportunities to convert a seemingly solemn occasion into a festive one. It was carnivalesque in a more specific sense because it involved a confrontation between the grotesque body and the classical body.[1] Hone's threadbare appearance was in marked contrast to the splendour of his prosecutors. His discourse was also grotesque because it resisted any attempts to seal it off or enclose it. His table was not covered with neatly arranged 'crimson bags' but littered with 'tattered volumes', which threatened to spill over into other areas of the courtroom. Similarly, his speeches refused to conform to classical notions of legal rhetoric. Despite frequent warnings that he was 'getting so far out of the case', his sprawling speeches continued to transgress the boundaries, or discriminations, which the prosecution tried to establish. Ellenborough thought that newspapers were 'trash' and that Hone made a 'hash' (p 100) of his speeches by trying to talk about them. The advice was ignored. Ellenborough was also powerless to stop pluralistic laughter ringing around, or engulfing, the court. The prosecution's plea that the individual reader, isolated in his closet, ought to be treated differently from readers who existed beyond the pale of polite culture was thrown out of court.

Hone's trials dramatized the conflict over reading relationships which was such an important feature of this period. The prosecution constructed the preferred reader as the head of a household who retires to the privacy of his closet to read in silence. He is located within the privileged private space of this room of his own, and yet this is also an equally privileged public space as it is one of the observation posts from which surveillance can be maintained. This reader is given the power to control the reading habits of children, servants and, it should be added, wives. Such a definition of household politics also functions, as Wollstonecraft and Hone himself demonstrated, as a model for national politics. The preferred reader indulges in a secretive activity, which hints at the dangerous, perhaps

1 My reading of Hone's trials has been influenced both by Mikhail Bakhtin, *Rabelais and His World*, Cambridge, Mass., 1968, and by Peter Stallybrass and Allon White's commentary on Bakhtin in *The Politics and Poetics of Transgression*, London, 1986. I am, at a more general level, very grateful to David Pirie for being such an attentive editor. I am also deeply indebted to Raymond Williams, who helped me to appreciate the importance of working-class writings.

even criminal, pleasures to be derived from it. This in turn helps to explain why it was regarded as essential to police the pleasures of those who were deemed to lack powers of discrimination.

Hone's campaign against a political franchise based on the privileges of the householder was closely related to his campaign to enfranchise those who occupied the position of poor relations within the reading public. The readers of his cheaply produced publications packed not just the courtroom itself, but also the streets around the Guildhall. They quite literally laughed the charges against Hone out of court. The formation of a noisy, partisan, festive community around a set of written texts provided a marked contrast to the notion of the reader as an isolated and yet powerful individual.

This essay has tried to stretch the kind of binding that seals off Romantic writings from available contexts. It has, to borrow another image from Hone's trial, untidied a table with its neatly arranged texts by scattering some 'tattered volumes' over it. These marginalized volumes are central to an understanding of the cultural mentality of the period. The construction of the marginal writer is inextricably linked to versions of the central, or major, author. The construction of marginal readers is also a way of defining the discriminating reader.

# LORD BYRON

## Malcolm Kelsall

Napoleon's army crossed the Belgian frontier on 15 June 1815. So rapid was the advance that the French alarmed even themselves. Marshal Ney withdrew from Quatre Bras unaware that only 4,000 raw infantry lay between him and Brussels. Wellington hesitated, uncertain where the main thrust might fall. He had not expected decisive events before July. Meantime the Duchess of Richmond went ahead with a grand Society ball. At supper with the Duchess, Wellington was handed a message. The Prussians had been repulsed from Fleurus near Charleroi. The battle now called Waterloo had begun.

> There was a sound of revelry by night,
> And Belgium's capital had gathered then
> Her Beauty and her Chivalry, and bright
> The lamps shone o'er fair women and brave men;
> A thousand hearts beat happily; and when
> Music arose with its voluptuous swell,
> Soft eyes look'd love to eyes which spake again,
> And all went merry as a marriage-bell;
> But hush! hark! a deep sound strikes like a rising knell!
>
> Did ye not hear it? – No; 'twas but the wind,
> Or the car rattling o'er the stony street;
> On with the dance! let joy be unconfined;
> No sleep till morn, when Youth and Pleasure meet
> To chase the glowing Hours with flying feet –
> But, hark! – that heavy sound breaks in once more,
> As if the clouds its echo would repeat;
> And nearer, clearer, deadlier than before!
> Arm! Arm! and out – it is – the cannon's opening roar!
>
> (*Childe Harold's Pilgrimage*, III. xxi–xxii)

There was a time when British schoolchildren might make an early acquaintance with poetry by learning this passage by heart. Waterloo was a famous victory, and Byron's lines could nurture patriotism. The verse is easy and obvious, clearly rhymed and rhythmic, without that obscurity of thought and diction which makes the national poet, Shakespeare, difficult of access, and without the impediments of learned allusion which choke the story of *Paradise Lost*. By memorizing such verses boys might become 'brave men' and girls grow into types of 'fair women' who support and inspire chivalry and the imperial *pax Britannica*.

Another passage by Byron on the same battle was less well known. In *The Vision of Judgment* he writes of the Recording Angel in heaven whose work has grown so great in time of war that 'Six angels and twelve saints were named his clerks':

> This was a handsome board – at least for heaven;
>     And yet they had even then enough to do,
> So many conquerors' cars were daily driven,
>     So many kingdoms fitted up anew;
> Each day too slew its thousands six or seven,
>     Till at the crowning carnage, Waterloo,
> They threw their pens down in divine disgust –
> The page was so besmear'd with blood and dust.
>
> This by the way; 'tis not mine to record
>     What angels shrink from: even the very devil
> On this occasion his own work abhorr'd,
>     So surfeited with the infernal revel;
> Though he himself had sharpen'd every sword,
>     It almost quench'd his innate thirst of evil.
> (Here Satan's sole good work deserves insertion –
> 'Tis, that he has both generals in reversion.)

(v–vi)

Like the verse of *Childe Harold* this too is simple – indeed the language is ostensibly less 'poetical', closer to 'the real language of men' (to adapt Wordsworth's phrase). The narration flows swiftly in *ottava rima*, speeded by the omission of the long, concluding alexandrine of the Spenserian stanza of *Childe Harold*. The tone is now sardonic, satirical. Waterloo is presented in a burlesque manner, but there is a serious undertow to the comic presentation. The carnage of battle provokes disgust in heaven, and, even in hell, abhorrence.

Only six years separate the publication of *Childe Harold*, III (1816) and *The Vision of Judgment* (1822). Byron's change of style is fundamental, and critical histories of the poet have repeatedly emphasized it: first, a 'Romantic' poet of tragic sensibility, then, as his 'hot youth' yielded to maturity, there emerges a neoclassical satirist whose cultural roots reach back through Pope to Horace and Juvenal. Byron himself drew attention to the distinction:

> As boy, I thought myself a clever fellow,
>     And wish'd that others held the same opinion;
> They took it up when my days grew more mellow,
>     And other minds acknowledged my dominion:
> Now my sere fancy 'falls into the yellow
>     Leaf,' and Imagination droops her pinion,
> And the sad truth which hovers o'er my desk
> Turns what was once romantic to burlesque.
>
> And if I laugh at any mortal thing,
>     'Tis that I may not weep; and if I weep,
> 'Tis that our nature cannot always bring
>     Itself to apathy . . .
>
> (Don Juan, IV. iii–iv)

The poet's distinction between 'romantic' and 'burlesque' has led modern academic commentary to emphasize these elements as a 'paradox' in Byron's writing, to concentrate on those contradictory elements which are 'ironic', and to discover a rapidly changing series of dramatic masks (personae) utilized by the poet on an existential and stylistic pilgrimage of self-discovery and development. Change is complex, and complexity is in vogue in the 'intertextuality' of critical and literary discourse.

Self-evidently, the two passages on Waterloo adopt very different perspectives on the battle, and, isolated from any kind of context, the most obvious thing about them is their disjunction of tone. One is emotionally excited by the spectacle of war, the other sardonically condemns. They are in 'paradoxical' relation, and appear to take 'contradictory' attitudes. But, on the other hand, it is equally obvious that poetry on Waterloo is not a form of 'discourse' operating in a vacuum. Both passages are reactions to history, and are themselves seeking to make history by shaping attitudes to a major event (perhaps *the* major event) in contemporary Europe. The verse in both cases is akin to oratory – 'a man speaking to men' (and the masculine viewpoint is emphatic). The simple, energized directness of the utterance aims to shape opinion in the public domain. The metaphysical wit appropriate (for instance) to a lyric by Donne, or the gnomic, visionary symbolism of a Blake song, would be indecorous here.

It is appropriate to ask, therefore, in what way this writing enters the world of affairs. What does even the very act of publication (becoming public) tell the reader about the nature of Byron's poetry? In what historical facts are the disjunctions of style grounded? Compare, thus, Byron's verse in *Childe Harold* with Donne's or Blake's intrusion upon the reader – Donne's verses inscribed in a thin ink on sheets of paper circulated among a coterie of wits, Blake's individually coloured engravings hovering between the public and private world in a few copies. But the publication of the third canto of *Childe Harold* is, like Waterloo itself, a major occurrence. Byron was regarded by many as the major English poet of the age, famous (by 1816, infamous) for liberal views, and, as a member of the British House of Lords, the familiar acquaintance of the leaders of the state. His publisher, John Murray, offered one of the most respectable imprints in Regency London (and the 'Mac' before 'Murray' had been dropped by his father lest it offend polite society!). The poem would be expected to sell tens of thousands. It was handsomely printed with generous margins on fine paper. For the libraries of the gentry there would be eventually the sweet savour and soft touch of leather bindings, the rich glow of marbled end-papers. *Exegi monumentum aere perennius* – a book is a monument more lasting than bronze.

The text is targeted, therefore, at an expected (and substantial) audience. The phrase 'a man speaking to men' may be refined. The poet is *Lord* Byron, and, thus, 'an aristocrat speaking', and not only to 'men' but 'women' also. Part of the enormous success of Byron's verse from the beginning depended on his stirring the emotions of his female readership – he had been the darling of Lady Oxford's circle in 1812 – and it is appropriate that the entrée to the battle is by way of the Duchess of Richmond's ball. Those in the know in high society would appreciate the concealed allusion in the phrase 'all went merry as a marriage-bell': the Prince of Orange was soon to become engaged to the Tsar's sister, Anna Pavlovna.

Compare the way *The Vision of Judgment* enters history. Byron has broken with the respectable Murray. His publisher is now the radical John Hunt (a man frequently prosecuted by the authorities). Working at Byron's elbow is John's brother Leigh, notorious for his virulent attacks on the Prince Regent and his hostility to Lord Castlereagh, the foreign secretary. In the same circle of writers are Shelley and Hazlitt, both of radical sympathies. Together they launch a part political, part literary journal entitled *The Liberal*. It ran for only four unsuccessful issues. In the first number, among translations of Goethe and Ariosto, a description of Pisa, epigrams against Lord Castlereagh, appeared *The Vision* – without Byron's name attached ('by Quevedo Redivivus'). John Hunt, the publisher, was successfully prosecuted for seditious libel. Byron remained out of the way in Italy. It is a very different basis from which to address the public than a big launch into high society from John Murray's. There is a loss of centrality, an exclusion from those centres of power and influence to which (as Burke wrote) an aristocrat was connected by lineage, marriage and friendship.

The change of style, tone, attitude between *Childe Harold* and *The Vision* thus has a context. Although the change is not merely the product of that context, none the less the more demotic voice in the later poem is related to its publication by a radical, and the lines are targeted at a potentially different audience than the Duchess of Richmond's class. To whom exactly Byron is speaking is problematical. It does not appear to be the woman reader – who had been in some measure alienated already by the ridicule of sentiment, sensibility and feminist attitudes in *Don Juan* (1818–); of this, more later. The centring of the consciousness of the poem in the Cabinet office in heaven (which is dominated by members of the so-called 'Tory' party) seems also to remove the poem from proletarian interests. Both sides at the battle of Waterloo are attacked, for Satan has the two generals 'in reversion': the Tory champion, the Duke of Wellington, and 'the child and champion of Jacobinism', Napoleon Bonaparte. The passage, noticeably, offers no positive alternative to the targets burlesqued. Exclusion from power may produce in an outsider a pathology of nihilistic opposition. In what way has Lord Byron, the darling of Lady Oxford's circle in 1812, become a sniper on his own class in fly-by-night journals from Italy in 1822?

The watershed had been 1816. On 25 April he left England for the Continent, never to return. Simple, biographical reasons are debts, sexual scandal and a disastrous marriage. The topic has been written to death. But the way he presented the act was grand and theatrical. He paraded in his verse (in *Childe Harold*) 'the pageant of his bleeding heart' (Arnold's phrase), and he was driven down to the Channel in a replica of Napoleon's travelling-coach. The flight from his duns and sexual scandal was turned, therefore, into a great gesture of opposition and defiance. His 'exile' from England is likened to that of the fallen idol of liberal Europe, now solitary upon St Helena, and his tragic portrayal of Waterloo in *Childe Harold* laments the fall of the emperor more than the triumph of the British. The governmental journals hounded him on his way with the usual charges: unsound moral and political principles ('Jacobinism' sexual and political) produced such disastrous consequences (understand, *sotto voce*, incest and homosexuality, to which modern commentators have added pederasty and even vampirism!). The poet preferred, however, to make the argument revolve upon the central historical event of the time. What was the significance of the eclipse of the child and champion of Jacobinism at the battle of Waterloo? Byron had made his life part of that history through his choice of symbolism.

That historical experience is fundamentally different from Romantics of Wordsworth's generation. Byron was one year old when the Bastille fell (1789). He never knew the frenzy of idealistic excitement the events of the nineties inspired, when human nature seemed made anew – 'Bliss was it in that dawn to be alive'. The great phenomenon of his youth and early manhood was Napoleon. There were not a few who admired the exploits of the First Consul, his defeat of the despotic monarchies of Europe, the establishment in the wake of French arms of new, liberal, constitutional governments in the liberated nations of Europe. Then came disenchantment. The First Consul became Emperor; the new order in Europe revealed itself as yet another dynastic empire; the needs of the French war machine provoked against the Emperor the very liberal forces he had once set free. Finally, the 'crowning carnage', Waterloo. Byron satirized in that phrase the monarchies (whose crowns were restored by the defeat of Napoleon) and Tory Wordsworth also, who had celebrated God's providence in the battle: 'Yea, Carnage is Thy daughter' (*Ode 1815*). Yet the tragedy is that, had the battle gone the other way, the phrase 'crowning carnage' would still have been appropriate, for Napoleon was no better now. 'I want a hero . . .' wrote Byron as the first words of his mock epic of the times, *Don Juan*. Napoleon, 'the Anakim of Anarchy', had become a lost leader.

If there was a time in Byron's life equivalent to Wordsworth's 'dawn' when 'to be young was very heaven', it had been in the year 1812 when he 'awoke and found himself famous'. The young (and irresistibly handsome) Lord Byron had returned from his Grand Tour of Europe (displaced by the war from the usual route across France to Italy, in his instance to the southern and eastern Mediterranean). Those exotic travels were recounted in the poetical journal of the first two cantos of *Childe Harold* (1812) – a sensational success – and were to underlie the exotic stories of a long series of verse romances beginning with *The Bride of Abydos* (1813) and *The Giaour* (1813), and continuing with *The Corsair* (1814) and *Lara* (1814). Young ladies of sensibility identified Byron with the heroes of his own verses, a fantasy he was not disinclined to encourage. On a more serious level, as a member of the House of Lords he linked his fortunes with those of the Whig party, at that time in opposition, but in excited daily expectation of being called to office by the Prince Regent (in vain). Byron spoke with passionate concern on the Luddite disturbances, manifesting at once those 'radical' sympathies which were soon to alienate his own class; but his castigation of 'Tory' oppression was not matched by any practical initiative to solve an intractable problem. He spoke too on Catholic emancipation and parliamentary reform, both classic Whig issues, but again without practical effect. Meantime the Prince Regent rejected his 'former friends', preferring the stability of a conservative administration to the insecurity of the Whig/Radical opposition, and Byron's party chiefs rapped the young man over the knuckles as a verbal hothead.

These are trivial events compared with what was unfolding in a world at war in 1812 (the year of the French retreat from Moscow), but it is the period of which Byron wrote in *Don Juan* when 'ambition was my idol', and that personal idol was 'broken' just as much as the 'pagod' Napoleon Bonaparte (whose initials, N. B., Byron eventually adopted as his own: Noel Byron). There are repeated attempts by Byron throughout his life to play the role of a man of action: in the English parliament of 1812, later as a conspirator with the nationalist secret society, the *Carbonari*, in Italy (1820–21), finally as a Philhellene and liberator of Greece. Every attempt ended in failure, even the famous adventure in Greece: Byron died of fever at Missolonghi (April 1824) before he could effect anything.

It is this period which was called 'an age of despair' by Shelley in the preface to *The Revolt of Islam*. The time extends from the catastrophe of Napoleon's Russian campaign to the death of the reactionary foreign minister Castlereagh (1822). At home it is the apogee of a repressive administration determined that the objectives of European war against 'Jacobinism' must take priority over reform. It seemed as if revolution were imminent. The Luddite riots and the seemingly military preparations of the populace before Peterloo are symptomatic of the pressures arising from beneath, which were to be contained by the suspension of Habeas Corpus (when necessary), the Six Acts, the systematic imprisonment of opposition journalists, who included Byron's friends Sir Francis Burdett and John Cam Hobhouse. Abroad, the 'legitimate' monarchies of Europe were restored, and nationalist and liberal movements repressed in Italy, Portugal and Spain.

Shelley wrote of these events that they produced an excess of morbidity in liberal minds, a pessimism which he sought to counter in his own verse: 'O Wind! if Winter comes can Spring be far behind?' 'Error' is of a 'transient nature' in the world, he claimed, and progressive Truth is like a force of Nature itself. The Truth will make men free. Hence the high destiny of poetry. He thought of Byron, and in 'Julian and Maddalo' Shelley's optimism is placed in debate against the bleak existential despair of Count Maddalo – a Byronic *alter ego*. The darkness of this aspect of Byronism is striking, emphatic, reiterated: in *Childe Harold*, III and IV (1816, 1818), in the metaphysical nihilism of *Manfred* (1817) and *Cain* (1821), in poems on political imprisonment – *The Prisoner of Chillon* (1816), *The Lament of Tasso* (1817) – and even in the nihilism of the comic 'Augustan' satirist's burlesques during the final years.

For many in the nineteenth century the essential voice of Byronism was found in passages of despair such as this:

> We wither from our youth, we gasp away –
> Sick – sick; unfound the boon, unslaked the thirst,
> Though to the last, in verge of our decay,
> Some phantom lures, such as we sought at first –
> But all too late, – so are we doubly curst.
> Love, fame, ambition, avarice – 'tis the same,
> Each idle – and all ill – and none the worst –
> For all are meteors with a different name,
> And Death the sable smoke where vanishes the flame.
>
> (*Childe Harold*, IV. cxxiv)

Although it would be reductive to claim of such lines that they are merely the reflection of Byron's personal history in the aftermath of events from 1812 to 1816, yet they fuel their despondency from experience of the times. Those words, 'Love, fame, ambition, avarice', are clearly directed at experiential matters of the poet's own frustrated career, and were taken as such by contemporary readers. Many identified the persona, Childe Harold, with the poet, and the technique of the narrative is to interweave matters of domestic biography with the great events of European history which fuel the poet's speculations as he voyages from the battlefield of Waterloo to Italy. There too hopes for freedom have (yet again) been extinguished by the return of a new barbarity to Europe: 'Some phantom lures, such as we sought at first –/But all too late . . .'

This despair is matched, however, by outbursts of faith and hope in the power of the human mind to resist evil as strong as anything offered by Shelley to combat the excess of morbidity in the age (witness the end of his *Prometheus Unbound*). A 'paradox' of By-

ronism is that the reiterated passages of surrender or alienation –
'Our life is a false nature: 'tis not in/The harmony of things' (*Childe
Harold*, IV. cxxvi) – are counterbalanced again and again by outbursts
of this kind:

> Yet, Freedom! yet thy banner, torn, but flying,
> Streams like the thunder-storm *against* the wind;
> Thy trumpet voice, though broken now and dying,
> The loudest still the tempest leaves behind;
> Thy tree hath lost its blossoms, and the rind,
> Chopp'd by the axe, looks rough and little worth,
> But the sap lasts, – and still the seed we find
> Sown deep, even in the bosom of the North;
> So shall a better spring less bitter fruit bring forth.
>
> (*Childe Harold*, IV. xcviii)

Clearly the general principle – 'Freedom' – has its specific context
here in the position of the poet in Europe in 1818. His is a passionate
commitment to the cause of liberalism in the face of the overwhelming success of the forces of reaction at the Congress of Vienna. That
'tree' which has lost its blossoms is, in one manifestation, the
Liberty Tree of the revolutionaries of 1790, and the verses have clear
analogies both to Shelley's, 'O Wind! if Winter comes can Spring be
far behind?' and to that famous, and moving, passage at the end of
Paine's *Rights of Man* in which he too likens the advance of
freedom to the first buds breaking in the earliest months of the year.
Those who, like Byron, had been aghast at the violence of the
French Revolution would note also the ominous quality of 'thunder-
storm'. The destructive cost of Freedom's battles had been immense,
and yet, yet, a better spring *must* come.

Like the disjunctive passages on Waterloo, these two latter examples, one of existential despair, the other of commitment to
Freedom, appear contradictory. The contradiction here is not manifest in style – they occur closely together in the same canto of the
same poem – but in attitude. An extraordinary morbidity in the one
(which recalls that Hamlet is a major archetypal figure for Romanticism) is contradicted by the compulsive potential energy of the
other. This is typically Byronic. Compare the sonnet usually printed
before *The Prisoner of Chillon* – 'Eternal Spirit of the chainless
Mind!/Brightest in dungeons, Liberty! thou art ...' – with the
ending of the narrative of imprisonment which follows, in which
the protagonist becomes obsessed with the imaginative creations of
the shackled mind, and when freed (through no energies of his own) is
alienated from the light. He regains his freedom with a sigh.

A common path for some modern critics has been to seek eventually to iron out these major contradictions within the poet by positing a spiritual and stylistic development – often in terms of different voices of progressive personae – and usually with its terminus in *Don Juan*, declared the poet's masterwork. The poet, despite his claim that he has declined 'into the sere and yellow leaf' (like the nihilistic king-killer Macbeth), has really matured, and his enhanced skill with language in the endlessly fascinating chatter of *Don Juan* is the stylistic correlative of the tolerant and assured morality of well-balanced middle age. It would be typical of this line of approach to compare the famous passage on vain ambition at the end of *Don Juan*, I (ccxvii *et seq.*) with the despair of *Childe Harold* and note that the poet, in middle age, now turns things into a joke. One has to get on living. So *carpe diem* – enjoy each day as it comes.

How true is this interpretation? If one turns again to that passage in *Don Juan* (IV. iii–iv) in which Byron describes the 'Childe' and the 'Don' (the child is father of the man), that relationship is described by the poet as relativistic rather than linear and progressive. Romance and burlesque, his two styles, weeping and laughing, his two philosophies, are inseparable functions. Rather than the process of life being developmental, it is one of decline (the termination of which is death). Early Imagination is preferred to Macbeth's sere Fancy, and the relation of both to 'sad truth' is problematical. Things are presented as existing only in terms of their relationships:

> And if I laugh at any mortal thing,
>     'Tis that I may not weep; and if I weep,
> 'Tis that our nature cannot always bring
>     Itself to apathy . . .
>
> (*Don Juan*, IV. iv)

Democritus (the laughing philosopher) and Heraclitus (who wept) are the comic and tragic masks of the dialectical drama of life.

Although one cannot explain that dialectical presentation merely by contextualizing it historically, none the less that conflict between opposing forces is the poetic equivalent both to Byron's own position as man of action without the chance of action, spokesman on the history of the times without an audience of his own kind – and also part of the whole 'contradiction' of the Romantic era: of the Revolution that devoured its children, of the child and champion of Jacobinism who became an emperor, of the battle to liberate Europe which brought back the *ancien régime*. Every action produces an equivalent reaction. One causes the other, nor can they be conceived except in relation. One despairs, and yet hopes; the melancholy cycle of things calls forth a tragic style; that tragedy is ridiculous and provokes laughter. One laughs even *because* things are so bad. In the 'comic masterpiece' *Don Juan* the battle of Ismail is the archetypal equivalent of Waterloo, and the two voices and styles come together typically thus:

> If here and there some transient trait of pity
>> Was shown, and some more noble heart broke through
> Its bloody bond, and saved perhaps some pretty
>> Child, or an aged, helpless man or two –
> What's this in one annihilated city,
>> Where thousand loves, and ties, and duties grew?
> Cockneys of London! Muscadins of Paris!
> Just ponder what a pious pastime war is:
>
> Think how the joys of reading a Gazette
>> Are purchased by all agonies and crimes:
> Or if these do not move you, don't forget
>> Such doom may be your own in after times.
> Meantime the taxes, Castlereagh, and debt,
>> Are hints as good as sermons, or as rhymes.
> Read your own hearts and Ireland's present story,
> Then feed her famine fat with Wellesley's glory.
>> (*Don Juan*, VIII. cxxiv–cxxv)

The 'voices' here are part sentimental, part satiric burlesque. The verse burns with *saeva indignatio*, and yet, at the end, there is a sense of despair. As the characters say in Paul Scott's *The Raj Quartet*, 'there is nothing we can do about it' – except, in Byron's case, express oneself in words, from exile, and by hole-in-the-corner publication.

The frustrations of the Byronic position ultimately become obsessive. Despite the superficial variety of style and mood, again and again the verse returns to a situation in which progress is blocked, or is to be achieved only at such cost that it is uncertain whether the price to be paid is worth the purchase. The motif is there from the beginning, even in the so-called 'romances' which, since McGann's edition, may be more profoundly seen as forms of displaced political and psychological allegory. Thus, the pirate chief of *The Corsair*, Conrad, has been driven into war against society by the tyranny of Turkish domination, and his resistance produces, as its correlative, personal and social criminality. The war between the two forces, tyrant and pirate, leads to no positive good, but all the sympathy of the poem is directed towards the Byronic hero – that gloomy yet sentimental figure of alienation derived originally from Milton's Satan:

> Yet was not Conrad thus by Nature sent
> To lead the guilty – guilt's worst instrument –
> His soul was changed, before his deeds had driven
> Him forth to war with man and forfeit heaven.

(I. 249–52)

The Sultan is murdered by a slave girl; the pirate band broken up in battle; the hero's faithful love (Medora) dies of grief, and Conrad disappears accompanied by the slave girl (Gulnare) only to re-emerge in *Lara* leading a proletarian rebellion against feudal tyranny. That fails, and he dies.

The pirate band of *The Corsair* is likened to a nest of scorpions, an image developed by Byron in *The Giaour* to express the essential guilt of his romantic heroes and their self-destructive quality:

> The Mind, that broods o'er guilty woes,
>    Is like the Scorpion girt by fire,
> In circle narrowing as it glows,
> The flames around their captive close,
> Till inly search'd by thousand throes,
>    And maddening in her ire,
> One sad and sole relief she knows,
> The sting she nourish'd for her foes,
> Whose venom never yet was vain,
> Gives but one pang, and cures all pain,
> And darts into her desperate brain . . .

(*The Giaour*, 422–32)

Again one may note the parallel with Paul Scott, for that image of the scorpion ringed with fire is dominant in the second volume of *The Raj Quartet*, and there too the relation between inner and outer, the psychological condition and the political, is an essential element in relating the individual to history. The blow that might be struck for Freedom is directed ultimately by the frenzied mind at itself, for that ring of fire, of hostile circumstance, about the imprisoned scorpion permits no escape: as Romantic Europe, so Imperial India.

The reiterated appearance of this kind of 'Byronic hero' is a leitmotif. In the romances it continues from the beginning through to *The Island* (1823), a poem about the failed mutiny on the *Bounty*. The figure is exploited as a form of *alter ego* in the poetical journal of travels *Childe Harold's Pilgrimage* (1812–18), as Byron reflects on the lessons of past and present history recalled by the landscape of

Europe, and is a basis for metaphysical questioning of the tyranny of the Christian religion in *Cain*. It is politicized in the tale of the guilty, failed revolutionary *Marino Faliero* (1821), and in *Don Juan* the pirate chief Lambro is another variant of the type. He is a Greek patriot who hates the Turks, but in despair at 'his country's wrongs' he has turned to prey on all mankind, and ends by destroying his daughter, the only being whom he loves. The pressures of psychological frustration and alienation teach the Hamlet-like hero of *Manfred*, facing the hell of his own imagination, that "'tis not so difficult to die'. What is difficult is to live in hope. The Romanticism of which Byron is a compelling voice is not, ultimately, about 'liberation'. The experience of the age had been the disappointment of the expectation that rebellion against 'tyranny' would produce freedom and happiness. On the contrary, it produced twenty-five years of 'carnage' and the restoration of the Bourbons. The problem was, after such experience, to find what basis for positive hope might there be. Romanticism is not a cant of instant liberation. It is an experience of learning about failure.

*The Vision of Judgment* (1821) may be used to illustrate the point more fully. Its historical subject is the reign of George III (1760–1820). It embraces, therefore, both the American and French Revolutions, and the fall of Napoleon. The particular occasion was the death of the king, and a panegyric upon him by the Tory Poet Laureate Robert Southey: *A Vision of Judgment*. In the Preface to his poem Southey attacked Byron and his circle as producing literature only fit for a brothel, and as constituting a Satanic school of poetry. It was the usual charge of sexual and political 'Jacobinism' and is not without foundation. The Byronic hero is undoubtedly derived from the Satanic hero of *Paradise Lost*. Byron's poem, therefore, has a clear and definite context, so much so that everything that happens in Byron is directly modelled on Southey. There is the same action and the same characters differently handled.

Ostensibly the poem is one of Byron's great defences of freedom, as the political character of the king is brought to trial at the gates of heaven:

> 'He ever warr'd with freedom and the free:
>    Nations as men, home subjects, foreign foes,
> So that they utter'd the word "Liberty!"
>    Found George the Third their first opponent . . .'
>
> (xlv)

Witness the New World and the Old, the oppressed Catholics in

Ireland, the imprisonment of Wilkes in the Tower for his freedom of speech. The invective against the king is matched by the debunking of Southey by ridicule. Here was a poet who had written in his hot youth a republican, regicide tragedy, *Wat Tyler*, now turned laureate of restored Bourbonism (and in abysmal 'spavined dactyls'). Neither heaven nor hell will listen to his twaddle, and he is ditched in the Lake District with that other renegade 'Wordswords'.

Such vigorous castigation of the Establishment made Byron a radical hero, but, in fact, the oratory produces no effect. George III is *not* convicted at his trial, and he enters heaven to join Louis XVI in praising God. The great attack on the king is spoken by an archetypal Byronic hero, but Satan is also the prince of *hell* who appears only at the rearward of the *angelic* band:

> But bringing up the rear of this bright host
>     A Spirit of a different aspect waved
> His wings, like thunder-clouds above some coast
>     Whose barren beach with frequent wrecks is paved;
> His brow was like the deep when tempest-tost;
>     Fierce and unfathomable thoughts engraved
> Eternal wrath on his immortal face,
> And *where* he gazed a gloom pervaded space.

(xxiv)

One may recall 'Yet, Freedom! yet thy banner . . . Streams like the thunder-storm . . .' The voice of opposition and rebellion is like that of a storm. Those 'frequent wrecks' may be easily allegorized in terms of the historical circumstances of the French Revolution, as might 'the deep when tempest-tost'. The outer disorder is matched by the inner psychological *angst* typical of the 'contradictory' voices of Byronism: 'Fierce and unfathomable thoughts engraved/Eternal wrath . . .' This is not Lucifer the light-bringer – enlightenment through revolution. He is the bringer of darkness: 'gloom pervaded space.' These are not mere literary tropes derived intertextually from *Paradise Lost*, nor is the *angst* that of the anxiety of literary influence. What Satan symbolically represents is the Romantic experience of history.

It is this figure who makes the great attack on George III, and one cannot separate the Satanic spokesman from what is spoken. Nor is that speech necessarily true, for it is made by the father of lies, and the invective is pitched 'over the top'. It is a point made by the archangel Michael, and the Minister of God is not ridiculed by Byron. On the contrary, substantial doubts about the integrity of

members of the court of inquiry gather round Satan's witnesses –
John Wilkes especially (libertine and exploitive manipulator of the
mob), and even the anonymous polemicist Junius. Michael asks
him:

> '. . .Thou wast
> Too bitter – is it not so? – in thy gloom
> Of passion?' 'Passion!' cried the phantom dim,
> 'I loved my country, and I hated him.
>
> 'What I have written, I have written: let
> The rest be on his head or mine!' So spoke
> Old 'Nominis Umbra'; and while speaking yet,
> Away he melted in celestial smoke.
>
> (lxxxiii–lxxxiv)

The last words spoken by 'the shade of a name' (the motto of
Junius's *Letters*) are those of Pontius Pilate about to crucify Christ.
They are appropriate words for hell, but call in question the status
of the champion of freedom. Moreover, he is stirred by personal
'hatred' and he vanishes, not into light, but combusts in the obscure
element of smoke.

The poem is structured, therefore, upon a dialectical tension in
which 'right' and 'wrong' are not absolutes, but contextualized by
circumstance and character. The major dialectic is that of the
constitution of eternity – the opposition between heaven and hell.
There is no concept in Byron of a 'marriage of heaven and hell' (as
in Blake). The forces of a Christian, reactionary heaven and a
libertine, libertarian, rebellious and destructive hell are in perpetual
antagonism. One may allegorize this locally as Tory against Whig,
supporters of the Bourbons against supporters of the French Revolution, but the poem places local history merely as an example of a
psychological and even a metaphysical eternity. Byron is both a
sceptic and believer in religion. The nature of things is founded on
dialectic, and without the dialectic (which implies no principle of
progress) there would be no things. If the poem carries a simple,
paraphrasable 'message', it is that perpetual antagonists might, at
least, respect the integrity of the other side. Byron describes the
meeting of Michael and Satan thus:

> He and the sombre, silent Spirit met –
> They knew each other both for good and ill;
> Such was their power, that neither could forget
> His former friend and future foe; but still
> There was a high, immortal, proud regret

> In either's eye, as if 'twere less their will
> Than destiny to make the eternal years
> Their date of war, and their 'Champ Clos' the spheres.
>
> (xxxii)

The struggle continues – and leads nowhere.

That too is the theme of the 'masterwork' *Don Juan*, but that poem changes so much in Byronism that it is both a summation and a new departure. One seismic shift is the virtual disappearance of the 'Byronic hero' as the symbolic protagonist. 'Donny Johnny', as the poet calls him, is, in a sense, a burlesque equivalent of the pilgrim figure of *Childe Harold*. His adventures take him on the Grand Tour of Europe, and on his travels he learns the different forms of government and the customs of many societies. He becomes cosmopolitan. But Johnny is neither a Satanic figure, nor even a Byronic *alter ego*, although the poet plays with the reader's expectation that he will be another chip off the old block. He is far closer to the protagonist of Scott's *Waverley* – a character to whom things happen in history, rather than a maker of things. He is caught up by events, and thus the theme is reinforced that 'there is nothing we can do about it'. The voice of protest rises still from time to time, but fragmented, on the periphery of the action, no longer located in a Corsair, a Doge of Venice (Marino Faliero) or Satan himself. It is the voice of the poet alone – a helpless, cynical, tolerant, middle-aged man on the sidelines.

The action of the poem is set in the 1780s and 1790s, at the advent of the French Revolution and the revolutionary wars. The poet's running commentary on Juan's adventures, however, is deliberately anachronistic, being set in the present, particularly with relation to his own years of fame in London, and his years of exile. He begins by locating himself in Spain, where Byron records that the soldiers of the defeated Bonapartists look out from their prison on the action. The signification of that is self-evident. This diachronic structure, therefore, allows Byron continually to compare then and now, and to show, pessimistically, how through a life of extraordinary (Satanic) upheaval all the changes have merely returned to the same point. The Bourbons were expelled, and the Bourbons are restored. 'Yet, Freedom! yet . . .' A lover of liberty may still express his detestation of Wellington's abandonment of the cause of liberty after Waterloo, Castlereagh's participation in the Congress System, the degeneracy of the Prince Regent. The nadir of the poem is reached at the battle of Ismail, the carnage of which parallels Waterloo. The battle stands as a type of all wars fought for dynastic ambition. Equally terrible, however, is the shipwreck canto (II), for the little society of men afloat on the ocean of eternity turns cannibal to survive, and (thus) dies. Only one man refuses to feed on his fellows, and lives. He is cast up on the shores of 'paradise' – an unspoilt island – but the man saved is Don Juan, who, like Satan, brings death with him to the Eve of the island (Haidée), and destroys this later Eden.

About the middle of the action Byron brings Don Juan to England. The clear intention is to contrast tyranny in Europe, which Juan has seen in Turkey and Russia, with the popular claim that Britain is the bastion of freedom. The climactic cantos of the poem (in its uncompleted form) locate Juan in high society, and especially at a political house party at Norman Abbey, a house whose 'Gothic' form is analogous to the Gothic constitution of 'Free Britons' – a commonplace analogy – and yet whose Norman name reminds one of the conquest of Britain by a military dictator. Thus one finds again a dialectical tension in Byron, for the owners of the house are both Norman conquerors and yet upholders of the 'free' constitution.

Had the poem been completed, the most probable plan left by Byron is that Juan (like himself) would have had to flee the country because of a sexual scandal – which is well in train when the poem breaks off. Juan was to leave England for France and join the 'liberated' French in the Revolution, his role that of Anarchasis Cloots, noted as 'the spokesman of the human race'. The real-life Anarchasis was guillotined by his own side during the Terror, and that was the end Byron planned for Juan. There would be no statue of stone to call him to account, expressive of the divine wrath of a Christian God. Instead the libertine apostle of liberty would find hell in the very freedom for which he had gone to fight.

This is to isolate only one major theme from a poem whose episodic narrative in desert island, harem, court and country house introduces continual variety, and where the digressive narrator (imitating Fielding, Swift and Sterne) will reflect as he goes on any subject that comes to mind: the passage of time and the troubles of indigestion, the philosophy of scepticism and the pleasures of sentiment. Like Cleopatra, *Don Juan* has infinite variety, although sometimes it rambles so much that it makes weary where most it satisfies.

To select any one passage, therefore, to illustrate a whole whose aim is variety is to risk contradicting a method founded on contradiction. None the less, the major thematic opposition of commitment and despair continually recurs, and, of necessity, one instance must represent multiplicity and multivalency. Since Britain is supposedly the home of Freedom, when Juan first lands (journeying from the court of the tyrant Catherine of Russia) he bursts out in a declamatory celebration of that Byronic cause. He is in a rhetorical flight of naïve idealism when he is interrupted by a 'Byronic hero' – a highwayman (a British 'Corsair'). Juan, who is a gentleman and hence armed, at once defends himself against this representative of 'the people's voice'. Faced with the choice of his 'money' or his 'life', he shoots the Byronic hero dead. So much for Anglo-Saxon liberty!

> 'And here,' [Juan] cried, 'is Freedom's chosen station;
>   Here peals the people's voice, nor can entomb it
> Racks, prisons, inquisitions; resurrection
> Awaits it, each new meeting or election.
>
> 'Here are chaste wives, pure lives; here people pay
>   But what they please; and if that things be dear
> 'Tis only that they love to throw away
>   Their cash, to show how much they have a-year.
> Here laws are all inviolate; none lay
>   Traps for the traveller; every highway's clear;
> Here' – he was interrupted by a knife,
> With – 'Damn your eyes! your money or your life!'
>
> (XI. ix–x)

In this passage the coupling of 'Freedom' with 'chaste wives' might well go unremarked, and, in isolation, it would seem inappropriate to emphasize the sexual implications, for the main thrust of the satire here is against Juan's naïve belief in British political cant. In the context of the poem as a whole, however, the sexual role of women, their liberty and libertinism, emerges as a major topic, one new in Byron's verse, and deeply disturbing in relation to Romantic representations of femininity. It is appropriate, therefore, that Juan's naïve oration raises the sexual issue, for cant about women, like political cant, is part of the discourse current in British society. The sexual politics of this poem invert notions of freedom by focusing upon the predatory and hypocritical women who seduce and use the helpless male libertine, Donny Johnny.

The socially approved stereotypes of the earlier poetry, now abandoned, were commonplace. Medora in *The Corsair*, for instance, is heroine as blancmange, a succulent dish tasted from time to time, then left pale, quivering and passive (before finally dissolving in death). Astarte, the unattainable beloved of *Manfred*, is the passive heroine idealized as the eternal feminine (*ewig weiblich*), part Venus figure, part Diana. She is dead, and appears in spirit form intoning the name of the hero. Such women are merely foils to the sentimentalized, criminal and dark Byronic protagonist who, in the imagination of Annabella Milbanke (Byron's wife), was to be tamed by the love of a chaste but sexually stimulated Christian bride. The continuation of the motif is obvious in the Brontës' creation of a Rochester and a Heathcliff.

It was in a brief comic fabliau, *Beppo* (1817), that Byron abruptly changed direction and tone by making the heroine the active 'liberated' figure who ends by running a husband and lover in tandem for her own profit and gratification. This was a direct affront to sentimental cant. It is equally an affront to contemporary feminism as represented, for example, by Mary Wollstonecraft. Her novel *The Wrongs of Woman* begins with the heroine imprisoned in a lunatic asylum by a tyrannical husband (and thus on the way to becoming the mad woman in the attic in *Jane Eyre*). As Catherine Morland (in *Northanger Abbey*) would appreciate, this is a just representation of the relation of Regency wives to their husbands in a patriarchal society — their essential virtue suppressed and their femininity displaced by the evil that men do. Suffering virtue is also sexy. Rape is a major subject of the eighteenth-century novel.

This stereotype of the oppressed woman in a patriarchal (thus tyrannical) society makes one crucial appearance in *Don Juan*, and the sexual politics of the role symbolically places the heroine in relation to the wider structures of political tyranny. In the desert island idyll the beautiful virgin Haidée is explicitly identified with Greece (an oppressed province of Turkey), and free love and the freedom of Greece are associated (in a manner reminiscent of Shelley's *The Revolt of Islam*). Thus Juan and Haidée in one another's arms are described as 'Half naked, loving, natural and Greek', and Byron's most famous lyric on freedom, 'The Isles of Greece', sung for them, begins with a celebration of female sexuality. Greece is the region where 'Burning Sappho loved and sung'. The lovers eventually are separated by the patriarchal figure of Lambro, who sells Juan into slavery, while Haidée dies of grief, pregnant with Juan's child.

Here, and here only, Byron seems to have wished to unite the sentimental heroine of his earlier romances with the oppressed figure essential to feminist polemic: 'Can Man be free if Woman be a slave?' (*Revolt of Islam*, II. xliii). As often occurs in Byron's late satiric verse, however, the poet is subversive of his own ideals even while (and because) most idealistic. For it is Haidée, not Juan, who is the seducer, and the island is ruled by her as a matriarch. The consequences are not paradisiacal. Lambro's patriarchy (his dowry for his daughter) is squandered in tipsy revelry. In a world at war, liaison with Juan, a penniless, naked adventurer, leaves the island unprotected and will prevent the necessary dynastic marriage which will secure family and folk. Even the 'Isles of Greece' lyric, when contextualized, emerges as the kind of sentimental ballad which appeals to Juan and Haidée in their cups and in bed, but neither of them has the will or the means to liberate Greece. It is no wonder the patriarch, Lambro, is angry.

This idyll of 'liberated' sexuality as a type of political freedom ('sexual Jacobinism') is offered only to be withdrawn. Juan is sold from the desert island as a slave to the sultan's harem. According to a Wollstonecraftian ideology it is the 'harem' which is the symbol of the general enslavement of woman to man, as slave to tyrant, and it is this system which reduces women to 'the love of pleasure and the love of sway'. Byron, as it were, adopts feminism's own satire on the feminine, but without offering an alternative. The society of women is organized as aristocratically as that of men and is ruled by a 'matriarch' and tyrant, Gulbeyaz, who knows all men have their price (a view more often attributed to the corrupting prime minister Sir Robert Walpole!). She buys men in the slave market, and has them drowned in sacks when she has finished with them.

There is strong likelihood that Byron is consciously playing with sexual roles. The beginning of the episode is a parody of the earlier *The Corsair*, but it is the man (Juan) who is now given the role of the slave girl (Gulnare) in that romance. Juan is dressed as a woman, threatened with castration, and sexually and politically humiliated by being asked to kiss the sultana's foot. Byron describes his hero in full drag:

> He stood like Atlas, with a world of words
> About his ears, and nathless would not bend;
> The blood of all his line's Castilian lords
> Boil'd in his veins . . .

> (V. civ)

Byron might have used the episode to show men what it was to be a slave like women. He does not. Instead what the poem describes is a situation in which women, in power, are just as tyrannical as men. It is mere cant to believe that in a world of 'masters' and 'slaves' the ruling class monopolize vice and the slaves, who wish for 'liberation', are custodians of virtue.

Change places and, handy dandy, the oppressed oppress. Such, after all, was one moral learnt from the French Revolution even by the optimistic Shelley, alienated by 'the atrocities of the demagogues, and the re-establishment of successive tyrannies in France' (*Revolt of Islam*, Preface).

Woman out of the harem (or the nunnery to which Juan's first love, Julia, is driven by a rival woman and a hypocritical husband) is represented by Catherine of Russia. For her, Man is a sexual object. Nor is she Woman as even *alma Venus genetrix* – generative sexual love. The carnage of the battle of Ismail is provoked by Catherine's *libido dominandi* – her lust for power – which is equal to her lust for men. Men die for the iron lady just as much as for the iron duke (Wellington).

The comparative structure of the poem invites the reader to contrast the free institutions of British society with the tyranny of the Continental powers. Hence Juan, liberated from Catherine's bed, apostrophizes Freedom on the English shore, and a liberal constitution is free also from the restrictions of the harem and the nunnery. Juan's invocation to 'chaste wives, pure lives' suggests the institution of Christian marriage repeatedly emphasized by conservative voices seeing a middle way between the old forms of Continental tyranny, but also the libertarian ethos of writers (like Byron and his circle) whom Southey judged fit only for a brothel. If Jane Austen castigated Henry Crawford severely, where, in the circles of hell, would one set the narrator of the adventures of Don Juan? The conservative 'mothers of the novel' of the time placed their security as women, and their happiness, in fidelity in marriage, the love of husband, in children at the domestic hearth and in a good income.

If there is an ideal figure of womanhood in the English cantos, it may be only the statue of the Virgin Mary with the infant Christ that presides over the ruins of Norman Abbey – expressive of an archaic faith. Possibly Aurora Raby, a mysterious, apparently pure and introspective woman whom Juan meets at the Abbey, may be intended to represent an ideal, glimpsed by Juan only to be lost, but the unfinished poem leaves suggestion insecure. What Byron *shows*, and describes at length in the cantos he completed, is a political system dominated by women (Wollstonecraft inverted). Power depends upon property, property upon marriage, and marriages are in the prerogative and power of women. Woman is more than 'liberated'. Aristocracy has become 'Gynocracy': petticoat government.

> You may see such at all the balls and dinners,
>   Among the proudest of our Aristocracy,
> So gentle, charming, charitable, chaste –
> And all by having *tact* as well as taste.

(XII. lxvi)

> They generally have some only son
>> Some heir to a large property, some friend
> Of an old family, some gay Sir John,
>> Or grave Lord George, with whom perhaps might end
> A line, and leave posterity undone,
>> Unless a marriage was applied to mend
> The prospect and their morals: and besides,
> They have at hand a blooming glut of brides.
>
> From these they will be careful to select,
>> For this an heiress, and for that a beauty;
> For one a songstress who hath no defect,
>> For t'other one who promises much duty;
> For this a lady no one can reject,
>> Whose sole accomplishments were quite a booty;
> A second for her excellent connexions;
> A third, because there can be no objections.
>
> (XV. xxxiii–xxxiv)

These predatory ladies toil not, neither do they spin, yet not even Solomon in all his glory was arrayed like one of these. Then, after marriage, begins the game of cuckoldry, and Juan is planned as the next victim. Lady Adeline has her eye upon him, but it is Lady Fitzfulke who will have him – whose name indicates the ancientness of the Norman blood she claims, and the main purpose of her life. This graphic social picture is the dramatic representation in action of the system of 'legitimacy' which the carnage of Waterloo restored throughout Europe – in its political form in the re-emergence of the Bourbons, in its sexual manifestation in the underwriting of dynastic property by the activity of Gynocracy. Hence the Duchess of Richmond's ball with which this essay began, where 'all went merry as a marriage-bell'. It is this society which will push Juan to his destruction. One form of 'hell' Byron considered to end the poem has already been discussed: a divorce scandal will drive him to France and his death in the Revolution. The other form of hell Byron said he had in mind was womankind. Juan was to be married into the system as a punishment. Marriage and divorce are the systole and diastole of the Gynocracy, the instruments of power by which women use, control or destroy men, their property and lives, even the freedom of Don Juan. And, like heaven and hell, men and women are 'married' for all eternity in this relationship. It is a disturbing argument. Byron outraged and provoked his age. That capacity to shock and disturb has not declined with the passage of time.

# 10

# SHELLEY

## Kelvin Everest

Shelley has always attracted controversy. From early in his own lifetime his actions and opinions were a frequent source of moral outrage for that incipient bourgeois self-righteousness which developed in the Regency, in an atmosphere of wartime cultural insularity and political reaction, and which came to dominate Victorian social life. Everything about Shelley stood to offend in this ethos. He was a man of exceptional intellectual gifts, which he exercised with an almost ascetic commitment across an unusually wide range of informed interests. These interests were set against the prevailing tide of English life in absolutely uncompromising terms. In a period of Anglican evangelicalism, Shelley was an atheist; in a period of political reaction, he was a democrat and, as he declared himself (in the autograph-album of a Swiss hotel), a 'lover of mankind'. He flouted, with youthfully extravagant abandon, all of the founding conventions and norms of his own massively powerful social class. It is, then, not surprising that Shelley attracted such hostility from his English contemporaries. The guardians of Establishment literary culture – and in particular the editors and reviewers of the influential Tory reviews – vilified Shelley. They saw him as a man whose political and religious opinions were an unforgivable betrayal of his own class. They also saw him as a man whose dangerous views provided the subject-matter for a formidable literary talent. This combination of judgements about Shelley was actually nearer the truth than a great many subsequent judgements. The question of Shelley's reputation is something to which we must return. It is scarcely possible to overestimate the extent of the distortions, misrepresentations, special pleadings and simple error which have combined to cloud understanding of his work and life.

The first thing, however, to make clear about Shelley's poetry is its extraordinary *range*, in literary kind, in tone, and in its great variety of occasions and contexts. In the nineteenth century Shelley was admired primarily as a lyric poet. His best medium was considered to be the short personal poem, concentrating the emotional complexity of private relationships and situations, as they bore the influence of time and change, in a remarkably subtle versification. Shelley's poetry in this manner was praised highly by the Victorians – to excess at times – and this was the kind of writing that Victorian readers had in mind when they ranked Shelley amongst the best poets in the language. Here for example is a characteristic lyric which was a favourite with anthologists, and which was included in Palgrave's *Golden Treasury*, not to mention the *Oxford Book of Nineteenth Century Verse*:

> The flower that smiles today
>   Tomorrow dies;
> All that we wish to stay
>   Tempts and then flies;
> What is this world's delight?
> Lightning, that mocks the night,
>   Brief even as bright. –
>
> Virtue, how frail it is! –
>   Friendship, how rare! –
> Love, how it sells poor bliss
>   For proud despair!
> But these though soon they fall,
> Survive their joy, and all
>   Which ours we call. –
>
> Whilst skies are blue and bright,
>   Whilst flowers are gay,
> Whilst eyes that change ere night
>   Make glad the day;
> Whilst yet the calm hours creep
> Dream thou – and from thy sleep
>   Then wake to weep.

This is a successful poem of its kind, and it succeeds in ways which are typical of Shelley's lyrical writing. The stanza form enables a series of variations on a complex set of metrical and rhyming demands, which are effected with apparent effortlessness. Shelley is particularly skilful in repeating short lines within a metrical scheme so that developments of mood and tone are registered in small but emphatic displacements of pattern (note for example the stressed first syllables in the first and second lines of the second stanza). The sentences settle to their grammatical resolution just as they complete each stanza, and the complexity of form and syntax is played off against a direct irony which gives the sense of a simple human emotion which is yet conscious of its causes: 'All that we wish to stay/Tempts and then flies'. There is too a characteristically uninsistent grace in the poem's deployment of a traditional poetic device, for the poem is of course written in the convention of *carpe diem*. The personal manner of the writing is thus grounded in a generalized literary idiom which, like the increasingly inclusive formulations of mood in the poem, suggests a universal context and resonance for personal experience.

But this poem is typical of Shelley's work in other ways too, which are perhaps less immediately recognizable. Until recently, all published versions of the poem incorporated a textual error – 'we' for 'these' in line twelve – which seriously obscures the argument. The poem is actually one of a great many lyrics retrieved from notebooks by Mary Shelley after her husband's sudden accidental death by drowning. She expended enormous labour on the task, and all readers of Shelley are permanently in her debt. But the notebooks are frequently very difficult to read, and, even when the semblance of a poem had been saved, Mary quite often felt obliged to introduce changes of punctuation, layout and even actual words, in order to clarify what she understood Shelley's sense to be. Another consequence of Mary's editorial work was that, in sometimes failing to recognize the real purpose and context of poems, she presented as personal lyrics a number of poems which, it now seems clear, Shelley had intended for a dramatic or consciously conventional speaker. 'The flower that smiles today' is such a lyric. Never published by Shelley, it was almost certainly written for the dramatic poem *Hellas*, about the Greek War of Independence, but not in the end used. In this context the poem has an impersonally ironic dimension quite lost when the poem is understood as an expression of private emotion.

Shelley was, then, rightly regarded in the nineteenth century as a lyric poet of the highest order, but the poems on which that reputation rested – the poems that were then, and still are, most frequently anthologized – are often read in forms and contexts never settled or intended by Shelley himself. The result has been an exaggerated emphasis on Shelley as a lyric poet of private emotional experience. This has been particularly misleading because Shelley's most original and distinctive writing is to be found in much longer and more obviously complex poems. These longer poems embrace an extraordinary variety of forms. There is the urgently direct and accessible manner of *The Mask of Anarchy*, a frankly political poem, or the carefully practical dramatic writing of *The Cenci*, Shelley's grimly serious five-act play (still performed from time to time) on the nature of evil. There is, at an opposite extreme, the playfully sophisticated 'Witch of Atlas', or the rapt and intense manner of *Epipsychidion*, with its strange fusion of autobiography and abstract symbolism. In contrast to these styles there is the wry and almost Byronic worldliness of 'Julian and Maddalo', and of the more relaxedly informal 'Letter to Maria Gisborne'. And Shelley can employ a much broader and more racy comic manner still, in the service of sharp literary and political satire, in 'Peter Bell the Third' and *Swellfoot the Tyrant*.

Most striking of all is the diversity of formal procedures which characterizes those long poems at the very centre of Shelley's achievement: *Prometheus Unbound*, *Adonais* and 'The Triumph of Life'. These marvellously original and rewarding poems display obvious similarities, in the consistency of various stylistic features, and in the sophisticated deployment of convention and genre in a way which subverts their established ideological connotations. But each poem also marks a new direction in the development of Shelley's career, offering new ways of negotiating and representing the general problems of human experience that were Shelley's main preoccupation throughout his life. Shelley was without doubt a highly self-conscious and self-critical artist, and he maintained a fundamental commitment to the *use* of his art in the service of human progress.

Why, then, has his critical reputation proved so unsteady in the twentieth century? For it is a fact that, of all the Romantic poets, Shelley has fared worst from the critics. Three problems propose themselves as important reasons for the continuing uncertainty of his critical stature. There is what we may call the biographical problem. There is the related problem of the wholly unsatisfactory nature of most existing *texts* of Shelley's poetry and prose. And, at the heart of all the arguments, there is the question of Shelley's politics.

The problem of politics is, or should be, unavoidable. The most influential critical attacks on Shelley, by T. S. Eliot (in *The Use of Poetry and the Use of Criticism*, 1933) and F. R. Leavis (in *Revaluation*, 1936), both claim strictly aesthetic criteria in their dismissals, while palpably applying moral sanctions grounded in an attitude to Shelley's social and political beliefs and the consequences of his efforts to live by them. Shelley's poetry is *radical* poetry. It seeks to represent the limitations and self-imposed evils of human history, past and present. It also seeks, where it can, to offer the possibility of a revolutionary transformation in human history, through the creative influences of imagination and rational understanding, leading to a fruitful control of the environment (Shelley's enduring and informed interest in science is well documented). The imagination is supremely important for Shelley. In his conception, it is the faculty by which we envisage a better form of human existence than the forms that actually exist or have existed. For Shelley it is also the faculty which enables sympathetic understanding and identification with others, and he therefore sees it as 'the prime agent of moral good' (the phrase is from the 'Defence of Poetry'). In practical political terms, Shelley was a materialist; the beneficial effects of imagination are to be understood as real modifications of human practices and institutions, and the ideal forms towards which human society is constantly made to evolve, through the purposive actions of its agents, exist nowhere but in human intelligence. As far as the ultimate mode of existence of absolute human values is concerned, Shelley remained resolutely sceptical – in the strict philosophical sense – throughout his life. He had nothing but scorn for the conventional forms of institutionalized religion, and in particular for those of Christianity. All of Shelley's major longer poems, and many of his best-known shorter ones, are written in a revolutionary spirit of opposition to the existing frame of things. Of course, the mood of the poetry alters with specific occasions and circumstances and, broadly speaking, the poetry darkens in mood as Shelley matures. This is, however, not to imply any suggestion of a conservative 'mellowing' in Shelley's mature commitments. He remained always, and fiercely, a radical.

These were the commitments which attracted hostility in Shelley's own lifetime, and they affect our own reading of his poetry in ways which run very deep; for the stylistic qualities in Shelley's poetry which have provided the basis for attack appear as 'limitations' primarily by the criteria of 'practical criticism'. These criteria, however, are hardly likely to do justice to a poetry like Shelley's, which apprehends the present reality of humanity in nature and society as a provisional condition which the poet has a moral duty to re-imagine in ways still compatible with the underlying laws of matter.

Leavis's *Revaluation* essay amply demonstrates the kind of attack on Shelley's verse which has been frequent over the last forty years (he is generalizing from his own reading of the 'Ode to the West Wind'):

Here ... we have the manifestation of essential characteristics – ... a general tendency of the images to forget the status of the metaphor or simile that introduced them and to assume an autonomy and a right to propagate, so that we lose in confused generations and perspectives the perception or thought that was the ostensible *raison d'être* of imagery ... [in which we recognize an] essential trait of Shelley's: his weak grasp upon the actual ... Shelley was not gifted for drama or narrative ... it is impossible to go on reading him at any length with pleasure; the elusive imagery, the high-pitched emotions, the tone and movement, the ardours, ecstasies, and despairs, are too much the same all through. The effect is of vanity and emptiness ... as well as monotony ... feeling in Shelley's poetry is divorced from thought ...[1]

These eloquent and influential judgements have been echoed and extended many times: in D. W. Harding's essay in the *Pelican Guide to English Literature* for example (still reprinted in recent editions after more than thirty years), or in such widely read and powerfully argued works as Donald Davie's *Purity of Diction in English Verse* (1952).

The particular kind of close reading involved in 'practical criticism' – the kind which dominated English studies in Britain and America for some forty years, from the 1930s on – derives from the work of I. A. Richards. In its most potent inflection, in the work of Leavis, it offers a literary-critical elaboration of the aesthetic imperatives and literary-historical consequences of T. S. Eliot's poetry and criticism. The emphasis in this dominant tradition has been on poetry as a form of human understanding with a special moral and cultural importance; a form of human understanding which can provide a uniquely subtle representation of reality. This reality is typically thought of as complex and ambiguous; and, in the kind of poem approved by the method of practical criticism, it is depicted in a way which enforces an integration of thought and feeling. For practical criticism, great poetry offers 'honesty and insight and wholemindedness', and these qualities are then considered to constitute the only true 'good life'. The successful poem, in representing these inner truths of experience, itself becomes a mode of existence for what is most valuable in human experience.

There are stylistic imperatives which flow from this view of poetry as a unique index to the qualities of a healthy consciousness ('healthy' is a word often used by Leavis in this context). One especially admired quality is an openness to complexities of thought and feeling, which is considered rightly apolitical and untheorized in

1 F. R. Leavis, *Revaluation: Tradition and Development in English Poetry*, London, 1936, pp 206–7, 210–11.

its moral outlook. Shakespeare and Keats (in a version laying stress on the doctrine of 'negative capability') are especially valued in this perspective. Great importance is also attributed to a sort of culturally indigenous propriety of diction and, connected with this, there is a central stress on poetry which fuses formal patterns with the tone and grain of a real speaking voice. The poetry most valued by practical criticism is thought of as being in touch with the language of the tribe, so to speak, which by implication is the prime source and carrier of those shared values and qualities of actual human experience which poetry can represent for the reader. In the most general terms, the criteria of practical criticism endorse what Hazlitt (in his essay on *Coriolanus*) claimed of the language of poetry, that it 'falls in naturally with the language of power'. Poetry is placed in a special position of responsibility towards the status quo; not simply in the sense of the prevailing political or class order, but, much more powerfully, in the whole range of forms of understanding and feeling which constitute consciousness within the given order of things. Poetry is then valued by practical criticism above all as the cultural form in which the eternal and immutable quality of the given order of consciousness is recognized and ratified.

A truly radical poetry, though, is of course seeking to combine a representation of what experience is actually like, with a representation of how it might be different, and better. We cannot expect to find the sentiments of a radical poetry echoing in the bosom as if they were already there, but never so well expressed. Radical poetry such as Shelley's is bound to attempt a recasting of known forms of experience in an imaginary order (which may of course be rationally grounded, though not empirically grounded). This imaginary order can then be brought into an oppositional and transformative relation to the real. While practical criticism is a way of reading which suits many important English writers, it is not especially suited to cope with the challenge of Shelley (though it does fit nicely with some of his work, such as for example parts of 'Julian and Maddalo', and some of his lyrical love-poems). It has indeed created a distorted and diminished version of Shelley, whose distinctive stylistic qualities could then be cast in a villainous role within the context of Leavis's diagnostic reading of the English poetic tradition as it weakened in the decades before the Modernist intervention.

If we now turn briefly to the biographical problems that have affected Shelley's reputation, we again meet the image of a villain, though the nature of the villainy in question has mutated from time to time. As we have already noticed, Shelley's contemporary literary culture was mostly hostile to his work, but it nevertheless sometimes recognized the direct subversive intention and forthright radical commitments of the poetry. After his death the situation changed. Shelley's literary remains and – for a significant period, at least – his reputation passed into the keeping of his widow and his friends. Mary Shelley was forbidden by Shelley's father, Sir Timothy, to publish any biography of her husband. Throughout a very long life Sir Timothy Shelley never forgave the unconventional and provocative behaviour of his son. He therefore threatened Mary's financial support, and that of her son, if she acted to promote Shelley's views and actions. She got round this prohibition by including in her 1839 edition of Shelley's poetry a number of 'Notes' which have a substantial biographical content. These Notes are intense in their admiration, and – anxious as Mary was somehow to atone for what seems to have been a rather cold relationship in her last months with her husband – they lay a strong stress on what Mary understood Shelley's good qualities to be. Their influence has been great, but it must be said that in some areas Mary did not understand Shelley's work especially well, and that in particular she simplified his moral and political outlook, and failed to understand the methods and purposes of his more difficult poetry. Shelley's reputation after his death was further shaped by four widely read biographical works, all by men who had known Shelley well, but only at certain periods and under certain circumstances. Each of these biographers – Thomas Jefferson Hogg, Edward Trelawny, Thomas Love Peacock and Thomas Medwin – had their personal reasons for presenting Shelley's character and behaviour in ways which helped them to offer satisfactory accounts of themselves and their own involvement in Shelley's affairs.

Later in the century, responsibility for the prevailing image of Shelley was assumed by frankly uncritical and misguided admirers. These included notably Jane, Lady Shelley, wife of Shelley and Mary's only surviving son (also called Percy), who of course had never herself met Shelley. These admirers fostered something akin to a 'Shelley-worship'. They assiduously promoted what they considered a favourable image of Shelley as an ineffectual dreamer and hopelessly unpragmatic idealist. Their distorted and partial version of Shelley attributed to him a kind of idealism which seemed to many readers reckless and viciously blind to real human costs. This image was then in its turn very influentially reacted against by twentieth-century writers and critics, who wished to think both of themselves and of their literary calling as altogether more hard-headed.

In fact it is necessary to understand the development of Shelley's reputation in its most important dimension as a function of much larger cultural developments, in which he came to have a representative role. In later Victorian experience Shelley virtually stands for an oppositional idealism, social, political and sexual, which – under the particular circumstances of late nineteenth-century industrial capitalism – was regarded as impossible to mediate in constructive social terms. And what is more, the attempt to mediate it could then only lead to undesirable consequences; as for example when Arnold's characterization of Shelley as 'an ineffectual angel, beating in the void his luminous wings in vain' (in the essay on Shelley in his *Essays in Criticism*) is picked up in the name and character of Hardy's Angel Clare in *Tess of the D'Urbervilles*. Indeed Shelley frequently provides the model for nineteenth-century representations of the socially alienated idealist (Will Ladislaw in *Middlemarch* is another striking example). It is one of the numerous ironies attendant upon this developing image of Shelley that his first conspicuously successful longer poem, *Alastor*, actually addresses itself to the self-destructive and socially undesirable consequences of a poetic idealism which is not socially mediated.

We have already touched on the problem of Shelley's *text* – that is to say, the printed form in which his poetry and prose has been generally available – in discussing the problems that should be borne in mind when reading lyrics such as 'The flower that smiles today'. But the problem of the text is a good deal more serious than that, and it has always existed in close connection with the problem of Shelley's distorted cultural image. For Shelley could not be allowed to be much of a conscious artist if he was to be denied any 'firm grasp upon the actual'. This requirement of the image was neatly served by the consequences of Shelley's sudden, early death, in exile. A great mass of Shelley's work, including many of the lyrics and also the longer works by which he has been best known, had to be retrieved from its uncertain state in notebook drafts. Additionally, the single most important volume of poetry actually published in Shelley's lifetime, *Prometheus Unbound*, was printed in England, without Shelley's supervision (he was in Italy, and received no proofs, although he asked for them), in a form absolutely riddled with sense-affecting error. In correcting the text, successive editors have assumed an extraordinary degree of licence because they have tended to assume that their own judgement, in matters of grammar, versification, indentation, titles, spelling, capitals, punctuation and even diction, was more to be trusted than Shelley's own. The situation has been complicated by the fact that so much of Shelley's writing *has* to be at least punctuated, and generally tidied for readers, because of its simple unreadiness for print as Shelley left it. Thus a text of Shelley has come into being which corroborated the attitudes to the poet which lay behind the very genesis of that text.

Only very recently have readers come to see Shelley more plainly. Most people who take a serious interest in his work now recognize its fundamental social engagement, its subordination of the personal to general issues of morality and social progress, its artistic variety and seriousness. It remains true that Shelley lived a dramatic and interesting life, and that his private experience itself necessarily becomes a document for interpretation. But the interpretation can nowadays at least be attempted on a basis of clear-sighted perspectives on what actually happened, and on the interests and attitudes that Shelley actually had. It is useful briefly to outline those aspects of Shelley's biography which have fuelled controversy over the years. Some survey of the issues is needed, because so much has been made of the ways in which Shelley's life may or may not be seen to dramatize the limitations of his intellectual outlook.

One particularly controversial topic has been the difficult question of Shelley's relationships with women. He has been attacked for his behaviour in this respect by people of the most widely divergent outlooks and moral convictions. Shelley married twice. His first marriage was an elopement. At the age of nineteen Shelley ran away with Harriet Westbrook, the sixteen-year-old friend of one of his sisters. Some months earlier he had been expelled from University College, Oxford, for circulating an implicitly atheistical pamphlet (*The Necessity of Atheism*). The elopement compounded a breach with his father which was never properly to heal, and which indeed was to widen in later years. Shelley's motives in the affair were undoubtedly very mixed, but it is certain that a rather immaturely reckless anti-authoritarianism came into it. It also seems the case – judging from comments Shelley made to friends some years after the event – that he wished to avoid the disgrace that would fall upon Harriet had she lived with him out of wedlock. It is also probable that Shelley believed himself at the time of the elopement (as he continued to do throughout his life) to be seriously, even terminally ill, and that he wished Harriet to benefit from an inheritance.

Nevertheless, for all the rashness of the elopement, the marriage at first went reasonably well. Harriet's prettiness and quietly rational manner won her the affection of people who were later to wield an influence on judgements of Shelley's subsequent conduct, notably

Robert Southey, whom the Shelleys came to know during their residence in the Lake District in 1811. Southey had been a fierce radical in his youth, but by the time of his meeting with the Shelleys he had become a pillar of Establishment literary culture and a spokesman for Tory values. At first he indulged Shelley's radicalism and atheism, and undertook to put him in the way of more sensible views. When this failed he took sternly against Shelley and became in the poet's imagination a sort of symbolic figure standing for the diseased and pernicious intelligence of the time-serving intellectual. Shelley's friend Thomas Love Peacock, the novelist, also knew and liked Harriet and allowed this to colour his account of Shelley in his influential *Memoir*, published many years after Shelley's death in response to Hogg's *Life*.

Two aspects of Shelley's relationship with Harriet have attracted especially sharp commentary, because they both can be made to imply that Shelley's views were either insincerely held, or that they led to misery for those who knew him, or both.

Firstly, Shelley has been frequently accused of hypocrisy in advocating sexual freedom in love, but reacting badly against the attempt by his friend Hogg to initiate an affair with Harriet quite soon after her marriage. Now it is unquestionable that Shelley was dismayed and deeply upset by Hogg's advances, but equally the records that survive make it clear that Shelley was annoyed not by the idea of a sexual liaison between his best friend and his new young wife, but by Hogg's manner in the business, that of a slily seducing Regency rake.

Secondly, commentators have been quick to seize upon Shelley's desertion of Harriet for Mary Wollstonecraft Godwin in 1814 (a second elopement, this time to the Continent), after three years of marriage to Harriet, as a callous and selfish action. These characterizations have been further fuelled and complicated by the appalling subsequent chain of events, which culminated in Harriet's suicide by drowning in the Serpentine, late in 1816. It has seemed possible to some to interpret Shelley's behaviour in this dreadful context as coldly feckless even to the point of murder, and this extreme view has been abetted by the coincidental circumstance that Mary Shelley's half-sister Fanny Imlay also took her own life at about the same time, for unconnected reasons which still appear to have involved her strong feeling for Shelley. Shelley's married life with Mary was also flawed and saddened by tragic deaths and by entanglements with other women. Mary herself seems to have blamed Shelley for the death of their one-year-old daughter Clara in Venice in 1818, and to have allowed this permanently to affect her subsequent private relationship with the poet. This in its turn appears to have contributed to the situation in which Shelley became closely involved – certainly emotionally, possibly sexually – with a series of women over the last five years of his life. These included notably Mary's half-sister Claire Clairmont, the Pisan heiress Emilia Viviani, and also Jane Williams, the common-law wife of Shelley's friend Edward Williams, who was to drown with him in 1822.

These biographical details, which so unhappily shadowed public and international developments in the post-Napoleonic years, are of course private matters. And yet the reader of Shelley is obliged to confront them because of the insistence in the poetry on moral and political ideas which have direct implications for personal as well as political conduct. Those who wish to disprove or reject or discredit the radical idealism of Shelley's outlook have found it hard to resist an appeal to the 'lessons' of his private life; do they not consistently go to show where views of this sort lead? This way of building a case against Shelley has recently taken a particularly unfortunate turn with the rise of feminism in European and Anglo-American arenas of literary debate. Shelley was a feminist; of that there can be no doubt. His longest poem, *Laon and Cythna*, assumes the central importance of sexual equality in any durable social revolution. 'Can man be free if woman be a slave?' asks the heroine, Cythna, in a passage crucial to the structure of the entire narrative (II. xliii). Shelley concerns himself in an explicit and unmistakable way with the oppression of women in history and in his own society, and gives extensive consideration in his writings of every kind to the problems of moral and political consciousness, and of viable political action, which are produced by that oppression. If we except Blake (and Blake's feminism is exceptional in a number of ways), Shelley is quite simply the only serious male writer of poetry in the earlier nineteenth century to confront with honesty and sustained effort the extremely difficult challenge of a feminist politics. Of course, his effort is shaped and limited by his historical experience, his background and education, and the intellectual traditions within which he worked and developed. These things are true for everybody. In Shelley's case, his feminism, as indeed his radicalism more generally, is all the more remarkable for the context which produced it.

It is, then, a piquant irony that Shelley should in recent years have come under attack from feminist critics who find his beliefs compromised or contradicted by the realities of his behaviour in personal relationships with women. This is a version of the reactionary argument against Shelley which appears peculiarly ill-judged and impoverished in historical imagination. This way of regarding Shelley has emerged partly as a consequence of the very greatly increased interest, in recent years, in Mary Shelley's own work as a writer – a development which would have delighted Shelley as much as it would have surprised Mary, who needed all Shelley's encouragement to take her own work seriously. It is important to take care that a rightly enhanced and detailed appreciation of Mary Shelley should not entail a reactive downward valuation of the man who, at her own request, helped her as an artist in whatever ways he could.

It is clear that, like everybody else, Shelley was far from being perfect. Particularly in his late teens and early twenties his sympathetic imagination could be impaired and blinkered by an impetuous zeal in extreme commitments, intellectual and political, of which he had yet to learn the cost. He was made to learn the cost by terrible personal tragedy and repeated bitter experience of failure and disappointment. He was devastated by his first wife's suicide: his friend Leigh Hunt said that it 'tore his being to pieces', and Claire Clairmont claimed that Shelley's enthusiasms were never again so fierce and free after the winter of 1816. His beliefs made residence in England very uncomfortable after 1817, when he was denied custody of his two children by Harriet because of the atheism of his youthful poem *Queen Mab*.

After his move to Italy in 1818, Shelley never really established a settled home, any more than he had done in England. His life was in a sense a long series of journeys punctuated by temporary residences, although he was settled in a constructive and supportive small community for a while – a couple of years – in Pisa until a few months before his death. He persistently reiterated the conviction that he was suffering from a serious illness, which might lead to an early death. It is by no means certain that this conviction was irrationally founded: Shelley clearly suffered often from real and severe illness. He had also to endure the pain of losing both his young children by Mary within fifteen months of arriving in Italy (the Shelleys' beloved William died in Rome in 1819, aged three and a half), and then of losing Mary's affection without relinquishing the emotional and other ties which still bound them, so that his other relationships were compromised and unhappy too. He had, in short, as good a set of reasons as anyone to appreciate the difficulties of sustaining his conviction in the desirability of human freedoms, and particularly political and sexual freedoms.

Indeed what is remarkable about Shelley is the *toughness* of his idealism, its survival and continuing development in the face of experience which many might have found crushing. He retained his unspiteful and much underrated sense of humour and fun. He worried over the contradictions of his republicanism and his feminism; what young male aristocrat of the Regency could not have found contradictions in such commitments? Above all, he continued to think and work and *write*, without audience, without any success by the customary criteria of the day, without any sense of achievable political goals in the short term. And it must be by this writing that we should nowadays judge Shelley. His private life, so interesting, so extraordinarily various and dramatic, finds its best record in the larger interests and preoccupations by which it is taken up in the poetry. Shelley had no monopoly on personal unhappiness, in marriage or anything else. It is not equitable that he should be judged in such terms simply because he never ceased to conduct his life by conscious ideals which his world refused.

It is fairer and more useful to consider the broad impersonal contexts of Shelley's thought and poetry. His work takes its fundamental orientations from the social-historical circumstances in which the second-generation English Romantics grew up. Three factors dominate these circumstances: the French Revolution, in its dual aspect of initial millennial promise followed by bitter disillusionment; the promise of Napoleonic republicanism with its long years of European war and the ultimate victory of reactionary monarchy; and the even longer years of chilling political reaction and oppression in England, which began in the 1790s, and which altered only with the breakup of the political consensus after Waterloo and the Congress of Vienna. Shelley inherited the revolutionary ideals of nineties English radicalism, but was born late enough to reject the pessimism and apostasy which by 1810 characterized the outlook of the first-generation Romantics, particularly Wordsworth, Coleridge and Southey, all of whom Shelley admired intensely as poets.

In his Preface to *Laon and Cythna* (1818; better known under the title of the revised and censored version, as *The Revolt of Islam*), Shelley gives acute consideration to these cultural and intellectual circumstances. The national unity enforced by wartime conditions in England was, by the time of Waterloo in 1815, under a serious threat of collapse into anarchic class war. Shelley understood this very well. The threat was countered time and again by savage repression, but radical hopes were still nourished by the unforgotten idealism and early promise of the French Revolution, and the intellectual traditions which lay behind it were of course still available. Shelley's early intellectual development as an atheist and republican was influenced primarily by two sources. He read widely in the French materialist philosophers and their populists, particularly Holbach and Volney. He also immersed himself in the indigenous republican and radical traditions which had flourished in England since the seventeenth century, and which had issued in a richly influential series of works produced in response to Burke's attack on the Revolution, *Reflections on the Revolution in France* (1790): notably Thomas Paine's *Rights of Man* (1791, 1792) and *The Age of Reason* (1794, 1795), and William Godwin's *Political Justice* (1793). Shelley's first long poem, *Queen Mab* (1813), displays the influence of these traditions so well that it became effectively a primer for working-class political movements in England throughout the nineteenth century.

*Queen Mab* remains a readable and profoundly interesting work, not least for its diverse and very lengthy prose notes. The poem's lucidly discursive style deals for the most part in religious and political ideas, and the direct and accessible manner still retains a certain polemical edge. Shelley himself came to dismiss the poem as too youthfully immature to do its causes much good, and it is true that the hard clarity of most of the verse is uneasily framed by a dream-vision machinery, adapted from Volney, Southey and Milton, which dissipates the force of the poem's intellectual thrust. Indeed this awkward combination of rational radicalism and a visionary poetic anticipates what some have seen as an unresolved tension which persists right through Shelley's career. But Shelley was also keen to be seen to set little store by *Queen Mab*, because he feared that its circulation in the early 1820s (in popular 'pirated' – unauthor- ized – editions) might prejudice future attempts to win custody of his children by Harriet in the English courts.

To the widely shared influences of French materialism and English radicalism Shelley added three further elements which transform his intellectual temper into its very distinctive and unusual form. He was impressed early by proto-feminist works such as James Law- rence's *Empire of the Nairs* (1811), but above all by the feminism of his second wife Mary's mother, Mary Wollstonecraft, who had died soon after giving birth to Mary in 1797 (after a brief marriage to Godwin). He also enriched the materialism of his early influences by a deep and informed interest in the sceptical tradition in philosophy, an interest which led him into an abiding interest in classical and especially Greek thought; this interest gives his atheism an impress- ively meditated and intellectually well-defended character, which is resolutely sceptical rather than dismissive about, for example, the questions of a first cause and an afterlife. Shelley did, however, always maintain an admiration for Jesus Christ, whom he thought of in historical terms as a kind of reformer whose message had been distorted. Thirdly, Shelley's grasp of English radical traditions was greatly invigorated by an almost intoxicated enthusiasm for Platonic forms of thought, particularly as these provided metaphors and formulations for the expression of ideas that were at the very heart of his outlook. Essentially, these ideas involved an insistence on the primacy of the human imagination, and on the fundamental necessity of conceptions of beauty and the ideal as the sources of that sense of the perfect which enabled continual striving towards better forms for human action and creativity. Shelley's Platonism nevertheless *is* metaphorical; he thought of the better world, by which present reality can be judged, as something which might one day be present to the senses, and embodied in actually functioning institutions.

There is in Shelley's work a contradictory blend of long-term radical optimism with an intensely passionate apprehension and representation of the given contingencies and experiences of 'sad reality'. This contradiction reflects larger tensions in the social and historical forces which helped to shape Shelley's thought and artistic practices. It is worth dwelling for a moment on some features of this social-historical context as they were more exactly specific to Shelley. The undeniable difficulty and contradictoriness of certain aspects of his thought and poetry may then at least be understood as of a piece with their shaping social and historical conditions.

Shelley's radicalism was a product of, as well as a reaction against, his aristocratic background and upbringing. Intellectually this radicalism begins in an accelerating movement away from the ideas and commitments of the Whig aristocracy, but Shelley's style of political idealism always retains a more or less discernible cast of aristocratic confidence. His easily established affinity with Byron is quite understandable. In the same way there is an abiding difficulty for readers in the literary sophistication and erudition of Shelley's manner, the product of an expensive English private education at preparatory school, followed by Eton and, if only for one term, Oxford. There is no embarrassment in Shelley's wholehearted deployment of his sophisticated literary intelligence, but there is a certain paradox in his use of it in the service of what is in the end a *popular* cause. He clearly bears the stamp of his own class, as a person and as a writer, but that very class happens also to be the prime target of his own revolutionary critique. This difficult situation helps to produce a range of stylistic and thematic preoccupations which are at once problematic and characteristic. There is for example the recurrent use of self-images in the poetry, where the attention is on the limitations and problems of distinctly Shelley-like protagonists. There is also a constantly recurring preoccupation with the death of such figures. In *Alastor* (1816) this death is the final register of a damning social irresponsibility on the part of the poet, whose failure to mediate his ideals for his society consigns him to oblivion. Shelley's perspective here on a Shelleyan protagonist is thus controlled and ironic, and this is the typical mode of his maturer work. There is nevertheless an inescapable and pervasive concern in Shelley's poetry with the difficulty of his personal relation to the forces acting for change in society.

The 'Ode to the West Wind' is a striking example. This most exciting and exhilarating of English lyrics, very beautiful in its fusion of wild headlong movement with tightly intricate formal control, is a celebratory invocation of the spirit of change in nature and society. This spirit sweeps inexorably through matter and mind, destructive and creative, and it is embodied in the poem in language suggesting Shelley's favourite volcanic imagery of revolutionary social change, and also in biblical language of apocalypse and resurrection. The poem's first three stanzas – each in formal terms elaborately modelled on an adaptation of Italian *terza rima* to English sonnet schemes – celebrate in turn the wind's effect on leaves, clouds and ocean, and affirm the revolutionary potential of the natural process in its social inflection (the leaves in line four suggest the peoples of the world; the Mediterranean languor shattered in stanza three associates with an overthrown imperial indulgence and complacency). But stanza four, opening with a personalized recapitulation of the action of the first three stanzas, registers a sense of dislocation from these great forces of nature and society on the part of the poem's speaker. A simple unity with the wind is remembered from boyhood, but has receded with the onset of adult experience and self-consciousness. As is often the case in Shelley, an exaggeratedly self-pitying image of self can appear irritatingly posed and self-regarding when not understood in its ironic context (that is to say, this limited sense of self will be transcended in the poem):

> If even
> I were as in my boyhood, and could be
>
> The comrade of thy wanderings over Heaven,
> As then, when to outstrip thy skiey speed
> Scarce seemed a vision – I would ne'er have striven

> As thus with thee in prayer in my sore need.
> Oh! lift me as a wave, a leaf, a cloud!
> I fall upon the thorns of life – I bleed –
>
> A heavy weight of hours has chained and bowed
> One too like thee: tameless, and swift, and proud.

(47–56)

Momentarily, the affinity between speaker and wind is articulated in the form of a metaphoric expression of lost and defeated energies, and this calls into question the effective role of the speaker as an agent of the forces for change represented in the wind. But the poem's magnificent closing stanza seizes on this very problem – the speaker's despondent consciousness of lonely disjunction from any effective agency of change in society – and makes his poetic articulation of the problem into a way of solving it. The completed poem itself becomes the mode of the poet's agency, in its embodiment of the revolutionary spirit of the wind. The poem's speaker affirms his newly established unity with the wind by identifying it with the breath of his utterance. This unity is also affirmed, in the midst of a complex movement of thought catching many associations and implications, by the introduction of a daring pun on the leaves of the first stanza and the leaves of the books through which the speaker's own revolutionary idealism will be rekindled in the intelligence of future generations:

> Make me thy lyre, even as the forest is:
> What if my leaves are falling like its own!
> The tumult of thy mighty harmonies
>
> Will take from both a deep, autumnal tone,
> Sweet though in sadness. Be thou, Spirit fierce,
> My spirit! Be thou me, impetuous one!
>
> Drive my dead thoughts over the universe
> Like withered leaves to quicken a new birth!
> And, by the incantation of this verse,
>
> Scatter, as from an unextinguished hearth
> Ashes and sparks, my words among mankind!
> Be through my lips to unawakened Earth
>
> The trumpet of a prophecy! O Wind,
> If Winter comes, can Spring be far behind?

(57–70)

The poem's concern throughout has been to represent a difficult relation between the individual human subject, limited by time, chance and circumstance, and the great movements of history. Here, in the closing stanza, it issues in a superbly eloquent affirmation of long-term possibility and optimism. The short-term perspectives, those which are inescapable for the individual subject, are more bleak (the tone is 'deep, autumnal'; the poet's hair – a further connotation for the leaves – is falling too). The revolutionary potential of the poem greatly exceeds any possible personal agency of the poet. The implicit irony in the famous last line is not accidental. It is always best when reading Shelley's poetry to *assume* a certain subtlety and self-consciousness, rather than to look for the sound-intoxicated and weakly emotional outpouring which has been unfairly associated with poems such as the 'Ode' for too long. Most of the mature verse which Shelley himself published is much more intelligent, demanding and self-critical than that. The 'Ode' is a remarkable poem precisely because its rich and beautiful qualities of sound and movement do not vitiate the poem's intellectual strength and subtlety.

Shelley's own literary criticism constantly affirms the fundamental interdependence of the artist and the social-historical circumstances in which art is produced. In a part of the Preface to *Prometheus Unbound* which Shelley added as a reply to accusations by reviewers that an earlier poem of his had plagiarized from the Lake poets, he acknowledged the substantial extent to which a writer could not escape from history: 'Poets, not otherwise than philosophers, painters, sculptors and musicians, are, in one sense, the creators, and, in another, the creations, of their age. From this subjection the loftiest do not escape.' For Shelley this inescapable interdependence gives to poets – in his admittedly broad sense of the word 'poet' – a uniquely important social function, for they articulate to human society its own nature, and they imagine for it different and better natures too. Shelley thinks of poetry in this broad sense as any product of the human imagination which, working upon the given materials of experience, fashions them into forms which more effectively realize their own potentiality for good. As a chorus of *Prometheus Unbound* puts it, speaking of the poet's calling:

> Nor seeks nor finds he mortal blisses,
> But feeds on the aërial kisses
> Of shapes that haunt thought's wildernesses.
> He will watch from dawn to gloom
> The lake-reflected sun illume
> The yellow bees i'the ivy-bloom,
> Nor heed nor see what things they be;

> But from these create he can
> Forms more real than living man,
> Nurslings of immortality! –

(I. 740–49)

Here the phenomenal world is sharply seen, but its meaning is produced by the poet's transformation of it into a representation of a mental ideal – 'shapes that haunt thought's wildernesses' – which is 'more real' in its perfection than the actual conditions which produce the ideal. The poet gives moral form and purpose to the onward rush of human development.

The 'Defence of Poetry', written towards the end of Shelley's life but not published until after his death, ends with an affirmation of this view of the poet:

The most unfailing herald, companion, and follower of the awakening of a great people to work a beneficial change in opinion or institution, is Poetry. At such periods there is an accumulation of the power of communicating and receiving intense and impassioned conceptions respecting man and nature. The persons in whom this power resides, may often, as far as regards many portions of their nature, have little apparent correspondence with that spirit of good of which they are the ministers. But even whilst they deny and abjure, they are yet compelled to serve, the Power which is seated upon the throne of their own soul. It is impossible to read the compositions of the most celebrated writers of the present day without being startled with the electric life which burns within their words. They measure the circumference and sound the depths of human nature with a comprehensive and all-penetrating spirit, and they are themselves perhaps the most sincerely astonished at its manifestations, for it is less their spirit than the spirit of the age.

We should note the relevance of this dialectical conception of poetry to Shelley's own case. It is obvious that any reading of Shelley which fails to recognize his high conception of the poet's social function, and of the historical nature of poetry, will seriously limit itself. But the dialectical frame of mind also helps us to understand the *kind* of poet that Shelley is. As he develops he constantly adopts, and then transforms from within, a great variety of received literary modes. Shelley appropriates and turns in new directions materials drawn from a literary culture and intellectual tradition which provide the determining conditions of his achievement. It is too little appreciated that to a large extent the elements of Shelley's style are derived from the current idioms of English Romantic literary culture.

Many features of his style which emerge early and remain relative constants are developed from popular contemporary literary forms.

Shelley makes habitual recourse to Gothic conventions, for example; he regularly uses melancholy landscapes and night-scenes, graves, ghosts, supernatural beings and events, and situations of extremity and duress. All these elements of his style derive in the first place quite simply from his youthful immersion in the contemporary productions of the fashion for such things. This immersion leaves him with stylistic mannerisms which are very noticeable in his earlier output – they are for instance still quite prominent in *Alastor*, and in the 'Hymn to Intellectual Beauty' (1816) – and which continue to resurface throughout his career, for instance in *Adonais*. The taste for exotic narratives, often involving the East, often involving a complicated journey over and underground, by foot or by boat, is another instance in which he draws on widely employed conventions of the period found, for example, ubiquitously in Southey's poetry (which Shelley seems to have known more or less by heart). This narrative manner tended to go with fairly light and quick-moving metres, in Southey certainly and also in Scott and Thomas Moore (and a host of others). This too Shelley took up and developed into his characteristic rapidity and fluency of verse movement within complex stanzaic forms.

His style also brings out the often overlooked continuing potency of post-Augustan conventions in the Romantic period. For example, a consciously poetic diction still survived and even flourished; Wordsworth's bold strictures in his Preface to *Lyrical Ballads* were not aimed at straw targets, but against still quite dominant practices. Shelley's taste for unusual grammatical demands within taxing combinations of metre and rhyme has much in common with later eighteenth-century poets trained in the classical languages. Even his habit of using elaborate sustained metaphors, with a tendency to introduce distinct but related subordinate metaphors within these, is an aspect of his difficulty for the modern reader which seems less unusual beside a great deal of post-Miltonic English verse of the eighteenth and early nineteenth centuries. Of course these elements were later fused, in Shelley, with a plainer and more idiomatic blank-verse manner absorbing the achievements in metre and diction of Wordsworth and Coleridge. *Alastor* marks a great advance in this respect, and *Prometheus Unbound* confirms Shelley's control of the form. His style also shows an increasingly sophisticated ability to work in adaptations of a Spenserian or Miltonic manner, and, in the later years, to adapt in remarkable ways the verse textures of classical and European writers, notably Dante and Calderón. Shelley's poetry undoubtedly appears difficult and almost quirkily mannered to the new reader, but its demanding originality nevertheless emerges from the given materials of the historical moment.

We have already noted the exceptional *range* which is a striking feature of Shelley's achievement as a writer. Shelley's openness to a great variety of poetic forms depends on a skilful versatility which was won by constant practice. His notebooks very clearly demonstrate the care which Shelley customarily took with his own verse. A new poem typically starts in a wild and tangled draft, is then worked over in various ways, and finally – we are speaking of finished poems – written out in a carefully considered way. The notebooks certainly look chaotic at first, but even when working on an almost illegible first draft Shelley's numerous revisions never scramble the metre (he uses indentation as a guide here), and where they affect the grammar he takes care, usually, to sort this out too (though he is less consistent in this respect). But Shelley's manifestly conscious artistry was always at the service of a restlessly experimental literary intelligence, which could never settle into any one formal idiom. This openness goes with the fundamentally *sceptical* cast of his intelligence. In Shelley fierce radical commitments and powerful emotional drives are given an inquiring and undogmatic intellectual grounding. This sceptical impatience with fixed forms – forms which yet provide the determining conditions of his writing – is a quality absolutely basic to the distinctive character of Shelley's poetry.

Take for instance the poem now known as 'England in 1819' (Mary's title):

> An old, mad, blind, despised and dying King;
> Princes, the dregs of their dull race, who flow
> Through public scorn, – mud from a muddy spring;
> Rulers who neither see nor feel nor know,
> But leechlike to their fainting Country cling
> Till they drop, blind in blood, without a blow;
> A people starved and stabbed in the untilled field;
> An army whom liberticide and prey
> Makes as a two-edged sword to all who wield;
> Golden and sanguine laws which tempt and slay;
> Religion Christless, Godless, a book sealed;
> A senate, Time's worst statute, unrepealed,
> Are graves from which a glorious Phantom may
> Burst, to illumine our tempestuous day.

This is one of the many powerful political poems that Shelley wrote in Italy in the last months of 1819, after receiving from England the news of the Peterloo massacre (the most important of them is *The*

*Mask of Anarchy*). 'England in 1819' is a sonnet, but Shelley's handling of the form gives to the poem a restless feeling of barely contained anger which refuses to settle to finished shape. The rhymes effectively constitute a sort of inverted Petrarchan sonnet fused with an adaptation of the Shakespearian couplet. The first six lines, on the royal family, are a self-contained unit like the Petrarchan sestet, and they end on a strong pause of grammar and sense. The poem's last eight lines have two rhyme sounds only, but they are so arranged as to produce a quatrain followed by two couplets; and the 'turn' of the sonnet, its change of mood and argumentative direction, is suspended until the very last moment, between the thirteenth and fourteenth lines. The grammar too turns on these last two lines. The poem is in fact a list of evils, nominated in their causes and effects, which, all governed by the verb 'Are' in line thirteen, the poem finally predicates as graves which – like the sleeping seeds of the 'West Wind' – may be the necessary precondition of rebirth into better form. The sense of the poem is that the darkest social and political conditions are the ones that force a revolutionary crisis, and it thus affirms a long-term political optimism much needed on the radical side in post-Napoleonic Europe.

The metaphoric structure is typical in its unfolding. The first line ironically suggests Lear behind the pathetic figure of the old king. George III was by 1819 incapably ill with a disease giving all the appearances of total madness, and had left his kingdom to the rule of his son George (Regent in 1819; he became George IV in 1820), and his variously feckless and loathsome brothers. The associations of 'dregs' and 'flow' are allowed to develop and multiply, producing the 'leechlike' image which produces in its turn the phrase 'blind in blood', completing the movement of associations in the metaphors and at the same time clinching a brutal political reference. And yet the feeling of the poem is in the end reserved and self-questioning. The force of 'Burst' is significantly modified by its auxiliary 'may', falling as it does weakly on the end of the line. The poem's strength of analysis and indignation is a way of perceiving a desperate situation, but *only* that. Perhaps there is no end in sight to the situation in England in 1819.

We often meet this kind of sceptical reserve in Shelley's writing, drawing back from absolute teleological propositions, and enacting this withdrawal in the form itself of the poetry. The contrast with Keats, and with *his* adaptations of sonnet form, is instructive here. Shelley's sonnets usually resist the sense of settled form; think again of the stanza used in 'Ode to the West Wind', or examine for example the rhyme scheme of 'Ozymandias'. Keats too, notably in his Odes, adapts and builds on the tradition of English sonnet-writing in his own stanza forms; each of his major Odes, in fact, uses a stanza which combines and rearranges elements from different types of sonnet. But the effects in Keats are very different from Shelley's. Keats achieves a beautifully arrested, sculptural kind of writing – a lyric equivalent of the statuesque stillness in the opening lines of *Hyperion* – which strikes the ear as perfectly finished and whole (read for example the fourth stanza of the 'Ode on a Grecian Urn', or the first stanza of the 'Ode to Autumn'). Shelley does not even try for this kind of writing; he is interested in process and possibility, and in the ways in which these may be represented. In Shelley's poetry present material and experiential realities are understood as the evanescent realizations of very long-term orders of being. Shelley's world is not static, and his art is thoroughly un-Keatsian; it has no concern to fix and hold experience up for contemplation. Experience for Shelley is always in developmental movement; it is always coming-to-be.

Shelley's poetic scepticism can be seen in a different mode in the 'Ode to Heaven', published with *Prometheus Unbound* in 1820. This poem in six nine-line stanzas presents three successive perspectives on the 'Heaven' of the title. The first, spoken in three stanzas by a 'Chorus of Spirits', triumphantly celebrates the splendour and endless fecund diversity of the material universe, invoked in the great dome of the open sky. It is a purely materialist celebration, which locates all meaning and value, through all history, in the ever-present physical realities of space and time. This chorus is followed by a single stanza spoken by 'A Remoter Voice', which repudiates the materialism of the opening chorus and asserts in its place the claims of a mental idealism which sees beyond the physical universe to the eternal and more perfect forms which underlie and inform it:

> Thou art but the mind's first chamber,
> Round which its young fancies clamber
> Like weak insects in a cave
>     Lighted up by stalactites;
> But the portal of the grave,
>     Where a world of new delights
>         Will make thy best glories seem
>         But a dim and noonday gleam
>         From the shadow of a dream.

This new perspective does not invalidate that of the first chorus, but its unresolved juxtaposition with it ironizes the claims of both materialist and idealist voices. And both voices are succeeded by a third, 'A Louder and Still Remoter Voice', which scornfully castigates the presumption of the earlier perspectives. The third voice asserts, with a kind of wondering imaginative scepticism, the ultimately imponderable and unknowable final cause and destiny of the universe. Indeed, in the immensity of spatial and temporal perspectives that it comprehends, this last perspective is eerily remote from human experience:

> What is Heaven? a globe of dew
> Filling in the morning new
> Some eyed flower whose young leaves waken
> > On an unimagined world.
> Constellated suns unshaken,
> > Orbits measureless, are furled
> > > In that frail and fading sphere,
> > > With ten million gathered there
> > > To tremble, gleam, and disappear!

The scepticism of the poem's vision is subtly enforced by its self-ironizing rhetoric, which subverts opposed modes of interpretation and systems of value without wholly invalidating them. The effect is of a 'Romantic irony', in which moral positives survive our consciousness of their limits. This ironic mode is frequent in Byron's poetry, for example in the funny and moving ironies of *Don Juan*; but Byron's purposes are of course comic and worldly, and in an altogether different register from Shelley's.

Shelley's greatest poem, *Prometheus Unbound*, embodies the whole range of qualities and preoccupations which we have noted, and orchestrates them into a grand and brilliantly original *tour de force*. The poem is a verse drama which completes Aeschylus's *Prometheus Bound*, but in a revolutionary re-plotting. Shelley has the immortal champion of humanity liberated from his torture, not by an agreed complicity with his tyrant, but by overthrowing tyranny. This overthrow is effected through an understanding of the processes and forces which establish and preserve evil in human power-relations. It is an almost overwhelmingly ambitious and complex theme, but the poem, while amongst the most demanding of works to come to terms with at first, succeeds to an astonishing degree in overcoming the technical problems Shelley sets for himself in it. The verse alternates blank verse with passages of lyrical writing which correspond loosely to the choric elements in Greek verse drama, Shelley's primary model for his poem. The blank verse is a richly impressive achievement, offering a subtle set of variations ranging in manner from a bleakly Hebraic and post-Miltonic sonority and seriousness – see for example Prometheus's opening speech in Act I, or Jupiter's speech in Act III, scene i – to the strange and delicate writing which characterizes the female characters, notably Asia and Panthea in the earlier scenes of the second act.

In a sense, the 'action' of *Prometheus Unbound* is straightforward. Act I opens with Prometheus's renunciation of his curse against the tyrant Jupiter. The renounced curse embodies Prometheus's long-preserved negatively defiant state of mind, which, Prometheus now realizes, has itself worked to perpetuate the power of his oppressor. Shelley's essential proposition here is that most social and political evils are generated by human intelligence, and are therefore subject to human control, although the institutionalized and deeply entrenched nature of human evil necessitates more than a change of attitude, and the renunciation of the curse must be understood only as a vital stage in the process of humanity's revolutionary self-understanding and transformation.

The drama associates conscious and rationally articulated understanding of one's true historical situation with maleness. Act I dramatizes a sort of desperate masculine recognition that postures of aggression, even when dropped and transcended, still leave a vacuum so far as purposive action is concerned, and a collateral danger that revolutionary upheaval may at any time issue in an inverted status quo which merely apes its predecessor, and perpetuates an endless cycle of tyranny, retribution and new tyranny. Prometheus's self-transformation must be fused with other external forces and deeply internal impulses before this cycle – so recently and devastatingly worked through in the history of the French Revolution – may be broken for good. The external forces include a radically activated and self-consciously unified people, and also a natural world understood as potentially infinite in nourishment and beauty, but evolving under laws which need to be comprehended and harnessed by humanity. Some of these conceptions are carried by the figure of Demogorgon. The internal impulses, which in the logic of the poem's action must hurry to merge with Prometheus before his defeat of Jupiter issues in inverted tyranny, are love and strong feeling. These Shelley associates with femaleness, primarily in Act II. The poem's vision of a revolutionary human consciousness thus works by seeking a creative combination of qualities which are striated and ranged in opposition by the gendering and socializing codes of his own time (which still correspond in many ways to those of our own present social experience).

The poem as a whole operates partly by dramatizing dialectical interactions between concepts and qualities which were understood as opposites in Shelley's day: male and female; reason and feeling; Hebraic and Hellenic; East and West (Prometheus is identified with the founding European civilization of Greece, Asia with the then newly known religions and civilizations of India and the Far East). These oppositions are at the same time worked in terms of metaphoric contrasts between winter and spring, night and day, frozen colourless rock and a verdurous prismatic warmth. The poem's great wealth of apparently incidental natural description effects temporal and seasonal transitions between Acts I and III: the change, for example, between the closing lines of Act I and Asia's first speech in Act II is a singularly beautiful but also very carefully engineered effect.

Shelley's *dramatic* sense in *Prometheus Unbound* is easy to underestimate. There is irony in the way in which a reformed Prometheus, unable in his newly redeemed consciousness to recall the specific terms of the curse he wishes to retract, calls up the image of his oppressor to repeat it for him, and thus painfully enacts again his own original self-cursing – for this is what his curse amounted to. And there is similarly sharp dramatic irony, coupled with acute social observation, in the representation of Mercury, in Act I, as the corrupt intellectual who knowingly throws in his lot with an evil regime for the sake of comfort and self-advancement. His cynical interrogation of Prometheus combines mock-pitying mock-bafflement at Prometheus's ostensibly futile heroism in resistance with a cunning attempt to wheedle out the secret which Prometheus holds at the expense of Mercury's master, Jupiter. There are numerous such ironies, operating locally within the text and at large in the very structure of the action – Jupiter is right, for instance, to embrace Demogorgon as his son and heir, but utterly wrong in his understanding of what he has spawned – which would require far more extensive discussion than is possible in the present context. But it must be insisted that the play is most profoundly conscious of its own formal possibilities, and of the extent and complexity of the basic problems with which it is concerned – the origin and destiny of evil, the nature of human agency in historical change, the relationship between mental categories and material reality. Indeed, understanding has long been limited by the sheer originality and strangeness of Shelley's formal conception. The sustained and elaborately worked-out deployment of volcanic imagery has been understood at all only relatively recently, and yet its presence is by no means decorative, but literally structural. The time-scheme of the action is most important. It is crucial to realize that considerable time elapses between the first and second acts, for instance (Panthea's descriptions of Prometheus to Asia in Act II, scene i, do not correspond to the action of the first act), for this has direct bearing on the kind of historical process which the play is envisaging. It is also inevitable that the action of Act II is later than, and contingent upon, the action of Act I (as Act III follows Act II). The various actions with their accumulating and merging consequences cannot coherently be thought of as co-instantaneous (as they frequently have been), because of the linear and dialectical nature of the revolutionary crisis in Shelley's analysis of it, in the play and elsewhere.

Several features of this extraordinarily rich poem remain misunderstood, indeed scarcely noticed: the reiterated preoccupation with prophecy and oracular pronouncement, for example, by which Shelley bridges physical and volcanic elements, and his concern with the mutually determining relationship of human consciousness and historical development; or the attempt to find a dramatic equivalent for the relationship between permanently existing (because immaterial) mental forms and temporary but material things, such as individual people or the natural world. In fact the very status of the 'characters' whose words and actions constitute the play makes a difficult and strange demand on the reader. Their mode of operation is sceptical and syncretic. They clearly identify with concepts of various kinds – Asia is love, her sisters are related forms of love, and so on – but they also identify with different past human attempts to imagine expressive forms for these concepts. Prometheus, for instance, is made at many points to suggest Christ too, and similarly Jupiter may suggest the God of the Old Testament, while the style or shaping of the play from moment to moment may invoke a Greek or Renaissance or Romantic idiom of understanding. It is of the essence of Shelley's intelligence that he should represent the great crisis of his own time in a way that at once universalizes and relativizes it.

It is appropriate to turn briefly, in conclusion, to *Adonais*. Readers have tended to agree that this is Shelley's best and most perfectly finished poem, an elegy for the dead John Keats which is given a powerful personal resonance. It is Shelley's own elegy too. It is a sophisticated and daring appropriation of a received literary idiom to startling new purposes, and the poem plays ironically on this fact. While following the conventional elegiac pattern of lament and inconsolable desolation in bereavement, gradually usurped by spiritual comfort which takes joy in the real immortality of the lost one,

Shelley's elegy resolutely avoids any connotation of the supernatural or transcendent in his handling of the developing mood. The poem assumes that Keats has been murdered by his socially and politically hostile reviewers, particularly those of the *Quarterly Review* (Shelley in fact mistakenly thought it was Southey); but this is not merely fanciful, or neurotically exaggerated on Shelley's part, but simply consistent with his pervasive assumption that Keats, living through his writings while alive, will live through them immortally once the obscuring clouds of the reviews have cleared. Shelley's own poem, in anticipating Keats's ascent to his true status, itself helps to bring it about. Like the 'Ode to the West Wind', Shelley's elegy is the agent of its own prophecy.

*Adonais* borrows heavily from the language and imagery of Platonism, but the poem does not endorse the Platonic conception of a really existent higher realm. Keats's immortality will take the form of endless mental reincarnations in the minds of idealistic young readers, as they come again and again to his poetry for the first time:

> The splendours of the firmament of time
> May be eclipsed, but are extinguished not;
> Like stars to their appointed height they climb
> And death is a low mist which cannot blot
> The brightness it may veil. When lofty thought
> Lifts a young heart above its mortal lair,
> And love and life contend in it, for what
> Shall be its earthly doom, the dead live there
> And move like winds of light on dark and stormy air.
>
> (388–96)

But the quality of the poem cannot be understood except in a careful attention to its intricate patterns of connecting imagery; strikingly, patterns of seasonal variation, especially in flowers, of light and its opposites, night and clouds and mists, together with its immutable incarnations, particularly in stars. These patterns animate the language of *Adonais* in every stanza, constantly enlarging its associations and scale of utterance, and in mutual exchange with the unfolding drama of the poem's argument.

It is easy nowadays to mistake at first the poem's highly literary and even learned idiom for an excluding élitism, particularly when a classical education no longer forms part of the average poetry reader's background. But few poems better repay fierce effort. The whole conception of the poem should be grasped as in graceful honour of its dead subject. *Adonais* differs from other English elegies – such as Milton's *Lycidas* or Arnold's 'Thyrsis' – in that the dead man is celebrated throughout as a more important poet than the author; which, indeed, is what Shelley really judged Keats to be. Thus the poem is a courteously elaborated compliment. It is in formal Greek dress because Keats had been sneered at as an uneducated Cockney guttersnipe. It is in Spenserian stanzas because Spenser was Keats's favourite poet when Shelley knew him. And *Adonais* is filled with remembrances, material or glancing, of Keats's own poems, beginning with the title itself. The name 'Adonais' offended Shelley's classicist friends as an apparently hybrid word making reference to the vegetation-season-god Adonis and to the Greek pastoral elegists associated with his name – Theocritus, Bion and Moschus. The title certainly includes these associations, but Shelley probably also intends to associate the 'fading melodies' of Keats with those at the end of his own 'Ode to a Nightingale'. The Greek word for a nightingale is $\dot{\alpha}\eta\delta\acute{o}\nu o\varsigma$ ($\dot{\alpha}\delta\acute{o}\nu o\varsigma$ in the Doric dialect), and it is appropriate that the poem should begin in a graceful classical pun alluding to Keats's poetry, when the poem itself is so deftly and ingeniously rich in such allusion. These allusions begin in the second paragraph of the Preface when Shelley says of the Protestant cemetery at Rome – resting-place not only of Keats but of Shelley's son William – that it 'might make one in love with death, to think that one should be buried in so sweet a place'. In the poem itself these references are very numerous, and function in a variety of ways. 'Mountain shepherds' come to mourn Adonais because Endymion was a mountain shepherd. Adonais could 'scale Heaven' like an eagle because Keats's masterpiece in Shelley's view, the *Hyperion* fragments, was an epic about the sun-god. Keats's spirit's sister is the nightingale; his limbs are washed from a lucid urn; and the 'many-coloured glass' that stains the white radiance of eternity commemorates the casement 'innumerable of stains' that broke the moonlight into colours over the dream-imprisoned Madeline in 'The Eve of St Agnes'.

The supreme irony which pervades *Adonais* is the relevance of its vision to Shelley's own career as a poet. There is a famous self-portrait in the poem, but this has been misunderstood. It is undoubtedly self-pitying and weakly defeated in manner, but this is dramatically appropriate, because it comes in the first movement of the poem, which is very dark in mood and unable to command any optimistic perspectives on the fate of Keats, let alone on the almost completely unsuccessful and unrecognized poet Shelley. It is in fact from the introduction of the self-portrait into the poem that its dominant mood starts to lift and its perspectives to alter. And yet, in the end, there is a radical ambivalence in Shelley's sense of his own achievement as a writer, as this is formulated in *Adonais*. The closing stanzas are triumphant in their willingness to embrace death as the entry to that kind of life which poetry enjoys. But for Shelley, uncertain and modest in his sense of his own abilities, welcoming the prospect of death can seem also like a brave acceptance of what he takes to be failure. Great poetry lives on, but the person simply dies. As ever, Shelley builds a sceptical reserve into the claims even of his best work.

# 11

## KEATS

### David B. Pirie

I

Keats lived in London, the political hub of a country in crisis; and the five years from 1815 to 1819, in which he composed very nearly all of his extant poems, were, for the society in which he lived and worked, momentous. In 1815 the long war with Napoleonic France was finally concluded at Waterloo, and the map of the European world was to be redrawn. That war had begun, two years before Keats was born, as a conflict between a revolutionary French regime, trumpeting its commitment to equality, and a reactionary British government, terrified that the infection of democracy might cross the Channel and subvert the English people. For a quarter of a century that hope or fear had dominated British politics.

By the time Keats was writing, whole areas of the country would have been ungovernable without a virtual army of occupation. Of the 155 new barracks built in England between 1792 and 1815, many had been sited not in the south, to prevent a French invasion, but in the disaffected areas of the Midlands and the north.[1] In his letters Keats attacks these 'extensive barracks which disgusted [him] extremely with government'; and argues that the 'worst thing' which 'Napoleon has done' is teach the British government and its 'Divine Right gentlemen . . . how to organize their monstrous armies'.[2] An elaborate system of spies gave the army some notable successes. Mass executions at Lancaster and Chester and York followed the show trials of Luddites – with fourteen men being hanged, in two batches of seven, on a single day at York in 1813; and in 1817 the cavalry were ready and waiting to ambush the Pentridge rebels as they made their armed march on the garrison city of Nottingham.

1 E. P. Thompson, *The Making of the English Working Class*, London, 1965, p 605.
2 *The Letters of John Keats 1814–1821*, ed. H. E. Rollins, 2 vols, Cambridge, Mass., 1958, i. 131–2, 397.

Nevertheless, throughout 1818 the numbers joining the protest marches and demonstrations, in hopes of gaining what we might now regard as minimal human rights, swelled, and the authorities were close to panic. Or perhaps they found it expedient to exaggerate the threat. Certainly Keats suspected that they were using the 'unlucky termination' of the French Revolution as a pretext for reversing the 'grand march of intellect' and the 'progress of free sentiments', for 'turning back to the despotism of the 16th Century'. According to Keats, the Government had 'made a handle of this event . . . to undermine our freedom'.[1]

With that plural first-person pronoun '*our*', Keats may merely be reminding the friend to whom this letter is addressed that, as intellectuals, they both value the freedom of expression which the Government's censorship laws were designed to repress. However, Keats may be identifying himself here, as he certainly is when using that trope on many other occasions in his verse and prose, with an infinitely larger group than his own, small, fairly well-educated circle of London friends. Keats often identifies his own first-person voice with the vast majority of his fellow-citizens – with all who were still disenfranchised; with those who, though in many cases still illiterate, were nevertheless increasingly vociferous in making their own demands; with those who, later in the nineteenth century, would be called the working classes but are here, in Keats's letter, still repeatedly described as 'the multitude' and 'the people'. One of my aims in this essay is to show how plural pronouns may have made many of Keats's poems sound, in their frequent use of 'we' and 'our' and 'us', more politicized to his contemporaries than they seem to us today – more obtrusively community-spirited, more knowingly egalitarian, perhaps even more brashly demagogic.

Keats was never rich enough to have a vote. He trained as a doctor – a profession of lower social status than today – because he assumed he would have to work for a living. His parents had earned theirs in the business of stabling other people's horses. To conservative reviewers at least, Keats's position in the social hierarchy was clear; as a would-be poet he was risibly low caste. Yet Keats himself seems to have sometimes feared that his literary ambitions might, in addressing a pampered élite, be taking him too far away from the majority. There is in some of his writings an audible anxiety that his

---

1 *Letters*, ii. 192–4. For Keats's belief that 'there is really a grand march of intellect' which, as society develops, gradually frees humanity from 'dogmas and superstitions', see *Letters*, i. 282.

relatively privileged life amongst the London intelligentsia might cut him off from the ordinary people of England, insulating him from the pain of their poverty and the effort of their struggle for human rights. As early as 1816 Keats promised to make his verse confront 'the agonies, the strife/Of human hearts' ('Sleep and Poetry', 124–5); but by 1819 the poet who knows he should be amongst 'those to whom the miseries of the world/Are misery and will not let them rest' fears that he and his cultured friends are still 'dreamers weak', and that they have no adequate answer to the accusing question, 'What benefit canst thou do, or all thy tribe,/To the great world?' (*The Fall of Hyperion*, i, 148–9, 162–8).

The guilt may have been triggered by specific news from the north. In August 1819, at a Manchester political rally, the yeomanry had been sent in, with sabres drawn, to attack tens of thousands of unarmed men, women and children. The coining of 'Peterloo' as the name for this massacre accused the repressive Tory government of still waging a war against its own citizens, long after the defeat of Napoleon and any threat from abroad. However embarrassed at his own inability to influence the outcome, Keats was in no doubt as to which side he wanted to win. As he followed events in 'The present struggle of the people in England' he observed that 'what has rous'd them to do it is their distresses' and decided: 'This is no contest between Whig and tory – but between right and wrong.'[1]

Although new, oppressive laws had invested the Cabinet with unprecedented power, Keats still managed, the year after Peterloo, to compose a poem of defiant optimism: 'In after-time . . .' This prophesies that the British people will eventually triumph. They will find the strength to overpower both of the key weapons wielded by the Government: its partisan lawcourts and its brutal army. The dissemination of ideas and information through the printing-press will, in spite of the savage censorship laws, eventually inspire the people to exercise their latent but gigantic power. Though Keats wrote the poem in 1820 he was already so ill that he would compose no more verse. As one of his friends remarked, when publishing 'In after-time . . .' as 'the last stanza, of any kind, that he wrote': 'it may be said, he died with his pen wielded in the cause of Reform.'[2]

1 *Letters*, ii. 193–4.
2 Charles Brown in *Plymouth and Devonport Weekly Journal*, 4 July 1839; quoted in *The Poems of John Keats*, ed. Jack Stillinger, Cambridge, Mass., 1978, p 484.

It could also be said that what may be his first poem,[1] written just seven years earlier, is devoted to the same cause. The sonnet 'On Peace', written after England's defeat of France in 1814, is an explicit plea for 'liberty'. The poem tells those European nations whose 'chains' were 'burst' by the French Revolution that they must demand a postwar settlement where they remain 'free', however much 'sceptred tyrants' try to make them cower in their 'former state'. In another early poem, 'Written on 29 May, the Anniversary of the Restoration of Charles II', Keats jeers at the public festivities that were still organized each year on that date, and at those 'Infatuate Britons' whose besotted reverence for monarchy makes them support the junketing. For liberals like Keats the date on which England had abandoned its idealistic republicanism was an occasion for sorrow and anger. It represented the nation's 'direst, foulest shame'. Far from celebrating the restored monarchy, the people should mourn and 'revere' those 'patriots' who had in earlier times tried to overthrow it. Such heroes, when their plots had been discovered, had been executed as traitors; but, to Keats's ear, the real treason could be heard now, in these royalist celebrations that sought to sanctify the squalor of the current Establishment. The great betrayal of a Commonwealth that might have built a just society was audible in every 'traitorous lying bell' rung at such anniversaries by the Tory government's great ally, the Church of England.

Even on an ordinary Sunday morning 'church bells' could provoke Keats into composing another subversive poem. His lines 'Written in Disgust of Vulgar Superstition' complain that the bell-ringer's 'melancholy round' stops 'the people' enjoying themselves. The church summons them, on their one day of rest, away from 'converse' with each other. Once lured into the service and 'hearkening to the sermon's horrid sound', people may be intimidated by the horror stories of hell-fire. The poem itself, however, aims for self-confidence, and prophesies eventual 'oblivion' for the Anglican propagandists.

---

1 Editors place it second in the sequence after 'Imitation of Spenser'. The latter, like 'On Peace', cannot be dated more precisely than some time early in 1814. Charles Brown did describe it as Keats's 'earliest attempt', but in the context of claiming that 'The Faery Queen . . . awakened his genius' and that 'enamoured of the stanza, he attempted to imitate it.' Brown then remarked that 'the "Imitation of Spenser" is in his first volume of Poems', so he may have meant only that it was the earliest of Keats's *published* poems ('On Peace' was first printed in *Notes and Queries* in 1904). See *The Keats Circle: Letters and Papers 1816–1879*, ed. H. E. Rollins, 2 vols, Cambridge, Mass., 1965, ii. 55–6.

II

None of the last four poems mentioned was published in Keats's lifetime. At a time when the Government often used the laws of blasphemous libel to suppress political writing, fear of prosecution could prevent a great range of work being published. But fear of conservative reviewers and the lost sales they could cause may have played as large a part.

What is far more extraordinary than Keats's self-censorship, at a time of such risks for writer and printer, is the behaviour of his sillier critics in the twentieth century. With the benefit of the entire *œuvre* before them, they have still tended to blind themselves to Keats's politics. Admittedly, few would now risk the unqualified nonsense of that Oxford professor of literature, Sir Arthur Quiller-Couch, who announced: 'Keats has no politics ... little social feeling. He is the young apostle of poetry for poetry's sake.' Many, however, still encourage an almost exclusive concentration on a relatively few poems – those that can, with suitably selective extracts from Keats's letters, be glossed as implying that the professor, though guilty of exaggeration, was right enough about the poems that matter.

One of the most popular candidates for such status is still the 'Ode on a Grecian Urn', from which he quoted the slogan 'Beauty is truth, truth beauty'. Put this in the context of an oft-used quotation from Keats's letters – where he suggests that great works of art make 'all disagreeables evaporate, from their being in close relationship with Beauty and Truth' – and Keats can seem to favour the kind of truth that took him as far as possible from the ugly realities of contemporary British politics. What has to be suppressed is the fact that the very same paragraph of the same letter has just celebrated the 'very encouraging' news about William Hone, the radical publisher who had just been found not guilty of libel. The opposite result – another success for the Government in its sequence of show trials designed to intimidate their critics into silence – would, Keats writes, 'have dulled still more Liberty's Emblazoning'; instead Hone has 'done *us* an essential service'. The same letter ends with Keats's report that his militantly subversive friend Shelley has followed up his notorious poem *Queen Mab* by publishing *Laon and Cythna*, a work that risks 'being objected to as much'.[1] It is in such politically charged contexts – at a time when both sides, in the struggle over

1 *Letters*, i. 191–4.

reform, had only literature to use as the medium of propaganda, and when the censorship laws were being applied with unprecedented viciousness – that Keats is triggered to explore the relationship of beauty to truth.

A less selective reading of this famous letter might relate it not only to the 'Urn' but also to one of Keats's most indisputably political poems, 'Nebuchadnezzar's Dream', which praises Hone as a 'Daniel' before whose truth the 'lying lips' of tyranny 'turn pale'.[1] But 'Nebuchadnezzar's Dream', like the letter's praise of Hone and so much of Keats's writing, is ignored by – perhaps censored from – most critical commentary. Keats wrote no fewer than 150 works in verse, and some of these are large-scale achievements: *Otho the Great* is a full-length, five-act play,[2] while *Endymion* is a narrative poem that runs to 4,000 lines. In prose too the productivity impresses: no fewer than 320 letters survive, the longest of which covers twenty-five pages of print; and the best of his letters, in shrewdness of thought, subtlety of emotion and the precision and energy of their style, lead some to value Keats's prose almost as much as his verse. Yet this output, so massive for an author who died when he was just twenty-five, is too often defined by reference to no more than a couple of dozen, arguably atypical, extracts.

Another passage from the letters, favoured by those who wish to construct Keats as an apolitical aesthete, celebrates 'the authenticity of the Imagination'. Here he describes himself as 'certain of nothing but of the holiness of the Heart's affections and the truth of Imagination – What the Imagination seizes as Beauty must be truth.'[3] However, for Keats, the heart's affections often compel an inclusive philanthropy – a compassion that demands change towards social justice; and his verse can deploy 'Imagination' itself as a key term in an essentially egalitarian rhetoric. *The Fall of Hyperion*, in its very opening lines, insists that the supposedly rare quality of

1 Critics who make much of Keats's 'development' should logically treat this letter, which was written in December 1817, as more relevant to 'Nebuchadnezzar's Dream' (which was also written in 1817, and probably in December) than to 'Ode on a Grecian Urn' (which was not composed until spring 1819 at the earliest). For Keats's knowledge and use of the legal and political events of 1817, see Aileen Ward, 'Keats's Sonnet, "Nebuchadnezzar's Dream"', *Philological Quarterly*, XXXIV. ii (April 1955), 177–88.

2 The play was to some extent a collaborative venture with Keats's friend Charles Brown. Brown reports supplying much of the plot (though not the incidents of Act V), while Keats's task was 'to embody it into poetry' (*The Keats Circle*, ii. 66).

3 *Letters*, i. 184.

'Imagination' is shared by all human beings, even those whose alien culture seems to us so primitive that we label them 'savage'. The tragedy, for Keats, is that the vast majority, unlike the few famous poets of the past whom we revere, have lacked the language-skills to record their experience for posterity. The 'pity' is that

> these have not
> Traced upon vellum or wild Indian leaf
> The shadows of melodious utterance.

Thus:

> bare of laurel they live, dream, and die;
> For Poesy alone can tell her dreams . . .

It is only 'the fine spell of words' that 'can save/Imagination' from 'dumb enchantment', that unjust silence to which the passage of time has condemned nearly all our ancestors.

Now these lines were almost certainly written in September 1819,[1] just after Henry Hunt, who had been the leading speaker at Peterloo less than a month earlier, made his 'triumphal entry into London'. The phrase comes from Keats's own eyewitness account, which focuses on the sheer scale of Hunt's popularity – the 'multitudes' who marched with him in his vast procession or lined the route to applaud him. Hunt's eloquence had, years ago, earned him the nickname 'Orator Hunt'; and it was the spellbinding vigour and clarity with which he voiced their own, barely articulate dreams of a juster society that mattered so much to his supporters. Many of these would themselves have been wholly illiterate and most would be so relatively uneducated as to have little confidence in their own verbal skills. Without such a voice to speak on their behalf, to 'save/ Imagination from . . . dumb enchantment', their aspirations would continue to be ignored by that culturally privileged, relatively rich minority who constituted most of Keats's own potential readership. These genteel readers would want to rationalize away the demands of the Manchester workers who had demonstrated at Peterloo. Such readers might also choose to interpret the cheers of the London mob, bellowing forth its loud-mouthed welcome, as evidence of a coarseness that was innate, proof that the common people were born to be irredeemably less subtle, less capable of judgement than those appointed to govern them; that those distinctions between the

---

1 Hunt made his 'triumphal entry' on 13 September (*Letters*, ii. 194); just over a week later, on the 21st, Keats sent the opening lines of *The Fall of Hyperion* to a friend (*Letters*, ii. 172).

short-sightedness of the many and the vision of the few – the distinctions that had justified earlier generations of working people being left disenfranchised – could still be drawn just as firmly amongst those who were alive in modern England.

So the opening passage of *The Fall of Hyperion*, after mourning the silenced majorities of the dead past, proceeds to attack any living pundit who still uses his privileged voice, in the contemporary debate, to silence others:

> Who alive can say,
> 'Thou art no poet; may'st not tell thy dreams'?
> Since every man whose soul is not a clod
> Hath visions, and would speak, if he had . . .
> . . . been well-nurtured in his mother tongue.
>
> (i. 11–15)

The English language did not belong to the conservative reviewers and their class allies – nor in fact to Keats, who, in his sonnet about the sonnet form, characteristically writes of '*our* English' ('If by dull rhymes . . .', 1). English belonged by a law as natural as genetic inheritance to everyone alive in England at the time; it was their 'mother tongue'. If a monstrous society had not deprived most of its citizens of a decent education, if instead it had ensured that their minds were as 'well-nurtured' as their bodies should be, then all would speak out of their own poetic souls.

### III

Now Keats would have met in works by the younger Wordsworth this egalitarian idea that a peasant was a silent poet, that an uneducated shepherd's emotions were at least as subtle and profound as those of the pampered minority who had the wealth and leisure for study. But the older Wordsworth, far from being the poet of social justice, now often seemed the high priest of a thoroughly antisocial nature-worship – a voice crying in the wilderness, 'Keep out. To enjoy this, I have to be alone!' By the time Keats published his first volume of poems, in 1817 at the age of twenty-one, an older generation of poets – like Wordsworth and Southey and Coleridge – were in their mid- or late forties. They were now congratulating themselves on having matured into Tories. They remembered their own misspent youth as one of naïve idealism. They themselves had then been gulled by the blissful but false dawn of the French Revolution into perpetrating far too much poetic nonsense. They too had ranted about the brotherhood of man and the desirability of radically altering society. Now, after the sour lesson of France had been fully learnt, verse should, they believed, be far more prudent. It should concentrate on the private intensities of individual experience – such as those one might feel when alone amongst 'wild unpeopled hills'.[1]

From a Tory reader's point of view such verse had at the very least a negative virtue: it could never seduce people into valuing each other so highly that they put social justice above loyalty to God and King. Its celebration of solitude would encourage no one to join the crowds at that series of political rallies which led to Peterloo – crowds who marched behind banners announcing that a changed society could only be achieved by working together, that the way to 'be Free' was 'to Unite'.[2] At best, for a conservative, literature that reverenced the unalterable forms of an ancient landscape might positively encourage faith in the long-established, traditional systems of government. It might suggest that natural laws, as permanent and unchallengeable as those that maintained the ascendancy of hill over valley, ensured that the ruling class must always rule over a labouring class that must always labour. Of course those natural laws might be seen as evidence of the Christian God who had created them; they might be understood as the self-imposed rules within which an omnipotent deity had originally moulded his mountains, as well as his divinely appointed monarchies. If so, the Church-and-State reader could see landscape verse as doubly loyal to timeless truths.

Back in 1798 Coleridge, summarizing his poem 'France: An Ode' (or 'The Recantation'), had already identified the formative events from which a fashion for the more introspective verse of solitary nature-worship had grown. Earlier poetry about 'Freedom' had proved so downright dangerous as to force the true poet towards a new definition, one that pinpointed the only kind of 'liberty' that in future it would be safe to explore. The French Revolution had, after all, declined, through 'The blasphemies and horrors of the Terrorists', into tyrannical imperialism. This, for Coleridge, proved that the 'grand ideal of Freedom' does 'not belong to men, as a society,

---

1 'The Old Cumberland Beggar', l 14. Other lines of this early poem conveniently demonstrate the extent to which Keats, though so exasperated by Wordsworth's politics, was often impressed by his poetry. In another passage politicians are rebuked for their patronizing attitude towards the poor and reminded that 'we all of us have one human heart' – a line Keats was still quoting with approval even after he had had to record his disgust at the older poet's 'sad, sad, sad' willingness to act as election agent for the Tory Lord Lowther (*Letters*, i. 299 and ii. 80).

2 Robert Walmsley, *Peterloo: The Case Reopened*, Manchester, 1969, p 152.

nor can possibly be ... realized, under any form of human government'; instead, feelings of true liberty are available only 'to the individual man, so far as he is ... inflamed with the love and adoration of God in Nature'.[1] Keats's first volume, *Poems* (1817), in this context of a lesson that history had supposedly taught a full twenty years earlier, was bound to strike many of its first readers as deviant; to conservative reviewers it could seem wilfully defiant. One section of the book, far from reporting lonely meditations, is devoted to epistles to friends.

In the first of these epistles, 'To George Felton Mathew', the poet, conventionally enough, hopes to 'find/Some flowery spot, sequestered, wild, romantic' (36–7); but, perversely, he does not want to go there alone – he is not seeking that solitude in which he might focus on Coleridge's 'God in Nature'. Instead the idea of the trip 'is vain' unless Mathew joins him. Then the countryside would become a shared viewpoint from which they can both care about society and swap radical versions of political history: 'Where we may soft humanity put on' (55), where 'We ... could tell/Of those who in the cause of freedom fell' (65–6).

The next epistle, 'To My Brother George', offers a comparable false lead. Here, ideal poets are at first described as those who 'Fly from all sorrowing far, far away' (20). He 'whose head is pregnant with poetic lore' might go out alone, on 'an evening ramble', and receive amazing visions (53–66). This, however, is not the high spot in a true poet's career. The 'richer far' moment comes later, when others will read his words and feel inspired to take political action:

> The patriot shall feel
> My stern alarum, and unsheathe his steel,
> Or in the senate thunder out my numbers
> To startle princes from their easy slumbers.
>
> (73–6)

The third epistle, 'To Charles Cowden Clarke', has a similarly explicit passage, praising its addressee for his libertarian view of history, in which 'the patriot's stern duty' is best exemplified by 'The hand of Brutus, that so grandly fell/Upon a tyrant's head' (69–72). Both of these poems pay their compliments to a modern patriot who defies tyranny: Leigh Hunt. In 'To Charles Cowden Clarke',

1  S. T. Coleridge, 'Argument' supplied for 'France: An Ode' when the poem (which had first been published on 16 April 1798) made its second appearance in the *Morning Post*, 14 October 1802. See *The Poems of Samuel Taylor Coleridge*, ed. E. H. Coleridge, Oxford, 1912, p 244.

Hunt is 'The wronged Libertas' (45); and the same nickname makes him synonymous with freedom in 'To My Brother George' (24).

However, this poem is more slyly subversive elsewhere. A later passage ridicules the massive army with which the Government was then trying to control its people; but this jeer emerges from an innocent-seeming description of wild poppies growing as weeds amongst a 'field . . . of oats'. These 'show their scarlet coats,/So pert and useless, that they bring to mind/The scarlet coats that pester human-kind' (127–30). It is such a discreetly localized protest – 'scarlet coats' is less defiantly obvious than 'redcoats' – that readers now can miss it entirely; but it exemplifies the kind of hints that were provokingly clear to conservative readers at the time. 'Even in their favourite descriptions of nature', complained one reviewer of the 1817 volume, liberal poets like Keats were 'too fond . . . of a reference to the factitious resemblances of society'.[1]

A different poem addressed 'To My Brother George' in the 1817 volume – a sonnet – devotes a dozen lines to celebrating the 'Many . . . wonders' of the natural world; but these descriptions, through anthropomorphic imagery and a borrowing from Shelley's notorious *Queen Mab*,[2] already anticipate the peculiarly human solidarity which will be privileged in the closing couplet:

> But what, without the social thought of thee,
> Would be the wonders of the sky and sea?

One of the 1817 sonnets does manage, in its first words, a reverent invocation 'O Solitude . . .', but even this ends by insisting that 'the highest bliss of human-kind' is that contradiction in terms, a solitude shared with someone else. Another sonnet describes, for its first ten lines, a Wordsworthian walk alone in the countryside. At first the poet thinks that the joy he feels while admiring the wild flowers cannot be surpassed; but in the last four lines this is exposed as a delusion and the poem's title – 'To a Friend . . .' – explained. The poet recalls an earlier occasion when he was given some garden flowers as a token of friendship. Those cultivated roses, once remembered, are recognized as in fact far superior to the wild flowers, because they speak, 'with tender plea', 'of truth and Friendliness unquelled'.

One contemporary reviewer of the 1817 poems described them as 'changeful . . . as much alive to the *socialities* . . . as to the

1 *Edinburgh Magazine and Literary Miscellany* (*Scots Magazine*), October 1817; reprinted in G. M. Matthews, *Keats: The Critical Heritage*, London, 1971, p 72.
2 See ll 10–12 (where the moon is 'half-discovered' in the 'revels' of 'her bridal night'), and line 4 (where 'feathery gold' echoes *Queen Mab*, ii. 16).

contemplative beauties of nature'.[1] At numerous points where the volume might strike us now as blandly devoted to the most innocuous topics, it would for its first readers have confirmed the reviewer's judgement; and it was a judgement on an issue that then mattered a great deal. At the time, to weigh a poem's commitment to the 'socialities' of 'humanity and Friendliness unquelled' relative to its faith in 'the contemplative beauties of nature' could function as a litmus test of its author's politics. Another 1817 sonnet, 'On Leaving Some Friends at an Early Hour', longs for 'a golden pen' with which repeatedly to 'write down' some 'line of glorious tone', and the explanation for this urgent need is at once odd and yet highly characteristic. The solitary poet, already missing the company of his friends and 'not content . . . to be alone', sees the act of writing as a means of reunion. The composition of verse, far from enacting some desirable escape from society, is useful precisely because it expresses his sociability and thus allows the poet to resume, at least in his mind's eye, his true place amongst his fellows.

## IV

Those of the 1817 poems that focus on personal friendship would belong logically enough, to the minds of their first readers, in the same volume as passages that articulate a more inclusive, more obviously political solidarity. Indeed the two are on occasion wholly inseparable, since some of Keats's friends were already notorious; and it was their denunciation of the Government that, in progressive circles, had earned them renown and, amongst more conservative readers, infamy. Right at the front of *Poems* Keats published an affectionate sonnet dedicating the entire volume 'To Leigh Hunt, Esq.', a name which, perhaps more than any other, was likely to enrage conservative reviewers. Leigh Hunt (though no relation of Henry Hunt, and less militant in his politics) was well known not just as a poet but also as a campaigning journalist. His verbal war against Establishment lies and lunacies had been conducted mainly in the sturdily liberal magazine that he edited, the *Examiner*. This had been regularly read by Keats as a schoolboy and had, according to a fellow pupil, 'laid the foundation of his love of civil and religious liberty'.[2] Keats did not actually meet his hero and become a regular

---

1 *Edinburgh Magazine and Literary Miscellany* (*Scots Magazine*), October 1817; reprinted in *Keats: The Critical Heritage*, p 72.
2 Charles and Mary Cowden Clarke, *Recollections of Writers*, London, 1878, p 124.

member of Leigh Hunt's circle (which included friends as radical as Shelley) until October 1816; but he had already written – nearly two years earlier – a poem praising Hunt for resisting the censorship laws and enduring two years in prison. This poem too, 'Written on the Day that Mr Leigh Hunt Left Prison', was boldly included in the 1817 volume. Here Keats announces that Hunt's offending article about the Prince Regent had involved no more – and no less – than 'showing truth to flattered state'. The government lackey, who for the time being can decide when such a man as 'kind Hunt' is 'shut in prison' and when he is released, has only an illusory power. That mere 'Minion of grandeur', like the current regime's entire 'wretched crew', is doomed to an unqualified death. By contrast, a libertarian intellectual of Hunt's stature, who even in prison felt so 'free' that 'he flew/With daring Milton', has an 'immortal spirit'. Unimpaired by these transient attempts to discredit his work, Hunt's 'fame' will survive.

These two sonnets would have been sufficient on their own to prevent right-wing reviewers mistaking Keats for some aloof aesthete, harmlessly musing in a world of his own. Unsurprisingly, he was attacked by contemporary commentators not as an isolated target but precisely because he seemed the spokesperson for a group. One reviewer of the 1817 volume devoted his first sentence to pointing out that Keats was 'a particular friend' of such notoriously liberal journalists as Leigh Hunt and William Hazlitt.[1] John Lockhart, in his extraordinarily vicious review of the volume, heard an essentially collective voice being flaunted, and saw *Poems* as another manifesto for an entire 'Cockney School' – one which he explicitly defined as a school not only of 'poetry' but also of 'politics'.[2] What led such reviewers to interpret not just the dedicatory sonnet to Hunt but the volume itself as a deliberate act of political defiance? One of the ingredients that provoked at the time might now seem no more than Keats's healthy disregard for mere snobbery: for instance he included no fewer than three poems addressed to his brothers, and thus announced that he felt no shame about his family and its relatively

1 *Edinburgh Magazine and Literary Miscellany* (*Scots Magazine*), October 1817; reprinted in *Keats: The Critical Heritage*, p 71.
2 John Gibson Lockhart (anonymously, using pseudonym of 'Z'), 'Cockney School of Poetry – No. IV', *Blackwood's Edinburgh Magazine*, August 1818; reprinted in *Keats: The Critical Heritage*, pp 109, 110, 97. Keats had already been described as representing an entire 'school' of poetry by the *British Critic* in June 1818 and, even earlier, by the *Edinburgh Magazine* in October 1817; see *Keats: The Critical Heritage*, pp 94 and 73.

humble status. Lockhart seems to have regarded such candour as proof of a vulgarity that had to be crushed. He chose to describe Keats's medical knowledge as qualifying him for no loftier role than that of a chemist's shop assistant. Such an upstart daring to attempt poetry at all was, to Lockhart, a radical impertinence. In this too, Keats, far from being harmlessly eccentric, was supposedly all too typical of a new mood that had infected the lower orders. Lockhart complained that now 'footmen' imagined they could 'compose tragedies', and that even 'farm-servants' were threatening to invade the privileged realm of literature.

Sometimes in this 1817 volume Keats seems to have been almost inviting such an attack. For instance, one sonnet suggests that England's semi-literate labouring masses, the unrecorded 'people of no name', have a moral intelligence and a moral energy that are actually superior to anything found amongst the propertied classes. The latter may like to claim that the city slums and the remote countryside are populated by simpletons; but in fact, the poem claims, it is in those very places, 'In noisome alley, and in pathless wood', that

> Oft may be found a 'singleness of aim'
> That ought to frighten into hooded shame
> A money-mongering, pitiable brood.
>
> ('Addressed to Haydon')

This is polemical role-reversal. In Burke's sneering phrase it had been the 'multitude' who were 'swinish'; now, in Keats's sonnet, it is the privileged few who are pigs. It is they who are reduced to a subhuman rabble; they who, in the 'Envy and Malice' of their greedy, 'money-mongering' competitiveness, are reduced by their herd-like instincts to a 'pitiable *brood*'; they who sometimes run back 'to their native sty' when shamed by some 'stout unbending champion' of justice. Conversely it is in fact the much-maligned multitude who are the ones still possessed of truly human vision and thus able to recognize such a champion. It is precisely amongst the supposedly *lower* orders that true '*High*mindedness' is now to be found. The instinct to recognize and cherish what is just – that 'jealousy for good' – and the co-operative tendency to target what will benefit all – a 'singleness of aim' – are common human traits; and thus should be sought, where they are still common, amongst the uncorrupted masses of the common people. It is they who can still identify and admire a real champion of humanity.

However, the poem goes on to imply that these 'unnumbered

souls', most of whom are still barely literate, are not yet well equipped to articulate their moral insight. Instead of writing, or even speaking, about their heroes, they must merely 'breathe' out a 'still applause'. Like those lost generations in *The Fall of Hyperion*, whose 'Imagination' could not be saved from 'dumb enchantment', they are a relatively silent majority; and yet their views matter. For the American revolutionaries it had been explicitly 'all men' who, having been 'created equal', had 'inalienable rights'; and, in *The Fall of Hyperion* the true poet is, by definition, 'a sage,/A humanist, physician to *all* men' (i. 189–90). For Keats the notion that a poet should represent himself in proud isolation, as implicitly superior to ordinary people, is deeply puzzling, and he repeatedly challenges it. At one point in *The Fall of Hyperion*'s allegorical dream sequence the poet drinks a potion, while 'pledging all the mortals of the world'; but he then finds himself apparently being singled out as worthy of special access to the truth. The absurdity of this arouses immediate protest:

> 'Are there not thousands in the world,' said I, . . .
> 'Who love their fellows even to the death;
> Who feel the giant agony of the world;
> And more, like slaves to poor humanity,
> Labour for mortal good? I sure should see
> Other men here; but I am here alone.'
>
> (i. 154–60)

These 'thousands' had already been anticipated in the poem that closes the 1817 volume, 'Sleep and Poetry'. There Keats's resolution to confront 'the agonies, the strife/Of human Hearts' is followed by a vision of the charioteer-poet joining a mass procession, where 'thousands in a thousand different ways' march forward. The poet's task is to concentrate, 'Most awfully intent', on the various sounds that they make, 'to listen' to – and record in writing – their 'numerous tramplings' (122–54). In a sonnet that was not to be published by Keats, though he wrote it as early as April 1817, he can afford to offer some more obviously militant trampling: a prophetic vision of the people crushing under foot all authoritarian regimes: 'A trampling down of . . . Turbans and crowns and blank regality'. However, this sonnet, 'On Receiving a Laurel Crown from Leigh Hunt', is explicitly about the poet's embarrassment at being treated as the laureate of liberty when he has done so little to deserve it. Keats feels he is still offering only 'wild surmises/Of all the many glories that may be'.

An almost identical phrase – 'wild surmise' – had been used six months earlier in a poem that Keats did publish in the 1817 volume:

the sonnet beginning 'Much have I travelled in the realms of gold'. This is now one of Keats's best-known works, but even here the modern reader may miss the complex political ambiguities that energize this poem's famous conclusion, and many of the most powerful passages of other poems that Keats himself chose to publish. On the one hand the sonnet does contain hints that its first readers would have recognized as implicitly subversive; but on the other it also exercises its own self-censorship, ensuring that those hints are prudently muffled. Furthermore the sonnet confesses its unease at remaining so circumspect. At its most paradoxical the verse can seem almost noisy in the very act of drawing attention to its own evasive silence.

The sonnet's opening gesture, however, might seem shockingly direct and frank. To a patrician reviewer its title – 'On First Looking into Chapman's Homer' – volunteers at least two scandalous admissions: firstly, the author grew up in such plebeian circumstances that he had not glanced at the classic text of Greek literature before; secondly, he is still so ignorant of Greek that even now he has come no closer than Chapman's translation. Open celebration of a discovery so belated and indirect challenges all the snobberies on which social hierarchy depends. Those who would jeer at the low-caste, under-educated members of a Cockney School might expect such cultural poverty to be blushingly disguised. Instead it is blandly displayed, almost as a badge of pride; and the bravado is reiterated within the poem itself. Line 8 attributes the novice reader's excitement not to the discovery of Homer's own voice – nor even to reading Alexander Pope's elegantly restrained translation – but to having first 'heard Chapman speak out loud and bold', in a version that was conventionally understood to be so much coarser than Pope's as to smack of the primitive.

Yet one likely reason for this sonnet having later been so often picked out for praise is, ironically enough, a latent élitism in the famous image that at first does seem to focus with awed reverence on the singularity of 'stout Cortez'. Two-thirds of the way through the poem that great leader is discovered, as a one-off hero complete with his proper name and his unique vision, epitomized in those 'eagle eyes' with which he alone 'stared at the Pacific'. He is gazing at the vast ocean that represents Nature at its sublimely large-scale best; and doubtless, like other European conquerors of popular myth, he is a sufficiently devout, heretic-slaughtering Christian to be now contemplating also the majesty of the God who created all this water. He has thus stationed himself, as the Coleridge of 'France: An Ode' would advise, in a pose that allows him to face Nature and God.

But to do so he has probably had to turn his back on innumerable human companions, all those other ranks who have obediently followed the general to this vantage point. Indeed the tableau may provoke the thought that it is, in a sense, they who have brought him here, and not the other way round. Without their assistance Cortez could never, working alone, have hacked for himself a path through jungle and hostile natives. It may be that a whole army of walk-on parts, of mere spear-carriers, has been necessary to carry the hero of this drama to its climactic scene – one in which he then looks away from them. They are apparently being ignored by their leader, oblivious to ordinary people in the reverie of his egotistical sublime. But – and this is surely the crucial point – they are not ignored by the poem. The sonnet's closing lines turn back from the singular Cortez to focus instead upon the plural mass of his followers – 'all his men' who 'look' not over the warlord's shoulder, at the Pacific, but 'at each other with a wild surmise – silent upon a peak in Darien'.

The sonnet thus reaches a conclusion so inconclusive, so untamed as to seem wild indeed; and just what the men have in mind must remain to some extent an enigma, one about which the curious reader too can only surmise. However, the direction of the sonnet's sudden swerve is clear – and challengingly so. It lurches away from the individual hero's awed meditation, and towards that far more restless, less controlled group-consciousness with which his people look, not to him, but to each other. They could be looking for information in their puzzlement; they could be seeking support in their fear; it is even possible that they are looking around, now that the general's back is turned, hoping to discover fellow conspirators – to see in other faces confirmation that they too are indulging in 'wild surmises' about what would happen if they were to trample down their leader's 'blank regality'. They could, in looking to each other, be looking forward to 'the many glories that may be' if only they could all nerve themselves to break ranks. The poem, which is itself 'Looking into' a book and can make only 'Chapman speak out', leaves them opaquely 'silent'. It cannot or will not – or perhaps it dare not – tell us more than that it is finally arrested, not by the singular warlord, but by the 'wild surmise' shared by his troops.

V

By the time the 1817 volume was published Keats had already begun a major narrative poem, *Endymion*, a work that does, at some points, merge the voice of its poetic storyteller – traditionally a figure of detached singularity – with that of thousands of others: a 'crowd', 'a multitude that reared/Their voices' in unison (i. 161–5). In attempting a more egalitarian, more plural voice, the poem opposed powerful literary conventions that were by contrast implicitly élitist. The fashion was for poetry that focused on the singularity of supposedly superior individuals. Even as liberal and optimistic a critic as William Hazlitt had recently complained that high literature, in any 'arguments on . . . the privileges of the few and the claims of the many',[1] seemed bound to side with the Establishment. The essay that supported this sobering proposition had made a deep impression upon Keats when he first read it, in the *Examiner*, the year before embarking on *Endymion*. According to Hazlitt, the plural 'many' are simply *too* many to be well served by current definitions of poetry. Poetry tends to concentrate on the untypical few or even on the unique individual. In fact 'the cause of the people is indeed but little calculated as a subject of poetry':

The principle of poetry is a very anti-levelling principle . . . Kings, priests, nobles, are its train-bearers . . . It puts the individual for the species, the one above the infinite many, might before right. A lion hunting a flock of sheep . . . is a more poetical object than they; and we even take part with the lordly beast, because our vanity . . . makes us disposed to place ourselves in the situation of the strongest party . . . There is nothing heroical in a multitude . . .

Hazlitt concludes that, ironically enough, '*poetical* justice' merely gives a bogus legitimacy to 'a noble or royal hunt, in which what is sport to the few is death to the many'. Some parts of *Endymion* seem precisely designed to reverse this pattern and to make poetry out of – and on behalf of – the many rather than the few. Much of the first book is devoted to crowd scenes which could evoke something 'heroical in a multitude'.

Moreover, if other poetry does tend to glamorize those in power as royal lions and to despise the masses as amorphous flocks of sheep, *Endymion* in the opening lines of Book III turns that tendency inside out. It invites us to identify not with a few princes or government ministers but with many hard-working farm labourers. The latter depend for their livelihood on the proper management of

1 'Coriolanus', first published in the *Examiner*, 15 December 1816, then in *Characters of Shakespeare's Plays* (1817); reprinted in *Works*, ed. P. P. Howe, 21 vols, London, 1930–34, iv. 214–16. The essay was attacked by William Gifford in the *Quarterly Review* (in January 1818: xviii. 458–66) and provoked Hazlitt to compose a riposte that Keats thought worth quoting at massive length in March 1819: see *Letters*, ii. 74–6.

sheep, but their efforts are wrecked by the ruffians of the ruling class. Those 'who lord it o'er their fellow-men' are represented by the poem's metaphors as vandals, and the England that they ravage as farmland. These lordly thugs release sheep into the hayfields during the summer; they thus destroy the feed-stuff that, come winter, will be essential to the flocks and to the peasant farmers, who indirectly feed themselves by tending these innately 'human pastures' (1–5). It is the Tory ministers themselves who truly resemble sheep at their most mindless. It is their own propagandist extravagances (like the inane public festivities described in ll 16–18), their childish indulgence 'in empurpled vests,/And crowns . . . Their tiptop nothings . . . their thrones' (11–15) that are 'baaing vanities' (3).

The emphatic repetition of 'they' and 'their' here – appearing seven times in only six lines (10–15) – firmly distances the privileged minority as aliens to be denounced, not role models to be emulated. This militant use of plural pronouns may also be inspired by Hazlitt's essay, which plays a ferocious game of 'them' and 'us', making its anger emphatic by italicizing the first-person pronouns:

The great have private feelings of their own, to which the interests of humanity . . . must curtsey. Their interests are so far from being the same as those of the community, that they are in direct and necessary opposition to them; their power is at the expense of *our* weakness; their riches of *our* poverty; their pride of *our* degradation; their splendour of *our* wretchedness; their tyranny of *our* servitude.

In *Endymion*'s extended metaphor the great run, like foxes with burning tails, through the fields to set the corn alight. They thus 'sear up and singe/*Our* gold and ripe-eared hopes' (7–8). That plural at the beginning of the line insists that the poet speaks with, and for, an entire community. Implicitly this community is the people of England suffering under the destructive policies of the current government. The poem's first readers are invited to identify with the people, to share their aspirations, to join in a single community of 'Our . . . hopes'.

It was this passage from *Endymion* that Lockhart chose as evidence for his accusation that the Cockney School's youngest pupil had already learnt 'to lisp sedition'.[1] Granted the savage sentences currently being dealt out for just such an offence, this was an

---

1 *Blackwood's Edinburgh Magazine*, August 1818; reprinted in *Keats: The Critical Heritage*, p 109.

intimidatingly serious charge. Another contemporary reviewer saw in the very same lines a loud enough echo of the French Revolution to describe them as 'jacobinical'.[1] Even Keats himself, saying that the passage would 'easily be seen' as an attack on the 'present Ministers' of the Tory Cabinet, had picked it out for a friend, from a poem of over 4,000 lines, as significant.[2] Nevertheless the challenge here is often dodged by modern criticism. Lines about contemporary England are represented as having nothing to do with the poem's main narrative, set in ancient Greece. As such, it is argued, they constitute such a clumsy digression that, in kindness to Keats, they should be forgiven and forgotten. In fact they belong intimately with the overall poem in at least two ways. Firstly, their extended metaphor represents the people of early nineteenth-century England as a farming community: shepherds, struggling to grow crops that can sustain their flocks through hard times, and having to contend with those who seek to wreck their efforts. In Book I the poem's overall narrative begins by describing, at elaborate length, a mass gathering of precisely that kind of agricultural community. Before we hear of Endymion himself we meet the multitudes of shepherds whose leader and protector he is meant to be. Secondly, that striking use of plural pronouns in the Book III passage is a motif of the poem's style throughout Book I – and indeed recurs to play a crucial role in numerous other Keats poems.

## VI

The personal pronouns that *Endymion* deploys in its famous opening passage are all plural. It is 'for *us*' that 'A thing of beauty' keeps 'A bower quiet'. In 'Spite of . . . the inhuman dearth of noble natures' in these 'gloomy days', and in spite of all that thwarts '*our* searching' for some route out of the current 'despondence', there is no need for anyone to turn away from the real world in some latently suicidal despair. A co-operative instinct ensures that '*we*' are 'wreathing/A flowery band to bind *us* to the earth'. So too the image of an appropriate afterlife for the heroes of the past is not concocted by the singular sensibility of the poet. The 'grandeur' of their 'dooms' is what '*We* have imagined'; just as the 'endless fountain of immortal drink', which relieves the arid present, is composed of 'All lovely

---

1 *British Critic*, June 1818; reprinted in *Keats: The Critical Heritage*, p 94.
2 Woodhouse's note to his own copy of *Endymion*, Berg Collection, New York Public Library; quoted in Miriam Allott, *The Poems of John Keats*, London, 1970, p 20.

tales that *we* have heard or read' (i. 4–23). In the following ten lines there are no fewer than seven further uses of 'we' or 'us' or 'our' before at last, in line 34, the poem makes its first use of 'I'.

This opening passage is widely accepted as having been inspired by Wordsworth's 'Prospectus' at the beginning of *The Excursion*. However, the differences are as striking as the similarities. They confirm Keats's insistence in a letter that his own 'poetical Character' is of that 'sort' which should be 'distinguished from the Words-worthian or egotistical sublime'.[1] Wordsworth's 'Prospectus' deploys the singular 'I' as the subject of the poem's opening sentence, and the word appears as early as the second line. That singular personal pronoun, in the form of 'I' or 'me' or 'my', occurs a dozen times in the first forty-six lines, until Wordsworth describes 'Beauty' as what 'waits upon *my* steps;/Pitches her tents before *me* as *I* move' (45–6).[2] This commitment to 'the individual mind that keeps her own/Inviolate retirement' (19–20) seems to have struck Keats as too fugitive and cloistered a virtue. In composing his own introductory sequence for *Endymion* he preferred plurals that could evoke a shared voice and a vision that is implicitly far more communal.

The narrative core of Keats's poem begins by describing the public meeting-place of all the men and women who live and work in a whole range of local villages (63–88). It is situated deep within 'A mighty forest', but approachable by many paths; and its central feature is an altar dedicated to worship of Pan, god of universal nature and, more specifically, divine protector of the flocks and crops upon which these sheep-farmers depend. Dawn is breaking on a day of festival when the community comes together. So instead of

1 *Letters*, i. 387. See also Keats's earlier support for J. H. Reynolds's admiration of the anonymous Robin Hood ballads and 'the old Poets' (including Shakespeare): 'it may be said that we ought to read our contemporaries, that Wordsworth etc. should have their due . . . but, for the sake of a few fine imaginative or domestic passages, are we to be bullied into a certain Philosophy engendered in the whims of an Egotist? Every man has his speculations, but every man does not brood and peacock over them . . .' (*Letters*, i. 223–4).

2 This of course exaggerates the difference. Wordsworth himself, even in this very passage, makes some telling uses of the plural pronoun; and it is a device which he uses with superb effect at crucial points of other poems, such as the closing lines of 'Elegiac Stanzas upon Peele Castle' or the 'Immortality Ode'. Moreover, Keats so admired *The Excursion* as a whole (see *Letters*, i. 203–5) that it is not likely to have been his own chosen example of that 'egotism, Vanity and bigotry' which he told his brothers made Wordsworth repellent (*Letters*, i. 237). For a recent account of Keats's intense and ambivalent attitudes to Wordsworth, see Jack Stillinger, 'Wordsworth and Keats', ch. 9 of *The Age of William Wordsworth*, ed. Kenneth R. Johnston and Gene W. Ruoff, New Brunswick, NJ, 1987.

hills whose solemnity derives from Wordsworthian silence and solitude, this landscape is already echoing the people's movement towards their rendezvous: '*Man*'s voice was on the mountains' (104).
In the next lines the poetry seems to delight in turning from the
soundless movements of the natural world – 'the silent workings of
the dawn' (107) – to the genial noisiness of the first people to arrive
for the meeting:

> . . . with joyful cries, there sped
> A troop of little children garlanded
> Who gathering round the altar seemed to pry
> Earnestly round, as wishing to espy
> Some folk on holiday. Nor had they waited
> For many moments, ere their ears were sated
> With a faint breath of music, which even then
> Filled out its voice . . .
>
> (i. 109–16)

These happily expectant first-comers, 'garlanded' and 'gathering
round', must recall the poem's opening invitation that '*we*', the
readers, should see *our*selves as 'wreathing/A flowery band to bind *us*
to the earth'. Their 'joyful cries' echo the insistence that 'A thing of
beauty is a joy' that works 'for *us*'. So we are encouraged to identify,
in the fullest sense, with their vision. As they eagerly listen for
sounds of others approaching, we must share their view that the
thing of beauty to which we should look forward most eagerly is the
gathering of the community for shared celebration.

At the precise moment when the main procession is about to come
in sight and '*we*/Might mark' them, the poem breaks off to make its
first appeal to the muse:

> And now, as deep into the wood as *we*
> Might mark a lynx's eye, there glimmered light
> Fair faces and a rush of garments white,
> Plainer and plainer showing, till at last
> Into the widest alley they all passed,
> Making directly for the woodland altar.
> O kindly muse, let not my weak tongue falter
> In telling of this goodly company,
> Of their old piety, and of their glee . . .
>
> (i. 122–30)

That use of 'we' stations the poet amongst the people, as the two
groups meet and merge. He is no isolated, rarefied 'genius', but has
the responsibility of speaking – 'telling' – on behalf of 'this goodly
company' to which he himself momentarily belongs, identifying with

them in collective spirit and common purpose. Nor is he immune from human vulnerability: his 'weak tongue' may 'falter' without the Muse's guidance. An appeal for such help may be conventional; but in this unconventionally belated position it suggests that what matters, more than any of the preceding subject-matter, is the appearance of the community as it meets. It is now, when faced by his most crucial task of doing justice to 'this goodly company', that he needs his descriptive power to be at its height.

The ensuing description stresses that this is a peasant community. Yet each 'crowd of shepherds', for all their 'sunburnt looks', enters in formal sequence, as a 'well trimmed' component of a co-ordinated procession (138–9). 'Leading the way' is a group of young women singing 'a shepherd song' (135–6); then the first 'crowd of shepherds', divided into one section carrying the tools of their trade and another playing the flute. 'Close after these' the 'venerable Priest' advances out of the forest 'full soberly/Begirt with ministering looks'. In one hand he holds a wine-vase that is 'milk-white', and in the other a basket of flowers that are 'whiter still' (147–57). We have already been told that each of the girls at the front of the procession holds 'a white wicker' (137), and, even earlier, our very first glimpse of the procession was 'a rush of garments white' (124).

To the more paranoid Tories amongst the poem's first readers this colour scheme for such efficiently marshalled ranks might suggest the opposite of innocence: white was firmly associated with the reform movement. Henry Hunt, its most publicized leader, always wore a huge white hat. He had been the chief speaker at the mass demonstrations that had led to the 'Spa Fields riots' in London in November and December of 1816. It was in that year and in the early months of 1817 that the radical movement established its pattern of elaborate marches through which relatively uneducated folk could make clear statements, displaying their growing numbers, their increasingly efficient organization, their shared sense of direction and their faith in their own leaders. White clothing was used to give their massed ranks some of the effect of an army in uniform or of a religious procession. At Peterloo, for instance, the marchers from Oldham included a contingent of two hundred women all dressed in white; and the same colour was adopted by the Committee of the Manchester Female Reformers, 'all handsomely dressed in white', their leader carrying a 'white silk flag'. Every man in Samuel Bamford's 6,000-strong contingent marching in from the Rochdale area wore 'a white Sundays' shirt'. The iconography of Hunt's London procession, which Keats himself would later witness, included 'The Committees, bearing white wands' and 'A white flag'.[1] This long-established symbolism was well understood by those conservative institutions for whom the rituals of democrats evoked the blasphemous rites of pagans. Church of England schools sent home any pupils who wore white hats just as firmly as they turned away those who were found wearing around their necks, instead of crucifixes, lockets containing portraits of Henry Hunt, or 'Saint Henry' as he was adoringly nicknamed. In broadside poems by Government propagandists, Hunt was attacked as a pseudo-priest. He supposedly 'preached' a 'treason sermon' and wanted the working people to worship him as 'their Lord'.[2]

The priest in *Endymion* is of course too old to be some coded portrait of Henry Hunt; his age is emphasized as much as his wisdom. So he anticipates that other old man who dominates the crucial episode of Book III, the still high-minded but now physically frail Glaucus. Now Glaucus himself could suggest William Godwin, whose radical publications had been a major influence back in the 1790s. Godwin had lived on, arguably keeping to his ideals – long after most of those who had once shared them had deserted the cause and left that 'inhuman dearth/Of noble natures' which abandoned Keats and his liberal contemporaries to such 'despondence', such 'unhealthy and o'er-darkened . . . searching' (i. 8–11). Keats, in respecting the elderly Godwin enough to read not only his radical master-work, *Political Justice* (1793), but at least two of his novels, was seeking to recover the inspiration of an earlier time; but he knew that even the most unswerving liberal of that generation was too old to act as an effective leader now. In *Endymion*'s Book III the tormented Glaucus has, for many wearying years of solitary confinement, been the guardian of a magic book: a powerful antidote to despair. It can remove 'a load of misery and pain' with the golden 'shine of hope', 'cheering' its reader 'to cope/Strenuous with hellish tyranny' (684–7). However, its pages can only liberate the younger generation if it is now used by one of their own number, someone youthful enough to deploy it with the vigour needed to ensure their 'enfranchisement' (299) – someone like Endymion himself,

---

1 Samuel Bamford, *The Autobiography of Samuel Bamford*, vol. II: *Passages in the Life of a Radical*, ed. W. H. Chaloner, London, 1967, pp 177–80; Thompson, *The Making of the English Working Class*, p 680.
2 Donald Read, *Peterloo and Its Background*, Manchester, 1958, p 54; Thompson, *The Making of the English Working Class*, p 624; Walmsley, *Peterloo: The Case Reopened*, p 130; Edgell Rickward, *Radical Squibs and Loyal Ripostes*, Bath, 1971, p 693.

who, in spite of his own reluctance, is indeed 'The youth elect' (710).

In Book I's description of the mass gathering it is not the aged priest but the young Endymion whose arrival is accompanied 'by a multitude that reared/Their voices to the clouds' (164–5). He is the official leader of these shepherd-folk. They all look to him as the figurehead through whom they can focus their shared aspirations, the guardian who will protect the health of the community. This is a responsibility that, almost at the end of the poem, Endymion will apparently accept:

> Through me the shepherd realm shall prosper well,
> For to thy tongue will I all health confide.

> (iv. 863–4)

But at the outset, here in Book I, Endymion seems to refuse his role. Far from encouraging optimism in his people, he allows them to see his own self-absorbed depression. His demeanour, to 'common lookers-on', suggests a self-indulgent fantasist – 'one who dreamed/Of idleness in groves Elysian' (176–7); and indeed much of his dream-journey through the rest of the poem can be interpreted as escapist. To the more sympathetic onlookers at the meeting his facial expression suggests 'A lurking trouble' (179) – a fear of the future which soon becomes infectious, so that the spectators too start to dread the coming winter:

> Then would they sigh,
> And think of yellow leaves, of owlet's cry,
> Of logs piled solemnly. Ah, well-a-day,
> Why should *our* young Endymion pine away?

> (i. 181–4)

Here, too, 'our' signals the narrator's own slide into identification with the farming community. No speech-marks intervene to make the anxious questions only theirs and not his. It is not just these old-world shepherds, but also the modern poet with his readers, who need to ask why so influential a figure, who might act as inspiring spokesperson for the popular will, should instead behave so dispiritingly.

In terms of the opening of Book III and the politics of contemporary England, why should any potential leader of liberal opinion, like the influentially gloomy Lord Byron for instance (or perhaps even the self-critical John Keats himself), ever allow the public to think that he has given up hope? Why should he seem so defeatist, so resigned to the success of those who destroy the summer's hay crop and to the defeat of those who work to ensure a satisfactory winter? Why can he not control – or at the very least hide from those whom he should encourage – 'the cankering venom' of his self-absorbed despair (i. 396)? In Endymion's own case, one answer may be that sexual love, rather than helping to quicken the larger loves through which a juster society can be built, has actually sapped political energy. Both theories, about the interaction of the erotic and the communal, are explored in one of Book I's finest passages (769–857). It may also be that Endymion, though an ancient Greek, has overdosed on a cultural fad of Keats's own day and read his way too often into what Book II calls 'The deadly feel of solitude' (284). Certainly his supposed search for the ideal woman, through the poem's later narrative, allows him to spend much time travelling alone; and if that journey amounts to Keats's diagnosis of escapism, it may be partly the challenge of human sexuality, in all its mundanity and messiness, which the protagonist hopes to evade, and not only his civic responsibilities for the welfare of the people assembled at the festival in Book I.

In spite of their sulky leader the massed gathering of men and women still manages a communal celebration at 'the woodland altar' (127) to which they have processed. The young prince may not yet be ready to inspire, but fortunately one survivor from a previous generation – that 'venerable priest' (149) – is still able to act as their spokesman. As soon as the priest prepares to address them, 'lifting up his aged hands' (195), then 'each look was changed/To sudden veneration' (186–7). This old man has the courageous optimism to remain unaffected by Endymion's gloom, perhaps because of the egalitarian assumptions that allow him to smile upon the entire congregation 'with joy from greatest to the least' (194).

His rousing speech begins with a wide-ranging series of vocatives. Not only does he address himself explicitly to women as well as to men (and indeed to children too), but also to the various local groups, some of which have come down from villages high in the mountains, others up from the valleys. There are contingents whose home villages are amongst gently rolling hills and others who have come all the way from the coast where they live at the 'ocean's very marge' (204). This is not the parochial meeting of a single community on its home territory; it represents that scale of unity amongst numerous small, remote communities of ordinary people – and that efficiency of long-distance co-ordination – which, in Keats's England, formed the dream of the radicals and the nightmare of the propertied classes. Already many on both sides of the political divide could recognize that momentum towards organization which, by the time of Peterloo, would allow just one of the contingents that marched towards the Manchester meeting to be composed of sections from no fewer than twenty different villages or little towns.

After these inclusive vocatives the priest proceeds to identify his audience with his own rousing voice, in the demagogue's essential trope of the first-person *plural* pronoun. He uses 'we' or 'our' or 'us' no fewer than eight times in only ten lines (213–22). It is '*we*' who should sing 'to *our* great god Pan', the guardian of '*our*' cattle and of '*our*' sheep and of '*our*' lands, whose representative is 'Endymion *our* lord'. The religious ritual is not to be articulated through the singular voice of the priest himself but through the collective voice of the entire crowd: it is to be '*our* solemnity' articulated in '*our* vows'. He speaks for and to a crowd, and it is as a crowd that they respond. It is explicitly by a 'chorus' that the Hymn to Pan is then sung (231).

## VII

The Hymn to Pan is indeed a hymn, not a solo. It is performed by a chorus of peasant farmers on behalf of all those at the mass gathering, and its words point to the sheer strength of numbers mustered to hear it: 'see . . . The many that are come' (i. 289–91). The hymn's rhetoric is the essentially plural one of communal solidarity: 'Hear *us*, great Pan' (246); 'Hear *us*, O satyr-king' (278). The pleas are for crops growing on '*our* village leas' (254), for protection against these crops being damaged by 'snouted wild-boars rooting tender corn' to 'Anger *our* huntsmen' (282–3). This of course anticipates the explicitly political opening of Book III, where it is the Tory government who are the destructive animals, running amok like 'fire-branded foxes' to devastate the fields of '*our* gold and ripe-eared hopes'. The plural pronouns of the hymn itself are clearly less explicitly political. Nevertheless they create a style which a conservative reader could describe fairly precisely as 'rabble-rousing'; since, as the hymn closes, 'the whole multitude' is indeed roused to 'shout' as loud as thunder (307–10).

Keats was imprudent enough to recite this hymn aloud at a famous dinner party in 1817. A fellow guest, William Wordsworth, seems to have interpreted it as a gesture towards contemporary politics and as such an insult to his own pious conservatism. He huffily decided 'to take it as a bit of Paganism for the Time'.[1] At the time everyone must have had a view on whether the Government's repressive legislation introduced earlier that year was really justified by a serious threat of violent revolution. As well as the panic induced by the mass demonstrations and public meetings, there was also the fear caused by terrorists: the members of the secret, subversive movement called Luddism which had in the previous years been launching attacks in the Midlands and the north. It *was* in this wilder countryside that the conspiracy had grown. In Nottinghamshire the clandestine rendezvous for Luddites was usually, like the mass meeting in *Endymion*, deep in the forest; but, according to one modern historian, 'it is noteworthy how many disturbances in the North originated in the moors' – 'moors in which discontented mobs could gather and hold secret meetings'.[2] So, at the time, Wordsworth was bound to feel jittery about strange sounds out on the 'barren moors', and those are exactly what Keats's recital of the 'Hymn to Pan' forced him, at one point, to hear.

The god is invoked as

> Strange ministrant of undescribed sounds
> That come a-swooning over hollow grounds
> And wither drearily on barren moors;
> Dread opener of the mysterious doors
> Leading to universal knowledge – See
> The many that are come . . .

> (i. 285–91)

To a conservative these lines could seem chillingly irresponsible. The arrogant humanism of revolutionary France was indeed still deluding far too many English radicals into pursuit of some 'myster-

---

1 *The Keats Circle*, ii. 143–4. Some scholars have argued that accounts of the incident are unreliable, either because the witnesses are not to be trusted or because their accounts have subsequently been misinterpreted: see, for instance, Robert Gittings, *John Keats*, London, 1968, pp 250–53, and Stillinger, 'Wordsworth and Keats'. However, Wordsworth left London 'rather huff'd' at not being treated as 'infallible', according to Keats. The remark is made in a letter of 8 April 1818 which then makes a resolution that 'we will have no more abominable rows'. The letter, according to B. R. Haydon, its recipient and the arranger of the infamous dinner, 'appears to allude here to the violent political and religious discussions of the set' (*Letters*, i. 265–6). Keats published the 'Hymn to Pan' in the *Yellow Dwarf*, 9 May 1818, just over three months after the dinner-party reading and about a fortnight after its publication as part of *Endymion* (*Letters*, i. 37, 44).

2 F. O. Darvall, *Popular Disturbances and Public Order in Regency England*, Oxford, 1934, p 51.

ious', non-Christian short cut to a so-called '*Universal* Knowledge', one justifying claptrap about the international brotherhood of man. The word 'universal' was a key term in the radical books and pamphlets that the Government was so ruthlessly trying to suppress. Tom Paine himself, in the runaway best seller of the revolutionary period, had defined the crucial conflict as that between what he called 'Mr Burke's doctrine of Church and State' and his own commitment to '*UNIVERSAL* RIGHT OF CONSCIENCE AND *UNIVERSAL* RIGHT OF CITIZENSHIP'. His insistence on these two 'universal' rights would be remembered by even the most cursory reader of *Rights of Man* since they had been picked out for emphasis by being printed in block capitals. Even a reader who had got no further than the book's dedication would have found Paine addressing George Washington with the 'prayer . . . that the Rights of man may become as *universal* as your benevolence can wish'.[1]

There would be no reassurance for conservatives in the fact that the chorus singing the hymn was composed not of contemporary British workers but of ancient Greek peasants. Modern radicalism had so often drawn on the models of ancient Greece, the supposed birthplace of democracy, that the Establishment was forced to retaliate, producing histories of Greece which could show the Athenian experiment as in fact a disaster – one that exposed 'the dangerous turbulence of democracy'.[2] Greek mythology supplied the very titles of some of the more extreme radical journals, such as the *Gorgon* or the *Medusa*.[3] In some contexts the most up-to-date political journalism and ancient Greek literature seem to function almost indistinguishably. Keats himself records in a letter that he has just been discussing the prospects in the then crucial Westminster by-election with two different friends – one who is 'as usual among his favourite democratic papers', and the other who (though he supposedly 'talks of nothing else but the electors of Westminster') is 'at present in Greek histories and antiquities'.[4]

Too respectful an interest in ancient Greece could also type one at this time as a libertarian in matters of sex. Greek sculpture and

1 David Powell, *Tom Paine: The Greatest Exile*, New York, 1985, pp 184, 189.
2 Richard Jenkyns, *The Victorians and Ancient Greece*, Oxford, 1980, pp 14–15; E. Rawson, *The Spartan Tradition in European Thought*, Oxford, 1969, p 357. See also Robert M. Ryan, 'The Politics of Greek Religion', in *Critical Essays on John Keats*, ed. Hermione de Almeida, Boston, 1990.
3 W. H. Wickwar, *The Struggle for the Freedom of the Press 1819–1832*, London, 1928, p 60.
4 *Letters*, ii. 63–4.

pottery had only recently begun to reach England in any quantity, the statuary from the Acropolis first going on display in 1817, when it inspired Keats's famous sonnet 'On Seeing the Elgin Marbles'. Two years later, in 1819, when Byron published the second canto of *Don Juan*, his poem could rely on a safely established association between nudity, guilt-free sexuality and the ancient Greeks. Its young hero and heroine, though unmarried, can happily fall into each other's arms to form 'a group that's quite antique/Half-naked, loving, natural and Greek' (II. cxciv). The same poem relied upon instant understanding of a joke about the nudity of Greek 'gods and goddesses' who strangely lack the 'pantaloons and bodices' needed to conceal the more indecent features of their anatomies. Juan's respectable mother wanted the lad to be taught 'classic studies', but, in view of the 'filthy loves' indulged in by the very divinities of that culture, she 'dreaded the mythology' (I. xli).

In 1820 a conservative reviewer complained that some modern writers were deploying Greek mythology precisely because of 'its grossness – its alliance to the sensitive pleasures which belong to the animal'. This attack is then directed specifically against Keats, who seems so obsessed with 'the "happy pieties" of Paganism' that he can 'write of scarcely anything else'.[1] The cited example is in fact the 'wild ecstasy' with which the orgiastic 'men or gods' in the first stanza of 'Ode on a Grecian Urn' complete their 'mad pursuit' of the 'maidens'. But many of *Endymion*'s first readers may have seen the erotic freedom that ancient Greece inspired being celebrated there too – in the hero's constant pursuit of enticing women and, more particularly, in his decisive act of liberation in Book III, which releases innumerable young couples into each other's arms and frees their sexuality from all stain by having a pagan goddess bless their passion in an elaborate ceremony.

To conservative readers a story that began with crowds of ancient Greeks worshipping their promiscuous gods was all too likely to include both sexuality outside marriage and populist politics. What for modern readers may be an agenda so hidden that the poems now seem utterly innocuous could, for Keats's contemporaries, reveal itself all too clearly as a celebration of everything that was subversive. For instance, that dedicatory sonnet to Leigh Hunt in the 1817 volume, though taken as a defiantly radical gesture by reviewers, contains no explicit reference to the politics for which Hunt was so

---

1 Unsigned review (by Josiah Condor) in *Eclectic Review*, September 1820; reprinted in *Keats: The Critical Heritage*, pp 236–7.

notorious. The one point of solidarity clearly being celebrated is merely that Hunt, like Keats, still reverences Greek gods when, in these benighted times, 'The shrine of Flora' is by most forgotten and 'Pan is no longer sought'. Who could be affronted by that? One answer is all those readers whose taste was offended by *any* reference in polite literature to a Greek god; and such readers were numerous, as we can tell from the huge sales for doubly bowdlerized versions of earlier English poetry. These had not just eliminated the sexual references, but had as meticulously censored out all references to the classical gods – as if these were equal and interrelated indecencies.[1]

So the fact that *Endymion*'s 'men in society', gathered to sing their Hymn to Pan, are not attending an explicitly political meeting but a religious one would, at the very least, have seemed indecisive. To some contemporary readers, subversive working-class movements, like Luddism with its infamous oaths of secrecy sworn on the Bible, were blasphemous pseudo-religions, adapting Christian ritual and rhetoric to do the Devil's work of treason. Back in the early 1790s, as Wordsworth would ruefully have remembered, the Bishop of Llandaff denounced egalitarianism as a primitive god whose worship involved limitless human sacrifice: 'I fly with terror from the altar of Liberty, when I see it stained with the blood of the aged, of the innocent, of the defenceless sex . . . streaming with the blood of the monarch himself.'[2] The religious imagery in which both sides described the reform movement lasted right through to 1819, when a newspaper described the crowds of labouring folk on their march towards a mass rally as a procession of 'willing votaries to the shrine of sacred liberty'.[3]

---

1 James Plumptre in *A Collection of Songs* (1805) offered versions in which the term 'Phoebus' in a lyric from Shakespeare's *Cymbeline* had been replaced by 'the sun' and a song from *The Tempest* had been cleansed of its references to both Ceres and Juno. Journalists of the Church and State party were lavish in their praise: the *Anti-Jacobin* begged Plumptre to translate more works on the same principle, which he obligingly did in the three volumes of *The English Drama Purified*. See M. J. Quinlan, *Victorian Prelude: A History of English Manners 1700–1830*, Columbia University Studies in English and Comparative Literature, New York, 1941, pp 229–37.

2 Richard Watson, Bishop of Llandaff, 'Appendix to His Late Sermon' (1793) as quoted by 'a Republican' (William Wordsworth) in his denunciation of Watson's 'extraordinary . . . Political Principles', 'A Letter to the Bishop of Llandaff' (composed 1793). *The Prose Works of William Wordsworth*, ed. W. J. B. Owen and Jane Worthington Smyser, Oxford, 1974, i. 33.

3 Read, *Peterloo and Its Background*, p 128.

## VIII

It was in 1819 that Keats wrote 'Ode on a Grecian Urn', and returned, in its fourth stanza, to the scene first explored in *Endymion*: the procession of an entire 'folk' towards a 'green altar' in the forest, where they are to hold their festival. However, the Urn's images are both more enigmatic and more ominous. Here the procession is led by an essentially 'mysterious priest'; and it is marching towards slaughter. Admittedly it is only 'that heifer lowing at the skies/And all her silken flanks with garlands dressed' who is certainly destined to perish in 'the sacrifice'; but the final, 'desolate' image is of human loss: 'streets' that 'evermore/Will silent be' because, from the ritual march that 'emptied' them, 'not a soul . . . can e'er return.'

The ode may have been composed as late as autumn 1819 as a response to (or perhaps a retreat from) the news of the August massacre in Manchester.[1] It was certainly written later than a remarkably similar mass rally – one led by the same radical orator, Henry Hunt, and held on the same site earlier in the year. Then too, remote villages and little towns had been virtually emptied as their inhabitants – men, women and children – marched away towards the assembly point on St Peter's Field. For at least two years before that the newspapers had been reporting huge protest demonstrations. Their scale reminded alarmist conservatives of the populist politics that had eventually displaced France's ruling class. In the 1780s the French monarchy had quailed, failing to halt a momentum that had eventually led to wholesale butchery – first in the Terror, and then through two decades of bloody international war. Arguably the English authorities were now justified in using maximal force; restraint would only mean far more lives having to be sacrificed later.

So in the questions that stanza IV of the ode asks about the procession, there could be some anxious bewilderment about present mass movements (as well as the more obvious curiosity about the dynamics of ancient societies). These questions are not about any singular motivation that may be hidden within the individual mind of the 'mysterious priest'; they are about plurals – about the sense of corporate identity shared by everyone in the procession. The poem

1 Jack Stillinger, in his authoritative edition of the poems, remarks that, though the Nightingale and Psyche odes can be allocated to spring 1819 and 'To Autumn' can be dated precisely at 19 September 1819, 'the *Grecian Urn* and *Melancholy* are dated only "1819" in reliable sources . . . each could have been written at any time during the year, even . . . after *Autumn*' (*The Poems of John Keats*, ed. Stillinger, p 466).

demands 'Who are these coming to the sacrifice?' It wants to know
their intended destination ('To what green altar'?), and to discover
their point of origin ('what little town'?), to learn the kind of terrain
in which they had worked to produce their shared livelihood. However, the silent Urn, offering no picture of their 'little town', cannot
reveal whether it had developed around a river-crossing, or beside
the sea, or high in the mountains, before being 'emptied of its folk
this pious morn'. It's worth registering how extreme a term the
poem deploys in 'emptied'; and how much it therefore means by
'folk'. It is awed by an alien way of life, in which the latent conflict
of brute egotisms has been resolved into unqualified unity of purpose
– a society able to march out with such an absolutely shared sense of
direction that it leaves not a single person behind.

Stanza IV closes in desolate acceptance that there is no one left
to answer the poem's yearning to understand, and perhaps no community able to satisfy the poet's own longing to belong. The sense of
exclusion is obviously apt enough if these figures are the centuries-
dead citizens of a now irrecoverably lost civilization – a culture
whose social solidarity has no equivalent in modern Europe. But,
oddly enough, it could be just as apt if the procession does have a
fairly precise contemporary equivalent. Keats and the ode's first
readers could also feel forlorn outsiders, even if they glimpse in this
ancient procession an image of England's labouring folk embarking
on the latest protest march. Some strange sense of solidarity, comparable to that of the Greek city-state, might be re-emerging in modern
England; but if so, it was not being experienced at first hand by
sophisticates like Keats and his friends and his likely readers. Instead
it was being enjoyed and enacted by masses of underprivileged,
barely literate people whose way of life could seem just as mysterious
as that of early Greeks and whose beliefs could remain just as
opaque. Some decades after the ode's composition Disraeli would
compose, in *Sybil*, a portrait of England, still so class-ridden, still
composed of tribes so foreign to each other as to justify the subtitle
'The Two Nations'. In Keats's own day some of the demonstrators
found even their own leaders' language confusingly foreign: one
poignant example is misinterpreting the extremists' talk of a 'provisional government' – one that could immediately replace the Tories
– as an all too credible demand for a regime that would stop
starvation and organize 'provisions' to feed the people.

The restless, complex tone of the fourth stanza is, of course,
entirely compatible with interpretations that prefer to keep the Urn
and all its images firmly distant in an ancient world, or safely

apolitical in a discussion of timeless aesthetic. But the poem, as it watches the folk move irrevocably beyond any further comprehension, offers a curious amalgam of response, in which fear jostles with admiration and with envy – and even with an odd kind of self-pity at one's own isolated irrelevance. These could seem even more appropriate if the procession does hint at those mass movements that had so recently convulsed France and were already threatening to alter England.

On either reading, the focus is clearly on community in stanza IV; and that's why the ode asks so wistfully what kind of place could allow this all-embracing community to develop. What the ode most achingly wants to find out is why the people went off on their procession. What was the set of shared beliefs that motivated such harmonious action? What was their joint intention? However, the very town in which such solidarity developed cannot now be identified, and so the undiscoverable streets in which its inhabitants met each other must stay silent. None of those inhabitants can ever come back from the past to explain the mysterious ritual's origin and purpose, to answer the poem's helpless 'why':

> And little town, thy streets for evermore
> Will silent be; and not a soul to tell
> Why thou art desolate can e'er return.

Faced by such a question, the Urn, as emblem of the sort of anti-historical, apolitical high art that contemporary reviewers favoured and that Keats himself felt under pressure to supply, can only remain silent.

According to the opening stanza the pot is a 'historian', but essentially 'sylvan'. As such it may be too much of a backwoodsman to know anything of what we might call social and political history: how people lived in 'little town' or larger city, how they developed their more co-operative system of values. Even if its claims as 'historian' are only those of a storyteller, 'sylvan' may suggest the unending seasonal cycle in which trees that shed their leaves in autumn will bloom again come spring. This 'leaf-fringed legend' certainly has to coil itself into a material circularity: it fits, like a snake biting its tail, around the actual 'shape' of the pot. Elsewhere Keats's verse spells out that, when 'a marble urn' is 'shifted round to see the other side', the rotation soon leads to the reappearance of the figures that had been 'first seen' ('Ode on Indolence', i). Here too, any story that a Grecian Urn's revolving imagery tries to tell about mortal individuals and their essentially linear lives – lives which all too certainly have an end as well as a beginning and a middle – may indeed be imprecise: 'A flowery tale', whose insubstantiality 'haunts about' the Urn's revolving 'shape'. Questions about that tale's accuracy or relevance to the realities of mortal existence seem to be hinted at in the interrogative grammar of lines 5–10. The ode equivocates as to whether these figures, who are so freely and painlessly displaying their uninhibited sexuality, can be 'mortals' at all (rather than 'deities' or 'gods'). It also asks where on earth they are pursuing their 'wild ecstacy') – 'Tempe' or 'Arcady' – or perhaps nowhere except, of course, on the fanciful surface of the potter's artefact, which, in expressing itself 'more sweetly than our rhyme', may be functioning less informatively.

But what strikes a conservative as an irrelevantly fanciful Utopia can seem to a radical a practical blueprint for that joyous future which society must one day achieve. What has been lost of primal innocence could one day be recovered. The hopes raised by the earliest stage of the French Revolution need not be seen as lost for ever at the end of some linear history's cul-de-sac. They may, in the fullness of time's revolving patterns, return. It is precisely the cyclical imagery of the seasons, in which winter's seemingly dead bare trees already contain spring's new leaves, that Shelley used at about the same time in 'Ode to the West Wind', to maintain, through the gloom of post-Waterloo Europe, hope of a juster, happier future.

Keats's own ode is restlessly equivocal about such optimism; but its third stanza does feel the appeal in the idea of 'boughs that cannot shed' their 'leaves' in any irrevocable sense, and of 'leaves' that will never 'bid the spring' a lasting 'adieu'. The poignant fear that this is only an artistic fiction, imaginable by poet and potter but unrealizable on earth, is triggered only by the intensity of Keats's own yearning that it might be more. A year before writing the ode Keats had described his own vision of an egalitarian Utopia in which 'every human might become great, and Humanity instead of being a wide heath . . . with here and there a remote Oak or Pine, would become a grand democracy of Forest Trees.'[1] Those who took to the streets at this time to demand democracy had been using precisely this imagery for years. In 1802 a protest march of workers had been 'preceded by twenty-four young blooming handsome women, each bearing a branch of a cotton tree'.[2] In one London

1 *Letters*, i. 232.
2 Thompson, *The Making of the English Working Class*, p 425.

procession watched by Keats himself, where many thousands of demonstrators had been marshalled into a sequence of symbolic groups, their hero, Henry Hunt, was preceded by 'some hundreds' of men 'bearing large branches of oak, poplar etc.'[1] At the front of Samuel Bamford's contingent marching towards Peterloo was a group of 'the most comely ... youths' each of whom had a whole 'branch of laurel held presented in his hand'.[2]

The ode's final stanza equips its 'men and maidens overwrought,/ With forest branches'; but it is their nakedly unashamed sexuality that is even more likely to have jarred the sensibilities of conservative readers. It was just such sexuality, they argued, indulged in so fecklessly by the masses, that produced overpopulation and the resultant poverty about which the liberals whinged. The destitution that the plebs blamed on government policy was, by this thesis, their own fault. Shelley thundered against the 'hardened insolence' of the proposal that 'the poor should be compelled ... to abstain from sexual intercourse while the rich are permitted to add as many mouths to consume the product of the labours of the poor as they please' (*A Philosophical View of Reform*); and Cobbett, in his famous 'Address to the Journey men and Labourers' of 1816 railed against the propaganda that made sex ugly and suggested that 'a young man, arm-in-arm with a rosy-cheeked girl, must be a spectacle of evil omen'. The ode, confronting the Urn's idyllic image of sexual desire freed from all risk of later disappointment, is more sceptical. These 'melodies ... Are sweeter' than any we have yet heard in the real world. The 'fair youth' may be the same figure as the 'Bold Lover' who, in his frozen excitement, is for ever 'winning near the goal' but 'never, never' able to complete his gesture of desire (11–18); or he may be a third figure – in which case the scene has the pathos and precariousness of a human triangle. By either reading the idealized stasis hints at a discrepancy between what can be imaged by a sufficiently imaginative artist and its very different referent in the dynamic actuality of 'human passion' (28). Movement may be of the essence in real life; the potter, in attempting something like the painter's 'still life', may be committed to a contradiction in terms.

However, the ode also embraces the hope, beloved of radicals, that there had been in ancient days – and could again be – a society in which people ordered their sexuality and their communities so much more joyously and justly as indeed to seem like gods. Perhaps it was

1   Ibid., p 680.
2   Bamford, *Autobiography*, p 197.

the fault of the repressive codes of modern Europe, with their superstitious propaganda about some original sin, that made human sexuality seem innately dissatisfying – an unslakeable thirst of 'burning forehead, and . . . parching tongue'. Perhaps only neurotic guilt led lovers, in moments of anticipated fulfilment, to feel 'sorrowful and cloyed' (28–30). Such self-abasement has, as its corollary, the servile acceptance of a social hierarchy in which it seems natural for the many to accept the superiority of a few; and both may be relatively modern superstitions. If we could learn how the apparently happier people of ancient Greece lived, we might be able to use such knowledge to liberate our own lives. To the poet of *Endymion* the Urn's images – not only of godlike, shame-free sexuality, but also of an entire community going walkabout together – can tantalizingly evoke just the kind of past that, if only we could understand it, could be an inspiration to the present.

It is indeed to the present that the ode, in its fifth and final stanza, returns, summoning its readers back to their own corporate self-consciousness by deploying plural pronouns. The Urn is now said to 'tease *us* out of thought'. The bleak prospect of 'old age' does not threaten only the poet, but 'this generation'. The passage of time will ensure that all those who have lived together in this same society, all who are now enduring and enjoying this same, shared historical moment, will eventually waste away. After they have perished a future generation will be faced by an altered set of challenges; but that 'other woe' is a gripping enigma, because it is bound to be so different, not from the idiosyncratic experience of Keats himself but from all the experiences that he is now sharing with his contemporaries. It will be 'other woe/Than *ours*'. These pronouns recall the first stanza's point that poetry does not belong just to its author. For Keats and his first readers, modern literature is '*our* rhyme', a shared experience, a joint responsibility. Now the medium of literature, unlike the circular, static and in some ways inevitably reductive Urn, can tell us something about the shared values and motivations of earlier communities. Keats and his readers do have articulate Greek texts to balance the silence of Grecian urns, and so do have some access to historical truth; and most of that truth is not about the idiosyncracies of some individual mind contemplating, in lofty isolation, God and Nature. Historical truth *is* about communities, shared experiences, co-operative ventures – what reactionaries like Coleridge had proscribed from poetry as the dangerous topic of 'men, as society'.

Of course the ode's fourth stanza has been about men *and* women as society – all the 'folk' who normally dwell in the now emptied little town. So the poem's last stanza can unite the genders into a single 'brede' of 'men and maidens', where both, in their shared pursuit of a common goal, are equally and indistinguishably 'overwrought'. They may be roused beyond self-restraint, sexually, as individual libidos; both 'men and maidens' compose '*this* generation', and both are equal partners in the fertile act that will breed the next. But they could be 'overwrought' as a community, impassioned like that 'whole multitude' in *Endymion* who greet the Hymn to Pan with a shout like thunder. By either reading, the Urn – and the poem that to some extent seeks to imitate it – is able to seem 'a friend to *man*', in an inclusive usage which clearly signals all women as well as all men. And we, as the poem's readers, are forced, by those first-person plural pronouns of 'us' and 'our', to acknowledge that all of us, equally, do belong to that special 'brede' of Man.

## IX

For Keats the bleak results of the French Revolution had not removed the obligations of philanthropy. Granted his belief that most contemporary religion was a fraud and that the Christian god, at least, was mere fantasy, man in general remained the highest subject that verse could address; and the poet should still approach humanity with respectful optimism. Recent European history did not justify the currently fashionable modes of murmuring self-analysis or of bombastic pessimism. In fact, at a time of such political turmoil, these were peculiarly irresponsible. Consider for instance the vehemence with which *The Fall of Hyperion* denounces 'all mock lyrists, large *self*-worshippers/And careless hectorers in proud bad verse' (i. 207–8). Elsewhere Keats suggests that behind the work of the more swaggeringly cynical author there is no true tough-mindedness. For all its vaunted realism the poetry of modish despair derives from a literally twisted mind – one that, with morbid selectivity, homes in only on such data as will sustain its own bitter thesis, and, in doing so, turns a blind eye to literature's greatest duty, which, for Keats, is to support and encourage:

> Darkness and worms and shrouds and sepulchres
> Delight it, for it feeds upon the burrs
> And thorns of life, forgetting the great end
> Of poesy, that it should be a friend
> To soothe the cares and lift the thoughts of *man*.
>
> ('Sleep and Poetry', 243–7)

Keats's objections to Byronic gloom are much like Shelley's. When liberalism is temporarily powerless against current regimes, poetry should not wallow in defeatist images of the present. Instead, like the 'trumpet of a prophecy',[1] it should offer positive images of a better world. It should intervene, like an active 'friend', to 'lift the thoughts of *man*'.

The Grecian Urn, if it is also to function as 'a friend to man' and thus fulfil the ode's description, perhaps has to offer some uplifting answer to the pessimism so endemic in 1819. Cynics at that time might insist on an absolute opposition between the search for truth and the pursuit of beauty, arguing that the latter, as proven by the French experiment, was unattainable on earth and could be imaged only where truth had been abandoned, in day-dream or fanciful work of art. It may be that the Urn is just such an artefact and that its identification of truth with beauty exposes it as peddling fantasy. But the ode itself may wish to support some senses in which Beauty and Truth are indeed wholly compatible. Perhaps in its closing lines some of the Beauty which the Urn recommends is to be understood as embracing Truths that pessimists in 1819 would dismiss as fantasies: those uplifting visions of how men and women might yet, in some more auspicious time, manage both their sexual desires and their needs of community far, far more satisfactorily – not in the escapist's dream of heaven but here 'on earth', which is 'all' that we 'know' and all that we 'need to know'.

The closing lines balance the proposition that 'Beauty is truth' with an equally unqualified claim that 'truth [is] beauty'. Perhaps those seemingly prosaic, historical truths about how other, often arguably happier, societies ordered their affairs in the past should no longer be seen as too drably factual to enter high art's realm of Beauty. Perhaps, too, the idea that sex is a natural human instinct should not go on being censored on the grounds of a bogus aesthetic that finds it too indelicate a truth to count as beautiful. There could even be the suggestion, in a poem that seems so equivocal about the silence with which it colludes, that one day 'our rhyme' may need to widen its definition of acceptable beauty to include even the ugliest truths about the suffering of the poor and the self-indulgence of the rich.

At first glance the Urn could seem a culpably 'Cold pastoral' in keeping its 'streets' so 'silent', a 'bride of quietness' wedded to

1 P. B. Shelley, 'Ode to the West Wind', l 69.

theories of art that the most repressive Tories favoured. The Prince
Regent himself, according to Hone's parody of an 1819 speech, was
demanding silence from England's noisy demonstrators and telling
them that 'their duty' was 'to be starved in quiet'.[1] However, the
Urn's very quietness, because it is at first so obtrusive and is then so
decisively abandoned in the direct speech of the closing lines, may
implicitly raise the very issues that a more discreet and lasting silence
would have suppressed. The beautiful Urn, inasmuch as it at least
provokes such curiosities, even where it cannot satisfy them, may be
supportive enough of humane compassion and of human optimism
to be indeed 'a friend to *man*'.

This word 'Man', for Keats's generation, still had the dangerous
power to evoke a radical egalitarianism. From Rousseau's 'Man is
born free; but everywhere is in chains' through to Wollstonecraft
and Paine 'vindicating' the 'rights of man', the word had been the
cornerstone of revolutionary rhetoric, and it could still function as a
shorthand rejection of hierarchy. 'Man' could seem an insistently
inclusive term, defining us all in terms of the species and denying
the titles and ranks that had divided humanity into the few with
rights and the many with duties. The bogus singularity evoked by
grandiose titles blinds the few to the truth of our shared humanity.
In *Hyperion*, Saturn is ignorant explicitly because he has the uniquely
singular status of being 'the king', and is thus 'blind from sheer
supremacy'. A mournful megalomaniac, he dreams that he has
suffered a personal defeat at the hands of an equally singular rival,
Jove. He misinterprets history in lunatic egotism, constantly describing his situation by use of the *singular* first-person pronoun. By
contrast, one of the lesser gods, Oceanus, sees clearly and reveals the
essentially plural – and essentially impersonal – truth: '*We* fall by
course of Nature's law, not force . . . of Jove' (ii. 181–2). In earlier
times, Oceanus continues,

>                    *we* the giant race,
> Found *ourselves* ruling new and beauteous realms.
> Now comes the pain of truth, to whom 'tis pain – . . .
> As heaven and earth are fairer, fairer far
> Than chaos and blank darkness, though once chiefs;
> And as *we* show beyond that heaven and earth . . .
> So on *our* heels a fresh perfection treads,
> A power more strong in beauty, born of *us*
> And fated to excel *us*, as *we* pass

1 Rickword, *Radical Squibs*, p 90.

> In glory that old darkness; nor are *we*
> Thereby more conquered than by *us* the rule
> Of shapeless chaos . . .
> . . . For 'tis the eternal law
> That first in beauty should be first in might;
> Yea, by that law, another race may drive
> *Our* conquerors to mourn as *we* do now.
>
> (ii. 200–231)

In these fourteen and a half lines, the plural first-person pronouns of 'we', 'us', 'ourselves' and 'our' are used no fewer than eleven times.

Keats, in his letters, sees British history not in terms of individual kings and queens but in terms of conflict between social groups and their beliefs. Progress is being halted by the Establishment's attempt to 'spread a horrid superstition against all innovation and improvement – The present struggle of the people is to destroy this superstition . . . the French Revolution put a stop to . . . the change for the better – Now it is in progress again.'[1] As in *Hyperion*, change is change for the better: the process of history, the succession of the generations, is naturally one in which those with lovelier ideas – such as brotherhood rather than hierarchy – have 'A power more strong in beauty' and are thus 'fated to excel'. What Oceanus specifically calls the 'truth' is synonymous with 'the eternal law/That first in beauty should be first in might'. These lines, published in the volume of 1820, only ten months after Peterloo, appeared in the same book that offered 'Ode on a Grecian Urn'; so they may well have been used by some to gloss the ode's own assertion about truth and beauty, and as a justification for regarding that too as some sort of contribution to the current 'contest . . . between right and wrong'.[2]

## X

Keats's five other great odes ('. . . to Psyche', '. . . to a Nightingale', '. . . on Melancholy', '. . . on Indolence' and 'To Autumn') were also written in 1819, and all but 'Indolence' published in that same volume issued in June 1820. The Odes do of course supply some support for those who favour a more solitary Keats. They are at least in part about the temptations of egotism, the enticements of despair, the desire for escape into a natural or aesthetic

1 *Letters*, ii. 193–4.
2 Ibid., ii. 194.

world far from the nagging challenge of humanity. The poet of the Odes does often yearn to turn his back on ordinary men and women, on their aspirations and on the appalling injustices that prevent most of them standing any chance of seeing their dreams come true. But the Odes do not record some permanent surrender to the allurements of the egotistical sublime; instead, at their most dynamically disturbed and disturbing, they enact a struggle *against* such temptations.

'Ode to a Nightingale', for instance, implicitly defines the entire breed of man as capable of unique emotional responsiveness. We are all capable of being intensely stirred by beauty, such as the nightingale's song. What we can all hear in it evokes some of the more poignant peculiarities of human consciousness, such as our ability to mourn the past and to fear the future. Unlike nightingales – and, as far as we know, unlike any other species in the ecosystem – we can be conscious of our own mortality. Such consciousness is dispiriting indeed when each of us plays the lonely game of caring only for her or his own individual experience. In stanza VI the first-person-singular's death-wish dream 'To cease upon the midnight with no pain' almost instantly becomes the nightmare indignity of being reduced to one insensitive lump of turf: 'Still wouldst thou sing, and I have ears in vain –/To thy high requiem become a sod'. But, however deaf the individual will become, the poem has already, in stanza III, invited us also to think in plural terms, of 'men' rather than a singular man, and their common pain *is* audible: 'where men sit' and *do* 'hear each other groan'. That larger, more plural view embraces a sense of the past, a history through which 'hungry generations tread' as relentlessly as the ordinary people of England are now doing, taking to the streets for their mass demonstrations against a Government whose callous ineptitude is imposing literal starvation. Thinking in these larger, less egotistical terms – of whole generations – attunes the ear to hear, in the prospect of death, a guarantee of ultimate equality. Death is the great leveller, obliterating the bogus distinctions of the social hierarchy. The voice, heard by the vulnerable first-person-singular poet in the transience of his own 'passing night', was also in fact 'heard/In ancient days by emperor and clown' (63–4). Clown, of course, in its characteristic early nineteenth-century usage, signals a social rank – the mere farm labourer at the opposite end of the social spectrum from the emperor. Both, the poem insists, hear 'the self-same song' (65). They have an equal sensitivity to such beauty, and are thus defined as existing equally as members of the same human species. The natural nightingale, like the aesthetic Urn, offers its beauty undiscriminatingly, as a 'friend to man'. If emperor and clown read aright they will hear, in the bird's song and in the poet's, 'our rhyme'.

Indeed, if the test of true humanity is how often one hears the song of a bird, the clown working out in the fields is, if anything, at an actual advantage over the emperor lolling about inside his palace. The vast majority of Keats's compatriots had not yet been shifted by the Industrial Revolution from field to factory. So the clown, as agricultural labourer, like those peasant farmers of *Endymion*, can typify the ordinary working people of England. In this context we can see why Keats was enraged by the poetry of Pope, who at one point argues explicitly for a poetic decorum which will reflect and maintain the gulf between clown and emperor:

> A vile conceit in pompous words exprest
> Is like a clown in regal purple drest.
>
> (*An Essay on Criticism*, 320–21)

Keats himself perpetrates just such a 'vile conceit' in the 'Autumn' ode, whose second, central stanza dresses up a whole series of farm labourers in the majesty of the season. It has been argued that stanza I's bees are England's workers and that the 'Cells' evoke the government gaols in which dissident labourers were languishing during that autumn of 1819.[1] But surely it is the central stanza II which typifies the plural, egalitarian Keats. It's there that the singular season is personified as a plural *group* of persons. There's not only the worker sitting inside on the granary floor, but also the gleaner, 'laden', after his productive labour in the field, with a heavy basket. He is discovered in mid-movement, struggling to maintain a steady balance as he crosses the stream. That as yet half-crossed stream is not necessarily a political Rubicon, but the precarious equipoise required suggests that this frozen snapshot cannot long remain still. It will very soon become a movie; and who knows where its resumed narrative may lead? As well as these two, there's that quietly vigilant figure 'by a cyder-press', watching 'the last oozings hours by hours'. We need not make this focus on 'last' things too apocalyptic; but that worker's 'patient look' might not be going to last for an indefinite number of hours (21–2).

As well as these three, we also have the indisputably ominous figure of the mower, the traditional emblem of time's remorseless

---

1 William Keech, 'Cockney Couplets: Keats and the Politics of Style', *Studies in Romanticism*, xxv (1986), 193–6.

movement, cutting down each generation to make way for the next. At present this labourer is temporarily exhausted, 'sound asleep'. But he sleeps on what is explicitly still only 'a *half*-reaped furrow'; so we know that the second half cannot survive his inevitable waking. Ready to his hand lies the reaping sickle – and if we were alarmist Tory readers in the England of 1819, our paranoia might see that not just as the tool of his humble trade but also as the weapon with which he might force 'the grand march of intellect' forward, insisting that 'first in beauty' shall be 'first in might'. Certainly it is only for the moment that his 'hook/Spares the next swath and all its twined flowers'; their death sentence will be carried out just as soon as he wakes. Those poor flowers, so fatally entangled amongst the crops, which for our future well-being we must ruthlessly cut down, evoke poignantly enough why Keats remained a liberal reformer rather than a militant radical. The short-term losses that the violent revolutionary accepts for long-term gains were such that, as the post-Peterloo crisis loomed in 1819 and newspapers carried articles such as 'Return of the Killed and Wounded at Manchester', Keats was willing to linger a precarious while longer in the arrested motion of 'Autumn's' stopped clock. The beautiful and yet brutal dynamism of the historical process could be relied on to press forward again soon enough.

To see whether Keats could ever have unambivalently supported the Luddites or the Pentridge rebels, with all the blood-letting that such conspirators perpetrated themselves and provoked from the authorities, we only have to look at what 'Autumn' does, in its first stanza, with the potentially lethal term 'conspiring'. The word is soothed into being no more than the intimacy of bosom friendship between season and sun. It is explicitly a 'maturing sun'. So what is relished by the poem as an almost static moment is in fact innately dynamic and will, in the fertility of time, give birth to the future. But the sun's interaction with autumn embraces, in so 'mellow' a 'fruitfulness', such an intimately 'close bosom friend' that this is the opposite of rape. The poem's hope – however precarious – is that from such tender lovemaking only love can be made. We need fear no monster of violence being born.

On the other hand, the workers of stanza II reveal that the process of history must inevitably be less personal, more plural than this; that the fields are not some pastoral parkland in which couples meet for leisurely, loving pleasure; the fields are where innumerable men and women labour until they are exhausted. They toil to produce food and yet, in 1819, remain another of those 'hungry generations' that a callous landed gentry underpays, counting on that wearied resignation in which some of stanza II's workers doze. And even if, when they get home from work, they have the strength left for a bit of sexual 'conspiring' with each other, they won't find themselves being pampered into romance by the trappings of what Keats's *Lamia* calls a 'purple-lined *palace* of sweet sin' (ii. 31). As that poem bleakly insists elsewhere, with yet another use of that characteristic pronoun:

> Love in a hut, with water and a crust,
> Is – Love, forgive *us*! – cinders, ashes, dust . . .

(ii. 1–2)

Keats's respect for the compelling forces of sexual love is, I believe, a major complication in – one might almost say a major inhibition to – his politics. In the climactic passage of *Hyperion*, just before the end of the poem, Apollo has a revelation. What he sees is roughly what we would call history; and he cries out:

> Knowledge enormous makes a God of me.
> Names, deeds, grey legends, dire events, rebellions,
> Majesties, sovran voices, agonies,
> Creations and destroyings, all at once
> Pour into the wide hollows of my brain

(iii. 114–18)

As 'rebellions' jostle 'Majesties', the medicine men of the revolutionary tribe, who claim to be 'sovran voices', may indeed herald the construction of fresh and healthier societies; but they achieve their 'Creations' of the new in intimate proximity to the 'agonies' involved in the 'destroyings' of the old. So the real enormity of this 'enormous knowledge' is that radical change, however just, however certain to serve ultimately the progressive 'march of intellect', is in the short term downright cruel. Those 'sovran voices' of revolution have no sovran remedy which allows a poet to be 'physician to all men'; on the contrary they require him to approve the deliberate wounding and killing of people on both sides. And even those who are to die in defence of the morally indefensible status quo are human beings. As such, they too were originally conceived in an act of love, and may now be precious not only to a parent or to their own child but also to some lover for whom this supposedly sacrificeable physique is the object of desire.

Keats often felt challenged to take a more active political role – felt, as he put it, 'ambitious of doing the world some good' or bound to work on what he called 'the liberal side of the question'.[1] But as a crucial passage of *Endymion* (i. 807–23) makes explicit, such ambition to intervene in public events is often defeated by what seems to be an opposite desire: the sexual and romantic aspiration to make love with just one other person.

XI

Even where Keats is decisively writing only about sexual love and not about politics, his poetry still implicitly opposes the lonely singularity of the 'egotistical sublime'. For instance the famous 'Bright star' sonnet devotes most of its lines to a syntactically negative clause, insisting that the poet, though wanting to be as 'steadfast' as the star, does not want to be as loftily isolated from humankind, does not aspire to the Wordsworthian solitude that threatens loneliness: '*Not* in lone splendour ... watching, with eternal lids apart,/Like nature's patient, sleepless Eremite'. The poem is rejecting the eternal vigilance of the egotistical sublime in favour of a serene sleep that literally depends on contact with another human being, 'Pillowed upon my fair love's ripening breast'. It seems predictable that another Keats sonnet, the one that actually addresses itself 'To Sleep', should invoke sleep as 'Shutting, with careful fingers and benign,/*Our* gloom-pleased eyes'.

It is similarly unsurprising, in the light of the 'Bright star' sonnet, that Keats's verse elsewhere sees sexuality, even in its most bitingly physical modes, as an essentially *human* story, constructed not by the singular lover but by a plural 'we', which stands at least for both partners and perhaps for the entire species. The summons at one point in 'Sleep and Poetry' is:

1  In September 1819, after reading in the *Examiner* about Henry Hunt's continuing post-Peterloo reform meetings, Keats wrote: 'I cannot help being very much pleased with the present public proceedings. I hope sincerely I shall be able to put a mite of help to the Liberal side of the Question before I die' (*Letters*, ii. 180). Specifically, Keats resolves to find work as a political journalist and 'write, on the liberal side of the question, for whoever will pay me' (Ibid., ii. 174, 176). Back in April 1818, Keats had claimed: 'I would jump down Aetna for any great Public Good' (Ibid., i. 267); and in June 1818 he had been inspired, by the landscape and people of Wordsworth's Grasmere, to feel with unprecedented intensity 'the glory of Patriotism, the glory of making by any means a country happier. This is what I like better than scenery' (Ibid., i. 307). 'Scenery is fine,' Keats had conceded in a letter earlier that year, 'but human nature is finer'; and the glory of walking through the English countryside was that one 'may meet with some of Edmond Ironside's descendents' or 'meet with some shadowing of Alfred in the shape of a gypsy, a huntsman or a shepherd' (Ibid., i. 242).

To woo sweet kisses from averted faces –
Play with their fingers, touch their shoulders white
Into a pretty shrinking with a bite
As hard as *lips* can make it, till, agreed,
A lovely tale of *human* life *we*'ll read.

(106–10)

Admittedly sex can be seen as fragmenting the community, breaking us up into myriad couples, each of whose shared experience is essentially private. Whether our favoured position in bed is to face each other or not, it usually involves both of us turning our backs on the public world. And yet Keats's inclusive use here of the plural pronoun in the context of sexuality does make a kind of sense. The complexity and intensity of human sex is not just often distinctly peculiar, it is also peculiar to our species; and at best it does allow us to read a lovely tale of essentially *human* life – one that reveals, beyond the clothing of social distinctions, that naked equality which is our true being. So even on this topic 'Sleep and Poetry' may be shrewd in choosing to speak as 'we' and deciding to reject the singular pronoun.

Keats's narrative of myth and magic in the classical world, *Lamia*, ends its Part I with an explicit acknowledgement of its plural audience. It suggests that at this point the readers may be tempted to long for escapist fantasy-verse, in which the loving couple could for ever be left alone with each other – safely 'Shut from the busy world' in their magical, erotic hideaway. ''Twould humour many a heart to leave them thus', *if* the audience did not accept that 'verse *must* tell,/For truth's sake' that of course the idyll did not last. The readers, however reluctantly, do accept that realistic narrative verse has to move on to recount 'what woe afterwards befell' (i. 394–7). Yet the contract with the audience involves not only this commitment to shared realism, but also to the shared fear that, in an age increasingly respectful of what we would now call science, a chilly reverence for fact may damage perception. The new fad for investigation and classification could drain all magic and colour from the world that we see. At the climax of *Lamia* it is not the poet alone but his plural audience too that asks the wistful question:

Do not all charms fly
At the mere touch of cold philosophy?
There was an awful rainbow once in heaven:
*We* know her woof, her texture; she is given
In the dull catalogue of common things.

(ii. 229–33)

The poem's stance is often, however, more ambivalent than this. The love affair – one that can only survive while Lycius avoids all his friends and neighbours, acting as if he has 'almost forsworn' the 'noisy world' (ii. 33) – is sometimes seen by the poem as almost pathological in its isolationism. Furthermore, the new, purpose-built 'palace' in which the lovers are 'enthroned' and 'regal drest' had a sinister equivalent in Keats's England. Its 'royal porch' and daz-zlingly 'wealthy . . . banquet-room' have much the same effect on the too-easily-impressed, 'marvelling' burghers of Corinth as the Prince Regent's flamboyantly extravagant building and banqueting had had on the worthies of Brighton. In fact the Corinthians do, at one point, come close to raising what was for a nineteenth-century English liberal a central question: whose work is producing the surplus that is here being so ostentatiously consumed? The guests enter Lycius's palace, 'wondering/Whence all this mighty cost and blaze of wealth could spring' (ii. 3, 31, 17, 133, 155, 173–90, 152, 197–8). Certainly the notion that a couple rich enough to organize such a feast might nevertheless deserve more sympathy than someone on a 'fast' is introduced, with a raised eyebrow, as 'a doubtful tale from faery land', one that may not be easy for the typical disenfran-chised English reader to credit – 'Hard for the non-elect to under-stand' (ii. 5–6).

XII

The marriage that proves so fatal in *Lamia* is never risked by any of the romantic couples in Keats's trio of medieval romances. Both *Isabella* and *The Eve of St Agnes* are essentially tales of forbidden sexuality where the poet's sympathies are largely with the young lovers. In both cases the authoritarian relatives who oppose the affairs, though representatives of supposedly civilized society, are in fact condemned by the poem as barbaric. However, Keats's famous imitation of a medieval ballad, 'La Belle Dame sans Merci', is far more ambiguous. Its dialogue form requires us to respond to two enigmatic voices as we try to understand their and the poem's attitude to the perhaps sinister and certainly seductive lady of the title. Moreover, the poem exists in two versions that are so different that interpretation of its sexual politics depends on the text chosen; as does any view of what attitude the poem adopts to the élite figures whose deaths it envisages: 'pale kings and princes too,/Pale warriors, death-pale were they all'. If the speaker of these words is himself a 'knight at arms', as he is in the most commonly printed version, we can assume that he has nothing but sympathy for the fate of his class allies. If, however, the speaker is by contrast a 'wretched wight' (a certainly pathetic and perhaps specifically destitute representative of the lowest rank in society), as he is in the only version that we know Keats approved for publication, his attitude to dead royalty and their soldiers is less certain.

The setting in both versions is autumnal, with the sedge already withered and the birds gone.

> The squirrel's granary is full,
> And the harvest's done.

Winter is clearly looming, and if this man 'Alone and palely loitering' is a mere 'wight' he could already be hungry. It need not just be lost love that has him looking 'haggard', with the colour in his face 'fading . . . Fast' and a pale 'brow' so visibly 'moist' as to suggest 'fever'. If it is partly through poverty that he is so frail, the 'latest dream' – offering the prospect of 'kings and princes', in spite of their usual control of 'granary' and 'harvest', ending up with 'starv'd lips' themselves – may not be an unqualified nightmare. Certainly the 'horrid warning' evoked as such lips 'gaped wide' is universal in its application, reminding us that death, to the medieval poets, was often the great leveller; that countless generations of once glamorously colourful 'kings and princes' have long ago become just as pale in death as the most pallid 'wight' amongst their subjects; and that the same fate will overtake the most apparently unchallengeable of current rulers. That prospect clearly lurks also in the last stanza of *The Eve of St Agnes*, where 'the Baron . . . And all his warrior-guests' are 'long be-nightmared' by dreams in which the 'coffin-worm' looms 'large', even as the young lovers, in defiance of all such authority, have 'fled away into the storm' (371–5).

Earlier in this poem Porphyro, in his clandestine visit to Madeline's bedroom, has played on her lute to wake her. The tune that he uses to rouse her from her erotic dream, moving her on to the reality of their first lovemaking, is 'an ancient ditty . . . In Provence call'd, "La Belle Dame sans Merci"' (289–92). Like that other 'Provençal song' that accompanies the 'Dance' of 'sunburnt' peasants in 'the warm South' ('Ode to a Nightingale', 14–15), the reference to a region of France may have been far more telling to readers brought up to believe, for the past twenty years, that they should be at war with all things French. Certainly we should understand that, in celebrating not only the folk-songs of the common people but those of the nation that for so long had been the foreign enemy, the very

title of 'La Belle Dame sans Merci' may have led its first readers to
hope or fear, depending on their politics, that it would indeed supply
a voice not to a genteel knight but to some ordinary 'wight'.

The version of 'La Belle Dame sans Merci' that does make the
male speaker a 'wretched wight' also gives him, in the poem's erotic
plot, a less helplessly passive role than he has in the better-known
text. Furthermore, it offers a less demonizing portrait of the mysterious lady who here has her own vulnerability for the reader to weigh
against that of the 'wight'. Their more even-handed process of
mutual seduction could reasonably be called lovemaking, however
sinister a conservative reader might find such behaviour on what is,
after all, their first meeting.

The sour prediction made by some reviewers that sexual libertarian-
ism tended to work hand in glove with subversive politics is more
certainly fulfilled in a section of *Isabella* that attacks the heroine's
brothers, not only for their literally murderous hostility to her love
affair but also for their equally lethal exploitation of their workers.
The relevant passage of the poem was denounced as 'bad taste' by
one contemporary reviewer and as 'insulting bravado' by another;[1]
and, as with Lockhart homing in on Book III of *Endymion*, it may
have been the flaunting of the plural first-person pronoun that
provoked. The poem's own rage against the arrogance of the capitalist
brothers, 'these money-bags' (142), reaches its climax in

> Why were they proud? again *we* ask aloud,
> Why in the name of Glory were they proud?
>
> (127–8)

The rhetoric of repetition, the populist use of colloquialism ('in the
name of Glory'), the rough insistence that the poem's questions be
asked 'aloud' and, above all, the claim, implicit in that 'we', of
intimidating numbers supporting the poet's protest: all these suggest
not the quiet, solitary meditations of the lone artist but the noisy
challenge of the demagogue, and even perhaps the roars of the
emboldened crowd to whom, and for whom, he speaks. 'Insulting
bravado' seems accurate enough.

The solidarity which those plural pronouns recommend as the
answer to callous capitalists seems logical, granted that capitalism's
victims are essentially plural. Just this one firm of businessmen

---

1 Anonymous review of 1820 volume, *Edinburgh Magazine and Literary Miscellany*
(*Scots Magazine*), August 1820 and October 1820; and anonymous review, *London
Magazine* (*Baldwin's*), September 1820; reprinted in *Keats: The Critical Heritage*,
pp 213, 220–22.

condemns many, many ordinary workers to terrible suffering. Stanza XIV, having reminded us that the owners consist of just '*two* brothers', continues:

> And for them many a weary hand did swelt
>   In torched mines and noisy factories,
> And many once proud-quivered loins did melt
>   In blood from stinging whip. With hollow eyes
> Many all day in dazzling river stood,
> To take the rich-ored driftings of the flood.
> . . . for them alone did seethe
>   A thousand men in troubles wide and dark . . .

$$(107-12, 117-18)$$

We scarcely need the 'once proud-quivered loins' of the now exploited Indians to feel the reasonableness of the poem's relating the brothers' repressive view of young love to their oppression of those whom they employ. The freedom that Keats favours is indivisible, based on a notion of human dignity which is equally degraded by the puritanical and the profit-obsessed.

Consider, however, the fertile precision with which Keats is choosing and using words when he describes those who have to sweat, 'In torched mines and noisy factories', as 'many a hand'. That hand contains a characteristic ambiguity. Each worker is partly no more than his sweating hand because, even as the poem denounces the capitalist exploiters, it understands their dehumanizing vision. They are not conscious sadists but blinkered imperialists, and simply cannot see the humanity of those whom they exploit. As moral amputees themselves, they chop all their workers down to mere factory hands. But the same word, in its precision about the body, can simultaneously insist on the humanity that the poem itself sees and that the reader is invited to recognize. The living creatures whose 'blood' is shed by 'stinging whip' may be abused by their employers as if they are animals; but it is not with paws but with human hands that they sweat.

There is in fact a larger ambiguity governing the whole passage. Hitherto I have had to oversimplify and suggest that the word 'them', in the lines above, can refer only to the 'two brothers', that it could not include the third sibling, Isabella – the apparently innocent heroine of this tale and, in the plot that has her lover murdered, the helpless victim of her brothers. In fact the grammar of the context allows – perhaps encourages – the reader to consider the possibility that it is also for Isabella's benefit that so many people sweat and suffer. She may know far less about the sources of her pampered existence than her siblings, and, as a female in a patriarchal society, she is clearly far less powerful than they are. Nevertheless she is a lady, born into a privileged, landowning family, whose imperialist ventures are now putting the natives of many distant territories to highly profitable work. As such she enjoys the same material lifestyle, in the same grand house, as her brothers. At no point in the poem does she seem prepared to elope with her low-caste lover and live on what little he and she could earn by their own efforts. The poem of course remains hugely sympathetic to her; but the alternative interpretation of the key pronouns allows it to suggest that wickedness is less a matter of individual personality than of the structures within which social or racial groups relate to each other.

Keats's verse is often praised for its 'sensuality' or 'sensuousness', and rightly so. But beware of any suggestion that the poetry's focus on the physical makes it less thoughtful or less thought-provoking. Keats's interest in the human body is an informed and committed attention to what all human beings (of whatever class or country) have in common. The insistence on our shared physicality is part of his egalitarian campaign against all the hierarchies by which we are divided.

Much of the glory of his own subversive version of the creation myth in the Hyperion poems is that, as humanity is born out of failed gods who are learning the painful lessons of defeat and vulnerability and mutual need, the transformation is not just cerebral or emotional but anatomical. The life to which these gigantic, statuesque beings are lumbering is recognizably human because of what happens to pulsing heart and palpable hand. There has been considerable debate as to which vanquished regime is represented in these bemused novices who are struggling to understand and even embody the energies of change. Could Saturn, who at first finds his defeat and new status as an ex-divinity so inconceivable, be the French king who was dethroned; or an English king who, in radical prophecy, will be; or a post-Waterloo Napoleon? Or as these fallen monuments debate the difficulties of hope and the enticements of defeatism, might they, in the reactionary Europe of 1819, seem more like would-be revolutionaries, whose idealistic vision of a godlike human nature was now arguably in ruins? Could it be the idols of radicalism, rather than those of reaction, who are imaged in these fallen monuments? It may be that the poet himself would have no more decisive answer than that, at best, he had striven to write as 'a Humanist, physician to all men'.

# 12

## ORIENTALISM

### Marilyn Butler

The palaces of kings are built upon the ruins of the bowers of paradise ... We have it in our power to begin the world over again.

Thomas Paine, *Common Sense*, 1776

For many readers the Romantic lyric poem is the archetypal poem, subjective, emotional, accessible; and the Romantic poet is the model for all poets. Interpreters of Romanticism, especially those writing in the late nineteenth or twentieth centuries, have often stressed that the places it conjures up are not our world, literal and external, but gorgeous representations of the poet's inner world, guarantors of the power of Imagination. Yet Romantic poets were also ambitious to play a part in the public sphere. Then they were dialogists rather than monologists, who engaged in furious debates with other writers about issues, and invented new genres or revived very old ones, in order to match times they perceived as uniquely heroic. Whether as visions of paradisal life or as waking nightmares, Romantic world-making had real-life, complex applications, far beyond what the individual writers could foresee. The poets may in reality have been at their most functional where they have come to seem most Romantic. This is most true of their poems on the East, commonly allegories of empire, and generally located where real-life empires persisted or were arising, in the terrain between Greece and India.

From the mid-seventeenth century, sophisticated French culture made the Arab world of the Middle East and north Africa fashionable for other Europeans. First a series of observant, amused and amusing travellers familiarized the Western public with visions of wealth and luxury: palaces, gardens, veiled maidens and iced sherbet typified Eastern court life, from Tunis in the west, via Cairo and Baghdad to Delhi, the capital of the Mogul empire. Then, in the first decade of the eighteenth century, the Frenchman Antoine Galland translated a motley multi-volume collection of stories he called the *Arabian Nights Entertainment*, which at once came out in English. Using this model the French developed the prose 'oriental tale', which with wit and style celebrated an idealized world of consumerist delights – a land of magic, ingenious contrivances, treasure, love-intrigue and powerful arbitrary caliphs. Accuracy to modern Middle Eastern realities played a minimal part in the development of this genre. Either the oriental tale dreamed up a land of heart's desire or (in the hands of dissident intellectuals, such as Voltaire) it sniped at court despotism nearer home. So the taste for oriental fiction, fantasy and satire preceded Orientalism, which became the term for the serious, broadly based modern study of Asian cultures, languages and religions.

The French literary historian Raymond Schwab dates the emergence of a fully fledged learned discourse about the East from 1770, when the Frenchman Anquetil du Perron published his translation of the *Zend-Avesta*, the Parsee holy book which enshrined the ancient Persian cult of Zoroaster. Schwab argues that late eighteenth-century culture can be thought of as the 'oriental renaissance' much as the period two to three centuries earlier is termed the 'classical renaissance'. In each case the recovery of an exciting body of very old knowledge acted, paradoxically, to rejuvenate a tired if younger culture.[1] Central European accounts of orientalism will on the other hand give a somewhat different emphasis, by focusing rather on the great flowering in nineteenth-century Germany of new academic disciplines such as (comparative) religion, including hermeneutics and the higher criticism, and the more secular humane specialisms, philology and historiography. But Schwab's insistence on an eighteenth-century point of departure, and on attributing the early leadership to French scholars working on the Middle East, does in fact better explain the content and manner of Romantic-period orientalist poetry in English, which draws richly on both Middle Eastern and Indian materials from the mid-1780s onwards, but also remains orientated towards France, the French Revolution and the Anglo-French world-power rivalry acted out in the Napoleonic wars.

The time of origin may seem a relatively minor point, since for many students of orientalism nowadays the phenomenon belongs

---

1 Raymond Schwab, *La Renaissance orientale*, Paris, 1950, English tr., New York, 1974.

classically to the nineteenth and early twentieth centuries, which is also the heyday of European worldwide imperialism. Considered as a 200-year-old body of Western scholarship relating to the East, orientalism can be viewed cynically, as the academic and cultural support-system of more openly utilitarian enterprises: the Western discovery, mapping, development, occupation and modernization of the non-European world. In 1978 the Palestinian-American literary critic Edward Said produced his seminal post-colonial study, *Orientalism*, which takes as its point of departure Napoleon Bonaparte's invasion of Egypt in 1798, accompanied by a cohort of research scholars briefed to open up Egyptian and Arabic learning and antiquities to Western eyes. For Said this starting-point symbolizes the covert *interestedness* of this whole field of scholarship, including its more abstruse or unworldly subdivisions: 'Orientalism can be discussed and analysed as the corporate institution for dealing with the Orient . . . by authorizing views of it, describing it, by teaching it, settling it, ruling over it; in short . . . as a Western style for dominating, restructuring and having authority over the Orient.'[1] Said sees travellers, soldiers, administrators, artists and poets, whether consciously or not, collaborating in a vast undertaking of geopolitical espionage.

As it happens, Edward Said has little to say about English Romantic poetry. He follows older textbooks in stating that English poets anticipate later French writers and artists (Flaubert, Nerval) in exploiting the East's associations with personal irresponsibility, sexual freedom and release. The examples he gives are poems long considered of lesser importance, such as Southey's religious epics or Byron's Turkish tales, which Said feels no need to analyse.[2] It is enough that works of their type, which he takes to be essentially private fantasy, bolster Western superiority by providing an Eastern *alter ego* – weak, sensuous, servile, effeminate – where the West is strong, free and manly.

In fact this is an old-established misconception about the poems in question. Taken as a whole, imaginative prose and poetry written in English on the East from the early 1790s represents an intellectually ambitious strand of Romanticism, associated with the imitation of high-cultural forms (Renaissance romance, classical history and tragedy, the Bible, Shakespeare), with public-sphere rather than

1 Edward Said, *Orientalism*, London, 1978, p 3.
2 Ibid., p 167.

domestic or local material, and above all with the period's hunger for essentialist, universal Knowledge. Romantic narrative poetry does not need to be let into Said's argument on special terms. Some at least powerfully confirms the thesis he adapts from the French cultural historian Michel Foucault, that a highly significant revision and categorization of Knowledge occurred in the late Enlightenment, and that this, like discourse generally, had a socio-political function: 'Men govern themselves and others by the production of truth . . . the establishment of domains in which the practice of true and false can be made at once ordered and pertinent.'[1]

Since 1978 Said's positions have been challenged from within cultural criticism; he has replied to objectors, and stirred up further controversy.[2] The two main complaints of fellow post-colonialists are that Said's account of Eastern culture is monolithic, and that the case he presents is partly Westernized. My own description of Romantic oriental poetry assumes that it is in fact legitimate to treat this as a Western discourse – far more than, from my perspective, Said does. On the other hand I find myself in agreement with Said's Eastern critics on the first point: his analyses of both Western and Eastern orientalism surely 'totalize' cultures in a way that rapidly ceases to be useful.

The oriental poems written in England over the four Romantic decades (1785–1825) display the ebb and flow of public opinion, as well as the self-examination and display of individual poets. They are rich in metaphor, allegory and myth. Some criticize empire, and other Western writers promoting it. Said's book is open to the basic critical objection that it erases all those meaningful differences of language, attitude and voice which writing concerned with and aimed at the public sphere actively brings out. In seeking to uncover his own political allegory in this writing, Said denies the allegories, and politics, already there. He claims that to write about Easterners as 'the Other' is to enforce demeaning stereotypes on individuals and nations. Yet this is not the only model for a literary reaching

---

1 Interview with Michel Foucault, in *After Philosophy*, ed. Kenneth Baynes et al., Cambridge, Mass., 1987, p 108.
2 For engagements with Said, see for example Homi Bhabha, 'Difference, Discrimination, and the Discourse of Colonialism', in *The Politics of Theory*, ed. F. Barker et al., Colchester, 1983, and 'Signs Taken for Wonders', *Critical Inquiry*, xii (1985), 144–65; Robert Young, *White Mythologies: Writing History and the West*, London, 1990, pp 126–56; sundry numbers of *Cultural Critique* (1986–9); Aijaz Ahmad, *In Theory: Nations, Classes, Literature*, London, 1992; and Said's own *Culture and Imperialism*, London, 1993.

outward. Critics of classical literature influenced by anthropology tend to argue quite the opposite, that Greek drama had an exploratory and positive part to play for its domestic audience precisely when it opened up 'other worlds', with their dangerous yet delightful possibilities.[1] The Foucault-derived model is reductive, finally, in its tendency to uniformity, for texts also struggle within themselves and with one another, and in the end it is their contradictions that are productive of change.

Poets, travel-writers, novelists undoubtedly belong in a discourse through which the British teach themselves about India and acquire the national will to be there. The long allegorical poem, creating an imaginary empire in the East, is a form which comes into existence in the 1790s and dies back from the 1820s (though adult prose fiction and adventure yarns flourish and grow). The form coincides with Britain's main period of Indian wars of conquest, effectively taking off in the decade 1795–1805, when the East India Company's bridgeheads in Bengal, Madras and Bombay were transformed into what became by 1807 an empire engorging most of the subcontinent south of the Himalayas. But these poems do not merely produce compelling, if fictional, images of rulers and states, and the modes by which power works. At times they dramatize practical political options which the individual citizen might hope to influence. Poetry can be proactive, and it can aim to subvert. As Britain transformed itself into an Eastern empire, most of the orientalizing poets, at least some of the time, imagined such empires as lightly allegorized, defamiliarized versions of the British state. An imagined overthrow 'otherwhere', the plot of poem after poem, stands for revolution anywhere, including the British empire, including metropolitan Britain – an entirely different proposition.

Merely to identify the extent and symbolic nature of oriental poetry in the Romantic period is to challenge some literary-historical orthodoxies, which for much of the nineteenth and twentieth centuries have grouped the best English Romantic poetry around the domestic, consolatory *œuvre* of Wordsworth. It also challenges a style of writing on Coleridge that stresses his debts to German philosophy and theology, the latter by now often sympathetic to Eastern religion. According to this latter line of thinking, Coleridge's 'Kubla Khan' is the archetypal English oriental poem, earning praise as an inward journey of discovery which taps the spiritual resources

1  See for example Froma Zeitlin, 'Thebes: Theatre of Self and Society in Athenian Drama', in Peter Euben, *Greek Tragedy and Political Theory*, Ithaca, NY, 1987.

associated with India.[1] 'Kubla Khan' is honoured for bringing at least some English poetry of the period into line with the German lyrics of Novalis and Hölderlin, who shared in German enthusiasm from the 1790s for an 'Indic' culture which uniquely fused poetry and religion. 'Kubla Khan' hints at a mysterious, numinous East, influenced quite possibly by German taste – all the more likely if it was written in August 1799, after Coleridge returned from his visit to Germany.[2] It takes more straining to read into it the next decade's 'high romanticism', by which Friedrich Schlegel and Friedrich Creuzer draw learnedly on Hindu literary and religious examples to support claims that, through symbol and myth, poetry enacts the primal union of spirit and matter.[3]

But it is arguable that in 'constructing' knowledge as an essentially spiritual field, more refined than the field of brute force, German academics were themselves not wholly innocent of cultural nationalism. What they (and their sympathizer Coleridge) did achieve was a challenge, on behalf of an abstracted intellectuality and a Christian, conservative ideology, to the materialism of the military powers France and Britain. This chapter surveys the domestic literary response to the same issue, as the Western powers squabbled over the domination of Europe and Asia in this, the crucial period at the threshold of empire.

## THE 1780s

In the early 1780s Englishmen were given to complaining how little the English had contributed to Western knowledge of India. Then came a remarkably quick flowering by two efficient, sophisticated

1 John Drew, *British Romantics and India*, Cambridge, 1987, claims that English writers from Coleridge to E. M. Forster regarded Indian wisdom as a source of spiritual truth; E. S. Shaffer, *Kubla Khan and the Fall of Jerusalem, 1770–1880*, Cambridge, 1975, pp 17–61, considers this poem a substantial contribution to German poetic orientalism and its academic form of expression, the 'higher criticism'.

2 For an impressive examination of the case for dating 'Kubla Khan' in 1799, never convincingly refuted, see Elisabeth Schneider's careful examination of its debts to Southey's materials assembled for *Thalaba* (*Coleridge, Opium and 'Kubla Khan'*, Chicago, 1953, pp 174–227). Given the nature of these materials, this argument militates against a heavily symbolic reading of 'Kubla Khan'. Compare with my less full discussion of 'Kubla Khan' as an orientalist text in 'Plotting the Revolution: Romanticism as Political Narrative', in *Romantic Revolutions*, ed. Kenneth Johnston et al., Bloomington, Ind., 1990, pp 133–57.

3 For a convenient selection from German academic mythologizing in the Romantic period see Burton Feldman and Robert D. Richardson, *The Rise of Modern Mythology, 1680–1860*, Bloomington, Ind., 1972, pp 215–40, and esp. pp 297–364.

groups, one at home and one in Calcutta. In a London where French high culture was supremely fashionable, the sceptical French approach to comparative religion or mythology and the collection of ancient sacred artefacts were all the rage. But when it came to information, the wealthy London circle of liberal Francophiles who formed the Society of Antiquaries and published its journal, *Archaeologia*, was more than matched by Sir William Jones's Asiatic Society of Bengal, founded 1784, which from 1789 distributed its papers Europe-wide in the journal *Asiatic Researches*. The first, élite group were concerned with sculpture, architecture and religion, while the second – doctors, soldiers, middle-class company employees – extended their interests more widely into all the arts and sciences. Jones (1746–94), greatest of British orientalists, to some extent linked the two groups, through his good connections in liberal Whig circles before he left for Calcutta in 1783 to take up an Indian judgeship.

British India consisted at this time of three unequal tracts of land. The largest, Bengal, was administered from the important trading post of Calcutta. The two other ports in British hands, Madras and Bombay, had smaller hinterlands. The East India Company, which owned the monopoly of trade with India, was governed in London by a Court of Proprietors, or shareholders, and a smaller, elective Court of Directors. The latter, the executive body, transmitted decisions on policy to a Governor (later Governor-General) in Bengal, who in turn headed a company administration which in 1800 employed approximately 4,500 soldiers and civilians in India.

The principle of governing territories overseas was a sensitive one and much disputed. Gibbon's *Decline and Fall of the Roman Empire* and Adam Smith's *Wealth of Nations*, two great works of 1776, the year of the American Declaration of Independence, both upheld the liberal-Whiggish view that rich possessions in the East would corrupt the State and damage the economy. The company's 'nabobs' were often represented satirically back home as crass profiteers, who fleeced the natives and returned to Britain to spend their fortunes. Influential statesmen, including Pitt, Fox and Burke, held that the balance of the British constitution would be upset if this source of wealth and power was left effectively in the hands of City merchants, or indeed in those of the king and his ministers, bypassing Parliament. This faction of the governing Whig aristocracy secured a partial victory in 1784 with an amended India Act which brought the company to some extent under parliamentary supervision. Burke, Windham and their friends later attempted to impeach for corruption one of the most notable of eighteenth-century Company servants,

Warren Hastings (1732–1818), after he returned home in 1785 from a thirteen-year stint as Governor.

England's 'oriental renaissance' figures within this power struggle. Its moment of origin here implicates it directly in the current political controversies about extending power over a distant people, or about importing corruption, or about the gulf between the two cultures – or about which sections of the wealthy classes were to govern Britain. In the 1770s and early 1780s almost all the important British contributions to knowledge of India were generated, mostly in Calcutta, under the direct encouragement or patronage of Hastings. Before Hastings's day the surgeon John Zephaniah Holwell contributed a volume containing four essays on the religion, folk festivals and chronologies of the Hindus of mid-eighteenth-century Bengal, *Interesting historical events, Relative to the provinces of Bengal, and the Empire of Hindostan* (1766–7). Colonel Alexander Dow appended two more essays on Hinduism to his translation from a seventeenth-century Persian original of a history of the Deccan (1772). The two most important works Hastings directly commissioned were Nathaniel Brassey Halhed's *Code of Gentoo Laws* (1776), a digest translated from Sanskrit via Persian, and Charles Wilkins's translation from Sanskrit of the sacred text, the *Bhagavadgita*, which Hastings had published in 1785 at the Company's expense.

The effort in the Hastings era in India itself thus went into ancient Hindu law and religion, and the ancient language in which both were written. The important works he commissioned were afterwards assimilated into the academic study of Indian traditions. But the rhetoric explaining this selection is worth attending to. Hastings himself, introducing the *Bhagavadgita*, praised 'a sublimity of conception, reasoning and diction, almost unequalled; and a single exception, among all the known religions of mankind, of a theology accurately corresponding with that of the Christian dispensation'.[1] He goes on to stress the practical contribution the Company's servants were making by informing the British and other Europeans about Hindu culture and language, and by eradicating an earlier impression of Indians as savages:

Every instance which brings their real character home to observation will impress us with a more generous sense of feeling for their natural rights, and teach us to estimate them by the measure of our own. But such instances can

1 Warren Hastings, preliminary letter to Charles Wilkins, *The Bhagvat-Gita, or Dialogues of Kreeshna and Arjoon*, London, 1785, p 10.

only be obtained in their writings: and these will survive when the British dominion in India shall long have ceased to exist.[1]

The imposing rhetoric in favour of timeless truths, a style which continues to be characteristic of orientalism, masks the extent to which law, religion and language were keys to practical administrative problems: the need to secure native co-operation and to work with a native infrastructure in order to govern a large territory like Bengal. Hastings needed to win approval for a controversial policy of Indianizing, which he was pursuing against the received wisdom both of his Company predecessors and of traditional Whigs and Tories at home. He advocated intervening in the politics of neighbouring Indian states, forming alliances with them, coercing them and even warring with them. Whatever he might say about the brevity of British dominion, he acted, in his wars of 1777–82, as though to make Bengal the nucleus of a new and major Indian state. Prosaically, Hastings had to convince the public at home that his Indian 'allies' were worth the money his deals and his campaigns were costing. He needed to undercut British chauvinism and parochialism by an appeal to the imagination, so that the idea of Britain as an Indian power became enticing, noble or merely safe. He also had to promote himself and his subordinates as civilized, cultivated gentlemen rather than buccaneers.

Of the two best books of Indian antiquities produced in England at this period, one, a comparative treatise on architecture by the painter William Hodges, had also benefited from Hastings's encouragement.[2] But the rich, cosmopolitan art-collectors who between 1780 and 1789 heard a spate of papers on Indian antiquities – men like Richard Gough, Richard Payne Knight, Sir William Hamilton and Charles Townley – were already ultra-liberal in the style of some of the disaffected French aristocracy. They were predisposed to admire Hinduism in a manner incompatible with Hastings's essentially soothing approach, as a type of paganism that offered to outdo Christianity in age, grandeur and sophistication. The papers read to the Antiquaries included some that presented Indian art at its most awe-inspiring and universal, such as the cave-temples of Elephanta and Salsette in the neighbourhood of Bombay. Others floated insolent comparisons: the phallus or linga so common in Indian sacred art was

1 Ibid., p 14.
2 William Hodges, *A Dissertation on the Prototypes of Architecture, Hindoo, Moorish and Gothic*, London, 1786. Hodges argues that non-classical architectural traditions are not inferior copies but 'the spontaneous produce of genius in different countries, the necessary effects of similar necessity and materials' (p 60).

understood by the antiquarian Richard Gough as an attempt to embody in physical imagery the attributes of God; this was, Gough added impudently, a conception of art as a symbolic language more profound than the representational art of monotheism.[1]

But the oriental poetry composed by William Jones himself, working in the intervals of his weightier researches in language, myth and law (the Hastings fields), shows how aristocratic orientalism could also accommodate itself to commercial and political needs in the period immediately prior to the French Revolution. With his eye apparently on the English drawing-room public, Jones wrote a series of odes addressing Hindu divinities. Many were female, most could be likened to familiar Greek and Roman opposite numbers; Jones for example points out that Lakshmi resembles Ceres. These poems plainly aren't translations; they are somewhat flat adaptations of the Pindaric ode, using Hindu local colour. The effect is to convey that Hindu poetry is very respectable and classical. Its pantheon of gods and goddesses seems unfamiliar only in being benign and responsible, bent on making crops grow rather than committing adultery. The high percentage of women deities is no accident, and in one of Jones's most charming poems, 'The Hindu Wife', they are reinforced by a story from the long ancient epic, the *Mahabharata*, in which Draupady saves her five husbands from the wrath of a magician by confessing that she was momentarily tempted by a handsome poet. For a sophisticated Western readership, a small, wealthy élite now semi-detached for reasons of snobbery from the Church and no more enthusiastic about monarchy, Hinduism gained charm from its dispersal of divine authority, its avoidance of a tyrant-god, its apparent lack of severity in sexual matters, and the relaxed, civilizing presence of a female element in its pantheon.

Jones's most famous and influential translation was a play, *Sacontala* (or *Sakuntala*), by Calidas (Kalidasa), whom Jones describes as 'the Shakespeare of India', and dates, too early, as a contemporary of Christ.[2] *Sacontala* appeared in English in 1789, and was translated

---

1 Richard Gough, *A Comparative View of the Antient Monuments of India*, London, 1785, p viii. Gough's argument echoes that of the Frenchman D'Hancarville and is reflected the following year in Richard Payne Knight's privately printed but soon notorious 'A Discourse on the Worship of Priapus', which Knight afterwards reissued in a more decorous version as *An Inquiry into the Symbolical Language of Ancient Art and Mythology* (1818). For English study of India in the two decades prior to the French Revolution see Mildred Archer and Ronald Lightbown, *India Observed: India as Viewed by British Artists, 1760–1860*, London, 1982, pp 8–31.

2 William Jones, *Collected Works*, ed. A. M. Jones, 6 vols, London, 1799, vi. 205. Kalidasa is now placed in the sixth century AD.

into German in 1791 by a sympathizer with the French Revolution, Georg Forster. The impact of the German version was especially marked. Herder praised the play as the epitome of Indian spiritual sublimity and richness. Friedrich Schlegel's shift from advocating classicism to modern or 'romantic' poetry in 1797 seems to coincide with reading *Sacontala*, and his poem *The Ages of the World* (1800) is full of its symbols of light, flowers and children. Goethe too was 'extravagantly impressed', and afterwards stated that it had influenced *Faust*; arguably, indeed, it gave him that work's formal structural principle, whereby the pantheistic, feminized Part II, a cosmos like that of *Sacontala*, balances the severe Hebraism of Part I.

Like many of Jones's literary translations, the play was originally a secular work, but in the West it was taken to have religious meaning. A king, Dushmanta, courts the girl Sacontala, who is half peasant, half nymph. He falls madly in love, gets her pregnant and then, mad again or spellbound, cannot remember her. She wanders off, forsaken, to have her child; years later he meets her, remembers and falls in love all over again. This resembles the plot also found in the stories of Cupid and Psyche and of Endymion and Cynthia, in which a mortal becomes deranged on meeting an immortal. Keats uses it repeatedly; 'nympholepsy', as Byron calls it in *Childe Harold*, IV, becomes a fashionable motif for the younger English Romantics and the lesser poets of the 1820s who immediately followed them. If the story is read as symbolizing a mortal's yearning after the ideal, as it certainly came to be interpreted in the course of the nineteenth century, it becomes evidence for the view that Romantic poetry is displaced theology. But Jones's Hindu variant enjoyed a vogue before the early Victorian religious revival, and the charm of his *Sacontala* surely lay in conveying to the French-revolutionary generation an image of the divine profoundly different from that of Hebraism, one that appears to admit the sexual drive as part of the divine nature.

Other works of the French Revolution period seem to have drawn on Jones's translations and his images, and to have aimed at a comparable blend of religious unorthodoxy and social acceptability. Erasmus Darwin's *Botanic Garden* (1791) also celebrates a sexual principle in the universe, and suggests that Hindu and Greek paganism is ultimately more 'natural' than Judaism. Shelley studied Jones and Darwin, and fed this late eighteenth-century style of religious demystification into his more openly tendentious equation of divine love and sexuality.

But if Jones calculated that the urbane public at which he pitched his message would decide British policy in the coming generation, he reckoned without the strengthening of religious orthodoxy at home and the influence of the middle and professional classes, affronted rather than beguiled by his land of libertarian love. Before 1800, the date at which most of his poems were first appearing in England, Jones's opponents at home were arguing that his presentation of Indian arts and learning was either too flattering or too historical and backward-looking. By creating an impression of India as a land of infinite riches and splendour, in theory educating the British public into tolerance and generosity, he was suspected of stimulating Western greed and of fostering conservatism, even the conservation of traditional India and its existing privileged classes – that is, of tacitly backing Hastings's policies.[1] Afterwards Mill would accuse him of inventing the India that was a land of happy children, by contrast with Europe as the continent of sad grown-ups, yet another reason for Westerners to take Indians over for their own good.

## THE 1790s

Constantin Volney's *Les Ruines* (1791) was translated into English as *The Ruins: or a Survey of the Revolutions of Empire* in 1792. Based on Volney's reflections as he visited ancient sites in Syria and Egypt in the 1780s, it is an imaginative impression of the history of the State, seen as a succession of *anciens régimes*. A French traveller meets a genie, who teaches him Rousseau's message that once, very early in human affairs, mankind was free, equal and non-competitive. After greed crept in, so did the lust for dominion and the desire to deceive and enslave. Rulers learnt to use religion, not as a means of interpreting nature, its earlier function, but as 'nothing more than a political expedient by which to rule the credulous vulgar ... Bold and energetic spirits ... formed vast projects of ambition.' Such a man 'was the Hebrew legislator [Moses], who, desirous of separating his nation from every other, and of forming a distinct and exclusive empire, conceived the design of taking for its basis religious

1 Jones's most powerful early critics were, in chronological order: (1) Thomas Maurice, *Indian Antiquities*, 7 vols, (1793–1800), for whom see text; (2) Francis Jeffrey, Scottish lawyer and editor of the *Edinburgh Review* (1802–29), who allowed little theology or mythology to be reviewed in his journal and was particularly prone to lampoon, or have lampooned, works on Eastern 'antiquities', though he covered travels, geography and politics; and (3) James Mill, *The History of British India*, 7 vols (1817), though Mill is equally dismissive of Maurice. For a fuller treatment of Jones (and Southey, Mill and Moore), see Javed Majeed, *Ungoverned Imaginings: James Mill's 'History of British India' and Orientalism*, Oxford, 1992.

prejudices, and of erecting round it a sacred rampart of rites and opinions'.[1] Volney bestows on his genie a historical analysis as encompassing as Marx's. Since human history has been a record of fraud, tyranny and imposition, in which priests have abetted rulers, the people should be taught to reread this old story with their eyes open. This technique of rereading the old plots, transvaluing them, taking them to a happy (that is, progressive) ending, is extraordinarily reusable within imaginative discourse – precisely a sphere in which English culture was strong, and moreover a sphere not subjected (unlike political polemic and the political speech) to censorship. Hence Volney's surprisingly strong presence in English literature, far beyond what his originality would have earned him, as the formal and tactical mentor of Blake and Godwin, Landor, Southey and Shelley.

In today's terms Volney was not so much the Marx as the Foucault of his day, a man who taught a totalizing theory which showed a generation how to overestimate the efficacy of Power. Sectors of the population of Western Europe and America were powerfully radicalized by arguments of this type. After Volney, Charles Dupuis's seven-volume analysis of religion as a perverted, mystified sun-worship, *L'origine de tous les cultes* (1795), impressed Jefferson and also survived in England in selections and adaptations for a century to come. Shelley's *Queen Mab* (1813), which is itself a free adaptation of Volney's *Ruins*, was pirated in 1821 and thereafter remained a radical classic, in circles such as the Chartists, until at least the 1880s.[2] The case against 'state religion' was quickly naturalized in England. Alexander Geddes, a Scots-born Roman Catholic priest, issued a new translation of the Old Testament in 1792, preceded by his derogatory observations about the Hebraism of the Old Testament as the religion of 'a stupid, carnal people'.[3] Tom Paine's theological tract *The Age of Reason* (1794) relays a more directly political message in Paine's wonderfully accessible English prose; by 1819, when the radical publisher Richard Carlile reissued Paine's works, it was for *The Age of Reason*, not *Rights of Man*, that the publisher was prosecuted. Geddes and Paine are, with

1 Constantin Volney, *The Ruins: or a Survey of the Revolutions of Empire* [1792], London, 1822, pp 282–3.
2 See E. P. Thompson, *The Making of the English Working Class*, Harmondsworth, 1964, pp 107–8; and Iain McCalman, *Radical Underworld*, Cambridge, 1988, pp 24, 79–82.
3 Alexander Geddes, *Prospectus of a New Translation of the Holy Bible* (1786), quoted in J. J. McGann, 'The Idea of an Indeterminate Text: Blake and Dr Alexander Geddes', *Social Values and Poetic Acts*, Cambridge, Mass., 1988, p 166.

Volney, almost certainly the mediators through whom William Blake picked up the vision of world history that inspires his two great series of epics of the French revolutionary years.

Blake's first series of prophecies – *America* (1793), *Europe* (1794) and *The Song of Los* (1795), the last of which subdivides into 'Africa' and 'Asia' – celebrate the coming of revolution to the four continents of the world. The old world is conceived on Volneyan lines as an evil empire maintained by 'priestcraft'. The secret power which governs things is personified in *America* by Albion's Angel, but afterwards by a figure based on Moses, traditionally the author of the first books of the Old Testament, whom Blake renames Urizen. In his first attempts at rendering revolution, such as the unfinished *The French Revolution* and *America*, Blake thinks rather literally in terms of an armed struggle. He soon recasts the conflict into an ideological one, to which the modern artist contributes by deconstructing and imaginatively (but always provisionally) reconstructing the old poetic forms, which have hardened into laws. *The First Book of Urizen* (1794) begins with the ominous subject 'Of the primeval priest's assumed power' and with the cramped figure of Moses engraving his brazen book, and continues by parodying the various 'mythemes', the Hebraic and pagan creation myths by which the nets of religion have been cast over the world's peoples. Blake gives a more or less standard mythographical account of this process in *The Marriage of Heaven and Hell* (1791–4), the work in which he promises that he will shortly write his own parodic 'Bible of Hell':

The ancient Poets animated all sensible objects with Gods or Geniuses, calling them with the names and adorning them with the properties of woods, rivers, mountains, lakes, cities, nations . . .

Till a system was formed, which some took advantage of & enslav'd the vulgar by attempting to realize or abstract the mental deities from their objects; thus began Priesthood . . .

And at length they pronouncd that the Gods had orderd such things.

Thus men forgot that All deities reside in the human breast.[1]

Only briefly and gnomically does Blake include in his account of world history the dispersal of Urizen's laws among the Africans and Asians: 'Black grew the sunny African/When Rintrah gave Abstract Philosophy to Brama in the East.' He certainly does not imagine either continent as potentially the home of its own enlightenment. When revolution flares in Europe, Asia's rulers scuttle out like spiders:

1 William Blake, *The Marriage of Heaven and Hell*, pl. 11; in *William Blake's Writings*, ed. G. E. Bentley, Oxford, 1978, i. 85.

The Kings of Asia heard
The howl rise up from Europe!
And each ran out from his Web;
From his ancient woven Den;
For the darkness of Asia was startled
At the thick-flaming, thought-creating fires of Orc.[1]

By Blake's heyday, the revolutionary years 1791–5, British public opinion was polarizing into loyalist and 'Jacobin', believer and 'infidel'. Before most of Jones's poetry was published his subtle case for a natural religion based on a secularized, aestheticized Hinduism was swept aside by stronger, more populist impulses: the alarmism of the orthodox, the fervour of the religious and the bourgeois French ideologues' polemic against priestcraft in any form. In the course of the 1790s Hinduism was re-presented in the new, intenser spirit of the times. Charles Grant, an able servant of the East India Company and a stout evangelical, is scarcely an obvious follower of Volney, but he sounds as if he knows his message. In 1792 Grant wrote a memorandum, his 'Observations on the State of Society among the Asiatic Subjects of Great Britain', for Henry Dundas, the minister under Pitt responsible for Indian affairs.[2] For Grant, Hindu law was not, as Hastings and Jones suggested, a social creed naturally rooted in immemorial village customs, but a monolithic religious system, Volney's 'priestcraft', upholding an irresistible, if abstracted, Power. The 'cruel genius' pervading Indian despotism was the ethos of Hinduism, with its idols and skull-draped shrines. It was Brahman priests' promotion of that fraud and imposture that had reduced the mass of the population to poverty and degradation:

Erected upon the darkest ignorance, and the boldest falsehood, it has been the work of ages to strengthen these foundations, and to keep the fabric impregnable. The understanding is chained and kept in perpetual imprisonment, like dreaded rivals for power in the East, who deprived of their eyes, and immured in dungeons, receive poisonous provisions from the gaoler's hands . . . In whatever regards the civil and personal, as well as the religious concerns of the Hindoos, the Brahmins . . . formed the religion, they are the exclusive depositaries of its ordinances . . . they are . . . authorized to assist in the government of public affairs, and in effect to control it . . . In short, a

1 Blake, *The Song of Los*, pl. 6, ll 1–6; in *Writings*, i. 191.
2 Grant (1746–1823), member of the influential Clapham Sect and near neighbour of the African administrator Zachary Macaulay, had served in India throughout the Hastings era and was severely critical both of the pro-Hindu campaign and of its underlying motive, British expansion. A moralist, he considered that the British presence in India had thus far done only harm to its population, and had even failed to profit the Company.

Hindoo, from the hour of his birth ... is subject to an accumulation of burdensome rites, with which the preservation of his caste, his credit, and place in society, are strictly connected ... The return he has for this unbounded subjection, is an indulgence in perpetual deviations, even from those few principles of morality which his religion acknowledges. It is thus that abject slavery, and unparalleled depravity, have become distinguishing features of the Hindoos.[1]

Since India was emerging as a classic instance of an unreformed despotism, the British had an obligation to undertake the enlightenment of the population – by which Grant ultimately hoped for its conversion to Christianity, but immediately stressed its education, through a determined new policy of teaching Indians the English language, in the 'arts and sciences' of advanced Europe. Grant was in short a pioneer among the evangelical administrators and empire-builders who, together with the utilitarians, made progressivism, humanitarianism, Anglicization and strong rule from London the principal features of India's government.

An increasingly powerful figure in the East India Company, Grant circulated his views privately but influentially, and they had wide support well before the Company's charter was next debated in 1813, as is demonstrated by the appearance of his 'Observations' as Appendix to the 1813 parliamentary debates. In 1793, however, it was the Anglican historian Thomas Maurice who retrieved the topic of India for the general public and brought it back within safe parameters. Jones had taken care to claim elaborately that the Hebraic chronology – that is, the primacy of the 'Mosaic' account of the world's creation – was safe from the investigations of the orientalists.[2] Maurice, along with many of Jones's more sophisticated readers, brushed aside those disclaimers and pointed out that the impression left by Jones's work as a whole was sceptical. He was backed in this view by Lord Wellesley, elder brother to the future Duke of Wellington and one of the most aggrandizing of early Governors-General. In 1800 Wellesley set up Fort William College at Calcutta to educate young recruits to the Company's service in more prudent and pragmatic fields: Indian vernacular languages, for example, rather than suspect orientalism.

For many British readers, among them policy-makers, Maurice's seven-volume *Indian Antiquities* (1793–1800), an elaborate and often

---

1 Charles Grant, 'Observations on the State of Society among the Asiatic Subjects of Great Britain', in *Parliamentary Papers, 1812–13*, x, Paper 282, pp 60–61, 66.
2 William Jones, 'On the Gods of Greece, Egypt and India' (1784); in *Works*, i. 229–80.

sensationally hostile representation of Hindu beliefs and art, replaced Jones's sunny Hinduism. Unorthodox discourses – orientalism of Jones's type, natural science of the schools of Erasmus Darwin and the geologist James Hutton – were being viewed with suspicion by 1795. Typical of the paranoia spread by the Terror, Maurice suspected a conspiracy out in British India between cunning Brahmans and cells of British revolutionary intellectuals ('illuminati') who liked to dabble in arcane knowledge. The same conspiracy theories were being featured in alarmist exposés of European cults such as Freemasonry, and in Gothic fiction such as Schiller's *Ghost-Seer* or Godwin's *St Leon*. Because freethinkers had posed Hinduism against Christianity, the godly now turned Christianity on Hinduism. No longer the site of a charming, innocent, even paradisal sensuousness, Hindu states were more likely to be deemed priest-ridden, cruel and despotic, and thus 'asking' for Western conquest.

Bonaparte, now the revolution's most successful general, invaded Egypt in 1798, heading an expedition which fully availed itself of the programme of demystification, followed by world revolution, spelt out by Volney and his kind. The French accidentally found an English fellow traveller in young Walter Savage Landor, who in 1796 came upon a plot for a narrative poem in an oriental tale published by Clara Reeve as an appendix to her *Progress of Romance* (1787). In Reeve's plot Charoba, Queen of Egypt in early biblical times, cunningly outwits the Iberian adventurer Gebir after he conquers her kingdom and demands that she share the throne with him. Landor's fine Miltonic poem *Gebir* parcs away the interesting feminist theme to replace it with an anti-colonialist fable probably intended for Britain rather than France. De Quincey, like Southey a dedicated reader of *Gebir*, certainly identified its Iberia (that is, Spain) with modern England, adding that Landor's drift in this poem was enough to make him 'a poet with whom the Attorney-General might have occasion to speak'.[1]

Gebir sets sail with his younger brother and their army to conquer an older and more sinister civilization: priest-ridden, corrupt and magical Egypt. Gebir falls in love with the Egyptian queen, his younger brother Tamar with a pastoral nymph. Tamar's affair prospers, and the poet prophesies that from this couple a Corsican hero will one day spring to become Europe's liberator. But Gebir,

1 'W. S. Landor', in *De Quincey's Collected Writings*, ed. D. Masson, Edinburgh, 1890, xi. 403–4; quoted in Nigel Leask, *British Romantic Writers and the East: Anxieties of Empire*, Cambridge Studies in Romanticism, Cambridge, 1993, p 26.

the would-be colonialist, is killed at what should have been his wedding, when Charoba innocently hands him a cloak that has been poisoned by her old nurse.

First readers found the narrative obscure, partly because it is densely written, partly because it can defy chronology for the sake of the right political allusion. In the third book, for instance, Gebir the ancient giant descends to the underworld in order to meet his father, but the ghostly monarchs he finds there include identifiable modern Europeans, including George III. The political sympathies of the author must also have been puzzling, for though evidently an admirer of Bonaparte he criticizes Gebir's project to invade an inhabited, advanced country such as Egypt. Landor must in fact have planned the poem, and may have completed it, before news of Bonaparte's campaign reached England. The air of topicality arose then by accident, but for contemporaries it remained a barrier.

Even without this difficulty Landor sends out puzzling ideological messages, in which the negatives register more clearly than the positives. Where Reeve aligned herself with a beleaguered nation, represented by a woman threatened with a forced marriage, Landor goes out of his way to damn the Egyptian court. Its dominant figures, the malign nurse Dalica and her sister Myrthyr, a witch, come straight from Volney. Dalica's visit to Myrthyr, one of the few members of an 'ancient race' left in a deserted city, effortlessly merges the poem's prevailing Latinism with contemporary Gothicism:

> With Time's first sickle they had marked the hour
> When at their incantation would the Moon
> Start back, and shuddering shed blue blasted light.
>
> (v. 16–18)

The nurse proceeds to give her sister an alienating account of the heroine's education and disposition. Even though Queen Charoba never conspires to kill her lover, the description of her childish amusements is disquieting:

> For I have often seen her with both hands
> Shake a dry crocodile, of equal height,
> And listen to the shells within the scales,
> And fancy there was life, and yet apply
> The jagged jaws wide open to her ear.
>
> (v. 121–5)

Landor's Egypt, populated by shadowy cultists and murderous

women, provides a model for Eastern court cultures in romances to come.

## THE 1800s

Robert Southey was the most prolific and influential English poet writing on the East through the wartime years, 1793–1815. While still at school in the 1780s he had the idea of writing a long poem on each major religion. He began the first, *Madoc*, which treats native British and native American religions, in 1794, the year that he and Coleridge planned to emigrate to the banks of the Susquehanna. Eventually the Islamic *Thalaba the Destroyer* appeared in 1801, the Mexican *Madoc* in 1805 and the Hindu *Curse of Kehama* in 1810.

With *Thalaba the Destroyer* the eighteenth-century Arabian-French prose oriental tale suddenly emerges in its full flowering as Romantic narrative poetry – which means that it is also an eclectic historical pastiche, most obviously medieval romance and Spenserian epic. Yet the first oddity to strike readers may have been its informal, folkloric features: the hero, an illiterate boy brought up as a herdsman among the Bedouin, and the metre, an unrhymed stanza in fact borrowed from the Greek chorus but sufficiently odd to madden critics even more passionately orthodox on metre than on religion and politics.

*Thalaba* was accessible and entertaining like few other long poems. It was intended, surely, for family reading, which is why its Spenserian twelve books are also twelve exciting episodes, each very different from the stories before and after. The plot takes its youthful hero across deserts, in pursuit of magicians who are trying to murder him; after Baghdad, to an underworld entered from the ruins of Nineveh; and to a paradisal but eventually sinister garden – in which he meets his childhood sweetheart again; then, after losing her, some yet grimmer, more threatening, emotionally disturbing trials, until he is travelling by dog-sled through a surreal mountain landscape towards his death. Variety, of setting and tone, is very important to the poem, which oscillates between extremes. The Gothic horror of the magicians' cave, Dom-daniel (Book II), succeeds the epitome of desire, the fabled illusory desert city of Irem (Book I), which becomes visible to a mortal very rarely, as a warning of death.

Even longer than the poem, the copious footnotes, a commonplace-book and near-encyclopaedia of Eastern travel literature, legends and story-types, could be put to one side, kept for separate study or enjoyed when the reader was older. The best of the entries are as compelling as the best of the episodes, and could evidently speak quite as eloquently to the imagination of other writers. A note to Book VIII elucidates the still relatively unfamiliar legend of the vampire by collecting together published reports of eighteenth-century visitations, two in the Balkans, one on a Greek island. The anthropological fullness of these accounts of popular religious practice – and their gruesome detail – surely fed or even created the persistent nineteenth-century craze for this Near Eastern apparition, which fully took off in England with Byron's *The Giaour* (1813), Mary Shelley's *Frankenstein* (1818) and John Polidori's *The Vampyre* (1819). In Book VII, the note to 'the Paradise of Sin' ruled by a magician called Alaodin relates it to similar reports of three such magical but sinister walled gardens, one in Cathay, another in either India or Abyssinia. A careful reading of this short anthology of the oriental paradise shows its likely role in the making of 'Kubla Khan'.[1]

*Thalaba*, designed to be rereadable, at least proved infinitely reusable. Scott declared that his own romantic historical poems were modelled on it. His prose fiction, with its positive and rich use of annotation, gains probably as much from Southey's use of humble characters as agents, and of superstition, legend and balladry as basic cultural materials. Nineteenth-century exotic adventure stories, especially fantasy such as George Macdonald's, clearly emerge indebted to the same rich vein of oral narrative. They also learn a semi-naturalized use of allegory, how to poeticize a novelistic story of bereavement, endurance, learning through experience.

In Southey's poem there emerges for the first time in its full flowering the nineteenth century's new anthropological interest in stories, their modes of transmission across cultural borders and their symbolic meanings; for the footnotes expand Southey's range of reference beyond what would be expected of an oriental tale, to include traces of archaic myth, originating in two striking cases from Greenland, and much comment on the archetypal nature of myths and religious beliefs and practices.[2] Even so, Southey also lays

1 See n 2, p 400.
2 Southey builds up the portraits of his romance's leading villains, the sister witches Khawla and Maimuna, from a great variety of sources, including the rich Jewish-Christian-Muslim archive of Solomon as a magician, north-African and Central American magic, and the German missionary David Cranz's valuably anthropological *History of Greenland* (1767), from which Southey derives the she-bear who visits Thalaba as he lies bound in Maimuna's cave (originally part of the initiation rites of a Greenland shaman). In the same work Southey found the legend he at first meant to use for the plot's climax, of a gigantic hag who squats in a cave deep

down the narrative paradigms of Romantic poetic orientalizing, above all the cunning juxtaposition of desire and terror, the exotic and the grotesque, a formula which in the next generation sold plenty of other people's poems, if never enough of his own.

*The Curse of Kehama* (1810) opens theatrically at the funeral in Delhi of an unpleasant Hindu prince, killed by the father of a low-caste girl he was trying to rape. The passing of this son and heir of the tyrant Kehama is marked by a cinematographic crowd-scene centred on the rite of suttee, during which two wives (one acquiescent, one reluctant) and innumerable passive slaves are burnt alive on the funeral pyre. The raja Kehama is a wicked despot whose vengefulness pursues the heroine (the proposed victim of rape) and her father throughout the plot. Kehama is also a rebel against the gods, for he aims to rule not only on earth but in heaven. Here the Hindu religion is systemically at fault, according to the description Southey gives in his Preface, since it is anarchic enough to allow the possibility that the gods could be successfully challenged by proud bad men.

Like Charles Grant in his 'Observations' Southey is concerned not so much with Hinduism's doctrines as with its social ethics. Southey surely knew Grant's paper, since in effect he served from 1802 as a spokesman for the same evangelical lobby on matters Indian to which Grant himself and William Wilberforce also belonged. Gradually, since the turn of opinion in the late 1790s against Hinduism and a policy of co-operation, press reports of suttee became more common; they served to fuel British indignation, like modern Western press reporting of punishment under Islamic law. It was through the press, tracts and the Gothicization of India in popular literature that Wilberforce and his supporters in the evangelical Clapham Sect mounted an extra-parliamentary campaign which in 1813 secured the amendment of the India Act and gave Christian missionaries the right for the first time to proselytize in British India.

While Southey's epics were canvassing polite readers, he was addressing a larger public by reviewing the unfashionable writings of Baptist missionaries based on the fringes of British India, in the *Annual Review* from 1802 and in the *Quarterly Review* from 1809. Southey gives a pragmatic reason in the *Quarterly* (vol I, 1809) for supporting a policy of proselytizing among the common people, a

---

under the sea, a principle of evil; the witch Khawla has some of her attributes. Second-generation Romantic orientalizing (that of the 1810s) tends to mask the dispersed ethnic origins of many of the genre's motifs.

course detested by upper-class readers, who had a snobbish aversion to lower-class sects such as the Baptists. In the great struggle between good and evil – Southey's understanding of the current issue between Britain and France – Indian hearts need to be won, since the French, only recently ousted from India by the British, are working diplomatically to get back there. Experience of counter-revolution in Brittany, Naples and most recently Spain had taught the old Jacobin Southey that the populace was less easy to rouse by inflammatory politics than by an appeal to its familiar code, religion. Where in the mid-1790s he indignantly adopted Volney's case against religion, he now utilized its argument for the Government side, and preached religion's utility as the best-tried instrument of social control.

While *Thalaba* was more referred to than any other oriental narrative poem, *Kehama* outdid it as a political intervention. After a decade and a half of practice as a popular poet, especially on Gothic themes, Southey's portrayal of Hinduism is powerful propaganda – Grant popularized and sensationalized. The great-occasion opening introduces a hierarchy far steeper than the European one upheld by Christianity.

In Delhi the lives of women, people of low caste and slaves are being forfeited to religious law, or to the whim of a wicked despot. After his son's cremation Kehama's regime becomes a claustrophobic charnel-house which begins to engulf the heavens, a world of man-made curses and spells, while the gods look on from far away. Grimmer even than the suttee in the first scene is the raja's curse in the second, which enlists the homely forces of nature to visit eternal punishment on the peasant who has offended him:

> I charm thy life
> From the weapons of strife,
> From stone and from wood,
> From fire and from flood,
> From the serpent's tooth,
> And the beasts of blood:
> From Sickness I charm thee,
> And Time shall not harm thee;
> But Earth which is mine,
> Its fruits shall deny thee;
> And Water shall hear me,
> And know thee and fly thee;
> And the Winds shall not touch thee
> When they pass by thee,

And the Dews shall not wet thee
   When they fall nigh thee:
   And thou shalt seek Death
   To release thee, in vain;
   Thou shalt live in thy pain
   While Kehama shall reign,
   With a fire in thy heart
   And a fire in thy brain;
   And Sleep shall obey me,
   And visit thee never,
And the Curse shall be on thee
   For ever and ever.

                                              (II. xiv)


Most commentators on Southey's politics emphasize that Toryism soon succeeded his boyhood Jacobinism. This can't mean that it
did so before 1800, or in any substantial way before *Thalaba*. By the
ordinary yardsticks derived from domestic politics – such as support
for the war with France – Southey sided with the Government, and
was thus a Tory, when he wrote *Kehama*. Yet his democratic
sympathies, more visible than Coleridge's during their youthful
collaboration, still to some degree survive his conversion; so do his
millenarian hopes of progress. Kailyal and Ladurlad, successors to
his earlier peasant protagonists Wat Tyler, Joan of Arc and Thalaba,
enable him to frame *Kehama* as an Indian class-struggle in which
readers' sympathies are enlisted on behalf of the poor. The situation
is complicated and ironized because Kehama, the evil emperor, is
manifestly a poetic figuring of Napoleon. By merging the Western
despot with the Eastern, Southey is able to retain the forms of his
first oriental romance, and tropes such as the illusory, deceitful
throne, built over dungeons or placed in a pseudo-paradise. The
folkloric protagonist traditionally battles against worldly power in
bad hands. The difference in 1810 is that it is a carefully selected
specific regime – a British India threatened by Hindu and French
subversion – that elicits Southey's story of heroic resistance.
   Southey places his herdsman-hero in *Thalaba* and his peasant
father and daughter in *Kehama* in novel-like plots, in effect invents
the modern-style genre of mid- to low-brow fantasy, in order to let
the reader realize empathetically the horror of living under a system
in which power is wielded through black magic or is indifferent to
human life. Kailyal and Ladurlad are decent, prosy, fully redeemable
human beings, who work their way towards salvation by their own
efforts, without outside human help. There is no sign of a foreign

worldly power coming to their aid. The outcome of their efforts may well have been intended, allegorically, as winning through to a personal salvation as Christian converts. Certainly Southey worked hard in his later years to avoid criticism from Christian clerics, and was glad when he got praise. The apparent decency and piety of protagonists like Ladurlad and Thalaba struck John Henry Newman favourably, as a believable, unsentimental heroism to which the author gave no false rewards.[1] All the same, what Southey's peasants achieve in society – defiance of Kehama, and a part in his death – reads like either a popular religious reformation or a popular uprising.

Southey's plots speak one language, socially an optimistic one, his images another. After the 1790s, Gothicism's device of burying rulers and priests in near-universal horror loses its original radical inflection. Temporarily *Kehama* may have joined the campaign to demonize Napoleon, now a monarch falsely sanctified by the Catholic Church. More widely and permanently, it traduced Hinduism and Hindus. The reproach against Southey and other evangelical campaigners is surely that in conditions of wartime paranoia they held up Hindu society as a uniquely illiberal social system. They and their lobby silenced those who, by co-operating with Hindu regimes, implied that India might at any time be restored to Hindu government. For want of such an implied alternative, the case against an oriental British empire, so well supported in Gibbon's day, virtually vanished from the public sphere.

Or did it? Apart from the opening, *Kehama*'s most memorable scene is probably the one in which Ladurlad discovers in a lost city beneath the sea a hall in which two lines of dead kings sit facing one another. It is in fact a moment which Rider Haggard borrows for his African novel of adventure, *King Solomon's Mines*. The spectacle arouses readers' fear of the Other, of the unimaginably old, or vast, or inexplicable, or dead – identifiably, by now, the mystified Western public's fear of the East. De Quincey's visions of Egyptian burial and entombment belong to just this genre. The poetic realization of such moments by Landor and Southey translate readily into nineteenth-century prose adventure yarns and fantasy, but it seems likely that their seed-time in poetry clarified their symbolic suggestiveness and emotional power. It was the poets who found ways of realizing an alienness that was imaginatively almost impossible to

---

1 J. H. Newman, from article in *London Review* (1829), reproduced in *Southey: The Critical Heritage*, ed. Lionel Madden, London, 1972, p 332.

cope with, and brought out real distaste for so troubling a region, an unknowable India with which the British had become dangerously enmeshed. Empire as a Western sickness, the theme of Conrad's *Heart of Darkness*, originates with the Romantics.

## THE 1810s

A genre made popular invites takeover. Southey's demonic India, constructed this way in the interests of a religious lobby, seems to trigger a vein of orientalism in which institutionalized religion itself serves as the main target. The new style of critical orientalism was launched by Sydney Owenson, afterwards Lady Morgan, the Irish novelist. Already known as the author of *The Wild Irish Girl* (1806), a slapdash, extravagant nationalist romance, Owenson turned to the East with *Woman: or Ida of Athens* (1809) and *The Missionary: An Indian Tale* (1811), novels set respectively in two contentious Eastern empires, the Turkish and the British. In each of Owenson's Eastern plots the spirit of the conquered nation is represented by a charismatic young woman leader, who is dominated, imposed on and to a degree betrayed by a masterful Western lover.

Owenson did not invent the figuring of nation as a woman, though she helped popularize and politicize it. In his influential mid-eighteenth-century Oxford lectures on the Old Testament (1754), Robert Lowth, future Bishop of London, had shown how collectively the very different books of the Bible constitute the chronicles of the ancient Jewish people, in parts rendered in great poetry, and freely using devices such as allegory and symbolism. It is Lowth who influentially suggests that the recurring figure of a mourning woman stands for a defeated city or people, Jerusalem or Israel as a whole. A few years later, in his effort to reshape the fragmentary traditional Gaelic poetry of the Scottish people, James Macpherson weaves into his epics attributed to the third-century poet Ossian, *Fingal* (1762) and *Temora* (1763), several episodes of solitary young women abandoned, raped, or searching for a lover on the field of battle. In prefatory essays both Macpherson and the Scottish academic Hugh Blair stress the similarity of primitive Celtic and Middle Eastern or biblical poetry. Macpherson also mentions their common use of the trope of the mourning woman, and indeed some of his fragments in which such women appear have authenticated Gaelic originals.

During the next decades Irish historians beginning with Sylvester O'Halloran, author of *A General History of Ireland to the Close of the Twelfth Century* (1774), speculatively traced the origins of the Celts to the East, sometimes India, sometimes the Middle East (e.g. Troy, Phoenicia) or North Africa (e.g. Carthage). This manoeuvre made Irish history venerable and culturally rich, yet oppositional, fugitive and subversive compared with the sanctioned genealogies of Church and State. The latter traced their lines back ultimately to Jerusalem and Athens (both now part of the Turkish empire), but by the prestigious official route, Europe's characteristic main line: first imperial Rome and then imperial London. Clara Reeve may or may not be thinking of Lowth's suggestive allegorical reading of the Bible's dispossessed women when in her 'History of Charoba' she makes her Egyptian Head of State, who is threatened with dispossession, a woman. She almost certainly thinks of Cleopatra, Dido and Zenobia of Palmyra, all (like Boadicea) resistance-leaders against the expanding power of Rome.

Though she does not develop for feminist purposes the woman as national figurehead, Reeve's *Progress of Romance* (1787) has its own agenda to question authority: the exaggerated prestige of masculine epic, traditionally concerned with war and affairs of State, compared with that of feminine romance, preoccupied with love and affairs of the heart. This should have brought her into conflict with a supposedly authoritative treatment of much of her field, Thomas Warton's *History of English Literature, 1100–1603* (1777–82); for Warton views romance as the sanctioned, mainstream form of a relatively stable, hegemonic English Catholic-and-Court culture, trickling down from the educated classes to the people via song, story and ballad. Warton, an Anglican and Tory, chooses dates that allow him to skirt internal wars and revolutions, and even full acknowledgement of the linguistic, ethnic and religious differences among the British. Waves of invasion by Celts, Anglo-Saxons, Danes, Norsemen and Normans had made the British a hybrid population in the eyes of Warton's many critics. Division, not homogeneity, shows in the persistent traces of paganism found in folk practices and legends, in the view that the early Church was already corrupted from the East, and in the Eastern sources now detectable in much European medieval romance.

The quarter-century after Warton's Anglocentric, metropolitan book saw a massive expansion in British and provincial studies. If the eighteenth-century age of revolutions hosted an Oriental Renaissance, it did the same for a Celtic Renaissance, and the two persistently claimed their connectedness against a London-based 'Englishness'. From the 1780s scholars of Irish, Welsh and Scots-Gaelic pre-medieval origins were for nationalistic reasons enforcing O'Halloran's stories of trade links, immigration, even ancient-world colonization of Ireland by Eastern peoples. The Celts' ancestors might have been Indians, or Jews of the patriarchal period. The Celtic languages allegedly have affinities with Hebrew; the Celtic mythology and pagan pantheon proves a common experience of Noah's Flood; one or all the Celtic branches were descended from the ten lost tribes of Israel. Religious sects and prophets emerged in the 1780s and 1790s advocating the British–Israelite connection; most of these were considered politically radical, some of the prophets dangerous.[1]

In 1798 Ireland erupted in a widespread and bloody rebellion, headed by the United Irishmen and supported by an invading French army. Robert Emmet attempted another rising in 1803. Continuing agrarian unrest, a mounting political campaign for Catholic emancipation, and bold criticism of Britain's war effort by an Irish journalist, Peter Finnerty, brought Ireland back into the headlines in 1811, and in early 1812 Percy Shelley was drawn to Dublin as a sympathizer and activist. It is partly because the question of Ireland – its persecuted religionists, its national consciousness – now began to merge with the modern politics and ancient histories of various peoples of the Orient that Eastern imperialism henceforth figured as the topic of a new style of political poetry.

On its own, to represent either Ireland or an Eastern nation as a forsaken woman does not seem a forceful patriotic gesture. Moore does it frequently in his immensely popular *Irish Melodies*, a ten-part series which began to appear in 1808. But his plangent offers to die for Erin (in 'When he, who adores thee, has left but the name') confine both lovers to the vicinity of the piano, and seem to detract

---

1 The wayward, potentially explosive Scots aristocrat Lord George Gordon in turn learnt Gaelic and adopted nationalist views, fomented anti-Catholic riots in London (1780) and became a convert to Judaism (1785). In 1787 William Blake's brother Robert drew and evidently studied 'the Druids', at a time when Blake himself was preoccupied with Hebrew patriarchs; from 1803 Blake returned to the theme of ancient Britain and its supposed identity with the Bible's patriarchal age, and he believed he was again in contact with the dead Robert. From 1792 the bardic ceremonials at the solstice, initiated by Edward Williams (Iolo Morganwg) first in London, afterwards at Cardiff, were identified both in Britain and France with French-revolutionary popular festivals. In 1795 Richard Brothers, self-styled 'Prince of Israel', preached a radical millenarianism according to which the French revolutionary wars would liberate Jerusalem; he was considered sufficiently dangerous to be locked up as a lunatic, like Gordon a decade earlier. For Gordon and the British Israelites, see Iain McCalman, *Grub Street in Revolution: Popular Romanticism, Science and Political Culture in Britain, 1780–1838*, Oxford, forthcoming; for the Welsh, Prys Morgan, *The Eighteenth-century Renaissance*, Llandybie, 1981; for a general account of myths of Eastern origins, Martin Bernal, *Black Athena: The Afroasiatic Roots of Classical Civilisation*, vol i, *The Fabrication of Ancient Greece, 1785–1985*, London, 1987.

from rather than enhance Ireland's stature. When male poets address any abstraction as female, the rule is to pose her, decorative but immobile, while she hears herself promised the earth. Once the writer imagining this situation is a woman, agency in the scene tends to pass to the woman character. Even in the domestic novel's standard proposal-scene, it's her answer (quite often no) that we attend to. Key evaluations of the suitor – his lifestyle, morals, attractiveness, overall merits – are elicited from her at such moments. The central sequence of Owenson's *The Missionary* confronts the priest and missionary Hilarion in Kashmir with the Hindu priestess Luxima. Quite unlike Moore's tender, unsuspicious lyrics, this is designed as a bruising encounter over two volumes, which for the reader undoes Hilarion's moral authority along with his complacency, even while the love affair still appears to be going according to (his) plan.

Owenson has taken care to prepare her British readers for an encounter that is cultural rather than personal, and demands analysis. The novel's Westerners are seventeenth-century Portuguese Catholics, some settled in Goa, circumstances which impede a British reader's automatic identification with the hero. Yet Hilarion, as an intellectual, a progressive, a sympathizer with India, is straightway linked with the most distinguished of travellers to modern British India. As the Missionary stands on shipboard off the Arabian coast, heading eastward, he begins a train of reflection which is a fairly close imitation of a famous passage by Sir William Jones: the opening paragraph of the Preliminary Discourse he delivered on 24 February 1784 to the first meeting of the Asiatic Society of Bengal. Jones, himself evoking and outbidding the *Discourses* of Sir Joshua Reynolds, President of the Royal Academy, strove for a comprehensiveness of vision that was truly world-scale:

When I was at sea last August . . . I found one evening that India lay before us, and Persia on our left, while a breeze from Arabia blew nearly on our stern . . . It gave me inexpressible pleasure to find myself in the midst of so noble an amphitheatre, almost encircled by vast regions of Asia, which has ever been esteemed the nurse of sciences, the inventress of delightful and useful arts, the scene of glorious actions, fertile in the productions of human genius, abounding in natural wonders, and infinitely diversified in the forms of religion and government, in the laws, manners, customs, and languages, as well as in the features and complexions of men. I could not help remarking how important and extensive a field was yet unexplored, and how many solid advantages unimproved . . .[1]

1 *First Discourse*, first published in *Asiatic Researches*, vol i (1789).

Owenson's imitation, a near parody, repeats phrases and parallels ideas only to exaggerate, unkindly, an element of self-aggrandizement, or even national advantage, that Jones probably never consciously meant. Hilarion's project is active, even militaristic; it soon diverges from knowledge:

through the clear bright atmosphere, the shores and mighty regions of the East presented themselves to the view, while the imagination of the Missionary, escaping beyond the limits of human vision, stretched over those various and wondrous tracts . . .

The mountains between Persia and India remind him of warrior hordes and the powerful genius, Tamerlane, who once led them. Then,

the Imposter of Mecca occurred to his recollection, with the scenes of his nativity and success. Bold in error, dauntless in imposition, enslaving the moral freedom while he subverted the natural liberty of mankind, and spreading, by the force of his single and singular genius, the wild doctrines he had invented, over the greatest empires of the earth, from the shores of the Atlantic to the wall of China; his success seemed even more wondrous, and his genius more powerful, than that of the Tartar conqueror. The soul of the Missionary swelled in the contemplation of scenes so calculated to elevate the ideas . . . and to recall the memory . . . to those events in human history, which stimulate, by their example, the powers of latent genius . . . and excite man to . . . found empires or to destroy them . . . He remembered that he, too, might have founded states, and given birth to doctrines; for what had Timur boasted, or Mahomet possessed, that had been denied to him?

(i. 36–42)

Thus introduced, Hilarion's mission contains the full range of Western motivations and practices upon the East, religious or secular, military or ideological – though a simplified psychology serves to underpin them, that of a man of huge energy, confidence and appetite for glory, the archetypal founder of empires. In this exemplary tale Hilarion arrives in India armed with a boundless will to dominate Indians and to compete successfully against his fellow Portuguese: he has the impact of a destructive force. A clash of cultures is worked out through the Missionary's relationship with Luxima, a breach of religious taboos on both sides, but especially rash and insensitive on Hilarion's. Their meeting is described in the style of timeless popular romance, familiar from modern pulp fiction, while it also evokes a fashionable theatrical tableau. It is one of those stylized scenes, associated with private performances by Emma

Hamilton and Germaine de Staël, which in drawing-rooms around 1800 enabled the 'attitudes' of representative characters to fix themselves in the onlooker's imagination:

Silently gazing, in wonder, upon each other, they stood finely opposed . . . she, like the East, lovely and luxuriant; he, like the West, lofty and commanding: the one, radiant in all the lustre, attractive in all the softness which distinguishes her native regions; the other, towering in all the energy, imposing in all the vigour, which marks his ruder latitudes . . . the one no less enthusiastic in her brilliant errors, than the other confident in his immutable truth.

The Christian and Heathen Priestess remained some time motionless, in look as in attitude . . .

Then Luxima breaks the spell by blushing – 'the woman stood too much confessed' – and the Missionary too is overwhelmed with confusion: 'he remained, leaning on his crosier, his eyes cast down on his beads, his lips motionless' (i. 149–51).

Owenson's denouement echoes Southey's cruel opening scene in *The Curse of Kehama* (of the previous year); but where he begins with a Hindu ritual which burns widows alive, she ends with the Christian religious practice of burning heretics, and her Hilarion is the intended victim. Owenson was certainly widely read, and admired particularly by Shelley. Already in the winter of 1811–12 he wrote a poem based on two Kashmiri lovers, 'Zeinab and Kathema', which centres on the woman Zeinab. Her name in Latin is Zenobia, after the patriot queen of ancient Palmyra; sure enough, she becomes a guerrilla in Britain and is hanged there. Owenson, it seems, pioneers three features common to many oriental poems of the next few years: an Irish–Eastern connection, a heroic woman as the focus for a defeated people's national consciousness, and a duel between major religions which is also a clash of national ideologies.

Byron's first, highly successful Turkish tale, *The Giaour* (1813), echoes, with variations, the second and third of Owenson's themes. When the action of the poem begins, its hero, the Western infidel or giaour, is already searching for his mistress Leila, one of the wives of Turkish Hassan, but he learns that on her husband's orders she has been sewn in a sack and dumped in the sea as a punishment for her adultery. *The Giaour* is one of the most powerful and exciting of Byron's narrative poems, thanks to its expressive plot. At the level of adventure story it turns on the sexual jealousy of the two men, representatives of the same caste though of different religions. At the level of allegory they fight over and kill a wholly silenced, passive woman, who can be seen as standing for the Greece both Christian Europe and Muslim Turkey now hope to possess.

If Byron is impressed by the Irish Owenson, he is equally indebted to Tom Moore, to whom he dedicated *The Corsair* (1814) – on the grounds that Moore was known to be writing an oriental poem, and that no one could be better qualified:

The wrongs of your own country, the magnificent and fiery spirit of her sons, the beauty and feeling of her daughters, may there [in the East] be found ... wildness, tenderness, and originality are part of your national claim of oriental descent, to which you have already thus far proved your title more clearly than the most zealous of your country's antiquarians.[1]

Many of the features of young-Romantic oriental poems are here summed up, under the heading of (originally) Irish national feeling. The poems will be written to establish a national case, along lines similar to those used by antiquarians to construct a national history; but they will also appear in dramatic or narrative form, resembling the traditional ballad's tales of love and war, and involving warlike men and beautiful women.

Byron's own early tales on Greek or Eastern Mediterranean nationalist themes fit this format, partly because he was influenced by Scott's success with romances influenced by Border ballads, and partly because he admired the more politicized tone of Moore's *Irish Melodies*. He comes nearest of all to Moore in his *Hebrew Melodies* (1815), songs written to the Western and Eastern synagogue melodies collected and offered to Byron by Isaac Nathan. Byron uses a blend of lamentation and fierce patriotic assertion not unlike Moore's for what he boasted were received as Zionist poems, but his more aggressive temperament ensures that the ferocity seems to sound louder. Set to Nathan's barbaric Eastern music, 'Jephthah's Daughter', which might logically have been classified among the lamentations, instead emerges as a song of triumph.

When after long delays it finally came, Moore's *Lalla Rookh* (1817) was written after all in a more polished oriental mode, reminiscent of the courtly eighteenth-century French treatment of the East. The publisher's unprecedented offer of £3,000 may have induced Moore to aim at critically approved polish rather than the deliberate archaism, naïvety and folk materials deployed by Southey, Scott and even Byron, in *The Giaour* and some of the *Hebrew Melodies*. A framed narrative suggesting both the *Arabian Nights Entertainment* and the *Canterbury Tales*, *Lalla Rookh* supposedly consists of the story Feramorz, a young poet, offers each evening to a

---

1 Dedication to *The Corsair*, in *Byron's Poems*, ed. J. J. McGann, Oxford, 1981, iii. 34.

Mogul princess as she travels from her father's court at Delhi to Kashmir, where she is to marry the king of mountainous Bokhara. Feramorz tells two long narratives, which have to be divided into episodes, and two much shorter ones; the short have a gossamer quality, for which Moore has over time become notorious, while the longer two are violent, tragic and in one case Gothic.

In effect Moore's longer stories are both fables of contemporary imperialism. Mokanna, the evil protagonist of 'The Veiled Prophet of Khorassan', has a historical Muslim original, but could reflect the hostile view of Muhammad, cited by both Gibbon and Sydney Owenson, that he may have been an unscrupulous impostor. Again, Mokanna could be the recently fallen Napoleon, who carved out an empire for himself with the aid of idealists for liberty, friends whom he finally forsook. 'The Fire-worshippers', long popular among liberal-minded British readers, still sufficiently known to be performed as a tableau in the Confederate city of Richmond, Virginia, during the American Civil War, celebrates the Persian and Zoroastrian resistance to the Arab and Muhammadan conquest of present-day Iran, as the Islamic armies swept eastwards towards Delhi. Feramorz's (Moore's) politics emerge here as firmly nationalist, on behalf of the religious freedom and political independence of a small nation, which, the wording of his introduction makes plain, could equally well be Ireland: 'Persians of the old religion ... many hundred years since, had fled hither from their Arab conquerors, preferring liberty and their altars in a foreign land to the alternative of apostasy or persecution in their own.' Still more explicitly, the mysterious but patriotic young storyteller in the frame incurs the furious criticism of the Court Vizier Fadladeen, in a satirical recycling of conservative English criticism of Moore's *Irish Melodies*.

The most distinguished and consistent of British poets writing on the East are Byron and Shelley. The East was their single greatest theme, and it is for this reason important for us to see how far their interest could have struck contemporaries as practically political, how far theorized and universal, how far primarily personal. Among the striking features of the situation around 1812, a convenient approximate starting-point for the careers of Byron and Shelley, one is that Britain had newly acquired, largely by conquest, a real empire in India. Second, a Parliament under pressure from a large middle-class religious lobby was about to direct the East India Company to accept Christian missions to India, a shift towards a policy of cultural assimilation. Third, Irish political activity, journalism, nationalist scholarship, fiction and poetry kept religion in the foreground as the key signifier of national consciousness. But, though the Irish link at first promised to radicalize the colonial issue for the British, it would also embarrass those English liberals (including Byron and especially Shelley) who saw the Catholic Church as the leading counter-revolutionary force in postwar Europe.

Byron begins his career as an Eastern writer in *Childe Harold*, II (1812), by considering the Turkish hold on Greece largely through the clash of two religious ideologies. His footnotes, unlike Southey's, are the fruit of personal observation as well as research. *The Giaour* and *The Bride of Abydos* (1813) benefit from the same cache of material but, possibly because this ran out, the three later Turkish tales are not footnoted. In the first three oriental poems both text and footnotes present information that compares Muslim rites and practices to Greek Orthodox ones or Christian dogma generally. As a secular-minded aristocrat Byron has little difficulty in adopting a pose of ironic detachment; in fact, in *The Giaour* particularly, he seems to prefer Muslim bigots to Christian bigots.

This is not the position of a mainstream revolutionary radical of the day, describing, in order to denounce, a religiously maintained system of empire; early Byron is noticeably unwilling to imagine a centre for empire other than the harem. But it is consistent with a call to Christian readers to support a policy of religious toleration and equal civil rights for subjected peoples, regardless of religion. Such a call in the Britain of 1812–13 reads not as radical but as Whiggish-liberal, the stance of the parliamentary Opposition. It tilts at the decision of 1813 to proselytize among the Indian masses and, without showing any zeal for Catholicism, comes out firmly against bigotry by those in power.

'I know thee not, I loathe thy race', observes the Muslim fisherman who narrates most of the first half of *The Giaour*, of the Christian infidel who is the central character. With his firsthand experience of a Christian Greece ruled by Muslim Turks, Byron in this group of tales tells a story his book-learned fellow poets do not, of the immense role played by religion in determining group identity – indeed, its inseparability from nationalism. Byron briefly celebrates a religious nationalist consciousness in his *Hebrew Melodies* – for instance, in the ecstatic death-song of 'Jephthah's Daughter', or 'The Vision of Belshazzar' or 'The Destruction of Sennacherib', better known by its opening line, 'The Assyrian came down like the wolf on the fold'. In his dedication of *The Corsair* to Moore he compliments his friend's patriotic zeal on behalf of Ireland, and his own song 'The Isles of Greece' expresses similar sentiments towards

Greece – when it is extracted from its ironized narrative context in Canto III of *Don Juan*, and from the drunken hack who performs it there. The irony in the end seems more Byronic than the fervour. Byron is not a nationalist poet at a length more sustained than an occasional lyric poem.

After *The Bride of Abydos* the Turkish tales shift from their religious preoccupation towards plots centring on more private, mysterious man–woman encounters. There is a sense in which Byron's many Eastern women – who range from the somnolent Dudù of *Don Juan*, Canto VI, to the freedom fighter Myrrha (*Sardanapalus*) and the arch-rebel Aholibamah (*Heaven and Earth*) – always to some degree represent a loved part of the earth and its people, in a way that none of Byron's individualistic male characters ever do. Conrad and Gulnare in *The Corsair*, Lara and Kaled in *Lara* (1814) are not orthodox lovers, in the first instance not lovers at all: it is the woman in each case who makes the passionate gestures, where before it was the man. Plainly both Gulnare and Kaled are Muslims, and the religious difference is an element in an already conflicted relationship, which readers surely ponder even while Byron leaves the point unstressed. In the verse novella *Beppo* (1818) Laura's husband comes home after many years of captivity a Turk and Muslim, but, this being easygoing Venice, he is able to resume possession of his wife and his religion after a small payment to the Church. Again, the novel-like *Don Juan* takes religion light-heartedly, although Juan's first three affairs, in different parts of the Mediterranean – with the Spanish Julia, the Greek-African Haidée and the harem slave Dudù – cross religious (and racial) frontiers, and are policed by religious conventions. But in Byron's three fine symbolic oriental dramas – *Sardanapalus* (1821), *Cain* (1822) and *Heaven and Earth* (1823) – a consistent and powerful new theme emerges, when the protagonists challenge religion in the name (more or less) of an unsanctioned love.

Byron's favourite late theme, that an apparently irregular life may be more truly moral than one that perfectly observes religious pieties, *can* anticipate the ironized drama of ideas of the late nineteenth century, by Ibsen, occasionally Schnitzler, often Shaw. A common intention to outrage the bourgeoisie explains why most of the characters, in his late world as in theirs, are complacently middle class – that is, by their own estimation, virtuous, pious and orderly people – while the protagonists who resist control – Juan, Sardanapalus and his mistress, Myrrha, Cain, the sisters Anah and Aholibamah, and Neuha and Torquil of *The Island* – are all wilder, more independent and driven by passion. In the early 1820s what would now be termed the religious right was mounting a strong campaign in the literary reviews and newspapers against non-respectable, sexually licentious and especially irreligious writing, with Byron and his friends, dubbed 'the Satanic school' by Southey in 1821, as the prime targets. Byron is in some ways responding to criticism in his humorously demonic *Don Juan* and the symbolic dramas, but his attack on institutional religion has now become much more careful, detailed and theologically grounded: he has found more to say about the moral legitimacy of the State (and its extension, a Christianizing empire) than ever before. In addition the *pressure* of public institutions on private lives is confronted, acted out – and politicized, in an essentially new way.

But can Byron really be claimed as a political modern? Definitions of political liberalism have changed so radically that modern readers often wonder how Byron can be termed either a liberal, or even a political, writer. In the twentieth century the word liberal is commonly associated with equality and democracy; Malcolm Kelsall in his study of Byron's politics convincingly shows classical liberal-Whig republicanism to be Byron's habitual political position, and this is the mind-set of the enlightened wing of Britain's eighteenth-century hereditary ruling class. By making the early skirmishes of the Greek war of independence in the Eastern Mediterranean look picturesquely archaic in *The Bride of Abydos, The Corsair* and so on, Byron avoided representation of a real revolutionary war. Usually Byron also avoids representing any leader of men as a parvenu or mere brigand; a partial exception is Haidée's father Lambro in *Don Juan*, Canto III (though he has become prosperous, and effectively rules his island). The real-life freedom fighter and pirate alluded to, Lambro Canzani, is named in the footnote to *The Bride of Abydos*, l 380, as, 'with Riga, the two most celebrated of the Greek revolutionaries'. Byron apparently goes out of his way not to glamorize low-born rebels – the populace in arms as witnessed on the streets of Paris in 1792–4 and in peasant Ireland in 1798. Kelsall and Nigel Leask account for this omission in terms of the appropriate discourse, Leask by drawing on Peter Burke's observation that throughout the classical humanist tradition, from Roman times, plebeian rebellion lay outside the limits of representation and 'low' people were not shown instigating political action.[1]

By falling in with classical-aristocratic representational practice,

1 Peter Burke, 'The Revolt of Masaniello' (1983), quoted in Leask, *British Romantic Writers*, p 44.

Byron and Shelley can appear to modern readers as exploiters of revolution rather than participants: both tend to turn it into a stage on which a very few aristocrats are the only qualified performers. The damage to their radical or even liberal pretensions is made all the greater by the sharp contrast between their patrician heroes and heroines and Southey's low-born ones. Since about 1980 Byron, even more than Shelley, has been subjected to a hostile scrutiny by cultural materialists. At its best this critical practice carefully uncovers the latent ideological implications of a text in its context; at worst it allows the critic to reconstruct a poetic context in the light of modern progressive opinion, typically feminism and post-colonialism. Even the subtle Jerome Christensen too sweepingly pronounces the Turkish tales 'misogynist'; that is a view qualified by Susan Wolfson and Caroline Franklin in their more discriminating examinations of the complex sexual politics of Byron's orientalism.[1] Feminists and post-colonialists hold up to scrutiny one favourite motif, the harem, richly represented in Byron's work (in *The Bride of Abydos, The Corsair, Don Juan*, Canto VI and *Sardanapalus*). By his overuse of this emblematic case of Eastern despotism and effeminacy, Byron allegedly betrays far from liberal attitudes: a contempt for female weakness and passivity, an association of the East with this degraded view of woman, and a voyeuristic, semi-pornographic curiosity towards what amounts to sexual abuse.

The danger of imposing modern precepts on past texts is that our language blots out the one in use at the time. Writing on harems, as on suttee, was used to whip up Western indignation against Eastern despotisms (and religions); so many wrote for this reason on the harem that others began to represent Western harem-watchers rather than the harem itself. Modern war-reporting of rape, torture and carnage generally seems voyeuristic, yet individual reports may not – may indeed seek to correct the voyeurism of others. We can best judge the pornographic and political impact of a single work by reading it *against* its genre, noticing where it gives more than what is generic or challenges genre-fed expectations. With public poetry, genre – a literary term – extends into discourse. Byron's readers and

1 'The death of Zuleika . . . does not merely represent misogyny (though of course it does); it allegorically renders the impossibility of confronting the strangeness of the Orient except in terms of the conventional homosocial, misogynist plot.' Jerome Christensen, *Lord Byron's Strength: Romantic Writing and Commercial Society*, Baltimore, 1993, p 118. Susan J. Wolfson, ' "Their She Condition": Cross-Dressing and the Politics of Gender in *Don Juan*', *ELH*, liv (1987); and Carolyn Franklin, *Byron's Heroines*, Oxford, 1992.

Byron already share a language for the Orient, pre-existent to Byron's own oriental writings: images, scenes and allegories attached to the notion of the East, or of the relationship 'metropolis-and-empire'. Genre is one element in a text's particular and necessary context, the circumstances of writing and publication another. Jerome McGann has given the context of Byron's poetry a new clarity of definition by his *Complete Poems*, with its weight of evidence on the texts, their individual composition- and publication-histories, and 'the contexts which surround and penetrate them'. McGann's own more recent Byron criticism focuses on the poet's exceptional aware-ness of context, and brings context back into his readings of the texts' self-deconstruction or flamboyant 'indeterminacy'.[1]

Byron professed scorn for any idea that he joined a genre already formed by others. When advising Moore to 'stick to the East; – the oracle, Staël, told me it was the only poetical policy', he also claimed that the field was at present empty of competition except for Southey's 'unsaleables'.[2] To be descending on a world of toiling professionals as an inspired amateur, to be inventing some-thing of his own, was necessary to his remarkable campaign of self-promotion. The sensational commercial success of Byron's own oriental narratives from *The Giaour* on sounds here as if it was calculated yet also opportunistic – Byronic enterprise. While claiming novelty, however, Byron combines the selling-points of the period's most successful poems so far – Scott's historical and picturesque series beginning with *The Lay of the Last Minstrel* and *Marmion* – with sensational Gothic details from Southey's disparaged *Thalaba*. Scott's guilty hero, Marmion, who has deserted his mistress and caused her death, suggests the Byronic hero, while his all-action ballad-like plots involving passion and feuding, set in a colourful past, establish the new format: heroic drama for a prosier, more commercial age, with the noble motivations and long speeches economically removed. Scott's world tends however to seem too like himself, well-disposed. At a stroke, by coming on as the guilty, misanthropic Childe Harold, Byron turns the wheel of fashion on from the medievalizing poetic Scott. From Southey he borrows *The Giaour*'s two nastiest signifiers of the religious imagination: the

1 J. J. McGann, '*Don Juan' in Context*, Chicago, 1976; 'The Book of Byron and the Book of the World', *Beauty of Inflections*, Oxford, 1985; and 'Hero with a Thousand Faces: The Rhetoric of Byronism', *Studies in Romanticism*, xxxi (1992), 295–314.
2 Byron to Moore, 28 August 1813; in *Letters and Journals of Lord Byron*, ed. L. Marchand, 12 vols, London, 1973–82, iii. 68.

Turkish fisherman's curse (that the Giaour will return from the grave as a vampire to 'suck the blood of all thy race') and the monk's guess that he is already possessed:

> On cliff he hath been known to stand,
> And rave as to some bloody hand
> Fresh sever'd from its parent limb,
> Invisible to all but him,
> Which beckons onward to his grave,
> And lures to leap into the wave.

(758, 826–31)[1]

From Byron's own day until very recently the commercialization of poetry he both satirized and used has served to deny him great-poet status. In 1982 Philip W. Martin presented a picture of a writer weakly tempted 'by an unsophisticated reading public', 'creating fantasies about himself' (including the fantasy that he is qualified to be a great poet) and as a result achieving 'a consciously produced artefact designed for the appeasement of a certain audience, a performance conducted under certain conditions'.[2] Since then these very gifts of visible self-creation, a performance centred on the performer, have come to seem the essence of Byron's fascination. He now tends to be congratulated on his ability to market himself, on his invention of an isolated, morbidly guilty persona who changes shape through 'seriality' – the brilliant device of fictionally renewing himself as a series of surrogates (Harold, the Giaour, Conrad, Lara, Manfred, on to the Cain and Lucifer who go off to contemplate the huge ghosts of extinct worlds in the second act of *Cain*). The persona is itself moulded by popular fiction and current scandal: the vampire, unwillingly sucking the blood of loved women, predominates in the Byronic hero during the first half of his career, Satan in the second.

Byron's glamorous, hugely publicized personality is no doubt the basis of his sexual magnetism, felt by those who read him and those who read about him. In the adulatory years from early 1813 to early 1816 he courted women's favour by creating heroes who had sincerely loved a woman and remained passionately faithful to her beyond the grave. When his marriage broke down and his promiscuity became public, the fictional and reported versions of Byron conflicted, but

---

1 Khawla, Southey's witch, uses a severed hand in her black-magic arts (*Thalaba*, Books II and IX), and the practice is extensively footnoted. See n 2, pp 414–15.
2 *Byron: A Poet before His Public*, Cambridge, 1982, pp 2–4.

not necessarily to his disservice: a reading woman could always think what his bride Annabella Milbanke once thought, that she alone understood him. Despite the duplicity of his self-presentation, however, Byron had a compelling, indeed most winning voice, heard as both strong and sincere. In his poems as in his letᵗ s he appears to speak to the reader, and to her or him alone. As ne moves in later verse from an essentially monologic to a dialogic mode he creates scenes between men and women, or sometimes men and men, that blend intensity with intimacy, tenderness and an unexpected naturalness – not merely between Juan and Julia or Laura and Beppo, in serio-comic works where changes of tone are needed, but in the dramas *Sardanapalus* and *Cain*, where the prevailing mood is grand. While he seems to many modern readers one of the least sincere of great poets, moment by moment Byron can be the most direct and focused, a man you have talked to. In the same way, equally paradoxically, he is the creator of inhabitable worlds.

So many modern critics, male and female, seem agreed that Byron's harem scenes are male fantasies that it would be rash to call the view wrong. Yet it must be obvious from the long-running romance career of the Sheikh that readers of women's romances also warm to the Eastern palace's opulence, coercion and female apartness. Nevertheless the harem does not figure in all Byron's tales, while two other elements do: swift, violent, almost wordless action, the expression of animal energy, and longer periods of still, obsessive grief, the man's virtual possession by the lost woman. Byron's strength is well explored by Jerome Christensen in his book devoted to the topic, as will rapidly translated. into action. The characters' power seems that of the writer; for many readers of either sex, empowerment is not only charismatic but accessible to anyone through fantasy. Moreover the subordination of this masculine power, in Byron's plots, to the hero's need, not for women in general but for one particular absent woman, seems to invite women, specifically, to appropriate the story. His spare detail and repetitive plotting leave silences for women readers to fill. As evidence of this, many of the best women writers of the first half of the nineteenth century – Hemans, Barrett Browning, Charlotte and Emily Brontë – owe debts to his powerful tone and compulsive world-creating.

Byron's lovers typically love on, undeterred by death; they have already defied the barriers of race, religion, class and law. The Giaour wants to spend eternity with Leila, washing in the sea. Manfred begs to be reunited with Astarte, his sister and mistress (whose name is mysteriously that of an Assyrian goddess, and her present abode the Zoroastrian underworld). Myrrha the Greek slave voluntarily undergoes the death of Hindu widows when they commit suttee, in order to remain with Sardanapalus the Assyrian king. Cain gives up the offer of joining the solitary Lucifer in eternity, in favour of finite human life with his sister-wife Adah.

The powerful will which Christensen identifies as Byron's strength would appear to express the poet's masculinity, and is in his earlier poems the property exclusively of the heroes. Later, however, it may be bestowed on a heroine who gains ascendancy over the men around her. Laura (in *Beppo*), Haidée (*Don Juan*) and Neuha (*The Island*) all exhibit unexpected power, taking charge at a crisis of the plot. In the first half of *Sardanapalus* Myrrha exemplifies the so-called masculine virtues of courage and decision, while the king stands for sociability and pleasure. These instances of female heroism are, however, on a merely human scale compared with that of Aholibamah, heroine of *Heaven and Earth*, who, as the instigator of a rebellion in Heaven, emerges as a female version of Milton's Satan, and hence as Byron's true *alter ego*. Moreover, where her ancestor Cain was necessarily a solitary rebel, Aholibamah is spokeswoman, moral leader, last survivor of the Cainites, apparently a group preferring to live outside the cruel laws an old, servile Noah is willing to implement. Remarkably more than Leila, her line is that of Owenson's Wild Irish Girl and Reeve's Charoba.

Responding to a religious critical faction who accused him of regressing to the early Christian (and Eastern-derived) heresy of Manicheism, Byron in *Heaven and Earth* bases his account of Noah's Flood not on Genesis but on the ancient but non-canonical Book of Enoch, written in Ethiopic and preserved in its entirety only in Abyssinia/Ethiopia until the 1780s. This alternative version relates that God determined to drown the earth when the beauty of the daughters of men drew the angels down from Heaven. Aholibamah's call to her angel-lover firmly declares an intellectual position, which is anti-ascetic, anti-idealist, nonconforming and equal:

> Samiasa!
> I call thee, I await thee, and I love thee.
> Many may worship thee, that will I not:
> If that thy spirit down to mine may move thee
> Descend and share my lot!

> (i. 92–6)

When he challenges the implications of some Hebraic stories Byron also questions strands in Christianity that view sexuality as corruption and woman as defiled. Similarly the drama *Cain* reviews the moral implications of the Old Testament's preference for Abel, who sacrifices a slaughtered lamb to God, over Cain, whose offering of the vegetable fruits of the earth is refused. Byron's return to the remote origins of Christianity exposes what is primitive, inhumane and irrational in its traditions – and, he hopes, the inadequacy in an individualistic age of a moral law grounded in fundamentalist belief or the habit of obedience.

Byron's richest orientalist work is his idiosyncratic, highly original drama *Sardanapalus*, in which the Eastern monarch enters dressed as a woman, and proceeds to question his State's stereotyped notions of civic, military, sexual and religious virtue – for later readers the more generalized categories of gender, race and class. Eventually he submits to the destiny appropriate to a king, leader and tragic hero: that is, he puts on armour, kills several of his enemies and finally, by killing himself, goes on (he supposes) to join his ancestors. Hitherto Sardanapalus has despised his ancestors, bloodthirsty barbarians descended from Nimrod, the Bible's mighty hunter.

Nineveh, over which Sardanapalus reigned, was not far from the Garden of Eden. A restored Eden is what Byron's king has in mind, a modern Utopia in which the citizens cultivate their gardens and live happily instead of getting drafted to die on the sands of India. But at the Assyrian court, a satirical mirror held up to modern imperial London, the talk of virtue is actually militaristic, practical-utilitarian or religious talk. (Though the religion is a form of sun-worship, its High Priest interprets his role as partly institutional and wholly political, like the *Quarterly Review*'s Anglican-evangelical critics.) No one could miss the application to London one year after George IV's accession, since the play is full of references to the king's divorce and to the scandalous parties he throws in his pavilion. The intention is hardly support of George, but exposure of the interestedness of London's increasingly influential religious lobby and, more generally, of the wide gulf between the behaviour of the modern Christian state and the teachings of the Prince of Peace.

Though Byron's oriental writings begin flamboyant, attention-seeking and openly self-serving, exerting a strength not harnessed to a specific political purpose, they end in dialogue with a much smaller, educated audience. For many readers *Sardanapalus* and *Cain* will never be as emotionally compelling as the suggestive Turkish tales. The more a work states, the less space it leaves for fantasy. Byron's role as one of the masters of European Eastern fantasy remains a separate achievement, hugely influential in ways impossible to measure, different in kind from the powerful assault of his symbolic dramas on the religious ideology sustaining British empire-building.

Shelley, the other leading orientalist poet, is consistently a more academic writer than Byron. His three long early poems – *Queen Mab* (1813), *Alastor* (1816) and *The Revolt of Islam* (1818) – all self-consciously revert to the orientalist themes and manner of the 1790s, the French-revolutionary decade. They could be said to rewrite Volney's *Ruins* and Southey's *Thalaba*, exposing some of the others' mistakes but more essentially reviewing them in the light of the failure of the French Revolution. Like both its precursor-works *Queen Mab* has copious notes, an anthology of the science and materialist thought of the Enlightenment; indeed it is likely to be the notes rather than the poem that made it a classic text for lower-class radicals after a cheap pirated edition appeared in 1821. The poem's opening line echoes the opening line of *Thalaba*; but the situation, the Fairy Queen's appearance to young Ianthe in order to give her a politicized history-lesson, draws on the opening scene of Volney's *Ruins*, where a genie appears to a French traveller among the ruins of Palmyra for the same purpose. Ianthe learns how from ancient times the world has been in the grip of evil, mostly Eastern, empires, that all over the world cruel religions have kept kings in power, and that 'priestcraft', backed by myths depicting divine cruelty, has everywhere sanctioned the arbitrary torture or killing of individuals. Where Southey in *The Curse of Kehama* has the emperor-magician Kehama torturing Ladurlad – he intends for ever – Shelley repeats the comparable legend that the Christian god inflicted an agonizing eternal life on Ahasuerus, the Wandering Jew, for refusing to let Christ rest at his door when on the way to his Crucifixion. The impact of invoking this victim of the Christian god's cruelty, 'a wondrous phantom, from the dreams/Of human error's dense and purblind faith' (vii. 64–5), is to deny the appropriateness of sending Christian missions to civilize the Hindus. Nevertheless Mab promises Ianthe that a Utopian future awaits mankind, a return to nature made possible by the enlightened science of an advanced age.

*Alastor* illustrates the way Shelley works consistently but not repetitively, refining his writing and excising what was too simple and doctrinaire in his own previous work. It is a sophisticated puzzle-poem, built out of the work of the previous generation, this time using the imaginative writers Wordsworth and Coleridge, Godwin and Wollstonecraft, and two orientalist texts in particular, Southey's *Thalaba* and Sydney Owenson's *The Missionary*. The fictional Poet-protagonist sounds as if he has written the Lake Poets' poetry and the novel – St Leon (1799) – in which Godwin incorporates Wollstonecraft's later thinking. But his wanderings seem to retrace the route followed by Thalaba, and to include two key incidents – Thalaba's departure from his Arabian home, leaving behind his intended bride, and her haunting of him after her death as a vampire. Material from Southey recurs in Shelley's poem in the same order as in Thalaba: scrabblings among Gothic body-parts near the beginning, a visit to an ancient city, and finally the arid mountain journey, partly by boat, which takes the hero to his death. Shelley does more than justice to Southey's descriptive powers in the passage in which he evokes Thalaba's journey at first spatially, through 'Many a wide waste and tangled wilderness', past pinnacles of ice and lakes of bitumen, into vast caves naturally pillared with crystal, their roofs glittering with gems; then back in time, to

> The awful ruins of the days of old:
> Athens, and Tyre, and Balbec, and the waste
> Where stood Jerusalem, the fallen towers
> Of Babylon, the eternal pyramids,
> Memphis and Thebes, and whatso'er of strange
> Sculptured on alabaster obelisk,
> Or jasper tomb, or mutilated sphynx,
> Dark Ethiopa in her desert hills
> Conceals.
>
> (108–16)

Shelley gives credit to Southey and to Thalaba, once his favourite poem, for its intimations of 'The thrilling secrets of the birth of time' (128) and for its almost tender fellow-feeling for small creatures – 'bright bird, insect, or gentle beast' (13). All the same, Southey has chosen to use the same form and story – that of the originally religious quest-romance – to bring out what is insidiously self-betraying in the modern intellectual's idealism. One tradition emerging in contemporary poetry, primarily associated with Wordsworth, Coleridge and Southey, automatically valorizes the subjective voice. Southey seemed to make his long narratives similarly monologic, when he sanctioned the actions of his hero no matter what sacrifices his career exacted from his loved ones. Shelley copies the quest but inverts or transvalues its meaning, by examining his quester's aims and 'visionary' aspirations sceptically, and, as the Poet becomes increasingly sick and lonely, suggesting that he is the victim of his own narcissistic fantasies.

However vague Thalaba might be as to time and place, it is full of travellers' thick descriptions of a region and its people. The allegorical plot moreover seems to figure a real politics and to anticipate a changed future. Owenson's *Missionary* is even more substantial in the way it uses its lovers to represent the clash of two religious cultures, connects gender with race inequality, and implies cross-reference to the treatment of Ireland, on England's doorstep. Shelley by comparison etherealizes his women characters and makes little use of the fact that they are Middle Easterners. Almost all critics of the poem agree on this: beginning with Mary Shelley, Percy Shelley's first important editor, they hold the poem itself to be narcissistic, that is, centred admiringly on Shelley himself.

Keats, not normally much of an orientalist, becomes one incidentally when in *Endymion* (1818) he seems to imitate and revise *Alastor*. Keats may well have read Shelley's poem as a yet more flagrant example of Wordsworthian egotism and abstraction from materiality, for his quester Endymion sets out not with an intellectual but a natural objective – winning a woman – and his vigorous adventures take him to more graphic, better-peopled places, such as a Gothicized marine underworld revamped from the one in *The Curse of Kehama*. The woman in the case is admittedly Cynthia the moon-goddess, but Keats materializes even her, by putting (yet another) Indian girl in Endymion's way. Not by leaving this girl but by loving her, he finds he has won Cynthia after all.

On one point, however, Keats reads as Shelley's ally, even follower. While hardly ethereal, he is equally literary. Keats's resistance to prosaic reference is a resistance to history and politics, science and economics, discourses or heavy 'themes' he thinks ugly in poetry. In subsequent works which came near to brushing against Shelley's and Byron's, such as the two *Hyperion* poems, he writes his own account of the fall of an Eastern empire, but in a form so displaced that it is hard to relate his concerns to politics. His fragmentary *Cap and Bells* relies on a reader's knowledge of Moore's *Lalla Rookh*, but again exploits the setting and the manner rather than the topical matter.

The pull to literariness was felt by all good poets in the postwar Regency years and, as a side-effect, their poems often seemed private. Shelley in *Alastor* had tackled a genuine ideological dilemma – the seductions of subjectivity – but he must have been troubled by the way the poem's essentially literary language forced him to repeat the alienated behaviour-pattern he objected to. His longest, most ambitious poem yet, *The Revolt of Islam* (1818), a censored version of the poem published at the end of 1817 as *Laon and Cythna*, in some respects completes the project of his early work and exorcizes its dominating preoccupation with the 1790s. As its Preface declares, it is a rethinking of the French Revolution, an apparent failure only, for the revolution is destined to repeat itself until it succeeds – yesterday in Europe, today in Asia. The firmly political Preface leaves little room for evading Shelley's political intentions. Yet, with his customary intellectuality, he does not so much imagine one revolution as theorize the course of all revolutions: a harsh despotism that drives the people to take up arms, followed in turn by militarization, internal war, massacre, disease, starvation, rape – then counter-revolution, with priests taking a lead, and yet more cruelty and repression.

Where *Alastor* speaks what Bakhtin calls a heteroglossia – a babble of voices which are in fact the identifiable voices of contemporary creative writers – the essentially visual collage in *The Revolt of Islam* recalls impressive but fleeting scenes out of a scattering of sources, the most salient of which already treat revolutions in the East. These new-old scenes include aerial journeys, a cave reached by an underwater journey, and two ceremonial attempts to put the hero and heroine to death by fire. In a very different style of cross-reference the sufferings of the Greek people evoke the documented horrors of France's civil war: the various provincial massacres, the Terror and the end-of-war privations which Percy and Mary Shelley saw in France in 1814 at first hand. Against the nightmarish backdrop of this series of confused events, the protagonists Laon and Cythna or Laon and Laone, brother and sister, lovers, move as both figureheads of revolution and its martyrs. Since the Turkish sultan is the despot they are fighting, they to some degree represent fighters for Greek independence, but Shelley as usual avoids real cultural particularity. He remains, like Volney, an internationalist, for whom progress and world revolution must come globally. His most resolute poem of revolution could raise suspicions that Shelley is an early Western ideologue doing what Said is accused of doing: assimilating the East into a specialized academic discourse. Moreover his neglect of the Irish parallel, so soon after *Lalla Rookh*, seems a surprising omission from the one-time Irish sympathizer.[1]

1 An immediate practical reason for his avoidance of Ireland was his reluctance to take up the cause of the Catholic Church; for his private wish to subvert Catholicism in Ireland even in 1812, see Richard Holmes, *Shelley: The Pursuit*, London, 1977, pp 121–2. Owenson's and Moore's Irish orientalizing generated religious opposition as well as political support, from a literary viewpoint most notably in the brilliant anti-Catholic Gothic novel, C. R. Maturin's *Melmoth the Wanderer* (1820), where the principal episodes feature the horrors of the seventeenth-century Spanish Inquisition and of contemporary Hinduism.

With one exception, *Hellas* (1821) – a drama written in support of Greek independence – Shelley's orientalism does move on an intellectual plane, abstracted from personality, local and topical detail, and fighting on the ground. When, after *The Revolt of Islam*, he largely divests himself of his 1790s discipleships, he becomes yet more philosophical, eclectically learned and universal. His beautiful 'The Witch of Atlas' (1820) is to my mind the most aesthetically satisfying of all the period's oriental allegories, shapelier than *Thalaba*, less sugary than Moore's 'Paradise and the Peri' (*Lalla Rookh*) and far more incisive than either. Shelley had been working on translations of the Greek 'Homeric Hymns', a suggestive form which must have reminded him of William Jones's syncretic and carefully doctored hymns to the Hindu pantheon. In 'The Witch of Atlas' Shelley invents a deity who, born in a pastoral landscape (the north-African Atlas Mountains) when the world is young, of a union between the Sun and one of the Oceanides, represents a primitive type of god-making, the deification of natural phenomena. As she grows up, the Witch is surrounded by heraldic creatures, culled from Richard Payne Knight's *Inquiry into the Symbolical Language of Ancient Art and Mythology* (1818).[1] Arrived at maturity, in parallel it seems with human thought, the Witch sends her creatures away – all but a silent hermaphrodite, who represents a high point of the ancient world's religious evolution, Plato's idea that we were all once androgynes and that human love represents a yearning to be whole again.

Mythological time is over, historical time has begun. Travelling over northern Africa in her Southeyan, originally Arabian magic car, the Witch looks down on the death of the bad but also the good, about which she can do nothing. Human beings by now pray to be granted some form of immortality; her answer is to tip the bodies of a deserving old couple out into the green world, to be reabsorbed into its matter. She comes last to Egypt, the ancient-world empire often thought of as especially corrupt, not just because of its primacy and its vast, intimidating monuments, but because in the centuries of the early Church it was a cockpit of competing Eastern religions and philosophy – the classic site for what Priestley called, in the title of one of his most influential books, *The Corruptions of Christianity* (1782). The Witch contemplates Egypt's cruelty, despotism and animal-worshipping cults, laughs and moves on. The joke is on those who think that righting the world's wrongs might be achieved by beautiful idealisms.

1 For Payne Knight's book, see n 1, p 404.

Either in 1819 or 1820 Shelley wrote a satirical essay 'On the Devil, and Devils', in reply to the accusations of Manicheism and even satanism against Byron and, where occasion offered (as with *The Revolt of Islam* and *Frankenstein*), against his friends. Shelley was probably writing the essay at the same time as *Prometheus Unbound* (finished August 1820); both involved carefully rethinking Milton's Satan, who, as God's great antagonist in the Hebraic system, was seen by Shelley as identifiable with Prometheus, antagonist to Jupiter or Zeus in the Graeco-Roman system.[1] Though he raises the problem of the attractiveness of Milton's Satan relatively circumspectly in the Preface to *Prometheus Unbound*, Shelley must have taken the outspoken 'On the Devil' to be fit only for private consumption. There he boldly observes, for example, that Satan is far less guilty in the poem than God, the cold-blooded victor, a point that makes him wonder if Milton was a Christian at the time of writing. Milton dared not be franker for, like modern Europeans, he lived under the constraint of a restored tyranny; Shelley co-opts him, in short, as the founder-member of the challenged Satanic school.

He proceeds to a rapid historical review of the occurrence of the figure of Satan in both ancient Hebraic and pagan writings – as a Chaldean invention, as the 'second Principle' of Zoroastrian sun-worship, and in the Bible. He concludes that it was not pagans or heretics but worshippers of the Hebrew One God that made most use of the Devil: they needed him to resolve monotheism's internal contradiction, that a benign omnipotent Deity has to be supposed ultimately responsible for evil. Shelley here uses an old accusation available to critics of religious orthodoxy at all times since the 1780s, and since 1817 spiritedly revived, of the Church's own weakness for incorporating pagan narratives, rites, customs, even Eastern heresy and idolatry.[2] The significance of the essay is that it acts as a witty but not unserious manifesto for the group of writers who indeed

1  See Marilyn Butler, 'Romantic Manicheism: Shelley's "On the Devil, and Devils" and Byron's Mythological Dramas', in J. B. Bullen, ed., *The Sun is God: Painting, Literature and Mythology in the Nineteenth Century*, Oxford, 1989, pp 13–39, esp. p 23 for the essay's date.

2  Francis Douce, collector, scholar and Shakespearian, was the most tireless reviser of the orthodox, canonical and Eurocentric Warton. Two of his Appendices to *Illustrations of Shakspeare*, (2 vols, 1807), on the 'Gesta Romanorum' and 'The Morris Dance', have as a theme the pervasive presence of oriental elements in English popular culture. For Douce's influence see also my essay 'John Bull's Other Kingdom: Byron's Intellectual Comedy', *Studies in Romanticism*, xxxi (1992), 287–8.

adopt Satan as a totem, most notably in *Prometheus Unbound* and in Byron's symbolic dramas, three of which feature Lucifer. Shelley's essay makes it clear that Lucifer's main appeal is his comic potential as an embarrassment to modern educated Christians; but another important source of embarrassment is that Satan is also a Middle Easterner, a reminder in conditions of complacent European ascendancy that there is no such thing as northern cultural purity.

Shelley's *Prometheus Unbound* (1820) goes out of its way to use an Eastern setting, the by now familiar mountain terrain of Romantic orientalizing, which incorporates both the lands ruled by the Ottoman regime and the new British empire in India. Prometheus himself and Jupiter, along with the pantheon of nature gods and goddesses who attend the heroine Asia, seem unmistakably Greek (or Graeco-Roman). In some myths Prometheus is indeed identified with Europe, but Shelley's clear wish to link him with Satan must complicate that question, just as the legend that Dionysus or Bacchus led an army to India makes the play's lesser divinities East–West hybrids too. Meanwhile Shelley has moved the action from Aeschylus' Caucasus Mountains, in Asia Minor, to the Indian Caucasus, the site of Hinduism's holy Mount Meru, overlooking Kashmir; Panthea, Asia's sister, is made a goddess of South India. The fall of empire which this plot once again enacts thus brings the new British empire fully within its geographical scope.

Like 'The Witch of Atlas', *Prometheus Unbound* tells a story of human mental evolution. The action opens when mankind's theology and political theory are in a primitive condition – Shelley's provocative analysis of that phase of human knowledge in which a single god, Jupiter, could be perceived as ruler of the ancient world, or God the Father as sole creator along the lines of the account in Genesis. In Act II human thought has developed and primitive monotheism given way to the more sophisticated and socially advantageous dualism. By allowing for the coexistence of two competing Principles, Good and Evil, a religion such as Persian Zoroastrianism externalizes warring impulses in the human mind.[1] By staging this eternal drama or dialogue, religion advances conceptually far beyond the dictates of an often arbitrary tyrant-god, to offer human beings moral choices, a proper basis for the individual moral life. Where it was common for Christian comparative religionists to portray pan-

1 See Shelley's 'Essay on the Devil, and Devils' for a psychological explanation for religious dualism; in *Shelley's Prose*, ed. D. L. Clark, Albuquerque, N. Mex., 1966, p 265.

theism as a primitive religious creed, superseded by a more moral monotheism, Shelley stages the opposite scenario in his arrangement and writing of Acts I and II. Asia, anxiously interrogating Demogorgon for religious answers, finds that he will only echo her questions, or what she indicates she already thinks. When this scene opens, Asia and with her the reader think of Demogorgon as vast, formless, ineffable, more intimidating even than Jupiter the anthropomorphic tyrant-god, because Demogorgon hints at something more ancient and unmanageable: the abyss. Asia emerges from their meeting puzzled and more human, but Demogorgon has dwindled into a Wizard of Oz, a projection of humanity able to tell us only what we expect to hear.

Throughout Acts I and II Prometheus and Asia have an uncertain status, for their parent-text or texts, a lost drama by Aeschylus and behind that the Greek myths, lead us to take them for gods. It only gradually becomes plain that they have no divine powers, no special knowledge. Yet, with the departure in Act III, scene i of the gods they formerly imagined – Ocean, Apollo, Jupiter – they grow in mental stature and can converse with Nature in a wholly new way. The last act and a half open into a cosmic republicanism, a mighty natural commonwealth operating under scientific laws of attraction and repulsion, the modern substitute for the old symbolic language of the gods. As Erasmus Darwin had already inventively shown in *The Botanic Garden* (1791), Herschel's mapping of the heavens and Hutton's *Theory of the Earth* had ushered in a cosmos which was (in Hutton's words) 'without trace of a beginning – without prospect of an end'. Archaic belief-systems would not necessarily require a violent overthrow, the play suggests; time and the march of mind was already delivering it.

Nigel Leask points out that *Prometheus Unbound* is by modern standards easily the most politically correct of Shelley's works.[1] Asia, both an Asiatic and a woman, is the more effective and advanced of the two protagonists. Moreover, Prometheus' release, with her help, in the Vale of Kashmir seems to undo symbolically the male deception and enslavement of the feminine East acted out in Owenson's *The Missionary*. But the presence of Owenson needs relating to the presence of a more recent orientalist text, of great authority, which Shelley also had to incorporate and revise.

James Mill's powerful utilitarian *History of British India* (7 vols, 1817) took eleven years to write. Trenchant, drastic, it adopts

1 Leask, *British Romantic Writers*, pp 135–54.

arguments marshalled by Charles Grant in the 1790s against both Hinduism and the earlier, sympathetic British policy towards Indian religion and traditional culture. Mill, once a fervent Presbyterian, now a leading Benthamite, develops the already powerful secular side of Grant's arguments, but in place of Grant's case for enlightened religion (that is, Christianity) he outlines a secular millenarianism, an ideology of rapid, unprecedented social progress under British rule. His topic is British India because, with the coming of the British, Indian history begins again. Mill thus cuts out most of Jones's historical agenda for orientalism, denigrating Indian learning and arts by sweepingly terming them backward and effeminate:

In some of the more delicate manufactures, however, particularly in spinning, weaving and dyeing, the Hindus ... no doubt surpass all that was attained by the rude Europeans. In the fabrication, too, of trinkets; in the art of polishing and setting the precious stones ... our rough and impatient ancestors did not attain the same nicety which is attained by the patient Hindus ... In point of manners and character, the manliness and courage of our ancestors, compared with the slavish and dastardly spirit of the Hindus, place them in an elevated rank ... The gothic nations, as soon as they became a settled people, exhibit the marks of a superior character and civilization to those of the Hindus.[1]

On the strength of his book Mill became Examiner at the East India Company headquarters in London's Threadneedle Street. In 1819 Shelley's close friend T. L. Peacock, hitherto a keen scholar of Welsh, ancient Greek and Zoroastrianism, competed successfully for the post of Assistant Examiner under Mill. In the autumn of 1819 he was still reading *British India* and, that November, spent a day walking with Mill, during which they had their first serious conversation. Peacock was evidently deeply impressed, for his attitude to traditional culture becomes henceforth cynical and modern.[2] Probably soon after this meeting he wrote an essay, 'The Four Ages of Poetry', which, using poetry as a criterion, describes the cultural progress of mankind to date. In the age of the primitive tribe poets flattered chiefs but also voiced early religious insights about the world. Under more polished courtly regimes poets became more sophisticated, more servile, better remunerated and intellectually

1 James Mill, *The History of British India*, ed. and abridged by William Thomas, Chicago, 1975, pp 246–7.
2 See Marilyn Butler, 'Druids, Bards and Twice-Born Bacchus: Peacock's Engagement with Primitive Mythology', in *Keats–Shelley Memorial Bulletin*, xxxvi (1985), 57–76, for the impact of Mill on Peacock's subsequent treatment of the remote past, particularly in *Misfortunes of Elphin* (1828).

more marginal. Nowadays pro-Government poets were still at work, but ambling up and down the hills of the remote Lake District, while the higher reaches of knowledge had passed for ever into other hands, those of 'mathematicians, astronomers, chemists, moralists, metaphysicians, historians, politicians and political economists'. In a short, loaded account of the popular narrative poetry of the present day ('Mr Scott digs up the poachers and cattle-stealers of the ancient border . . . Lord Byron cruizes for thieves and pirates on the shores of the Morea . . . Mr Wordsworth picks up village legends from old women and sextons . . .') Peacock picks out nostalgia and cultural regressiveness as the common factor: the verse 'a modern-antique compound of frippery and barbarism', the poet 'a semi-barbarian in a civilized community'.[1]

Many modern commentators have thought Peacock not serious here, but he surely was serious, and Shelley believed it. He was nevertheless puzzled and nettled, since his own clothes were being stolen: Peacock thus far had studied literary antiquities, while Shelley read widely in modern science and materialist or sceptical philosophers. When Peacock sent him the essay, he replied with his most important prose work, *A Defence of Poetry*, in which he denies the marginality of modern poetry. But by choosing this line of argument he accepts Mill's and now Peacock's premise, that poets' writing must belong to contemporary discourse and, if serious, must also aim to be useful. A surprising utilitarian attack elicits a utilitarian reply.

Not by coincidence, surely, Shelley's own orientalist poems of the next months, 'The Witch of Atlas' and *Prometheus Unbound*, are progressivist on terms that tacitly suggest a desire to incorporate the best of Mill while refuting the worst. The worst is the harsh, arrogant tone represented in the passage from Mill quoted above, trumpeting a masculine, militaristic and Eurocentric world-view; the best, the conviction that the modern world is moving on from its old religious and court culture, which has been either frivolous or slavish, into a symbolically egalitarian order in which the master discourse is science. By clothing Mill's progressivism and scientism in transcendent poetry in the last acts of *Prometheus Unbound* Shelley in effect completes his Defence. He has rebuked Mill by a temporal scheme which shows that in the religious era it was the East rather than the West that made the highest contribution to

1  T. L. Peacock, 'The Four Ages of Poetry', in *Peacock's Works*, ed. H. F. B. Brett-Smith and C. L. Jones, Halliford edn, viii, London, 1934, pp 24, 19–20.

human development, and that a feminine culture may signify wisdom and strength. But he can't be said to challenge; indeed here he provides an idealizing cover for James Mill's policy, now becoming Britain's Indian policy. Anglicization, the creation of an educated secular middle class, agrarian improvement, trade and commerce, improved communications, would deliver Mill's rational, prosperous new age – some way short of Shelley's millennium but equally capable of being described as a progressive modern state achieved with the help of science.

Shelley grew up a sympathizer with revolution. His discipleship to Godwin, even more than to Volney, meant that he hoped change would come through enlightenment rather than violence. In the effort to promote change and a better world, exalted poetry such as his own played a part. The East also played a part, because it was not only imaginatively but literally a world of almost limitless potential. Within the past generation a wide variety of scholars and poets had given Europe and Asia a common past (linguistic, religious, cultural, old-regime political) and thus a common destiny: liberation. In the very period that the grand narrative of evolutionism was emerging in the natural sciences, more modest stories of uneven human development, a race's progress or stasis or even extinction, began to take shape in the emerging fields of ethnography and cultural history. Parts of the population of the British Isles might have a dark ancestry; these (the Celts) faced loss of identity, the death of their group; the Catholic and thence the Anglican Church was surely in part an Eastern Church. A similar long perspective taught that the world was in flux, and necessary change held out the hope of general progress.

The large areas of agreement, indeed the basic similarity of outlook, between the radicals Volney, Grant, Southey, Mill and Shelley underscores the fact that, for the British, India in particular became the site in which diverse experiments in Western progressivism might be worked out. Why call Grant and Southey progressives? Because their writing on India is centrally concerned with its transformation; they or their friends make similar cases for social amelioration at home. The ideas of all five can be condemned as Eurocentric, and for inviting a massive, indeed unrealizable, European intervention in Asian affairs – the very notion of which has deeply offended nineteenth- and twentieth-century nationalist and religious sentiment. Yet the same evolutionary model – in first its Volneyan, afterwards its Marxian, version – quickly took root among Third World revolutionaries, and originally provided the language they still use against narrowly based regimes, whether colonial, post-colonial or indigenous.

Intellectuals in the long tradition of the French Revolution have tended to measure radicalism by its degree of commitment to social progress rather than to the autonomy of small nations. If these five could all accept colonialism, given the right social policies, were they hypocrites or self-deceivers, always really working on behalf of European aggrandizement? Were they better or worse thinkers about Romantic India than Landor, Byron or Moore, who can all sound more simply critical of foreign occupation? The balance of insight and altruism just about comes down, it seems to me, on the side of the progressives. In either case, not to attend to the variety of motive and of social philosophy in this generation of writers is to impose an untenable uniformity on the English Romantic poetry addressing the East, or, simply, not to hear what is being said.

# BIBLIOGRAPHY

## 1 'Events... have made us a World of Readers': Reader Relations 1780–1830

### The history of book making

*(i) the technological aspect*

Feather, John, *A History of British Publishing*, London, 1988. A useful, standard modern survey.

Plant, Marjorie, *The English Book Trade: An Economic History of the Making and Sale of Books*, 3rd edn, London, 1974. Esp. chs 13–21, which cover such topics as the application of mechanical power to printing, the volume of production, the cost of books, and copyright.

Twyman, Michael, *Printing 1770–1970: An Illustrated History of Its Development and Uses in England*, London, 1970. A generously illustrated social history of printing.

*(ii) the socio-history of texts*

Couturier, Maurice, *Textual Communication: A Print-Based Theory of the Novel*, London, 1991. A blending of literary theory with the historical analysis of communications and the changing circumstances of book production.

McGann, Jerome J., 'Keats and the Historical Method in Literary Criticism', *Modern Language Notes*, xciv (1979), 988–1032.

———'The Text, the Poem, and the Problem of Historical Method', *New Literary History*, xii (1981), 269–88 (partly on Byron).

Both these essays are reprinted in McGann's *The Beauty of Inflections: Literary Investigations in Historical Method and Theory*, Oxford, 1985, pp 17–65 and 111–32. Here and elsewhere, McGann demonstrates the useful application of a new bibliographical and socio-historical contextualization to the study of Romantic poets.

———*The Textual Condition*, Princeton, 1991.

## The reading public

Altick, Richard D., *The English Common Reader: A Social History of the Mass Reading Public 1800–1900*, Chicago, 1957. Comprehensive, densely detailed and very readable, this is the classic study.

James, Louis, ed., *English Popular Literature 1819–1851*, New York, 1976. A lively and informative introduction which explores interrelated developments in publishing, education and popular literature in the period. The well-illustrated anthology covers almanacs, criminal broadsheets, popular journalism and graphic satire.

Kaufman, Paul, *Libraries and Their Users: Collected Papers in Library History*, London, 1969. Includes several essays on book distribution in the period.

Klancher, Jon P., *The Making of English Reading Audiences: 1790–1832*, Madison, Wis., 1987. More narrowly focused than Altick on the socio-political implications of reading and on the shaping powers of periodical literature, Klancher's study draws on the theoretics of Bakhtin, Foucault, Jameson and Marx to illuminate the new middle-class, radical and mass readerships of the early nineteenth century.

Leavis, Q. D., *Fiction and the Reading Public*, London, 1932. An enormously important study and itself the inheritor of certain Romantic conceptions of reading.

Lovell, Terry, *Consuming Fiction*, London, 1987. On the status of the novel and the market for fiction.

Ong, Walter J., *Orality and Literacy: The Technologizing of the Word*, London, 1982. Already a classic, this study explores some of the profound changes in our thought processes and social structures which are the result, at various stages of history, of the development of speech, writing and print.

Stone, Lawrence, 'Literacy and Education in England, 1640–1900', *Past and Present*, xlii (1969), 69–139. The major article to propound the theory of rising literacy in the early industrial period, it has been challenged by, among others, Michael Sanderson, 'Literacy and Social Mobility in the Industrial Revolution in England', *Past and Present*, lvi (1972), 75–104.

Summerfield, Geoffrey, *Fantasy and Reason: Children's Literature in the Eighteenth Century*, London, 1985.

Varma, Devendra P., *The Evergreen Tree of Diabolical Knowledge*, Washington, 1972. Contains much information on circulating libraries.

## *Radical writings, the press and the reading debate*

Aspinall, Arthur, *Politics and the Press, c.1780–1850*, London, 1949.

Butler, Marilyn, ed., *Burke, Paine, Godwin, and the Revolution Controversy* [Cambridge English Prose Texts], Cambridge, 1984. This provides a useful selection of and commentary upon opposed radical and conservative writings from the pamphlet war of the 1790s.

Hone, J. Ann, *For the Cause of Truth: Radicalism in London 1796–1821*, Oxford, 1982. A detailed historical monograph.

McCalman, Iain, *Radical Underworld: Prophets, Revolutionaries, and Pornographers in London, 1795–1840*, Cambridge, 1988. Mc-Calman broadens the inquiry of conventional histories of radicalism by drawing on spy reports and popular literary and religious movements to illuminate connections between underground revolutionary-republican groups and London's other underworlds.

Smith, Olivia, *The Politics of Language 1791–1819*, Oxford, 1984. Analysing the linked political and linguistic challenge from the radical literati and the self-educated in the period, Smith examines contemporary redefinitions of the nature of language and the distinct concerns of a vulgar and politically motivated reading audience.

Spinney, G. H., 'Cheap Repository Tracts: Hazard and Marshall Edition', *The Library*, 4th ser., xx (1940), 295–340. Spinney traces Hannah More's involvement with the counter-revolutionary cheap-reading programme and provides an itemized chronology and bibliography (not always accurate) of the Cheap Repository Tracts from their inception in March 1795.

Thompson, E. P., *The Making of the English Working Class*, rev. edn, Harmondsworth, 1968. This is the classic (and controversial) study, covering the formation of a working-class identity in the period 1780–1832. See, in particular, chs 1–5, which explore those continuing popular traditions in the eighteenth century which influenced the radical agitation of the 1790s, and chs 15 and 16, which survey the 'heroic age of popular Radicalism' (1815–19) and the consolidation of working-class consciousness in the 1820s and 1830s.

Webb, R. K., *The British Working-Class Reader 1790–1848: Literacy and Social Tension*, London, 1955, esp. chs 1 and 2.

Wickwar, William H., *The Struggle for the Freedom of the Press 1819–1832*, London, 1928.

*Magazines, reviews and newspapers*

Adburgham, Alison, *Women in Print: Writing Women and Women's Magazines from the Restoration to the Accession of Victoria*, London, 1972, esp. chs 8–16. This is an entertaining account, though patchy and prone to error in its scholarship and irritatingly unannotated.

Asquith, Ivon, 'The Structure, Ownership, and Control of the Press, 1780–1855', in *Newspaper History from the Seventeenth Century to the Present Day*, ed. George Boyce, James Curran and Pauline Wingate, London, 1978, pp 98–116.

Clive, John, *Scotch Reviewers: The 'Edinburgh Review', 1802–1815*, Cambridge, Mass., and London, 1957. A history of the political and cultural influence of the *Edinburgh Review*, based on a close analysis of its first fifty numbers.

Harrison, Stanley, *Poor Men's Guardians: A Record of the Struggles for a Democratic Newspaper Press, 1763–1973*, London, 1974, chs 2–5.

Hayden, John O., *The Romantic Reviewers 1802–1824*, Chicago, Ill., and London, 1969. Covers the general background to and the reviewing policies and practices of the major periodicals, and their critical reception of twelve major writers. Useful appendices and bibliography.

Morgan, Peter F., *Literary Critics and Reviewers in Early Nineteenth-Century Britain*, Beckenham, 1983. Covers the literary criticism of some of the more famous contributors to the *Edinburgh Review*, *Quarterly Review* and *Westminster Review*.

Reiman, Donald H., ed., *The Romantics Reviewed: Contemporary Reviews of British Romantic Writers*, 9 vols, New York, 1972. Includes many articles reprinted photographically, with short introductory notes.

Roper, Derek, *Reviewing before the 'Edinburgh' 1788–1802*, London, 1978. Surveys the reviewing of poetry, prose fiction, political, religious and historical writings in the fifteen years before the *Edinburgh Review*.

Sullivan, Alvin, ed., *British Literary Magazines: The Romantic Age, 1789–1836*, Westport, Conn., 1983. A comprehensive, alphabetical reference guide to and critical evaluation of periodicals published in the period, it concludes with a useful comparative chronology of social and literary events and key dates in the history of the literary journal.

Ward, William S., *Literary Reviews in British Periodicals 1798–1820: A Bibliography*, 2 vols, New York, 1972.

———*Literary Reviews in British Periodicals 1821–1826: A Bibliography*, New York, 1977.

———*Literary Reviews in British Periodicals 1789–1797: A Bibliography*, New York, 1979.

### Author–publisher–public relations

Collins, A. C., *The Profession of Letters: A Study of the Relation of Author to Patron, Publisher, and Public, 1780–1832*, London, 1928. An anecdotal, old-fashioned survey, Collins's study is none the less a mine of interesting detail and still a source for much current interpretation.

Halévy, Elie, *History of the English People in the Nineteenth Century, 1: England in 1815*, 1st English paperback edn, London, 1961. First published in French in 1913, Halévy's account of the institutions and culture of Regency Britain remains one of the most detailed. See esp. Part 3, ch 2.

Jack, Ian, *English Literature 1815–1832*, Oxford, 1963, esp. ch 1, 'The Literary Scene in 1815', and ch 15, 'The Literary Scene in 1832'.

Williams, Raymond, *Culture and Society 1780–1950*, London, 1958, chs 1–3. A probing account of the relations between artistic and social development in Britain in the period.

### Reading pictures

Brewer, John, *The Common People and Politics, 1750–1790s*, London, 1987.

Dickinson, H. T., *Caricatures and the Constitution, 1760–1832*, London, 1987.
Brewer and Dickinson contribute two volumes to Chadwyck-Healey's seven-volume collection, *The English Satirical Print, 1600–1832*. Providing rich visual documentation, these cartoons and caricatures are often narrowly topical (and therefore not always immediately accessible to the modern reader) in their attacks on political, royal, social and economic abuses.

Fox, Celina, 'Political Caricature and the Freedom of the Press in Early Nineteenth-Century England', in *Newspaper History from the Seventeenth Century to the Present Day*, ed. George Boyce, James Curran and Pauline Wingate, London, 1978, pp 226–46.

George, M. Dorothy, *English Political Caricature: A Study of Opinion and Propaganda*, 2 vols, Oxford, 1959, esp. vol ii, *1793–1832*. This is still the indispensable book on the subject.

Rickword, Edgell, ed., *Radical Squibs and Loyal Ripostes: Satirical Pamphlets of the Regency Period, 1819–1821. Illustrated by George Cruikshank and others*, Bath, 1971. It contains a selection of William Hone's political collaborations with Cruikshank, an influential partnership in the history of illustrated political journalism.

## 2 Politics and the Novel 1780–1830

*Texts used for quotation in the main essay have been asterisked.

*Fiction up to 1814: select texts*

*Bage, Robert, *Man as He Is*, 4 vols, London, 1792 [Garland facsimile, 1979].

————*Hermsprong, or Man as He is Not* (1796), ed. Peter Faulkner [World's Classics], Oxford, 1985.

*Brunton, Mary, *Self-Control* (1811), ed. Sara Maitland [Mothers of the Novel], London, 1986.

*————*Discipline* (1814), ed. Fay Weldon [Mothers of the Novel], London, 1986.

Edgeworth, Maria, *Castle Rackrent* (1800) and *Ennui* (1809), ed. Marilyn Butler [Penguin Classics], London, 1992.

*————*Belinda* (1801), ed. Eva Figes [Mothers of the Novel], London, 1986.

*————*The Absentee* (1812), ed. Brander Matthews [Everyman's Library], London, 1960 (also contains *Castle Rackrent*).

————*Tales and Novels* [the 'Longford Edition'], 12 vols, London, 1893.

*Godwin, William, *Caleb Williams* (1794), ed. Maurice Hindle [Penguin Classics], London, 1988.

Hays, Mary, *Memoirs of Emma Courtney* (1796), ed. Sally Cline [Mothers of the Novel], London, 1987.

*Holcroft, Thomas, *Anna St Ives* (1792), ed. Peter Faulkner [Oxford English Novels], London, 1970.

*————*The Adventures of Hugh Trevor* (1794–7), ed. Seamus Deane [Oxford English Novels], London, 1973.

Inchbald, Elizabeth, *A Simple Story* (1791), ed. J. M. S. Tompkins [Oxford English Novels], London, 1967.

————*Nature and Art*, 2 vols, London, 1796.

*Moore, John, *Mordaunt* (1800), ed. W. L. Renwick [Oxford English Novels], London, 1965.

More, Hannah, *Coelebs in Search of a Wife*, 2 vols, London, 1808.

Morgan, Lady, *The Wild Irish Girl* (1806), ed. Brigid Brophy [Mothers of the Novel], London, 1986.

*————*O'Donnel: A National Tale*, 3 vols, London, 1814 [Garland facsimile, 1979].

Opie, Amelia, *The Father and Daughter*, London, 1801.

*————*Adeline Mowbray* (1804), ed. Jeanette Winterson [Mothers of the Novel], London, 1986.

————*Temper, or Domestic Scenes*, 3 vols, London, 1812.

*Smith, Charlotte, *Desmond*, 3 vols, London, 1792.

*————*Marchmont*, 4 vols, London, 1796.

————*The Young Philosopher*, 4 vols, London, 1798.

*West, Jane, *A Gossip's Story*, 2 vols, London, 1796.

*————*A Tale of the Times*, 3 vols, London, 1799.

————*The Infidel Father*, 3 vols, London, 1802.

*Wollstonecraft, Mary, *Mary* (1788) and *Maria* (1798), ed. Janet Todd, [Penguin Classics], London, 1992. Also includes Mary Shelley's *Matilda* (written 1819–20, published 1959).

## Sir Walter Scott

*The Letters of Sir Walter Scott, 1787–1832*, ed. H. J. C. Grierson, 12 vols, London, 1932–7.

*Waverley Novels* [the *Magnum Opus*], 48 vols, Edinburgh, 1829–33. All subsequent collected editions have followed the *Magnum*. Additional notes and introductions can be found in several Victorian/Edwardian sets, such as the Border Edition, ed. Andrew Lang, 24 vols, 1901. A completely new Edinburgh Edition of the Waverley Novels, based normally on first edition texts, is currently in preparation. The first batch of novels – *The Black Dwarf, Kenilworth* and *The Tale of Old Mortality* – appeared in August 1993.

*Waverley* (1814), ed. Claire Lamont [World's Classics], Oxford, 1986.

*Old Mortality* (1816), ed. Angus Calder [Penguin Classics], Harmondsworth, 1975.

*The Heart of Midlothian* (1817), ed. Claire Lamont [World's Classics], Oxford, 1982.

*The Bride of Lammermoor* (1819), ed. Fiona Robertson [World's Classics], Oxford, 1991.

*Redgauntlet* (1824), ed. Kathryn Sutherland [World's Classics], Oxford, 1985.

*The Two Drovers and Other Stories*, ed. Graham Tulloch [World's Classics], Oxford, 1987.

Beiderwell, Bruce, *Power and Punishment in Scott's Novels*, Athens, Ga., and London, 1992.

Brown, David, *Walter Scott and the Historical Imagination*, London, 1979.

Corson, James C., *Notes and Index to Sir Herbert Grierson's Edition of the Letters of Sir Walter Scott*, Oxford, 1979. Effectively a Scott encyclopaedia.

Crawford, Thomas, *Walter Scott*, Edinburgh, 1982. The best short study.

Daiches, David, 'Scott's Achievement as a Novelist', in *Literary Essays*, Edinburgh, 1956, pp 88–121. A seminal essay.

Devlin, D. D., *The Author of Waverley*, London, 1971.

Ferris, Ina, *The Achievement of Literary Authority: Gender, History and the Waverley Novels*, Ithaca, NY, and London, 1991.

Gordon, Robert C., *Under Which King?*, Edinburgh, 1969.

Johnson, Edgar, *Walter Scott: The Great Unknown*, 2 vols, London, 1970. The most complete modern biography, incorporating critical chapters.

Lockhart, J. G., *Memoirs of the Life of Sir Walter Scott, Bart.*, 7 vols, Edinburgh, 1837–8. Classic life by Scott's son-in-law; most recent edition, ed. A. W. Pollard, 5 vols, London, 1900.

Lukács, Georg, *The Historical Novel* (1937), tr. Hannah and Stanley Mitchell, London, 1962. See esp. ch 1, 'The Classical Form of the Historical Novel'.

McMaster, Graham, *Scott and Society*, Cambridge, 1981. Scott's novels in political context.

Millgate, Jane, *Walter Scott: The Making of the Novelist*, Edinburgh, 1984. Accomplished account of Scott's authorial guises and relationship with his earliest readers.

————*Scott's Last Edition*, Edinburgh, 1987. The story of the *Magnum Opus*.

Scott, Paul Henderson, *Walter Scott and Scotland*, Edinburgh, 1981. Single-mindedly argues a Scottish 'nationalist' Scott.

Shaw, Harry E., *The Forms of Historical Fiction: Sir Walter Scott and His Successors*, Ithaca, NY, 1983.

Welsh, Alexander, *The Hero of the Waverley Novels*, New Haven, 1963; republished 'With New Essays on Scott', Princeton, 1992.

Wilt, Judith, *Secret Leaves: The Novels of Walter Scott*, Chicago, 1983.

## Thomas Love Peacock

*The Works of Thomas Love Peacock, ed. H. F. B. Brett-Smith and C. E. Jones [the 'Halliford Edition'], 10 vols, London, 1924–34.

*Headlong Hall and Gryll Grange (1816, 1861), ed. Michael Baron and Michael Slater [World's Classics], Oxford, 1987.

*Nightmare Abbey and Crotchet Castle (1818, 1831), ed. Raymond Wright [Penguin Classics], Harmondsworth, 1974.

Burns, Bryan, The Novels of Thomas Love Peacock, London, 1985.

Butler, Marilyn, Peacock Displayed: A Satirist in His Context, London, 1979. An admirable account of Peacock in his political milieu.

Dawson, Carl, His Fine Wit, London, 1970.

Madden, Lionel, Thomas Love Peacock, London, 1967.

McKay, Margaret, Peacock's Progress: Aspects of Artistic Development in the Novels of Thomas Love Peacock, Uppsala, Sweden, 1992.

Mills, Howard, Peacock, His Circle and His Age, Cambridge, 1969.

Mulvihill, James D., 'Thomas Love Peacock's Crotchet Castle: Reconciling the Spirits of the Age', Nineteeth Century Fiction, xl (1985), 253–70.

Sage, Lorna, ed., Peacock: The Satirical Novels [Macmillan Casebook], London, 1976.

## General works on the novel

Blakey, Dorothy, The Minerva Press 1790–1820, London, 1939. Bibliographical history of the largest publisher of fiction in the period.

Block, Andrew, The English Novel 1740–1850: A Catalogue, London, 1939; new and revised edn, 1961. Still the most comprehensive list of titles, though an accurate modern guide is a desideratum.

Colby, Robert A., Fiction with a Purpose, Bloomington, Ind., 1967. The first two chapters describe precursors of Waverley and Mansfield Park.

Gregory, Allene, The French Revolution and the English Novel, New York, 1964. First published in 1915; still useful as an overview.

Jones, Ann H., Ideas and Innovations: Best Sellers of Jane Austen's

*Age*, New York, 1986. Includes interesting chapters on Hamilton, Opie, Brunton and others.

Kaufman, Paul, *The Community Library: A Chapter in English Social History, Transactions of the American Philosophical Society*, NS, LVII, vii, Philadelphia, 1967. Authoritative account of contemporary circulating libraries.

Kelly, Gary, *The English Jacobin Novel 1780–1805*, Oxford, 1976. An informed study; chapters deal with Bage, Inchbald, Holcroft, Godwin.

————*English Fiction of the Romantic Period, 1789–1830*, London, 1989.

Kiely, Robert, *The Romantic Novel in England*, Cambridge, Mass., 1972.

Pickering, Samuel, Jr., *The Moral Tradition in English Fiction 1785–1850*, Hanover, NH, 1976. Useful for More and evangelicals.

Schofield, Mary Ann, and Macheski, Cecilia, eds, *Fetter'd or Free? British Women Novelists, 1670–1815*, Athens, OH, 1986. Several relevant essays, including Diana Bowstead's excellent 'Charlotte Smith's *Desmond*: The Epistolary Novel as Ideological Argument' (pp 237–63).

Spender, Dale, *Mothers of the Novel*, London, 1986. Feminist survey of previously neglected ground. Includes chapters on Inchbald, Smith, Wollstonecraft, Opie, Brunton.

Taylor, John Tinnon, *Early Opposition to the English Novel: The Popular Reaction from 1760 to 1830*, New York, 1943. Wider scope than title indicates.

Tompkins, J. M. S., *The Popular Novel in England: 1770–1800*, London, 1932.

# 3 Jane Austen: Questions of Context

## I Editions

*The Novels of Jane Austen*, ed. R. W. Chapman, 5 vols, Oxford, 3rd edn 1975.

*Minor Works*, ed. R. W. Chapman, *The Works of Jane Austen*, vi, Oxford, 1954.

*Volume the Second* [a facsimile edition], ed. B. C. Southam, Oxford, 1963.

*Sanditon* [a facsimile edition], ed. B. C. Southam, Oxford, 1975.

*Sir Charles Grandison* [a facsimile edition], ed. B. C. Southam, Oxford, 1980.

*Jane Austen's Letters*, ed. R. W. Chapman, Oxford, 1948.

*Jane Austen's Letters to Her Sister Cassandra and Others*, ed. R. W. Chapman, Oxford, 3rd edn 1979.

The complete novels of Jane Austen, published in the Penguin Classics series, 7 vols, is the most widely used and useful of paperback editions.

## II Biography

The main family biographies are:

Austen, Caroline, *My Aunt Jane Austen: A Memoir*, ed. R. W. Chapman, Alton, 1952.

Austen, Henry, 'Biographical Notice of the Author', published as preface to *Northanger Abbey* and *Persuasion*, London, 1818.

Austen-Leigh, J. E., *A Memoir of Jane Austen*, London, 1870.

Austen-Leigh, W. and R. A., *Jane Austen: Her Life and Letters*, London, 1913.

Later studies include:

Chapman, R. W., *Jane Austen: Facts and Problems*, Oxford, 1948. Still the most useful of short biographies, though the critical approach is dated and there are one or two inaccuracies.

Halperin, John, *The Life of Jane Austen*, Brighton, 1984.

Honan, Park, *Jane Austen: Her Life*, London, 1987. Includes new material and a survey of biographical studies to date.

Kaplan, Deborah, 'The Disappearance of the Woman Writer: Jane Austen and Her Biographers', *Prose Studies*, vii (1984), 129–47. Discusses, from a feminist viewpoint, the many problems of the Austen biography.

III *Bibliography*

Roth, Barry, and Weinsheimer, Joel, *An Annotated Bibliography of Jane Austen Studies, 1952–1972*, Charlottesville, Va., 1973.

Gilson, David John, *A Bibliography of Jane Austen*, The Soho Bibliographies, xxi, Oxford, 1982. This is a comprehensive survey, with brief descriptive notes, of virtually everything published on Austen up to 1982.

'Jane Austen Studies', listed annually in the Reports of the Jane Austen Society. Provides an annual update on the main bibliography and makes the 'Reports' essential reading for serious students of Austen.

IV *Critical studies*: *Books*

Bradbrook, Frank, *Jane Austen and Her Predecessors*, Cambridge, 1967.

Brown, Julia Prewett, *Jane Austen's Novels: Social Change and Literary Form*, Cambridge, Mass., 1979.

Butler, Marilyn, *Jane Austen and the War of Ideas*, Oxford, 1975.

Duckworth, Alistair, *Jane Austen and the Improvement of the Estate*, Baltimore, Md., 1971.

Evans, Mary, *Jane Austen and the State*, London, 1987.

Fergus, Jan, *Jane Austen and the Didactic Novel*, London, 1983.

Kirkham, Margaret, *Jane Austen, Feminism and Fiction*, Brighton, 1983, and New York, 1986.

Roberts, Warren, *Jane Austen and the French Revolution*, New York, 1979.

Smith, Leroy W., *Jane Austen and the Drama of Woman*, London, 1983.

Southam, B. C., *Jane Austen's Literary Manuscripts*, London, 1964.

Tanner, Tony, *Jane Austen*, London, 1986.

V *Critical studies*: *Articles*

Brown, Lloyd W., 'Jane Austen and the Feminist Tradition', *Nineteenth-century Fiction*, xxviii (1973), 321–38.

Fowler, Marian, 'The Courtesy-Book Heroine of *Mansfield Park*', *University of Toronto Quarterly*, 1974, 31–5.

———'The Feminist Bias of *Pride and Prejudice*', *Dalhousie Review*, lvii (1977), 47–64.

Honan, Park, 'Jane Austen and the American Revolution', *University of Leeds Review*, xxviii (1985–6), 181–95.

Jones, Myrddin, 'Feelings of Youth and Nature in *Mansfield Park*', *English* (Autumn 1980), 221–32.

McDonnell, Jane, '"A little spirit of independence": Sexual Politics and the Bildungsroman in *Mansfield Park*', *Novel*, xvii (1984), 197–214.

Newman, Karen, 'Can This Marriage be Saved: Jane Austen Makes Sense of an Ending', *ELH*, l (1983), 693–710.

Pickrel, Paul, '*Emma* as Sequel', *Nineteenth-Century Fiction*, xl (1985–6), 135–53.

——'Lionel Trilling and *Emma*: A Reconsideration', *Nineteenth-century Fiction*, xl (1985–6), 297–311.

## VI *Collections of essays*

Grey, John David, managing ed., A. Walton Litz and Brian Southam, consulting eds, *The Jane Austen Companion*, New York, 1986. Includes short essays on a variety of topics, both biographical and critical. A useful guide to the whole range of Austen studies.

Lodge, David, ed., *Jane Austen: Emma*, Macmillan's Casebook Series, London, 1968. This and the other Casebooks listed below provide useful introductions to the critical literature on each novel.

Monaghan, David, ed., *Jane Austen in a Social Context*, London, 1981.

Southam, B. C., ed., *Jane Austen: The Critical Heritage*, 2 vols, [1811–70; 1870–1940], London, 1968 and 1987.

——*Jane Austen: Northanger Abbey and Persuasion*, Macmillan's Casebook Series, London, 1976.

——*Jane Austen: Sense and Sensibility, Pride and Prejudice and Mansfield Park*, Macmillan's Casebook Series, London, 1976.

—— (ed.), *Critical Essays on Jane Austen*, London, 1968.

Todd, Janet, ed., *Jane Austen: New Perspectives*, Women and Literature, NS, iii, New York, 1983.

## VII *Critical studies relevant to the literary context of the Austen novels*

Barker, Gerard A., *Grandison's Heirs: The Paragon's Progression in the Late Eighteenth-Century English Novel*, Newark, Del., 1985.

Cottom, David, *The Civilized Imagination: A Study of Ann Radcliffe, Jane Austen and Sir Walter Scott*, Cambridge, 1985.

Gilbert, Sandra M., and Gubar, Susan, *The Madwoman in the Attic: The Woman Writer and the Nineteenth-Century Literary Imagination*, New Haven and London, 1979.

Girtwith, M., *Madame de Staël, Novelist: The Emergence of the Artist as Woman*, Illinois, 1978.

Moers, Ellen, *Literary Women*, New York, 1976.

Okin, Susan Moller, *Women in Western Political Thought*, Princeton, 1979, and London, 1980.

Poovey, Mary, *The Proper Lady and the Woman Writer: Ideology as Style in the Works of Mary Wollstonecraft, Mary Shelley, and Jane Austen*, Chicago, 1984.

Spencer, Jane, *The Rise of the Woman Novelist from Aphra Behn to Jane Austen*, Oxford, 1986.

## 4 William Blake

### I Editions

*The Illuminated Blake*, ed. David V. Erdman, London, 1975.

*The Complete Poetry and Prose of William Blake*, ed. David V. Erdman, New York, 1982.

*William Blake: Complete Writings*, ed. Geoffrey Keynes, Oxford, 1972.

*William Blake: The Complete Poems*, ed. Alicia Ostriker, Harmondsworth, 1977.

### II Critical and biographical studies

Ault, Donald D., *Visionary Physics: Blake's Response to Newton*, Chicago, 1974.

Beer, John, *Blake's Humanism*, Manchester, 1968.

Bentley, G. E., *Blake Records*, Oxford, 1969.

Bindman, David, *Blake as an Artist*, Oxford, 1977.

Crehan, Stewart, *Blake in Context*, Dublin, 1984.

Frye, Northrop, *Fearful Symmetry: A Study of William Blake*, Princeton, 1947.

Gillham, D. G., *Blake's Contrary States: The 'Songs of Innocence and of Experience' as Dramatic Poems*, Cambridge, 1966.

Glen, Heather, *Vision and Disenchantment: Blake's 'Songs' and Wordsworth's 'Lyrical Ballads'*, Cambridge, 1983.

Hagstrum, Jean H., *William Blake: Poet and Painter*, Chicago, 1964.

Harper, George Mills, *The Neoplatonism of William Blake*, Chapel Hill, NC, 1961.

Hilton, Nelson, *Literal Imagination: Blake's Vision of Words*, Berkeley, Calif., 1983.

Hilton, Nelson, and Vogler, Thomas A., eds, *Unnam'd Forms: Blake and Textuality*, Berkeley, Calif., 1986.

Hirsch, E. D., Jr., *Innocence and Experience: An Introduction to Blake*, New Haven, 1964.

Larrissy, Edward, *William Blake*, Oxford, 1985.

Lindsay, Jack, *William Blake: His Life and Work*, London, 1978.

Mitchell, W. J. T., *Blake's Composite Art: A Study of the Illuminated Poetry*, Princeton, 1978.

Ostriker, Alicia, *Vision and Verse in William Blake*, Madison, Wis., 1965.

Paley, Morton D., *Energy and the Imagination: A Study in the Development of Blake's Thought*, Oxford, 1970.

Phillips, Michael, ed., *Interpreting Blake*, Cambridge, 1978.

Raine, Kathleen, *Blake and Tradition*, 2 vols, Princeton, 1968, and London, 1969.

Schorer, Mark, *William Blake: The Politics of Vision*, New York, 1946.

Thompson, E. P., *Witness against the Beast: William Blake and the Moral Law*, Cambridge, 1993.

# 5 *Wordsworth*

## I *Editions*

Wordsworth revised most of his major poems in later life, and, although he remained a first-rate craftsman and effected many local improvements, the majority view now is that on the whole the original texts are to be preferred as more daring and less conventionally elegant.

A convenient selection, containing most of the important shorter poems in their earliest versions, along with the 1805 *Prelude*, is the Oxford Authors *William Wordsworth*, ed. Stephen Gill, Oxford, 1984. The Penguin Poetry Library *William Wordsworth*, ed. Nicholas Roe, London, 1992, includes 'The Ruined Cottage' and 'The Two-Part Prelude', and many of the shorter poems in their original published versions.

The Oxford Paperbacks complete *Poetical Works*, ed. Thomas Hutchinson, Ernest de Selincourt, Oxford, 1969, gives revised texts, as does John O. Hayden's Penguin *Poems*, 2 vols, Harmondsworth, 1977.

The pioneering critical edition in five volumes published by Oxford University Press under the editorship of Ernest de Selincourt and Helen Darbishire (1940–49; rev. 1952–9) is still worth consulting, though it is being gradually replaced by an elaborate edition (the Cornell Wordsworth) from Cornell University Press.

The best separate edition of *The Prelude* in its preliminary 1799 two-book form, and with parallel 1805 and 1850 texts, is the Norton Critical Edition, ed. Jonathan Wordsworth, M. H. Abrams and Stephen Gill, New York, 1979. There is also a Penguin parallel text edition, ed. J. C. Maxwell, Harmondsworth, 1971.

There are good annotated editions of the 1798 and 1800 *Lyrical Ballads*, ed. R. L. Brett and A. R. Jones, London, 1963; and of the 1805 edition, ed. Derek Roper, Plymouth, 1968, 2nd edn 1976; and by Michael Mason, London, 1992. *The Salisbury Plain Poems of William Wordsworth* have been edited by Stephen Gill in the Cornell Wordsworth series, Ithaca, NY, and Hassocks, 1975. *Wordsworth's Poems of 1807* have been edited by Alun R. Jones, Basingstoke, 1987. Texts prepared for the forthcoming Cambridge *Wordsworth* were published in 1985 by Cambridge University Press in advance form, ed. Jonathan Wordsworth: '*The Ruined Cottage*', '*The Brothers*', *and* '*Michael*' and '*The Pedlar*', '*Tintern Abbey*', *and* '*The Two-Part Prelude*'.

The standard edition of Wordsworth's prose is *The Prose Works of William Wordsworth*, ed. W. J. B. Owen and Jane Worthington Smyser, 3 vols, Oxford, 1974.

## II *Biography*

There are two first-rate biographies: Mary Moorman, *William Wordsworth: A Biography*, 2 vols, Oxford, 1965; and Stephen Gill, *William Wordsworth: A Life*, Oxford, 1989. An edition of *The Letters of William and Dorothy Wordsworth*, aiming at definitiveness, has been published by Oxford's Clarendon Press (7 vols, 1967–89). Its principal recent editor, Alan G. Hill, has produced the helpful *Letters of William Wordsworth: A New Selection*, Oxford, 1984. See also *Journals of Dorothy Wordsworth*, ed. Mary Moorman, Oxford, 1971.

## III *Critical studies*

Wordsworth has in general been well served by his critics, and there are far too many excellent critical studies to mention here. The books in this list have been selected to cover as wide a range as possible, but with particular emphasis on the political element in the poet's work.

Alexander, J. H., *Reading Wordsworth*, London, 1987. A short introductory study of the poetry of the great decade.

Averill, James H., *Wordsworth and the Poetry of Human Suffering*, Ithaca, NY, and London, 1980. A well-written but quite advanced analysis of Wordsworth's relationship to the sentimental tradition.

Bate, Jonathan, *Romantic Ecology: Wordsworth and the Environmental Tradition*, London, 1991. Relates Wordsworth with vigorous intelligence to a pressing current concern.

Beer, John, *Wordsworth and the Human Heart*, London and Basingstoke, 1978. A perceptive and humane tracing of the significance of the favourite word 'heart' through the poetry.

Chandler, James K., *Wordsworth's Second Nature: A Study of the Poetry and Politics*, Chicago and London, 1984. Argues for Burke's influence on Wordsworth as early as 1797, and charts carefully the similarities and differences between the two writers.

Coleridge, Samuel Taylor, *Biographia Literaria* (1817: numerous later editions). From Chapter 14 onwards this is primarily the first full critical study of Wordsworth, and still indispensable.

Danby, J. F., *The Simple Wordsworth: Studies in the Poems, 1797–1807*, London, 1960. A good general introduction to the shorter early poems, sensitive and approachable.

Davies, Hugh Sykes, *Wordsworth and the Worth of Words*, ed. John Kerrigan and Jonathan Wordsworth, Cambridge, 1988. A subtle study concentrating fruitfully on Wordsworth's unique way with words.

Ferry, David, *The Limits of Mortality: An Essay on Wordsworth's Major Poems*, Middletown, Conn., 1959. A somewhat unyielding but often suggestive analysis in terms of the 'mystical' and 'sacramental'.

Friedman, Michael H., *The Making of a Tory Humanist: William Wordsworth and the Idea of Community*, New York, 1979. Unusually sensitive use of Freud and Marx to produce often brilliant readings.

Glen, Heather, *Vision and Disenchantment: Blake's 'Songs' and Wordsworth's 'Lyrical Ballads'*, Cambridge, 1983.

Hartman, Geoffrey H., *Wordsworth's Poetry: 1797–1814*, New Haven and London, 1964. A now classic 'apocalyptic' reading of the highest distinction.

Hazlitt, William, 'Mr Wordsworth', in *The Spirit of the Age* (published anonymously in 1825: numerous later editions). A highly readable early assessment by Keats's mentor, irreverent and perceptive.

Jones, John, *The Egotistical Sublime: A History of Wordsworth's Imagination*, London, 1954. A helpful general study, concentrating on 'solitude and relationship'.

Levinson, Marjorie, *Wordsworth's Great Period Poems*, Cambridge, 1986. Exposure of the ideologies believed to underlie 'Tintern Abbey', 'Michael', the Immortality Ode and 'Peele Castle'.

McFarland, Thomas, *William Wordsworth: Intensity and Achievement*, Oxford, 1992. A work of passionate and profound scholarship, engaging sharply with fashionable criticism, such as the preceding item.

McMaster, Graham, ed., *William Wordsworth*, Harmondsworth, 1972. A first-rate selection of criticism, from Wordsworth himself to the date of publication.

Perkins, David, *Wordsworth and the Poetry of Sincerity*, Cambridge, Mass., 1964. A penetrating and wide-ranging study, primarily theoretical.

Pirie, David B., *William Wordsworth: The Poetry of Grandeur and of Tenderness*, London, 1982. A humane and committed response to the impersonal and the personal in Wordsworth's poetry.

Purkis, John, *A Preface to Wordsworth*, London, 1970, 2nd edn 1987. A lucid introduction to the intellectual background.

Roe, Nicholas, *Wordsworth and Coleridge: The Radical Years*, Oxford, 1988. An expert guide through the sometimes bewildering complexities of the two young poets' political connections and allegiances.

Simpson, David, *Wordsworth and the Figurings of the Real*, London and Basingstoke, 1982. An approachable post-structuralist reading.

————*Wordsworth's Historical Imagination: The Poetry of Displacement*, New York and London, 1987. A less achieved study than the preceding item, but important for its tentative exploration of possible political implications, sometimes in unlikely texts.

Thomas, Gordon Kent, *Wordsworth's Dirge and Promise: Napoleon, Wellington, and the Convention of Cintra*, Lincoln, Nebr., 1971. A sound study of the *Cintra* pamphlet.

Todd, F. M., *Politics and the Poet: A Study of Wordsworth*, London, 1957. A sensible and straightforward introduction to the political Wordsworth.

Turner, John, *Wordsworth: Play and Politics – A Study of Wordsworth's Poetry, 1787–1800*, London, 1986. The general thesis is elusive, but this is a study with many useful local insights.

Williams, John, *Wordsworth: Romantic Poetry and Revolutionary Politics*, Manchester, 1989. A clear exposition of Wordsworth's debt to the English republican tradition.

Wordsworth, Jonathan, *The Music of Humanity: A Critical Study of Wordsworth's 'Ruined Cottage', incorporating texts from a manuscript of 1799–1800*, London, 1969. A pioneering study of 'The Ruined Cottage', emphasizing Wordsworth the humanist.

## 6 Coleridge

### I *Editions*

#### Poetry

The standard complete edition of Coleridge's poems is *Complete Poetical Works*, ed. E. H. Coleridge, 2 vols, Oxford, 1912. The poems are reprinted without the dramas in a single paperback. This will be superseded by the forthcoming edition of the poems by J. C. C. Mays for the *Collected Works*, mentioned in the section on 'Prose', below. The most comprehensive selection for students to work with is the Everyman edition of the *Poems*, ed. John Beer, London, 1974.

#### Prose

*Collected Letters*, ed. E. L. Griggs, 6 vols, London, 1956–71.

*The Notebooks of Samuel Taylor Coleridge*, ed. K. Coburn, 6 vols, London, 1957–.

The standard edition of the prose, nearing completion, is *The Collected Works of Samuel Taylor Coleridge*, Bollingen Series lxxv, 14 vols, London and Princeton, 1969–. The *Biographia Literaria* in this edition is now in paperback. The corrected edition by J. Shawcross, 2 vols, Oxford, 1954, has a still useful Introduction, and George Watson's Everyman edition, London, 1965, is also handily in paperback.

Other useful selections and individual volumes include:

*Inquiring Spirit: A New Presentation of Coleridge from His Published and Unpublished Prose Writings*, ed. K. Coburn, Toronto, 1979.

*The Oxford Authors – Coleridge*, ed. H. J. Jackson, Oxford, 1985.

*Shakespearean Criticism*, ed. T. M. Raysor [Everyman], 2 vols, London, 1960.

*Aids to Reflection*, London, 1825.

*Specimens of the Table Talk of the Late Samuel Taylor Coleridge*, ed. H. N. Coleridge, 2 vols, London, 1835.

*On the Constitution of the Church and State*, ed. John Barrell [Everyman], London, 1972.

II  *Critical studies and biographies*

Bate, W. J., *Coleridge*, New York, 1973.

Beer, J., ed., *Coleridge's Variety: Bicentenary Studies*, London, 1974.

———*Coleridge's Poetic Intelligence*, London, 1977.

Butler, M., *Romantics, Rebels and Reactionaries*, Oxford, 1981.

Bygrave, S., *Coleridge and the Self*, London, 1986.

Calleo, D., *Coleridge and the Idea of the Modern State*, New Haven, 1966.

Christensen, J., *Coleridge's Blessed Machine of Language*, Ithaca, NY, 1981.

Coburn, K., ed., *Coleridge: A Collection of Critical Essays*, Englewood Cliffs, NJ, 1967.

Coleman, D., *Coleridge and 'The Friend'*, Oxford, 1988.

Cornwell, J., *Coleridge, Poet and Revolutionary 1772–1804*, London, 1973.

Empson, W., 'Introduction', in *Coleridge's Verse: A Selection*, ed. with D. Pirie, London, 1972.

Everest, K., *Coleridge's Secret Ministry: The Context of the Conversation Poems, 1795–8*, Brighton, 1979.

Fruman, N., *Coleridge: The Damaged Archangel*, New York, 1971.

Gravil, R., and Lefebure, M., eds, *The Coleridge Connection: Essays for Thomas McFarland*, London, 1990.

Gravil, R., Newlyn, L., and Roe, N., eds, *Coleridge's Imagination*, Cambridge, 1985.

Hamilton, P., *Coleridge's Poetics*, Oxford, 1983.

Hazlitt, W., 'My First Acquaintance with Poets' (1823) and 'Mr Coleridge' (1825) in *Selected Writings*, ed. R. Blythe, Harmondsworth, 1970.

Holmes, R., *Coleridge: Early Visions*, Harmondsworth, 1990.

Leask, N., *The Politics of Imagination in Coleridge's Critical Thought*, London, 1988.

Lefebure, M., *Samuel Taylor Coleridge: A Bondage of Opium*, London, 1974.

Levinson, M., *The Romantic Fragment Poem: A Critique of a Form*, Chapel Hill, NC, and London, 1986.

McFarland, T., *Coleridge and the Pantheist Tradition*, Oxford, 1969.

McGann, J., 'The Ancient Mariner: The Meaning of Meanings', in *The Beauty of Inflections*, Oxford, 1985.

Mill, J. S., 'Coleridge', in *Mill on Bentham and Coleridge*, ed. F. R. Leavis, London, 1950.

Newlyn, L., *Coleridge, Wordsworth and the Language of Allusion*, Oxford, 1986.

Pirie, D., 'A Verse Letter to [Asra]', in *Bicentenary Wordsworth Studies*, ed. J. Wordsworth, Ithaca, NY, and London, 1970.

Prickett, S., *Coleridge and Wordsworth: The Poetry of Growth*, Cambridge, 1970.

———*Romanticism and Religion: The Tradition of Coleridge and Wordsworth in the Victorian Church*, Cambridge, 1976.

Roe, N., *Wordsworth and Coleridge: The Radical Years*, Oxford, 1988.

Shaffer, E., '*Kubla Khan*' and *the Fall of Jerusalem*, Cambridge, 1975.

Spivak, G., 'The Letter as Cutting Edge', in *In Other Worlds: Essays in Cultural Politics*, New York and London, 1987.

Wellek, R., 'Coleridge', in *The Romantic Age*, in *A History of Modern Criticism 1750–1950*, vol 2, New Haven, 1955.

Wheeler, K., *Sources, Processes and Methods in Coleridge's 'Biographia Literaria'*, Cambridge, 1980.

———*The Creative Mind in Coleridge's Poetry*, London, 1981.

## 7 *Representing the People: Crabbe, Southey and Hazlitt*

I *Editions*

*Poems by George Crabbe*, ed. A. W. Ward, 3 vols, Cambridge, 1905.

*Selected Letters and Journals of George Crabbe*, ed. T. C. Faulkner and R. L. Blair, Oxford, 1985.

*Poems of Robert Southey*, ed. M. H. Fitzgerald, Oxford, 1909.

*The Complete Works of William Hazlitt*, ed. P. P. Howe, 21 vols, London, 1930.

*The Letters of William Hazlitt*, ed. H. M. Sikes, W. H. Bonner and G. Lahey, New York, 1978.

The writings of Crabbe and Hazlitt are available in selections: see George Crabbe, *Selected Poems*, Manchester, 1986, and *Tales 1812 and Other Selected Poems*, ed. H. Miller, Cambridge, 1967; William Hazlitt, *Selected Writings*, ed. Ronald Blythe, Harmondsworth, 1970, and William Hazlitt, *Selected Writings*, ed. Jon Cook, Oxford, 1991. There is no readily available selection of Southey's work in print, but see *A Choice of Robert Southey's Verse*, ed. Geoffrey Grigson, London, 1970. Otherwise these authors are best read in the collected editions cited above, but in the case of Crabbe see also the recently published *The Complete Poetical Works*, ed. N. D-. Champneys and A. Pollard, 3 vols, Oxford, 1988.

II *Biography*

For a biography of Crabbe, see René Huchon, *George Crabbe and His Times*, London, 1907; for Southey, see Edward Dowden, *Southey*, London, 1874; for Hazlitt, see Percy Howe, *Life of William Hazlitt*, London, 1922, and, most recently, Stanley Jones, *Hazlitt: A Life from Winterslow to Frith Street*, Oxford, 1989.

III *Critical studies: individual writers*

*Crabbe*

Edwards, Gavin, *George Crabbe's Poetry on Border Land*, Leicester, 1990.

Haddakin, Lilian, *The Poetry of Crabbe*, London, 1955.

Hatch, Ronald B., *Crabbe's Arabesque: Social Drama in the Poetry of George Crabbe*, Montreal and London, 1976.

Nelson, Beth, *George Crabbe and the Progress of Eighteenth Century Narrative Verse*, London, 1976.
New, Peter, *George Crabbe's Poetry*, London, 1976.
Pollard, A., ed., *Crabbe: The Critical Heritage*, London, 1972.

*Southey*

Cornell, Geoffrey, *Robert Southey and His Age*, Oxford, 1960.
Curry, Kenneth, *Southey*, London and Boston, 1975.
Madden, L., ed., *Southey: The Critical Heritage*, London, 1972.

*Hazlitt*

Albrecht, W. P., *Hazlitt and the Creative Imagination*, Lawrence, Kan., 1965.
Bromwich, David, *Hazlitt: The Mind of a Critic*, Oxford and New York, 1983.
Kinnaird, John, *William Hazlitt, Critic of Power*, New York, 1978.
Park, Roy, *Hazlitt and the Spirit of the Age*, Oxford, 1971.

## IV Critical studies: Literary and historical background

Aers, David, Cook, Jon, and Punter, David, *Romanticism and Ideology*, London and Boston, 1981.
Barrell, John, *The Dark Side of the Landscape*, Cambridge, 1980.
———*Literature in History: An Equal, Wide, Survey*, London, 1983.
Bhabha, Homi, ed., *Nation and Narration*, London and New York, 1990.
Butler, Marilyn, *Romantics, Rebels and Reactionaries*, Oxford, 1981.
Dickinson, H. T., *Liberty and Property*, London, 1977.
Empson, William, *Some Versions of Pastoral* (1935), Harmondsworth, 1966.
Sales, Roger, *English Literature in History, 1780–1830: Pastoral and Politics*, London, 1983.
Thompson, E. P., *The Making of the English Working Class* (1963), Harmondsworth, 1968.
Williams, Raymond, *The Country and the City*, London, 1973.

## 8 *Poor Relations: Writing in the Working Class, 1770–1835*

Barrell, John, *The Idea of Landscape and the Sense of Place 1730–1840: An Approach to the Poetry of John Clare*, Cambridge, 1972.

Hackwood, F. W., *William Hone: His Life and Times* [1912], New York, 1970.

James, Louis, *Print and the People 1819–1851*, London, 1976.

Klaus, H. Gustav, *The Literature of Labour: Two Hundred Years of Working-Class Writing*, Brighton, 1985.

Landry, Donna, *The Muses of Resistance: Labouring-class Women's Poetry in Britain*, Cambridge, 1990.

McCalman, Iain, *Radical Underworld: Prophets, Revolutionaries and Pornographers in London, 1795–1840*, Cambridge, 1988.

Rickword, Edgell, ed., *Radical Squibs and Loyal Ripostes: Satirical Pamphlets of the Regency Period*, Bath, 1971.

Sales, Roger, *English Literature in History 1780–1830: Pastoral and Politics*, London, 1983.

Shiach, Morag, *Discourse on Popular Culture: Class, Gender and History in Cultural Analysis, 1730 to the Present*, Cambridge, 1989.

Smith, Olivia, *The Politics of Language 1791–1819*, Oxford, 1984.

Thompson, E. P., *The Making of the English Working Class*, Harmondsworth, 1968.

Vicinus, Martha, *The Industrial Muse: A Study of Nineteenth Century British Working-Class Literature*, London, 1975.

Vincent, David, *Bread, Knowledge and Freedom: A Study of Nineteenth Century Working Class Autobiography*, London, 1982.

Accessible anthologies which reprint some working-class poetry include:

Barrell, John, and Bull, John, eds, *The Penguin Book of English Pastoral Verse*, Harmondsworth, 1982.

Lonsdale, Roger, ed., *The New Oxford Book of Eighteenth Century Verse*, Oxford, 1984.

Although it covers a later period, Brian Maidment's anthology of working-class poetry, *The Poor House Fugitives: Self-Taught*

*Poets and Poetry in Victorian Britain*, Manchester, 1987, is also recommended. Those wishing to find out more about working-class autobiographies are recommended to consult John Burnett, David Vincent and David Mayall, eds, *The Autobiography of the Working Class: An Annotated Critical Bibliography, Volume One: 1790–1900*, Brighton, 1984.

# 9 *Lord Byron*

## I *Editions and Biography*

The standard edition of Byron's poetry is Jerome J. McGann, ed., *Lord Byron: The Complete Poetical Works*, 7 vols, Oxford, 1980–93. *The Letters and Journals* have been edited by Leslie A. Marchand (12 vols, London, 1973–82), whose *Byron: A Biography* (3 vols, London, 1957) is the best account of the life. Equally good is Andrew Nicholson, *Lord Byron: The Complete Miscellaneous Prose*, Oxford, 1991. These are all expensive. Cheaper substitutes are the Oxford Standard Authors *Byron*, ed. Jerome J. McGann, Oxford, 1986; and Leslie A. Marchand's abbreviated *Lord Byron: Selected Letters and Journals*, London, 1982, and *Byron: A Portrait*, London, 1971. The Penguin *Don Juan*, ed. T. G. Steffan, E. Steffan and W. W. Pratt, Harmondsworth, 1973, is first class.

## II *Bibliography*

The standard bibliographies are: Oscar José Santucho, *George Gordon, Lord Byron: A Comprehensive Bibliography . . . 1807–1974*, New Jersey, 1977; and John Clubbe in *The English Romantic Poets: A Review of Research and Criticism*, ed. Frank Jordan, New York, 4th edn, 1985.

## III *Critical studies*

There are numerous critical introductions: Andrew Rutherford, *Byron: A Critical Study*, Edinburgh, 1961; M. K. Joseph, *Byron the Poet*, London, 1964; Leslie A. Marchand, *Byron's Poetry*, Boston, 1965; Paul Trueblood, *Lord Byron*, New York, 1969; John D. Jump, *Byron*, London, 1972; Bernard Blackstone, *Byron: A Survey*, London, 1975; Malcolm Kelsall, *Lord Byron*, Scribner's British Writers IV, New York, 1981.

More difficult and intellectually challenging are: George M. Ridenour, *The Style of 'Don Juan'*, New Haven, 1960; Paul West, *Byron and the Spoiler's Art*, London, 1960; William H. Marshall, *The Structure of Byron's Major Poems*, Philadelphia, 1962; Robert F. Gleckner, *Byron and the Ruins of Paradise*,

Baltimore, 1967; Paul Elledge, *Byron and the Dynamics of Metaphor*, Nashville, 1968; Jerome J. McGann, *Fiery Dust: Byron's Poetic Development*, Chicago, 1968; and *'Don Juan' in Context*, London, 1976; Michael Cooke, *The Blind Man Traces the Circle*, Princeton, 1969; Peter J. Manning, *Byron and His Fictions*, Detroit, 1978; Bernard Beatty, *Byron's 'Don Juan'*, London, 1985; and, with Vincent Newey, eds, *Byron and the Limits of Fiction*, Liverpool, 1988; Frederick L. Beaty, *Byron the Satirist*, Illinois, 1985; Mark Storey, *Byron and the Eye of Appetite*, London, 1986; Daniel P. Watkins, *Social Relations in Byron's Eastern Tales*, London and Toronto, 1987; Frederick R. Shilstone, *Byron and the Myth of Tradition*, Lincoln, Nebr. 1988; Frederick Garber, *Self, Text and Romantic Irony: The Example of Byron*, Princeton, 1988; Peter W. Graham, *'Don Juan' and Regency England*, Charlottesville, Va., 1990; Jerome Christensen, *Lord Byron's Strength: Romantic Writing and Commercial Society*, Baltimore, 1993.

Useful collections of essays are: Paul West, ed., *Byron: A Collection of Critical Essays*, Englewood Cliffs, NJ, 1963; Edward E. Bostetter, ed., *Twentieth Century Interpretations of 'Don Juan'*, Englewood Cliffs, NJ, 1969; Andrew Rutherford, ed., *Byron: The Critical Heritage*, London, 1970; John Jump, ed., *'Childe Harold's Pilgrimage' and 'Don Juan': A Casebook*, London, 1973. The Byron bicentenary in 1988 produced three noteworthy collections of essays: Andrew Rutherford, ed., *Byron: Augustan and Romantic*, Basingstoke, 1990; Alice Levine and Robert N. Keane, eds, *Rereading Byron*, New York, 1993; and the special Byron number of *Studies in Romanticism*, XXXI, iii (1992).

The best introduction to Byron in his historical and political context is Carl Woodring, *Politics in English Romantic Poetry*, Cambridge, Mass., 1970. William St Clair has written a fine account of the Greek War of Independence, *That Greece Might Still be Free*, London, 1972. Malcolm Kelsall examines Byron's Whig affiliations in *Byron's Politics*, Brighton, 1987. Sexual politics are examined by Louis Crompton, *Byron and Greek Love*, London, 1985, on Byron's homosexuality; and Caroline Franklin, *Byron's Heroines*, Oxford, 1992.

# 10 Shelley

## I Editions

There is at present no satisfactory standard edition of Shelley's
complete works. The Longman 'Annotated Poets' edition of
the *Complete Poems*, ed. G. M. Matthews and Kelvin Everest,
provides a reliable modern text of the poetry, arranged in
chronological order and with full annotation for all poems. At
present only volume one is available (published in 1989);
volumes two and three are scheduled for publication in 1996
and 1999. The first volume of the Longman edition includes
an Introduction which surveys the history of the text of
Shelley's poetry, and describes the characteristics of each of
the major editions published since Shelley's death. The
Oxford Standard Authors edition of the *Poetical Works*, ed.
Thomas Hutchinson, 1904, rev. G. M. Matthews, 1970, still
in the meantime provides the least unsatisfactory currently
available text of Shelley's complete poetry. This edition also
includes all of Mary Shelley's notes to the poems.

Shelley's works in prose are currently being edited for Oxford
University Press by E. B. Murray, in two volumes. The first
of these appeared in 1993; until the appearance of the second,
the reader must rely on the relevant volumes of the 'Julian'
edition of Shelley's works, ed. Roger Ingpen and Walter
Peck, 1926–30, or on David Lee Clark's collection *Shelley's
Prose, or The Trumpet of a Prophecy* (1954, corrected edn
1967, new edn 1988). Both of these collections, but more
particularly Clark's, are extremely unreliable in their texts,
datings and notes. They are also both far from complete. H.
B. Forman's four-volume edition of 1880 is in many respects
superior to any subsequent text, but it is not easy to find.
Shelley's two youthful Gothic novels, *Zastrozzi* and *St
Irvyne*, have been reissued from time to time, most recently
in a World's Classics edition by Stephen C. Behrendt (1986).

The standard edition of Shelley's letters is *The Letters of Percy
Bysshe Shelley*, ed. F. L. Jones, 2 vols, Oxford, 1964. This
too is an edition which has come to seem increasingly unsatisfactory. It omits quite a large number of the letters now
known to survive, and makes more mistakes and modifications

in the text than are acceptable by modern standards. A new edition is currently planned, under the editorship of Mary Quinn.

Interested readers now have access to the exceptionally complex manuscript materials underlying many of Shelley's texts, by consulting the volumes in two scholarly series published by Garland: 'The Manuscripts of the Younger British Romantics' (including three volumes of Shelley material), and 'The Bodleian Shelley Manuscripts', both under the general editorship of Donald H. Reiman. A further rich source of information and commentary is the eight volumes so far published of *Shelley and His Circle*, ed. Kenneth N. Cameron (vols i–iv, 1961–70) and Donald H. Reiman (vols v–viii, 1973–86).

## Other editions

There are some good selections of Shelley's poetry. *Shelley's Poetry and Prose*, ed. Donald H. Reiman and Sharon B. Powers, New York and London, 1977, is a very full selection with good texts, helpful notes and an excellent annotated bibliography; it also includes two of Shelley's most important prose works and a selection of critical essays on the poetry. The 'Everyman' *Selected Poems*, ed. Timothy Webb, 1977, has a reliable text and a good bibliography, but it is severely limited by space, as is the New Oxford English Series *Selected Poems and Prose*, ed. G. M. Matthews, 1964, which has an excellent long introduction and good notes. Also recommended is *Shelley: Alastor, Prometheus Unbound, and Adonais*, ed. Peter Butter, London, 1970; this text includes all of the poems in the three most important volumes of verse published by Shelley in his own lifetime, with very helpful notes and some interesting critical views. It is still worth consulting the notes in C. D. Locock's two-volume edition of the *Poems*, published in 1911.

## II *Biography*

The standard scholarly biography is by Newman Ivey White, *Shelley*, 2 vols, New York, 1940, although this work is now in many respects out of date. Richard Holmes, *Shelley: The Pursuit*, London, 1974, is lively, readable and well-informed, but it is unreliable in its critical judgements, and, in its anxiety not to offer anything remotely akin to 'Shelley-worship', it can be far-fetched in matters of detailed biographical interpretation, and rather too hostile to its subject. Biography of Shelley is a complex subject in itself, and anyone seriously interested in the life should consult, in addition to all of Shelley's writings, the letters and journals of his wife Mary Shelley and her stepsister Claire Clairmont, and the letters and journals of their close friends the Gisbornes and the Williamses: *The Letters of Mary Wollstonecraft Shelley*, ed. Betty T. Bennett, 3 vols, Baltimore, 1980–88; *The Journals of Mary Shelley*, ed. Paula R. Feldman and Diana Scott-Kilvert, 2 vols, Oxford, 1987 (this edition identifies Shelley's contributions, and gives full annotation for the important lists of reading kept by the Shelleys); *The Journals of Claire Clairmont*, ed. Marion Kingston Stocking, Cambridge, Mass., 1968; and *Maria Gisborne and Edward E. Williams., Shelley's Friends: Their Journals and Letters*, ed. F. L. Jones, Norman, Okla., 1951. Also of great importance are the influential early accounts of Shelley by those who knew him. Of these the most sympathetic and (as far as they go) the most reliable are two books by Leigh Hunt, *Lord Byron and Some of His Contemporaries* (1828), and his *Autobiography* (3 vols, 1850), and Thomas Love Peacock's 'Memoirs of Shelley', first published in *Fraser's Magazine* from June 1858 to March 1862. Peacock's 'Memoirs' were written in response to T. W. Hogg's *Life of Shelley*, (2 vols, 1858; two further manuscript vols have been lost), which is distorted by Hogg's own bias and purposes but still an entertaining and very interesting source. The same is true of E. J. Trelawny's *Recollections of the Last Days of Shelley and Byron* (1858), which was revised as *Records of Shelley, Byron and the Author* (2 vols, 1878).

Contemporary reviews of Shelley are collected in Newman Ivey White, ed., *The Unextinguished Hearth: Shelley and His Contemporary Critics*, Cambridge, 1938; the 'Critical Heritage' volume on Shelley, ed. James Barcus, London, 1975, is dependent on White and contributes little that is new. For the early development of Shelley's reputation, see Sylva Norman, *The Flight of the Skylark*, London, 1954.

## III  *Critical studies*

Good introductions to Shelley include the introductory essays in the 'Everyman' *Selected Poems* by Timothy Webb, and in the 'New Oxford' selection by G. M. Matthews. Also recommended for new readers are: Desmond King-Hele, *Shelley:*

*His Thought and Work*, 2nd edn, 1971; G. M. Mathews, *Shelley* (in the British Council 'Writers and Their Work' series, 1970), which includes an excellent bibliography; David B. Pirie, *Shelley*, Buckingham, 1988; Donald H. Reiman, *Percy Bysshe Shelley*, London, 1969; and Timothy Webb, *Shelley: A Voice Not Understood*, Manchester, 1977.

The range of critical writing on Shelley is vast. For an excellent guide through it see Frank Jordan, ed., *The English Romantic Poets: A Review of Research and Criticism*, 3rd edn, New York, 1972, with an essay by Donald H. Reiman, and 4th edn, 1985, with a long and richly detailed essay by Stuart Curran which is inclusive up to the mid-eighties. For a list of articles see the bibliography in the 'Everyman' *Selected Poems*, ed. Timothy Webb. Three useful collections of critical essays on Shelley are: G. M. Ridenour, ed., *Shelley: A Collection of Critical Essays*, Englewood Cliffs, NJ, 1965; Patrick Swinden, ed., *Shelley: Shorter Poems and Lyrics*, London, 1976; and R. B. Woodings, ed., *Shelley: Modern Judgements*, London, 1968. The following list includes a selection only of the best critical books on Shelley's poetry and thought.

Allott, Miriam, ed., *Essays on Shelley*, Liverpool, 1982.

Baker, Carlos, *Shelley's Major Poetry: The Fabric of a Vision*, Princeton and Oxford, 1948.

Bloom, Harold, *Shelley's Mythmaking*, New Haven and Oxford, 1959.

Butter, Peter, *Shelley's Idols of the Cave*, Edinburgh, 1954.

Cameron, Kenneth Neill, *The Young Shelley: Genesis of a Radical*, London, 1950.

———*Shelley: The Golden Years*, Cambridge, Mass., 1974. Provides the best up-to-date review of biographical problems in Shelley, and is also particularly good on the political context.

Chernaik, Judith, *The Lyrics of Shelley*, Cleveland, OH, 1972. Includes an important selection of lyrics newly edited from manuscript sources.

Cronin, Richard, *Shelley's Poetic Thoughts*, New York, 1981.

Curran, Stuart, *Shelley's 'Cenci': Scorpions Ringed with Fire*, Princeton, 1970.

———*Shelley's Annus Mirabilis: The Maturing of an Epic Vision*, San Marino, Calif., 1975.

Dawson, Paul, *The Unacknowledged Legislator: Shelley and Politics*, Oxford, 1983.

Everest, Kelvin, ed., *Shelley Revalued: Essays from the Gregynog Conference*, Leicester, 1983.

——*Percy Bysshe Shelley*, Essays & Studies Series, Cambridge, 1992.

Foot, Paul, *Red Shelley*, London, 1980. Not a scholarly book, but a fiercely committed and readable account of Shelley's radicalism.

Hogle, Jerrold, *Shelley's Process: Radical Transference and the Development of His Major Works*, Oxford, 1989. Demanding but exciting and far-reaching account of Shelley from a perspective informed by contemporary literary theory in the United States.

Keach, William, *Shelley's Style*, London, 1984.

Leighton, Angela, *Shelley and the Sublime: An Interpretation of the Major Poems*, Cambridge, 1984.

O'Neill, Michael, *The Human Mind's Imaginings*, Oxford, 1989.

Pulos, C. E., *The Deep Truth: A Study of Shelley's Scepticism*, Lincoln, Nebr., 1954. Important study of the intellectual heritage and contexts of Shelley's thought.

Robinson, Charles E., *Shelley and Byron: The Snake and Eagle Wreathed in Fight*, Baltimore, 1976.

Scrivener, Michael, *Radical Shelley: The Philosophical Anarchism and Utopian Thought of Percy Bysshe Shelley*, Princeton, 1982. Detailed study of the social and historical contexts of Shelley's radicalism.

Sperry, Stuart M., *Shelley's Major Verse: The Narrative and Dramatic Poetry*, Cambridge, Mass., 1988.

Wasserman, Earl R., *Shelley: A Critical Reading*, Baltimore, 1971. Difficult but richly rewarding.

Webb, Timothy, *The Violet in the Crucible: Shelley and Translation*, Oxford, 1976.

Wilson, Milton, *Shelley's Later Poetry: A Study of His Prophetic Imagination*, New York, 1959.

# 11 *Keats*

## I *Editions*

There are three one-volume editions of the complete poems. All are available in paperback versions. For the general reader the best is probably John Barnard's skilfully annotated edition, published by Penguin Books in 1973. Even fuller notes are provided by Miriam Allott in her edition, published by Longmans in 1970. Where there is controversy as to exactly what Keats wrote, the most reliably accurate text is likely to be that edited by Jack Stillinger in *The Poems of John Keats*, Harvard University Press, 1978.

All three editions order the poems according to the supposed chronology of their composition; they thus cannot reproduce the juxtapositions and sequences that Keats's first readers experienced. For instance, in the sequence Keats chose for the poems that he published in the 1820 volume, it was immediately after experiencing 'Robin Hood' that the reader began 'To Autumn'. It is highly illuminating to look at accurate reproductions of the three volumes that Keats himself published: *Poems* (1817), *Endymion* and *Lamia . . . and Other Poems* (1820). All are available in the *Revolution and Romanticism* series of reprints, ed. Jonathan Wordsworth, Oxford, 1988–90.

The detailed problems confronting a textual editor of Keats's verse are explained in Stillinger's poem-by-poem account, *The Texts of Keats's Poems*, Cambridge, Mass., 1974. For the texts of the Odes, see the usefully illustrated *The Odes of Keats and Their Earliest Known Manuscripts* by Robert Gittings, London, 1971.

All Keats's extant letters are available in a superbly annotated edition: *The Letters of John Keats 1814–1821*, ed. H. E. Rollins, 2 vols, Cambridge, Mass., 1958. For relevant letters by his friends, see *The Keats Circle: Letters and Papers 1816–1879*, ed. H. E. Rollins, 2 vols, Cambridge, Mass., 1965. See also *The Letters of Charles Armitage Brown*, ed. Jack Stillinger, Cambridge, Mass., 1966.

The complete works, including Keats's letters and other prose (such as his theatre reviews), are available in 'The Hampstead

Edition': *The Poetical and Other Writings of John Keats*, ed. with Notes and Appendices by H. Buxton Forman, rev. with additions by Maurice Buxton Forman, 8 vols, New York, 1970.

## II *Biography*

Bate, Walter Jackson, *John Keats*, Cambridge, Mass., 1964.

Gittings, Robert, *John Keats*, London, 1968.

Chilcott, Tim, *A Publisher and His Circle: The Life and Work of John Taylor, Keats's Publisher*, London, 1972.

## III *Bibliography and concordance*

MacGillivray, J. R., *Keats: A Bibliography and Reference Guide*, Oxford, 1949.

Hearn, R., *Keats Criticism since 1954: A Bibliography*, Salzburg, 1981.

*A Concordance to the Poems of John Keats*, ed. M. G. Becker, R. J. Dilligan and T. K. Bender, New York and London, 1981.

## IV *Critical studies: Books*

### (*i*) *introductory books*

The best recent survey of Keats's writings is John Barnard's *John Keats*, Cambridge, 1987. Often subtle enough to interest the most sophisticated reader, but consistently lucid and informative.

More elementary introductions include Timothy Hilton's heavily illustrated *Keats and His World*, London, 1971; William Walsh's *Introduction to Keats*, London, 1981; and Cedric Watts's *A Preface to Keats*, London, 1981.

### (*ii*) *general books*

The most consistently interesting book-length essay is probably Christopher Ricks's *Keats and Embarrassment*, Oxford, 1974.

Also useful are: Douglas Bush, *John Keats: His Life and Writings*, London, 1966; John Jones, *John Keats's Dream of Truth*, London, 1969; M. R. Ridley, *Keats's Craftsmanship: A Study in Poetic Development*, London, 1963; Stuart Sperry, *Keats the Poet*, Princeton, 1974; Jack Stillinger, *The Hoodwinking of Madeline and Other Essays on Keats's Poems*, Chicago and London, 1971; and Helen Vendler, *The Odes of John Keats*, Cambridge, Mass., 1983.

For a challengingly radical application of recent literary theory, see Marjorie Levinson, *Keats's Life of Allegory: The Origins of a Style*, Oxford, 1988: brilliant but eccentric and sometimes obscure. Jeffrey Baker's *John Keats and Symbolism*, Brighton, 1986, and David Pollard's *The Poetry of Keats: Language and Experience*, Brighton, 1984, also make use of modern theoretical approaches.

## (iii) specific topics

On Keats and politics there is still remarkably little. However, excellent (if brief) essays are to be found in 'Keats and Politics: A Forum', *Studies in Romanticism*, xxv (1986), 171–229. See also Jerome J. McGann's essay, 'Keats and the Historical Method in Literary Criticism', reproduced in his book *The Beauty of Inflections: Literary Investigations in Historical Method and Theory*, Oxford, 1985; Marilyn Butler, 'The War of the Intellectuals from Wordsworth to Keats', ch. 6 of *Romantics, Rebels and Reactionaries: English Literature and Its Background*, Oxford, 1981; and Vincent Newey, '"Alternate Uproar and Peace": Keats, Politics and the Idea of Revolution', *The Yearbook of English Studies*, xix (1989), 265–89.

Useful studies of Keats's writings in relation to other, specified subjects include the following. Medical training and practice in early nineteenth-century England: Hermione de Almeida, *Romantic Medicine and John Keats*, Oxford, 1991; ancient Greece: Martin Aske, *Keats and Hellenism*, Cambridge, 1985; early nineteenth-century literary criticism: David Bromwich, *Hazlitt: The Mind of a Critic*, Oxford, 1983; the visual arts: Ian Jack, *Keats and the Mirror of Art*, Oxford, 1967; twentieth-century verse: James Land Jones, *Adam's Dream: Mythic Consciousness in Keats and Yeats*, Athens, Ga., 1975; music: John A. Minahan, *Word Like a Bell: John Keats, Music and the Romantic Poet*, Kent, OH, 1992; theatre, and theatre criticism: Bernice Slote, *Keats and the Dramatic Principle*, Lincoln, Nebr., 1958; Shakespeare: R. White, *Keats as a Reader of Shakespeare*, London, 1987. For an influential defence of Keats's 'vulgarity', see John Bayley, 'Keats and Reality', *Proceedings of the British Academy*, xlviii (1962), 91–126.

## v Critical studies: Collections of Essays

Contemporary reviews of Keats's published volumes (and much other nineteenth-century criticism of his writings) are reproduced in *Keats: The Critical Heritage*, ed. G. M. Matthews, London, 1971. See also Lewis M. Schwartz, *Keats Reviewed by His Contemporaries: A Collection of Notices for the Years 1816–1821*, Metuchen, NJ, 1973.

Anthologies of earlier modern criticism include: *John Keats: A Reassessment*, ed. Kenneth Muir, Liverpool, 1959; *Twentieth Century Interpretations of Keats's Odes*, Englewood Cliffs, NJ, 1968; *John Keats, Odes: A Selection of Critical Essays*, ed. G. S. Fraser, London, 1971.

More recent anthologies include *Keats, The Narrative Poems: A Selection of Critical Essays*, ed. John Spencer Hill, London, 1983; *Modern Critical Views: John Keats*, ed. Harold Bloom, New York, 1985; *Critical Essays on Keats: Poems and Letters*, ed. Linda Cookson and Bryan Loughrey, London, 1988; and *Critical Essays on John Keats*, ed. Hermione de Almeida, Boston, 1990.

# 12 Orientalism

*Select Primary Texts, Romantic Period*

Beckford, William, *Vathek* (1786). An oriental tale.

Beddoes, Thomas, *Alexander's Expedition down the Hydaspes and the Indus to the Indian Ocean* (1792). Poem.

Blake, William, *The Marriage of Heaven and Hell* (1791–4); *The Song of Los* (1794); *The First Book of Urizen* (1794).

Burke, Edmund, *Writings and Speeches of Edmund Burke*, general ed. Paul Langford, Vol VI, *India: The Launching of the Hastings Impeachment, 1786–88*, ed. P. J. Marshall, Oxford, 1991.

Byron, George Gordon, Lord, *Childe Harold*, Cantos I and II (1812); *The Giaour* (1813); *The Bride of Abydos* (1813); *The Corsair* (1814); *Lara* (1814); *The Siege of Corinth* (1815); *Hebrew Melodies* (1815); *Manfred* (1817); *Beppo* (1818); *Don Juan* (1819–23); *Sardanapalus* (1821); *Cain* (1821); *Heaven and Earth* (1823); *The Island* (1823).

Coleridge, Samuel Taylor, 'Kubla Khan' (written 1797–9).

Douce, Francis, *Illustrations of Shakspeare* (2 vols, 1807), Appendices.

Edgeworth, Maria, 'Lame Jervas', in *Popular Tales* (1804); *Ennui* (1809).

Gough, Richard, *A Comparative View of the Antient Monuments of India* (1785).

Grant, Charles, 'Observations on the State of Society among the Asiatic Subjects of Great Britain', in *Parliamentary Papers, 1812–13*, Paper 282.

Hamilton, Eliza, *Letters of a Hindoo Rajah, to which is prefixed a Preliminary Dissertation on the History, Religion and Manners of the Hindoos* (1797). Novel.

Hastings, Warren, *see* Wilkins.

Hodges, William, *A Dissertation on the Prototypes of Architecture, Hindoo, Moorish and Gothic* (1786).

Jones, William. Poems, dramas and translations, many first published in *Collected Works*, ed. A. M. Jones (6 vols, 1799); *Asiatic Researches*, 1789–.

Keats, John, *Endymion* (1818); *Hyperion* (1820); *The Cap and Bells* (written 1820).

Landor, Walter Savage, *Gebir* (1798).

Lawrence, James, *The Empire of the Nairs, or The Rights of Women, an Utopian Romance* (1811).

Maturin, C. R., *Melmoth the Wanderer* (1820). Novel.

Maurice, Thomas, *Indian Antiquities* (7 vols, 1793–1800).

Mill, James, *The History of British India* (7 vols, 1817).

Moore, Thomas, 'The Tale of the Blanket' (prose fragment, 1805); *Irish Melodies* (10 series, from 1808); *Lalla Rookh* (1817), esp. 'The Veiled Prophet of Khorassan', 'The Fireworshippers' and the prose frame in which the verse tales are set; *The Epicurean* (1827) (historical novel, north African setting).

O'Halloran, Sylvester, *A General History of Ireland to the Close of the Twelfth Century* (1774).

Owenson, Sydney (afterwards Lady Morgan), *Woman: or Ida of Athens* (1809); *The Missionary* (1811).

Reeve, Clara, *The Progress of Romance* (1787). With 'Charoba: An Arabian Tale'.

Shelley, Mary, *Frankenstein* (1818); *The Last Man* (1824).

Shelley, P. B., *Queen Mab* (1813); *Alastor* (1816); *The Revolt of Islam* (1818); *Prometheus Unbound* (1820); 'The Witch of Atlas' (1820); *Hellas* (1821); 'On the Devil, and Devils' (1819–20), prose essay.

Southey, Robert, *Thalaba the Destroyer* (1801); *Madoc* (1805); *The Curse of Kehama* (1810); reviews of *Reports* of Baptist missionaries, *Annual Review* (1802–4) and *Quarterly Review*, i (1809).

Volney, Constantin, *Les Ruines* (1791); English tr., *The Ruins: or a Survey of the Revolutions of Empire* (1792).

Wilkins, Charles, tr., *The Bhagvat-Gita, or Dialogues of Kreeshna and Arjoon* (1785). With preliminary letter by Warren Hastings.

## Select Secondary Works

Ahmad, Aijaz, *In Theory: Nations, Classes, Literature*, London, 1992.

Archer, Mildred, and Lightbown, Ronald, *India Observed: India as Viewed by British Artists, 1760–1860*, London, 1982.

Barker, Francis et al., eds, *Europe and Its Others*, 2 vols, Colchester, 1985.

Barrell, John, *The Infection of Thomas de Quincey: A Psychopathology of Imperialism*, New Haven and London, 1990.

Bayly, C. A., *Indian Society and the Making of the British Empire*, New Cambridge History of India, Cambridge, 1988.

———*The Raj: India and the British, 1600–1947*, London, 1990.

Bernal, Martin, *Black Athena: The Afroasiatic Roots of Classical Civilisation*, Vol I, *The Fabrication of Ancient Greece, 1785–1985*, London, 1987.

Bhabha, Homi, 'Difference, Discrimination, and the Discourse of Colonialism', in F. Barker et al., eds, *The Politics of Theory*, Colchester, 1983.

——'Signs Taken for Wonders', *see* Barker, *Europe and Its Others* (above) and *Critical Inquiry*, xii (1985), 144–65.

—— ed., *Nation and Narration*, London, 1990.

Butler, Marilyn, 'Druids, Bards and Twice-Born Bacchus: Peacock's Engagement with Primitive Mythology', *Keats–Shelley Memorial Bulletin*, xxxvi (1985), 57–76.

——'Romantic Manicheism: Shelley's "On the Devil, and Devils" and Byron's Mythological Dramas', in J. B. Bullen, ed., *The Sun is God: Painting, Literature and Mythology in the Nineteenth Century*, Oxford, 1989, pp 13–39.

——'Plotting the Revolution: Romanticism as Political Narrative', in Kenneth Johnstone et al., eds, *Romantic Revolutions*, Bloomington, Ind., 1990, pp 133–57.

——'John Bull's Other Kingdom: Byron's Intellectual Comedy', *Studies in Romanticism*, xxxi (1992), 281–94.

Christensen, Jerome, *Lord Byron's Strength: Romantic Writing and Commercial Society*, Baltimore, 1993.

Crompton, Louis, *Byron and Greek Love: Homophobia in Nineteenth-Century England*, London, 1985.

Drew, John, *British Romantics and India*, Cambridge, 1987.

Embree, Ainslie, *Charles Grant and British Rule in India*, London, 1962.

——*Imagining India: Essays in Indian History*, Delhi, 1989.

Feldman, Burton, and Richardson, Robert D., *The Rise of Modern Mythology, 1680–1860*, Bloomington, Ind., 1972.

Franklin, Caroline, 'Haidée and Neuha: Byron's Heroines of the South', *Byron Journal*, xviii (1990), 37–49.

——*Byron's Heroines*, Oxford, 1992.

Green, Martin, *Dreams of Adventure, Deeds of Empire*, New York, 1979.

Headrick, Daniel R., *Tools of Empire: Technology and European Imperialism in the Nineteenth Century*, New York and Oxford, 1981.

Inden, Ronald, *Imagining India*, Oxford, 1990.

Kabbani, Rana, *Europe's Myths of Orient: Devise and Rule*, London, 1986.

Kejariwal, O. P., *The Asiatic Society of Bengal and the Discovery of India's Past*, Delhi, 1988.

Kelsall, Malcolm, *Byron's Politics*, Hassocks, Sussex, 1988.

Kopf, David, *British Orientalism and Bengal Renaissance*, Berkeley, 1969.

Leask, Nigel, *British Romantic Writers and the East: Anxieties of Empire*, Cambridge Studies in Romanticism, Cambridge, 1993.

Majeed, Javed, *Ungoverned Imaginings: James Mill's 'History of British India' and Orientalism*, Oxford, 1992.

Marchand, Leslie, *Byron: A Biography*, 3 vols, New York, 1957.

——ed., *Letters and Journals of Lord Byron*, 12 vols, London, 1973–82.

Martin, Philip W., *Byron: A Poet before His Public*, Cambridge, 1982.

Mason, Philip, *The Men Who Ruled India*, London, 1985.

McCalman, Iain, *Grub Street in Revolution: Popular Romanticism, Science and Political Culture in Britain, 1780–1838*, Oxford, forthcoming.

McGann, J. J., ed., *Byron: The Complete Poetical Works*, 7 vols, Oxford, 1981–93.

——*Fiery Dust*, Chicago, 1968.

——*'Don Juan' in Context*, Chicago, 1976.

——'The Book of Byron and the Book of the World', *Beauty of Inflections*, Oxford, 1985, pp 277–83.

——'Hero with a Thousand Faces: The Rhetoric of Byronism', *Studies in Romanticism*, xxxi (1992), 295–314.

Parry, Benita, 'Problems in Current Theories of Colonial Discourse', *Oxford Literary Review*, ix (1987), 51–2.

Pratt, Mary Louise, *Imperial Eyes*, London, 1992.

Said, Edward, *Orientalism*, London, 1978.

——*Culture and Imperialism*, London, 1993.

Schneider, Elisabeth, *Coleridge, Opium and 'Kubla Khan'*, Chicago, 1953.

Schwab, Raymond, *La Renaissance orientale*, Paris, 1950.

Shaffer, E. S., *Kubla Khan and the Fall of Jerusalem, 1770–1880*, Cambridge, 1975.

Spivak, Gayatri, 'Can the Subaltern Speak?', in Cary Nelson and L. Grossberg, eds, *Marxism and the Interpretation of Culture*, London, 1988.

Stokes, Eric, *English Utilitarians and India*, Oxford, 1959.

Viswanathan, Gauri, 'The Beginnings of English Literary Study in British India', *Oxford Literary Review*, ix (1987), 2–26.

Willson, A. Leslie, *A Mythical Image: The Idea of India in German Romanticism*, Durham, NC, 1984.

Young, Robert, *White Mythologies: Writing History and the West*, London, 1990.

# TABLE OF DATES

Dates of literary works are those of publication, unless otherwise described. Where works were published significantly later than their completion, they have been listed under both their year of composition and of publication, with cross-references in both cases.

1770   James Bruce discovers source of the Blue Nile. James Cook
         discovers Botany Bay, Australia.
       James Hogg b. William Wordsworth b. Thomas Chatterton
         d. (b. 1752)
       Edmund Burke, *Thoughts on the Cause of the Present
         Discontents*; Oliver Goldsmith, *The Deserted Village*
1771   Richard Arkwright introduces first spinning-mill.
       Walter Scott b. Dorothy Wordsworth b. Thomas Gray d. (b.
         1716) Tobias Smollett d. (b. 1721)
       James Beattie, *The Minstrel*, Book I; Henry Mackenzie, *The
         Man of Feeling*
1772   Warren Hastings becomes Governor of Bengal. Judge
         William Murray, in Somerset trial, decides that a slave
         becomes free when in England. William Blake begins
         apprenticeship as engraver.
       S. T. Coleridge b. David Ricardo b.
       William Jones, *Poems... from the Asiatic Languages*
1773   Boston Tea Party. Conflict over taxation between British
         colonists in America, threatening secession, and London
         government. Samuel Johnson and James Boswell tour
         Scotland.
       Francis Jeffrey b.
       Oliver Goldsmith, *She Stoops to Conquer*; John Wheatley,
         *Poems*
1774   Escalating conflict between English colonists in America and
         London government. Quebec Act to secure support of
         colonists in Canada for Britain. Warren Hastings becomes
         Governor-General in India. Joseph Priestley discovers
         oxygen. Perpetual copyright eliminated under new English
         law; cheap reprints possible.
       Robert Southey b. Oliver Goldsmith d. (b. *c.*1730)

James Beattie, *The Minstrel*, Book II; John Langhorne, *The Country Justice*; Sylvester O'Halloran, *A General History of Ireland to the Close of the Twelfth Century*

1775   War against American colonists: British defeated at Lexington, victorious at Bunker Hill. 29,000 German mercenaries hired by London government. James Watt perfects his invention of the steam engine.

Jane Austen b. Charles Lamb b. W. S. Landor b. M. G. ('Monk') Lewis b. J. M. W. Turner b.

Samuel Johnson, *A Journey to the Western Isles of Scotland*; Richard Brinsley Sheridan, *The Rivals*

1776   (4 July) American colonists' Declaration of Independence. Cook's third voyage to Pacific.

John Constable b. David Hume b. Sydney Owenson (Lady Morgan) b.

John Cartwright, *Take Your Choice*; Edward Gibbon, *Decline and Fall of the Roman Empire* I; Thomas Paine, *Common Sense*; Adam Smith, *Inquiry into the Nature and Causes of the Wealth of Nations*

1777   British army surrenders to Americans at Saratoga.

Thomas Campbell b.

Thomas Chatterton, *Poems supposed to have been written at Bristol in the 15th century, by Thomas Rowley* (posthumous publication); Joseph Priestley, *Disquisition Relating to Matter and Spirit*; Richard Brinsley Sheridan, *The School for Scandal*; Thomas Warton, *History of English Literature 1100–1603* (–1782)

1778   James Cook discovers Hawaii and charts Pacific coast of America.

Humphry Davy b. William Hazlitt b. Jean Jacques Rousseau d. (b. 1712) Voltaire d. (b. 1694)

Fanny Burney, *Evelina*; Thomas West, *A Guide to the Lakes in Cumberland, Westmorland and Lancashire*

1779   British, in India, begin war against Mahrattas (–1782); in west Africa, attack French Senegal, take Goree. Spain and Britain at war: siege of Gibraltar (–1783). French, in West Indies, take St Vincent and Grenada. Samuel Crompton invents spinning-mule, crossing water-powered spinning-frame (patented 1769 by Richard Arkwright) with the multiple-thread spinning-jenny (invented by James Hargreaves *c*.1764); Lancashire mill owned by Richard Arkwright destroyed by rioting workers.

Thomas Moore b. David Garrick d. (b. 1717)

William Cowper, *Olney Hymns*; Samuel Johnson, *Prefaces Biographical and Critical to the Works of the English Poets* (–1781); Richard Brinsley Sheridan, *The Critic*

1780    Newgate prison burnt in Gordon ('No Popery') Riots, witnessed by George Crabbe and William Blake. Yorkshire petition for parliamentary reform. First Sunday newspapers in London: the *British Gazette* and *Sunday Monitor*. Population of England and Wales about 7½ million: had been about 5 million in 1700.

John Wilson Croker, Tory politician and reviewer of Keats, b. William Hone b.

Second, substantially expanded edn of Thomas West's *Guide to Lakes* (1778)

1781    British army surrenders to Americans at Yorktown. In India, British capture Dutch settlement at Negapatam, Madras. Warren Hastings deposes Raja of Benares, seizes treasure of the Nabob of Oudh.

George Crabbe, *The Library*; Edward Gibbon, *Decline and Fall of the Roman Empire* II; Immanuel Kant, *Critique of Pure Reason*; Jean Jacques Rousseau, *Confessions*

1782    British–American peace talks in Paris. Spanish capture Minorca from British. James Watt patents double-acting rotary steam engine. Josiah Wedgwood develops pyrometer for checking temperature in pottery furnace.

Robert Bage, *Mount Henneth*; Fanny Burney, *Cecilia*; William Cowper, *Poems*; William Gilpin, *Observations on the River Wye*; Joseph Priestley, *A History of the Corruptions of Christianity*; J. Warton, *Essay on the Genius and Writings of Pope* (first version 1756)

1783    Peace of Versailles: independence of US conceded. Pitt becomes Prime Minister (–1801). Henry Bell perfects copper cylinder for calico printing. Sir William Jones takes up appointment as judge in Calcutta.

William Blake, *Poetical Sketches* (printed but not published; copies distributed privately by author); George Crabbe, *The Village*

1784    Pitt's India Act puts East India Company under some parliamentary control. Building of Brighton Pavilion, for Prince Regent, begins (–1827). Henry Cort introduces puddling process for manufacture of wrought iron. Andrew Meikle invents threshing machine. Vincent Lunardi ascends by balloon in England.

Leigh Hunt b. Samuel Johnson d. (b. 1709)

Robert Bage, *Barham Downs*; Charlotte Smith, *Elegiac Sonnets*; William John Wesley, *Deed of Declaration* (defining Methodism)

1785 Warren Hastings, Governor-General of India, resigns and returns to England. Edmund Cartwright perfects power loom and wool-combing machine. Robert Ransome patents cast-iron ploughshare.

Thomas De Quincey b. Thomas Peacock b.

James Boswell, *Journal of a Tour to the Hebrides*; Edmund Burke, *Speech on the Nabob of Arcot's Debts*; William Cowper, *The Task*; George Crabbe, *The Newspaper*; Charles Wilkins (tr.), *The Bhagavad-Gita*

1786 Lord Cornwallis appointed Governor-General of India. Raja of Kedah surrenders Penang to Britain.

William Beckford, *Vathek*; Robert Burns, *Poems Chiefly in the Scottish Dialect*; William Gilpin, *Observations of Picturesque Beauty in Mountains and Lakes of Cumberland and Westmoreland*; Richard Payne Knight, 'A Discourse on the Worship of Priapus' (privately printed but widely circulated; republished in 1818 as *An Enquiry into the Symbolical Language of Ancient Art and Mythology*); Helen Maria Williams, *Poems, in Two Volumes*

1787 United States Constitution defined. Turkey declares war on Russia. William Wordsworth goes to Cambridge University (–1791).

Robert Bage, *The Fair Syrian*; Clara Reeve, *Progress of Romance*; Mary Wollstonecraft, *Thoughts on the Education of Daughters*; Ann Yearsley, *Poems on Various Subjects*

1788 Botany Bay prison colony founded in Australia. Warren Hastings impeached for corrupt administration in India (proceedings opened by Burke). George III's first attack of insanity. Centenary celebrations of accession of William of Orange, 6 June 1688, 'The Glorious Revolution'. First issue of *The Times. Analytical Review* founded by Joseph Johnson.

George (Lord) Byron b. Edmund Kean b. Thomas Gainsborough d. (b. 1727) Charles Wesley d. (b. 1707)

Robert Bage, *James Wallace*; Edward Gibbon, *Decline and Fall of the Roman Empire* III–V; Immanuel Kant, *Critique of Practical Reason*; John Lemprière, *Classical Dictionary*;

Hannah More, *Thoughts on the Importance of the Manners of the Great to General Society*; Charlotte Smith, *Emmeline, or, The Orphan of the Castle*; Mary Wollstonecraft, *Mary: A Fiction* and *Original Stories from Real Life*

1789    Storming of the Bastille (14 July); abolition of French feudal system; Declaration of the Rights of Man. Richard Price addresses London Revolution Society, praising the French 'ardour for liberty' (the speech that provoked Burke to write *Reflections*, 1790); Norwich Revolution Society founded. The *Bounty* mutineers settle on Pitcairn Island. First steam-powered cotton factory in Manchester. Robert Ransome founds Orwell Works for production of agricultural implements and machinery.

Jeremy Bentham, *Introduction to the Principles of Morals and Legislation*; William Blake, *Songs of Innocence* and *The Book of Thel*; William Lisle Bowles, *Fourteen Sonnets*; Erasmus Darwin, *The Loves of the Plants*; Sir William Jones, *Sacontala, or the Fatal Ring: an Indian Drama*; Gilbert White, *Natural History of Selborne*

1790    French king forced to accept new constitution abolishing nobility and titles. Parliament decides to retain Test and Corporation Acts (legislation against Dissenters). Work on Firth–Clyde and Oxford–Birmingham canals begins. First steam-powered rolling mill in England. William Wordsworth tours France and Alps.

Adam Smith d. (b. 1723)

Archibald Alison, *Essays on the Nature and Principles of Taste*; William Blake, *The French Revolution* (printed 1790–91 for Joseph Johnson but not published); James Bruce, *Travels to Discover the Source of the Nile*; Edmund Burke, *Reflections on the Revolution in France* (sells 30,000 copies in first two years); Ann Radcliffe, *A Sicilian Romance*; Charlotte Smith, *Ethelinde*; Helen Maria Williams, *Julia: A Novel*, and *Letters Written in France in the Summer of 1790*; Mary Wollstonecraft, *A Vindication of the Rights of Men* (published anonymously); Ann Yearsley, *Earl Goodwin*

1791    French royal family captured attempting to leave country. 'Church and State' loyalist mob in Birmingham burn Priestley's house and laboratory. Sheffield Society for Constitutional Information founded in December (2,500 members, incl. 600 militant activists, by June 1792).

Parliament rejects bill proposing abolition of slave-trade. William Wordsworth's second visit to France. Samuel Taylor Coleridge goes to Cambridge University (–1794). William Godwin and Mary Wollstonecraft meet at Joseph Johnson's.

John Wesley d. (b. 1703)

William Bartram, *Travels through North and South Carolina*; Elizabeth Bentley, *Genuine Poetical Compositions*; James Boswell, *Life of Johnson*; Edmund Burke, *Appeal from the Old to the New Whigs* and *Letter to a Member of the National Assembly*; Erasmus Darwin, *The Botanic Garden*; Elizabeth Inchbald, *A Simple Story*; James Mackintosh, *Vindiciae Gallicae: Defence of the French Revolution and Its English Admirers against . . . Burke*; Hannah More, *An Estimate of the Religion of the Fashionable World*; Thomas Paine, *Rights of Man* I; Ann Radcliffe, *The Romance of the Forest*; Joseph Ritson, *Ancient Popular Poetry*; Charlotte Smith, *Celestina*

1792    In India, British defeat Tipu sultan in Mysore. France declares itself a republic; radical Jacobins seize power from more moderate Girondists; first guillotine in Paris. French defeat invading armies of Prussia and Austria at Valmy, conquer Austrian Netherlands. Whigs found Society of the Friends of the People. London Corresponding Society (founded January) in September sends 'Address' to French Legislative Assembly incl. 'Frenchmen, you are already free and Britons are preparing to become so'; by December over forty reform societies spread throughout country; 160 delegates to reform convention in Edinburgh – one speaker, for reading out an address from the United Irishmen, convicted of sedition and transported to Botany Bay; Association for the Preservation of Liberty and Property against Republicans and Levellers founded. Thomas Paine in revolutionary Paris, charged in English court with sedition and, in his absence, sentenced to death. Warren Hastings acquitted. Mary Wollstonecraft goes to France. William Wordsworth returns from France, after Annette Vallon has given birth to his illegitimate daughter.

P. B. Shelley b. Joshua Reynolds d. (b. 1723)

Robert Bage, *Man as He Is*; Thomas Dermody, *Poems*; William Gilpin, *Three Essays: On Picturesque Beauty, On Picturesque Travel, and on Sketching Landscape*; Thomas

Holcroft, *Anna St Ives*; Thomas Paine, *Rights of Man* II (published 17 Feb., banned 21 May, but perhaps 200,000 copies distributed in first year); Samuel Rogers, *The Pleasures of Memory*; Friedrich Schiller, *The Robbers* (tr. A. F. Tytler); Charlotte Smith, *Desmond*; Constantin Volney, *The Ruins: or a Survey of the Revolutions of Empire*; Mary Wollstonecraft, *A Vindication of the Rights of Woman*; Arthur Young, *Travels in France*

1793    French king and queen executed; beginning of 'Terror' in Paris. Britain and France at war, 1 Feb.: war lasts, apart from two brief interludes (beginning spring 1802 and spring 1814) until summer of 1815. English and Scottish 'Jacobins' attending 2nd Edinburgh convention prosecuted for sedition and convicted. Thomas Spence founds radical weekly, *Pig's Meat; or Lessons for the Swinish Multitude*.
John Clare b. Felicia Hemans b.
William Blake, *The Marriage of Heaven and Hell* (engraved), and *America* (rewritten, engraved and advertised in a prospectus with *Innocence, Thel, Marriage, Visions of the Daughters of Albion, Songs of Experience*); M. J. Condorcet, *Esquisse d'un tableau historique des progrès de l'esprit humain*; George Dyer, *The Complaints of the Poor People of England*; William Godwin, *An Enquiry Concerning Political Justice*; Thomas Maurice, *Indian Antiquities* (–1800); Hannah More, *Village Politics*; Charlotte Smith, *The Old Manor House*; Jane West, *Advantages of Education*; William Wordsworth, *Descriptive Sketches* and *An Evening Walk, Letter to the Bishop of Llandaff* (pub. 1876), writes first version of *Salisbury Plain*; Arthur Young, *The Example of France: a Warning to Britain*

1794    Rebellion in Poland, led by T. A. Kosciusko, crushed by Russians. In France, Danton, Robespierre, St Just and many others executed. At Sheffield open-air meeting, 5,000–6,000 English democrats demand peace with France and parliamentary reform; Habeas Corpus law, protecting citizen from arbitrary imprisonment, suspended; forty-one radicals, incl. Thomas Hardy, Thomas Holcroft, John Thelwell, John Horne Tooke, arrested and charged with high treason; juries refuse to convict; Government abandons trials. Harvest failure contributes to food prices at record high. Samuel Coleridge and Robert Southey plan to emigrate and found ideal 'pantisocratic' society in America.

William Jones d. (b. 1746)

William Blake, *Songs of Innocence and of Experience*, engraves
*Europe* and *First Book of Urizen*; Thomas Chatterton, new
edn of Rowley poems; S. T. Coleridge, *Monody on the
Death of Chatterton*; S. T. Coleridge and Robert Southey,
*Fall of Robespierre*; Erasmus Darwin, *Zoonomia or the
Laws of Organic Life*; William Godwin, *Things as They
Are*, or *The Adventures of Caleb Williams*; Thomas
Holcroft, *The Adventures of Hugh Trevor* (–1797); William
Payne Knight, *The Landscape*; Thomas Paine, *The Age of
Reason* I; William Paley, *Evidences of Christianity*; Uvedale
Price, *Essays on the Picturesque*; Joseph Priestley, *The
Present State of Europe Compared with Antient Prophecies*;
Ann Radcliffe, *The Mysteries of Udolpho*; Charlotte Smith,
*The Banished Man*; Robert Southey, *Wat Tyler* (pub.
1817); Mary Wollstonecraft, *Historical and Moral View of
the Origin and Progress of the French Revolution*

1795    Holland surrenders Ceylon to British. British army occupies
Cape of Good Hope. Mungo Park explores route of Niger
River. Bad harvest makes food prices even higher. George
III's coach stoned at opening of Parliament; Pitt brings in
'Two Acts', new, repressive laws against treasonable
conspiracy and assembly: meetings of more than fifty
people banned. London Corresponding Society organizes
mass open-air meetings at Copenhagen Fields, London.
Speenhamland system of poor relief introduced. Methodist
secession from Church of England. S. T. Coleridge gives
political lectures in Bristol attacking new laws; William
Wordsworth meets S. T. Coleridge and Robert Southey.
Mary Wollstonecraft leaves France, returns to London.

Thomas Carlyle b. John Keats b. James Boswell d. (b. 1740)

William Blake, *Los* (engraved); Maria Edgeworth, *Letters of
Julia and Caroline*; W. S. Landor, *The Poems of W.S.L.*;
Hannah More, *Cheap Repository Tracts* (–1798, 2 million
copies distributed in first year); Thomas Paine, *The Age of
Reason* II; Joseph Ritson, *Robin Hood: a collection of all
the ancient poems, songs and ballads now extant relative to
that outlaw*; Charlotte Smith, *Montalbert*; Robert Southey,
*Poems*; Helen Maria Williams (tr.), Bernardin de St Pierre's
*Paul et Virginie*

1796    French take control of northern Italy. Spain declares war on
Britain. Edward Jenner develops vaccination against

smallpox. Home Office surveillance of William
Wordsworth and S. T. Coleridge (suspected of spying for
France).
Robert Burns d. (b. 1759).
Jane Austen, *Pride and Prejudice* (pub. 1813) begun; Robert
Bage, *Hermsprong, or Man as He is Not*; Edmund Burke,
*Letters on a Regicide Peace, Thoughts on Scarcity* and
*Letter to a Noble Lord*; Fanny Burney, *Camilla*; S. T.
Coleridge, *Poems on Various Subjects* and *The Watchman*
(periodical); Mary Hays, *Memoirs of Emma Courtney*;
Elizabeth Inchbald, *Nature and Art*; M. G. Lewis, *The
Monk*; John Lucas, *Miscellanies in Verse*; Regina Maria
Roche, *Children of the Abbey*; Walter Scott (tr.), G. A.
Burger's *The Chase* and *William and Helen*; Charlotte
Smith, *Marchmont*; Robert Southey, *Joan of Arc*; Jane
West, *A Gossip's Story*; Mary Wollstonecraft, *Letters
Written... in Sweden, Norway and Denmark*

1797    French defeat Austrians at Rivoli, advance to Vienna;
Venetian republic abolished. Napoleon appointed
commander of army to invade England; failure of French
landing in Wales. British navy mutinies, April; mutineers
surrender, June: Richard Parker and thirty-five other
sailors hanged. *Anti-Jacobin or Weekly Examiner* founded
(–July 1798). British government issues first copper coins
and first one-pound notes. William Godwin and Mary
Wollstonecraft married.
Mary Wollstonecraft Godwin (later Mary Shelley) b.
Edmund Burke d. (b. 1728) Mary Wollstonecraft d. (b.
1759)
Jane Austen begins *Sense and Sensibility* (pub. 1811); Thomas
Bewick, *A History of British Birds*; Robert Buchanan,
*Poems*; Ann Radcliffe, *The Italian*; Robert Southey, *Poems*,
incl. 'Poems on the slave trade', 'Botany Bay Eclogues',
'The Pauper's Funeral', 'To Mary Wollstonecraft'; William
Wilberforce, *Practical View of the Religious System of
Professed Christians Contrasted with Real Christians*;
William Wordsworth, *The Borderers* (pub. 1842), writes
'The Ruined Cottage' (later revised and printed as *The
Excursion*, Book I, 1814)
1798    France conquers Switzerland and Egypt, captures Rome,
seizes Malta, annexes left bank of Rhine; French fleet
defeated at Battle of the Nile. Rebellion in Ireland; French

army landed in Ireland to aid rebels. British government introduces 10 per cent wartime tax on all incomes over £200. Habeas Corpus law, protecting citizen from arbitrary imprisonment, suspended again (see 1794) (–March 1801). Wordsworths and Coleridge go to Germany (–1799). Byron, aged ten, becomes Lord. *Anti-Jacobin Review* founded. *Philosophical Magazine* founded (–1826).

Jane Austen, *Northanger Abbey* (pub. 1818); Jeremy Bentham, *Political Economy*; S. T. Coleridge, *Fears in Solitude, written in 1798 during the alarm of an invasion; to which are added France: an Ode, and Frost at Midnight*; S. T. Coleridge and William Wordsworth, *Lyrical Ballads* (published anonymously); William Godwin, *Memoirs of the Author of A Vindication of the Rights of Woman*; Elizabeth Inchbald, *Lovers' Vows*; W. S. Landor, *Gebir*; M. G. Lewis, *The Castle Spectre*; Thomas Malthus, *Essay on the Principle of Population*; James Plumptre, *The Lakers, A Comic Opera*; Charlotte Smith, *The Young Philosopher*; Mary Wollstonecraft, *The Wrongs of Woman, or Maria* (posthumous pub.); William Wordsworth, *Peter Bell* (pub. 1819)

1799    Kingdom of Mysore shared out between Britain and Nizam of Hyderabad. French army, under Napoleon, invades Syria, besieges Acre, defeats Turks at Abukir. Napoleon becomes Consul. Britain joins Russo-Turk alliance. Alessandro Volta invents electric battery. Royal Institution founded. London Corresponding Society prohibited. Six Acts to repress democrats. Formation of unions outlawed. Wordsworths and S. T. Coleridge return to England.

Thomas Campbell, *The Pleasures of Hope*; George Canning and John Hookham Frere, *Poetry of the Anti-Jacobin*; William Godwin, *St Leon*; William Jones, *Collected Works* (6 vols, posthumous pub.); Mungo Park, *Travels in the Interior Districts of Africa . . . in the years 1795, 1796 and 1797*; Robert Southey, *Poems*; Adam Walker, *A System of Familiar Philosophy*; George Walker, *The Vagabond*; Jane West, *A Tale of the Times*; William Wordsworth completes early two-book version of *The Prelude*

1800    French defeat Austrians at Marengo, conquer Italy. British capture Malta. Food riots in many English counties. Owen founds New Lanark factory. First iron-frame printing-press built.

T. B. Macaulay b. William Cowper d. (b. 1731)

William Blake completes *Vala, or the Four Zoas*; Robert
Bloomfield, *The Farmer's Boy*; Humphry Davy, *Researches,
Chemical and Philosophical*; Maria Edgeworth, *Castle
Rackrent*; Elizabeth Hamilton, *Memoirs of Modern
Philosophers*; Hannah More, *Strictures on Modern System
of Female Education*; Mary Robinson, *Lyrical Tales*;
William Wordsworth writes 'Preface to *Lyrical Ballads*'
(pub. 1801, in second edn of *Lyrical Ballads*, described
inaccurately as '1800')

1801  Toussaint L'Ouverture frees slaves in Santo Domingo.
British drive French out of Egypt, which returns to being
under Turkish control. Nelson defeats Danes off
Copenhagen. Act of Union, joining Great Britain and
Ireland, comes into force. Union Jack becomes official flag
of UK. George III's refusing to approve act for
Emancipation of Roman Catholics leads to Pitt's
resignation. Food prices rise; hunger increases. 'Black
Lamp' conspiracy amongst workers in West Yorkshire (–
1802). Population of England and Wales approximately 9
million (had been about 7½ million in 1780); 25 per cent
now town-dwellers (had been only 15 per cent in 1750).

John Henry Newman b. Robert Bage d. (b. 1720)

S. T. Coleridge and William Wordsworth, *Lyrical Ballads*
(2nd edn); Maria Edgeworth, *Angelina, Belinda* and *Moral
Tales*; James Hogg, *Scottish Pastorals*; Thomas Moore,
*Poetical Works of the Late Thomas Little Esq*; Amelia Opie,
*Father and Daughter*; Robert Southey, *Thalaba the Destroyer*;
John Thelwall, *Poems Chiefly Written in Retirement*

1802  John Truter and William Somerville explore Bechuanaland.
French crush Toussaint L'Ouverture's rebellion of negro
slaves. Peace of Amiens: truce with France 27 March–16
May 1803. West India Docks, London, built. New
legislation on apprentices forbids the employment in cotton
mills of children under nine years old and limits working
day to twelve hours, though the provisions of the new act
are openly flouted for some years to come. Society for the
Suppression of Vice formed. *Edinburgh Review* founded.
William Cobbett's weekly *Political Register* founded
(–1835). John Debrett publishes *Peerage* (*Baronetage*
follows in 1808). William Wordsworth visits Annette
Vallon and his daughter in France, marries Mary
Hutchinson.

S. T. Coleridge, 'Dejection: An Ode' (in *Morning Post*, 4 October, Wordsworth's wedding day and his own wedding anniversary); W. S. Landor, *Poetry by the Author of Gebir*; William Paley, *Natural Theology*; Walter Scott, *Minstrelsy of the Scottish Border* (–1803); Jane West, *The Infidel Father*

1803    British army under Arthur Wellesley (later Wellington) wins Second Marathan War against Sindis of Gwalior; British capture Delhi. In London, Colonel Despard and supporters executed for treason: Anglo-Irish Jacobinism crushed (May). Peace of Amiens collapses (May): war with France resumes. Henry Shrapnel invents artillery shell. Caledonian Canal begun. William Blake charged with assault and seditious speech.

Edward Bulwer-Lytton b.

Erasmus Darwin, *The Temple of Nature; or, The Origin of Society, A Poem with Philosophical Notes*; William Hayley, *Life and Posthumous Writings of William Cowper*; William Kenrick (tr.), Rousseau's *Eloisa*; Joseph Lancaster, *Improvements in Education*

1804    Napoleon crowned emperor, makes preparations for invasion of England. War between Britain and Spain begins. East India Company wins war against Holkar of Indore. British and Foreign Bible Society founded in London. William Pitt again Prime Minister (–1806). William Blake tried and acquitted. S. T. Coleridge goes to Malta as secretary to British High Commissioner (–1805). P. B. Shelley at Eton (–1810).

Benjamin Disraeli b.

William Blake, *Milton*; Ann Candler, *Poetical Attempts*; Maria Edgeworth, *Popular Tales*; Amelia Opie, *Adeline Mowbray*

1805    Napoleon crowned King of Italy in Milan Cathedral. British naval victory at Trafalgar. French defeat Russian and Austrian armies at Austerlitz. Medical and Chirurgical Society founded. Byron goes to Trinity College, Cambridge.

Henry Cary (tr.), Dante's *Inferno*; William Godwin, *Fleetwood or the New Man of Feeling*; William Hazlitt, *An Essay on the Principles of Human Action*; Christian Milne, *Simple Poems*; Walter Scott, *Lay of the Last Minstrel* (sells 21,300 copies in first five years); Robert Southey, *Madoc*; Ann and Jane Taylor, *Original Poems for Infant Minds*;

Mary Tighe, *Psyche*; William Wordsworth completes 13-book *Prelude* (extensively reworked and published 1850)

1806   French defeat Prussians at Jena, reach Berlin and Warsaw, close Continental ports to British shipping. William Pitt dies. C. J. Fox dies. Work begins on building of Dartmoor Prison. First steam-powered textile mill in Manchester. S. T. Coleridge returns to Britain.

Elizabeth Barrett (later Browning) b. J. S. Mill b. Charlotte Smith d. (b. 1749)

Lord Byron, *Fugitive Pieces* (printed privately); Maria Edgeworth, *Leonora*; Jane Marcet, *Conversations on Chemistry, Intended More Especially for the Female Sex*; Thomas Moore, *Epistles, Odes and Other Poems*; Lady Morgan, *The Wild Irish Girl*; Amelia Opie, *Simple Tales*; Charlotte Richardson, *Poems*; Mary Robinson, *The Poems* (3 vols); Mary Saxby, *Memoirs of a Female Vagrant*; William Wordsworth, *The Waggoner* (pub. 1819)

1807   France invades Portugal. Russia withdraws from war against France. Sierra Leone and Gambia made British colonies. Slave-trading in British ships banned. Humphry Davy isolates sodium and potassium. Geological Society founded. First public gas-lighting in London.

Lord Byron, *Hours of Idleness*; George Crabbe, *Poems*, incl. 'The Parish Register'; William Hazlitt, *Reply to Malthus*; Charles and Mary Lamb, *Tales from Shakespeare*; Charles Maturin, *The Fatal Revenge*; Thomas Moore, *Irish Melodies*; Lady Morgan, *Lays of an Irish Harp*; Sydney Smith, *The Letters of Peter Plymley*; William Wordsworth, *Poems in Two Volumes*

1808   French invade Spain. British army lands in Portugal. Henry Crabb Robinson sent by *The Times* to Spain for reports on the Peninsular War: first war correspondent. British government abandons Portuguese in Convention of Cintra. Humphry Davy isolates magnesium. John Dalton begins *New System of Chemical Philosophy* (completed 1827), The *Examiner* (–1881) founded by Leigh Hunt.

William Blake begins *Jerusalem* (completed 1820); Elizabeth Hamilton, *Cottagers of Glenburnie*; Felicia Hemans, *Poems*; Charles Maturin, *The Wild Irish Boy*; Hannah More, *Coelebs in Search of a Wife*; Walter Scott, *Marmion*

1809   British expedition to Walcheren in Low Countries fails disastrously. In Peninsula, British defeated at Corunna

(January), victorious at Salamanca (July). French capture
Vienna. British capture Martinique and Cayenne from
French. Proposal for parliamentary reform rejected by
House of Commons. National Society for the Education of
the Poor in the Principles of the Established Church
founded. Lord Byron travels through Portugal, Spain,
Malta, Albania, Greece. *Quarterly Review* founded.

Charles Darwin b. Alfred Tennyson b. Thomas Holcroft d.
(b. 1745) Joseph Johnson d. (b. 1738) Thomas Paine d. (b.
1737) Anna Seward d. (b. 1747)

Robert Barker, *The Genuine Life*; Joseph Blacket, *Specimens
of Poetry*; William Blake, *A Descriptive Catalogue*; Lord
Byron, *English Bards and Scotch Reviewers*; S. T. Coleridge
periodical, *The Friend* (June–March 1810); Lady Morgan,
*Woman, or Ida of Athens*; David Ricardo, *The High Price
of Bullion, Proof of the Depreciation of Bank Notes*;
Charlotte Richardson, *Poems . . . composed during . . . illness*;
William Wordsworth, *Tract on the Convention of Cintra*

1810 British resist French offensive in Portugal, seize Guadeloupe,
last French colony in West Indies. French take Holland.
George III's madness admitted. Durham miners' strike.
London riots in support of Francis Burdett and
parliamentary reform. S. T. Coleridge lectures on
Shakespeare, quarrels with Wordsworth (friendship not
resumed until 1812). Lord Byron in Greece and Turkey
(–1811).

Elizabeth Gaskell b.

James Cock, *Simple Strains*; George Crabbe, *The Borough*;
William Edwards, *A Collection of Poems*; William Hazlitt,
*New and Improved Grammar of the English Tongue*; Walter
Scott, *The Lady of the Lake* (sells 20,000 copies in first
year) and (ed.) Anna Seward's *Poetical Works*; P. B.
Shelley, *Original Poetry by Victor and Cazire* (published
then withdrawn), *Zastrozzi, St Irvyne, Posthumous
Fragments of Margaret Nicholson*: Robert Southey, *The
Curse of Kehama*; William Wordsworth, *Guide to the Lakes*
(first version, as Introduction to Wilkinson's *Select Views
of Cumberland etc.*)

1811 British occupy Java. Prince of Wales begins Regency.
Industrial depression, as France's Continental System
(blockade) and Britain's retaliatory Orders in Council close
American as well as European markets for English

products. Government census shows four-fifths of entire population are manual workers. Hampden Clubs (pressure-groups for democracy) founded. From February, Luddite attacks on machines and mills (and general food riots) in Midlands and North. In November, Nottingham garrison reinforced by further 2,000 troops. P. B. Shelley expelled from Oxford University for publishing *The Necessity of Atheism* (with T. J. Hogg); sells copies of poem (now lost) to raise money for Peter Finnerty (journalist sentenced to eighteen months' imprisonment for exposing Government negligence in Walcheren expedition); marries Harriet Westbrook. Leigh Hunt prosecuted for article in *Examiner* denouncing severity of military punishments, 'One Thousand Lashes'. S. T. Coleridge lectures on Shakespeare and Milton. John Keats apprenticed to surgeon. Lord Byron returns to England. W. M. Thackeray b.

Jane Austen, *Sense and Sensibility;* (begun 1797); Mary Brunton, *Self-Control*; Leigh Hunt, *The Feast of the Poets*; Charles Lamb, 'On the Tragedies of Shakespeare'; James Lawrence, *Empire of the Nadirs*; Lady Morgan, *The Missionary: An Indian Tale*; Anna Seward, *Letters*, (6 vols, posthumous pub.)

1812   US declares war on Britain. French invade Russia, burn Moscow but are in retreat by October. Wellington's army enters Madrid. Anti-Luddite frame-breaking act (opposed in Lord Byron's first parliamentary speech) becomes law in February: death penalty for arranging oaths of allegiance to secret societies. In May, Prime Minister Spencer Perceval assassinated in House of Commons; the event openly celebrated by crowds of demonstrators in London and Nottingham; Lord Liverpool becomes Prime Minister. Luddite attacks increase. Eight infantry and four cavalry regiments operating in north-west England: 100 dissidents imprisoned at Lancaster (eight death sentences) and Chester (fifteen death sentences). Food riots in Bristol, Plymouth and Cornwall as well as northern England. P. B. Shelley, agitating in Dublin, under investigation by Home Office – his correspondence being opened, his servant arrested for distributing leaflets; meets William Godwin.

Robert Browning b. Charles Dickens b.

Lord Byron, *Childe Harold's Pilgrimage* I and II, *The Curse of Minerva*; Henry Cary (tr.), Dante's *Purgatory* and *Paradise*; George Crabbe, *Tales in Verse*; Humphry Davy, *Elements of Chemical Philosophy*; Maria Edgeworth, *Tales of Fashionable Life*; Felicia Hemans, *Domestic Affections and Other Poems*; Amelia Opie, *Temper, or Domestic Scenes*; P. B. Shelley, *An Address to the Irish People* and *Proposals for an Association*

1813    India Act amendment: Christian missionaries to proselytize in India. French defeated at Leipzig, expelled from Holland. British, victorious under Wellington at Vittoria, invade France. Further mass trials and executions of Luddites: eighteen sentenced to death at York, only one commuted to transportation for life. Leigh Hunt imprisoned for libel (prose disrespectful of Prince Regent) (– 1815). William Wordsworth accepts government pay as Distributor of Stamps. Robert Southey becomes Poet Laureate after Walter Scott refuses the appointment. P. B. Shelley in Ireland again.

Jane Austen, *Pride and Prejudice*; Lord Byron, *The Giaour*, *The Bride of Abydos*; S. T. Coleridge's play *Remorse* produced in London; James Hogg, *The Queen's Wake*; Mary Russell Mitford, *Narrative Poems on the Female Character in the Various Relations of Life*; Robert Owen, *A New View of Society*; J. C. Prichard, *Researches into the Physical History of Man*; P. B. Shelley, *Queen Mab*; Robert Southey, *Life of Nelson*

1814    Napoleon defeated and exiled to Elba; Louis XVIII takes French throne as hereditary right; Congress of Vienna reimposes authoritarian governments in Europe. Inquisition re-established in Spain. Peace of Ghent arranges peace between Britain and US. Lord Hastings, Governor-General of India, declares war on the Gurkhas of Nepal. Cape Province becomes a British colony. George Stephenson constructs first practical steam locomotive. First steam warship developed in Britain. Steam printing-machine invented. Edmund Kean appears in first major role at Theatre Royal, Drury Lane; P. B. Shelley elopes with Mary Godwin.

Jane Austen, *Mansfield Park*; Mary Brunton, *Discipline*; Fanny Burney, *The Wanderer*; Lord Byron, *The Corsair* (10,000 copies sold on first day of publication), *Lara*; Maria Edgeworth, *Patronage*; Leigh Hunt, *Feast of the*

*Poets*; Thomas Malthus, *Observations on the Effect of the Corn Laws*; Lady Morgan, *O'Donnel: A National Tale*; Walter Scott, *Waverley*; P. B. Shelley, *A Refutation of Deism*; William Wordsworth, *The Excursion*

1815    Napoleon escapes (March); Louis XVIII flees; British and Prussians victorious at Waterloo (18 June); Napoleon exiled to St Helena; 'Holy Alliance' of European royal families; Michel Ney executed for work as Napoleon's general at Waterloo. Humphry Davy invents the miners' safety lamp. Landowners succeed in passage of Corn Bill. Income tax ended (reimposed 1842). Since 1792, 155 new barracks built in England, many in Midlands and North. Apothecaries' Act passed. William Blake, in poverty, engraves designs for Wedgwood's chinaware catalogues. Lord Byron marries. John Keats writes sonnet celebrating Leigh Hunt's release from prison, enters Guy's Hospital as student.

Anthony Trollope b.

Lord Byron, *Hebrew Melodies*; James Doaning, *Narrative . . . in Easy Verse*; T. R. Malthus, *An Inquiry into the Nature and Progress of Rent*; Robert Owen, *Address to the Inhabitants of New Lanark*; David Ricardo, *The Influence of a Low Price of Corn on the Profits of Stock*; Walter Scott, *Guy Mannering*; William Wordsworth, first collected edition of *Poems, White Doe of Rylstone*

1816    Postwar slump. Three mass protest meetings at Spa Fields in London, all addressed by Henry Hunt, lead to riots (November) and armed march on Tower (December). Agricultural workers riot in East Anglia. Demonstrations and disturbances in towns of Midlands and North. Sir Francis Burdett and Westminster Committee begin campaign to extend suffrage to middle-class payers of direct taxes; opposed not only by Tories but by radicals (such as Henry Hunt, William Cobbett) wanting manhood suffrage. Cobbett begins issuing leading articles from *Political Register* as mass-circulation, stamp-duty-evading cheap pamphlets: ('Twopenny Trash'), beginning with 'Address to the Journeymen and Labourers'. Elgin Marbles exhibited. Lord Byron separates from wife, leaves England, never to return; in Geneva, meets P. B. Shelley, Mary Godwin and Claire Clairmont (Mary's stepsister); P. B. Shelley and Mary Godwin return to England; Harriet

Shelley's suicide; P. B. Shelley marries Mary
Wollstonecraft Godwin. John Keats completes medical
education; first published poem in *Examiner*.
Charlotte Brontë b. Richard Brinsley Sheridan d. (b. 1751)
Jane Austen, *Emma*; Lord Byron, *Poems, Prisoner of Chillon,
The Siege of Corinth, Childe Harold's Pilgrimage* III;
William Cobbett, *Political Register* (including special-issue
best seller, 'Address to the Journeymen and Labourers of
England, Scotland and Ireland'); S. T. Coleridge,
*Statesman's Manual, Christabel and Other Poems, Lay
Sermons* I; William Hazlitt, *Memoirs of Thomas Holcroft*;
Margaret Holford, *Margaret of Anjou*; Leigh Hunt, *The
Story of Rimini*; Lady Caroline Lamb, *Glenarvon*; Charles
Maturin, *Bertram*; Thomas Peacock, *Headlong Hall*; Walter
Scott, *The Antiquary* and *Old Mortality*; P. B. Shelley,
*Alastor and Other Poems*; William Wordsworth,
'Thanksgiving Ode' (for victory at Waterloo)

1817   Prince Regent attacked by stone-throwing demonstrators after
opening of Parliament (January). Henry Hunt and
Lancashire delegates to London reformers' meeting
succeed with motion demanding universal suffrage against
moderates wanting only household suffrage; 50,000
signatures on petition to Parliament. Committee of House
of Lords reports that Hampden Clubs are part of
'traiterous conspiracy . . . for . . . general insurrexion . . .
and division of property . . . and that such designs . . .
extended widely in some of the most populous and
manufacturing districts'. Habeas Corpus law again
suspended. Sections of 1795 Treason Acts renewed to
forbid 'Seditious Meetings' (including any gathering of
fifty or more not licensed by magistrates), revive death
penalty for words that might lead to disaffection amongst
armed forces; some democratic societies forced into hiding.
William Cobbett flees abroad; his 'Address to the
Journeymen and Labourers' pamphlet (1816) sells 200,000
copies by end of 1817. William Hone founds *Reformists'
Register* and *Black Dwarf*, is prosecuted for blasphemous
parodies. *Sherwin's Political Register* (later the *Republican*)
founded. *Blackwood's Edinburgh Magazine* founded. The
'blanketeers' protest-march from St Peter's Field,
Manchester, to London: approx. 5,000 challenged by
cavalry at Stockport (200 arrested); some reach Ashbourne,

Derbyshire (March). Pentridge rebellion: Derbyshire and Nottinghamshire workers make an armed march on garrison city of Nottingham (June); Jeremiah Brandreth and other leaders hanged and beheaded (7 November). Princess Charlotte, Prince Regent's only legitimate child, dies (6 November). P. B. Shelley often at Leigh Hunt's, where he meets John Keats: all three, with William Hazlitt, to be objects of John Lockhart's attack 'On the Cockney School of Poets' (begins in October issue of *Blackwood's Magazine*). Atheism of *Queen Mab* prevents P. B. Shelley being allowed custody of his children by Harriet.

Jane Austen d. (b. 1775)

Lord Byron, *Manfred*; S. T. Coleridge, *Biographia Literaria, Sibylline Leaves, Lay Sermons* II; William Godwin, *Mandeville*; William Hazlitt, *Characters of Shakespeare's Plays, The Round Table*, 'What is the People?'; William Hone, *Political Litany*; John Keats, *Poems*; James Mill, *The History of the British in India*; Thomas Moore, *Lalla Rookh*; Lady Morgan, *France*; Robert Owen, *Report to the Committee on the Poor Law*; Thomas Peacock, *Melincourt*; David Ricardo, *Principles of Political Economy and Taxation*; Mary and P. B. Shelley, *History of a Six Weeks Tour*; P. B. Shelley, *A Proposal for Putting Reform to the Vote, Laon and Cythna* (early version of *The Revolt of Islam*; published then withdrawn), *An Address . . . on the Death of the Princess Charlotte* (mourning death of Pentridge rebels, pub. 1843), 'Hymn to Intellectual Beauty'; Robert Southey, *Wat Tyler* (written 1794, pirated by radical publishers); Elizabeth Spence, *Letters from the North Highlands*

1818  Britain takes control of the Rajput States and Poona. Radical publisher Richard Carlile prosecuted. 1,500 petitions for reform from towns throughout country (700 from 300 towns in 1817). Spinners' and weavers' strikes: 60,000 looms idle. William Wordsworth working as election agent for richest landowner in Lake District, Tory Lord Lonsdale, whose candidate for the Westmorland parliamentary seat is opposed by Westminster Whig liberal, Henry Brougham. Shelleys leave England, join Lord Byron in Italy. John Keats attends William Hazlitt's lectures on the English poets; travels through Lake District to Scotland on walking tour; his *Endymion* condemned by

John Lockhart (continuing the attack 'On the Cockney
School of Poets' in *Blackwood's Magazine*) and by
*Quarterly Review*; death of Keats's brother Tom from
tuberculosis. John Wade's radical *Gorgon* founded.
Emily Brontë b. Karl Marx b. Warren Hastings d. (b. 1732)
M. G. 'Monk' Lewis d. (b. 1775)
Jane Austen, *Northanger Abbey* (written 1798) and *Persuasion*
(written 1816), both published posthumously; Lord Byron,
*Beppo, Childe Harold's Pilgrimage* IV; William Cobbett, *A
Grammar of the English Language*; S. T. Coleridge, *The
Friend* (rev., 3 vols); Susan Ferrier, *Marriage*; Henry
Hallam, *A View of the State of Europe during the Middle
Ages*; William Hazlitt, *Lectures on the English Poets*; Leigh
Hunt, *Foliage*; John Keats, *Endymion*; Richard Payne
Knight, *An Enquiry into the Symbolical Language of Ancient
Art and Mythology* (new version of 'A Discourse on the
Worship of Priapus', (1786); Thomas Moore, *National
Airs* I (–1827), *Fudge Family in Paris*; Thomas Peacock,
*Nightmare Abbey*; Walter Scott, *The Heart of Midlothian,
Rob Roy*; Mary Shelley, *Frankenstein*; P. B. Shelley, *The
Revolt of Islam*, 'Ozymandias'

1819  East India Company establishes British settlement in
Singapore. Peterloo massacre (16 August): peaceful
demonstration by 60,000–100,000 unarmed working men,
women and children, meeting in St Peter's Fields,
Manchester (but drawn from towns and villages
throughout north-west England) attacked by militia cavalry
with drawn sabres; 11 dead, over 400 injured; Prime
Minister and Prince Regent send thanks to magistrates
responsible, praising 'their prompt, decisive and efficient
measures for the preservation of the public peace'. 'Six
Acts' to prevent protest meetings and press freedom, incl.
Blasphemous and Seditious Libel Act; popular periodicals
redefined as newspapers, liable for fourpenny stamp duty
and thus too expensive for workers. In September, Henry
Hunt and followers process into London, watched by
300,000 spectators (incl. John Keats) lining streets. Richard
Carlile imprisoned for 'seditious' publications incl. Tom
Paine's *The Age of Reason* (1794–5). The *Indicator* founded
by Leigh Hunt (–1821).
George Eliot b. John Ruskin b. future Queen Victoria b.
Lord Byron, *Don Juan* I and II; George Crabbe, *Tales of the*

*Hall*; William Hazlitt, *Lectures on the English Comic Writers, Political Essays*; William Hone, *Political House that Jack Built*; John Keats, *The Fall of Hyperion* (pub. 1856); John Lockhart, *Peter's Letters to His Kinsfolk*; John Polidori, *The Vampyre*; J. H. Reynolds and P. B. Shelley, *Peter Bell the Third*; Walter Scott, *The Bride of Lammermoor*; P. B. Shelley, *The Mask of Anarchy* (pub. 1832), 'Julian and Maddalo' (pub. 1824); William Wordsworth, *Peter Bell* (written 1798) and *The Waggoner* (written 1806)

1820 Revolution in Spain and Portugal. Rebellion in Naples; Byron involved with Italian revolutionaries. Death of George III; succeeded by Prince Regent as George IV (–1830); new king, wishing to dissolve marriage, tries to prevent wife, Caroline, being recognized as queen; Caroline has popular support. Cato Street conspiracy to assassinate government ministers; leaders executed. First iron steamship. John Keats's play *Otho the Great* rejected by Drury Lane; advised to leave England for health, goes to Rome. *London Magazine* founded.

Anne Brontë b.

William Blake, *Jerusalem: The Emanation of the Giant Albion* (begun *c*. 1808); Thomas Bowdler, *The Family Shakespeare*; Thomas Brown, *Lectures on the Philosophy of the Human Mind*; John Clare, *Poems Descriptive of Rural Life*; John Galt, *Ayrshire Legatees*; William Godwin, *Of Population*; William Hazlitt, *Lectures on the Dramatic Literature of the Age of Elizabeth, Lectures on the English Poets*; William Hone, *The Man in the Moon*; John Keats, *Lamia, Isabella, The Eve of St Agnes and Other Poems*; Charles Lamb, 'Essays of Elia' in *London Magazine* (–1822); T. R. Malthus, *Principles of Political Economy*; Charles Maturin, *Melmoth the Wanderer*; Amelia Opie, *Tales of the Heart*; Thomas Peacock, *Four Ages of Poetry*; Walter Scott, *Ivanhoe, The Abbot*; P. B. Shelley, *Swellfoot the Tyrant* (published and suppressed), *The Cenci*, 'Ode to the West Wind', *Prometheus Unbound*, 'The Witch of Atlas' (pub. 1824), *A Philosophical View of Reform* (pub. 1920); Robert Southey, *Life of Wesley*; William Wordsworth, *The River Duddon: A Series of Sonnets* and *Vaudracour and Julia* (written 1804)

1821 Simón Bolívar, in war to liberate Venezuela, defeats Spanish army at Carabobo. Peru, Guatemala, Panama, Santo Domingo declared independent from Spain. Greek revolution begins. Austrian armies sent to crush revolt in Naples and revolution in Piedmont. Queen Caroline dies; anti–Government demonstration at funeral; troops open fire, kill two. Michael Faraday establishes principles of electromagnetic power. Lord Byron joins Shelleys in Pisa.

Elizabeth Inchbald d. (b. 1753) John Keats d. (b. 1795)

Joanna Baillie, *Metrical Legends of Exalted Characters*; Elizabeth Bentley, *Poems*; Lord Byron, *Marino Faliero, The Prophecy of Dante, Sardanapalus, The Two Foscari, Don Juan* III–V, *Cain*; John Clare, *The Village Minstrel*; William Cobbett, *Cottage Economy*; Thomas De Quincey, *Confessions of an English Opium Eater* (serialized in *London Magazine*); John Galt, *Annals of the Parish*; William Hazlitt, *Table Talk* (–1822); James Mill, *Elements of Political Economy*; Robert Millhouse, *Vicissitudes*; Sir William Edward Parry, *Journal of a Voyage for the Discovery of a North-west Passage*; Augustus Charles Pugin, *Specimens of Gothic Architecture*; Walter Scott, *Kenilworth*; P. B. Shelley, *Adonais, Epipsychidion* (published anonymously), *A Defence of Poetry* (pub. 1840), unauthorized pub. of *Queen Mab* (written 1813); Robert Southey, *A Vision of Judgement*

1822  Castlereagh commits suicide. Liberals – Canning and Peel – join Tory Cabinet. First iron railway bridge, designed by Stephenson, Stockton–Darlington line. Brazil becomes independent of Portugal. Greeks proclaim independence; Turks invade Greece. Leigh Hunt in Italy to found, with Lord Byron and Shelleys, the *Liberal*; in first of only four issues (October), Byron's *Vision of Judgement* published; John Hunt prosecuted for its publication. Weekly *Mirror of Literature, Amusement and Instruction* founded.

Matthew Arnold b. P. B. Shelley d. (b. 1792), drowned returning from meeting re the *Liberal*

Lord Byron, *The Vision of Judgement*; John Galt, *The Provost, The Entail*; James Hogg, *Poetical Works* (4 vols); Thomas Peacock, *Maid Marian*; Samuel Rogers, *Italy*; Walter Scott, *The Fortunes of Nigel, Peveril of the Peak*; P. B. Shelley, *Hellas*; William Wordsworth, *Ecclesiastical Sketches*

1823  Byron sails for Greece with army to support liberation from

Turkey. Mechanics' Institutes founded in London and Glasgow. Over 100 crimes redefined as no longer incurring death penalty. First issue of the *Lancet*, the *Phrenological Journal* (–1847) and the *Quarterly Magazine*.

Ann Radcliffe d. (b. 1764)

William Buckland, *Reliquae Diluvianae . . . Organic Remains . . . in . . . Geological Phenomena, Attesting the Action of an Universal Deluge*; Lord Byron, *Don Juan* VI–XIV, *The Island*; George Crabbe, *Poems* (7 vols); John Franklin, *Narrative of a Journey to the Polar Sea*; William Hazlitt, *Liber Amoris*; James Hogg, *The Three Perils of Woman*; Charles Lamb, *Essays of Elia*; Thomas Moore, *Fables for Holy Alliance*; Walter Scott, *Quentin Durward*; Mary Shelley, *Valperga*

1824　First Burmese War; British seize Rangoon. Combinations Act repealed; unions permitted.

Wilkie Collins b. Lord Byron d. (b. 1788)

Lord Byron, *Don Juan* XV–XVI; William Cobbett, *History of Protestant 'Reformation'* (–1826); William Godwin, *History of the Commonwealth of England*; James Hogg, *Private Memoirs and Confessions of a Justified Sinner*; W. S. Landor, *Imaginary Conversations of Literary Men and Statesmen* I and II; Thomas Medwin, *Conversations of Lord Byron*; Walter Scott, *Redgauntlet*; P. B. Shelley, *Posthumous Poems* (incl. 'Julian and Maddalo', 'The Witch of Atlas', *The Triumph of Life*)

1825　Defeat of Decembrist rebellion in Russia. New laws in France make sacrilege a capital offence and compensate aristocrats for financial losses in Revolution. First passenger (and first steam locomotion) railway opened, Stockton–Darlington. Michael Faraday discovers benzene.

Henry Brougham, *Observations on the Education of the People*; Thomas Carlyle, *Life of Schiller*; S. T. Coleridge, *Aids to Reflection*; William Hazlitt, *The Spirit of the Age*; James Mill, *Essays on Government*; Walter Scott, *Tales of the Crusaders*

1826　University College, London, founded (opened 1828). Society for the Diffusion of Useful Knowledge formed. Zoological Society founded. First railway tunnel: Liverpool–Manchester line. Machine-breaking by unemployed weavers.

Elizabeth Barrett, *An Essay on Mind, with Other Poems*;

James F. Cooper, *The Last of the Mohicans*; Benjamin Disraeli, *Vivian Grey*; John Galt, *Last of the Lairds*; Thomas Hood, *Whims and Oddities* I; Robert Millhouse, *The Song of the Patriot*; Walter Scott, *Woodstock*; Mary Shelley, *The Last Man*

1827    Turks take Athens; then Greeks win at Navarino. *Philosophical Magazine or Annals of Chemistry* (–1832) founded.

William Blake d. (b. 1757)

John Clare, *The Shepherd's Calendar*; John Keble, *The Christian Year*; Thomas De Quincey, 'On Murder Considered as One of the Fine Arts'; James Taylor, *Miscellaneous Poems*; Alfred and Charles Tennyson, *Poems by Two Brothers*

1828    Wellington becomes Prime Minister. Test and Corporation Acts repealed: Roman Catholics can be offered official appointments. Thomas Arnold becomes headmaster of Rugby School.

George Meredith b. D. G. Rossetti b.

Edward Bulwer-Lytton, *Pelham*; S. T. Coleridge, *Poetical Works*; Sir John Franklin, *Journal of a Second Expedition to the Polar Sea*; William Hazlitt, *Life of Napoleon* I–II; Leigh Hunt, *Lord Byron and Some of His Contemporaries*; W. S. Landor, *Imaginary Conversations* III; John Lockhart, *Life of Burns*; Sir William Edward Parry, *Narrative of an Attempt to Reach the North Pole*; Walter Scott, *Tales of a Grandfather* I and *The Fair Maid of Perth*

1829    Turkey concedes Greek independence. Suttee banned in British India. Catholic Emancipation Act. George Stephenson's 'Rocket' wins engine competition.

Humphry Davy d. (b. 1778)

James Hogg, *The Shepherd's Calendar*; W. S. Landor, *Imaginary Conversations* IV–V; Thomas Peacock, *The Misfortunes of Elphin*; Walter Scott, *Tales of a Grandfather* II, Collected Edition of Waverley novels (–1833); John Shipp, *Memoirs* I; Robert Southey, *Sir Thomas More, or Colloquies on the Progress and Prospects of Society*; Alfred Tennyson, 'Timbuctoo' (wins Cambridge University poetry competition)

1830    Revolution in Paris. In England, 'Captain Swing' rising: food riots, machine-breaking, arson and other terrorist attacks on landowners by farm workers (–spring 1831). George IV dies; William IV becomes king (–1837). Lord Grey (Whig) takes over as Prime Minister from Tory Wellington. Official opening of Liverpool–Manchester railway. Britain now has over 4,000 miles of canals (first commercial canal 1760). Geographical Society founded.

Christina Rossetti b. William Hazlitt d. (b. 1778)

Edward Bulwer-Lytton, *Paul Clifford*; William Cobbett, *Rural Rides* I, *Twopenny Trash* (–1833); S. T. Coleridge, *On the Constitution of the Church and State*; Charles Crocker, *The Vale of Obscurity, The Levant and Other Poems*; Ebenezer Elliott, *Corn Law Rhymes*; John Galt, *Lawrie Todd*; William Hazlitt, *Life of Napoleon* III–IV; Felicia Hemans, *Songs of the Affections*; John Jones, *Attempts in Verse*; Charles Lyell, *Principles of Geology* I; Thomas Moore, *Letters and Journals of Lord Byron*; Walter Scott, *Tales of a Grandfather* III; Mary Shelley, *Perkin Warbeck*; Alfred Tennyson, *Poems, Chiefly Lyrical*

1831   Cholera epidemic, originated in India (1826), reaches central Europe (hits Scotland 1832). Polish rebellion defeated by Russians. Darwin sets off on first voyage in the *Beagle* (–1836). Arrests of 'Swing' dissident labourers total 1,976: 19 executed, 481 transported. Brunel designs Clifton suspension bridge. Populations of Liverpool and Manchester have increased by 40 per cent in decade since 1821.

Benjamin Disraeli, *The Young Duke*; James Hogg, *Songs by the Ettrick Shepherd*; Thomas Peacock, *Crotchet Castle*; Jane Somerville, *Mechanism of the Heavens*

1832   Britain takes the Falkland Islands. Reform Bill enfranchises upper middle classes, almost doubling electorate, but only from 2.6 per cent of total population to 4.7 per cent.

Lewis Carroll (Charles Lutwidge Dodgson) b. George Crabbe d. (b. 1754) Walter Scott d. (b. 1771)

Edward Bulwer-Lytton, *Eugene Aram*; John Herschel, *A Preliminary Discourse on the Study of Natural Philosophy*; Leigh Hunt, *Poetical Works*; Charles Lyell, *Principles of Geology* II; Harriet Martineau, *Illustrations of Political Economy* (–1834); George Petrie, *Equality: A Poem*; P. B. Shelley, *The Mask of Anarchy* (written 1819); Alfred Tennyson, *Poems*

1833   Abolition of slavery in British Empire.

Hannah More d. (b. 1745)

Robert Browning, *Pauline*; Hartley Coleridge, *Poems*; Charles Dickens, *Sketches by Boz*; Charles Lamb, *Last Essays of Elia*; Charles Lyell, *Principles of Geology* III; William Whewell, *Astronomy and General Physics Considered with Reference to Natural Theology*

1834    South Australia Act allows establishment of colony. Poor Law Amendment Act: aid to destitute reduced, no assistance for able-bodied men unless living in workhouse. Charles Babbage invents principle of computer.

William Morris b. S. T. Coleridge d. (b. 1772) Charles Lamb d. (b. 1775), T. R. Malthus d. (b. 1766)

Edward Bulwer-Lytton, *The Last Days of Pompeii*; Charles Cole, *Political and Other Poems*; *The Poetical Works of the Rev. George Crabbe: with his Letters and Journals, and His Life, by his Son* (8 vols); Maria Edgeworth, *Helen*; James Hogg, *The Domestic Manners and Private Life of Sir Walter Scott*; P. M. Roget, *Animal and Vegetable Physiology*; Mary Somerville, *On the Connexion of the Physical Sciences*

1835    Melbourne (Australia) founded. First railway development 'mania' (–1837). Municipal Corporation Act transforms local government.

William Cobbett d. (b. 1762) Felicia Hemans d. (b. 1793) James Hogg d. (b. 1770)

Robert Browning, *Paracelsus*; Edward Bulwer-Lytton, *Rienzi*

1836    Charles Darwin returns from the Galapagos Islands. The People's Charter demands universal suffrage and vote by ballot.

William Godwin d. (b. 1756)

Thomas Carlyle, *Sartor Resartus*; Charles Dickens, *Pickwick Papers* (–1837); Asa Gray, *Elements of Botany*

1837    William IV succeeded by Victoria. Electric telegraph patented.

Algernon Swinburne b.

Thomas Carlyle, *History of the French Revolution*; Charles Dickens, *Oliver Twist* (–1838); William Whewell, *History of the Inductive Sciences*

# Index

Page references to the Table of Dates are in *italic*

# READ MORE IN PENGUIN

In every corner of the world, on every subject under the sun, Penguin represents quality and variety – the very best in publishing today.

For complete information about books available from Penguin – including Puffins, Penguin Classics and Arkana – and how to order them, write to us at the appropriate address below. Please note that for copyright reasons the selection of books varies from country to country.

**In the United Kingdom**: Please write to *Dept. EP, Penguin Books Ltd, Bath Road, Harmondsworth, West Drayton, Middlesex UB7 0DA*

**In the United States**: Please write to *Consumer Sales, Penguin USA, P.O. Box 999, Dept. 17109, Bergenfield, New Jersey 07621-0120*. VISA and MasterCard holders call 1-800-253-6476 to order Penguin titles

**In Canada**: Please write to *Penguin Books Canada Ltd, 10 Alcorn Avenue, Suite 300, Toronto, Ontario M4V 3B2*

**In Australia**: Please write to *Penguin Books Australia Ltd, P.O. Box 257, Ringwood, Victoria 3134*

**In New Zealand**: Please write to *Penguin Books (NZ) Ltd, Private Bag 102902, North Shore Mail Centre, Auckland 10*

**In India**: Please write to *Penguin Books India Pvt Ltd, 706 Eros Apartments, 56 Nehru Place, New Delhi 110 019*

**In the Netherlands**: Please write to *Penguin Books Netherlands bv, Postbus 3507, NL-1001 AH Amsterdam*

**In Germany**: Please write to *Penguin Books Deutschland GmbH, Metzlerstrasse 26, 60594 Frankfurt am Main*

**In Spain**: Please write to *Penguin Books S. A., Bravo Murillo 19, 1° B, 28015 Madrid*

**In Italy**: Please write to *Penguin Italia s.r.l., Via Felice Casati 20, I-20124 Milano*

**In France**: Please write to *Penguin France S. A., 17 rue Lejeune, F-31000 Toulouse*

**In Japan**: Please write to *Penguin Books Japan, Ishikiribashi Building, 2-5-4, Suido, Bunkyo-ku, Tokyo 112*

**In South Africa**: Please write to *Longman Penguin Southern Africa (Pty) Ltd, Private Bag X08, Bertsham 2013*

# READ MORE IN PENGUIN

## LITERARY CRITICISM

### A Lover's Discourse  Roland Barthes

'*A Lover's Discourse* . . . may be the most detailed, painstaking anatomy of desire we are ever likely to see or need again . . . The book is an ecstatic celebration of love and language and . . . readers interested in either or both . . . will enjoy savouring its rich and dark delights' – *Washington Post Book World*

### The New Pelican Guide to English Literature  Edited by Boris Ford

The indispensable critical guide to English and American literature in nine volumes, erudite yet accessible. From the ages of Chaucer and Shakespeare, via Georgian satirists and Victorian social critics, to the leading writers of the twentieth century, all literary life is here.

### The Structure of Complex Words  William Empson

'Twentieth-century England's greatest critic after T. S. Eliot, but whereas Eliot was the high priest, Empson was the *enfant terrible* . . . *The Structure of Complex Words* is one of the linguistic masterpieces of the epoch, finding in the feel and tone of our speech whole sedimented social histories' – *Guardian*

### The Art of Fiction  David Lodge

The articles with which David Lodge entertained and enlightened readers of the *Independent on Sunday* and the *Washington Post* are now revised, expanded and collected together in book form. 'Agreeable and highly instructive . . . a real treat' – *Sunday Telegraph*

### Vamps and Tramps  Camille Paglia

'Paglia is a genuinely unconventional thinker . . . In this collection she is best on homosexual politics, the betrayal of feminism and the sterility of American academe. Taken as a whole, the book gives an exceptionally interesting perspective on the last thirty years of intellectual life in America, and is, in its wacky way, a celebration of passion and the pursuit of truth' – *Sunday Telegraph*